Operations management
Planning and control of operations and operating resources

Operations management
Planning and control of operations and operating resources

Richard J. Schonberger
College of Business Administration
University of Nebraska

 1981

BUSINESS PUBLICATIONS, INC.
Plano, Texas 75075
IRWIN-DORSEY LIMITED
Georgetown, Ontario L7G 4B3

ISBN 0-256-02442-1
Library of Congress Catalog Card No. 80–69796

Printed in the United States of America

1 2 3 4 5 6 7 8 9 0 H 8 7 6 5 4 3 2 1

preface

Operations Management is a textbook that introduces students to the planning and control of operations and operating resources in any type of firm. The text addresses the production/operations management (P/OM) topics that are required by the accrediting agency for the nation's schools of business (The American Assembly of Collegiate Schools of Business). The text is suitable as well for the introductory production planning and control course in an industrial engineering curriculum.

The five chapters on production and inventory management (Chapters 2, 3, 4, 5, and 6) present, in an integrated fashion, much of the material covered in the five exams leading to professional status as a Certified Production and Inventory Manager (CPIM). The CPIM exams and certification are administered by the American Production and Inventory Control Society.

The book covers standard topics of modern P/OM, but its modes of presentation are a bit different. Four aspects of the book's style of presentation are:

1. A distinction between operations and operating resources, and a central model carried forward through the book to reiterate the distinction and integrate the chapters.
2. Depth of presentation.
3. A blend of science and practicality.
4. Application-oriented problems and cases that help students to relate, to integrate, to discover, and, in general, to gain useful insights.

A bit more may be said about each of these aspects of the book's style.

Distinctions and integrative model

Some years ago an article entitled "The Resources Management Movement: The Coming Death of Production Management Education" appeared in the *Academy of Management Journal*. It was written by a doctoral student named Richard Schonberger. The field has not developed in quite the naive way prophesied in the article. But develop it has! And toward resources management. *Material* requirements planning, *capacity* requirements planning, *resource* requirements planning, and Wight's broader notion of *manufacturing resource* planning—these developments made the 1970s an era of change in

P/OM that seems unparalleled unless one goes back to the Taylor and Gilbreth era.

Resources, or means, or capacity management has received increasing attention in P/OM research and textbooks. This book carries the idea forward. The title emphasizes operating resources; within the book the functions of operating resources management are grouped to comprise about half of an operations management model—a model that serves as a focal point for each chapter.

Depth

The typical P/OM course includes a sizable breadth of topics, concepts, and techniques. P/OM textbooks have gotten fatter, and instructors must either selectively omit a number of topics or find themselves flitting from topic to topic too quickly for students to attain mastery. My way of dealing with the problem has been *(a)* to leave out what seems less essential and *(b)* to treat what is essential in more depth than there is usually room for in P/OM books.

Leaving out topics requires making some difficult choices, and the responsibility for any poor choices is all mine. If I followed a principle in making choices about topical coverage, the principle probably was that production/operations management is not the same as operations research (OR). Other recent P/OM textbooks also seem to have steered away from OR. One reason is improved understanding of the uniqueness of P/OM. Another reason is that to an increasing extent OR has become an early tool course in business and engineering curricula.

Added depth of coverage largely concerns *reasons* for using or not using a given concept or technique. Effort is made not to oversell P/OM concepts and techniques, but rather to show the need for careful choice and for fitting the technique to the situation. A P/OM course is a *management* course, and when and where to use a managerial technique seem to warrant space in the course.

Science and practicality

This book gives little emphasis to the art of operations management. Artfulness is probably a blend of instinct, common sense, and aptitude in the experienced operations manager. More suitable for study in a book is the science of operations management. By science we do not mean mathematical models or algorithms. Those have an important but not an exclusive place in this book. Rather, the science of operations management is a systematic approach. A systematic approach may employ mathematical models, algorithms, heuristics, or procedures, and the chapters include a mix of all of these. In some chapters mathematical approaches dominate because the approaches have been proven to work in the firm; Chapter 9, Quality Assurance, is a good example. By contrast, proven procedural approaches dominate in Chapter 8, Methods, Processes, and Work Measurement: The subject matter of that chapter is nonmathematical (beyond basic arithmetic) but highly systematic.

Like most recent P/OM books, this one considers the delivery of services as well as the manufacture of goods. Better understanding of manufacturing management has led us to a better understanding of what *service* operations management is—and is not. We know, for example, that all of the P/OM *functions* apply to both services and manufacturing. But many of the sophisticated *techniques* of manufacturing management do not apply in the services environment, except by force fit. There is little to be said about services in a discussion of, say, material requirements planning, because MRP plans manufacturing inventories. For a different reason, there is not much to be said about services in a chapter on quality assurance. While quality is often of the essence in services, formal QA techniques (such as statistical quality control) require objective measures of quality. In services, measures of quality are not only subjective opinions, but they must also be gleaned from clients/customers with a varying willingness to be randomly sampled. On the other hand, a sizable number of P/OM techniques are useful in both manufacturing and services. For example, in Chapter 2, Demand Forecasting and Order Acceptance, services and manufacturing examples are given nearly equal weight.

Application-oriented problems and cases   The problems at the ends of chapters are a mixture of types, but in general they emphasize realistic applications. Many have multiple parts, just as problems in a real organization do. The problems are grouped by topics, and some are presented in ways that permit multiple answers; with only one answer some students may choose not do their own work, which compromises the value of doing the assignment.

I would like to acknowledge those who contributed ideas and other support to the book. First, I want to thank University of Nebraska colleagues who provided advice and criticism: Sang Lee, Gary Green, Les Digman, and Paul Wyman. I am most indebted to five gentlemen who, in reviewing the manuscript, set me straight on numerous key issues: Ed Davis, University of Virginia; Russ Morey, Western Illinois University; Jim Dier, University of Texas; Roy Williams, Memphis State University; and John Anderson, University of Minnesota. I also thank Bob Hall, Indiana University, for sharing with me some of the lastest thinking of the Repetitive Manufacturing Group of APICS; and Ray Lankford, Plossl and Lankford, Inc., for his helpful advice on capacity planning.

The office staff—Joyce Anderson, Jane Chrastil, and several others—also deserve thanks. They not only met tight typing schedules but also made artful sense out of many of my crude drawings.

Finally, my most sincere appreciation goes to my wife, Nancy, who begrudged none of my efforts. She encouraged me all the way. Really, she did.

Richard J. Schonberger

A NOTE TO THE STUDENT

What can you, the student, expect to learn about operations management by using this basic operations management textbook? The following provides a general idea.

After completing your studies, you should:

Thoroughly understand that . . .
  Every organization has an operations function—transformation of operating resources into goods or services.
  Successful operations are meticulously planned and controlled.

Have a general knowledge of the components of the operations function:
  Translation of item demand into master schedules, process plans, and detailed schedules.
  Translation of aggregate demand into plans for fixed capacity (plant and equipment) and adjustable capacity (labor, materials, and tools).
  Maintenance and control of operating inputs and outputs.

Clearly understand how and where quantitative models (most of which you have learned about in previous studies) can be helpful to operations management staff.

Have a working knowledge of the large variety of procedural models that are unique to the operations management field—for example, order-processing procedures, material requirements planning, statistical quality control, time standards, and assembly-line balancing.

Be easily able to identify the major types of operations—repetitive, job, project, and hybrids—and have a general understanding that operations management tools and techniques are not universal but depend on type of operation.

contents

Operations management
Planning and control of operations
and operating resources

Introduction to operations/operating resources management

ADVANCE PLANNING   ACTION PLANNING   CONTROL

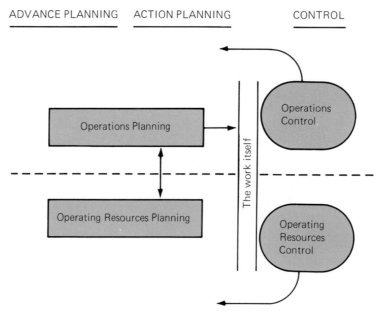

CHAPTER 1
Functions of operations/operating resources management

Part One, the introduction to this book, consists of a single chapter, Chapter 1, on the functions of operations/operating resources management. A dashed horizontal line in the chart on the opening page of Chapter 1 divides operations management from operating resources management. The distinction is emphasized in the book. Operations *are the dominant objectives. Any tendencies of* operating resourses *providers to pursue their own parochial interests are disruptive. Operating resources serve no purpose other than support for operations objectives: providing goods and services.*

The chart on the opposite page for Part One indicates that operations planning and operating resources planning each divide into an advance-planning and an action-planning zone. Operating plans emerge from the action-planning functions. The operating plans (planning package) are forwarded, and the work itself begins. The control zone on the right side of the chart refers to control over operating outputs and resource inputs. Information for control is fed back to the planners for corrective action.

FUNCTIONS OF OPERATIONS/ OPERATING RESOURCES MANAGEMENT

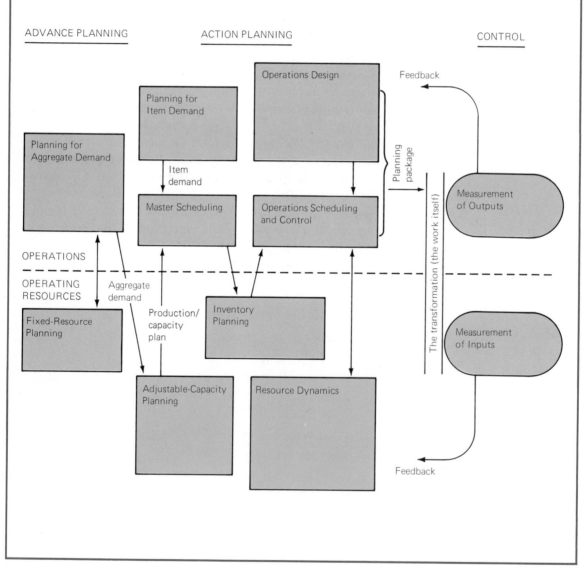

This is a book about managing ends and means. Productive *operations*, resulting in goods and services, are the ends, and *operating resources* are the means.

Much of getting jobs done today is technological. The engineer (or designer) designs the good or the service and perhaps also designs ways to provide it. The manager facilitates this. This book concerns the management role, that is, the management of operations and operating resources.

Management of operations and operating resources is a matter of planning, supervision, and control. Supervision is not included in this book, because it is a *general* function, not one that is unique to operating personnel. Being a general function, supervision is best examined in general studies in organizational behavior and personnel administration.

PLANNING AND CONTROL: TOOLS AND MODELS

Thus the focus of this book may be narrowed to planning and control. There is much to say about both. Packed into the modern course in operations management (or production management) are a large variety of planning and control tools. These studies are less conceptual than are most courses in management or administration. Instead more emphasis is placed on techniques—graphic, mathematical, and procedural.

The graphic tools are the heritage of the pioneers of scientific management, whose work began around the turn of the century. They used numbers for measurement but did not rely much on mathematical approaches. Work sequence charts are one prominent example of a graphic tool. A very general example is shown in Figure 1–1. There are many variations and many meanings assigned to the arrows and circles (or other geometric figures) in a work sequence chart, and the variations are referred to by many names, including flowchart, block diagram, network, lead-time chart, gozinto chart, and assembly diagram.

Various mathematical and statistical tools were pulled together during World War II as the foundation for operations research (OR). Linear programming and statistical probability distributions are examples of OR (mathematical) and statistical tools, respectively, that some readers may be familiar with. OR was

FIGURE 1–1
A graphic tool:
The work
sequence chart

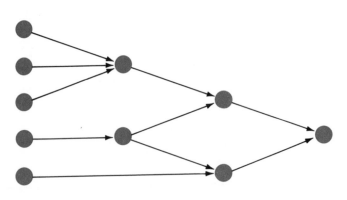

developed as an approach to highly complex decision making. Managing operations and operating resources sometimes involves complex problems of that sort. Therefore, this book incorporates a good many of the mathematical tools of the operations researcher.

The graphic and mathematical tools are often referred to as *models*. The idea is that the operations manager creates a model or likeness of the reality that is being dealt with. Mental processes in decision making may also be thought of as modeling. Operations managers who rely excessively on mental models tend to take a "fire-fighting" instead of a planning approach to their jobs.

Decision models are tangible and explicit. They provide a vehicle for a planning approach to operations management. This is normally desirable, because one may reflect on an explicit model at some length without the risk and cost of trial-and-error or fire-fighting approaches. Graphs and charts provide a focal point for discussion, and mathematical models may be manipulated or "solved."

But operations management is by no means dominated by mathematical and statistical approaches. Procedural techniques, the third kind of tool, have been a prime focus for operations management since antiquity. Major works such as building the pyramids surely owe much of their success to clever people who developed standard procedures for performing the operations and for providing resources.

Procedural techniques are standard routines or sets of decision rules directed toward improving the efficiency of recurring operations. In some industries these are commonly known as standard operating procedures, or "SOPs." Computer programmers refer to them as algorithms. Indeed as we automate recurring operations, the first step is to define the operations in plain English as SOPs; tighten the logic, and you have decision rules; structure the decision rules, and you have algorithms; finally the algorithm may be programmed in a computer language.

An inventory procedure might be to reorder when stock-on-hand drops below a day's supply. A purchasing procedure might be to advertise for bids when the order is for over $1,000. Sets of procedures may be strung together to guide the accomplishment of a complex or multistep task. There are general classes of procedures that tend to work in a wide variety of organizational settings. Therefore, standard procedural approaches may be studied in a book on operations management and may be custom-tailored to fit a given work situation.

Sometimes it is possible to try out a set of procedures using numbers to represent work activities or resources. The procedures may be changed and tried again to see what procedural set works best—using numbers rather than real work flows and real resources. This way of testing procedures is known as simulation, and when many numbers are needed to simulate properly, computer-assisted simulation may be used.

Decision models and procedures serve to simplify or "routinize" the operations management function. Demands for the attention of higher-level operations managers are overwhelming unless decision making can be made somewhat routine. Application of many of the routines—graphs, math models, procedures—may be assigned to lower-level employees. These include lower-paid managers, staff professionals, technicians, clerks, and operators. The result is fewer gaps in operations management, and at a lower cost than the pay rate of the manager ultimately responsible. The goal is better management at lower cost.

Planning and modeling are associated with the notion that management may often be treated as a science. While there is still much art in management, the artful side resists pinning down. Management science is more amenable to study and is especially well developed in the operations side of the organization. Therefore the focus in this book is on models for operations planning and control and operations management as a science.

FUNCTIONS OF THE ORGANIZATION

Managing operations and operating resources is one function found in any organization. There are other equally important functions. One way of looking at the whole organization is that of Figure 1–2.

It is common to look at organizations—any organizations—as having three basic functions that must be managed. As is shown in Figure 1–2, these are money, demand, and operations. These are said to be *line* functions. They tend to be the first departments that form when an organization grows large enough to departmentalize. They may be known as the accounting department, the marketing department, and the production department. Other departments that form later are generally regarded as *staff* departments. They provide advice and support for the line departments. Typical staff departments include personnel, quality control, engineering, purchasing, production control, and information systems.

Why should money, demand, and operations be basic but not, say, personnel or engineering? Consider this illustration. Suppose you buttonholed an employee at random coming out of a place of business and asked, "What is the purpose of this business?" The reply might well be, "To make a profit." Or it might be, "To satisfy a customer demand." Or it might be, "To produce

FIGURE 1–2
Basic or generic (line) departments

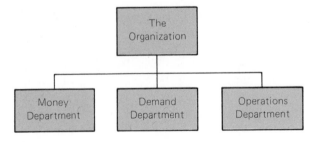

products or services." These replies relate to money, demand, and operations. It is far less likely that the reply would be, "To employ people"—a personnel function—or, "To design products and services"—the engineering function. The latter may more reasonably be considered as supportive—hence staff rather than line.

Figure 1–3 shows the three basic functions as pieces of the total "management pie." A gray area is shown where managing operations overlaps with managing money on the one hand and managing demand on the other.

Finance and accounting concern managing money. This includes assessment of proposals to invest in operating resources. The focus is on finding proposals that maximize return on investment or net dollar benefits. Managers of operating resources also must assess investment proposals, but from a narrower perspective. They deal with productive capacity and capability, with efficiency of the asset, and with cost minimization. The focus in this book will be more on those factors and less on profitability for the organization as a whole. This serves to minimize duplications with courses in finance and accounting.

The marketing function involves managing demand. This includes planning the mix of goods and services. This means planning which products, how many of each, and when they are to be available. The same questions face managers of operations and operating resources, but the emphasis is different. From the marketing standpoint the question is, "What products will the customer want?" From the operations standpoint the question is, "What customer demands are within our capacity to produce?" With those natural differences in focus, studies in operations need not duplicate studies in marketing.

FIGURE 1–3
The total "management pie"

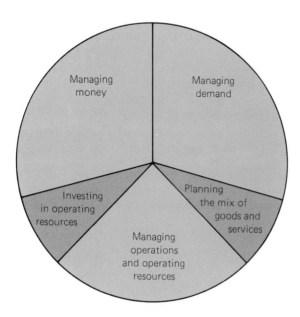

OPERATIONS AND OPERATING RESOURCES MANAGEMENT FUNCTIONS

Twenty years ago there were predecessors of this kind of textbook with titles like *Industrial Management* and *Manufacturing Management*. Later the term *production management* became more common.

Concepts and techniques for managing production in factories have been found to be useful in government and services as well. A journal article, "Production-Line Approach to Service," discusses an example.[1] The author describes the thorough use of planning and control techniques in producing McDonald's hamburgers. Today the applicability of operations management techniques in government and services is widely recognized, and such applications are found in all the chapters of this book.

With the newer emphasis on any kind of work, not just manufacturing, the terminology has changed. Production sounds too much like manufacturing. The more neutral term *operations* is being used increasingly. The management task of concern here, then, is management of operations, which includes management of operating resources.

There is a reason for keeping in mind the distinction between operations (ends) and operating resources (means). A brief story may help to illustrate. The author worked for a time in various planning and analysis jobs for the U.S. Navy. The jobs entailed numerous orientations and interviews with high-level managers of shore-based commands. Many of these meetings began with a commanding officer or department head stating the mission of the command, which was always, "Support the fleet." Many of the managers kept placards on their desks or walls proclaiming the same simple message. Keeping this message in prominent view helped avoid mixing up priorities in the vast bureaucratic organization that is the U.S. Navy. The thousands of people in these shore-based commands were to understand that they serve the fleet, not the other way around. They serve the fleet largely by helping to provide operating resources, but the operating resources people are the first to go if there is a budget cut or if they serve poorly.

When the distinction between operations functions is widely understood, there are likely to be more harmonious working relationships among operations management people. It becomes less likely that a foreman will say to a plant engineer or buyer: "Wait a minute. Aren't you supposed to be helping me?"

Functional model

It is not reasonable to put the management-of-operations chapters in one part of this book and the management-of-operating-resources chapters in another. The operations planning and control sequence seems to dictate that the topics be intermixed. This planning and control flow pattern and chapter coverage is represented in Figure 1–4.

---

[1] Theodore Leavitt, "Production-Line Approach to Service," *Harvard Business Review*, September–October 1972, pp. 45–52.

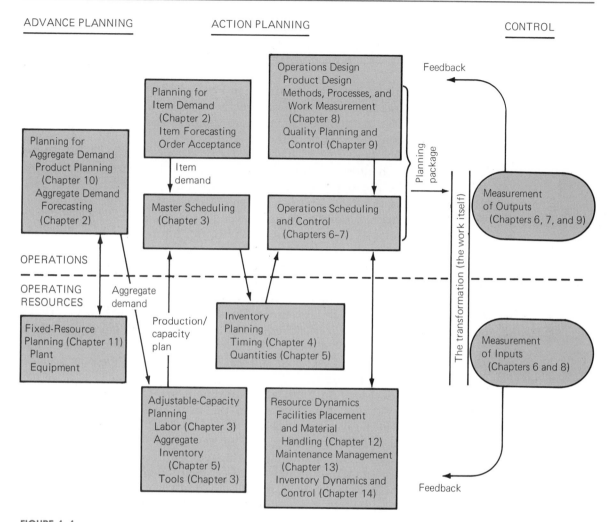

ADVANCE PLANNING   ACTION PLANNING   CONTROL

FIGURE 1-4
Operations/
operating
resources
management—
Functional
model

The figure is referred to as a functional model of operations/operating resources management.[2] Those functions that are best associated with operations are above the horizontal dashed line; those best associated with operating resources are below the line. The functional model is discussed in general terms and then in more detail below.

The functions, in blocks, are connected by arrows. The arrows represent certain key information flows. Vertically the functions group into zones of

---

[2] It is tempting to refer to Figure 1–4 as a model of the operations/operating resources management *system.* The temptation is resisted because the term *system* should probably be reserved for an operating entity, not a set of functions. The model in Figure 1–4 is far too abstract to be put to use as a system of management.

advance planning, action planning, and control. Advance planning is longer range and strategic. Action planning is shorter range and tactical. Control involves keeping a close match between the work itself and the advance and action plans.

The arrows in the center of the model in Figure 1–4 include the operations management functions that are most directly involved with the flow of goods and services. The planning becomes more detailed and complete as action planning functions take place, in the general sequence shown by the arrows. Those center functions in the chart are covered early in the book as Part Two (including Chapters 2 through 7). The operations design function is shown in a block at the upper right in the figure. Operations design (which is Part Three, Chapters 8 and 9) includes designs of product, process, and quality. These designs may be developed upon acceptance of customer orders. They may also be developed in advance and filed away for future use, which improves service to customers by cutting out design time before production can begin. Thus, operations design is not shown as part of the detailed operations planning sequence in the center of Figure 1–4.

Advance planning, at the left in the model, concerns strategic planning of the product line and fixed resources (Part Four, Chapters 10 and 11). These strategic plans are approved infrequently, and their implementation often takes years. They are not directly related to flows of goods and services, but they set limits on the kinds of goods and services the organization may provide for months or years to come.

Long-range decisions on plant and equipment are followed by decisions on location, layout, and handling within the plant, which are taken up in Chapter 12 (of Part Five, Resource Dynamics). Resource dynamics involves the life cycle of operating resources: acquisition, deployment, maintenance, and disposal. Chapter 13, Maintenance Management, covers maintenance of plant and equipment. Acquisition (purchasing), maintenance (care and storage), and disposal of materials and tools are examined in Chapter 14. (But dynamic planning for labor, the other operating resource, is left to personnel-oriented textbooks.) Resource dynamics must dovetail with detailed operations schedules; that is, the operating resources must be delivered when they are needed in productive operations.

The control zone at the extreme right in Figure 1–4 includes measurement of outputs and measurement of inputs. These measurements provide data for comparing actual outputs and resource usage with planned outputs and inputs. Measurement data are fed back to the planners, who may decide to adjust the plans. Since measurement is closely related to planning, measurement and control are included in the relevant planning chapters (Chapters 6 through 9).

Not shown in Figure 1–4 are informational links with other major functions such as finance and marketing. To do this would require a complicated grand model of informational links to all sectors. But ties to other major functions are discussed from time to time in the book.

Descriptions of functions

Each of the blocks in the functional model is considered separately below. A number of terms and concepts are briefly introduced and may be a lot to comprehend at this point. But the terms, the concepts, and the functional model are thoroughly examined and referred to in later chapters.

Planning for aggregate demand. Planning for aggregate demand, in the upper left of the functional model is the function that sets operations management in motion. The function consists of planning a line of goods and services for which there is or will be sufficient demand. Product planning has to do with types of goods and services, and aggregate demand forecasting has to do with quantities.

Fixed-resource planning. The downward arrow between the leftmost blocks in Figure 1–4 indicates that aggregate demand triggers fixed-resource planning. The logic is simple: There is no sense in laying out capital for plant and equipment without customer demand for the goods and services that those fixed resources might produce. But the arrow is two-headed. An existing organization already has its plant and equipment, and the organization seeks a volume of business that will amortize the costs of those fixed resources. Thus, the upward-pointing arrowhead tells us that the firm should develop products and generate demand that match the capabilities of existing plant and equipment.

Adjustable-capacity planning. Aggregate demand refers to demand for a group of products that share a certain group of operating resources, such as a machine shop. The adjustable resources (e.g., labor, materials, and tools) in the group of operating resources may be planned for on the basis of an aggregate demand forecast, usually for a period of a few months. (While labor, materials, and tools may be built up or depleted within a few months, fixed resources—plant and equipment—often take years to place in service.) The adjustable-capacity plan (see Figure 1–4) may specify a number of shifts or days per week in which the plant will operate. The plan can be expressed as a percent of maximum (fixed) capacity (e.g., a capacity plan may call for the plant to operate two shifts, seven days a week, which is 67 percent of maximum—three-shift—capacity). The capacity plan may be converted to units of output, which is referred to as the production plan.

Production/capacity planning may involve analysis of various options for fitting the required production to medium-range swings in demand. Seasonal demand is a common case. Options to be analyzed may include seasonal hiring, part time, shift work, overtime, layoffs, cross-training, reassignments, subcontracting, inventory buildup, backordering, and so forth. A goal is to come up with a production/capacity plan that minimizes total capacity costs.

Inventory is shown in two places in Figure 1–4. It is shown as a resource that is planned for in the aggregate—an element of the organization's capacity plan. Inventory is also planned in detail in connection with operations to meet the master production (or services) schedule.

Planning for item demand. Item demand refers to specific models, styles, sizes, and so forth, of goods and services. Detailed operations planning cannot go far without some degree of planning for item demand. Item demand consists of customer orders and/or a forecast of customer orders. Operations managers have to accept, modify, or deny customer orders in the light of other orders already stacked up; this is the order-acceptance part of planning for item demand. And goods may be produced in anticipation of customer orders; anticipating customer orders is the purpose of item forecasting.

Master scheduling. The master schedule shows the plan for timed completions of end products or services or major modules for which there is demand. In Figure 1–4 item demand is shown as a necessary input to master scheduling. In the model the arrow labeled "production/capacity plan" is intended to show that the master schedule is limited by capacity.

Inventory planning. For some human services operations there is little inventory to plan. But for some goods producers inventory planning is a major activity. The end products or modules found on the master schedule may divide into a variety of subassemblies and parts, which must be planned to be available at the right times (timing) and in the right amounts (quantities).

Operations scheduling and control. Every part, subassembly, and assembly is a separately planned order. The orders may be scheduled and controlled as jobs, lots, batches, or repetitive production runs. The model of Figure 1–4 shows three inputs into operations scheduling and control: the inventory plans for the items to be scheduled and controlled, an indication (from resource dynamics) of availability of resources, and operations design information.

Operations design. Operations design includes design of the product or service; design of methods, processes, and work measurement; and design of quality planning and control activities. Design of the product or service is largely an engineering design function or its counterpart in services (e.g., a dietitian in food service). For purposes of this book, engineering design is not separately discussed but is assumed as an external input to operations planning.

Figure 1–4 shows that operations design information and operations schedules comprise a planning package. The planning package is dispatched to the work force, and transformation of inputs into outputs begins. As the work proceeds, it is measured (see the two measurement blocks at the right in the model) and compared with the plan. These are the control functions. When plans go awry, revised plans must be issued or supervisors must employ motivational techniques to get back on course. This may be called a control cycle, with plans fed forward and progress information fed back so that revised plans may be fed forward and progress information fed back, and so forth, until the work is completed.

The lower feedback loop in Figure 1–4 represents information feedback on usage of inputs or resources. For example, there might be feedback on waste and idleness. This is a special concern if the resource is costly (e.g., platinum or a computer). We should keep in mind that the upper feedback loop, which refers to operations outputs, is more vital, because ends—on-time production with good quality—take precedence over means.

Resource dynamics. Operating resources—plant, equipment, tools, labor, and materials—have a life cycle. They are acquired, deployed, maintained (or simply stored), and eventually disposed of. (In the case of labor, the terms are *hiring, assigning, training,* and *releasing,* but dynamic planning for labor is omitted in this book.) A diagram of the life cycle is shown below.

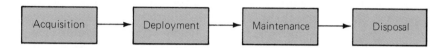

The life-cycle stages are referred to in Figure 1–4 as resource dynamics. There is a two-headed arrow between resource dynamics and scheduling. This signifies the need for resource deliveries to dovetail with operations schedules. Included in upcoming discussions of resource dynamics are plant location, plant layout, and material handling. These are related in that they are each concerned with minimizing resource-movement distance and cost. Other topics are maintenance of equipment and inventory dynamics and control, which includes purchasing, receiving, storage, and disposal.

OPERATIONS MANAGEMENT ENVIRONMENTS

The operations management environment is found widely in society. There are operations management environments at different levels in the organization, for different types of operations, and run by different types of people. These three aspects of the operations management environment—levels, operations, and people—are considered next.

Levels

The functional model of Figure 1–4 is intended to be general enough to apply to any organizational unit. Every organizational unit and subunit has its own operations to perform and its own particular operating resources to manage. A personnel department, for example, has a line of services that it offers. Personnel services should be properly planned and forecasted in the aggregate and by type; resource support should be carefully planned and managed; operational methods, timing, and scheduling should be developed; and systematic feedback on quantity, quality, and resource usage should be established. The same goes for a marketing department, an engineering department, or any other department.

Operations

While the functional model is general, the decision models and analysis techniques of operations management are not. They depend on types of operations. For example, certain models and techniques apply to high-volume, or *repetitive,* production. Much of goods manufacturing is of this type. At the opposite extreme are the fine arts and crafts. The artist and the craftsman do nicely without the aid of operations management models and analytical techniques.

A builder is neither a repetitive producer nor an artist, although we often desire that our buildings include some artful or unique features. There is a need for better management of such partly unique endeavors. Large-scale endeavors of this type are known as *projects;* for example, construction projects and research and development (R&D) projects. If small-scale, they are known as *jobs;* for example, painting a room or performing surgery on a patient.

Besides the three basic types of production—repetitive, project, and job—there are two notable hybrids: One is what some refer to as *job-lot* production, a hybrid of job and repetitive operations that is important in both consumer and industrial products manufacturing. The second is what we shall call (for lack of a simpler term) *limited-quantity large-scale* production, a hybrid of project and repetitive operations. The three basic and two hybrid types of operation are diagramed, with examples, in Figure 1–5. In the following discussion of the figure a few other terms are introduced. A variety of terms are necessary to distinguish among the great diversity of processes and operations, products and services, and firms and industries.

FIGURE 1–5
Five types of operations

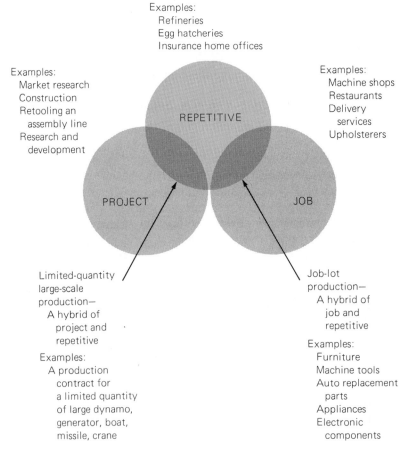

Examples:
Refineries
Egg hatcheries
Insurance home offices

Examples:
Market research
Construction
Retooling an
   assembly line
Research and
   development

REPETITIVE

Examples:
Machine shops
Restaurants
Delivery
   services
Upholsterers

PROJECT

JOB

Limited-quantity
large-scale
production—
   A hybrid of
   project and
   repetitive

Examples:
   A production
   contract for
   a limited quantity
   of large dynamo,
   generator, boat,
   missile, crane

Job-lot
production—
   A hybrid of
   job and
   repetitive

Examples:
Furniture
Machine tools
Auto replacement
   parts
Appliances
Electronic
   components

Repetitive. Three examples of repetitive operations are given in Figure 1–5: refineries, egg hatcheries, and insurance home offices. Processing large volumes of the same type of insurance policy application or claim form is surely a repetitive operation, and the insurance example is listed in order to show that services providers as well as goods producers can be classed as repetitive. But repetitive goods production is far more common. An enormous variety of goods are repetitively produced, and it is instructive to consider two subtypes of repetitive operations.

While refineries and egg hatcheries are both repetitive, they differ in an important way. Refining operations deal with a material that pours. Egg hatcheries have procedures to assure that the material does not pour! In statistics studies there are terms to describe things that do or don't pour. Things that pour are said to be *continuous* variables, and they may be counted in fractional parts. Things that do not pour are said to be *discrete* variables, and they are counted only in whole units.

Firms that process materials that pour are often referred to simply as the *process* industry (short for continuous-flow process). Liquids, gases, grains, flakes, and pellets are made by the industry. Makers of nails, toothpicks, pens, and even flashlight batteries sometimes consider themselves part of the process industry. Such products may be planned, scheduled, counted, and controlled by volume rather than by unit or piece. The process industry tends to be highly capital intensive. Refineries and chemical plants, for example, are highly mechanized. Labor is a small portion of product cost; plant and equipment (capital) is a large portion of cost. In this type of operation there are relatively few day-to-day production control problems, but there is important advance planning of fixed resources to be done.

Repetitive production of discrete items is planned, scheduled, counted, and controlled by natural unit or piece. A wide variety of products are of this type. Some, like eggs, require much handling but little processing. Others, like chairs and circuit breakers, require extensive parts fabrication followed by assembly into finished goods (the *fabrication/assembly* industry). Discrete production operations tend to require more human assistance and so may not be as highly mechanized as continuous operations. Many products, like spaghetti and noodles, are in an early state of continuous flow but later are chopped or formed into pieces and packaged in discrete units.

The method of counting or measuring materials—continuously or discretely—is of importance in a few spots in this book. But the circle labeled *repetitive* in Figure 1–5 is not divided into a continuous zone and a discrete zone, because the figure's main purpose is to type by size and volume rather than by method of counting. Job operations, considered next, are low-volume in contrast to high-volume repetitive operations.

Job. Examples of job operations in Figure 1–5 are machine shops, restaurants, delivery services, and upholsterers. That three of the four are services providers is deliberate, because the services sector is mostly job-oriented. Repetitive processing of insurance forms, discussed earlier, is an uncommon exception. Job shops are also plentiful in the goods manufacturing sector. One type of industrial job shop makes special parts in small volumes for assembly into final products. Industrial job shops also repair equipment and make tooling. While standardization (to the point of automation) is an aim in repetitive operations management, flexibility is essential in job operations management, because the mix of jobs changes daily, hourly, or even more often.

Project. Projects are large in size: A single project typically takes months or years to complete. Repetitive production of a product may also run for months or years, but each repetitively made unit is completed in minutes, hours, or days. Both job and project operations are low-volume endeavors (a project is usually unique—a unit of one), but projects are large, whereas jobs are small.

Examples of projects in Figure 1–5 are a market-research project, a construction project, a project to retool an assembly line, and a research and development (R&D) project. In the project environment, the total number of projects is usually small, but each is composed of a large, diverse mix of small jobs or activities to be accounted for.

Limited-quantity large-scale. The shaded zone of intersection between repetitive and project in Figure 1–5 represents the hybrid, limited-quantity large-scale operations. The listed examples are production contracts for a limited quantity of large dynamo, generator, boat, missile, or crane. Since multiple units are produced, this is not the same as project production. The quantity is not large enough to settle into a standardized operations management routine, as in repetitive production.

Job-lot. The interface between repetitive and job is an extra-special case. It is sometimes called job-lot production. Most goods-producing firms fall into that zone of overlap. Within the important zone are three kinds of goods producers:

1. Those that *make to stock* intermittently. Intermittent means off and on (rather than highly repetitive). Each successive lot may be for a different product or a different model, style, or size. Lots of each product can be planned and scheduled, perhaps in rotation, based on rates of depletion of the firm's *stock* of each item. Some appliance manufacturers make their own brand-name goods in this manner.

2. Those that *make to order* in quantity. Quantities are rather large but limited (not highly repetitive). Planning and scheduling may not be done very far in advance since the producer depends on an uncertain flow of customer *orders*, as in job operations. Some electronic component producers operate in this enviornment.

3. Those that *make parts to stock* and *assemble to order*. Furniture and machine-tool manufacturers are good examples. They usually stock frames and subassemblies, which are assembled in various patterns based on customer preference when orders are booked.

Combinations of the above three environments are common. For example auto-replacement parts producers usually make their own brand-name goods to stock and also bid on large orders in which another supplier's brand name will be used. (A strategy is to bid low when outside orders are needed and to bid high or not bid otherwise.)

Planning and control requirements. The five types of operations that have been described differ mainly in *volume* of units processed and *size* of the operation to produce the unit or units. The volume-size combinations seem important for our purposes, because each of the five resulting types of operation calls for a rather different set of planning and control techniques. The specific techniques are taken up throughout the book. A few summary remarks about them follow.

1. Repetitive operations require elaborate advance planning but are comparatively easy to control. Simple, inflexible rules and rather rigid standards of performance will suffice.
2. Job-oriented operations are variable from job to job. Waiting lines are common, and priority-ordering schemes are needed. It is necessary to keep a variety of excess resources on hand to handle short-run changes.
3. Project-oriented operations change as the project progresses, and there are large numbers of operations in progress at any given time. Planning and control of sequence of operations are critical.
4. Limited-quantity large-scale production requires controls to keep track of the progress of units in various stages of completion. Scheduling should allow for learning improvements from one unit to the next.
5. Job-lot operations involve standard components which are steadily monitored. Major periodic shifts from one end product to another related end product call for careful planning to translate end products into exact needs for components.

People

In very small organizations a single operating manager may have responsibility for virtually all of the functions in Figure 1–4. At the other extreme, in very large organizations, especially goods producers, the operating manger may have line responsibility for the transformation and virtually nothing else. What happens to all of the functions? They are gradually "staffed off." That is, staff specialists are hired to help plan and control operations and operating resources.

The staff specialists start out working for the line manager; as staff specialists become more numerous, they cluster into new staff (advisory) departments of their own. Figure 1–6 describes some common tendencies to staff off most of the operations management responsibilities. Production control, engineering, and quality assurance departments may inherit operations planning and progress monitoring duties. A master scheduling group may take over scheduling end products and services. Purchasing, personnel, maintenance, and other special departments form to execute plans for adjustable resources, based on aggregate planning decisions by an excecutive group. Facilities planning and capital budgeting groups perform detailed planning for fixed resources, based

FIGURE 1-6
Diffusion of line
responsibilities
("staffing off") as
organization
grows

Function	Responsibility
The transformation	Direct responsibility of the line (e.g., manufacturing or operating managers)
Planning operations and monitoring progress	Often staffed off wholly or partly to production control, engineering, and quality assurance groups
Scheduling end products and services	Usually staffed off to a master production scheduling group (which might include representatives of manufacturing, production control, marketing, and finance)
Planning and controlling adjustable resources (labor, materials, and tools)	Usually staffed off to an executive group for aggregate planning and to staff specialists (e.g., purchasing, personnel, and maintenance) for execution and control of plans.
Planning fixed resources (plant and equipment)	Usually staffed off to high-level finance/executive committee for decisions and to facilities planning/capital budgeting specialists for detailed planning
Demand planning	Usually staffed off to high-level executive committee for planning and to product development, marketing, and forecasting groups for execution of plans

on finance and executive committee decisions. And product development, marketing, and forecasting groups perform detailed demand planning, based on executive committee guidance.

In the next section, the clustering of responsibilities into staff departments is examined further, with specific examples.

ORGANIZATION STRUCTURES FOR OPERATIONS MANAGEMENT

It would make things simple if one could point to a certain block on the organization chart and say, "That's where you find the management of operations and operating resources." No such luck. Operations/operating resources management functions are scattered about the organization chart. (Similarly, the management of people is scattered about the chart and is in no way limited to a personnel department.)

The industrial organization

Figure 1–7 is an illustration of the degree of scatter of the functions. Operations management functions and subfunctions are in the center. At the top is a typical organization chart for a goods manufacturer. (It may be a bit presumptuous to say "typical," because organization charts vary a good deal.) The departments from the organization chart are repeated around the perimeter of the operations management model. Relevant department activities are also listed, and arrows point to allied functions within the model at the center of the chart.

Certain organizational tendencies deserve comment. The three line depart-

FIGURE 1–7: Operations management model and sample organization chart

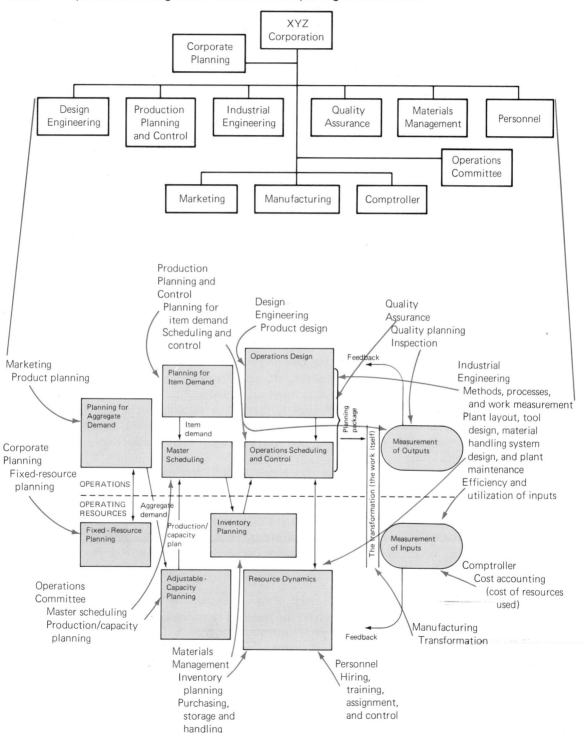

ments—marketing, manufacturing, and comptroller—are shown on the lower row of the organization chart. The main role of marketing is to assess demand and to help plan the line of products and services; the comptroller's main concern is with cost of resources; and the manufacturing superintendent's role is to implement operating plans. These three line managers also constitute the operations committee. Production/capacity planning and master scheduling require cooperative decision making by this committee.

A high-level corporate planning group has final responsibility for planning fixed resources, since plant and equipment have long-range effects on the corporation as a whole.

Six staff advisory departments are shown on the middle row of the organization chart. Design engineering is totally committed to design of products; quality assurance is concerned with quality planning and control, including inspection. Personnel has responsibilities in human resource dynamics: hiring, training, assignment, and control of the work force—topics that are generally beyond the scope of this book.

Industrial engineering (IE) has major roles in managing facilities and tools and in measuring the efficiency and utilization of operating resources. Efficiency of human resources is based on methods and time standards (work measurement) determined by IEs.

The other two departments, production planning and control (PP&C) and materials management, are wholly devoted to operations management. PP&C focuses on planning for item demand and operations scheduling and control; materials management has responsibility for inventory planning and inventory dynamics, that is, purchasing, storage, handling, and disposal. In some firms materials-management functions are included in the production control or PP&C department. (For brevity it is often named production control instead of production planning and control.) The two together comprise a sizable department. Its function centers on day-to-day production and inventory scheduling.

In general, it may be concluded that PP&C has central responsibility for short-range management of ends (outputs) and IE has central responsibility for medium-range management of means (resource inputs). But for the organization providing services instead of manufacturing goods, this does not hold true. Since service providers are not "industrial" and do not "produce," there may be no industrial engineering department and no production control department.

The service organization

Operations/operating resources management is scattered more widely about the organization chart for services than for goods organizations. A chart like that for an industrial organization (Figure 1–7) will not be presented for a services example. Service enterprises are too diverse for there to be an organization that could in any sense be considered as typical. Two particular characteristics of operations management in service organizations deserve comment.

One is that the line department providing the service may be commonly found as a staff department in a manufacturing organization. Examples are firms that provide engineering, accounting, employment, and maintenance services. Each of these is a staff specialty contributing product design and operating resources services in a manufacturing organization. They are line departments in charge of operations when they exist as services firms.

The second characteristic is that some functions that are separate specialties in manufacturing become the combined responsibility of a person or a small group in a services organization. Part of the reason is simply that services organizations are often too small for much specialization. Chefs and physicians tend to take responsibility not only for service operations themselves but also for product design, methods and processes, and quality assurance. In large services organizations operations management takes on more of a manufacturing flavor. Large banks, insurance companies, fast-food chains, and postal services hire industrial engineers and management analysts to design layouts, study methods and processes, set time standards, and compute efficiency and utilization of resources. Large data-processing shops sometimes have both a production-control and a quality-control department.

Organization structure: A compromise

Some conclusions may be drawn from the above discussions of organization structures. One conclusion is that operating organizations are not structured to suit the operations/operating resources management function. Nor should they be. Organizations are designed so that resources cluster together around common objectives, one of which is the production or operations objective. But some resources needed in operations—space, supplies, forecasting experts, operations researchers, the maintenance work force—may also serve marketing, the comptroller, personnel, and so forth. The organization is not put together by simple and obvious associations. The organization structure is a compromise.

Another conclusion is that an operations/operating resources management cluster is more likely to stand out in the organization chart of a goods than a services producer. This is reasonable: In goods manufacturing there is a lot of attention to planning and controlling the output and also the productive resources. While there is growing emphasis on these factors in service organizations, services do not have a full range of raw-material, work-in-process, and finished-goods inventories to be concerned with; catering to the customer's immediate need is dominant, and this is likely to shape organization structures in service enterprises.

A final conclusion is that organization structure is not a "given." It should be planned with care, just as operations and operating resources should be. Technologies are subject to change—sometimes rapid change, as with information processing technology. Usually, changing technology means changing responsibilities. Responsibility clusters—that is, organizational units—should therefore evolve. The tie between technology and organization structure is explored further in selected future chapters.

SYSTEMS IN OPERATIONS MANAGEMENT

At one time, operations management books (and their predecessors) paid much attention to tools, little to systems. In other words, each technique or tool was discussed separately from each other technique or tool. It tended to stand alone. One reason for separate treatments is that there are many tools, many kinds of organization, and many options. A few industries have managed to chain together some of the tools to form cohesive, efficient systems. But there is not enough room in a general textbook to present industry-by-industry operations management systems.

Over the years it has become increasingly possible to treat some of the subject matter of operations management in terms of integrated systems. A computer-based project planning and control approach, known as the program evaluation and review technique (PERT) or the critical path method (CPM), was developed in the 1950s. While PERT/CPM is not a fully integrated system of operations management, it is a step in that direction—for project operations.

An even more comprehensive systems approach has been developed for the production and inventory control area in job-lot operations. These developments began moving forward in the 1960s. A high point was the formation of the American Production and Inventory Control Society (APICS). Joseph Orlicky, Oliver Wight, and George W. Plossl, whose works are referenced in several places in this book, were instrumental in developing new computer-based technologies in production and inventory control; APICS has served as the torchbearer to spread their message throughout industry.

The term *system* has been around far longer than computers have been in use, and many fine management systems or subsystems do not involve computers. Modern production and inventory control systems, however, do rely a good deal on computer power. The keystone of the new concepts being promoted by APICS is a computer-based method called material requirements planning (MRP). There has been an outpouring of other new methods related to MRP; these include methods in production planning, master production scheduling, capacity planning and control, scheduling, dispatching, and priority planning—most of the topics in Part Two of this book.

These methods serve to join together some of the elements of the operations management function; they extend farther to forge badly needed links to the marketing function and materials suppliers. These new systems make it possible for medium and large producers to enjoy the kind of coordination that used to be possible only in smaller firms.

The APICS methods are now well known or in use in most of the larger and many of the medium and smaller goods producers in the industrial world. Considerable attention is given to these concepts in later chapters.

SUMMARY

The management of operations and operating resources supports the producing end of the business. It is one of three basic functions of any organization, the other two being marketing (or demand) management and money management. Managing operations involves planning, control, and supervision.

In this book the emphasis is on planning and control tools. These include graphic and mathematical models for decision making and procedural techniques for recurring operations. Choice of the correct tool depends partly on type of operation: repetitive, job-oriented, project-oriented, or a hybrid type of operation.

A distinction may be made between managing operations and managing operating resources. Operations are central, and providers of operating resources are hired as specialists whose purpose is to help those in operations.

Operations/operating resources management includes a number of functions. The triggering function is advance planning for aggregate demand for a line of goods and services. Advance planning of fixed resources is a closely related function.

Action planning begins with two functions: (1) planning for item demand and (2) planning production rate and adjustable capacity level, that is, labor, aggregate inventory, and tools. A master schedule of deliveries of end items may be developed from item-demand projections and the production/capacity plan. Master scheduling is followed by inventory planning, the function that determines the need for parts to go into the end items. The next function is operations scheduling and control of parts orders. Two functions that support operations scheduling and control are operations design and resource dynamics. Operations design provides for design of product, method and time, and quality control procedures. Resource dynamics assures deliveries of the right operating resources at the right time.

The control functions proceed after the planning package (operations design and schedule data) has been forwarded to the work force and the work has begun. Measurement of outputs and resource usage (inputs) is compared with plans and standards, and corrective action may be taken when there are variances.

It is unlikely that operations/operating resources management will take shape as one or two self-contained blocks of related functions on an organization chart. Organization structure is a compromise, and resources serving operations management may also serve marketing, finance, personnel, or another function. Therefore, operations management functions tend to be scattered about the organization chart to some extent.

A recent integrating influence has been the development of operations management *systems*, which are most advanced in job-lot manufacturing. These systems center on computerized material requirements planning but also extend into new methods for planning and controlling capacity and schedules.

This book is organized around five parts, the first of which consists of this introductory chapter. Part Two consists of six of the action-planning chapters, from item-demand planning and production/capacity planning through operations scheduling and control. Part Three includes Chapters 8 and 9 on operations design. Part Four includes two chapters, 10 and 11, on advance planning of product line and fixed resources. Part Five, Resource Dynamics, includes the final three chapters, 12, 13, and 14.

REFERENCES

A reference list appears at the end of each chapter. The lists provide limited help for further research. The book lists are intended to lead the student to the various parts of the library that hold material on a given topic. Thus a list might include one book with a management (HD) Library of Congress call number, one with an industrial engineering (T or TA) number, one with a management accounting (HF) number, and so forth. That will help get you to the right shelf, where there are likely to be other books on the same topic. Also included are lists of magazines, journals, and professional societies that are useful for people who have operations management interests.

For more recent books, Library of Congress call numbers are given. *These may or may not be valid for your library.* There has been a nationally organized effort to standardize Library of Congress call numbers in university and college libraries, but it has not been in operation long.

Books

Anderson, E. J., and G. T. Schwenning. *The Science of Production Organization.* Wiley, 1938.

Buffa, Elwood S. *PLAID Series Programmed Learning Aid for Production and Operations Management.* Irwin, 1973.

Carson, Gordon B., Harold A. Bolz, and Hewill H. Young. *Production Handbook.* Ronald, 1972 (TS155.P747).

Daniells, Lorna M. *Business Information Sources.* University of California Press, 1976 (HF5351.D375X).

Greene, James H., ed. *Production and Inventory Control Handbook.* McGraw-Hill, 1974 (TS155.P74).

Ireson, W. G., and E. L. Grant, eds. *Handbook of Industrial Engineering and Management.* 2d ed. Prentice-Hall, 1971 (T56.17).

Lindemann, A. J., Earl F. Lundgren, and H. K. von Kaas. *Encyclopaedic Dictionary of Management and Manufacturing Terms.* 2d ed. Kendall/Hunt, 1974 (HD19.L5).

Maynard, H. B., ed. *Handbook of Modern Manufacturing Management.* McGraw-Hill, 1970 (HD31.M377).

Periodicals (Societies)

Business Periodicals Index, an index of articles published in a limited number of business magazines and journals.

Decision Sciences (American Institute for Decision Sciences), an academic journal for all areas of business decision making.

Engineering Index, an index of articles published on engineering, including production engineering, in a large number of periodicals.

Interfaces (Institute for Management Science), a journal aimed at the interface between management scientist and practitioner.

Management Science (Institute for Management Science), an academic journal.

Production and Inventory Management (American Production and Inventory Control Society), a practitioner's journal.

Technical Book Review Index.

PROBLEMS

Note: Asterisked (*) problems require more than mimicry. They require judgment, and you should include discussion of reasons, assumptions, and outside sources of information.

Routinization

*1. It is clear that all of us use technology to "routinize" life's daily tasks: feeding, transportation, buying, bill-paying, and so on. Try to think of ways in which the *management* of those tasks may be routinized. Think in terms of models, information, and organization for planning and control. The disorganized person who doesn't plan and doesn't control is like what type of manager?

Kinds of operations

2. Listed below are various types of organizations. For each one, try to decide what its main kind of operation is: repetitive, job, project, limited-quantity large-scale, or job-lot. Discuss each.

Medical clinic	Cafeteria	Commercial fishing
Crane manufacturing	Book printing	Grocery checkout
Auditing	Petroleum refining	Farming
Architecture	Purchasing	Mowing grass on campus
Shoe repair	Bottling	Law practice
Radio manufacturing	Construction	Welding shop

*3. Why is it that operations management tends to be more highly developed in repetitive than in job or project operations?

Planning and control models

4. As organizations grow, their productive character may change, for example, from job-shop (custom) to repetitive or job-lot or from project to repetitive. Describe how this might happen for a type of organization of your own choosing. Also describe the accompanying changes in the management of operations/operating resources; that is, why would different kinds of planning and control models be called for?

Demand planning

*5. What kinds of organization/industry have a need for extremely long-range demand forecasting? Why? What kinds have a need for extremely short-range forecasting? Why?

Operations planning and control

*6. Do you put planning packages together for your own life's activities (trips, school assignments, meals, dates, etc.)? Describe each element of the planning package in terms of one of your own activities.

Capacity use rate

*7. News stories about businesses sometimes include statements like, "The firm is operating at 80 percent of capacity." What kind of planning results in the rate of capacity use? How may the rate be measured? Find a news story that discusses rate of capacity use, and summarize what you learn (or surmise) about this kind of planning. (Or, alternatively, telephone a local manufacturing firm to learn what you can about how that firm sets its capacity use rate.)

Feedback   *8. What kinds of feedback is the very small business most interested in? That is, what *results* are of special interest? What kinds of feedback information are common in larger firms but not in small firms? Illustrate by referring to a particular very small firm you know of.

FIGURE 1–8: Partial organization chart, ABC Power Company

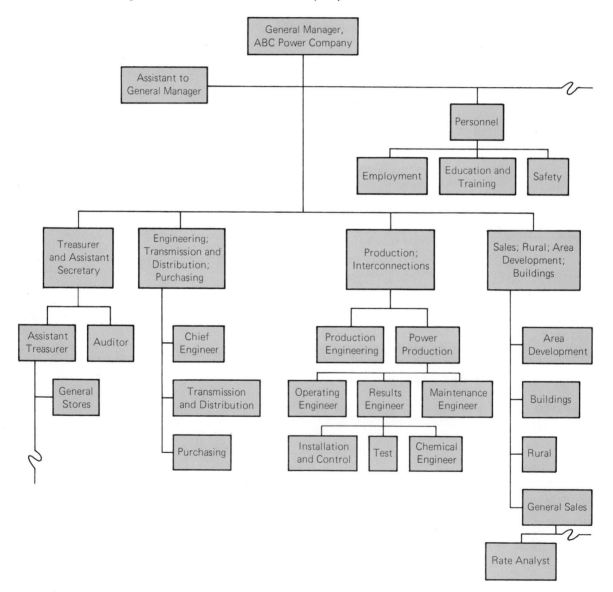

Operations management investment

*9. How does competition affect operations/operating resources management? Consider, for example, some of the most successful firms in the highly competitive fast-food, lodging, and grocery industries. What do the successful firms do in operations/operating resources management that their less successful competitors (maybe some that went under!) do not do?

Organization structures

*10. Think of five diverse examples of nonprofit organizations. For each, describe what its three line management functions (money, demand, and operations management) would consist of.

*11. Obtain an organization chart that shows enough detail to identify the operations/operating resources management functions. Identify those functions and explain your reasoning in a way similar to the way in which this was done in the chapter discussion of organization structures. Do you believe the organization structure properly provides for clustering of common operations management responsibilities? Why or why not?

*12. A partial organization chart for a company that provides services (instead of goods) is shown in Figure 1–8. The organization chart is for a hypothetical firm called ABC Power Company, a provider of electric power and allied services. (The chart is similar to one obtained from a real power company.) On separate paper, develop a chart similar to the chart of Figure 1–6 for a goods producer. Your task is to relate blocks on the organization chart to blocks on the functional model of operations/operating resources management (Figure 1–4). Explain your reasoning.

Production and inventory control

*13. Think of cases in which you were given exaggerated delivery promises on goods you had ordered. Why is it so common for the seller to be unable to say with reasonable accuracy when the goods will arrive? Think especially of reasons pertaining to the operations/operating resources management function.

IN-BASKET CASE*

Topic: Production Control Organization

To:

From: Plant Superintendent, Auto Accessories Corp.

None of our production control people belong to any kind of professional organization. I'm sure there is one (or some), and I wonder if we are missing anything by not having members. Please study the matter for me and write a report.

---

*Instructions for this in-basket case as well as those in each of the other chapters are as follows:

IN-BASKET CASE INSTRUCTIONS

The in-basket case is an information-search case study of a hypothetical operations/operating resources management problem assigned by your hypothetical "boss," the instructor. The assignment is a type that might appear in the in-basket of an employee in (usually) a staff position.

This is *not just* a knowledge-gaining library research project. It's a problem-solving project that requires finding information and then applying it, plus your own reasoning powers, to the problem and situation. A good study includes the following:

1. Good library work on the given management technique(s).
2. Practical information on the application (i.e., the firm, industry, situation, and/or craft).
3. Good integration of the two kinds of information ("solving the problem").

While there is no way that you can get detailed facts about the hypothetical firm you are working for, you can at least get generally available data about firms in that line of work. Think of it as a preliminary study after which detailed facts and figures could be obtained, if warranted. You can present sample calculations or arguments using the best available data. Best estimates are OK where actual data (such as costs) are unavailable, but try not to make imaginative assumptions. Also, discuss the validity of your sources of data.

Use your own wits in seeking information. Note: The boss has the course textbook on his bookshelf and thus will not be satisfied with a report that merely draws from that single source. But start by looking there before you turn to other sources, such as periodicals, indexes, handbooks, card catalogs, and local business people. To impress the boss with your thoroughness, you may wish to keep a journal of your search activities. If you can't find much, you could at least show how hard you tried.

Discussion of sources of information should be integrated with your assertions throughout the report (full citations: names, titles, dates, page numbers, etc.). This serves as authoritative support and adds credibility (as well as being needed for the company's files for possible future reference). Also, a good report is full of examples, illustrations, sample calculations, comparisons, contrasts, and so on. You should expect to become something of an expert in the matter your assignment deals with. If you interview someone, become an expert first—*before* the interview.

Your boss will tell you how long the report should be and when it is due.

Translating demand into operations

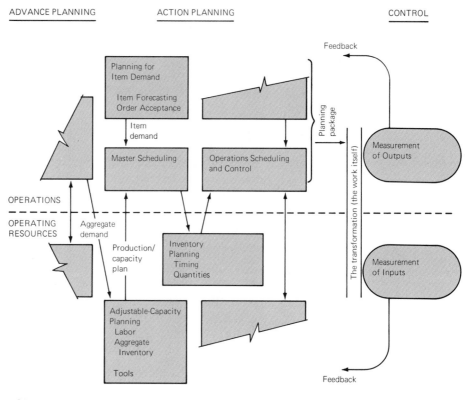

ADVANCE PLANNING

ACTION PLANNING

CONTROL

Feedback

Planning for
Item Demand

Item Forecasting
Order Acceptance

Item demand

Planning package

Measurement
of Outputs

Master Scheduling

Operations Scheduling
and Control

OPERATIONS

OPERATING
RESOURCES

Aggregate demand

Production/
capacity
plan

Inventory
Planning
Timing
Quantities

The transformation (the work itself)

Measurement
of Inputs

Adjustable-Capacity
Planning
Labor
Aggregate
Inventory

Tools

Feedback

In Part Two we begin examining each of the functions of operations/ operating resources management, specifically the action-planning functions. These functions involve the central issues in operations management—the issues that most directly relate to the flow of goods and services. Those functions are grouped in the center of the chart on the opposite page for Part Two. They are planning for item demand, adjustable-capacity planning, master scheduling, inventory planning, and operations scheduling and control—which is roughly the order of planning for the flow of goods and services. Parts Three, Four, and Five cover support functions that feed the central action-planning functions.

Three of the action-planning functions are above the dashed line in the chart on the opposite page: planning for item demand, master scheduling, and operations scheduling and control. These above-the-line functions pertain to planning the operating ends. The two action planning functions below the line, adjustable-capacity planning and inventory planning, provide for operating resources, the means. There is close interaction among the functions above and below the dashed line—a master-slave interaction, so to speak.

The five functions of Part Two are covered in six chapters. Chapter 2 on planning for item demand deals with customer demand for end products and services. For convenience, Chapter 2 also includes aggregate demand forecasting, a longer-range and more strategic type of planning. Chapter 3 covers both operating resources (capacity planning) and operations (master scheduling). A goal is to get a close match between capacity inputs and production outputs. Chapters 4 and 5 discuss inventory planning: timing of inventory orders in Chapter 4 and quantities to be ordered in Chapter 5. Inventories (parts or finished goods) are planned in order to fill the orders represented on the master schedule. The topic of Chapters 6 and 7 is scheduling and control of the work itself: fabricating and assembling the inventories that were planned for, providing customer service and so forth. Repetitive, job, and job-lot operations are discussed in Chapter 6, Operations Scheduling and Control. Special scheduling and control techniques for project and limited-quantity large-scale production are treated in Chapter 7, PERT/CPM and LOB Systems. Measurement of production outputs and resource inputs is a part of the control functions covered in Chapters 6 and 7.

chapter 2

DEMAND FORECASTING AND
ORDER ACCEPTANCE

PLANNING FOR
AGGREGATE DEMAND

Product planning

AGGREGATE DEMAND
FORECASTING

PLANNING FOR
ITEM DEMAND

ITEM FORECASTING
ORDER ACCEPTANCE

ADVANCE PLANNING   ACTION PLANNING   CONTROL

Planning for
Item Demand

Operations Design   Feedback

Planning for
Aggregate
Demand

Item
demand

Planning package

Measurement
of Outputs

Master
Scheduling

Operations Scheduling
and Control

OPERATIONS

OPERATING
RESOURCES   Aggregate
demand

The transformation (the work itself)

Fixed - Resource
Planning

Production/
capacity
plan

Inventory
Planning

Measurement
of Inputs

Adjustable -
Capacity
Planning

Resource Dynamics

Feedback

Great Expectations is the title of a novel by Dickens. Great expectations are also the reason for operating any sort of organization. In this chapter these become a question: *How great* are our expectations of demand for our products and services?

Expected demand is the sum of (1) orders already booked, entered, and accepted; and (2) the promise (forecast) of upcoming orders or sales. Expected demand may be stated in terms of items (i.e., item demand) and also in terms of logical demand groupings (i.e., aggregate demand). The forecasting of item and aggregate demand and the acceptance of booked orders are the topics of this chapter.

The importance of demand-forecasting and order-acceptance information is suggested in the chart on the chapter title page. The chart shows three types of demand information that are important to other operations management functions. The arrow pointing downward from aggregate demand forecasting represents long-range demand information. Long-range forecasts are a basis for occasional outlays of large amounts of capital for fixed resources (plant and equipment). The arrow labeled *aggregate demand* is the key information input into the adjustable-capacity planning function. Aggregate demand information indicates how much labor, inventory, and tools to stock the plant with. The arrow labeled *item demand* is one of two key inputs into master scheduling (i.e., planning the priority-order and timing of particular goods and services); the other is the arrow labeled *production/capacity plan*, which is based largely on aggregate demand.

Coordinated forecasting and order acceptance is coming to be known as *demand management*. The idea is that operations managers should play an active, not a passive, role in regard to demands on productive capacity. By involving themselves in demand forecasting and order acceptance, operations managers gain the information needed to plan capacity to match requirements.

The initial section in this chapter explains the nature of demand forecasting. The three remaining sections discuss forecasting methods, the forecasting environment, and order acceptance.

DEMAND FORECASTING

Demand forecasting is easily confused with other popular—and specialized—uses of the general term *forecasting*. Some of the various meanings of forecasting are explained below.

If you should ask a librarian for reading materials on forecasting, you should expect to receive lore on weather forecasting. That is the popular meaning of forecasting.

If you look up forecasting in the subject card catalog in a library, you will find mostly readings on economic forecasting, for example, readings on the forecasting of gross national product and disposable personal income. Economic forecasting is a second meaning of forecasting, and it has some bearing on the topic of this chapter.

A third meaning of forecasting is demand forecasting. That is the topic of concern here.

A fourth meaning is sales forecasting. This has somewhat the same meaning as demand forecasting except that the word *sales* implies private enterprise; the word *demand* is better for our purposes, since it would also apply to the public services sector. Also, marketing managers and operations managers have different outlooks: The marketing outlook is one of *sales to the customer;* the operations outlook is one of *demands for production* and for the *operating resources to produce.* (Subject card catalogs in libraries tend to include more under the sales-forecasting than the demand-forecasting designation.)

A fifth, less common use of the term *forecasting* is in phrases like "personnel forecast," "materials forecast," and "tool forecast." Those uses concern means or resources as opposed to ends, that is, the products and services. We shall avoid using forecasting in this way. Instead, when we discuss resources, the term we use will be resource *planning.*

Still other terms associated with forecasting include *time-series analysis, econometrics,* and *trend projection.* These are a few of the methods of forecasting, and they are discussed later in the chapter.

In large national corporations demand forecasting is often a three-pronged process. This is shown in Figure 2–1. The sales force produces one set of forecasting figures. Economists look at how the economy is likely to affect the organization's demand, which gives another set of figures. And statisticians or computerized statistical routines project past demand trends, thus giving a third set of figures. Then top management may review all three sets and overrule them all. It may prefer to trust its own experience and judgment. Even so, the three sets of figures would surely have helped to sharpen its judgments about future demands. Each of the three is explained below.

FIGURE 2–1
Three determinants of demand forecast

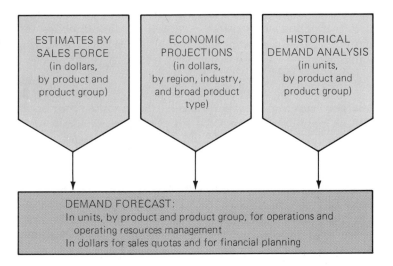

ESTIMATES BY SALES FORCE
(in dollars, by product and product group)

ECONOMIC PROJECTIONS
(in dollars, by region, industry, and broad product type)

HISTORICAL DEMAND ANALYSIS
(in units, by product and product group)

DEMAND FORECAST:
In units, by product and product group, for operations and operating resources management
In dollars for sales quotas and for financial planning

Sales force estimates

Sales force estimates are compiled partly for the purpose of setting sales quotas for the sales staff, in dollars. Managers may periodically request individual sales estimates of each salesperson. The separate estimates may be consolidated at district levels, regional levels, and national levels. Test marketing may yield further data on probable sales of certain items.

Dollar sales forecasts may be easily, though not necessarily reliably, converted into unit demand forecasts. A forecast must be in units if it is to be useful for operations and operating resources management.

Economic projection

Economic projections may also be helpful. For example, any firm offering goods and services related to homemaking surely is interested in national economic projections for housing starts. Economic projections range from educated guesses of an economist or a panel of economists to computer projections based on mathematical equations. Economic forecasting based on sets of mathematical equations processed by computers is a field known as econometrics.

The econometrician builds forecasting models by such methods as statistical regression analysis. A simple approach is to use a single regression equation. For example, suppose that farm machinery demand is to be forecasted. The econometrician tries out various possible causes of change in farm machinery expenditures. Past data on different sets of causal factors are put into a computer for regression tests. The set of causal factors that works best on past data may be used to forecast future demand. The forecast equation would have the causal variables (e.g., good crops, machinery prices, advertising) on the right side of the equation and the demand projection (the dependent variable) on the left side.

A single regression equation may not be accurate enough, because causes of demand may be complicated by interrelationships. For example, demand for machinery may indeed be affected by price and advertising, but price probably goes up when there are more advertising expenses. It may be prudent to set up and test factors that affect price, which results in a second regression equation. Perhaps a third regression equation should be set up to test causal factors affecting advertising. A system of simultaneous regression equations may emerge. A forecast of farm machinery is based on solving the simultaneous equations.

Historical demand analysis

Available data on past demand for goods and services tend to be profuse in larger firms that keep careful records. In some other organizations recorded data on past demand may be nil. This is most likely in small organizations or in small departments within larger organizations.

Where records are nil, historical demand analysis still gets done, but it is totally judgmental: The manager or department head reflects on his past experience and comes to a decision on what future demands to expect. This is likely to result in rough forecasts. Lack of accuracy in the demand forecast will surely mean idle resources at some times and failure to meet customer demands at other times. The failure of many small businessmen to keep even minimal demand records may be a key reason for business failure. The small firm, often poorly financed, can ill afford to badly misjudge demand.

If demand records are kept, statistical analysis may be used. The object is to find and to project into the future underlying patterns of demand for each product or service. This is a bit like a search for the Holy Grail. You won't find it. But in searching for it, you may expect to gain insights. In demand forecasting, this means making smaller prediction errors than would have been made without the search.

The forecasting methods discussed in this chapter are proven and widely used. It will be seen, however, that computers and statistical forecasting routines are only tools. Judgment is still the more important element. Judgment is needed to access the situation, to select the proper analysis methods, to test the reasonableness of the results, and to revise and reanalyze when necessary. This is not just a platitude that applies equally to all topics in the book. Examples and cautionary remarks throughout this chapter reemphasize the key role that judgment plays in forecasting.

HISTORICAL PROJECTION METHODS

Historical projection methods are aimed at extending past demand into the future. The projection methods discussed here are the mean, trend, seasonal, moving average, exponential smoothing, leading indicator, correlation, and simulation.

The mean, trend, and seasonal analysis methods may be used to project several periods into the future. These methods are well suited to, though not limited to, longer-term forecasting, often a year or longer. They may be used in the *rolling-forecast* mode. A rolling forecast is one that is redone or rolled over at intervals—every quarter, every six months, or every year, for example.

Moving average and exponential smoothing are used for projecting just one period at a time. They are well suited to short-term projection, typically one week, one month, or one quarter into the future. However, the next-period projection may be used (at some risk) as the projection for later periods as well. In that case, the techniques could provide long-term as well as short-term forecasts; each period they would automatically roll over. Leading indicator, correlation, and simulation may apply to short- or long-term forecasting.

In all of the methods except correlation, demand is examined on a time scale; these are often called time-series analysis methods. Several of the methods may be used to examine a given time series. This is sometimes called component analysis, because each method attempts to isolate a component of past demand.

Components of demand

Three general components of demand are shown in Figure 2–2. These components are a long-term demand pattern, a short-term demand pattern, and

FIGURE 2–2
Three
components of
demand

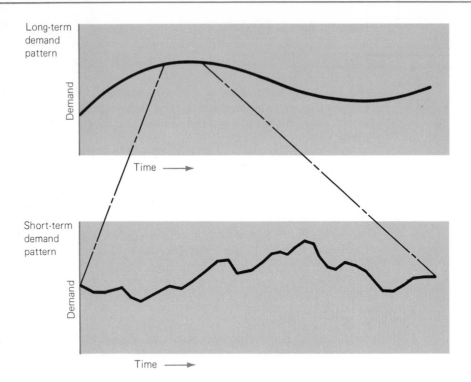

Long-term
demand
pattern

Short-term
demand
pattern

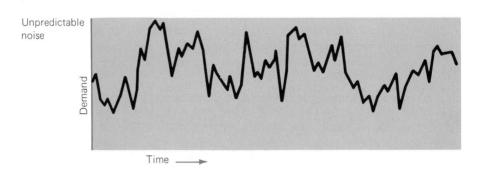

Unpredictable
noise

what may be called noise. As the figure shows, there is an underlying long-term demand pattern, a slowly changing function. Each segment has short-term ups and downs; these may be tracked by using moving average or exponential smoothing. The other demand component is unpredictable noise. The analyst would not try to predict or dissect it—just as the physicist would not try to predict or dissect electronic white noise that is everywhere in space.

Actual demand is related to forecasted demand as follows:

$$\text{Actual demand} = \text{Long-term forecast}$$
$$+ \text{ Long-term forecast error}$$
$$+ \text{ Short-term forecast}$$
$$+ \text{ Short-term forecast error}$$
$$+ \text{ Noise}$$

The forecaster attempts to cut down the forecast errors. One way is by using good analysis methods. Another is by gathering together a good data base. A third is by exhaustive processing of the data, using the analysis methods. All cost money. A firm acquires good analysis methods by hiring well-trained analysts. The data base requires a costly information system. And the processing cost, by computer or calculator, increases with thoroughness. It is easy to see that cost puts a limit on forecast accuracy. Even if there weren't these costs, there would still be forecast inaccuracy due to noise.[1]

A number of forecasting methods have been devised to reduce forecast error. Three methods of long-term forecasting are considered first. These methods—the mean, trend, and seasonal analysis—may make use of shorter-term records of actual demand. Since the long-term forecast is the aggregate of the short term, a long-term forecast may at the same time yield a shorter-term forecast. Short-term forecasts—by moving average and exponential smoothing—are considered in later sections. Since the short-term forecasts go only one period at a time, they do not show anything about the long term.

Mean

The simplest time series is the arithmetic mean. Where demand is steady and not inherently seasonal, the simple mean may be suitable for forecasting. Consider the example below.

**EXAMPLE 2–1
Data Services
and the mean**

Data Services, Inc., offers computer programming commercially. Three years of past quarterly demand, in hours of programmer time, are given in Figure 2–3. No strong trend or seasonal pattern is evident from the graph. If first-quarter demand is high one year, it looks as likely to be low the next. The same goes for the other quarters. The up-and-down movement seems random. And one would not reason that programming should be a service having some sort of seasonal demand pattern. What should the forecast be for upcoming quarters in 1979? Perhaps it should be the mean, 437. That may be the best way to minimize forecast error for so nondescript a demand.

Trend

Some would look at Figure 2–3 and see something other than the mean as the forecast basis. For example, in the last seven quarters the trend is downward. Perhaps that 7-quarter downward trend is more logical as a forecast basis than the 12-quarter mean. Perhaps the Data Services example ought to be reconsidered.

---

[1] Maybe the truth is that so-called noise represents our ignorance. Even so, it is probably composed of so large a number of causal variables that we had best treat it with benign neglect.

FIGURE 2–3
Demand
forecast by
arithmetic
mean—Data
Services, Inc.

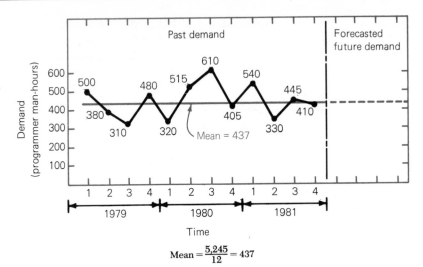

$$\text{Mean} = \frac{5,245}{12} = 437$$

Note: Do *not* assume that this forecast method is a good one for Data Services. There may be better ones.

EXAMPLE 2–2
Data Services
and "eyeball"
trends

Figure 2–4 is an "eyeball" projection of the seven-quarter trend for Data Services. The trend line is moving Data Services toward out-of-business status. The trend downward may be reasonable for the first quarter of 1982. But surely, if Data Services is a sound enterprise, business will turn upward. *This* trend line seems invalid for forecasting several periods into the future.

For a better forecast, better demand data would be helpful. Let us assume that 20 instead of 12 quarters of past demand data are available. The demand history is displayed in Figure 2–5.

Quite a different pattern emerges. The long-run trend is definitely upward. With

FIGURE 2–4
Seven-quarter
"eyeball"
trend—Data
Services, Inc.

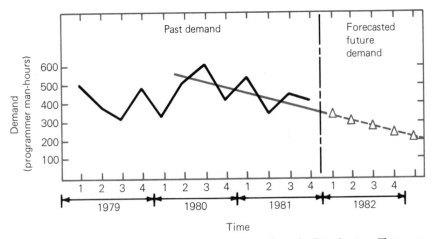

Note: Do *not* assume that this forecast method is a good one for Data Services. There may be much better ones.

FIGURE 2–5
Twenty-quarter
"eyeball"
trend—Data
Services, Inc.

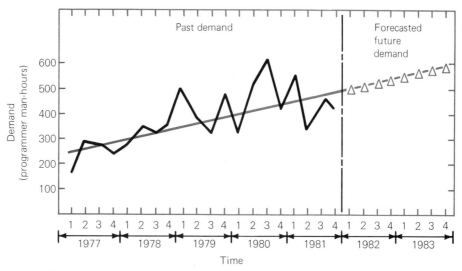

Note: Do *not* assume that this forecast method is a good one for Data Services. There may be better ones.

a straightedge, the eyeballed upward trend line is drawn and projected two years (eight quarters) into the future. The 1983 quarterly forecasts are now in the range of 500 programmer-hours instead of the 300 range resulting from only a seven-quarter trend projection (in Figure 2–4).

Another interpretation of the 20 quarters of demand data is that they describe a slow curve. Figure 2–6 shows such a curve projected by the eyeball method through 1983. The 1982–83 forecast is now between the two previous straight-line forecasts. This projection is for a leveling-off at about 450.

FIGURE 2–6
Twenty-quarter
"eyeball"
curve—Data
Services, Inc.

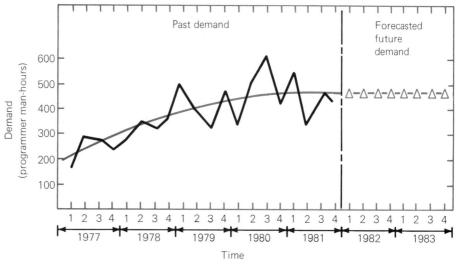

Note: Do *not* assume that this forecast method is a good one for Data Services. There may be better ones.

The curving projection looks valid. In other cases a straight-line projection may look valid. In any case the managers may use the graphic projection only to sharpen their own judgment. For example, the managers of Data Services, Inc., may have other information about their customers that leads them to a more optimistic forecast than the projected 450. Even where such outside information seems to overrule historical projection, the projection is worth doing. It is quick and simple.

Now let us turn to a method that is less quick, less simple. The reader who has studied statistics may have wondered about the crudity of the eyeball method. The precise way is to project mathematically, using regression analysis. The least-squares technique of regression analysis (see chapter supplement) results in the formula for the straight line of best fit. (The least-squares method may also be modified so that it yields a formula for a curving line of projection instead of a straight line.)

While the least-squares method is more accurate than the eyeball method, it is sometimes unnecessary. Some rules of thumb on which method to use are:

1. Use the eyeball method if only one or a small number of products/services are to be forecasted.
2. Use least squares—run on a calculator or a computer—if a lot of products/ services are to be forecasted.

While the eyeball method is generally accurate enough for something so speculative as forecasting, drawing graphs for eyeball projections is time-consuming. The eyeball method would take many hand-drawn graphs if there were a large number of products. Least squares takes a good deal of setup time, but after that it goes fast, especially with a programmable calculator or computer. Computer-based forecasting routines are advantageous in that they are generally able to print out mathematical formulas as approximations of the demand pattern, graphic projections, and tabular listings. Thus, least-squares regression is valued not for its forecasting accuracy but because it aids in routinizing some of the steps in forecasting.

Seasonal

A seasonal index is the ratio of the demand for a particular season to the demand for an average season. Thus, if demand is for 100 units in an average season and demand for the summer season is 80, the summer-season index is $80/100 = 0.8$. Some sort of averaging process is used to arrive at the 100 per season figure. The term *season* should not be limited to spring, summer, fall, and winter. The forecaster looking for seasonality may wish to consider a rainy season, a holiday season, a hunting season, or any other period that comes once a year.

Seasonal index calculations. The Metro Movers example is a good one to extend to seasonal analysis since the moving industry is known to be highly seasonal. Metro Movers' seasonal demand pattern is examined below for the four seasons, spring, summer, fall and winter. This is not quite the same as the four quarters. The first fiscal quarter is January–February–March; by contrast, the winter season is usually December–January–February. For a mover it makes more sense to use seasons than quarters because of the heavy surge in demand in June–July–August—during school vacations.

EXAMPLE 2–3
Metro Movers and seasonal indices

There is no need to look at actual demand data to know that a moving company has a seasonal demand. It is common sense. Even so, a good starting point in seasonal analysis is scrutiny of the demand graph.

The graph of past quarterly demand for Metro Movers is shown in Figure 2–7. It is clear that summer demands are by far the highest in every year. Also, fall demands are generally the lowest. The seasonal index measures how much higher and how much lower. Figure 2–8 shows calculations of seasonal indices for the 16 available past demands.

FIGURE 2–7
Seasonal demand history—Metro Movers

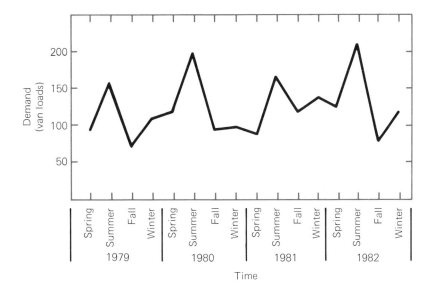

These seasonal indices are rearranged by year and season in Figure 2–9. The three values for each season need somehow to be reduced to a single index. The index for fall is steadily rising, from 0.61 to 0.73 to 0.96; that is not sufficient reason to expect it to continue to rise, especially since the other seasons do not show trends. Thus, the projections of the seasonal indices for 1983 are the means of each column.

Seasonally adjusted trends. Metro Movers may now use the seasonal indices in fine-tuning its forecasts of demand for each coming season. For example, suppose that Metro Movers expects to move 480 vans of goods next year, based on projection of the mean of past years' demands. It would be naive to divide 480 by 4 and project 120 vans in each season. Instead,

1. Divide 480 by 4 = 120 vans in an average season.
2.   120 × 0.85 = 102 vans forecasted for spring 1983.
3.   120 × 1.46 = 175 vans forecasted for summer 1983.
4.   120 × 0.76 = 91 vans forecasted for fall 1983.
5.   120 × 0.93 = 112 vans forecasted for winter 1983–84.
       Yearly total = 480

FIGURE 2–8
Seasonal index calculations—Metro Movers

(1) Time	(2) Actual demand	(3) Mean seasonal demand (basis four-period MA)*	(4) Seasonal index (col. 2/ col. 3)
Spring 1979	90		
Summer 1979	160		
Fall 1979	70	115	0.61
Winter 1979	120	125	0.96
Spring 1980	130	132	0.98
Summer 1980	200	132	1.52
Fall 1980	90	124	0.73
Winter 1980	100	114	0.88
Spring 1981	80	115	0.70
Summer 1981	170	125	1.36
Fall 1981	130	136	0.96
Winter 1981	140	147	0.95
Spring 1982	130	146	0.89
Summer 1982	210	138	1.52
Fall 1982	80		
Winter 1982	120		

* This four-period moving average is centered on the middle of a given season, that is, 1½ months into the season. It includes demands going back six months and forward six months from that point. Thus, the first figure in column 3 is based on demands for the last 1½ months of spring 1979; all of summer, fall, and winter 1979; and the first 1½ months of spring 1980. So,

$$\frac{(90/2 + 160 + 70 + 120 + 130/2)}{4} = 115$$

This is a bit cumbersome, but it assures that no one season is weighted more heavily than any other. (There is another way to get the same figures: Calculate ordinary four-period moving averages; then average each successive pair of those figures. This process is demonstrated in some other textbooks, usually under the heading "centered moving average.")

Note: Do *not* assume that this forecast method is a good one for Metro Movers. There may be better ones.

FIGURE 2–9
Summary and projection of seasonal indices—Metro Movers

		Spring	Summer	Fall	Winter	
Past	1979			0.61	0.96	
	1980	0.98	1.52	0.73	0.88	
	1981	0.70	1.36	0.96	0.95	
	1982	0.89	1.52			
Future	1983	0.85	1.46	0.76	0.93	⟵ Mean of each column

It takes a few more steps if the basic demand projection is an up or down trend instead of a level line. For example, assume that Metro Movers again projects 1983 demand at 480 vans; this time it is based on historical projection of an upward trend of about 2.5 percent per quarter. The 480 is the sum of four quarterly demands, at a 2.5 percent upward slope:

116—spring 1983
119—summer 1983
121—fall 1983
<u>124—winter 1983–84</u>
480

Now the seasonal adjustments are:

116 × 0.85 = 99 vans forecasted for spring 1983.
119 × 1.46 = 174 vans forecasted for summer 1983.
117 × 0.76 = 89 vans forecasted for fall 1983.
120 × 0.93 = 112 vans forecasted for winter 1983–84.

A comparison of the last two cases, without trend and with trend, is shown in Figure 2–10. The figure shows what might be expected: Trend effects, which are so important in the long run, tend to be overshadowed in the short run by seasonal (or other) influences.

FIGURE 2–10
Seasonal adjustment of level and upward projection— Metro Movers

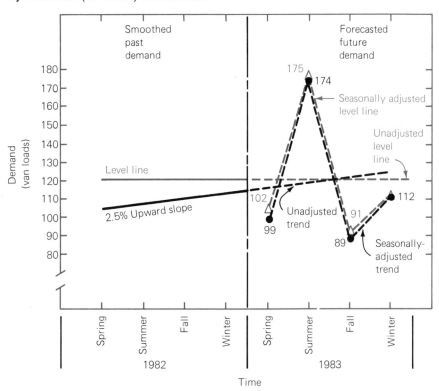

Note: Do *not* assume that these forecast methods are good ones for Metro Movers. There may be better ones.

Seasonality and "pipeline filling." Goods that are new or back in the market after interruption generally should not be forecasted based on seasonality logic. The reason is the "pipeline" phenomenon: When the product hits the market, its demand may rise slowly and then become very heavy until the wholesale/retail pipeline is filled; then demand may go slack for a time until consumers become fully aware of and respond to the product. A simple moving average (to be covered next), unadjusted for seasonality, may be the best forecasting method during this transitional period. Later, when product demand reaches a steadier state, seasonal indexing refinements may be added.

Moving average

The moving average (MA), which became popular in the 1960s, is simply the mean of a given number of the most recent actual demands. The given number may be called the time span of the MA. Like other time-series methods, the moving average smooths the actual historical demand fluctuations by reducing variation—hopefully, variation from forecast error. In an extension known as the weighted moving average, extra weight is placed on more recent actual demands in the time span. Time span, smoothing effects, and weighted MA are explained in more detail below.

Time span. The proper time span for forecasting a certain item by MA may be determined by analysis. The following example shows how.

EXAMPLE 2–4
Metro Movers and moving average

Metro Movers has good records on the number of van loads it has moved per week. A part-time student employee (S.E., for short) offers to analyze the data in order to develop a moving-average (MA) forecasting system. The manager accepts his offer.

Demand data for the last 16 weeks are shown on the left in Figure 2–11. On the

FIGURE 2–11
Demand data and moving average (MA)— Metro Movers

Week	Demand (van loads)		Three-week MA
1	6		9.0
2	8		10.7
3	13		11.7
4	11		12.7
5	11		12.7
6	16		11.7
7	11		8.7
8	8		10.0
9	7		10.7
10	15		12.0
11	10		8.7
12	11		8.3
13	5		8.7
14	9		11.0
15	12		
16	12		

Sample calculation for week 1: $\dfrac{6+8+13}{3} = 9.0$

FIGURE 2–12
Three-week
moving average
(MA) and MAD—
Metro Movers

(1) Week	(2) Actual demand	(3) Forecasted demand (three-week MA)	(4) Forecast error (col. 2 − col. 3)	(5) Absolute sum of forecast errors*
1	6			
2	8			
3	13			
4	11	9.0	2.0	2.0
5	11	10.7	0.3	2.3
6	16	11.7	4.3	6.6
7	11	12.7	−1.7	8.3
8	8	12.7	−4.7	13.0
9	7	11.7	−4.7	17.7
10	15	8.7	6.3	24.0
11	10	10.0	0.0	24.0
12	11	10.7	0.3	24.3
13	5	12.0	−7.0	31.3
14	9	8.7	0.3	31.6
15	12	8.3	3.7	35.3
16	12	8.7	3.3	38.6

$$\text{MAD} = \frac{38.6}{13} = 3.0 \text{ vans per week}$$

* *Absolute sum* means the sum of the digits only, ignoring whether they are plus or minus.

Note: Do *not* assume that this forecast method is a good one for Metro Movers. There may be better ones.

right in Figure 2–11 is S.E.'s calculation of three-week MAs. A sample calculation for week 1 is shown below the figure.

Next, S.E. calculates the forecast error that would have resulted if he had been using this MA forecast in the past. See Figure 2–12. It can be seen that the three-week MA for weeks 1, 2, and 3 becomes the forecast for week 4. Actual demand in week 4 turns out to be 11, so the forecast error is $11 - 9 = 2$. That is a shortage or underestimate of two vans for that week. Then the MA for weeks 2, 3, and 4 becomes the forecast for week 5. The forecast error is $11 - 10.7 = 0.3$. The process continues, the average moving (or rolling over) each week, dropping off the oldest week and adding the newest; hence, a moving average.

Column 5 cumulatively sums the absolute values of the forecast errors from column 4. The total forecast error, 38.6, is divided by the number of weeks, 13. The result, 3.0 vans per week, is the average or mean forecast error. In forecasting circles this measure of average forecast error is widely known as the mean absolute deviation (MAD).

Suppose that S.E. decides to try a different time span, say six weeks. The six-week MA, forecast errors, and MAD calculations are shown in Figure 2–13.

The mean error of 2.4 is better than the previous 3.0. S.E. could try other MA time spans and could perhaps reduce the error further. (In a larger firm with many products, searching for the best time span is a job for the computer.)

FIGURE 2–13
Six-week moving
average (MA)
and MAD—
Metro Movers

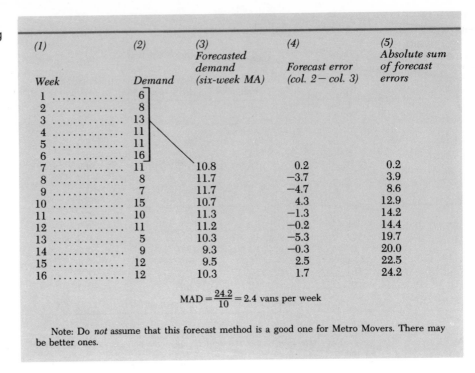

(1) Week	(2) Demand	(3) Forecasted demand (six-week MA)	(4) Forecast error (col. 2 − col. 3)	(5) Absolute sum of forecast errors
1	6			
2	8			
3	13			
4	11			
5	11			
6	16			
7	11	10.8	0.2	0.2
8	8	11.7	−3.7	3.9
9	7	11.7	−4.7	8.6
10	15	10.7	4.3	12.9
11	10	11.3	−1.3	14.2
12	11	11.2	−0.2	14.4
13	5	10.3	−5.3	19.7
14	9	9.3	−0.3	20.0
15	12	9.5	2.5	22.5
16	12	10.3	1.7	24.2

$$\text{MAD} = \frac{24.2}{10} = 2.4 \text{ vans per week}$$

Note: Do *not* assume that this forecast method is a good one for Metro Movers. There may be better ones.

MA time spans generally should be long where demands are rather stable (e.g., for toilet tissue). They should be short for highly changeable demands (e.g., for houseplants). Most users of MA are producers of durable goods, and durable goods tend to have stable demand patterns in the short run. Therefore, longer time spans, say 6–12 periods, are common.

The time span that results in the lowest MAD would be the best choice for actual use in forecasting future demands. But keep in mind that we prove it based on past data. As long as we think that the future will be similar to the past, this is fine. If we are quite sure that the future will be different, then there is little point in expending much time analyzing past demands.

Smoothing effects. History-based forecasting analysis methods like MA attempt to wash out some of the forecast error from historical demand data. The effect is to produce a series of forecast values that are smoother—less variable—than the historical time series. These smoothing effects are illustrated in Figure 2–14 for the three-week and six-week data in the MA example. The actual demand pattern, taken from Figure 2–11, exhibits some extreme high and low spikes. The three-week MA data pattern, taken from Figure 2–12, has spikes that are much less pronounced. And the six-week MA data pattern, taken from Figure 2–13, is smoothed to look like gently rolling hills. Taken to the extreme, the 12 weeks of actual data would be smoothed to a single flat prediction line—no peaks or valleys—which is the mean (discussed

FIGURE 2-14
Smoothing
effects of the
moving average

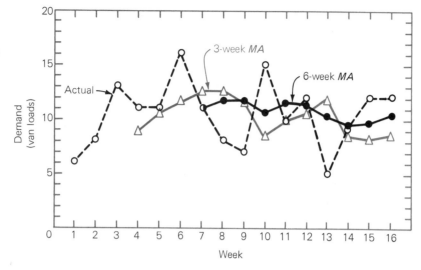

earlier). The "correct" amount of smoothing—the correct MA time span—is that which results in the least error (smallest MAD).

Weighted moving average. A weakness of the simple moving average is that it places as much weight on the oldest as on the most recent demands. One way to deal with this problem is to adopt a weighting scheme. One such scheme is shown in the following extension of the Metro Movers example.

EXAMPLE 2-5
Metro Movers
and weighted
moving
average

Figure 2-15 for Metro Movers is segmented into separate time spans in order to show the weighting process more clearly. In this scheme the most recent of the three weeks in each time span is weighted (multiplied by) ³⁄₆; the middle week is more distant in the past and therefore deserves less weight—²⁄₆; the most distant week is weighted least at ¹⁄₆. The weights add up to ⁶⁄₆, or 1, as they must. (If the weights added up to more than 1, the result would be forecasts with a high bias; less than 1 would yield a low bias.)

Other weighting schemes could be used. The weights could, for example, be ¹⁄₆, ²⁄₆, and ³⁄₆ (which correctly adds up to ⁶⁄₆). This would put even more emphasis on recent data and less on distant data. The combination of time span and weighting scheme that results in the lowest MAD may be sought and then adopted for future forecasting.

The forecast errors in Figure 2-15 may be compared with the forecast errors for the same four weeks for the simple MA in Figure 2-12. The simple three-week MA results in a total forecast error of 14.3 (7.0 + 0.3 + 3.7 + 3.3) for the last four weeks. The weighted MA results in a smaller total forecast error, 13.7. This will often be true. It is a common tendency because recent demands are often more indicative of the immediate future than are past demands; therefore it seems best to weight recent data more heavily.

(1)	(2)	(3)	(4)	(5) Weighted three-week MA forecast (sum of col. 4)	(6)	(7)
Week	*Actual demand*	*Weighting factor*	*Weighted demand*		*Forecast error*	*Absolute sum of forecast errors*
10	15	1/6	15/6			
11	10	2/6	20/6			
12	11	3/6	33/6			
13	5			68/6, or 11.3	−6.3	6.3
11	10	1/6	10/6			
12	11	2/6	22/6			
13	5	3/6	15/6			
14	9			47/6, or 7.8	1.2	7.5
12	11	1/6	11/6			
13	5	2/6	10/6			
14	9	3/6	27/6			
15	12			48/6, or 8.0	4.0	11.5
13	5	1/6	5/6			
14	9	2/6	18/6			
15	12	3/6	36/6			
16	12			59/6, or 9.8	2.2	13.7

$$\text{MAD} = \frac{13.7}{4} = 3.4$$

Note: Do *not* assume that this forecast method is a good one for Metro Movers. There may be better ones.

FIGURE 2–15
Weighted three-week moving average—Metro Movers

Sometimes, however, this does not hold true. Sometimes the very fact that a lot was demanded in the most recent weeks tends to mean that less will be demanded in the near future. One explanation is that buyers may become partly sated after a period of high demand; they may hold off for a while, thereby resulting in a period of low demand. This helps to explain why MA methods are sometimes considered too crude for use in forecasting the most vital products or services of some organizations.

Exponential smoothing

Many firms that adopted the MA technique in the 1950s saw fit to change to exponential smoothing in the 1960s or 1970s. Exponential smoothing calculations seem very different from the weighted MA process; in result, the two methods are very similar.

In exponential smoothing (ES) the forecast for next period equals the forecast for last period plus a portion (α) of last period's forecast error:[2]

Next forecast = Last forecast + α(Last demand − Last forecast)

For example, assume that the last forecast was for 100 units but that only 90 were demanded. If α is set at 0.2, then the ES forecast is:

---

[2] Some people prefer to transform it into this equivalent form:

Next forecast = α(Last demand) + $(1 − \alpha)$(Last forecast)

$$\text{Next forecast} = 100 + 0.2(90 - 100)$$
$$= 100 + 0.2(-10)$$
$$= 100 - 2$$
$$= 98$$

ES example. This forecast of two units less than last period makes sense because the last period was overestimated. Thus, ES results in lower forecasts where you have recently overestimated, and it results in higher forecasts where you have underestimated. This is shown for the Metro Movers data in the example below.

EXAMPLE 2–6
Metro Movers
and
exponential
smoothing

Exponential smoothing, where $\alpha = 0.2$, is shown in Figure 2–16. Data from Metro Movers, Example 2–4, are used. In ES there must be a start-up forecast. In this case it is 10.6 for week 12. Following the suggestions of Brown,[3] the start-up value here is the simple mean of past demand data. The past demand data, for weeks 1–11, are taken from Figure 2–11.

(1) Week	(2) Actual demand	(3) Forecast	(4) Forecast error	(5) Smoothing adjustment [(0.2) (col. 4)]	(6) Exponentially smoothed forecast (col. 3 + col. 5)	(7) Absolute sum of forecast errors in col. 4	
12	11	10.6	0.4	0.1	10.7		Start-up phase
13	5	10.7	−5.7	−1.1	9.6	5.7	ES
14	9	9.6	−0.6	−0.1	9.5	6.3	forecasting
15	12	9.5	2.5	0.5	10.0	8.8	phase
16	12	10.0	2.0			10.8	

$$\text{MAD} = \frac{10.8}{4} = 2.7 \text{ vans per week}$$

Note: Do *not* assume that this forecast method is a good one for Metro Movers. There may be better ones.

FIGURE 2–16
Exponentially
smoothed
demand
forecasts—Metro
Movers

The underestimate for start-up week 12 was slight, only 0.4 unit. Multiplying that 0.4 by the 0.2 smoothing constant yields an adjustment of 0.1, rounded off. Adding that 0.1 to the old forecast of 10.6 yields 10.7 as the forecast for next week, week 13.

In week 13 the 10.7 forecast exceeds actual demand of 5; the error is −5.7. That times 0.2 gives an adjustment of −1.1. Thus, the next forecast, for week 14, is cut back by −1.1 to 9.6. And so on.

---

[3] Robert Goodell Brown, *Smoothing, Forecasting, and Prediction of Discrete Time Series* (Prentice-Hall, 1963), p. 102 (TA168.B68).

Figure 2–16 results may be compared with the three-month MA results in Figures 2–12 and 2–15. Simple MA forecast errors for the last four weeks from Figure 2–12 sum to 14.3 (7.0 + 0.3 + 3.7 + 3.3). Weighted MA forecast errors from Figure 2–15 are better at 13.7. ES forecast errors in Figure 2–16 sum to still less, 10.8 (week 12 is not counted). This is by no means a fair comparison since the number of demand weeks is so small and since ES has not run long enough for the artificial start-up forecast to be "washed out." Yet it is indicative of the tendency for exponential smoothing to be more accurate than moving average forecasts.

In testing for the proper value of α, the mean absolute deviation is again helpful. Using past demand data, the MAD could be calculated for $\alpha = 0.1$, $0.2, \ldots 0.9$. The α yielding the lowest MAD could then be adopted. It is common to use an α in the range of 0.1 to 0.3. The reason is the same as that mentioned earlier for using longer MA time spans: Most larger firms using ES are manufacturers of durable goods having rather stable short-run demand patterns. A small α, such as 0.2, fits this situation well. A small α means a small adjustment for forecast error, and this keeps each successive forecast close to its predecessor. A large α, say 0.7, would result in new forecasts that more closely follow the large up-and-down swings of actual demand. This would be suitable for the less stable demand pattern of a luxury good or service.

ES compared with MA. It may appear that the next-period ES forecast is always based solely on what happened last period with no regard for all preceding demand periods. Not so. Metaphorically, if the forecast for next period, F_N, is the son, then the father is F_{N-1}, the grandfather is F_{N-2}, the great-grandfather is F_{N-3}, and so forth. The current sibling, F_N, has inherited a portion, α, of the error attributable to the father, F_{N-1}; a smaller portion of the error attributable to the grandfather; and so forth.

This creates a mathematical series. It could be shown that the series takes a form that would have the following results: In the case where $\alpha = 0.2$,

0.2 is the weight assigned to the F_{N-1} error;

$(0.2)(0.8)$ is the weight assigned to the F_{N-2} error;

$(0.2)(0.8)^2$ is the weight assigned to the F_{N-3} error;

$(0.2)(0.8)^3$ is the weight assigned to the F_{N-4} error;

or, in general, $(\alpha)(1 - \alpha)^t$ is the weight assigned to the F_{N-t} error.

The pattern of decreasing weights for $\alpha = 0.2$ is plotted on the chart in Figure 2–17. Also plotted are the calculated weights for $\alpha = 0.5$, along with the weights used in Figures 2–12 and 2–15 for a simple and a weighted three-month moving average.

The figure shows that the MA weights (connected by dashed lines) cover only the MA time span, three months. The ES weights (connected by solid lines) extend back into the past indefinitely. The figure also shows that MA weights of ⅜, ⅔, and ⅙ plot on the chart close to ES with $\alpha = 0.5$.

It is possible to construct a weighted MA that closely approximates ES.

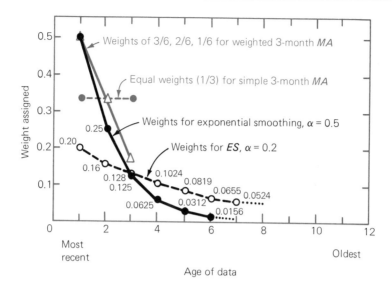

FIGURE 2-17
Weights for simple and weighted MA and for ES

But why bother? The word *exponential* and the symbol α may tend to frighten off those who "don't speak mathematics." But ES is actually simpler and less expensive to perform than any MA process. ES involves one small formula, while MA requires adding all the past demands in the time span. A greater advantage of ES as compared with MA is in data storage. Only the latest ES forecast need be saved; by contrast, all the data in the most recent time span must be saved for MA forecasting. This is a major factor for the large firm that forecasts for a large number of separate products/services. Computer data storage is costly.

The main strengths of both ES and MA are that they are simple and automatic. Thus, they are suitable for computer programming. Simplicity and automaticity are also weaknesses. That is, the methods are sometimes too simple—or crude; and they are sometimes too automatic—or inflexible. A cafeteria chain might be willing to turn over the demand forecasting for bread, salad, and desserts to a computer using a moving-average method. But for expensive meat entrées, it might prefer to project demand by combining analysis techniques with a strong dose of judgment and experience. A business can afford to devote more individual attention and analysis to its costliest product.

Enhanced ES and other advanced methods

There are a number of ways to enhance exponential smoothing. For example, there are double ES, triple and multiple ES, and ES with a tracking signal. These are not treated in this book, but a few words on their purposes are in order.

Double ES is like simple ES except that it adds variables so that the smoothed forecast will keep up more closely with an upward or downward trend. The trend is specified in the general form of a straight-line equation, $Y = a +$

bx. Simple ES does not follow trends very well. Or rather, it follows trends, but with a lag. Thus double ES may be preferable for demands that exhibit trends.

Triple and *multiple ES* allow use of higher-order time-series variables. These are suitable where demands exhibit cyclic patterns instead of straight-line trends.

A *tracking signal* may be added to any ES process. A tracking signal is just a continuous check on the average forecast error. If that average—expressed in terms of the MAD or standard deviation—gets too large, it triggers a shift to a new smoothing constant. If the new smoothing constant performs worse, it may trigger a shift back to the original smoothing constant. While it is a bit hard to express this procedure mathematically, it is not hard to program a computer to do it. (Tracking-signal algorithms are common exercises in some computer science classes.)

More advanced methods that search for underlying cycles and time series are beyond the scope of this book. They involve autocorrelation, polynomial extrapolation, spectral analysis, and other statistical processes. Such methods are of more interest to the economist or the stock market analyst than to the operations manager.

Leading indicator

A superior kind of forecasting tool is the leading indicator. Changes in demand may be preceded by changes in some other variable. If so, the other variable is a leading indicator. The leading indicator is helpful if the patterns of change in the two variables are similar (i.e., they correlate) and if the lead time is long enough for action to be taken before the demand change occurs.

Few firms are able to discover a variable of this type—one that changes with demand but leads it significantly. The reason is probably that demand for a given good or service usually depends on (is led by) a number of variables rather than by one dominant variable. The search for such a variable can be costly and futile. Therefore most of the work with leading indicators has centered on national economic forecasting instead of local demand forecasting. Nevertheless, the leading indicator should be part of the demand forecaster's tool kit, since it is a valued predictor in those cases where it can be isolated.

One story about leading indicators has been widely circulated. It is said that the Rothschild family reaped a fortune by having advance news of Napoleon's defeat at Waterloo. Nathan, the Rothschild brother who was located in England, is said to have received the news via carrier pigeon. On that basis he supposedly bought depressed war-effort securities and sold them at a huge profit after the news reached England.[4]

The leading indicator in this case was news of the war, and it led prices of securities. The Rothschilds' astuteness was not in realizing this, for it was

---

[4] One historian disputes the stories, asserting that the Rothschilds made more money during the war than at its end and that the news was forwarded by a courier in a Rothschild ship, not a carrier pigeon. Virginia Cowles, *The Rothschilds: A Family of Fortune* (Knopf, 1973), pp. 47–50 (HG 1552.R8C66).

common knowledge; rather it was in their development of an information network to capitalize on the knowledge. A costly information system like that set up by the Rothschilds can provide highly accurate information fast. By contrast, personal judgment as a basis for action is cheap but tends to be less accurate and to be hindsight rather than foresight. That is, our personal judgment often does not lead events.

Thus, it is best for leading indicators to have long lead times as well as accuracy. This requires good information systems. The following example demonstrates this.

EXAMPLE 2–7
State Jobs Service and leading indicators

Mr. H. Hand, manager of the Metro City office of the State Jobs Service, sees the need for better demand forecasting. The problem has been that surges in clients tend to catch the office off guard. Advance warning of demand is needed in order to plan for staff, desks, phones, forms, and even space.

One element of demand is well known: Many of the job seekers are there as a result of being laid off by Acme Industries. Acme is by far the largest employer in Metro City. Mr. Hand is able to obtain Acme records on layoffs over the past year. The layoff data are plotted on a time chart along with the Jobs Service office's data on job applicants. The chart is shown in Figure 2–18. The chart shows job applicants ranging from a high of 145 (in period 8) to a low of 45 (in period 20). Layoffs at Acme range from a high of 60 (in periods 6 and 7) to a low of zero (in several periods).

Plotting the points seems well worth the effort, because Mr. Hand notes a striking similarity in the shapes of the two plots. Furthermore, the layoffs plot seems to lead the applicants plot. For example, the high of 145 applicants occurred two weeks after the high of 60 layoffs; and the low of 45 applicants occurred two weeks after layoffs spiked downward to zero. Weeks 1, 3, 17, 21, and 22 are other places on the layoff plot where a two-week lead appears; and the lead is close to two weeks in weeks 11–15.

Does a two-week lead make sense? Or could it be coincidence? Mr. Hand feels that it makes sense. He bases this on the impression that laid-off Acme people tend

FIGURE 2–18
Layoffs at Acme and job applicants at Jobs Service— With time scale

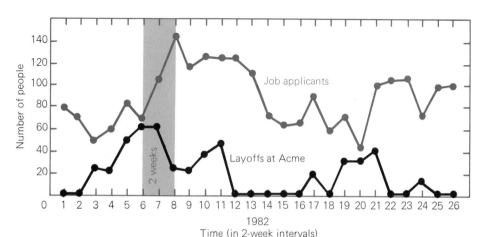

to live off their severance pay for a time—two weeks seems reasonable—before actively seeking another job.

Mr. Hand therefore takes the final steps: (1) He establishes an information system. It is simply an agreement that every two weeks Acme will release the number of its laid-off employees to the Jobs Service office. (2) He establishes a forecasting process based on that layoff information and the two-week lead pattern of Figure 2–18.

How good is Mr. Hand's leading indicator? (1) By one measure, the supporting information system, it is very good! Getting the layoff data from Acme is cheap and highly accurate. (2) In terms of lead time, it is not so good. Two weeks' notice is not much for the purpose of adjusting resources on hand. (3) In terms of validity, the leading indicator *seems* good, but how may we measure "good"? One answer is: Measure it by the correlation coefficient. That is the next topic.

Correlation

Correlation means degree of association. The *correlation coefficient, r,* is a measure of degree of association. The value of r ranges from 1.0 for perfect correlation to 0.0 for no correlation at all to -1.0 for perfect negative correlation. In positive correlation a rise in one attribute occurs along with a rise in the other; in negative correlation a rise in one occurs along with a fall in the other. To calculate r a number of pairs of values are needed. The chapter supplement provides a formula and sample calculations. The following extension of the Jobs Service office example shows one way of using r in connection with forecasting.

EXAMPLE 2–8
State Jobs Service and correlation coefficient

Mr. Hand's inspection of Figure 2–18 revealed a two-week lead of layoffs at Acme over applicants at the Jobs Service office. To see how well these are correlated, Mr. Hand calculates the correlation coefficient, r. His first step is to plot points on a scatter diagram, Figure 2–19. This is a plot of layoffs at Acme for period $N-2$ matched with applicants at the Jobs Service office for period N. The data are taken from Figure 2–18. For example, the first point plotted is 0,50. That is taken from Figure 2–18, where, for period 1, layoffs is 0 and two weeks later applicants is 50. Each other point is plotted in the same way. The points tend to run along a broad band moving upward at a nearly 45-degree angle, as shown by the shading in Figure 2–19. This is the pattern of a positive correlation. (Negative correlations go downward left to right.)

Now the method shown in the chapter supplement is followed to give the correlation coefficient, r. It is $+0.78$. That is a reasonably good correlation. It supports Mr. Hand's visual impression that layoffs at Acme is a helpful leading indicator.

In the Jobs Service example the amount of lead was determined visually. The two variables were plotted on the time scale in Figure 2–18, and brief inspection showed that the two curves were generally two weeks apart. Sometimes the amount of lead is hard to see; and where there are many potential leading indicators to check out, manual plotting and visual inspection become tedious. In such cases computers may take over. It is simple for the computer

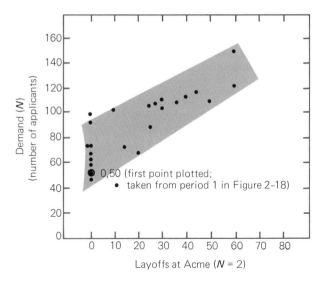

FIGURE 2–19
Correlation of layoffs at Acme ($N-2$) with demand at Jobs Service (N)

Demand (N) (number of applicants)

0,50 (first point plotted; taken from period 1 in Figure 2-18)

Layoffs at Acme ($N = 2$)

to calculate r for a number of different lead periods. The one with the best r may then be selected.

What about a lead period of zero? That would exist where a pair of events occur at the same time.[5] Even if the correlation is perfect ($r = 1.0$), it *appears* that it is of no help in forecasting: No lead time means no forewarning and therefore, it might seem, no *fore*casting. This impression is not correct. Correlation with no lead *can* be valuable *if* the indicator (independent variable) is more predictable than demand is.

As an example, a phone company in a large city may know that new residential phone orders correlate nearly perfectly with new arrivals in the city—with no lead time. There is probably value in knowing this, because in most large cities careful studies are done to project population increases. Fairly reliable projections of new residences may be available. The phone company need not spend a lot of money projecting residential telephone installations; instead, the city's data on new residences may be used. For these reasons most large firms are indeed quite interested in establishing good correlations, even without lead time.

Multiple regression/correlation is an extension of simple regression and correlation. In this method multiple causal variables may be analyzed. The result is a formula with demand on the left side of the equal sign and each of the causal variables, properly weighted, on the right. For example, the phone company may look for other predictors besides new residences. Level of savings in local thrift institutions and amount of phone advertising are possibilities. A multiple regression equation might be put together with three causal vari-

---

[5] The introductory statistics course usually focuses on this type of simple correlation—with no lead time.

ables in it: new residences (N), savings (S), and advertising (A). Then computer processing using past data would yield the parameters for each of the three causal variables. As an example, the equation to forecast next month's demand (D) for phone installations might be:

$$D = 0.36N + 2.81S + 0.89A$$

Since advertising effects may take awhile, advertising could be treated as a leading indicator. Perhaps it could be shown that advertising leads demand by one month. The revised multiple regression equation might appear as:

$$D = 0.41N + 2.70S + 0.88A_{n-1}$$

Much more has been done with multiple regression/correlation in economic forecasting than in demand forecasting. The method, which is complex and requires a computer, is beyond the scope of this book. The approach has often proven futile at the level of the firm; however, multiple regression has frequently been used for large utilities or large public agencies whose demand is likely to be affected by a number of broad socioeconomic variables.

For example, in a magazine article about power rates, it is noted that "an econometric approach . . . which most utilities use, involves multiple regression analysis to determine the sensitivity of electricity demand to such variables as economic growth and inflation."[6] The gist of the article is that the utilities have a preference for the econometric approach because it tends to show a high demand growth rate, which helps justify rate boosts. A simpler trend analysis approach, recommended by a consulting group to the Illinois Commerce Commission, tends to show lower demand rate increase. In the article the consultants' approach is called an "engineering approach" in which "categories of residential electricity users are multiplied by expected use of air conditioners, refrigerators, and other appliances."

Forecasting by simulation

Trend and seasonal analysis, moving average, and exponential smoothing are standard forecasting tools, especially for durable goods manufacturers. A computer is not needed for these techniques, but most firms have computerized them for efficiency reasons. The modern computer, however, provides the firm with computational power to run *forecasting simulations*. Forecasting simulation has the potential to surpass, in accuracy, the capabilities of any of the individual forecasting techniques.

In each trial, the forecasted values are subtracted from a set of actual demands from the recent past, giving simulated forecast error. The forecast method yielding least error is selected by the computer. The simulations are run every forecasting period, and the best method is recommended only for that forecast. For each successive forecast a new simulation is done, and a new technique may be its basis. (By contrast, the search for a time span or a smoothing constant—for a moving average or exponential smoothing—is performed as an occasional review rather than every forecasting period).

---

[6] "Why It's Tougher to Justify Rate Boosts," *Business Week*, November 7, 1977, p. 56.

One ardent advocate of forecasting simulation is Bernard T. Smith, inventory manager at American Hardware Supply.[7] The forecast simulation system devised by Smith applies to 100,000 hardware products. Each is simulated every month for the next three months. In Smith's system seven forecast techniques are simulated. Each of the seven is simple for buyers and other inventory people in the company to understand.

For example, one of the seven forecast techniques is a simple three-month sum, which is not quite the same as a three-month moving average. The simulation for that method uses historical demand data for only the past six months. The past six months takes in the two most recent three-month periods. To illustrate the simulation, let us assume that demand for giant-size trash bags was 500 in the last three-month period and 400 in the period before that. In a three-month-sum forecast method, the latest three-month sum is the forecast for the next period. Therefore the computer simulation treats 400 as the forecast for the three-month period in which actual demand was 500. The simulated forecast error is $500 - 400 = 100$ trash bags. That forecast error is converted to a percent error so that it may be compared with six other computer-simulated methods for forecasting trash bags. The percent error is $1 - (400/500) = 0.20$, or 20 percent.

Six other simple, easy-to-understand methods (including simple trend and simple seasonal) are simulated to see what percent error results. If the three-month-sum method turns out to have a lower percent error than the other six simulated methods, then the computer will use the three-month-sum method to make the next forecast. The forecast would be 500 for the next three months, and for next month the forecast is simply $500/3 = 167$ trash bags. The forecast rolls over (is recomputed) each month. The computer prints out the forecast for each of the 100,000 items, but buyers may overrule the printed forecast if they do not believe it.

THE FORECASTING ENVIRONMENT

The preceding section included warnings not to assume that the given technique is a good one—for that particular case. We may now examine some of the reasons for exercising caution. The hazardous business of forecasting is best practiced with a full understanding of the forecasting environment. The following discussion includes four selected aspects of the forecasting environment: aggregate forecasting, forecast error in out-periods, and forecasting in selected industries and in support organizations.

Aggregate demand forecasting

The nature of forecasting is such that we expect demand forecasts to be wrong. If our average forecast error is high, we end up with too many of the items or resources that are overforecasted and too few of the items or resources that are underforecasted.

---

[7] See Bernard T. Smith, *Focus Forecasting: Computer Techniques for Inventory Control* (CBI Publishing, 1978) (HD55.S48).

FIGURE 2–20
Item-forecast
versus group-
forecast
accuracy

Item	Third-quarter forecast	Third-quarter actual	Error	Percent error
Bracket	1,280	1,600	+320	25.0
Doorknob	20,300	23,200	+2,900	14.3
Hinge	15,120	18,660	+3,540	23.4
Vise........................	32,010	22,210	−9,800	30.6
Tool case	7,880	7,960	+80	1.0
Grate	41,290	36,920	−4,370	10.6
Average item forecast error (MAD)				17.5
Group totals	117,880	110,550	+7,330	6.2

Happily, the average error is likely to be far less for a group of items than for the average item within a group. This is seen in Figure 2–20, which shows six items in a small group. A third-quarter forecast and third-quarter actual demand are given for each item. The error is the difference between actual and forecast amounts. The percent error is the absolute error (no minus signs) divided by actual demand. The average of the percent errors for the six items is 17.5 percent. But the average error for the items as a group is only 6.2 percent.

The result of forecasting for whole product groups is the aggregate demand forecast, which could be measured in pieces, pounds, and so on, or perhaps converted to capacity units like labor-hours or machine-hours. Aggregate demand forecasts are useful in planning for adjustable capacity (e.g., work force and inventories). (See the chart on the chapter title page.) The purpose is to adjust capacity to fit forecasted aggregate demand. The capacity-demand matching process works well only if product groupings are set wisely; this is explained in a later chapter. The point here is simply that it *is* possible to avoid large overcommitment or undercommitment of resources; the way to avoid such costly errors is to rely on the lower error rates of group forecasts.

Item forecasts have a different purpose. Item forecasts are an input into the master-scheduling function. The high level of inaccuracy of the item forecast is a challenge that the master scheduler must live with, because the master schedule is by item, not by group of items. The group-forecasting concept can, however, be applied in a small way to improving item-forecast accuracy. The idea is to compute seasonal indices for groups of items that follow similar demand patterns. Then apply the group seasonal indices to the individual items in the group when item forecasting is done. The principle is: Seasonal indices are more accurate for groups than for separate items.[8]

---

[8] Glenn Dalhart, "Class Seasonality—A New Approach," in *Forecasting*, 2d ed., (American Production and Inventory Control Society, 1979), pp. 11–16.

Forecast error in out-periods

Forecasts are more accurate for shorter periods of time. This makes intuitive sense, and it can be shown by an example, Figure 2–21. The demand forecast is set at 500 (column 2). Only a sample of weeks is included for illustration: weeks 2, 5, 10, 15, 20, and 25. Cumulative actual demand (column 3) is simply number of weeks times the weekly forecast of 500. That is, column 3 = (column 1) × (column 2). Cumulative actual demand figures were made up but are realistic. Cumulative error (column 5) is actual (column 4) minus forecast (column 3). The error as a multiple of the weekly forecast is the error in column 5 divided by the forecast, 500. The result is a pattern of rising error as the forecast encompasses more weeks of demand.

Knowing this does not mean that longer-range forecasting is futile. There must be such forecasts for resource planning purposes. They must project as far into the future as the planning lead time for the given resource.

Two useful principles follow from the knowledge that shorter forecasts are more accurate:

1. As time passes, forecasts should be refined by interjecting newer data and rolling the forecast over.
2. The planning and control systems that are sustained by the forecast should be segmented, if possible, according to the need for forecast accuracy.

As an example of both points, some goods producers master-schedule product modules and components based on projections of 52 weeks; the master schedule is refined every month based on latest revised forecasts plus actual orders. Final assembly of end products is based on shorter-range projections, maybe for only a few days or weeks.

Since part and module schedules are based on longer-range forecasts, they are subject to large errors. But parts and modules are not so costly as end products, and there is some flexibility as to what end products parts and modules may be assembled into. Since the more costly and inflexible end products are assembled based on short-term assembly schedules, the error is small.

This reasoning is reexamined in a later chapter.

FIGURE 2–21
Cumulative forecast error, picture frames

(1)	(2)	(3)	(4)	(5)	(6)
	Weekly	Cumulative	Cumulative		Error as a multiple of
Week number	demand forecast	demand forecast	actual demand	Cumulative error	weekly forecast
2	500	1,000	1,162	162	0.3
5	500	2,500	2,716	216	0.4
10	500	5,000	5,488	488	1.0
15	500	7,500	8,110	610	1.2
20	500	10,000	11,250	1,250	2.5
25	500	12,500	14,010	1,410	2.8

Forecasting in selected industries

The competition affects the kind of forecast required. In some industries there are competitive pressures to meet customer demand immediately from stock. Examples are auto replacement parts, consumer goods, and cafeteria foods. These are make-to-stock/ship-to-order businesses. They require that everything from raw materials to finished goods be based on demand forecasts.

At the other extreme are industries that have very long manufacturing lead times. These are the heavy-capital-goods firms that are project-oriented. Examples are ships, locomotives, missiles, and heavy construction. These are make-to-order firms. Such firms generally maintain no inventories, not even for raw materials. They have a need only for long-term forecasting—as the basis for planning fixed capacity. Raw material acquisition and production of goods are based on firm contracts rather than on forecasts.

Figure 2–22 illustrates the two extreme types of industry plus two in-between. As is shown, it is customer lead time that dictates how much forecasting is required.

The first of the in-between industries is the class referred to as the job shop. Job shops, including foundries, hospitals, and restaurants, forecast for

FIGURE 2–22
Demand lead times and forecasts required

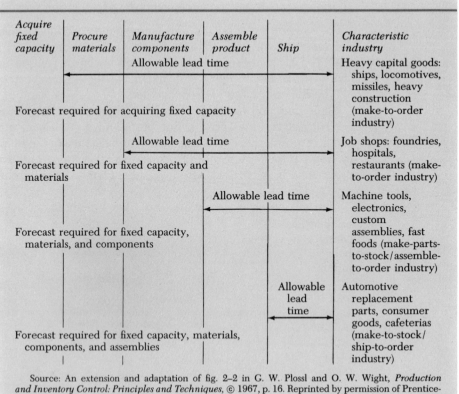

Source: An extension and adaptation of fig. 2–2 in G. W. Plossl and O. W. Wight, *Production and Inventory Control: Principles and Techniques,* © 1967, p. 16. Reprinted by permission of Prentice-Hall, Inc., Englewood Cliffs, New Jersey.

fixed capacity and for raw materials. These firms make to order but from materials on hand.

The other in-between type of industry is that which produces components (plus raw materials and fixed capacity) based on forecasts. But assembly and shipment await firm customer ordering. Examples are machine tools, electronics, custom assemblies, and fast foods. (Fast-food establishments often precook or preassemble ingredients based on forecasts). These are assemble-to-order firms.

The figure may give the impression that in a given firm up to four different types of forecasts could be required: one for fixed capacity, one for raw materials, one for components, and one for product assembly. Modern production and inventory control, based on time-phased material planning, is able to cut this to two or three forecasts: a long-range forecast for fixed capacity and a shorter-range forecast that links parts to components and perhaps to product assembly.

Forecasting in support organizations

The common view seems to be that forecasting should be done by those with responsibility for basic products/services. This would limit forecasting to items earning revenue. Or, for non-revenue-producing organizations, forecasting would be restricted to major-mission items; for example, in social work the key factor is number of eligible clients.

This view of forecasting appears to be too narrow. The view here is that *all* managers should forecast. Putting it another way, all staff services and nonrevenue items should be forecasted—in addition to forecasting for revenue and major-mission items. An example may help to show why forecasting is necessary in support departments.

EXAMPLE 2–9 Apex Steel Cabinet Company

O. R. Guy is the new president of Apex. One of his first acts is to create the Department of Management Science and to assign corporate forecasting to it. Corporate forecasting applies to the firm's revenue-earning products: its line of steel cabinets.

M.S. Department analysts arrive at a forecast of a 10 percent increase in total steel cabinet sales for next year. Mr. Guy informs key department heads that they may consider 10 percent budget increases to be their targets for planning departmental budgets. Protests come at Mr. Guy from several directions. Most notable are the following three:

1. *Engineering chief:* "Mr. Guy, I hate to protest any budget increase. But I'd rather wait until I need it. The Engineering workload often goes down when cabinet sales go up. That's because Marketing pressures us less for new product designs when sales are good. But then in some years of good sales we have a lot of new design and design modification work. This happens when several key products are in the decline phase of their life cycles. So you can see that our budget should not depend strictly on corporate sales."

2. *Personnel chief:* "We are the same way, Mr. Guy. The Personnel workload depends more on things like whether the labor contract is up for renewal. Sure, we need to do more interviewing and training when corporate sales go up. But we have

bigger problems when they go down. Layoffs and reassignments are tougher. Also, when sales go down, we may get more grievances."

3. *Marketing chief:* "Well, I hate to be the crybaby. But it's Marketing that bears most of the load in meeting that 10 percent forecasted sales increase. I was going to ask for a 20 percent budget increase—mainly for a stepped-up advertising campaign. I don't dispute the M.S. projection of a 10 percent sales increase. The market is there; we just need to spend more to tap it."

Based on these three comments, Mr. Hand rescinds his note about a 10 percent targeted budget increase. He then informs managers at all levels in the firm that they are expected to formally forecast their key workloads. This becomes the basis for their plans and budgets. The M.S. Department is assigned to serve as adviser for those managers requesting help.

To explain what is meant by key workloads, Mr. Guy provides each manager with a simple forecasting plan developed by the chief of personnel. This plan is shown in Figure 2–23.

The plan in Figure 2–23 provides for forecasting *in units of demand* as much as possible. The alternative is to skip this step and directly plan for staff, equipment, and other resources. This is the approach taken for item 7 in Figure 2–23, miscellaneous workloads. Some of the methods—trend projection and judgment—may be used in this approach. But it is not demand forecasting; it is supply, or resource capacity, forecasting.

FIGURE 2–23
Forecasting plan—Personnel Department, Apex Company

Workloads	Forecast basis
1. Hiring/interviewing	Number of job openings—based on data from other departments
	Number of job applicants—based on trend projection and judgment
2. Layoffs and reassignments	Number of employees—based on data from other departments
3. Grievances	Number of stage 1, 2, and 3 grievances, estimated separately—based on trend projection and judgment
4. Training	Number of classroom hours
	Number of OJT hours
	Both based on data from other departments
5. Payroll actions	Number of payroll actions—based on number of employees and judgment on impact of major changes
6. Union contract negotiations	Number of key issues—based on judgment
7. Miscellaneous—all other workloads	Not forecasted in units; instead resource needs are estimated directly based on trends and judgment

Skipping the demand-forecasting step is the easy way. It is also less precise. The precise approach is to forecast demand in units. Independently of that, the standard time per unit may be determined—very precisely if the product is a key one. Then the unit forecast may be multiplied by the standard time to give staffing needs. And the unit forecast may be multiplied by material factors, space factors, and so on, to give the projected needs for other resources. The cost of all these resources then becomes the budget.

Mr. Guy in the example thus seems to be following a rational approach in requesting demand forecasts of all managers. It would be a mistake, however, to expect every manager to employ extensive—and expensive—record keeping and historical data analysis. For lesser demands, a less formal approach should be satisfactory.

ORDER ACCEPTANCE

When things are going well, operations is able to produce and deliver what marketing sells. To keep things going well, operations management must play an active role in customer ordering. It is poor policy for the operating department to simply put into backlog any orders that sales is able to "scare up." Instead, there should be a well-devised order-acceptance system.

Order acceptance by operations management serves as its commitment in the close partnership that marketing and operations should have. Speedy notice of this commitment can provide salespeople with sound information to use in making sales and delivery agreements. In return, the sales force may be able to gear its selling activities more toward operating capacity. That is, it may push sales of items that help to keep slack shops busy and ease off on items that would strain other shop capacities.

Order acceptance is complementary to demand forecasting. In fact, an accepted order differs from a forecasted order only in that the accepted order is more certain. Order acceptance, along with item and aggregate forecasting, provides for a coordinated approach to demand management.

The sequence of order processing is shown in Figure 2–24. The first step is *order booking*. That is, an order is booked by sales. The second step is *order entry*, in which the order is entered into the organization's order-processing system. Order entry may include credit checking, documenting pertinent customer data, and assigning an internal order number. The third step is to determine *total requirements*: Orders for common end products (or services) are totaled, and they may have to be restated in production terms; this may mean translating sales models (end products) into manufacturing end items or major modules. Total end-item requirements are then compared with the master production schedule (MPS), which was based largely on forecasts rather than actual orders. End-item requirements that are covered by the MPS constitute accepted orders. Then, in the fourth step, *order acceptance*, sales may be so informed and may pass the word along to the customer (step five).

In the next few order-processing steps, customer identification is lost. In

FIGURE 2-24
The order-
processing
sequence

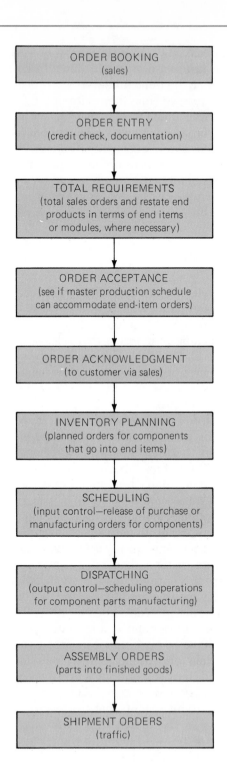

ORDER BOOKING
(sales)

ORDER ENTRY
(credit check, documentation)

TOTAL REQUIREMENTS
(total sales orders and restate end
products in terms of end items
or modules, where necessary)

ORDER ACCEPTANCE
(see if master production schedule
can accommodate end-item orders)

ORDER ACKNOWLEDGMENT
(to customer via sales)

INVENTORY PLANNING
(planned orders for components
that go into end items)

SCHEDULING
(input control—release of purchase or
manufacturing orders for components)

DISPATCHING
(output control—scheduling operations
for component parts manufacturing)

ASSEMBLY ORDERS
(parts into finished goods)

SHIPMENT ORDERS
(traffic)

the sixth step, *inventory planning,* end-item orders are exploded into component parts requirements, which results in manufacture and purchase orders for parts, but common parts go into various end items ordered by various customers. *Scheduling* is the seventh step: Scheduling releases the parts manufacturing orders, controlling the release rate so as not to overload the shops. *Dispatching* is the eighth step: Dispatching controls the priorities of parts orders as they queue up in certain work centers to have certain operations done.

Finally, in the ninth step, *assembly orders,* the customer order reemerges as the basis for orders for the final assembly of end items (and accessories) into finished goods or end products. *Shipment orders,* geographically consolidated, constitute the tenth and last step in the figure.

In the past little attention was paid to the order-acceptance function. At least there was little concern about planning and organizing for it. Instead it was treated as a problem—a special case to worry about when promised deliveries could not be met. Today some firms are beginning to set up systematic procedures for order acceptance (or order promising, as a few are calling it). Computers help, mainly by calculating the amount of workload that results from orders that are booked by sales. If there are excessive workloads in certain centers of capacity, orders may have to be rejected or modified.

SUMMARY

The demand forecast, in units (not dollars), triggers many of the other activities in managing operations and operating resources. The forecast provides advance notice so that changes may be planned for.

The demand forecast may be based partly on national economic forecasts. Sales force estimates and market research are also helpful. Historical analysis of demand patterns is a third basis for demand forecasts.

Tools of historical demand analysis include the simple mean, trend, and seasonal analysis. These are multiperiod projection techniques, and they are useful in medium- and long-term projection. The least-squares technique of trend projection may be used where precision is desired or where there are many products/services to be forecasted. Calculators or computers are helpful in routinizing the calculation process. Seasonal indices may be combined with trend projection to produce improved forecasts sensitive to seasonal influences.

Period-by-period projection tools include moving average and exponential smoothing. These are useful tools for short- and medium-term projection. The MAD (mean absolute deviation) is a useful statistic to test different MA and ES options using actual demand data from past periods. The option with the lowest MAD would be the most suitable.

Other forecasting techniques include leading indicators and correlation. Leading indicators are hard to find but valuable when found. A leading indicator is any known variable that proves to rise or fall in the same way, as, but in advance of, product demand. Correlation coefficients may be used to test how well changes in a leading indicator correspond with changes in the product demand that it leads. Correlation (without lead) may be valuable if the independent variable is more predictable than your own demand.

With computers, recent demand data may be used to simulate several forecast methods. The best forecast may then be automatically selected by the computer, and the simulation is repeated every forecast period for every item being forecasted.

The forecast environment helps to determine the type of forecast required. Item forecasts tend toward high error rates but are necessary for master scheduling. Forecasts for product groups are more accurate, and they can help to show aggregate needs for work force and inventories.

Forecasts are more accurate for the near future than for out-periods. Out-period forecasts should therefore be updated as time moves forward. Also, less accurate out-period forecasts should serve as the basis for scheduling cheaper, more flexible goods; costly end-product production should be based on more accurate short-term forecasts where possible.

In industries with long customer lead times, only long-term forecasts for fixed capacity are required. Shorter-lead-time industries require more extensive forecasting, perhaps for materials, components, and assemblies.

The manager of a given organization unit should take care of his own demand forecasting rather than relying totally on forecasts for the larger organization of which his unit is a part. His unit's demand may follow patterns that are quite different from the patterns of other units in the same firm.

The last step in the demand planning process is to combine forecasted demand for each product/service with existing customer orders. To do this step right, it should include an evaluation. That is, the impact of customer orders on operating capacity should be evaluated. This provides an order acceptance—a commitment to honor the customer order. Order acceptance opens the way for improved communications and trust between operations and marketing people.

REFERENCES

Books

Box, G. E. P., and G. M. Jenkins. *Time Series Analysis, Forecasting, and Control*. Holden-Day, 1970 (QA280.B67).

Brown, R. G. *Smoothing, Forecasting, and Prediction of Discrete Time Series*. Prentice-Hall, 1963 (TA168.B68).

Butler, William F., Robert A. Kavesh, and Robert B. Platt, eds. *Methods and Techniques of Business Forecasting*. Prentice-Hall, 1974 (HB3730.M42).

Chambers, J. C., S. K. Mullick, and D. D. Smith. *An Executive's Guide to Forecasting*. Wiley, 1974 (HF5415.2.C38).

Forecasting. 2d ed. American Production and Inventory Control Society, 1979.

Gross, Charles W., and Robin T. Peterson. *Business Forecasting*. Houghton Mifflin, 1976.

Wheelwright, S. C., and S. Makridakis. *Forecasting Methods for Management.* Wiley, 1973 (HD69.F58W5).

PROBLEMS

Note: **Asterisked (*) problems require more than mimicry. They require judgment, and you should include discussion of reasons, assumptions, and outside sources of information.**

1. Huckleberry Farms, Inc., has three years of monthly demand data for its biggest seller, Huckleberry Jam. The planning director aims to use the data, given below, for demand forecasting.

Cases of Huckleberry Jam

	Three years ago	Two years ago	Last year
January	530	535	578
February	436	477	507
March	522	530	562
April	448	482	533
May	422	498	516
June	499	563	580
July	478	488	537
August	400	428	440
September	444	430	511
October	486	486	480
November	437	502	499
December	501	547	542

a. Calculate a six-month moving-average *forecast* (applicable to the *future*). What time period in the future is this forecast applicable to?

b. Which of the following MA time spans is best: three months, six months, or nine months? Prove your answer by calculating mean absolute deviations (MAD), using data *for the last 12 months only.* (If suitable computer facilities and software are available to you, use the full 36 months' data.)

c. Calculate a weighted five-month moving-average *forecast* (applicable to the *future*), using a reasonable weighting scheme of your own design. Using the *past eight months' data only,* determine the MAD for your weighted MA design.

d. If the most recent forecast—for December of last year—was 495, what is the next exponential smoothing (ES) forecast? use $\alpha = 0.3$. What time period in the future is this forecast applicable to?

e. Which of the following alphas is best for ES forecasting: 0.1, 0.3, or 0.5? Prove your answer by calculating MADs, using monthly data *for the last three months only.* In each case, assume that 570 was the ES forecast for September of last year.

f. Although the given data are monthly, Huckleberry also needs a forecast for next quarter and next year. Manipulate the monthly data (create new tables of data) so that they are useful for a quarterly and an annual forecast. Now compute a quarterly and an annual MA forecast, using a three-period (*not* three months in this case!) time span. And compute a quarterly and an annual ES forecast, using $\alpha = 0.3$ and assuming that the last period forecast was (1) 1,596 for quarterly and (2) 5,990 for annual.

g. Plot the data on a scatter diagram, with time as the horizontal axis (use graph paper, or else take some care in creating a substitute on ordinary lined paper). Now use the eyeball trend projection method to produce a forecast (not adjusted for seasonality) for Huckleberry Jam for the next 12 months. Either a straight or curving line may be used—whichever fits best. Write down each of the 12 forecasted values. (If suitable computer facilities and software are available to you, verify your plotted trend line by processing the data on the computer.)

*h. Most consumer products show some degree of demand seasonality? What kind of seasonality pattern would you expect for Huckleberry Jam? Why? *After responding to the preceding question,* examine the three years' history to see if the data tend to follow your reasoning. You may find it helpful to plot the three sets of 12-month data "on top of each other" on a graph to see if there is a pattern of seasonality. Now comment further on Huckleberry's demand patterns.

i. Select any 3 of the 12 months, and calculate seasonal indices for those 3 months for each year. Follow the method of Figure 2–8, modified so that the basis is a 12-month moving average. Now develop projected (next-year) seasonal indices for each of the three months. (If suitable computer facilities and software are available to you, develop seasonal indices for the full 12 months.)

j. Combine your results from *h* and *i*, that is, your trend projection with your seasonal indices. What are your seasonally adjusted trend forecasts for next year?

2. Seal-Fine Sash Company has three years of quarterly demand data for its standard "bedroom" window unit. The production control manager uses the data, given below, for demand forecasting.

Number of window units

	Three years ago	Two years ago	Last year
Winter	190	215	401
Spring	147	210	510
Summer	494	755	925
Fall	773	1,088	1,482

a. Calculate the three-quarter moving-average *forecast* (applicable to the *future*). What time period in the future is this moving average for?

b. Which of the following MA time spans is best: three quarters or four quarters? Prove your answer by calculating mean absolute deviations (MAD), using all 12 quarters of data. (If suitable computer facilities and software are available to you, process the data by computer rather than manually.) Do the MAD values seem to show that MA is a suitable method for the quarterly forecasting of Seal-Fine's window units? Explain.

c. Calculate a weighted three-quarter moving-average *forecast* (applicable to the *future*), using a reasonable weighting scheme of your own design. Using the *past eight quarters' data only,* determine the MAD for your weighted MA design.

d. If the most recent forecast—for fall of last year—was 1,550, what is the next exponential smoothing (ES) forecast? Use $\alpha = 0.2$. What time period in the future is the forecast applicable to?

e. Which of the following alphas is best for ES forecasting: 0.1, 0.3, or 0.5? Prove your answer by calculating MADs, using quarterly data *for the last three quarters only.* In each case, assume that 540 was the ES forecast for winter of last year. Do the MAD values seem to show that ES is a suitable method for quarterly forecasting of Seal-Fine's window units? Explain.

f. Plot the data on a scatter diagram, with time as the horizontal axis (use graph paper, or else take some care in creating a substitute on ordinary lined paper). Use the eyeball trend projection method to produce a forecast (not adjusted for seasonality) for the window units for the next four quarters. Now combine the data in such a way as to yield yearly forecasts for the next three years. Either a straight or curving line may be used—whichever fits best. Write down each of the forecasted values. (If suitable computer facilities and software are available to you, verify your plotted trend line by processing the data by computer.)

*g. What kind of seasonal demand pattern would you expect for Seal-Fine's product line? Explain. *After responding to the preceding question,* examine the three years' history to see if the data tend to follow your reasoning. You may find it helpful to plot the three sets of quarterly data "on top of each other" on a graph to see if there is a pattern of seasonality. Now comment further on Seal-Fine's demand patterns.

h. Select any two of the four quarters, and calculate seasonal indices for those two quarters for each year. Follow the method of Figure 2–8. Now develop projected (next-year) seasonal indices for each of the two quarters. (If suitable computer facilities and software are available to you, develop seasonal indices for all four quarters.)

i. Combine your four-quarter trend projection from *f* with your seasonal indices from *h*. What are your seasonally adjusted trend forecasts for next year?

3. Anderson Theaters owns a chain of movie theaters. In one city, a college town, there are several Anderson Theaters. There is interest in finding out exactly what influence the college student population has on movie attendance. Student population figures have been obtained from local colleges. These, along with movie attendance figures for the past 12 months, are given below:

Month	1	2	3	4	5	6	7	8	9	10	11	12
Students*	8	18	18	18	15	9	11	6	17	19	19	13
Attendance*	14	15	16	12	10	8	9	7	11	13	14	17

* In thousands. The student figures are monthly averages.

a. What is the correlation coefficient? (Solve by computer if convenient. Or use the manual method in the supplement.)

b. Is this correlation analysis useful for Anderson Theaters? Discuss fully.

Forecast error   4.   Planners at the county hospital are preparing a staffing plan and budget for next quarter. The listing below is computer data on labor-hours in various departments for last quarter. The trouble is, the average forecast error looks very high. Is the forecast error too high, or could next quarter's computer forecast be useful as the basis for a quarterly staffing plan? Perform any necessary calculations, and discuss.

Class	Last quarter labor-hour forecast	Last quarter labor-hour actual
Anesthesia	130	208
Cardiopulmonary	210	175
Emergency	650	589
Obstetrics	380	391
Pathology	90	68
Physical therapy	110	71
Radiology	200	277
Surgery	810	950

5.   According to one business news story, five- and ten-year plans, based partly on forecasts, were instituted in many a firm in the early 1960s, but many were abandoned or neglected in the early 1970s. Some executives stated that the plans simply were not used.

Can any of this disillusionment be explained based on forecast error tendencies? Explain.

Forecast lead   6.   Below is a list of a variety of organization types. Figure 2–22 shows that forecasts
time/purpose   may be required for planning (1) fixed capacity, (2) materials, (3) components, and (4) assemblies. Refer to the concepts presented in the figure in order to match up the types of organizations listed below with the four purposes. Briefly explain your match-ups.

Furniture manufacturing	Roller-skating rink
Clothing manufacturing	Natural gas distributor
Air conditioning/heating contractor	Orthodontist
Highway construction	A church parish
Airframe manufacturing	Sound system manufacturing
Commercial printing	Small appliance manufacturing
Tractor manufacturing	Toy manufacturing

Who should   *7.   At Apex Steel Cabinet Company, Personnel was the first department to separately
forecast?   forecast its key workloads—see Example 2–9 in the chapter. Mr. Guy, the president, wants key workload forecasting extended to other departments. Your assignment is to prepare logical workload lists and forecast bases, similar to Figure 2–23 in the chapter, for the following departments or sections: Public Relations, Advertising, and Data Processing.

Order   *8   Describe the order-processing sequence for a real organization that you are famil-
acceptance/   iar with, or visit an organization to collect the necessary data. You may wish to
order   supplement your description with a flowchart of some kind.
processing

IN-BASKET CASE*

Topic: Econometric Forecasting—Construction Co. (Housing)

To:

From: General Manager, Central States Home Builders, Inc.

Our firm is one of the largest in the area, but like the other home builders, we suffer from large swings in consumer demand for housing. I am wondering if it would be worthwhile for us to subscribe to one of the nationally known econometric forecasting services in order to better anticipate the ups and downs. I don't know anything about the costs or the range of their forecasting services— maybe these services wouldn't be very helpful to a house builder. Please do a study of the matter and report back to me.

*See instructions at end of problems section, Chapter 1.

supplement to chapter 2

LEAST SQUARES AND CORRELATION COEFFICIENTS

In this supplement two related techniques are examined. Both concern the straight line that most closely fits a set of plotted data points:

1. The least-squares technique, considered first, is a method of developing the equation for the straight line of best fit.
2. The correlation coefficient, considered last, measures how well a given straight line or line of regression fits a set of plotted data points.

Least squares   The general formula for a straight line is:

$$Y = a + bX$$

For any set of plotted data points, the least-squares method may be used to determine values for a and b in the formula that best fits the data points; a is the Y-intercept, and b is the slope. The least-squares formulas for a and b are:

$$a = \frac{\Sigma Y}{N} \quad \text{and} \quad b = \frac{\Sigma XY}{\Sigma X^2},$$

where

$\Sigma Y =$ Sum of the Y-values for all plotted points
$N =$ Total number of plotted points
$\Sigma XY =$ Sum of the product of X-value times Y-value for all plotted points
$\Sigma X^2 =$ Sum of squares of X-values for all plotted points

The two formulas and the resulting line of best fit are illustrated in a forecasting example, considered next.

EXAMPLE S2–1
Least-squares trend line, Data Services

In the last seven quarters, demand, in programmer-hours, was as follows at Data Services, Inc.:

510	600	400	520	340	440	420

What is the trend line?

Solution:

A table simplifies computation of a and b values. In the table the fourth quarter, in which 520 was the demand, is treated as the base period. It is numbered as period

0. The three previous periods are numbered −1, −2, and −3; the three succeeding periods are numbered +1, +2, and +3. The small numbers simplify calculations. The Y-values are the seven demand figures. The table is given below.

Y	X	X²	XY	
510	−3	9	−1,530	
600	−2	4	−1,200	
400	−1	1	−400	
520	0	0	0	← Base period
340	+1	1	+340	
440	+2	4	+880	
420	+3	9	+1,260	
Sums 3,230	0	28	−650	

Since

$$a = \frac{\Sigma Y}{N} \text{ and } b = \frac{\Sigma XY}{\Sigma X^2},$$

$$a = \frac{3,230}{7} = 461$$

$$b = \frac{-650}{28} = -23.2$$

The formula for the line of best fit is:

$$Y = 461 - 23.2 X$$

The formula may be used to forecast, say, the next quarter. With the base period (fourth quarter) numbered 0, the next (eighth) quarter is numbered +4. Then,

$$Y = 461 - 23.2 \,(+4)$$
$$= 461 - 93$$
$$= 368 \text{ programmer-hours}$$

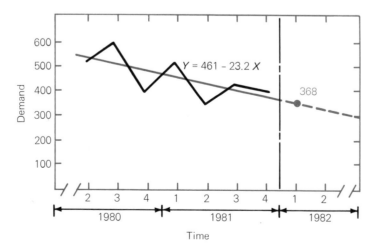

FIGURE S2–1
Seven-quarter least-squares trend—Data Services, Inc.

Figure S2–1 summarizes the results of the least-squares computations and the forecast for next quarter. Dates are put on the figure to make it agree with the dates for Figure 2–4 in the chapter. It may be seen that the least-squares trend is very nearly the same as the eyeball trend of Figure 2–4.

Correlation coefficients

The coefficient of correlation, r, ranges from 1.0 for perfect correlation to 0.0 for no correlation at all. An r of 1.0 applies to the case where all plotted points are on the straight line of best fit.

One formula for r is:

$$r = \sqrt{1 - \frac{\Sigma (Y - Y_f)^2}{\Sigma (Y - \overline{Y})^2}},$$

where

Y = Any given Y-value among the plotted points
Y_f = Corresponding Y-value for calculated points along the line of best fit (or line of regression)
$\overline{Y}$ = Mean Y-value

This formula applies when the sample size (number of plotted points) is reasonably large. When the line of best fit has not been calculated, the following formula permits direct computation of r:

$$r = \frac{N\Sigma XY - (\Sigma X)(\Sigma Y)}{\sqrt{N\Sigma X^2 - (\Sigma X)^2} \sqrt{N\Sigma Y^2 - (\Sigma Y)^2}}$$

Small sample size. When the sample size is small, adjustments for degrees of freedom are necessary. For a sloping straight trend line, a formula that includes the adjustments is:

$$r = \sqrt{1 - \frac{\Sigma (Y - Y_F)^2/(N - 2)}{\Sigma (Y - \overline{Y})^2/(N - 1)}}$$

This version of the formula applies to the Data Services, Inc., example presented in the above section on the least-squares method. The Data Services example is extended here to demonstrate calculation of r.

EXAMPLE S2–2
Correlation coefficient, Data Services

In Example S2–1, the formula for the line of best fit for seven quarters of programmer-hour demand was calculated as:

$$Y = 461 - 23.2X$$

The seven quarters of past data yielding the formula were given as:

510   600   400   520   340   440   420

What is the coefficient of correlation, r?

Solution:

A table simplifies the computation of *r*. The Y_F values in the table are computed from the line-of-best-fit formula. For example, the first Y_F is for period −3 (since period 4 was treated as the base period). Then,

$$Y_F = 461 - 23.2(-3)$$
$$= 461 - 69.6 = 391$$

$\overline{Y}$ is simply

$$\frac{\Sigma Y}{N} = \frac{3,230}{7} = 461$$

Other values necessary to calculate *r* are given in Figure S2–2.

FIGURE S2–2
Working figures
for computing, *r*,
Data Services

	Y	Y_F	$Y - Y_F$	$(Y - Y_F)^2$	$\overline{Y}$	$Y - \overline{Y}$	$(Y - \overline{Y})^2$
	510	531	−21	441	461	49	2,401
	600	507	93	8,649	461	139	19,321
	400	484	−84	7,056	461	−61	3,721
	520	461	59	3,481	461	59	3,481
	340	438	−98	9,604	461	−121	14,641
	440	415	25	625	461	−21	441
	420	391	29	841	461	−41	1,681
Sums	3,230			30,697			45,687

By substitution,

$$r = \sqrt{1 - \frac{30,697/5}{45,687/6}} = \sqrt{1 - \frac{6,139.4}{7,614.5}}$$
$$= \sqrt{1 - 0.81} = \sqrt{0.19}$$
$$= 0.44$$

An *r* of 0.44 is not high. This means that the line of best fit is not a good predictor. (But it may be the best available.)

Larger sample size. Two alternative formulas were given for computing *r* when the sample size is reasonably large. An extension of Example 2–8 in the chapter serves to demonstrate the second of the two formulas.

EXAMPLE S2–3
Correlation
coefficient,
Jobs Service

In Example 2–8 layoffs at Acme two weeks earlier are plotted against job applicants at the Jobs Service office. Figure 2–18 shows the correlation visually. What is the calculated coefficient of correlation, *r*?

Solution:

A table simplifies the computations. Figure S2–3 provides the necessary totals to solve for *r*. All *X* and *Y* values are taken from Example 2–8. Since there are 24 data items, $N = 24$. The second formula for *r* is repeated below.

FIGURE S2–3
Working figures
for computing *r,*
Jobs Service

Number of applicants Y	Layoffs at Acme (N− 2) X	Y²	X²	XY
50	0	2,500	0	0
60	0	3,600	0	0
80	25	6,400	625	2,000
65	20	4,225	400	1,300
110	50	12,100	2,500	5,500
145	60	21,025	3,600	8,700
115	60	13,225	3,600	6,900
125	25	15,625	625	3,125
120	20	14,400	400	2,400
120	35	14,400	1,225	4,200
110	45	12,100	2,025	4,950
70	0	4,900	0	0
60	0	3,600	0	0
65	0	4,225	0	0
90	0	8,100	0	0
55	0	3,025	0	0
70	20	4,900	400	1,400
45	0	2,025	0	0
100	30	10,000	900	3,000
105	30	11,025	900	3,150
105	40	11,025	1,600	4,200
70	0	4,900	0	0
95	0	9,025	0	0
100	10	10,000	100	1,000
Sums 2,130	470	206,350	18,900	51,825

$$r = \frac{N\Sigma XY - (\Sigma X)(\Sigma Y)}{\sqrt{N\Sigma X^2 - (\Sigma X)^2}\ \sqrt{N\Sigma Y^2 - (\Sigma Y)^2}}$$

By substitution,

$$r = \frac{24(51,825) - (2,130)(470)}{\sqrt{24(18,900) - (470)^2}\ \sqrt{24(206,350) - (2,130)^2}}$$

$$= 0.78$$

An *r* of 0.78 is rather high. Layoffs at Acme may be considered a good leading indicator.

chapter 3

CAPACITY PLANNING AND MASTER SCHEDULING

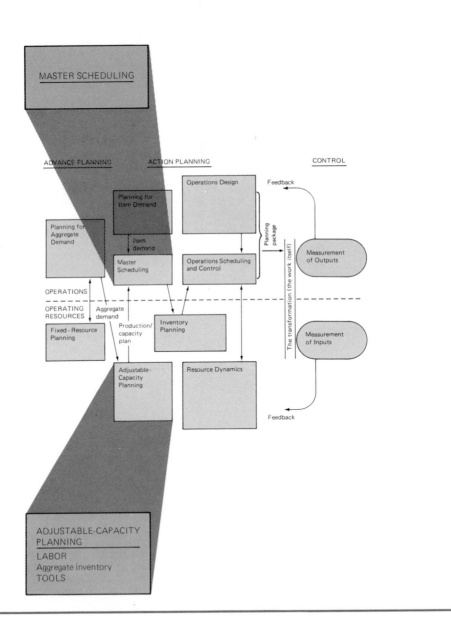

Does aggregate demand match gross production capacity? This is the question in production/capacity planning. Can unit ("disaggregated") demand by met by existing capacity? This is a central issue in master scheduling. Production/capacity planning and master scheduling are the subjects of this chapter. Matching capacity to workload in individual work centers is a related issue, but it is too early to discuss that detailed level of capacity management. It is reserved for a later chapter (Chapter 6) under the heading "work-center loading and capacity control."

PURPOSE OF CAPACITY PLANNING AND MASTER SCHEDULING

There are two main objectives of capacity planning and master scheduling. The objectives are meeting demand and utilizing capacity. The master schedule shows a key part of the plan for meeting item demand. Production/capacity planning has the objective of keeping overall capacity utilization at a high level.

Capacity utilization may be expressed as a percent of available hours that capacity is in productive use. Available hours may be single-shift or multiple-shift, and may refer to labor-hours, machine-hours, tool-hours or other special categories like passenger-seat-hours on a bus. Capacity utilization is a critical concern because of the cost of idleness of the resources in the given unit of capacity. Formal measurement of capacity is discussed in more depth in Chapters 6 and 8.

Matching capacity and demand

The title page for this chapter highlights the two blocks from the functional model (from Figure 1–4) that are of interest in this chapter. The necessary inputs, covered in the last chapter, are the arrows labeled aggregate demand and item demand. Aggregate demand forecasts are needed for production planning and adjustable-capacity planning.

Production planning sets forth rates of output to meet aggregate demand. Rates of output translate into plans for the adjustable elements of capacity: labor, aggregate inventories, and tools. Work force and inventory levels may be adjusted in response to swings in aggregate demand. Other responses include the use of subcontracting, temporary labor, rented tools, and marginal facilities; slower customer service; and off-peak pricing.

Production planning yields an aggregate capacity plan. The aggregate plan sets forth the intensity of use of fixed capacity. Intensity of use may be measured by throughput of products or services or by direct labor hours. We may read in the newspaper that a local plant is running at 80 percent of capacity. This means that the firm is achieving 80 percent of maximum throughput, or is operating at 80 percent of maximum direct labor or machine hours. (Throughput may convert directly into labor or machine hours.)

Item demand—orders and/or forecasts for particular items—is needed for master scheduling of items. Master scheduling is constrained by availability of capacity. The arrow labeled production/capacity plan on the chapter title page indicates the need for the capacity-planning function to precede the master-scheduling function.

The chart on the chapter title page indicates that aggregate inventory and tool planning are a part of adjustable-capacity planning. Aggregate inventory planning techniques are closely related to techniques for planning inventory quantities by item; the two topics are discussed together in Chapter 5, Inventory Planning—Quantities. Tool planning in the aggregate is mentioned in this chapter, and tools as inventory items are considered in Chapter 14, Inventory Dynamics and Control.

Capacity-demand matching model

Capacity-demand matching has been considered in the broad terms of the functional model on the chapter title page. We now turn to the details. Figure 3–1 presents a capacity-demand matching model. There is enough detail in the model to explain the complex case of a manufacturer that fabricates and assembles in the job-lot mode. Later a reduced version of the same model is presented for a service organization. The whole of Figure 3–1 is discussed below. More detailed discussion is included later.

In Figure 3–1, blocks 1, 2, and 3 concern demand planning in the aggregate and blocks 4, 5, and 6 concern demand planning for specific end products or services. Block 1 refers to aggregate policies, such as permissible use of overtime and subcontracting. Production planning, block 3, is setting production rates to meet forecasted aggregate demand (block 2), subject to aggregate policy limitations. The arrow labeled aggregate capacity plan represents the capacity needed to meet the production plan.

Blocks 4 and 5, actual customer demand and forecasted item demand, may be combined as total requirements (block 6) for specific items.[1] Some of those requirements may be for finished goods. The long arrow from block 6 to block 9, final-assembly schedule, represents such requirements. Final-assembly schedules tend to be very short range, based on recent actual customer orders where possible. Some of the total requirements in block 6 are for components only (e.g., demands for service parts). The arrow from block 6 to block 10, inventory planning, represents component demands. Finally, some of the requirements in block 6 are translated into needs for *end items*, a term that often means major modules or subassemblies. The arrow from block 6 to block 7, trial master schedule, represents end-item demands.

The trial master schedule is put together in order to meet end-item requirements, subject to aggregate capacity limits. The dashed arrow from block 7 to block 3 indicates that production planning and aggregate capacity planning may be revised in order to match more closely with end-item demands in the master schedule.

A final master production schedule (MPS) of end items emerges (block 8).

---

[1] There is a move afoot within the American Production and Inventory Control Society (APICS) to promote use of the term *demand management*. Demand management refers to the activities that impose production requirements on the organization. In Figure 3–1 blocks 2, 4, 5, and 6, plus the arrow from 8 to 4, would be considered demand management activities.

FIGURE 3–1
Capacity-demand matching process

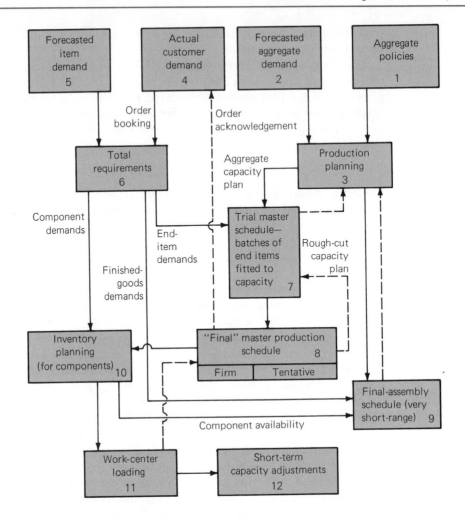

A dashed arrow from block 8 to block 7 is labeled rough-cut capacity plan. This is a quick check on capacity requirements in one or a few critical work centers. The firm portion of the MPS cannot be easily changed, because parts for these end items would be on order. The tentative portion is easily changed.

End items on the MPS are made from component parts. Orders for those parts are planned in block 10, inventory planning. Block 11, work-center loading, refers to workloads in the work centers resulting from parts that are to be made rather than bought. If workloads are too heavy or light, the MPS may be changed, which changes the parts orders, which changes loads in the parts-manufacturing work centers. The dashed line from block 11 to block 8 represents such revision of the MPS.

The final block is short-term capacity adjustments (block 12). Overtime, layoffs, or similar adjustments may be needed to take care of workload-capacity mismatches that remain after all preceding attempts to achieve a balance.

In the remainder of the chapter concepts and techniques that apply to the capacity-planning and master-scheduling blocks (blocks 1, 2, 3, 7, and 8) are discussed.

PLANNING FOR AGGREGATE DEMAND

Figure 3–1 shows two inputs to production planning. One is aggregate policies (block 1); the other is forecasted aggregate demands (block 2). Each is explained below. (Aggregate inventory is discussed in Chapter 5.)

Aggregate policies

Aggregate policies are based on high-level strategies. The following are some examples:

A municipal power company may have a strategy of providing employee security in order to gain a stable work force (low turnover). This might translate into aggregate policies to absorb surges in demand without much short-term hiring and layoffs. For example, one policy could be to maintain excess work force, especially linesmen and installers. Another policy might be to subcontract some of the excess demands for repairing downed lines and so forth.

A bowling proprietor may have a strategy of high capacity utilization. A supportive aggregate policy (or tactic) is lower prices for daytime bowling.

A food wholesaler may have a strategy of very fast service to retail grocers. Supportive aggregate policies might include the use of shift work, weekend hours, overtime, and cross-trained workers for interdepartmental worker loans. A supportive inventory policy would be to maintain large inventories.

Any kind of organization might adopt the strategy of keeping a tight rein on internal service costs. One aggregate policy for this would be to use service pools: typing pools, motor pools, and labor pools, for example. These are usually less costly than assigning the service units to individual departments— but service quality and response time may suffer.

The examples point out common kinds of aggregate policies. The following is a more complete list:

Hiring and layoffs	Maintenance work as a filler
Overtime and extra shifts	Use of marginal facilities
Part-time and temporary labor	Renting space or tools
Cross-training and transfers (of people or work) between departments	Subcontracting
	Refusing, backordering, or postponing work
Labor pools	Building inventories
Motor pools	Peak/off-peak price differences

Aggregate policies (as well as underlying strategies) are set by top officers, including high-level managers in operations and operating resources. Examples are the general manager or plant superintendent, chief of purchasing, chief of plant maintenance, chief of inventory control, and chief of production control.

Aggregate policies may be expressed as minimums, maximums, or ranges and may be priority-ordered. For example, a set of priority-ordered policies aimed at maintaining a level permanent work force might be:

1. Inventory buildup, up to 10 percent above predicted demand.
2. Use of temporary labor, up to 5 percent of excess demands (after inventory depletion).
3. Use of overtime, up to 5 percent, for further excess demands.
4. Reduction of customer service beyond that.

With such specific policies production planning is straightforward.

Forecasting aggregate demand

In Chapter 2 a distinction was made between unit forecasting and aggregate forecasting. The reasons for this split may now be more fully explained. As Figure 3–1 shows, forecasting demand, by unit (block 5), is needed for planning specific components and end products or services. Forecasting aggregate demand, by product groups (block 2), has the broader purpose of setting production rates.

We know from Chapter 2 that forecasting by product groups can be more accurate than item forecasting. The challenge is to form meaningful product groups. Normally it is best to group by common labor processes, common machine processes, or dominant routings. These groups make up units of capacity that can be separately staffed, subcontracted, set up, inventoried, and so forth.

The forecast for a product group should account for seasonal and promotional surges and extend across several time periods. A forecast period of a few weeks may be enough in services. This is especially true in services that use mostly unskilled labor; such labor is usually plentiful and therefore adjustable over short time periods. A forecast period of several months or quarters is needed where skilled labor is used or for goods producers. Goods make a difference, since they may be inventoried. One-week forecast periods are desirable in many firms for group forecasts, but one-month periods may be sufficient for firms employing highly stable skilled labor.

The forecast of aggregate demand provides data for production/capacity planning (block 3 in Figure 3–1), considered next.

PRODUCTION/CAPACITY PLANNING—BASIC CONCEPTS

The production plan sets forth planned rates of production (see block 3 in Figure 3–1). The rates of production may be set by considering:

1. Available capacity.
2. Planned end-item inventory levels.
3. Planned backlogs of end items.

If orders are processed on demand, there can be no backlogs, and number 3 would not apply. For services providers and make-to-order goods producers, the output is not inventoriable, so number 2 would not apply. But number 1, available capacity, is always of concern.

Available capacity may be compared with planned production rates for large capacity (or product) groups. This level of capacity planning may be referred to as aggregate capacity planning; the planning of demands on capacity in individual work centers is a more detailed level of planning, considered in later chapters.

In very small firms or firms with a single, narrow product line, a single aggregate capacity plan may be sufficient. For example, a company that makes unfinished furniture may have laborers who are cross-trained to operate any woodworking machine or tool. The aggregate forecast might be translated first into labor hours and then into number of workers needed. Since workers are cross-trained, there is no need to subdivide the plan into capacity groups.

In most firms two or more logical capacity groups may be identified for aggregate capacity planning. In a firm making *finished* furniture, woodworkers might form one logical group, wood finishers a second group, and upholsterers a third. In this case the forecast should show how much aggregate demand there is for woodworking, for wood finishing, and for upholstering. Then the right amount of aggregate labor can be planned in each of the three capacity groupings.

Production/ capacity planning in simple organizations

A simple example of production and capacity planning follows. It is simple in that it is for a services organization that does not have many work centers or an inventoriable product.

EXAMPLE 3–1
Production/ capacity plan, janitorial service

Bright Way Janitorial Service has established four categories of capacity:

1. Wet processes (mopping, buffing, etc.).
2. Dry processes (vacuuming/dusting).
3. Glass cleaning.
4. Special cleaning (e.g., stripping).

These categories were set because they define four separate kinds of worker/equipment processes. Each may be forecasted based on historical data. Bright Way uses the forecasts, along with its labor, service, and pricing policies, to arrive at a production/capacity plan for a four-week period, by week.

The forecast and the production/capacity plan are updated (rolled over) every two weeks. The short forecast interval is suitable because hiring and training require less than two weeks. Updating the production/capacity plan need not be done every week, because there is a staff of irregular workers on call. They serve as a cushion against inaccurate forecasting.

Bright Way has a strategy of seeking "higher-quality" customers, paying a bit higher wage, and gaining a somewhat more stable workforce than its competitors. In support of that strategy the following aggregate policies have developed:

Labor:
   Priority 1—18–22 percent full-time labor, no overtime.
   Priority 2—65–75 percent part-time labor.
   Priority 3—8–12 percent irregular laborers.
   Priority 4—20 percent of full-time and part-time staff cross-trained for possible temporary transfer to secondary work category.
   Priority 5—subcontract (make advance agreements) for excess short-term demands, where possible.
Service (responsiveness):
   Priority 1—maintain all schedules for regular customers.
   Priority 2—next-week response to new customers—up to limits of staffing—for routine cleaning, that is, work categories 1, 2, and 3.
   Priority 3—work special cleaning demands into the schedule as soon as possible without disrupting regular schedules.
Pricing: No pricing incentives. This policy subject to change if competition warrants it.

With those policies as a basis, Bright Way's production/capacity plan for the next four weeks is as shown in Figure 3–2. The plan shows forecasted labor-hours of demand for each work category and for each week. The forecasted labor-hours are assigned to full-time, part-time, overtime, and irregular labor. In this four-week period there is no planned need for subcontracting. The totals at the bottom include percentages. These fit the percentage goals that Bright Way set in its aggregate policies.

For example, in week 1 the total forecasted demand for category 1 (wet processes) is 1,240 labor-hours of business. Janitorial staff assignments for that demand are: 240 labor-hours of full-time labor, 860 of part-time labor, and 140 of irregular labor. Since 240 + 860 + 140 = 1,240, the plan meets forecasted demand with no need for subcontracting.

Forecasted demand for all four work categories in week 1 totals 3,835 labor-hours. To meet that demand without subcontracting, the plan calls for 800 labor-hours full-time, 2,690 part-time, and 335 irregular. In percentages full-time labor is 21 percent, which falls within the priority 1 goal of 18–22 percent; part-time is 70 percent, which is within the priority 2 goal of 65–75 percent; and irregular is 8.7 percent, which is within the priority 3 goal of 8–12 percent.

All priorities are met in week 1. The production plan is to do the full amount of business that the demand forecast indicated is available. The capacity plan is the planned labor assignments, which are expressed in four different capacity groupings, that is, work categories 1–4.

In weeks 2, 3, and 4 hiring is called for because forecasted demand is on the increase. Since hiring is normaly possible in less than two weeks, this plan provides the necessary lead time.

FIGURE 3-2
Four-week group forecast and production/capacity plan—Bright Way Janitorial Service

Work category	Labor type	Labor-hours, by week							
		1		2		3		4	
		Forecasted	Assigned	Forecasted	Assigned	Forecasted	Assigned	Forecasted	Assigned
1	Full-time	1,240	240	1,160	240	1,100	240	1,100	240
	Part-time		860		860		860		860
	Irregular		140		60				
	Subcontract								
2	Full-time	1,900	400	2,000	400	2,280	480	2,450	520
	Part-time		1,320		1,320		1,400		1,480
	Irregular		180		280		380		450
	Subcontract								
3	Full-time	480	120	480	120	480	120	480	120
	Part-time		360		360		360		360
	Irregular								
	Subcontract								
4	Full-time	205	40	300	40	240	40	380	40
	Part-time		150		220		200		270
	Irregular		15		40				70
	Subcontract								
	Totals	3,835		3,940		4,100		4,410	
	Full-time		800 (21%)		800 (20%)		880 (21%)		920 (21%)
	Part-time		2,690 (70%)		2,760 (70%)		2,820 (69%)		2,970 (67%)
	Irregular Sub-contract		335 (8.7%)		380 (9.6%)		380 (9.3%)		520 (12%)
	Projected hiring	—	—	4 PT		2 FT 3 PT		2 FT 2 PT	

We have not considered the methods of forecasting and analysis of production planning options that Bright Way might have used. The purpose has been just to show the inputs (policies and forecasts) and the outputs (the production plan). The production plan is really just a staffing and hiring plan for Bright Way. For a goods producer the planning would be far more complicated since inventory options would be added.

Bright Way's plan specifies aggregate labor in the four work categories and the number of people to be hired each period. It does not show what work categories they must be hired into and trained for. That would be detailed planning. Also not shown are needs for cleaning equipment and supplies. Bright Way might project these needs by using equipment and supplies multipliers for each work category.

Chase-demand versus level-capacity plans

In the example just discussed, Bright Way forecasted four weeks in advance. This is not typical of janitorial services. Most janitorial services plan only one week in advance; they pay the minimum wage, hire almost any applicant, and accept large turnover rates. Bright Way aims to be different. Its prices and wages are higher; it selects employees with care; it gives raises based on reliability and longevity; and it specializes in cleaning in "higher-quality" locales, such as banks. Therefore, it plans, forecasts, and hires farther in advance.

Compared with the capacity planning of almost any other kinds of enterprise, Bright Way's capacity planning seems decidedly reactive, "catch-as-catch-can." But compared with its janitorial-service competitors, Bright Way seems to be farsighted. The typical janitorial service follows what is often called a *chase-demand* strategy of capacity planning. For the janitorial-service industry Bright Way may be said to follow more of a *level-capacity* strategy. The two strategies are contrasted in Figure 3–3.

FIGURE 3–3
Chase-demand and level-capacity strategies in janitorial service firms

	Relatively level-capacity (Bright Way)	Chase-demand (competitors)
Labor-skill level	Low	Very low
Wage rate	Low	Very low
Working conditions	Pleasant	Mediocre
Training required per employee	Low	Very low
Labor turnover	Moderate	High
Hire-fire costs	Moderate	High
Error rate	Low	Moderate
Type of budgeting and forecasting required	Short run	Very short run

Source: Adapted from a similar figure (but for a brokerage firm) in W. Earl Sasser, R. Paul Olsen, and D. Daryl Wyckoff, *Management of Service Operations* (Allyn and Bacon, 1978), p. 304 (HD9981.5.S27).

In the chase-demand strategy the labor force rises and falls with demand. There is not enough planning lead time to groom a well-trained, well-paid, stable work force. The first six entries under chase-demand in the figure reflect this reliance on a transient work force. It follows that planning is very short run.

Bright Way's relatively level-capacity strategy provides for more lead time to select and train a stable, better-paid work force. The planning horizon is a bit longer, though still short run as compared with that of other industries.

Chase-demand is the capacity-planning partner of a quick response marketing strategy. On the other hand, level capacity is the partner of a quality-of-service marketing strategy. There may be a competitive niche for both strategies in a given locale.

PRODUCTION/CAPACITY PLANNING FOR GOODS PRODUCERS

The importance of production/capacity planning tends to be greater for goods producers than for service providers. Goods producers tend to be more capital intensive, which means high costs when fixed capacity is idle. And goods producers have an inventoriable product. While inventories provide extra options for balancing capacity with aggregate demand, they complicate the analysis and introduce an extra cost factor: the cost of idle inventories.

Discussion of aggregate inventory planning is deferred until the Chapter 5 treatment of inventory planning. Four other techniques of production/capacity planning for goods producers are discussed in this section:

1. Learning-curve planning.
2. The quarterly ordering system.
3. Group-forecasting-based approaches.
4. Transportation method.

The first three are practical, usable approaches for certain operating environments. The fourth is a restrictive cost-analysis approach that is somewhat lacking in practical value but is instructive as a way of showing cost relationships in production/capacity planning.[2]

Learning-curve planning

As people learn, their time to do a given task decreases. In industry this is known as the learning-curve phenomenon, and it applies not only to direct labor but also to those who support the direct-labor effort. Where the learning-curve effect is significant, planning production rates and capacity plans should

---

[2] Another approach that is widely used for instructive purposes is the linear decision rule (LDR) approach. And a new and still developing practical approach is resource requirements planning (RRP), which is a computer-assisted method of simulating master production scheduling alternatives in order to project loads on capacity groupings. These techniques, while important, are reserved for an advanced course.

FIGURE 3–4
Eighty percent
learning curve

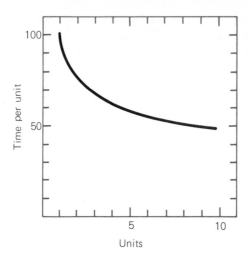

allow for it. With learning effects, production rates may increase over time with no change in capacity level, or capacity levels may be reduced over time without reducing production rates.

The learning-curve phenomenon was observed in airframe manufacturing as far back as 1925.[3] In subsequent years aircraft manufacturers found a dominant learning pattern, the 80 percent learning curve: The second plane required 80 percent as much direct labor as the first; the fourth required 80 percent as much as the second; the tenth, 80 percent as much as the fifth; and so forth. The rate of learning to assemble aircraft was concluded to be 20 percent between doubled quantities.

Graphically an 80 percent learning curve appears as shown in Figure 3–4. Mathematically, the learning curve follows the general formula

$$Y = aX^b,$$

where

$$Y = \text{Labor-hours per unit}$$
$$X = \text{Unit number}$$
$$a = \text{Labor-hours for first unit}$$
$$b = \frac{\text{Logarithm of learning-curve rate}}{\text{Logarithm of 2}}$$

In production/capacity planning by the learning curve, labor requirements over time are calculated. An example follows.

---

[3] The commander of Wright-Patterson Air Force Base was reported to have observed it in 1925: Winfred B. Hirshmann, "Profit from the Learning Curve," *Harvard Business Review,* January–February 1964, p. 125.

EXAMPLE 3–2
Learning-curve
planning,
Bellweather
Electric, Inc.

Bellweather has a contract for 60 portable electric generators. The labor-hour requirement to manufacture the first unit is 100 hours. With that as a given, Bellweather planners develop an aggregate capacity plan, using learning-curve calculations. A 90 percent learning curve is used, based on previous experience on generator contracts.

Using the general formula, the labor requirement for the second generator is:

$$Y = aX^b$$

$$Y = (100)(2)^{\left(\frac{\log 0.9}{\log 2.0}\right)}$$

$$= (100)(2)^{\left(\frac{-0.0457}{0.3010}\right)}$$

$$= (100)(2)^{-0.152}$$

$$= (100)(0.9)$$

$$= 90 \text{ hours}$$

It would not have been necessary to go through the calculations for the second unit, since, for a 90 percent learning curve, there is 10 percent learning between doubled quantities.

For the fourth unit,

$$Y = aX^b = 100(4)^{-0.152} = (100)(0.81) = 81$$

This result may be obtained more simply by

$$(100)(0.9)^2 = (100)(0.9)(0.9) = (100)(0.81) = 81$$

For the eighth unit,

$$Y = aX^b = 100(8)^{-0.152} = (100)(0.729) = 72.9$$

This result is also obtained by

$$(100)(0.9)^3 = (100)(0.9)(0.9)(0.9) = (100)(0.729) = 72.9$$

This way of avoiding logarithms works for the 16th, 32d, 64th, etc., units—for any unit that is a power of 2; but for the 3d, 5th, 6th, 7th, 9th, etc., units, the logarithmic calculation is necessary.

Cumbersome logarithmic and exponentiation operations may be performed easily on a good hand-held electronic calculator. Where multiple calculations are necessary—Bellweather has 60 values to compute—it might be better to spend 15 minutes writing and running a short computer program to print out a listing of results.[4]

Figure 3–5 displays some of the results of the learning-curve calculations. With these figures Bellweather may match its labor assignments to the decreasing per unit labor-hour requirements. Completions of finished generators can be master-scheduled to increase at the 90 percent learning-curve rate.

---

[4] Learning-curve tables have been widely used in the past, especially in federal contracting agencies and in the aerospace industry. (Tables may be found in R. W. Conway and Andrew Shultz, Jr., "The Manufacturing Progress Function," *Journal of Industrial Engineering*, vol. 10, no. 1 (January–February 1959), pp. 39–54.) Today it is probably faster for the using organization to run calculations on an interactive computer terminal or an electronic calculator than to bother with tables.

FIGURE 3–5
Labor-hour
requirements for
generator
manufacturing,
Bellweather
Electric

Generator number	Labor-hours required	Cumulative labor-hours required
1	100	100.0
2	90	190.0
3	84.6	274.6
10	70.5	799.4
20	63.4	1,460.8
30	59.6	2,072.7
40	57.1	2,654.3
50	55.2	3,214.2
60	53.7	3,757.4

Learning-curve concepts are important today in any firm engaged in large-scale limited-quantity production: airplanes, earthmovers, and so on. (Learning curves are also important today for setting prices on goods whose costs fall rapidly—such as digital watches and electronic calculators—but this is not a production/capacity-planning topic.)

The learning curve is of little use in production/capacity planning of other kinds of goods, especially job-lot production of consumer and industrial goods. In these cases production/capacity planning has evolved in response to market forces, which is discussed next.

Evolution in production/ capacity planning

Following World War II, consumer waiting lists for refrigerators, washing machines, rubber tires, and so forth, were often a year or two long. For the manufacturer, such order backlogs provided long planning lead times. The *quarterly ordering system* came into use. The firm merely decided what items and components it would produce next quarter, and resources needs were thoroughly planned to fit that production. The plans remained generally accurate for the whole quarter, since the order backlog provided secure demand.

The backlogs were whittled down as the consumer pipeline gradually filled up with goods. In the late 1950s and early 1960s a new era of short backlogs and stiff competition emerged. Without the luxury of long backlogs, manufacturers turned to item forecasting as a basis for quarterly ordering. Means, trends, and moving averages were used to predict end-item and component demands, and the demands were loaded (scheduled) into appropriate work centers.

But item-forecasting accuracy is basically poor. When greater-than-predicted demands for certain items occurred, rush orders were put into the system or existing orders were moved forward on the schedules. Expediters ("parts chasers") were hired to handle "hot lists" and to pull the rush jobs through. That they could do. What expediters could not do anything about was the overloads that the rush jobs caused in some work centers. Other jobs would need to be late to make way for the rush jobs. At the same time, lower-than-predicted demands caused slowdowns in certain other work centers. The pattern of overloads and underloads, plus many late orders, became common. Quarterly ordering, when based on *item* forecasting, didn't work.

In Chapter 2 we learned that item forecasts are less accurate than group forecasts. The next advance in production/capacity planning was based on that fact. To overcome some of the problems of expediting-based systems, better plans based on *group forecasts* came into use.

Quarterly ordering is still in limited use, and indeed it works very well for the firm fortunate enough to have long backlogs of customer demands. Quarterly ordering is simple enough not to require an example, but two examples of group-forecasting-based approaches are examined. One is for make-to-order plants, and the other is for make-to-stock plants.

Production/ capacity planning in make-to-order plants

The following example of production/capacity planning in a make-to-order plant focuses on order backlogs and lead times. The method follows a two-step process:

1. Identify broad capacity groups or similar processes—following the principle that forecasts are more accurate for larger groupings.
2. Develop a production/capacity plan based on projecting recent total demands into the future and on backlog and lead-time policies.

EXAMPLE 3–3
Production/ capacity planning, tail and exhaust pipe plant

Hot Pipes Division of International Industries makes tail pipes and exhaust pipes for the aftermarket. (That means replacement parts.) Orders are rather small and diverse, and Hot Pipes does not retail its own brand name. Therefore, it is strictly a make-to-order plant.

An aggregate capacity plan, to cover a number of weeks, is needed. Fine-tuning is possible on a day-to-day basis; that is, Hot Pipes can do a limited amount of overtime work and labor borrowing on a daily basis. But the regular work force must be hired and trained in advance—and planned for, using production planning methods.

Make-to-order planning is difficult in view of lack of order lead time. Still, a quick and simple projection of recent data into the future is helpful.

Step 1. Step 1 is to identify broad capacity groupings. Tail pipes and exhaust pipes seem to be the two key groups that are logical for separate capacity plans: They are built in separate areas of the factory with different equipment and different worker skills. Capacity may be measured in *pieces* for both groupings.

Step 2. In step 2, demands for recent past periods are totaled and capacity (piece) requirements are developed, based on projecting the demand pattern into the future.

Figure 3–6 shows past demands for tail pipes on the left and two capacity options on the right. Option 1 provides for 1,800 pieces per week—100 less than the mean demand for the past eight weeks. The deviations range from +700 to −1,400 pieces per week. Option 2 provides for 300 less pieces per week than option 1. The deviations range from +100 to −3,500 pieces per week.

The first option results in excess capacity in four of the eight weeks: weeks 2–5. The second results in excess capacity in only one of the weeks: week 2.

The projected backlogs are quite opposite: For option 1 the backlog reaches 1,400 pieces in the seventh week. That is nearly a one-week backlog at the planned production

FIGURE 3–6
Capacity/
backlog options
for tail pipes

Week	Recent weekly demands		Option 1: 1,800 pieces per week		Option 2: 1,500 pieces per week	
	Pieces	Cumulative pieces	Cumulative	Deviation	Cumulative	Deviation
1	1,800	1,800	1,800	0	1,500	−300
2	1,100	2,900	3,600	+700	3,000	+100
3	1,800	4,700	5,400	+700	4,500	−200
4	1,950	6,650	7,200	+550	6,000	−650
5	2,300	8,950	9,000	+50	7,500	−1,450
6	2,800	11,750	10,800	−950	9,000	−2,750
7	2,250	14,000	12,600	−1,400	10,500	−3,500
8	1,200	15,200	14,400	−800	12,000	−3,200

$$\text{Mean demand} = \frac{15,200}{8} = 1,900 \text{ pieces per week}$$

rate of 1,800 pieces per week. For option 2 the backlog reaches 3,500 pieces—over two weeks' backlog—in the seventh week.

Two weeks' backlog means a two-week lead time for Hot Pipes' customers. For its rather competitive industry, that may be unacceptable. Thus, Hot Pipes may decide to pay for the excess capacity of option 1 in order to keep planned backlogs and lead times down to within a week.

In the simplified example above, options such as extra shifts and subcontracting were not considered. Overtime, labor borrowing, and similar very short-range adjustments should normally *not* be considered in the production/capacity-planning stage; those are measures to be taken when all other capacity planning fails (see block 12, short-term capacity adjustments, in the model of Figure 3–1).

For this method, the assumption is that orders may be backlogged and worked off in later periods. Note that backlogs are carried forward by the cumulative totals.

In some firms an unmet order is a lost order; backlogs are not carryable. This tends to be the case in transportation, restaurants, lodging, and similar fast-reaction-oriented industries. For such industries production/capacity planning may also be based on recent demands. But the demands would not be cumulative; therefore negative deviations are lost sales, not backlogs.

Production/ capacity planning in make-to-stock plants

Production/capacity planning in a make-to-stock plant begins with the same two steps as in the make-to-order case: Identify groups, and develop production rates to fit projected group demands. That may complete the plan, but more often the firm will add a third step: Refine the production rates to provide for desired inventory levels. Occasionally there is a fourth step: Refining the plan by examining how production loads onto individual shops or departments. All four steps are presented in the following example.

EXAMPLE 3–4
Production/
capacity
planning,
electronics
plant

Step 1. For production/capacity-planning purposes, Quark Electronics divides its productive processes into three product groups. These are identified simply as groups 1, 2, and 3. Each group covers a large number of products, some end products, and some assemblies and parts.

The reason for the division into three groups is seen in Figure 3–7. There are three dominant process-flow paths, or routings. The three routings wind through the four shop areas and include 13 of the 16 work centers in the four shops. A number of products do not exactly fit any of the three routings. But enough do to provide a solid basis for production/capacity planning.

Aggregate demand may be forecasted for each product group identified; then both man-hour and machine-hour requirements may be roughly matched against product demand.

Step 2. The next step is to develop a production/capacity plan based on desired work force utilization. Figure 3–8 shows a forecast and a trial production plan for product group 1. The plan provides for an even 10,200-piece-per-week production rate for the four weeks covered by the forecast. All different kinds of pieces are counted. Still, Quark planners feel that pieces is a meaningful measure for producing an aggregate capacity plan. Product groups 2 and 3 should be similarly planned.

FIGURE 3–7
Common
routings, Quark
Electronics

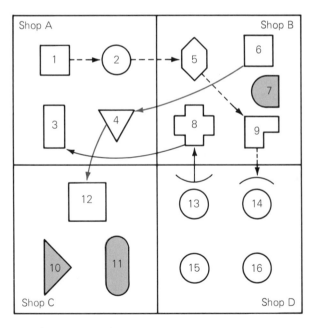

Key: Product group 1: – – – – – – – ▶
        Product group 2: ————————▶
        Product group 3: ————————▶
        Work centers not included in common routings: ▭

Note: Machines 13, 14, 15, and 16 are identical.

FIGURE 3–8
Triai production
plan, product
group 1

Week	Pieces through product group 1				
	Forecast		Trial production plan		
	Pieces per week (000)	Cumulative	Pieces per week (000)	Cumulative	Inventory
0					14.0
1	10.0	10.0	10.2	10.2	14.2
2	10.0	20.0	10.2	20.4	14.4
3	10.4	30.4	10.2	30.6	14.2
4	10.4	40.8	10.2	40.8	14.0

The plan appears to provide a good balance between forecasted demand and planned capacity. They are equal at 40,800 cumulative pieces.

Step 3. The third step is to refine the production plan to provide for desired inventory levels. As Figure 3–8 shows, the beginning inventory is 14,000 pieces and the ending inventory (week 4) is also 14,000 pieces. Sometimes a change in inventory level is desired. For example, the firm may desire an inventory buildup, perhaps in anticipation of a seasonal or promotional surge in demand. If so, the planned production rate would need to be increased above the 10,200 pieces per week shown in the trial production plan. The planned rate would be decreased if the firm desired to work off some inventory.

Inventory levels would also be examined for product groups 2 and 3. Production/capacity planning could stop there. But a more exacting plan may be derived by calculating effects on each shop, by labor-hours and by machine-hours; shop-level capacity planning is considered next.

Step 4. A more exacting aggregate plan requires converting group capacity into smaller capacity units. Conversion factors of some sort are needed. If group capacity were in labor-hours (or machine-hours), then perhaps historical percentages could be used to translate group hours into shop hours. In the case of Quark Electronics, the group capacity plan is in pieces per week. Therefore, labor-hours and machine-hours per piece are suitable as conversion factors. These factors may be historical and not overly exact.

Figure 3–9 shows, for week 1, how such conversion factors may be used to convert planned pieces to labor-hours and machine-hours for each shop. Dividing planned pieces per week by the standard rates gives required labor-hours and machine-hours.

Sample calculations are shown at the bottom of the figure for the results in shop A, group 1. The labor rate of 200 pieces per hour is divided into the planned production rate of 10,200 pieces per week; the result is 51 labor-hours required in week 1. Similarly, the 41 machine-hours required in week 1 are derived by dividing 10,200 pieces per week by the machine rate of 250 pieces per hour.

After the calculations are completed, total labor-hours and machine-hours may be summed for each shop. The totals are compared with single-shift shop capacities, and the difference is the shortage of labor-hours or machine-hours. (Shop capacities are based on number of people or machines times 40 hours regular time per week less nonavailable time, such as break time, and delay time.)

FIGURE 3-9
Production plan
converted to
labor-hours and
machine-hours,
Quark Electronics

	Shop A	Shop B	Shop C	Shop D
Week 1: labor-hours				
Group 1..............................	⑤①	68		46
Group 2..............................	36	58	83	
Group 3..............................	50	80		40
Total labor-hours required	137	206	83	86
Labor-hour capacity	160	200	80	80
Shortage of labor-hours	−23	+6	+3	+6
Week 1: Machine-hours				
Group 1..............................	④①	37		51
Group 2..............................	29	29	21	
Group 3..............................	50	20		27
Total machine-hours required	120	86	21	78
Machine-hour capacity	120	100	36	100
Shortage of machine-hours	0	−14	−15	−22

Sample calculations (for circled figures):
  Given:
    Standard labor rate in shop A = 200 pieces per hour.
    Standard machine rate in shop A = 250 pieces per hour.
    Trial production rate for group 1 = 10,200 pieces per week.
  Therefore:
    Labor-hours required = 10,200/200 = 51.
    Machine-hours required = 10,200/250 = 41.

Few serious capacity problems are indicated by the results in Figure 3–9. The minus results indicate excess capacity, but only for shop A labor is this much of a concern. There is a greater amount of excess machine-hours, but this may be thought of as a normal margin for error, since machines constitute "fixed" capacity that cannot be added to on short notice.

The 23 hours of excess labor in shop A could be dealt with by cutting the work force. Or Quark planners could make out a revised production plan with more pieces in group 1, 2, or 3—whichever would cause the least additional labor-hours in the already overloaded shops B, C, and D.

The same procedure would extend to weeks 2, 3, and 4. The calculating burden may be eased by using a computer. But it is not necessary to achieve a highly refined match between required and available capacity since this is only an aggregate plan.

Transportation method

In using the transportation method in production/capacity planning, production labor costs are included. The options are to use inside labor—your own work force—or to subcontract to an outside firm (outside labor). Further options, in the case of inside labor, are regular time and overtime.

Also usually included in using the transportation method are two inventory costs. One is carrying cost: Where capacity in a given time period is short, that period's demand may have to be produced in an earlier period; if so, there is a cost to carry the goods until the period in which they are demanded. The other cost is backorder cost: Instead of producing in advance of demand, you may produce late; if so, the goods are said to be backordered, and the backorder cost is the cost of lost goodwill from the customer who has been "put on hold."

An example. Costs for various capacity options may be matched with demand, period by period. A transportation matrix simplifies the process. An example follows:

EXAMPLE 3–5
Transportation method in production/ capacity planning, Quark Electronics

One of Quark's products is a ROM (read-only memory) board. It is used in microcomputers. The production/capacity planning horizon used by Quark for the fast-changing ROM market is just four months. Capacity options and their costs are given below. Backordering is an option also. But Quark analysts prefer not to include backordering since backorder costs are so speculative. Thus backorders are not allowed in the analysis, even though Quark actually does backorder.

Cost data:

Regular-time cost per unit . . . . $ 80
Overtime cost per unit   120
Subcontract cost per unit   130
Carrying cost per unit per period   5

Capacity data and demand-forecast data in ROM boards, for the next four months, are:

| Month | *Capacity (000)* | | | *Demand forecast (000)* |
	Regular time	*Overtime*	*Subcontract*	
July	23	5	10	30
August*	12	3	10	35
September	21	5	10	20
October	24	5	10	35

* Two-week factory shutdown for vacation.

Quark expects to have 5,000 units in stock on July 1. The planned ending inventory (October 31) is 8,000 units.

These data are placed in a transportation matrix, Figure 3–10. The bottom and right edges contain demand and capacity figures. Note that the ending inventory of 8,000 is added to the October demand of 35,000, giving a total October figure of 43,000—abbreviated as 43. The unused capacity column is necessary because demand sums up to only 128, which is 16 short of the 144 sum for available capacity.

Costs are placed above the slash (/) in each cell. July regular-time production costs $80 per unit for July demand. But the cost is $85 per unit for August demand, because the July production would have to be carried for a month at a $5 per unit carrying cost. All other cell costs follow similar reasoning.

A minumum-cost production plan may be found by inspection for this simple problem. More difficult problems may be solved by a standard transportation-method algorithm, not presented here. (A transportation algorithm is presented in Chapter 12 as part of a plant-location example.) Figure 3–11 is the minimum-cost solution.

The solution is easy to derive by starting in the upper left corner. July demand is satisfied first: five units of beginning inventory is a given, at a cost of zero. The $80 cost per unit for July regular-time production is next cheapest; all 23 units of regular-time capacity are taken. The total is 5 + 23 = 28 so far; 2 more units are needed to meet the demand of 30. The cheapest source of those two units is July overtime at $120 per unit.

August demand, also 30, is next. First, all 12 units at $80 per unit are taken from August regular-time production. All three August overtime units at $120 are also taken. Next cheapest is not August subcontract ($130) but July overtime at $125; three units of July overtime capacity remain and are taken. The total August demand of 30 requires

FIGURE 3–10
Initial transportation matrix, Quark Electronics

		Demand forecast				Unused capacity	Available capacity
		July	August	September	October		
	Beginning inventory	0 / 5	5 /	10 /	15 /	0 /	5
Capacity	July: Regular	80 /	85 /	90 /	95 /	0 /	23
	Overtime	120 /	125 /	130 /	135 /	0 /	5
	Subcontract	130 /	135 /	140 /	145 /	0 /	10
	August: Regular		80 /	85 /	90 /	0 /	12
	Overtime		120 /	125 /	130 /		3
	Subcontract		130 /	135 /	140 /	0 /	10
	September: Regular			80 /	85 /	0 /	22
	Overtime			120 /	125 /	0 /	5
	Subcontract			130 /	135 /	0 /	10
	October: Regular				80 /	0 /	24
	Overtime				120 /	0 /	5
	Subcontract				130 /	0 /	10
	Demand	30	30	25	35 + 8 = 43	16	144

| | | Demand forecast | | | Unused capacity | Available capacity |
	July	August	September	October		
Beginning inventory	0 / 5	5	10	15	0 /	5
July: Regular	80 / 23	85	90	95	0 /	23
Overtime	120 / 2	125 / 3	130	135	0 /	5
Subcontract	130	135 / 2	140	145	0 / 8	10
August: Regular		80 / 12	85	90	0 /	12
Overtime		120 / 3	125	130	0 /	3
Subcontract		130 / 10	135	140	0 /	10
September: Regular			80 / 22	85	0 /	22
Overtime			120 / 3	125 / 2	0 /	5
Subcontract			130	135 / 2	0 / 8	10
October: Regular				80 / 24	0 /	24
Overtime				120 / 5	0 /	5
Subcontract				130 / 10	0 /	10
Demand	30	30	25	35 + 8 = 43	16	144

(left margin label: **Capacity**)

FIGURE 3–11
Final transportation matrix, Quark Electronics

12 more units; 10 come from August subcontract at $130, and 2 come from July subcontract at $135. Note that a carrying cost of $5 per unit is included in the three units of July overtime and the two units of July subcontract.

September demand is low and is met simply: 22 units of September regular time and 3 units of September overtime.

October demand is high and, like August demand, requires some advance production in September to meet it. Carrying costs for two units of September overtime and two units of September subcontract are incurred.

Lastly, the unused capacity column is filled in—by inspection.

The total cost of this production plan is the sum of units times the cost per unit for each cell in the matrix:

$$
\begin{array}{r r r}
000 & & 000 \\
5 \times \$ & 0 = \$ & 0 \\
23 \times & 80 = & 1{,}840 \\
2 \times & 120 = & 240 \\
3 \times & 125 = & 375 \\
2 \times & 135 = & 270 \\
12 \times & 80 = & 960 \\
3 \times & 120 = & 360 \\
10 \times & 130 = & 1{,}300 \\
22 \times & 80 = & 1{,}760 \\
3 \times & 120 = & 360 \\
2 \times & 125 = & 250 \\
2 \times & 135 = & 270 \\
24 \times & 80 = & 1{,}920 \\
5 \times & 120 = & 600 \\
10 \times & 130 = & 1{,}300 \\
8 \times & 0 = & 0 \\
8 \times & 0 = & 0 \\
\hline
\text{Total cost} & = \$11{,}805, & \text{or } \$11{,}805{,}000
\end{array}
$$

Since all cost options have been considered, this aggregate plan costing $11,805,000 is optimal. However, the plan and the cost are not entirely realistic. One obvious defect is the omission of backorders. Example 3–6, a continuation of Example 3–5, addresses the backordering option.

EXAMPLE 3–6
Sensitivity of production/ capacity plan to backorder cost, Quark Electronics

A management-science technique that is useful where costs cannot be estimated accurately is *sensitivity analysis*. The cost of lost customer goodwill resulting from backordering is such a cost. In applying simplified sensitivity analysis, a range of costs may be tried to see their effects on the plan. Quark tries just two costs, an extreme high of $50 per unit and an extreme low of $1 per unit.

Sensitivity analysis will show that at the $50 cost the production plan would not change; it is far cheaper to produce a month early and incur a $5 per unit carrying cost than to produce a month late and incur a $50 per unit backorder cost. On the other hand, at the $1 cost backordering saves money and alters the aggregate plan. This is shown in Figure 3–12. Four cells, identified by shading, are affected: Two units move out of the $135 and $125 shaded cells and into the $121 and $135 shaded cells. Savings are $4 per unit times 2,000 (abbreviated as 2) units, which equals $8,000. However, that $8,000 is minuscule when compared with the $11,805,000 total cost of the initial aggregate plan.

Quark concludes that backorders may be disallowed for production-planning purposes with little loss of validity. This does *not* prevent Quark from using backorders when actual (as opposed to forecasted) demand surges occur—as they surely will.

Uses and limitations. The elegance or simplicity of the transportation method makes it attractive as a tool for *learning* about the trade-offs involved in production/capacity planning. It is a limited tool for practical *use* because of:

Difficulties in cost estimating.

Uncertainties in capacity and demand forecasting.

Omission from the model of options that individually have minor effects but collectively may have major effects.

In the latter category are such options as hiring, firing, layoffs, reassignment, cross-training, partial shipments, shipment of substitutes, refusing orders, and use of marginal facilities.

FIGURE 3–12
New production plan with backorder cost at $1 per unit, Quark Electronics

		Demand forecast				Unused capacity	Available capacity
		July	August	September	October		
	Beginning inventory	0 / 5	5	10	15	0	5
Capacity	July: Regular	80 / 23	85	90	95	0	23
	Overtime	120 / 2	125 / 3	130	135	0	5
	Subcontract	130	135	140	145	0 / 10	10
	August: Regular	81	80 / 12	85	90	0	12
	Overtime	121	120 / 3	125	130	0	3
	Subcontract	131	130 / 10	135	140	0	10
	September: Regular	82	81	80 / 22	85	0	22
	Overtime	122	121 / 2	120 / 3	125	0	5
	Subcontract	132	131	130	135 / 4	0 / 6	10
	October: Regular	83	82	81	80 / 24	0	24
	Overtime	123	122	121	120 / 5	0	5
	Subcontract	133	132	131	130 / 10	0	10
	Demand	30	30	25	35 + 8 = 43	16	144

For these reasons not many organizations are likely to make regular use of the transportation method in their production/capacity planning. Rules of thumb, company policies, educated guesses, and so forth, may be more widely used. But if an organization does not regularly use the transportation method, it might still try it occasionally as a rough check on its aggregate policies and assumptions. Just as sensitivity analysis helped Quark to see that backorders need not be planned for, occasional transportation-method analysis may suggest to a firm that, for example, the costs of overtime or subcontracting have become excessive.

MASTER SCHEDULE

Two major planning streams merge to form the master production schedule, or MPS (block 7 in Figure 3–1). One stream is item-demand planning (input planning). The other is production/capacity planning (output planning). This is shown below.

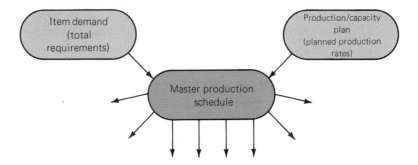

The MPS, in turn, drives short-range planning and control in many functional areas: Detailed scheduling, hiring, training, budgeting, financial planning, accounting, inventory control, purchasing, material handling, and subcontracting are prominent examples. Let us take another, closer, look at the model of Figure 3–1 as it applies to MPS development.

Item demand

Figure 3–1 shows two source blocks for planning item demand: actual customer demand in block 4 and forecasted demand in block 5. Block 4 refers to actual customer orders *booked*. As was pointed out in Chapter 2, a booked order may be a sale on paper, but it is not (or should not be) a production commitment until it is accepted by production control. Production control's order acknowledgment tells sales that the booking has been accepted, partially accepted, rescheduled, postponed, or rejected.

Advance-booked orders from dealers and warehouses sometimes specify basic models but not options. In that case production control would need to forecast the options. That is a secondary aspect of item forecasting, block 5. The primary aspect is forecasting end products for periods beyond those that actual customer orders account for. The item-forecasting methods presented in Chapter 2 apply. For goods producers, the forecast for aggregate demand may be by months, but for item demand it is more likely to be by weeks. The reason is that item-forecast totals are used to create the MPS, and one-week time periods (often called time buckets) are thought to be a suitable basis for most production scheduling in many goods-producing organizations.

Actual customer demand and forecasted orders are merged in block 6. The result is the total product mix demanded, which may be made up of final assemblies, major modules or end items, and independently needed components. For goods producers the requirements may cover an advance period of 6–12 months.

Covering end-item demand

The master production schedule is the plan for covering customer demands for end items. That is, the MPS is the schedule for producing the product mix of major modules, assemblies, or, sometimes, complete products. For a goods producer the MPS is not the same as the total factory requirements. Some reasons are:

The total factory requirements are uneven from period to period, but the MPS must smooth out demands to fit planned aggregate capacity.

Some of the end items may already be on hand or in process.

It may be economical to batch some of the demands into reasonably sized lots.

The MPS may cover major modules or end items, with a separate short-run schedule for their final assembly (block 9 in Figure 3–1).

Some of the total factory requirements are for independently needed components, such as service parts. These demands bypass the MPS and go directly to inventory planning for components (block 10).

Feedback controls

Trial master production schedules are developed before the final version. One object is to get a reasonable fit between the trial MPS and planned production rates (the aggregate capacity plan). That is the meaning of the dashed line from block 7 back to block 3 in Figure 3–1. A second object is to test the trial MPS to see that it does not overload bottleneck work centers; this test, referred to as rough-cut capacity planning, is shown by the dashed arrow from block 8 to block 7 in Figure 3–1. The pairs of arrows, one solid and one dashed, between blocks 3 and 7 and between blocks 7 and 8 indicate closed-loop control over the MPS.[5] Closed-loop control keeps the MPS honest, so to speak.

The "final" MPS (block 8) emerges after suitable trials. The firm portion

---

[5] Closed-loop control between blocks 3 and 7 may be achieved through use of computer-based resource requirements planning simulations. See Joseph Orlicky, *Material Requirements Planning* (McGraw-Hill, 1975), pp. 240–51 (TS155.8.O74).

covers the total lead-time period. Since lead time covers the period in which plans are in motion, schedules need to be more stable for that zone. Still the "firm" schedule may be changed. The tentative portion covers future time buckets. Penalties for changes that far out in the future are slight; thus, changes in the tentative part of the MPS are to expected.

Another dashed feedback line, block 8 to block 4, was mentioned earlier. It is the master scheduler's order acknowledgment. Traditionally in industry, communication from production to sales has been poor. The sales staff bears the burden, because they cannot give the customer reliable delivery promises. But modern, well-designed production and inventory control systems, with feedback-controlled MPSs as the hub, are finally able to provide decent order acknowledgment and order-status information. The competitive advantages should be impressive.

The final-assembly schedule (block 9), applicable for goods producers but not services producers, may or may not be the same as the MPS. Where it may be the same is in the firm with a small product line, simple products, or large specially designed products. Examples are lawn mowers, hand tools, vacuum cleaners, clocks, and large turbines or weapons systems.

The two schedules are not likely to be the same for the manufacturer of complex products assembled from standard components with a variety of options. Vehicles, machines, furniture, electronic equipment, and many other products are of this type. The MPS for major modules must be set long before the final-assembly schedule is prepared. Also, the MPS may extend months into the future; the final assembly of components into final products may be scheduled only a few days in advance.[6]

The final-assembly schedule is based on actual customer (or warehouse) demand for finished end products; but it is constrained by component availability as given in the MPS. The three arrows leading into block 9 in Figure 3–1 represent the three inputs—actual orders, component availability, and capacity availability—that determine the very short-run final-assembly schedule. The dashed line feeding back to production planning (block 3) applies only to production planning for the final-assembly work center. This provides closed-loop feedback control to keep the final-assembly schedule honest; that is, it assures that assembly labor is there when needed.

Disaggregation and rough-cut capacity planning

At this point some clarifying remarks are in order. Earlier we saw capacity planning applied first at the aggregate or product-group level and then disaggregated into a more exacting aggregate capacity plan by examining capacity effects at the shop or department level. Figure 3–13 shows these two levels of capacity planning, plus further disaggregation—down to the level of the work within the shop or department.

One type of capacity planning at the work-center level is rough-cut capac-

---

[6] This and the preceding paragraph paraphrase Orlicky, ibid., pp. 234–35.

FIGURE 3–13
Disaggregation
in capacity
planning

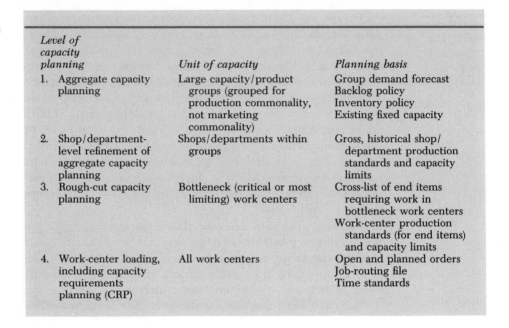

Level of capacity planning	Unit of capacity	Planning basis
1. Aggregate capacity planning	Large capacity/product groups (grouped for production commonality, not marketing commonality)	Group demand forecast Backlog policy Inventory policy Existing fixed capacity
2. Shop/department-level refinement of aggregate capacity planning	Shops/departments within groups	Gross, historical shop/department production standards and capacity limits
3. Rough-cut capacity planning	Bottleneck (critical or most limiting) work centers	Cross-list of end items requiring work in bottleneck work centers Work-center production standards (for end items) and capacity limits
4. Work-center loading, including capacity requirements planning (CRP)	All work centers	Open and planned orders Job-routing file Time standards

ity planning (see dashed arrow from block 8 to block 7 in Figure 3–1), which is discussed in the next section of this chapter. Rough-cut capacity planning is applied to bottleneck work centers only.

Another type is work-center loading, which includes a computer-based procedure known as capacity requirements planning (CRP). Work-center loading applies to all work centers. It is based on detailed job information: what jobs or orders (for component parts) are open or planned, what work centers they are routed through, and how long they take in each work center (time standards). Work-center loading is not presented until Chapter 6, because it depends on inventory planning and job planning, which are covered in Chapters 4, 5, and 6.

Rough-cut capacity planning does not depend on plans for component orders and thus may be considered here. A rough-cut capacity plan is valuable if one or a few work centers are especially worrisome, that is, are bottleneck work centers. Often the bottleneck is a particularly expensive machine, such as a drying oven. The bottleneck could be a certain scarce labor resource, such as a tool and die maker or an underwater welder. The rough-cut capacity-planning procedure is to convert trial MPS quantities into workload requirements in the bottleneck work center(s). Requirements may be expressed in pieces, pounds, machine-hours, labor-hours, or (frequently) machine cycles per time bucket. If requirements exceed capacity in a bottleneck work center, the MPS quantity may have to be reduced or moved to a later time bucket. The following is a simple example.

EXAMPLE 3–7
Rough-cut
capacity
planning—
Molded hoses

Ajax Rubber Co. produces V-belts and molded rubber hoses for automobiles and other vehicles. The master scheduler has prepared a trial MPS, and a portion of it is shown in Figure 3–14. This portion pertains to molded hoses. All hoses except size XL (extra large) are cured in ovens that are the most critical bottleneck work center in the plant. Therefore, the master scheduler makes sure that the MPS is not overstated for that work center. (Note: Figure 3–13 refers to a "cross-list of end items requiring work in bottleneck work centers." For Ajax, that list would include all molded hoses except for extra-large models.)

In the hose-curing work center, cut lengths of extruded rubber are placed on mandrels that protrude from racks which may be rolled into curing ovens. Maximum oven capacity is 760 rack-loads per week.

The number of mandrels per rack depends on the hose model number, but it averages 34 per rack. For rough-cut capacity-planning purposes, that average is good enough to be used as a production standard for converting trial MPS quantities to workload requirements. The conversion is made in Figure 3–14B.

The results of the conversion show an overload in the first week: 801 rack-loads required compared with 760 rack-loads maximum capacity. The master scheduler might be able to shift some of the workload from the first to the second week to correct the overload.

Master schedule—Simplified example

A simplified example of the steps leading to a master production schedule follows. The example is simplified in that it is for services rather than goods. Thus, the master schedule and the final-assembly schedule coincide. Or putting it differently, there is a master *services* schedule but no final-assembly schedule—since services are not assemblies.

FIGURE 3–14
Trial MPS,
molded hoses

A. Total hoses requiring SM cure	Week beginning . . .			
End item	109	116	123	130
Hose 201XL*	800			320
Hose 208S		300		300
•	•	•	•	•
•	•	•	•	•
•	•	•	•	•
Hose 618MM	560		560	
Total hoses	28,020	22,160	20,600	23,080
Less XL* hoses	−800	0	0	−320
Total requiring SM cure	27,220	22,160	20,600	22,760

*XL (extra-large) hoses are not processed in the SM (small/medium) curing ovens, which are the most critical bottleneck work center.

B. Conversion to number of curing racks				
Hoses to SM cure	27,220	22,160	20,600	22,760
Divided by conversion factor	34	34	34	34
Workload requirements (rack-loads)	801	652	606	669

EXAMPLE 3–8
Master scheduling in Department of Management, Funk University

Each teaching department in the College of Business Administration at Funk University must prepare a master schedule. The master schedule consists of one schedule for each course and covers the next few terms. The master schedule is prepared twice each term: One version is prepared based on preregistrations; an updated version is based on general registration data.

The master-scheduling process is illustrated in Figure 3–15. There are eight blocks in the figure. They are the same as blocks 1 through 8 in the general capacity-planning model of Figure 3–1. The example is for one teaching department, the Department of Management. All other departments would follow the same steps, but the aggregate forecast groups (block 2) would be different. The Department of Management's courses—perhaps 40–50 offerings—cluster nicely into three "product" groups. These are:

1. Quantitative/management information systems (MIS)/production operations management (POM).
2. Behavioral/personnel.
3. General mangement/business policy.

These groups are not intended to correspond to clusters of *demand* (though student demands may cluster that way). Rather the purpose is to form natural units of *capacity*. That is, the courses in a given group should be similar enough to enable a corresponding group of faculty members to trade off on teaching assignments. The groupings shown would by no means be perfect. Someone whose specialty is personnel administration may, for example, have a secondary interest in general management instead of in behavior. Still the groupings should be adequate for the purpose. That purpose is to arrive at a capacity plan that is reasonable for matching against total course requirements (block 6) in order to produce a trial master schedule of course offerings (block 7).

An aggregate capacity plan emerges from block 3. The unit of service in a teaching department has a rather invariable "standard time" requirement. For example, the standard three-hour course takes a standard 45 semester hours or 30 quarter hours of class time. Since resource needs are quite predictable, the capacity plan is complete at this point. (Not so for the typical goods producer, which would need to refine the capacity plan via blocks 10, 11, and 12 of Figure 3–1.)

A control on the capacity plan is aggregate policies (block 1). Policies generally exist about class sizes (i.e., faculty-student ratios), classroom space, teaching loads (per faculty member), use of teaching assistants, and utilization of faculty skills. The last has to do with the extent to which faculty will be assigned to teach in their strong areas versus their weaker areas of expertise. Production planning (block 3) includes trade-off analysis, because the aggregate policies are in partial conflict with one another and also with the forecasted group demands (block 2). The capacity plan, then, is a compromise.

While blocks 1 through 3 deal with aggregate demand and capacity, blocks 4 through 6 deal with unit demand, course by course. Actual demand, consisting of registrations by course, comprises block 4. Block 5 is forecasted demand; this is predicted registrations, by course, based on historical patterns plus other knowledge.

In block 6 course requirements for the next few terms are assembled into a list. This "shopping list" is matched against what is available in the capacity plan. The result is the trial master schedule of course offerings for the next few terms. The

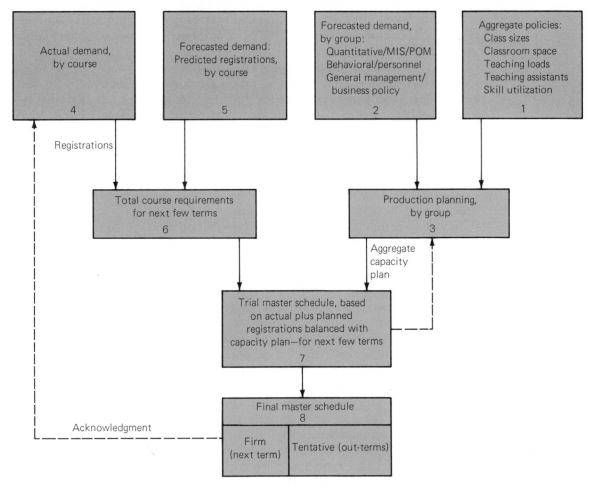

FIGURE 3–15
Master scheduling, Department of Management

feedback arrow from block 7 to block 3 of Figure 3–15 indicates closed-loop control: It makes the master schedule an honest reflection of capacity to meet demands by adjusting the aggregate capacity plan until there is a fit.

Finally a master schedule emerges (block 8). It is firm for the current lead-time period, which is the upcoming term. It is tentative for all future terms. When the master schedule is set within the department, acknowledgment is sent out from Funk University's registrar to students who have registered. Their registration for a given course is either confirmed or denied; if denied, a substitute may be offered.

SUMMARY

The aim in production/capacity management is to achieve a good match between capacity and demand. The time period is medium range, for example, weeks or months. Over that time range capital assets—plant and equipment—

are mostly fixed. Thus, capacity/demand matching concerns more adjustable resources; these include the work force, inventories, and subcontractors. Other ways of adjusting to aggregate demand include use of marginal facilities, slower customer service, and off-peak price adjustments.

Aggregate policies may be set as guidelines for employing these capacity adjustments, and aggregate demand for logical capacity groupings may be forecasted. Production planning is then performed in order to set aggregate capacity levels. Production-planning options are few in service industries; there are many more options in goods-producing enterprise because of the complicating effects of inventories.

Two recognizable planning strategies are chase-demand and level-capacity. Chase-demand provides responsive service but at a cost of fluctuating capacity levels. Level-capacity has opposite traits.

Increased competition complicates production/capacity planning. Competition forces cuts in delivery times. This means less time to react and more need for advance planning of capacity levels. Learning-curve planning is helpful in the case of large end products. Options for production/capacity planning in make-to-order plants may be tested by matching recent demand data with various production levels; effects on order backlogs and lead times are revealed. Production/capacity planning in make-to-stock operations may go a few steps further: Inventory buildup or depletion effects and labor-hour and machine-hour effects may be calculated and appraised for each capacity grouping. It is also possible to seek a minimum-cost production/capacity plan via a variation of the transportation method; the method may include regular-hour labor cost, overtime labor cost, subcontracting cost, inventory carrying cost, back-order cost, and other costs. Sensitivity analysis may be performed, especially on costs that are uncertain.

The MPS is based on actual orders plus item forecasts. In some cases MPS demands suggest the need for more capacity, and this may trigger further production planning. A trial MPS may overload a bottleneck work center. Rough-cut capacity planning is aimed at discovering such potential overloads so that the final MPS may be adjusted to correct the overload condition. The firm portion of the final MPS is not often changed, but the tentative portion— for out-periods—may be changed easily without affecting work in progress.

REFERENCES

Books

Berry, William L., Thomas E. Vollman, and D. Clay Whybark. *Master Production Scheduling: Principles and Practice.* American Production and Inventory Control Society, 1979.

Orlicky, Joseph. *Material Requirements Planning.* McGraw-Hill, 1975 (TS155.8.O74).

Plossl, G. W., and O. W. Wight. *Production and Inventory Control: Principles and Techniques.* Prentice-Hall, 1967 (HD55.P5).

Sasser, W. Earl, R. Paul Olsen, and D. Daryl Wychoff. *Management of Service Operations.* Allyn and Bacon, 1978 (HD9981.5.S27).

Periodicals (societies)

Production and Inventory Management (American Production and Inventory Control Society); numerous articles on capacity management.

PROBLEMS

Note: Asterisked (*) problems require more than mimicry. They require judgment, and you should include reasons, assumptions, and outside sources of information.

Production Planning

1. City Sod is a small business that sells and lays sod (rolled strips of grass). The owner has devised a forecasting procedure based on demand history from previous years plus projection of demand in recent weeks. The forecast for the next six weeks, in labor-hours of sod laying, is:

    860   880   900   920   930   940

    Currently City Sod has a staff of sod layers consisting of 4 crew chiefs and 15 laborers. A crew chief lays sod along with the laborers but also directs the crew.

    The owner has decided on the following staffing policies:

    (1) A two-week backlog will be accumulated before adding staff.
    (2) Plans are based on a 40-hour workweek; overtime is used only to absorb weather or other delays and employee absences or quits.
    (3) The ideal crew size is one crew chief and four laborers.
        a. Devise a hiring plan for the six-week period covered by the forecast. In your answer, assume the following:
          (1) There is a current backlog of 1,200 labor-hours of sod-laying orders.
          OR
          (2) You decide on the current backlog, but make it between 1,139 and 1,241 labor-hours.
        b. Does City Sod follow more of a chase-demand or a level-capacity strategy of production planning? Explain.

2. Bright Way Janitorial Service (Example 3–1 in the chapter) is considering a shift from a level-capacity to a chase-demand strategy of production/capacity planning. Bright Way managers know that chase-demand would greatly simplify production/capacity planning. Explain why this is so. What new management problems would chase-demand tend to create?

Learning-curve planning

3. Iridion, Inc., has been awarded a contract to produce 200 of a new type of rail-driven passenger car for a large city. Based on Iridion's previous experience in guided rocket manufacturing, an 80 percent learning curve is planned for the passenger-car contract. The first passenger car takes 1,400 direct-labor hours to make.
        a. If the city pays Iridion's accumulated direct-labor costs after the fourth unit, how many direct-labor hours should the city expect to pay for at that time?
        b. The actual direct-labor usage for the first eight units produced is as follows:

    1,400   1,206   1,172   1,145   1,101   1,083   1,033   1,005

Would you recommend that Iridion stay with its planning estimate of an 80 percent learning curve? Explain?

c. Same as part *b*, except for the following changes in actual direct-labor usage:

| 1,400 | 1,089 | 887 | 801 | 728 | 684 | 600 | 586 |

4. Bellweather Electronics (Example 3–2 in the chapter) already has a production plan for the generator contract. It is shown in Figure 3–5, and it is based on a projected 90 percent learning curve. Bellweather planners have decided to prepare a contingency plan based on the possibility of an 80 percent learning curve.

    a. Prepare and run a computer program resulting in a listing similar to that of Figure 3–5, but based on an 80 percent learning curve. *Or*, perform the calculations on a hand calculator and prepare the listing manually.

    *b. Devise a master schedule *on a time scale* that Bellweather could use to produce the generators following a level-capacity strategy. Show the number of generators to be completed every four weeks until all 60 are done. Use the 90 percent learning-curve data from Figure 3–5, and assume a generator-shop capacity of 100 labor-hours per week. Also, assume that generators are produced one at a time in a single work bay.

    *c. Follow the instructions for *b* above, but use an 80 percent learning curve. Comment on the number of weeks to complete the contract at an 80 percent versus a 90 percent learning-curve rate.

Production Planning— Make-to- order

5. Coast Limited Railways has a car-repair yard in Kansas City to repair the line's own cars. In the six most recent months, Kansas City's car-repair workload has been:

Month	Cars
1	83
2	72
3	71
4	90
5	49
6	56

    a. Coast Limited headquarters has directed that Kansas City plan for a capacity level not to exceed cumulative demand by more than half a month's average demand during the six-month planning period. Prepare the capacity plan, following the backlogging method of Example 3–3 in the chapter. Explain the positive and negative deviations.

    *b. What important factors in *a* above could be analyzed in terms of dollars?

    *c. Is it necessary that this production-planning method be based on *cumulative* demand and planning figures? If it were Coast's policy to divert all excess orders to independent repair yards, would cumulative calculations be suitable? Explain and illustrate by an example.

6. Concrete Products, Inc., makes reinforced concrete structural members (trusses, etc.) for large buildings and bridges. Each order is a special design, so no finished-goods inventories are possible. Concrete members are made by using molds that are bolted onto huge "shake tables." A shaking or vibrating action causes the wet concrete to pack, without air pockets, around reinforcing steel in the

molds. Concrete Products uses a chase-demand strategy of hiring labor to assemble the molds, fill them with concrete, and later disassemble them. If it takes a week to hire and train a laborer, how can Concrete Products make the chase-demand strategy work well? The following is a representative sample of recent workloads, in labor-hours on the shake tables:

Week	Labor-hours
1	212
2	200
3	170
4	204
5	241
6	194
7	168
8	215
9	225

Production planning— Make-to- stock

7. The production control staff of Quark Electronics, Example 3–4 in the chapter, is preparing alternative trial production plans.

   a. The production rate for a second trial plan is set at 15,300 pieces per week (50 percent greater than in the first trial) for product-group 1. The production rates for groups 2 and 3 are unchanged. Calculate labor-hour and machine-hour effects for week 1 only. (That is, redo Figure 3–9, using 15,300 pieces for product-group 1.) Is the second trial plan feasible? Or does it seriously overload capacity?

   b. A third trial production plan is simpler to prepare. The simpler method is based on a single forecast in pieces, which is the composite of the three product-group forecasts. This requires a single average labor rate and a single average machine rate for each shop—instead of separate rates for each of the three product groups. Assume that for week 1 the composite forecast is for 50,000 pieces and that the shop production rates are:

Rate (pieces per hour)	Shop A	Shop B	Shop C	Shop D
Labor	300	222	650	830
Machine	500	750	2,000	600

   Prepare the trial production plan for week 1 (similar to Figure 3–9 in the chapter). Compare the results of the third trial production plan with those of the first. Where has accuracy been lost in the third plan? In spite of this loss of accuracy, why might the production control chief prefer plan 3 (that is, where has there been a gain in precision)?

   c. In what sense are all of Quark's production plans aggregate capacity plans?

8. Gulf Tube and Pipe Co. prepares monthly production/capacity plans for three capacity areas, one of which is the pipe-forming, -cutting, and -welding (FCW) processes. The forecasted FCW demand for next month is given below.

Week	Forecasted lineal feet (000)
1	6,000
2	5,800
3	5,400
4	4,600

The present inventory is 16 million lineal feet.

a. Devise a production plan, following a chase-demand strategy, that results in an ending inventory of 14 million lineal feet.

b. Devise a production plan, following a level-capacity strategy, that results in an ending inventory of 14 million lineal feet.

c. The following rule of thumb is used for purposes of capacity planning: Two workers are required for every million lineal feet produced. Develop two capacity plans (i.e., work force), one using data from part a and the other using data from part b.

d. Citing data from parts a through d, explain the contrasting effects on inventories and labor of chase-demand and level-capacity strategies.

Transportation method

9. Zap Foundry makes high-precision subcontracted castings. To beat the competition Zap has imposed a price penalty upon itself for castings that cannot be completed in the same month that they are booked: Zap's price is lowered by $1 per direct-labor hour for every month of delay. This $1 price penalty/incentive may serve as its backorder cost. Other cost data are:

Regular time .... $10 per direct-labor hour
Overtime .... $15 per direct-labor hour

Capacity-and demand-forecast data, in direct-labor hours, for the next three months are:

	Capacity		
Month	Regular time	Overtime	Demand forecast
1	600	150	940
2	700	150	750
3	680	150	500

a. For a beginning backlog of 300 direct-labor hours, determine the optimum (minimum-cost) production plan, using the transportation method; plan for an ending inventory of 150. How much does the plan cost?

b. Zap is mainly a make-to-order subcontractor, but a popular casting is sometimes made to stock. Finished-goods carrying costs have never been calculated or applied to production planning. Is ignoring carrying costs—for those occasional make-to-stock lots—a severe inaccuracy? Try to answer the question via a simple sensitivity analysis and the transportation method.

10. Mountain Steel Co., a producer of metal streetlamp poles and related products, plans capacity three months into the future. For the next three months forecasted demand and capacity options are as follows (in labor-hours):

Sources of Capacity	Month 1	Month 2	Month 3
Demand forecast	1,850	1,650	1,750
Labor, regular shift	1,600	1,500	1,600
Overtime	200	180	280

The cost of labor averages $50 per hour regular shift and $75 per hour overtime. Inventory carrying cost is estimated at $2 per labor-hour of inventory carried. Backorder cost is estimated at $3 per labor-hour.

    a. If the beginning inventory is 40 and the planned ending inventory is 60, what is the capacity plan for the three months? Develop the plan, using the transportation method.

    b. Could the quarterly ordering system be used in this firm? Discuss.

Master scheduling

11. Devise a master scheduling diagram similar to Figure 3–15, but for draftsmen in an engineering firm. Explain your diagram.

12. Devise a master scheduling diagram similar to Figure 3–15, but for a maintenance department. Assume that maintenance includes janitorial crews and repairmen such as plumbers and electricians but does not include construction or remodeling. Explain your diagram.

Rough-cut capacity planning

13. At Gulf Tube and Pipe Co. the master scheduler has developed a trial master production schedule. Lately the growing demand for pipe products has strained capacity in the pipe-cutting work center. The work center consists of a single Dynacut cutoff machine, with a single-shift daily capacity of 120,000 lineal feet. The master scheduler has been running a rough-cut capacity plan to assure that the MPS quantities do not overload the Dynacut machine. Engineering has provided the master scheduler with a list of all end-item numbers that require cutoff, and those items are starred in the trial MPS shown (partially) below.

End-item number	Week				
	1	*2*	*3*	*4*	*5*
0263	400	—	—	—	—
0845*	—	300	—	—	300
0997*	300	—	—	300	—
1063	—	200	800	—	—
. ...	.	.	.	.	.
. ...	.	.	.	.	.
. ...	.	.	.	.	.
Totals for *-items (000 of lineal feet)	600	680	470	550	590

    a. Assuming a five-day-per-week single-shift operation, what does rough-cut capacity planning suggest should be done?

    b. Can you tell from the data given what Gulf's production/capacity planning strategy is (i.e., level-capacity or chase-demand)? Explain.

*14. In general registration at your college, registering for classes probably requires you to pass through several work centers. Which work center would you consider to be a bottleneck? Do you think the registrar's office would find the rough-cut capacity-planning idea useful in planning for that bottleneck work center? Explain. You will probably need to consider what the MPS would consist of in this case. (If you prefer, you could answer this question using drop-and-add or another administrative procedure, instead of general registration.)

IN-BASKET CASE*

Topic: Aggregate Planning—Moving Co.

To:

From: President, Metro Movers, Inc.

   We have the problem of seasonal demands. We've never done a very good job of adjusting to this. Now I understand there are "aggregate planning" techniques aimed at coping with imbalances of demand and resource capacity. Please investigate the possibility of adapting the aggregate planning idea to our situation, i.e., planning for trucks, drivers, labor, supplies, etc., in the face of typical seasonal demand factors in the moving business.

*See instructions at end of problems section, Chapter 1.

CASE

Richards Industries

   Richards Industries is a producer of high-grade molded plastic tanks for farm and industrial uses. Production/capacity planning is based on a sales forecast that is expressed in dollars. Total dollars of demand for the year is translated, via a conversion factor, into total number of laborer days. If the forecast for next year (spring and summer sales) is high, the tank producing season is scheduled to begin in August; or if not so high, in September.

   Production is phased in: first one shift; then after two or three weeks, two shifts; and later, three shifts. Thus, a major planning decision is the timing of production shift work. Richards builds inventories of finished tanks for shipment in winter and spring. Sales have been growing 35 percent annually.

   Richards makes 26 sizes of tank. A 55-gallon tank is considered small, and a 1,500-gallon tank is considered large. Tank production capacity is 2,000 tanks per week.

   Current staffing is 17 people per shift: 14 needed to man five rotational molding stations, plus 3 extra to allow for absenteeism. Besides absenteeism, turnover is high: 175 percent in 1978 (down from 400 percent two years earlier). It takes only one day to one week to train a new worker, and workers are paid the minimum wage. Each worker produces an average of $58,000 in annual sales, as opposed to $45,000 per worker in the plastics industry as a whole. An innovative rotational-molding process is a key ingredient in the firm's past successes.

   Is Richards doing a good job of production/capacity planning?

chapter 4

INVENTORY PLANNING–TIMING

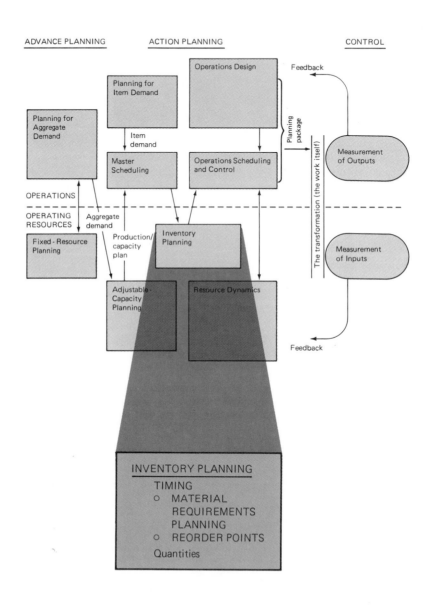

ADVANCE PLANNING ACTION PLANNING CONTROL

INVENTORY PLANNING

 TIMING
  o MATERIAL
   REQUIREMENTS
   PLANNING
  o REORDER POINTS
 Quantities

In the most general sense an inventory is any idle resource. Strictly speaking, then, concepts of inventory management apply to inventories of:

Capital goods—plant and equipment, often referred to as facilities.

Manufacturing materials—materials that go into manufactured items.

Support materials—often referred to as MRO, for *m*aintenance, *r*epair, and *o*perating supplies.

Work-in-process (WIP) inventories—materials in a partial stage of completion.

Finished goods—materials, parts, modules, end items, or final assemblies for external customers, sometimes called distribution inventories.

Tools—implements used to perform work; can include reference information, the tool of the professional.

Labor—even the work force may be considered as an inventory.[1]

Planning for capital goods, labor, and tools is discussed in other chapters. Planning for capital goods is a unique problem since capital goods are fixed resources. Labor and tools are unlike materials in that materials flow in and out of the organization. It is the inventories that *flow*—that is, materials—that are discussed in this and the next chapter. Planning for material inventories takes up two chapters because material flows are so dominant a part of operations management. It is not uncommon for material inventories to absorb over half of a firm's total expenditures. There may be thousands of items to manage and hundreds of thousands of inventory transactions per year.

The central concern of inventory planning is to provide items at the right time and in the right quantities. Timing is the more serious concern, and it is considered next. Quantities—or lot sizing—is considered in Chapter 5.

TIMING OF ORDERS

In the manufacturing sector, planning the timing of component-parts orders is coming to be known as priority planning. Most manufactured end products are made from many component parts, and planning for the parts to be available at the right time is largely a matter of arranging the orders for parts in priority sequence, according to when the parts will be needed.

In a later chapter we shall learn about priority control—the dispatching function—which is necessary in order to keep priorities up to date. We begin by considering various procedures for setting order priorities in order to get parts orders started in the first place.

MRP versus ROP

We are all aware of a major advance in *retail* inventory *control* in the 1970s: the computer-based control afforded by point-of-sale terminals. What

---

[1] The airlines, for example, maintain inventories of pilots during slack periods. The pilots are under contract and must be paid (at least partially) whether or not they have flights. Their idleness pay may be considered as an inventory carrying cost.

the layman is largely unaware of is a major advance in the same decade in *manufacturing* inventory *planning*. It is called material requirements planning (MRP), and it is also computer-based.[2]

MRP is a procedure for time-phasing component-parts orders. Another time-phasing approach known as time-phased order point (TPOP) is often used along with MRP. MRP/TPOP is an alternative to the traditional method of timing orders, the reorder point (ROP). The major difference between MRP/TPOP and ROP may be stated concisely:

MRP/TPOP *plans future orders.*

ROP *determines the next order.*

We see that MRP/TPOP is future-oriented. ROP is present-oriented; that is, it determines if there is a need right *now* to release the next order.

Another important difference between MRP and ROP is that MRP provides data that permit planning adjustable capacity farther into the future. The output of computer-based MRP can serve as an input to capacity requirements planning (CRP), which is discussed in Chapter 6.

MRP/TPOP was developed for the special case of dependent demand. The following discussion of dependent and independent demand serves to point out further distinctions between MRP/TPOP and ROP.

Dependent demand

Demand for a given item is said to be dependent when the item is to go into or become part of another item. Component parts go into what are referred to as *parent* items. A tuner, for example is a component part that goes into the parent radio receiver. Treating parts demands as being dependent makes good sense only if it is easy or economical to see what particular parent items are to receive the parts. An auto tire in a service station cannot be planned as a dependent-demand item, because there is no advance knowledge about parent demand; that is, there is no schedule of customer cars needing tires, so there is no schedule of types of tires needed to go into those cars.

Demand for most manufacturing stocks are dependent on demands for parent items. A multilevel product structure forms a dependency chain. That is, demand for a raw material depends on demand for the fabricated part; demand for the fabricated part depends on demand for the subassembly; demand for the subassembly depends on demand for the major module; and demand for the major module depends on demand for the complete end-item assembly.

Sometimes the dependency chain is short. In pottery manufacturing, demand for potters' clay and glazing chemicals depends on demand for pots. That is the extent of it. With so short a product structure there is less need for computer-based MRP as a means of planning for minimum inventories.

In other cases the dependency structure is long. Raw metal stock may be

---

[2] MRP was implemented in a few firms in the 1960s, but it enjoyed explosive growth in the 1970s.

FIGURE 4-1
Applications of
three techniques
for timing orders

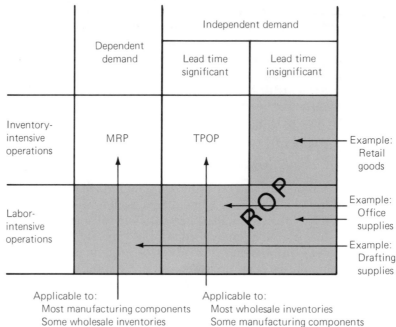

cut into a gear that goes onto a shaft that fits into a gearbox that combines with an engine that is assembled into a vehicle. There may be 10,000 parts with such dependency relationships in the vehicle. The MRP idea is to plan the quantity and timing of each component in order to meet the demand for the parent item.

Figure 4–1 summarizes the application areas for which MRP, TPOP, and ROP are best suited. As the figure shows, MRP is applicable to most manufacturing components, but it is especially helpful where there are multilevel product structures.

The figure also shows that MRP is applicable to some wholesale inventories. An example would be a situation in which the wholesaler acts as an agent taking orders for hard-to-get or expensive goods. For such items the wholesaler's orders might depend on planned order schedules from a few retail customers. While this is a rather rare case, it helps to show the scope of the MRP concept: It is a concept based on the idea of dependency rather than on a certain kind of firm.

Staff departments in a manufacturing company (labor-intensive operations) could also be said to rely on components with dependent demand. For example, demand for engineering drawings is dependent on orders for items. But engineers' drawing supplies amount to so small a portion of engineering costs that the supplies would normally not be planned via MRP. Thus, the lower left portion of Figure 4–1 is shaded, and this indicates that reorder point is the likely method of timing orders. Perhaps the MRP concept will make inroads into service inventories at some time in the future.

Independent demand

Demand for a given item is said to be independent where there is no clearly identifiable parent or parents or where parent-item demand cannot be determined economically. This is the tendency when, for example, many small orders make up total demand for a given item. Lack of parent-item demand data rules out MRP. Time-phased order point (TPOP) or reorder point (ROP) must be considered.

ROP is a reactive approach. The ROP idea is for the next order to be based on stock depletion in the recent past—since future need is unknown ("steering the boat by observing the wake").

For a cabinetmaker, glue and screws would be treated as independent-demand items. They go into certain cabinets (parent items), but it is not very economical to try to order glue and screws for specific cabinets. Instead glue and screws may be ordered when stocks get low: the reorder-point method. Orders for fine woods for cabinets, on the other hand, may be planned as dependent-demand items, with the timing of wood orders coordinated with cabinet job-order schedules (the MRP idea).

In Figure 4–1 the independent-demand column is subdivided based on lead-time significance. Where lead time is relatively insignificant, there is no need to try to plan more than the next order; ROP may therefore be used. For example, liquor stores, fast-food businesses, and service stations can often replenish low stocks in a day or less.

Time-phased order point (TPOP) is like ROP in that it is based on an item forecast rather than on parent-item demand. TPOP is suitable where lead time is relatively insignificant. For example, it generally takes days, weeks, or even months for wholesalers' inventories to be replenished. The longer lead times make it desirable to plan orders well in advance. Therefore, in the TPOP approach the timing of orders is based on *forecasted* demand for the component item itself.

Besides wholesale inventories, some manufacturing components may be planned via TPOP. For example, service parts (spare parts) may be considered as independent-demand items and thus may be planned using TPOP. Demand for components that go into the service parts, in turn, depends on forecasted demand for the parent service parts. Thus, TPOP for service parts may be married to MRP for lower-level components. TPOP feeds MRP.

Planned orders

Planning is thought to be a hallmark of good management. MRP/TPOP plans weeks or months into the future, whereas ROP plans only the next order. Thus, MRP/TPOP is thought to be an important step forward. Indeed, one may predict that future advances in inventory management will include enlarging the planning zone (unshaded) in Figure 4–1. Ways may be found to extend the MRP/TPOP concept of planned orders into the retail sector and perhaps into services as well. The supermarket would rather not have some 30,000 square feet packed with inventory. The time may come when the grocer will begin offering discounts on expensive grocery items like meats to customers who will provide the grocer with a timetable of future orders. That would allow the grocer to shrink the inventory of meats. The last link in the planning chain would be forged, an inventory planning chain that links consumer to grocer to wholesaler to meat-packer to feeder to rancher. At each stage that is able to manage in the advance-planning mode, inventories are cut, thereby lowering cost.

MATERIAL REQUIREMENTS PLANNING

With MRP it is possible to *plan for* zero inventories. Zero inventories are possible when material deliveries are timed so that they are available at the place of need precisely when they are needed. MRP does not provide for achieving that goal but may plan for it. It is a matter of timing.

MRP time-phasing

An example may help to demonstrate time-phasing in MRP.

EXAMPLE 4–1 MRP for a caterer

Imagine that you are a caterer. Assume that you have a master schedule of parties to cater every night for the next two weeks. Your inventory policy is zero inventories (except for incidentals like seasonings). To plan for zero inventories, you consult menus for every food dish to be provided for every one of the catering orders in the next two weeks. Menu quantities times number of servings equals gross requirements. Let us say that salami gross requirements are as shown in Figure 4–2A. Salami is required in the quantities shown on days 3, 6, 11, and 13.

You normally order salami from a butcher shop two days ahead of time. That is, purchase lead time is two days for salami. Therefore you plan to release salami orders as is shown in Figure 4–2B. Each planned order release is two days in advance of the gross requirement shown in Figure 4–2A.

The schedule of planned order releases is correctly timed and in the exact quantities

FIGURE 4–2
Planned-order-release determination—Salami

A. Gross requirements schedule

Day	1	2	3	4	5	6	7	8	9	10	11	12	13	14
Gross requirements (slices)	—	—	100	—	—	320	—	—	—	—	80	—	510	—

B. Planned order releases

Day	1	2	3	4	5	6	7	8	9	10	11	12
Planned order releases (slices)	100	—	—	320	—	—	—	—	80	—	510	—

needed. It is a material requirements plan for one of the components that go into the foods to be catered. It is a plan for zero inventory, and zero inventory is achieved if the butcher delivers the salami orders in the planned two days. If deliveries come a day early, then inventory builds. Also, if an order of salami arrives on time but a customer cancels the catering order that the salami was to go into, inventory builds. Such supply and demand uncertainties cause some inventory when MRP is used, but MRP cuts inventory considerably from what it is when the producer (caterer) *plans* to have components in stock.

MRP computer processing

It should be clear that MRP is a simple idea. The MRP calculations for salami were easy too, because there is only a single level of dependency from salami slices to a master schedule of catered food dishes. From the earlier discussion of dependent demand, recall the case of raw metal (1), cut into a gear (2), fit onto a shaft (3), placed in a gearbox (4), installed in an engine (5), assembled into a vehicle (6). That is five levels of parts below the end item (vehicle). The timing and quantities of parts to be ordered at each level are dependent on needs for parts by the parent item directly above. Planned-order-release calculations must cascade, that is, proceed from the first level to the second to the third, and so on. Cascading calculations are sufficient reason for computers, especially for products containing thousands of parts.

But cascading (level-by-level) calculations are not the only complication. The same raw metal that is cut into a gear might also go into a number of other parent items that ultimately become the given vehicle. Furthermore, the raw metal and perhaps the gear, the shaft, the gearbox, and the engine may go into other parent items that ultimately become various other vehicle types. Finally, dependent demands (i.e., demands that descend from parent items) for parts at any level must be consolidated with independent demands. Independent demands arise, for example, from orders for spare parts (service parts). Computers are needed to total and properly time-phase all of these requirements for the same part.

Computer power makes MRP practicable. Figure 4–3 shows the three necessary inputs and one key output of an MRP computer run. The inputs are a master production schedule, an item master file, and a bill-of-materials file. In the following discussion of each, the key MRP output, a planned-order-release listing, is also discussed.

Master production schedule. The *master production schedule* (MPS) is the action input. The MPS provides the end-item schedule, which drives MRP. In most firms using MRP the MPS has weekly time buckets (periods) extending 52 weeks (a year) into the future. The MPS is normally updated once a month. As days go by during the month, the MPS gets increasingly out of date. That is, toward the end of the month some of the scheduled quantities turn out to be out of line with orders that marketing is actually booking. The MPS might be updated during the month to correct for this or other problems. More often, the MPS is left as it is, and inaccuracies are dealt with via the

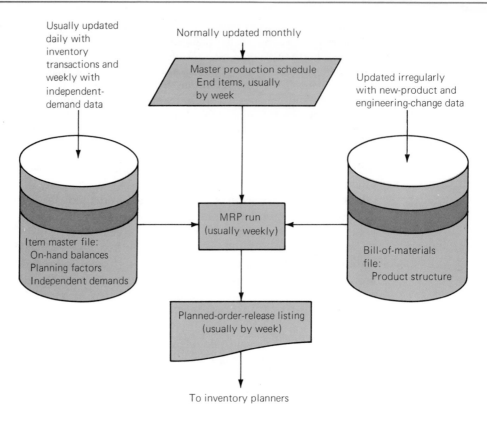

weekly MRP runs, by component-parts schedule changes and by dispatching and shop-floor control measures.

Item master file. The item master file is a file that holds reference data (rather than acting as driver, as the MPS does). The reference data in the file includes on-hand stock balances and planning factors for every component item. The on-hand balance is simply the quantity that is supposed to be in storage. The stock balance on hand may be verified by periodically counting what is in storage. The balance is kept up to date by posting transactions (receipts, issues, new items, etc.) to the master file.

The on-hand balance is necessary in the MRP computation of net requirements. In an MRP run gross requirements for a given part are computed. Then net requirements are computed, thus:

$$\text{Net requirements} = \text{Gross requirements} - \text{On-hand balance}$$

In the earlier example of the caterer, stock balances were not introduced. The example is changed and extended here to allow for an on-hand stock balance. Since a caterer would hardly use computerized MRP, the salami is changed to salamite, a chemical compound. In industry, MRP is usually run weekly rather than daily, and the gross requirements for salamite are changed from a 14-day to a 14-week schedule.

EXAMPLE 4–2
MRP for a
chemical
product

Let us say that 220 units of salamite is the on-hand balance at time zero (the start of week 1). The gross requirements are as shown in Figure 4–2, but with the days changed to weeks. The net requirement in week 3 is:

$$\text{Net} = \text{Gross} - \text{On-hand}$$
$$= 100 - 220 = -120$$

The net requirement is −120, which means that an excess of 120 is projected to be the stock balance at the end of week 3, after 100 have been used to cover the week 3 gross requirement. In weeks 4 and 5 the stock balance stays at 120. In week 6 the net requirement is:

$$\text{Net} = 320 - 120 = 200$$

Now the net requirement is a positive 200; in MRP a positive net requirement is covered by a planned order. The planned order quantity is 200, and the planned order release is two weeks earlier (since the planned lead time, LT, is two weeks).

The planned order release for 200 in week 4 is exactly enough to cover the net requirement of 200 in week 6.

Figure 4–4A shows MRP computation results as a five-row table for the salamite example. This type of table might be available for reference on a computer cathode-ray tube terminal or as printed output. The net-requirements row usually would not be shown since net requirements are working figures, not final MRP results. (The schedule-receipts row, empty in this example, is explained later.)

In the table we see that the on-hand balance is worked off as of week 6. In week 6 the projected shortage of 200 is indicated by the +200 net requirement and also by the −200 on-hand balance. The planned order release for 200 in week 4 prevents the negative on-hand balance, and so the −200 is crossed out and replaced by the final balance of zero. The on-hand balance stays at zero through the remaining eight weeks.

Planning factors stored in the item master file include lead time, lot size, safety stock, and so forth. Unlike stock balances, the planning factors in the file seldom need to be updated. In Example 4–2 the lead time (LT) of two weeks would have been extracted from the item master file. A lot size, Q (for quantity), may also be found in the file. The following modified example provides for a fixed order quantity, Q, instead of ordering just what is needed, as in Example 4–2.

EXAMPLE 4–3
MRP for a
chemical
product—Fixed
order quantity

Assume that salamite is produced in a vat that holds 500 units. Even though 500 units is not likely to be the net requirement, it seems economical to make the salamite in full 500-unit batches. The excess above the net requirement is carried as a stock balance.

Figure 4–4B shows the MRP computation results for the case of a fixed order quantity, Q, equal to 500 units.

FIGURE 4-4
MRP Computations—Salamite

A. MRP with a stock balance

Week	1	2	3	4	5	6	7	8	9	10	11	12	13	14
Gross requirements			100			320					80		510	
Scheduled receipts														
Stock balance on hand (220)	220	220	120	120	120	0 (~~−200~~)	0	0	0	0	0 (~~−80~~)	0	0 (~~−510~~)	0
Net requirements	−220	−220	−120	−120	−120	+200	0	0	0	0	+80	0	+510	0
Planned order releases				200 $\underset{LT=2}{\underbrace{}}$					80 $\underset{LT=2}{\underbrace{}}$		510 $\underset{LT=2}{\underbrace{}}$			

Explanation:
1. 220 are on hand at end of week 2 and beginning of week 3.
2. Net = Gross − On-hand = 100 − 220 = −120.
3. On-hand at end of week 3 is excess, 120.

B. MRP with fixed order quantity

LT = 2 Q = 500

Week	1	2	3	4	5	6	7	8	9	10	11	12	13	14
Gross requirements			100			320					80		510	
Scheduled receipts														
On hand (220)	220	220	120	120	120	300 (~~−200~~)	300	300	300	300	220	220	210 (~~−290~~)	210
Planned order releases				500							500			

The computer calculates net requirements as in part A, but in part B net requirements are left off, so that only the computed results are shown. A net requirement of 200 is calculated for week 6, and the computer plans an order two weeks earlier (since LT = 2). The order is for $Q = 500$, the fixed order quantity, which brings stock on hand in week 6 to +300. The on-hand balance drops to 220 in week 11 and to −290 in week 13. The computer acts to prevent the negative balance in week 13 by planning an order for 500. The planned order release is in week 11, which eliminates the negative balance in week 13 and leaves 210 units to spare.

Clearly, fixed order quantities compromise the MRP goal of low or zero inventories. The debate about what order-quantity policy to use is reserved for the next chapter.

Bill-of-materials file. A *bill of materials* (BOM) is not the kind of bill that demands payment. Bill of materials is industry's term for a structured list of component parts that go into a product. The BOM names the parts that are detailed on the engineer's blueprints.

Like the item master file, the computerized BOM file serves as a reference file for MRP processing. In an MRP system, BOMs must be accurate and must be stated in terms of the same end items that are found on the master production schedule.

The BOM file keeps track of what component parts and how much of each go into a unit of the parent item. In each MRP run the computer (1) calculates planned order timing and quantity for the parent item, (2) consults the BOM file to see what goes into the parent, and (3) translates the parent's planned order requirement into gross requirements for each component. As an example of the calculation, if there are three of a certain component per parent, the gross requirement for that component will be equal to triple the planned order quantity for the parent. (The grand total of gross requirements for the component would also include requirements derived from other parents and from independent demands.) A continuation of the salamite example serves to demonstrate the role of the BOM file.

EXAMPLE 4–4
MRP for a
chemical
product with
two levels

Planned order releases for salamite have been calculated. The computer consults the BOM file to find what goes into salamite. The first ingredient is a chemical compound known as sal. There are two grams of sal per unit of salamite. Therefore the planned order quantities for salamite are doubled to equal gross requirements for sal. This simple translation of salamite orders into sal needs is shown in Figure 4–5. (The salamite data come from Figure 4–4B.)

Net requirements and planned order releases may now be calculated for sal, as is shown in the figure. The the computer does the same for the next ingredient or component of salamite.

The bill-of-materials file in which salamite and sal might be found could have a structure similar to Figure 4–6. Salamite is shown as a level 2 subassembly that goes into a level 1 subassembly, which combines with other level 1

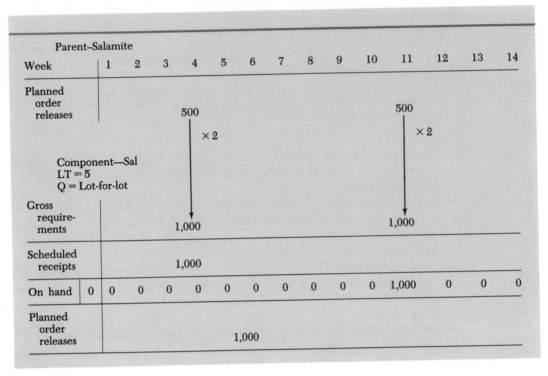

FIGURE 4–5
BOM reference data and scheduled receipts in MRP

items to form an end item. The MRP processing sequence begins at the end-item level (zero) and works its way down through the BOM structure. The figure shows that Sal is made from level 4 parts (or perhaps subassemblies that are made from level 5 parts).

It is cumbersome to develop the MPS and to forecast MPS requirements if there are a large number of products in the BOM file. For that reason some engineering BOM numbers may be judiciously combined into modular bills and pseudobills (or superbills). Engineering bills are often streamlined in this and other ways at the time that MRP is introduced into an organization. The process is referred to as restructuring the bills of materials.[3]

Scheduled receipts

Another MRP factor is scheduled receipts. Returning to Figure 4–5, we see that in week 4 there is a scheduled receipt of 1,000, which is the gross-requirement quantity in week 4. A scheduled receipt represents an *open order* instead of a planned order. That is, an order for 1,000 has already been released, for make or buy, and it is scheduled to be delivered in week 4. Since the lead time is five weeks, it appears that the order would have been released, opened, and scheduled last week.

---

[3] See Joseph Orlicky, *Material Requirements Planning* (McGraw-Hill, 1975), "Product Definition," ch. 10 (TS155.8.O74).

FIGURE 4-6
Sample BOM or
product structure

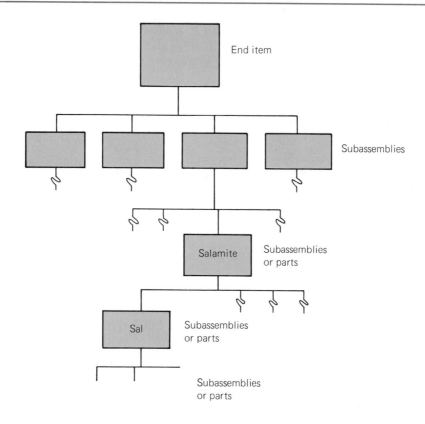

Let us examine the events that change a planned order into a scheduled receipt. The sketch below is a partial MRP for sal as it might have appeared on Monday morning this week.

		1	2	3	4	5	
Gross						1,000	
Scheduled receipts							
On hand	0	0	0	0	0	0	
Planned order releases		1,000					

Anytime that a planned order release appears in the first time bucket, action to schedule the order is called for. Therefore, sometime on Monday the scheduler writes up a shop order to make 1,000 grams of sal. The effect of scheduling the order is to remove it from the planned-order-release row and to show it as a scheduled receipt, as is shown below:

		1	2	3	4	5	
Gross						1,000	
Scheduled receipts						1,000	
On hand	0	0	0	0	0	0	
Planned order releases							

Next time the computer runs the MRP program the scheduled receipt for 1,000 grams will be included. The order is shown as a scheduled receipt each week until the shop delivers the 1,000 grams. (But the order could get canceled or changed in quantity or timing. Also the shop may produce more or less than the planned quantity of 1,000 grams.) Upon delivery of the 1,000 grams. the computer will have the following transactions to process:

1. Add 1,000 to on-hand.
2. Deduct 1,000 from scheduled receipts and from gross requirements.
3. Deduct 1,000 from on-hand to signify delivery of the 1,000 grams to the shop where it is needed for manufacture of the parent item, salamite.

The possibility of scheduled receipts calls for adding one more term to the formula for net requirements:

$$\text{Net requirements} = \text{Gross requirements} - \text{On-hand} - \text{Scheduled receipts}$$

Other MRP features

More advanced examples of MRP processing are included in the chapter supplement. The examples demonstrate other MRP features, including:

Multiple parents
Scrap allowances
Time-phased order point (TPOP)
Safety stocks

Computer program packages for MRP, which are widely available, allow for these and other features. The computer package must be able to find where a component part goes into more than one parent (multiple parents) and consolidate requirements. Scrap allowances may be handled by increasing the planned-order-release quantity by the usual or expected scrap loss amount, but not increasing the scheduled-receipts amount. That is, order extras but do not expect them to be received (in usable condition). TPOP-derived demands must be consolidated with parent-item demands to equal gross requirements for components at any level in the product structure. Safety stock is an extra inventory amount above the net requirement. Most MRP packages allow for safety stocks to be entered as planning factors in the item master file and preserved as minimum planned stock balance on hand in MRP computations. (But some authorities feel that component safety stocks are undesirable in MRP; see the chapter supplement.)

The computational steps in MRP processing may now be summarized, with inclusion of the above-mentioned other MRP features:

1. *Compute gross requirements,* by time bucket. At level 1, gross requirements are based on requirements extended downward from the MPS. At lower levels, gross requirements in a given time bucket equal outside independent demand plus planned-order-release quantities for the parent parts in the same time bucket. The quantity extended downward from the parents is multiplied by the *quantity per* (often one).

2. *Compute net requirements* by subtracting on-hand balance and scheduled receipts from gross requirements plus safety stock (if any). This is done one time bucket at a time, beginning with the first.

3. *Compute planned order quantity.* A planned order is needed to cover a net requirement. A positive net requirement is the indicator. That is, when a positive net requirement is found in step 2, a planned order release *for at least that amount* is needed. Fixed order quantities or other order-batching policies may result in planned order quantities larger than net requirements. A scrap allowance also makes the planned order quantity larger than the net requirement.

4. *Compute planned-order-release timing.* The planned-order-release time is computed by subtracting the lead time from the time period in which the positive net requirement occurs.

5. *Convert planned orders to open orders.* Time passes, and planned orders move toward the first time bucket. When a planned order is in the current period (first time bucket), inventory planners may *open* an order. That is, the planned order is converted to an open (active) order. The open order is processed by purchasing if it is a buy order, by production scheduling if it is a make order. The next MRP run then deletes the planned order and shows its quantity in the *scheduled-receipts* row, properly offset for lead time.

REORDER POINT

The reorder point (ROP) is probably as old as man (maybe older, since some animals, such as squirrels, exhibit manlike behavior in replenishing low stocks). The ROP and its variations provide for reordering when stocks get down to some low level. Let us look at some of the ROP variations.

Perpetual system

The classic ROP is a *perpetual* inventory system. This means that every time an issue is made (perpetually), the stock balance is checked to see whether it is down to the ROP. If it is, an order is placed. In the small informal case, it is the physical stock level that is perpetually examined. In the more formal case, it is the stock record balance that is examined.

Reorder points are all around us. We may reorder (go get) postage stamps when our stock is down to three. There used to be a perforated tab on the side of Kleenex boxes; the customer was to tear out the tab and then follow ROP-like instructions—something like, "When the Kleenex gets down to here, that's the time to buy two more boxes of Kleenex." (You were not only being told the reorder point; you were also being told that your lot size should be two boxes.)

Two-bin system

In small stockrooms a version of perpetual ROP called the *two-bin system* is often used. Two adjacent storage bins are assigned to hold a single item. Users of the stockroom are told to withdraw from bin 1 first. The rule is that when the first bin empties, an order is placed. The second bin contains the ROP, a quantity intended to cover the lead time for filling the order.

There are many variations. In a forms storeroom, a colored sheet of paper may be inserted in a stack of forms on a shelf to show when the ROP (second "bin") has been reached. Indirect material or free stock like washers, screws, and nails is often placed in trays on the shop floor; a painted line partway down inside the tray can designate the ROP (second "bin"). Transistors, diodes, and so on, are often stored in corrugated boxes on shelves; a small box in the larger box may be used to contain the ROP (second "bin"). Figure 4–7 shows some of these two-bin variations.

The two-bin system works best where a single person is in charge of the stockroom or is in charge of a daily check to see which items are down to the ROP. Otherwise people will get too busy to note the need for an order; each person can conveniently blame the next person when the second bin is emptied without anyone having reordered.

If the two-bin system exists in a firm that has partial computer control of inventories, prepunched order cards can be placed near bin 2. Then, when bin 2 is entered, it is an easy matter to initiate the reorder: Just pull a prepunched card. The card would contain identifying data; nothing need be written down. People are less likely to "forget" to order when ordering is so simple.

ROP calculation

The ROP (the quantity in bin 2) may be set by judgment and experience or by an ROP formula. Usually one's judgment would tend to follow the concepts on which the basic ROP formula is based. The formula is:

$$ROP = DLT + SS = (D)(LT) + SS,$$

where

ROP = Reorder point
DLT = Demand during lead time
SS = Safety stock
D = Average demand per time period
LT = Average lead time

Demand during lead time may be computed using a recent average demand amount and a recent average lead time. An explanatory example follows.

FIGURE 4–7
Two-bin system variations

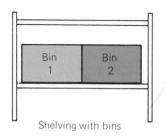

Shelving with bins

Rule: Use from bin 1 first: when empty, reorder

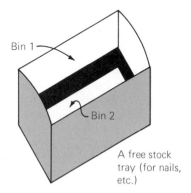

A free stock tray (for nails, etc.)

Rule: When down to black zone, reorder.

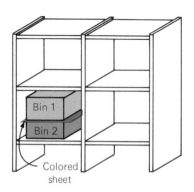

Colored sheet

Open shelving (for forms)

Rule: When down to colored sheet, reorder .

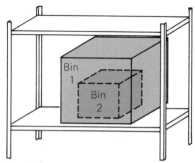

Open shelving with small box inside larger box

Rule: When small box must be broken open, reorder.

EXAMPLE 4–5
ROP
calculation,
fuel oil
example

Assume that a building heated by fuel oil averages 600 gallons consumed per year and that the average lead time is two weeks. Thus,

D = 600 gallons per year
LT = 2 weeks/52 weeks per year = 0.04 year
$DLT = (D)(LT) = (600)(0.04) = 24$ gallons

Then, if safety stock is 40 gallons,

$$\text{ROP} = \text{DLT} + \text{SS} = 24 + 40$$
$$= 64 \text{ gallons}$$

Replenish-
ment cycle

Use of the ROP may be shown by a graph. Figure 4–8 is a common form of a graph for illustrating ROP replenishment cycles. An explanatory example follows:

EXAMPLE 4–6
Replenishment
cycles for
discrete
demand,
radiator cap
example

Radiator caps are issued in discrete units; that is, there cannot be an issue of half a radiator cap. (By contrast, a continuous item like fuel oil can be issued in fractional parts of a gallon.) Figure 4–8 shows two replenishment cycles for radiator caps. The graph shows a stairstep depletion pattern; and it shows early and late order arrivals, including a case in which backordering occurs.

In the first cycle radiator caps are being issued at a slow pace, slower than past average demand, that is. Then in the fourth time period there is a spurt. Just into the fifth time period stock on hand drops below the ROP. An order is placed. During lead time, stock issues start out slowly, then speed up in periods 6 and 7. All radiator caps are gone by the beginning of period 7, and still orders come in.

The shading indicates orders unfilled because of the stockout condition. Orders accepted when stock is out are said to be *backorders*. They are usually filled first when stock does arrive.

In this case the stockout is caused by the late spurt in demand plus slow delivery; the actual lead time is shown to be greater than average. It is a case in which safety stock did not fully protect because of the combination of high demand and slow delivery.

The second cycle begins when the order arrives in period 7. The order quantity or lot size, Q, brings the stock level up from zero to Q units, and the backorders are immediately filled, dropping the stock level somewhat. Stock depletion is at about an average rate through period 10. In period 11 there is a surge in demand for radiator caps. The surge in demand continues into period 12, and it reduces stock to below the ROP. An order is placed.

This time, delivery is faster than average (see actual LT as compared with average LT) and there is little demand during the lead-time period. This combination of events results in little use of the DLT quantity and no use of the SS amount. Stock is high when the order quantity, Q, arrives. The order arrival pushes the stock level up to near the maximum, which is the ROP plus Q.

Safety-stock
influences

Safety stock provides protection against stockout. Safety stock is influenced by a number of factors. Figure 4–9 lists some of the factors in three categories: demand protection, supply protection, and internal factors.

FIGURE 4–8
ROP
Replenishment
cycles, radiator
cap example

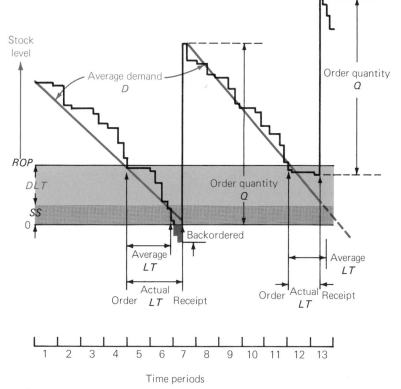

Note: When the depletion line is horizontal, time is passing with no stock depletion; a vertical segment shows a depletion.

Under *demand protection,* demand variability (factor 1 in the figure) is usually thought to be the most important safety-stock factor. Demand is usually variable, and safety stock protects for variability on the high side of mean demand.[4]

Confidence in the demand estimate (factor 2) refers mainly to the amount of past data or experience. If the item has been in stock for years, its mean demand and demand variability may be estimated with confidence. If not, more safety stock is needed.

Exposure to stockout (factor 3) is the amount of time that stock is low and in danger of running out. Exposure could be measured in number of days

---

[4] Another name for safety stock is *reserve*. This alternative term may be especially familiar to the public in view of the energy crisis and publicity about oil reserves and natural gas reserves. But, as Tom Bethal points out in a magazine article, the general public thinks that the term *natural gas reserves* means total quantity in the earth. Bethel notes that in the gas industry gas reserves are proven (drilled) inventories and that these inventories are based on recent demand forecasts (and, presumably, demand variability). If that is true, then gas reserves are safety stocks; more wells may be drilled to keep the safety stocks in line with demand forecasts. Tom Bethel, "The Gas Price Fixers," *Harper's,* June 1979, pp. 37–44+.

FIGURE 4–9
Factors
influencing
safety stock

Demand protection	*Supply protection*	*Internal factors*
1. Demand variability	4. Lead-time variability	7. Consequences of stockout
2. Confidence in	5. Confidence in lead-	8. Item cost
demand estimate	time estimate	9. Obsolescence
3. Exposure to stockout	6. Security of supply	10. Scrap rate
		11. Space requirements

per year that an item is down to one day's supply or less. It is often sufficient to measure exposure in number of order cycles per year instead of in time (days). The idea is that more order cycles mean more chances to run out—when stock gets low near the end of each cycle. Thus, if stock is ordered often (in small lots), more safety stock is needed.

Factors 4 and 5, under *supply protection,* are like 1 and 2. More lead-time variability or less confidence means more safety stock.

Factor, 6, security of supply, is especially important when there are raw material shortages. (The shortages of 1974 were especially severe.) A sole-source supplier or suppliers with troubles also raise the issue of security of supply. Larger safety stocks provide general protection. Stockpiling, a purchasing action, is a more extreme measure.

Consequences of stockout (factor 7) is an *internal factor.* A stockout sometimes has little effect. On the other hand, lack of a particular bolt could shut down an assembly line; if that is likely, safety stock is needed.

If item cost (factor 8) is very high, you cannot afford to invest in safety stock. If it is low, safety-stock protection is obtained cheaply.

High risk of obsolescence (factor 9) is like high item cost: You do not want much of such items in safety stock. A high scrap rate (factor 10) has the opposite effect: The potential for scrap may call for more safety-stock protection.

The final factor (11) is space requirements. Bulkier items require more space, and therefore fewer of them are desirable for safety stock.

Safety stock is often expressed in terms of days', weeks', or months' supply. Then safety-stock protection among items may be compared. A firm that has a safety stock of 10 cases of nails for an annual demand of 60 cases has a two-month's supply in safety stock. The simple calculation is:

$$\frac{\text{Safety stock}}{\text{Periodic demand}} = \frac{10 \text{ cases}}{\dfrac{60 \text{ cases}}{12 \text{ months}}} = \frac{10}{5} = 2 \text{ months' supply}$$

Equivalently

$$\frac{10 \text{ cases}}{\dfrac{60 \text{ cases}}{52 \text{ weeks}}} = \frac{10}{1.15} = 8.7 \text{ weeks' supply}$$

Statistical safety stock

In some firms supply protection (factors 4, 5, and 6 in Figure 4–9) is up to the purchasing department; internal factors (factors 7–11) are accounting and production department concerns, and inventory planning has the responsibility for demand protection (factors 1, 2, and 3). Inventory planning may want a streamlined, perhaps computerized, process for determining safety stocks to provide the proper level of demand protection. One such process is based on statistical service levels, considered next.

Statistical service levels. The cost of a stockout to the firm is often obscure. An approach that avoids wild estimates of stockout cost is the concept of statistical service levels. Under this concept the firm sets a service-level target. The target is expressed as a frequency of running out of stock. For example, if the service level is 0.98, that means customer orders would be filled 98 percent of the time, with a stockout 2 percent of the time.

TABLE 4–1
Safety factors for various service levels based on mean absolute deviation of normally distributed demand

Service level (percent of order cycles without stockout)	MAD safety factor	Service level (percent of order cycles without stockout)	MAD safety factor
50.00%	0.00	98.00	2.56
75.00	0.84	98.61	2.75
80.00	1.05	99.00	2.91
84.13	1.25	99.18	3.00
85.00	1.30	99.38	3.13
89.44	1.56	99.50	3.20
90.00	1.60	99.60	3.31
93.32	1.88	99.70	3.44
94.00	1.95	99.80	3.60
94.52	2.00	99.86	3.75
95.00	2.06	99.90	3.85
96.00	2.19	99.93	4.00
97.00	2.35	99.99	5.00
97.72	2.50		

The table is based on an assumption that demand variability is normally distributed. Source: G. W. Plossl and O. W. Wight, *Production and Inventory Control: Principles and Techniques,* © 1967, p. 108. Reprinted by permission of Prentice-Hall, Inc., Englewood Cliffs, New Jersey.

A method has been devised for converting the service level to a *safety factor* that may be multiplied by the mean absolute deviation (MAD) of past demand to give safety stock. The MAD is a measure of unpredictability or error (or noise) in the forecasting system. Safety factors for a range of service levels are given in Table 4–1. A formula for using the table is:

$$\text{Safety stock} = \text{Safety factor} \times \text{MAD}$$

As an example, assume that mean demand for bread at your house is 100 slices per order cycle but that demand varies by a MAD of 40 slices. If a

TABLE 4–2
MAD adjustment
factors for lead
time in excess of
forecast interval

When forecast interval = 1 and lead time is	MAD is multiplied by:
2	1.63
3	2.16
4	2.64
5	3.09
6	3.51
8	4.29
10	5.01
12	5.69
15	6.66
20	8.14

Source: Adapted from G. W. Plossl and O. W. Wight, *Production and Inventory Control: Principles and Techniques,* © 1967, p. 112. Reprinted by permission of Prentice-Hall, Inc., Englewood Cliffs, New Jersey.

service level of 94.52 percent is desired, it calls for a safety factor of 2.00—from Table 4–1. Therefore:

$$\text{Safety stock} = 2 \times 40$$
$$= 80 \text{ slices (or about 4 loaves)}$$

Service levels and adjustment factors. The statistical safety-stock formula needs to be modified when the lead time for an item is longer than the forecast period. The MAD is based on an average forecast period, but in longer lead times more demand variability is likely. The MAD must be adjusted upward. The amount of the adjustment can be precisely determined by a simulation procedure that is beyond the scope of this discussion. A set of adjustment factors that offer reasonable precision is given in Table 4–2. The modified safety stock, then, is:

$$SS = (MAD)(MAD \text{ adjustment factor}) (SF)$$

The following example demonstrates.

EXAMPLE 4–6
Safety stock
based on
demand
variability

Household Supply, Inc., is the mail-order arm of a large retail chain. The replacement parts business at HHS is subject to largely independent demand; replenishment of HHS stocks is therefore controlled by exponentially smoothed forecasts and reorder points. For instance, one replacement item is cutting-cord reels for its lawn edger-trimmer (known as the Weedzapper). Relevant data for calculating the ROP are:

Forecast for next month = 400 reels
Mean abolute deviation of demand = 200 reels
Estimated lead time = 2 months
Planned service level = 95%

From Table 4–1 the safety factor (SF) for a 95 percent service level is 2.06. From Table 4–2 the MAD adjustment factor, based on a lead time of twice the forecast interval, is 1.63. Therefore,

$$ROP = (D)\ (LT) + (MAD)\ (MAD \text{ adjustment factor})\ (SF)$$
$$= (400)\ (2) + (200)\ (2.06)\ (1.65)$$
$$= 800 + 680 = 1,480 \text{ reels}$$

This means that when the stock gets down to 1,480 reels, the cutting cord should be reorderd. The ROP of 1,480 provides for 800 reels to cover the average demand during lead time (DLT) and 680 reels of safety stock (SS), which protects against demand variability.

The MAD may be calculated by the computer, using stored data on actual demands for a given item. Safety-stock determination is thus reduced to simple computer computations, and the SS computation combines easily with DLT computations to produce ROPs for each item stocked. ROPs based on the latest demand and lead-time history and the latest service-level policy can be listed at any time. The lists can be scanned by inventory planners, who may manually change some safety stocks in light of some of the other ten safety-stock factors given in Figure 4–9.

Periodic system

Another type of reorder-point system is the periodic system. In the perpetual system the ROP is a quantity; in periodic, the ROP is a point in time. Periodic reordering is just what the name implies: Reordering is done at regular intervals.

Often the periodic system of *timing* orders is combined with maximum-minimum *quantity* criteria. For example, a grocery store might periodically reorder laundry soaps, with two days as the order interval. The maximum shelf space for one item, say Whiter-White Detergent, might be four cases. In that case the maximum inventory level is probably four cases. The desired minimum might be one case. The periodic system would work like this:

1. Check stock of Whiter-White on Monday, Wednesday, Friday, and so on.
2. If shelf stock is below one case, reorder enough to bring the stock as close to four cases as possible without exceeding four cases.
3. If stock is above one case, reorder zero cases.

Note that the minimum is really a reorder-point *quantity* used in conjunction with the reorder-point interval; the maximum governs what the lot size shall be to bring stock up to the maximum level.

Lead times are usually short (e.g., one day) in the grocery business. In most other businesses lead times are longer, and the quantity ordered under the periodic system should probably include factors other than just maximum inventory. Let us consider an elaborate example.

EXAMPLE 4–7
Periodic
reordering with
long lead times

Assume that an inventory planner in a manufacturing firm reorders a certain type of wire once a month and that the lead time is one month. The amount ordered, Q, might be:

$$Q = EOQ + DLT + SS + AL + BO - OH,$$

where

EOQ = Economic order quantity
DLT = Demand during lead time
SS = Safety stock
AL = Allocated quantity, i.e., quantity earmarked for a particular use
BO = Backorder quantity
OH = On-hand balance

Assume further that EOQ = 400 and DLT = 50 and that on the date of periodic reordering SS = 20, AL = 15, BO = 30, and OH = 30. What this means is that 30 are on hand, including the safety stock of 20; 15 of that 30 on hand are allocated to a customer who has not yet taken delivery; and 30 are backordered for another customer who apparently does not want to take the remaining 15 as a partial delivery. Thus, today's order is for:

$$Q = 400 + 50 + 20 + 15 + 30 - 30 = 485$$

If normal events take place, 50 units will be demanded during lead time. That 50, plus the AL of 15 and the BO of 30, equals net demand of 95. Deduct the 30 on hand, and the current demand equals 65 when the order of 485 arrives. Immediate coverage of that current demand reduces the balance to 420, and that is exactly what is desired: 400 as the EOQ in addition to 20 as the safety stock.

MRP/ROP COMPARISON

Most people who go through the MRP learning process grasp the mechanics of MRP quickly, and they easily see the difference between applied MRP and applied ROP. Or do they? There are some subtleties that bear closer scrutiny.

The ROP system as used in manufacturing is actually likely to be what may be called an *ROP/shortage-list system*. ROP/shortage list was in wide use before computers; it was an early and successful application on unit-record equipment (which used punched cards, tabulators, and printers); and it was an early and successful application on computers—well before computer-based MRP came along.

Computer-based inventory planning in factories includes several common steps, regardless of whether MRP or ROP/shortage list is used:

1. A master production schedule is set up manually and loaded into the computer.
2. A computer file containing bills of materials is referred to for each end item on the MPS.
3. A computer program explodes BOMs into gross parts requirements.
4. On-hand balances in the computerized item master file are subtracted from gross requirements.

5. The result is called *net requirements* in MRP and a *shortage list* in the ROP/shortage-list system.[5]

There are major differences in *how* the above steps are used in MRP and ROP/shortage list. Key differences are:

1. In MRP the five steps are used to plan net requirements for (usually) 52 weeks into the future. In ROP/shortage list the five steps are used to plan a shortage list for only the current time bucket (e.g., next week).

2. In MRP the steps are used to plan virtually all parts for fabrication. In ROP/shortage list the steps are used *only to plan exceptions:* ROP "plans" the vast majority of parts orders, and exceptions—parts badly needed for the current time bucket—appear on the latest shortage list.

The following example serves to illustrate these points.

Example 4–8
Component parts planning, MRP versus ROP/shortage list—Pencil sharpener module

Figures 4–10 and 4–11 show two methods of planning orders for parts to go into a pencil sharpener module. Figure 4–10 shows an assembly diagram for the module, a shavings receptacle, and it includes a step-by-step example of how parts might be ordered for the module, using the ROP/shortage-list system. Figure 4–11 is a contrasting step-by-step discussion of the same planning situation, except that MRP is used.

FIGURE 4–10
Inventory planning via ROP and shortage lists, pencil sharpener module

ROP/shortage-list steps

1. Over the weekend, the computer explodes the bill of materials for each end item appearing *next week* on the master production schedule. The result is a *parts-shortage list.* A portion of the explosion process is shown below for a module that goes into a pencil sharpener.

	Parts needed	−	Parts available		=	Parts short
			In stock	On order		
Subassembly	600 Shavings modules			600		
Component parts	600 Molded plastic shavings receptacles		500			100
	600 Stamped metal end plates		1,500			
	1,200 Screws		1,400			

---

[5] Old-timers would refer to the ROP/shortage-list approach as "bill-of-materials explosion." Since MRP also includes BOM explosion, that term is no longer precise enough.

FIGURE 4–10
(continued)

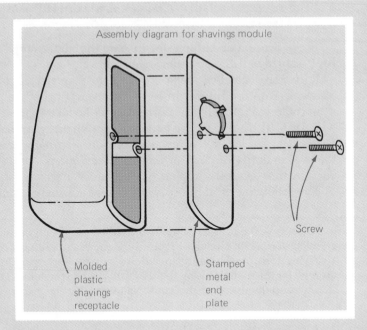

Assembly diagram for shavings module

Screw

Molded plastic shavings receptacle

Stamped metal end plate

2. On Monday morning the parts-shortage list becomes a *hot list*. Expediters rush through a make order (or buy order) for hot items—the receptacles in this case.

Hot list
1. Receptacle → Shop order   or   Purchase order

3. The receptacles are made (or bought) in a lot of 200 units.
4. Production counts (or purchased-part counts) are recorded as receipts in computer inventory records, thus increasing the balance in stock by 1,200 receptacles and 600 shavings modules (less any that are scrapped).
5. All parts are withdrawn from storage and delivered to the work center where they are assembled.
6. Parts issued are recorded in inventory records, thus decreasing the balance in stock by 600 receptacles, 600 end plates, and 1,200 screws (plus any extras needed.)
7. Stock record balances are compared with ROPs and:
   End plates are down to 300, which is below the ROP of 400, and are therefore put on order in the lot size of 1,200 (a normal order, not a special).

FIGURE 4–10
(concluded)

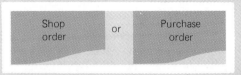

Screws are already on order, in the lot size of 10,000, as a result of reaching the ROP of 2,000 last week.

Shavings receptacles are above ROP of 400 and are not ordered.

Shavings module is a make-to-order part and therefore is not replenished by ROP.

Summary of transactions processed

Part	ROP	Lot size	Transaction	Receipts	Issues	On order	On hand	Balance
Shavings module	*	*	Beginning balance				0	0
			Assembly order			600	0	600
			Production count	+600			600	600
Shavings receptacle	400	1,200	Beginning balance				500	500
			Hot-list order			1,200	500	1,700
			Production (buy) count	+1,200			1,700	1,700
			Issue for assembly		−600		1,100	1,100
End plate	400	1,200	Beginning balance				900	900
			Issue for assembly		−600		300	300
			Below ROP; place order			1,200	300	1,500
Screw	2,000	10,000	Open order from last week			10,000	1,400	11,400
			Issue for assembly		−1,200	10,000	200	10,200

* A make-to-order part.

In summary . . .

Parts are reordered in two ways:

1. *The ROP way.* This is the normal way for perhaps thousands of component parts. It is based on stock depletion and perpetual comparison with ROP.
2. The *hot-list way.* This is for the special exceptions—parts that the ROP process didn't provide on time or in the right amount. The hot list is revealed by the process of exploding the BOM.

Note: The hot list may also include parts that have reached their ROP and are on order but that need speeding up (which shows up via BOM explosion). For example, the screw for the shavings module reached its ROP last week. The order is in process, but the stock on hand is getting very low; the order could end up on the next hot list.

FIGURE 4–11
Inventory
planning via
MPS-MRP, pencil
sharpener
module

MRP steps

1. Over the weekend, the computer explodes the bill of materials for each end item on the master production schedule for the *next 52 weeks.* MRP processing results in *planned order releases.* A portion of the MRP process is shown below for a module that goes into a pencil sharpener.
2. When the planned order release—for the shavings receptacle in this case—becomes current, the order is scheduled and released to production (or purchasing).
3. Steps 3–6 are the same as in Figure 4–10.
4.
5.
6.
7. Stock record balances are used in next week's MRP run in computing net requirements.

In summary . . .

All parts orders are planned, in the needed quantities and offset for lead time, via MRP.

Sample MRP outputs

Shavings module LT = 1 week		*Week*								
		1	*2*	*3*	*4*	*5*	*6*	*7*	*8*	· ·
Gross requirements		0	0	0	0	600	0	0	0	· ·
Scheduled receipts										
On hand	0	0	0	0	0	600	0	0	0	· ·
Planned order release					600					

Shavings receptacle LT = 2 weeks; $Q = 1,200$					From POR, shavings module					
Gross requirements		0	0	0	600	0	0	0	0	· ·
Scheduled receipts										
On hand	500	500	500	500	1,100	1,100	1,100	1,100	1,100	· ·
Planned order release			1,200							

FIGURE 4–11
(continued)

End plate
LT = 2 weeks;
Q = 1,200

From POR, shavings module

Gross requirements		0	0	0	600	0	0	0	0	· ·
Scheduled receipts										
On hand	900	900	900	900	300	300	300	300	300	· ·
Planned order release										

Screw
LT = 3 weeks;
Q = 10,000

From POR, shavings module

Gross requirements		0	0	0	600	0	0	0	0	· ·
Scheduled receipts										
On hand	1,400	1,400	1,400	1,400	800	800	800	800	800	· ·
Planned order release										

A major difference is made apparent in step 1 of the two figures: Each calls for an MPS and exploding the BOM. But in Figure 4–10 the result is a parts-shortage list for next week only, and in Figure 4–11 it is planned order releases for 52 weeks.

Next compare step 2. On Monday morning the shortage list becomes a hot list, which is turned over to expediters. But on Monday morning in the MRP case, planned order releases that are in the current time bucket (number 1) are calmly turned over to scheduling (for made parts) or purchasing (for bought parts).

Step 3 through 6 are the same in the two figures. Parts are made or bought (step 3). Parts made or bought are counted, and the count is entered as an addition to the on-hand balance in the item master file (step 4). Parts needed to go into a parent (the shavings module in this case) are withdrawn from storage and delivered to the proper work center (step 5). Parts issued are deducted from the on-hand balance in the item master file (step 6). With these steps all inventory records are updated for next week's run.

Step 7 is very different in the two figures. In ROP/shortage list, stock record balances are used for comparison with reorder points for every part in the item master file. (This may be done every day.) The usual ROP rule is followed: If the balance is below the ROP, order it. The ROP order is not based on parent-item needs but on past usage. In MRP, stock record balances are used in next week's computer run to compute net requirements for parts to go into parents at a future date. Stock record balances serve a reference-file purpose in both MRP and ROP/shortage list, but in ROP the reference data may trigger a current *reaction* but not future *planning*.

ROP/shortage-list transactions are summarized below the seven steps in Figure 4–10, and samples of MRP outputs are shown below the steps in Figure 4–11. The ROP/shortage-list summary shows a beginning balance for the parent and each component. Orders, receipts, and issues are the transactions that change the status of the item in inventory records. Three types of orders are noted: (1) The shavings receptacle appears on a shortage list and becomes a hot-list order. (2) The end-plate balance goes below its ROP in the current period and becomes an ROP order. (3) The screw balance fell below its ROP last week, and it is an open order this week.

The samples of MRP outputs show a planned order release for 600 of the parent (module) in a *future* time bucket, week 4 in the example. That quantity becomes the requirement for each of the three parts.

The summary at the bottom of Figure 4–10 shows why some writers have referred to this parts-ordering system as a push-pull system: Orders for parts that have hit their ROPs are formally *pushed* out to the shop and to vendors, and hot orders for parts appearing on shortage lists are informally *pulled* through by expediters. (But in smaller firms without data-processing power, expediters do not have the benefit of a shortage list. They *discover* shortages in the stockroom when they try to assemble the parts—referred to as staging—to meet a due date.)

Figure 4–11 shows that in MRP a planned order matures (step 2)—that is, it moves toward the current week instead of being pushed out to production on short notice. In MRP, orders are formally pushed onto production, but gently and with advance planning. A few orders may still have to be pulled by informal expediting. But the more common way of handling urgent orders is to formally reschedule them—via MRP weekly updating—thereby avoiding expediting.

LOT REQUIREMENTS PLANNING

Brief comment must be given to *lot requirements planning,* which is sort of a hybrid of MRP and ROP/shortage list. Lot requirements planning was developed in the punched-card tabulating equipment era, that is, in the late 1950s prior to the first business computers. The method calls for putting the MPS and BOM onto punched cards. End-item *lot quantities* on the MPS are exploded (by runs through the tab equipment) into parts requirements—just as is done in MRP. But timing of orders is *not* calculated. The inventory planner receives printouts showing which component parts should be ordered and when the corresponding end-item lot is due on the MPS. The planner then guesses and manually calculates when to release component-part orders. The planner also manually adjusts component order quantities in light of parts already in stock.

Lot requirements planning requires a modest amount of machine calculations, and the calculations do not involve an item master file, which in MRP can be a very large file. The file is not needed since stock-on-hand and lead-time data are not employed in the calculations. In short, lot requirements planning provides modest results for a modest computational cost. Lot requirements planning may be suited today for producing items like fishing rods or brooms, which have few components and levels. Today, however, a minicomputer or a microcomputer, instead of tab equipment, would provide calculating power.

SUMMARY

The chief concern in planning item inventories is the timing of orders. The traditional planning model is the reorder point (ROP). In recent years a new model, material requirements planning (MRP), has emerged. MRP is revolutionizing the planning of dependent-demand inventory items.

MRP applies especially to end items with dependent demand consisting of several levels of component parts. Fabrication is the typical setting. Independent demand is commonly found at retail and wholesale and in many services.

MRP is computer-based planning. Three input files are necessary to run MRP: A several-month master production schedule (MPS) of end-item requirements acts as the driver. A bill-of-materials (BOM) file provides reference data on the product structure of each end item; that is, it shows what component parts must be planned for. An item master file provides reference data on each of the component parts: on-hand balance, lead time, lot size, safety stock, service-part forecast, and so forth.

MRP processing consists of computing the net requirements of each component part in the end items' BOMs, including consolidating all demands for the same part. Net requirements are expressed in terms of quantity and timing. Planned orders of the appropriate lot size and offset for lead time are generated as the end result of MRP processing. Inventory planners may then act to release the most current planned orders to purchasing and manufacturing.

For independent demands an MRP-using firm may employ the time-phased order point (TPOP), which is a forecast-based approach that blends in with MRP. Safety stock may be included in net requirements for either MRP or TPOP; more uniform stockout protection may be had by allowing safety stock at the end-item (MPS) level but not at the component-parts levels.

Manufacturers that have not implemented MRP are likely to plan inventory orders via ROP plus periodic parts-explosion and -shortage lists. ROP is routine and can be computerized; it can also be run visually, using what is known as the two-bin system. The ROP process is simply to perpetually check on stock level for a given item and to reorder it when stock level drops below the ROP. The ROP quantity includes average demand during lead time plus a safety stock. The safety stock guards against demand surges (among other things), and it may be mathematically related to historical variability of demand and to desired service. Another ROP version is the periodic system in which stock is checked and orders are placed at periodic intervals rather than perpetually watching the stock level.

ROP tends to provide more stock than necessary for most items, but it will result in shortages of other parts. The reason is the ROP is tied to past demand, not to future projections and actual orders. Periodic parts-explosion and -shortage lists, usually computer-generated, show what parts will be short for the upcoming period's master production schedule. Expediters may then try to overcome the shortages.

REFERENCES

Books

Fuchs, Jerome H. *Computerized Inventory Control Systems.* Prentice-Hall, 1976 (TS160.F8).

Love, Stephen F. *Inventory Control.* McGraw-Hill, 1979 (HD55.L68).

New, Colin. *Requirements Planning.* Gower Press, 1973, (TS160.N48).

Orlicky, Joseph. *Material Requirements Planning.* McGraw-Hill, 1975 (TS155.8.O74).

Plossl, G. W., and O. W. Wight. *Production and Inventory Control.* Prentice-Hall, 1967 (HD55.P5).

Periodicals (societies)

Journal of Operations Management (American Production and Inventory Control Society); research rather than applications articles.

Journal of Purchasing and Materials Management (National Association of Purchasing Management).

Production and Inventory Management (American Production and Inventory Control Society); numerous articles on inventory planning.

PROBLEMS

Note: **Asterisked (*) problems require more than mimicry. They require judgment, and you should include discussion of reasons, assumptions, and outside sources of information.**

MRP, BOM, and item master file

1. Acme Wood Products Corp. makes wooden picture frames. One size is 10″ × 12″, and it is made with three finishes: oak-stained, walnut-stained and mahogany-stained. The parts needed for final assembly and finishing are (for each frame) two 10-inch and two 12-inch wood pieces and four corner brackets. Inventory planning is by MRP. Lot sizes are 1,000 for wood parts and 5,000 for brackets.
   a. Construct the BOM structure. You need not limit yourself to the given data.
   b. What should go into the item master file? Be as specific as possible, given the above data. But you need not limit yourself to the given data.
   c. Assume that for every oak-stained frame, two walnut-stained and three mahogany-stained frames are made. Also assume that gross requirements for ten-inch wood pieces in the next five weeks are: 0, 600, 0, 240, and 300. Compute all parent-item planned orders based on these gross requirements for the wood pieces (Work backward.)
   d. Based on the gross requirements information from part c, compute the planned-order-release schedule for 10-inch wood pieces (no other item). Assume a current on-hand balance of zero and a lead time of one week.
2. The sketch below is of the two main parts of a transparent-tape dispenser: molded plastic housing and roll of tape. A master production schedule for the dispenser is shown below the sketch.
   a. Draw a structured bill of materials for the tape dispenser. Include the main parts and one level of parts below that.
   b. Assume that lead times are one week for the roll of tape and two weeks for the spool (mounting ring). Beginning on-hand balances are zero for the roll of tape and 3,000 for the spool. Draw the MPS, with MRPs for the roll of tape and the spool below it. (Do *not* include housing and wound transparent

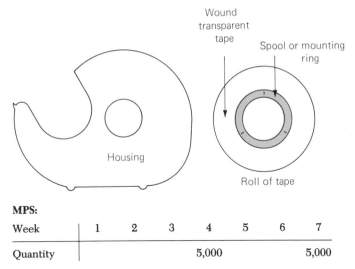

Housing

Wound
transparent
tape

Spool or mounting
ring

Roll of tape

MPS:

Week	1	2	3	4	5	6	7
Quantity				5,000		5,000	

tape.) Compute gross requirements, scheduled receipts (if any), on-hand balance, and planned order releases for the roll of tape and the spool. Use lot-for-lot order quantities. Show your results in the usual MRP display format.

  c. Explain your entries or lack of entries in the scheduled-receipts row for both the roll of tape and the spool.

  d. Assume that the rolls of tape are sold separately as well as being a component of the tape dispenser. Make up a forecast of independent (external) demand for rolls of tape for each of the seven time buckets. Merge your forecast of independent demand with the dependent demand from the parent item. Also assume an on-hand balance of 2,000 for the roll of tape and a scheduled receipt of 4,000 in week 2 for the spool. Recompute the MRPs as in part *b.* What could be the explanation for the *quantity 4,000* as a scheduled receipt in week 2?

3. Assume that you are employed by a company that makes a type of simple chair (you decide on the chair's design). MRP is to be the method of inventory planning for the chair.

  a. Draw a bill-of-materials structure for the chair. Briefly explain or sketch the type of chair.

  b. Develop an eight–ten-week MPS for the chair.

  c. Develop MRPs for three or four of the chair's components, with the following restrictions:

   (1) Include level 1 and level 2 components (e.g., a chair arm might be level 1 and the raw material to make the arm might be level 2).

   (2) Make your own assumptions about lead times, order quantities, and beginning inventories.

   (3) (Optional—feature explained in chapter supplement): Include a safety stock for one of the parts.

        Your answer should be realistic; no two students should have the same answer.

4. Same as preceding problem, except that your product is a ball-point pen.

5. Select a product composed of fabricated parts (*not* a product referred to in the chapter explanation of MRP or in preceding MRP problems). In *one page,* develop an MPS for the product, plus a level 1 MRP for a major module and a level 2 MRP for a part that goes into the level 1 module. Include the following in your plan:

   a. An 8–10-week planning period.

   b. Draw the MPS at the top of your page, with time buckets for the two levels of parts MRPs lined up below it. The material requirements plans for the parts should include four rows: one for gross requirements, one for scheduled receipts, one for on-hand balance, and one for planned order releases. Make up the following data: realistic quantities for the MPS; beginning on-hand balances, lead times, and order quantities for each part, but make one order quantity fixed and the other lot-for-lot; and one or more scheduled receipts based on a previous order, already released (be careful about the timing and quantity of scheduled receipts).

   c. For level 1 and level 2 parts, calculate the timing and quantities of gross requirements, scheduled receipts, on-hand balance, and planned order releases. Display results on your charts.

      Optional for part c—features explained in chapter supplement):

      (1) Include a safety stock for one of the parts.

      (2) Include a scrap allowance for one of the parts.

      (3) Include demands from an external source (rather than from parent planned order releases) for one of the parts.

Replenishment cycle

6. Fuel oil is one source of heat in a Northern university. Average fuel demand in winter is 6,000 gallons per month. The reorder point is 640 gallons; the average lead time is two weeks; and the order quantity is 8,000 gallons.

   a. How many orders are there in an average five-month winter season?

   b. What is the demand during lead time? What is the safety stock?

   c. Draw a graph showing three replenishment cycles for the fuel oil. Construct the graph so that:

      (1) In the first cycle, delivery takes more than two weeks (with normal demand during lead time).

      (2) In the second cycle, delivery takes less than two weeks (with normal demand during lead time).

      (3) In the third cycle, lead time is average, but demand during the lead-time period is low.

   Note: Since fuel-oil usage for heating is continuous (not discrete), your line showing actual usage should waver downward rather than follow a stairstep pattern downward.

Safety stock

7. The following is a list of inventory items that might be found in various locations in a hospital. For each item, pick what you feel are the two most dominant factors that should influence safety stock for the item. (Factors influencing safety stock may be found in Figure 4–9.) Also state whether you feel that the item should have a high, medium, or low safety stock, as measured in weeks' supply. Explain.

Toothpicks   Pillows
Disposable hypodermic syringes   Rare blood

X-ray film   Aspirin
Coffee cups (pottery)   Soap solution for mopping floors
Daily newspapers (for sale)   Prosthetic devices (artificial limbs)

Statistical ROP

8. A beer distributor reorders when a stock item drops to a reorder point. Reorder points include statistical safety stocks with the service level set at 95 percent. For PBR beer, the forecasted usage for the next two weeks is 500 cases and the mean absolute deviation of demand has been 110 cases (for a two-week period). Purchase lead time is one week (a five-day workweek).

    a. What is the safety stock? How many working days' supply is it?

    b. What is the ROP?

    c. How many times larger would the safety stock have to be to provide 99 percent service to PBR customers? How many working days' supply does the 99 percent level provide?

    *d. Statistical safety stock protects against demand variability. What two other factors do you think are especially important as influences on size of safety stock for this item, PBR beer? Explain.

9. Brown Instrument Co. replenishes replacement (service) parts based on statistical reorder point. One part is a 40-mm. thumbscrew. Relevant data for the thumbscrew are:

    Planned stockout frequency = Once per year
    Planned lead time = 1 week
    Forecast for next week = 30
    Batch size = 300
    Mean absolute deviation of demand = 20

    a. What is the reorder point? (Hint: Convert planned stockout frequency to service level.)

    b. What would the ROP be if lead time were four weeks instead of one?

Reordering methods

10. An auto muffler shop reorders all common mufflers and the like once a week—on Tuesday mornings. (Rarely needed mufflers are not stocked.) Two of the biggest-selling mufflers are muffler A and muffler B. Each is ordered if stock is below three, and enough are ordered to bring the supply up to ten. Under this reordering system the average inventory of each is about eight. It takes two days to replenish.

    A reorder-point policy with a service level of 90 percent is being considered as a replacement for the present policy. To see whether ROP would reduce costly inventories, the following data are provided:

	Muffler A	Muffler B
Item cost	$7	$39
Daily usage (average)	2	2
Mean absolute deviation of daily usage	1.2	1.2

    a. What kind of reorder policy is the present one? Are there names for it?

    b. What safety stocks and ROPs would there be for mufflers A and B under an ROP policy?

    c. Should the muffler shop go to an ROP system? Stay with the present system? Devise a hybrid system? Discuss, including pros and cons.

**ROP/
shortage list**

11. One of the products manufactured by a maker of hand tools is a pliers. There are four parts, shown in the accompanying illustration. The parts are ordered by ROP/shortage list. At a given point in time the status of each part is as shown below; reference data are also given.

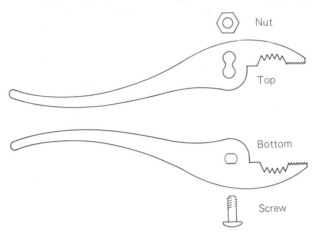

Item	Inventory status	ROP	Q	LT
Nut..................	8,000 on hand, none on order	4,000	10,000	10 days
Top	2,200 on hand, none on order	2,000	5,000	10 days
Bottom	3,800 on hand, none on order	2,000	5,000	10 days
Screw...............	1,700 on hand, 10,000 ordered two days ago	4,000	10,000	5 days
Pliers	2,700 on hand, none on order	3,000	3,000	5 days

   a. Describe all the ordering actions needed.

   b. Give the new status for each part after the ordering actions from part *a* have been carried out and completed.

   c. What are some advantages of ordering pliers by ROP/shortage list, as compared with MRP?

IN-BASKET CASE*

Topic: Material Requirements Planning (MRP)—Soft Drinks

To:

From: General Manager, Midwest Soft Drink Co.

   Now and then I hear the term *material requirements planning (MRP)* bandied about. It apparently is some sort of system or technique for planning the materials needed for some sort of job or type of production. We do a less-than-ideal job of ordering containers and ingredients for our bottling function, and I'd like you to investigate to see if MRP would be useful for us.

---

* See instructions at end of problems section, Chapter 1.

supplement to chapter 4

MRP/TPOP LOGIC

In this supplement MRP and TPOP are more fully explained. The examples are more realistic than the simple cases presented in the body of the chapter, and MRP/TPOP logic, including ways of treating certain special problems, is examined more closely.

Discussion centers on planning parts for bicycle manufacturing. The bicycle example is introduced in the first section and carried through three more topic sections:

1. BOM for a bicycle.
2. MRP processing—multiple parents and scrap allowances.
3. Time-phased order point logic.
4. Safety stock in MRP.

BOM for a bicycle

Figure S4–1 is a partial bill of materials for a bicycle. There is enough room to show only a sample of the 300-odd component parts that would go into such a bicycle. The complete BOM breaks down into as many levels as are necessary to get to the *purchased* part. The breakdown of the front and

FIGURE S4–1: Partial bill of materials for a bicycle

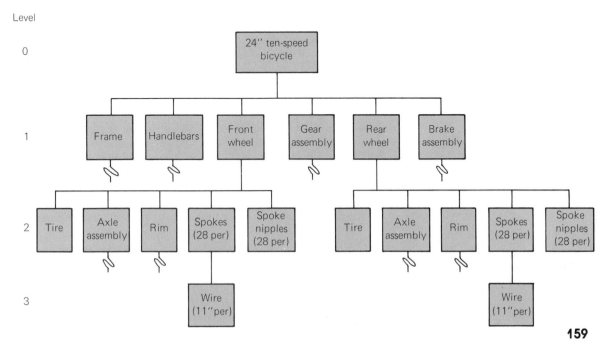

159

rear wheels illustrates: Each wheel has a tire, an axle assembly, a rim assembly, 28 spokes, and 28 nipples (28 per wheel); and each spoke is fabricated (cut, bent, and threaded) from raw wire stock, 11 inches per spoke. The nipple is a second-level purchased part, and the wire is a third-level purchased item. Both spoke nipples and wire stock occur at two locations in the BOM; they would also occur in the BOMs for other bicycle sizes. Data-processing power is helpful in totaling the quantities needed for these kinds of parts that occur in multiple locations. (This is true with or without MRP.)

MRP processing—Multiple parents and scrap allowances

In this section the MRP method of consolidating gross requirements for a component that has multiple parents is examined. Also, the method of including a scrap allowance is explained.

EXAMPLE S4–1 MRP processing, bicycle spoke nipples

Figure S4–2 shows the generation of gross requirements for spoke nipples and the translation of those requirements into planned order releases. In the figure, planned order releases for front and rear wheels are given for three sizes of bicycles, 20-inch, 24-inch, and 26-inch. Requirements for wheels would have been derived from master production schedules (level 0) for all bike models. Planned order releases for spoke nipples emerge after higher levels of MRP processing have been completed.

Figure S4–2 shows how orders for more than one parent are consolidated to become gross requirements for a next-lower-level part. The requirement for nipples in week 5 is based on $84 + 60 + 24 + 24 = 192$ wheels. At 28 nipples per wheel the gross requirement is $192 \times 28 = 5,376$. For week 6 the basis is $36 + 36 + 72 + 84 = 228$ wheels. The gross requirement is 228×28, which equals 6,324. (Front-wheel and rear-wheel planned orders may be unequal because of extra demands for one or the other as service parts, to make up for scrap losses, and so forth.)

The 2,500 nipples on hand at week 0 continue to be on hand (in stock) through four weeks. In week 5, 5,376 are needed, but only 2,500 are available; there is a projected shortage of 2,876. The possibility of a shortage triggers the following: The MRP program subtracts the purchase lead time (LT), three weeks, from week 5, giving week 2; an order must be released then to avert the shortage in week 5. The lot size is lot-for-lot, that is, no batching of orders. Therefore the quantity ordered is 2,876 plus 2 percent scrap allowance, which equals 2,934 to be ordered. The shortage of 6,324 in week 6 triggers a planned order in week 3. The quantity is 6,324 plus 2 percent for scrap, which equals 6,450.

Note the treatment of the 2 percent scrap factor: The planned-order-release amount includes the 2 percent so that the extra amount will be placed on order. The net requirements—what you hope to receive—do not include it, since you expect 2 percent to be unfit for meeting parent-item needs.

Time-phased order point logic

TPOP logic is the same as MRP logic—actually TPOP becomes MRP—after gross requirements are computed. So it is only the computation of gross requirements for TPOP that need be explained. As has been mentioned, MRP is for dependent demands, and TPOP is for independent demands.

Planned order releases:

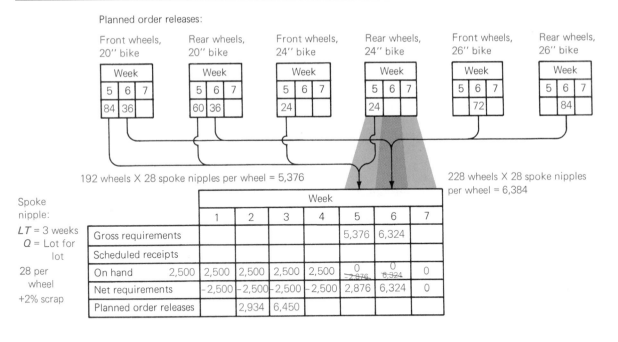

Spoke nipple:		Week						
LT = 3 weeks		1	2	3	4	5	6	7
Q = Lot for lot	Gross requirements					5,376	6,324	
	Scheduled receipts							
28 per wheel	On hand 2,500	2,500	2,500	2,500	2,500	0 ~~-2,876~~	0 ~~6,324~~	0
+2% scrap	Net requirements	-2,500	-2,500	-2,500	-2,500	2,876	6,324	0
	Planned order releases		2,934	6,450				

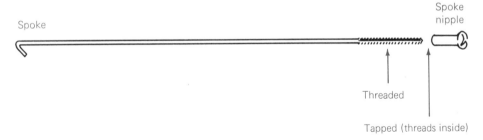

FIGURE S4–2
MRP generation of planned order releases, spoke nipple example

TPOP may be provided for as a subroutine in updating of the item master file. The TPOP subroutine is likely to consist mainly of a demand forecasting routine (algorithm). For example, the subroutine may project trends, perhaps with seasonal adjustments. Exponential smoothing (ES) could be used to save on past demand data storage. But if ES is used, the ES projection for next period is also the forecast for periods 2, 3, 4, and so on, all the way out through the six-month or year planning horizon. Not very accurate, but ES has not been touted as being accurate; rather, ES is expedient. If most of the gross requirements for a component part are independent demands, then ES should probably be avoided in favor of a multiperiod pattern-projection (trend, seasonal, etc.) method. TPOP may be illustrated by a continuation of the bicycle spoke example.

For a bicycle manufacturer, most of the gross demand for spokes would probably be dependent demands from planned orders for wheels. Some independent demands are also likely. Examples are demands for spokes from parts wholesalers or from other bicycle manufacturers that do not make their own spokes.

It is not common for buyers to make their requirements known to producers very far in advance. This means that the producer—the bicycle maker in this case—must forecast. Let us assume that ES is used to forecast independent demand for 11-inch spokes. The most recent forecast is for 800. That quantity, 800, is used as the forecast for the next 52 weeks. Figure S4–3 shows the 800-per-week TPOP source of independent demand at the upper left. At the upper right is the MRP source of dependent demand. The two sources of demand merge and comprise gross requirements for spokes. The independent-demand quantities, 800 per period, are extended directly; the single dependent demand of 672 is computed from the planned order of 24 wheels times 28 spokes per wheel. From this point on, MRP logic applies.

To summarize the difference between MRP and TPOP, MRP demands are *dependent* and are *calculated* based on parent-item needs, while TPOP demands are *independent* and are *forecasted*.

Figure S4–3 includes one other planning factor, a safety stock, SS. Safety stock is considered next.

Safety stock in MRP

Safety stock is a cushion or reserve. It protects against unplanned surges in demand and other uncertainties.

Discussion in the body of the chapter indicated that safety stock is basic to ROP systems. It is not so basic to MRP/TPOP. In fact, Orlicky recommends that safety stock generally be avoided at component levels in MRP. Instead

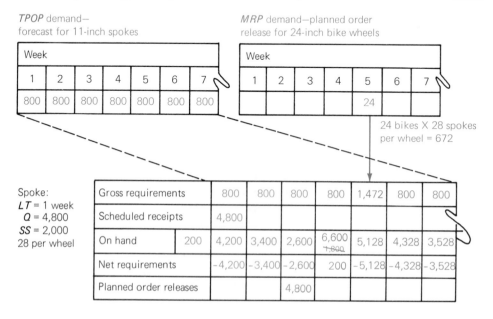

TPOP demand—forecast for 11-inch spokes

Week						
1	2	3	4	5	6	7
800	800	800	800	800	800	800

MRP demand—planned order release for 24-inch bike wheels

Week						
1	2	3	4	5	6	7
				24		

24 bikes X 28 spokes per wheel = 672

Spoke:
LT = 1 week
Q = 4,800
SS = 2,000
28 per wheel

Gross requirements		800	800	800	800	1,472	800	800
Scheduled receipts		4,800						
On hand	200	4,200	3,400	2,600	6,600 ~~1,800~~	5,128	4,328	3,528
Net requirements		–4,200	–3,400	–2,600	200	–5,128	–4,328	–3,528
Planned order releases				4,800				

safety stock may be provided at the MPS level; since component orders are linked to the MPS, safety stock in the master production schedule is considered to provide a balance of safety at all lower BOM levels. To add more safety stock at component levels tends to unbalance the protection. Worse, it tends to erode people's confidence in MRP, because people know there is a safety stock to fall back on when MRP plans are not followed.

Still MRP can be designed to allow for safety stock at component levels, and it appears that many MRP-using firms do carry some amount of safety stock for certain components. Safety stocks are most often used for purchased parts that have long lead time, that are hard to get, or that are obtainable from only one (perhaps unreliable) source.[1] Safety stock at the MRP component level may be illustrated by continuing the bicycle spoke example.

EXAMPLE S4–3
MRP safety stock, bicycle spokes

Referring back to Example S4–2, we see that Figure S4–3 shows the generation of gross requirements for spokes. The figure also shows the translation of gross requirements into planned order releases, with safety stock allowed for.

Safety stock (SS) is given as 2,000, and the on-hand balance is well below that at week 0. Being below the safety stock is a matter for mild concern but not alarm. After all, safety stock is not worth having around if it is never used.

The scheduled receipt of 4,800 in week 1 is to be expected in view of the low on-hand balance. That order for 4,800 spokes would have been released in an earlier period. Receipt of 4,800 and issue of 800 (to cover week 1 gross requirements) leaves an on-hand balance of 4,200. The on-hand balance drops by 800 in each of the next three weeks. That leaves the on-hand at 1,800 in week 4; since 1,800 is below the 2,000-unit safety stock, an order is planned for receipt in week 4. The lot size, Q, is 4,800, and lead time, LT, is one week. Thus, the planned order release is for 4,800 spokes in week 3, which keeps the planned on-hand balance from going below the safety stock of 2,000 in week 4.

How would safety stock ever be used when you plan always to be above it? *Unplanned* events will take care of that—unplanned events like hot orders booked too late to plan for.

---

[1] According to Orlicky, these are legitimate exceptions, but they can be overused. Joseph Orlicky, *Material Requirements Planning* (McGraw-Hill, 1975), pp. 78–80 (TS155.8.O74).

chapter 5

INVENTORY PLANNING–QUANTITIES

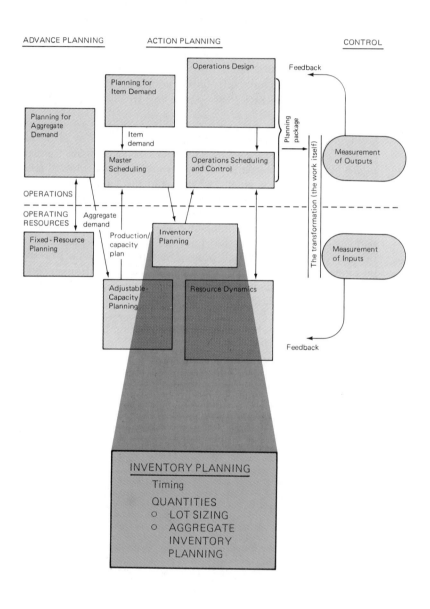

Planning for inventory quantities is presented in four parts. The first part concerns the importance of inventory quantity decisions and how they are related to timing decisions. The second part is on lot sizing, which means the size of the lot in the inventory order. The third part is on probabilistic lot-size/reorder point; the discussion deals with techniques for planning quantity and timing as an interrelated pair. The fourth part, on aggregate inventory planning, takes up the impact of overall policies on inventory quantities as well as techniques to control inventory quantity in the aggregate.

Since this chapter is the second of two on inventory planning, the relationship between the two chapters is discussed first.

TIMING/QUANTITY RELATIONSHIPS

There is a close, if not vital, relationship between the timing of inventory orders and the quantity of the orders. For one thing, the quantity must be decided whenever an order is planned (the timing of its release). For another, wrong timing and wrong quantity have similar adverse effects. Each may affect customer service, inventory carrying cost, order-processing cost, and capacity control. The effects are shown in Figure 5–1.

Late orders

The first column of Figure 5–1 shows adverse effects of late orders. One adverse effect is that customer service is poor when orders are late. The "customer" may be a parent inventory item in need of parts as well as an individual or an organizational customer. Another adverse effect is excessive order-processing or setup costs. Such costs arise when a late order triggers corrective action to expedite, look for another source, interrupt a job already set up, and so on. A third adverse effect is poor capacity control. Late orders may idle some capacity elements or may generate new orders for substitute items, thereby creating workloads, perhaps overtime, for certain capacity units.

FIGURE 5–1
Adverse effects of wrong timing and quantity

Effects \ Planning production and purchase orders	Wrong timing		Wrong quantity	
	Order is late	Order is early	Too large	Too small
Customer service	Poor	—	—	Poor
Inventory carrying cost	—	Excessive	Excessive	—
Order-processing (setup) cost	Excessive	—	—	Excessive
Capacity control	Poor	—	Poor (if manufacturing inventory)	Poor

**Early orders
and too large
quantities**

The second and third columns of the figure show adverse effects of orders that are too early and too large. Excessive inventory carrying cost is the most apparent effect. Carrying costs may be reduced by careful planning of inventory order quantities. Lot-sizing methods help control carrying costs for separate items, and aggregate inventory policies help provide overall control of carrying costs.

A subtle effect of an excessive quantity is poor capacity control. As Figure 5–1 indicates, that adverse effect applies only to manufacturing inventories: Large manufacturing lot sizes tend to cause lumpy demand for component parts, which results in unbalanced demands on capacity.

**Too small
quantities**

The fourth column mentions adverse effects of orders that are too small. Poor customer service (to parent item or human customer) is apparent. Partial orders can often help to placate the customer. Another possible adverse effect is excessive order-processing cost: There might be a need to reorder for the shortage, and in the long run small quantities mean more orders, increasing the order cost. Order-processing costs are a factor in some of the lot-sizing methods. Poor capacity control is another possible effect: Lack of enough parts may idle people, and in the long run small order quantities mean more orders, more exposures to stockout, and more capacity idled for lack of parts. (Exposure to stockout is discussed in Chapter 4.)

An objective of inventory planning is to minimize the kinds of adverse effects summarized in Figure 5–1. Planning for inventory timing was examined in the previous chapter. The next sections of this chapter explain various methods for planning inventory quantities.

LOT SIZING

Lot sizing refers to the order-quantity or lot-size or batch-size decision. Lot-size alternatives arise for *stocked* items; for one-time purchases lot size is not at issue.

Lot sizing is generally not as important as order timing. You can order too much or perhaps even too little but still provide service to the customer or user. But a late order may be worthless. Lot sizing is more a matter of economics than of service. Lot-sizing methods usually focus on controlling the costs of carrying inventory and processing orders. As the preceding section and Figure 5–1 suggest, lot sizing may also affect service and capacity control. These effects are examined below for three lot-sizing methods: lot-for-lot, part-period, and economic order quantity.

Lot-for-lot

Lot-for-lot is the simplest lot-sizing approach. Lot-for-lot simply means no batching of orders. In lot-for-lot, orders are frequent and order-processing costs are high, but planned inventory—and therefore carrying costs—are zero. From the narrow perspective of a single inventory item lot-for-lot seems uneconomical because of the high order-processing costs. But lot-for-lot has advantages for the system as a whole, especially as part of an MRP system. For groups of related inventory items frequent orders, via lot-for-lot, tend to smooth out purchasing or fabricating workloads; large batches, on the other hand, tend to cause lumpy workloads. An example will illustrate.

EXAMPLE 5–1 Lot-sizing effects on workloads, chain manufacturing example	The two parts of Figure 5–2 show contrasting effects of lot-for-lot versus batched orders. Figure 5–2A shows a smooth demand pattern for four styles of chain, and the smooth demand/production pattern is carried downward through the two levels to the purchased-part level (steel rod). Thus, the purchasing/receiving workload (for steel rod) is level and invariable; the workload for cutting two-inch pieces and five-inch pieces in one or more cutting work centers is level and invariable; and the workload to produce four styles of chain in fabrication work centers is level and invariable. Such even workloads make it possible to keep the work centers running at nearly full capacity and without sporadic overtime.

It is obvious that order batching will transform smooth demands and even loads (workloads) into a lumpy demand/load pattern. Not only that, but the lumpiness is amplified downward through bill-of-materials levels. This is shown in Figure 5–2B. At the finished-chain level, batching results in lot sizes varying from 0 to 20. Batching at the cut-piece level results in lot sizes varying from 0 to 40. And batching at the steel-rod level results in lot sizes varying from 0 to 60.

Comparing Figure 5–2A and Figure 5–2B, we see that lot-for-lot has a clear advantage from the standpoint of yielding smooth workloads. An *apparent* advantage of lot-for-lot is fewer setups. That is, batching in part B results in a stop-and-go production pattern, and each new batch requires a setup. For example, there are three setups for the steel rod in part B, but the smooth production pattern in part A seems to call for only one setup. The impression is deceptive, because this is an exaggerated case. Lot-for-lot usually would provide for alternating setups of small orders for different parts, and long-run setup cost would be high. The next two techniques, part-period and economic order quantity, provide for controlling setup cost.

Part-period	The part-period algorithm (PPA) is aimed at minimizing average cost per time bucket of ordering and carrying inventory.[1] While lot-for-lot has the broad objective of minimizing lumpiness in demand for sets of related parts, PPA is concerned only with the inventory costs of a single part. PPA is robust, however, in that it operates well for lumpy as well as smooth planned demand for a given part.

PPA makes use of an *economic part-period* (EPP) factor. The EPP is the quantity that would make setup cost equal to carrying cost if the item is carried in stock for one period. The EPP computation is

$$EPP = \frac{S}{CC},$$

where

---

[1] PPA is also known as the least-total-cost (LTC) method.

A. Lot-for-lot ordering

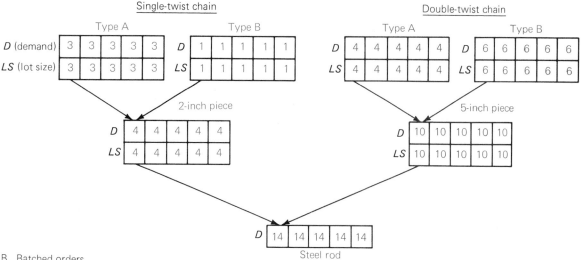

B. Batched orders

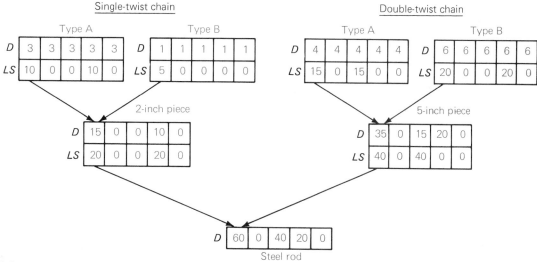

FIGURE 5-2
Lot-for-lot versus batched ordering

S = Setup cost
CC = Carrying cost per period

The part-period algorithm calls for successively computing cumulative part-periods of inventory carried for each lot-size option. The selected lot size is that whose part-period total most nearly equals, but does not exceed, the EPP.

A part-period of inventory means one part carried for one period or time bucket. (Part-period does *not* mean part *of* a period.) Twelve part-periods could be four parts carried for three periods or three parts carried for four periods or any other similar multiple of twelve.

PPA is demonstrated in the following example.

EXAMPLE 5–2
Part-period
algorithm

Net requirements for the next six weeks for a certain manufactured part are: 20, 0, 20, 25, 35, 10, 10. If setup cost is $600 per lot and carrying cost is $10 per unit per week, what lot size is recommended by PPA?

Solution:

1. Calculate EPP.

$$EPP = \frac{S}{CC} = \frac{\$600}{\$10} = 60$$

2. Calculate cumulative part-periods carried, beginning with the first period, for each lot-size option. Stop when EPP is reached. Calculations follow:

Trial	Trial lot size = Parts produced in period 1	Period (week)	Parts required	Part-period calculation	Cumulative part-periods
1	20	1	20	20 parts × 0 weeks carried = 0	0
2	20	2	0	0 parts × 1 week carried = 0	0
3	40	3	20	20 parts × 2 weeks carried = 40	40
4	65	4	25	25 parts × 3 weeks carried = 75	115

In the fourth trial the EPP, 60, is exceeded. Therefore, select the previous lot size, 40, which covers net requirements for weeks 1–3. Repeating for the next three weeks gives a second lot size of 70, which covers net requirements for weeks 4 and 5. (Computation of this lot size is reserved as an end-of-chapter problem.)

The results of the PPA calculations are summarized below:

	Period						
	1	*2*	*3*	*4*	*5*	*6*	*7*
Net requirements	20	0	20	25	35	10	10
Planned order (lot size)	40			70			*

* Not computed because of lack of net requirements for periods 8 and beyond.

PPA, like lot-for-lot, provides for variable lot sizes, in which the calculated lot size is equal to projected net requirements. This is in contrast to fixed-lot-size methods (like economic order quantity, discussed next), in which any excess in the produced lot must be carried in stock until the next requirement occurs. Another advantage of PPA, not obvious from the above example, is that PPA serves to minimize the sum of setup and carrying costs.[2]

---

[2] Actually PPA does not *exactly* minimize these costs. The reason why not is explained in Joseph Orlicky, *Material Requirements Planning* (McGraw-Hill, 1975), pp. 128–29. (TS155.8.O74).

Economic order quantity

The economic order quantity (EOQ) is one of the oldest tools of management science; a basic EOQ formula was developed by F. W. Harris in 1915. The newer PPA method is actually an offspring of EOQ. And like PPA, EOQ is concerned with the inventory costs of a single part: It seeks to minimize the sum of period setup and carrying costs for the part.

Unlike PPA, EOQ does not provide varying lot sizes to match varying projected demand. Instead, EOQ is based on the past average demand. Recall from the discussion in Chapter 4 that reorder point (ROP) is also based on past average demand, whereas MRP is based on future projected demand. EOQ and ROP have been a knife-and-fork-like pair.

Costs of inventory. The period inventory costs that EOQ seeks to minimize are of three types: order-processing cost, carrying cost, and item cost. Each is further explained below.

1. *Order-processing cost.* In a given period of time, say a year, an item may be reordered once, or twice, or three times, and so on. If it is ordered once, the lot size is large enough to cover the whole year's demand; if it is ordered twice, a half year's demand is the lot size; and so on.

The costs of processing an order include clerical costs of preparing the purchase order or manufacturing order. If it is a purchase order, costs of order expediting and processing the invoice are included; if it is a manufacturing order, the dominant cost may be machine setup cost. As before, let S represent the average cost of processing an order (S stands for *s*etup). Also, let Q (for *q*uantity) be the lot size and D be average annual demand for a given item. Then, for the given item:

$$\frac{D}{Q} = \text{Number of orders per year}$$

$$S\left(\frac{D}{Q}\right) = \text{Annual cost of processing orders}$$

Demand, D, could cover a period other than a year. For example, if D represents average monthly demand, then $S(D/Q)$ equals monthly cost of processing orders.

2. *Carrying cost.* Carrying cost is the cost to finance inventory and hold it in storage. Thus, carrying cost increases as number of units in storage increases. If a given item is reordered infrequently in large lots, its carrying costs will be large; if it is ordered often in small lots, its carrying costs will be small.

The finance-cost component of carrying cost refers to the capital tied up in inventory. It is an interest or opportunity cost. More visible are the holding costs. These include storage facilities, insurance, inventory taxes, handling, and losses from shrinkage and obsolescence. Total carrying costs per period divided by total dollar value of inventory yields what is known as the annual inventory-carrying-cost rate, I. One such rate may be established for all items carried in a given firm. To compute annual carrying cost for a single item, we need the unit cost, C, for the item. Then,

IC = Cost to carry one unit for one year

For any given lot size, Q, annual carrying cost equals annual cost to carry one unit times average units in stock, $Q/2$. Symbolically we have, for a given item:

$$IC\left(\frac{Q}{2}\right) = \text{Annual carrying cost}$$

Why is average inventory equal to $Q/2$? Because the average is, logically, halfway between planned maximum inventory, Q, and minimum inventory, zero (or half the sum of the maximum and the minimum). Safety stock can push maximum inventory above Q, but by a constant amount they may be ignored in lot-size analysis.

3. *Item cost.* The annual cost to make an item, or the total price paid for it, is, in the most basic EOQ model, treated as a constant. You pay the same per year whether it is bought in small or large lots. Thus, the annual item cost, demand (D) times cost (C), may be omitted in basic lot-size analysis. Quantity discount possibilities will be introduced later.

EOQ calculations. Since item cost is omitted, there are just two annual costs that vary with lot size: annual order-processing cost and carrying cost. The EOQ must minimize the sum of these costs. You may realize that algebraically the minimum occurs where

Annual order-processing cost = Annual carrying cost

Substituting and collecting terms yields a basic EOQ formula, as follows:[3]

$$S\left(\frac{D}{Q}\right) = IC\left(\frac{Q}{2}\right)$$

$$Q^2 = \frac{2DS}{IC}$$

$$Q = \sqrt{\frac{2DS}{IC}}$$

Basic EOQ may be illustrated graphically. Figure 5–3 is a general form of the graph. It shows the EOQ at the minimum total annual cost, which is also where annual carrying cost equals annual order-processing cost. As has been discussed, annual order-processing cost decreases and annual carrying cost increases with larger lot sizes.

Notice that the minimum cost is shown in a shaded zone. In that zone, which is fairly large horizontally, total annual cost does not deviate much

---

[3] The EOQ formula may also be derived by calculus. The method is to differentiate total annual cost with respect to Q and to solve for Q at minimum total cost.

FIGURE 5–3
Graph of annual
inventory cost
and lot sizes

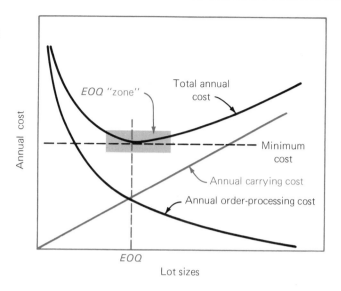

FIGURE 5–4
Effects on EOQ of
errors in carrying-
cost rate

Carrying-cost rate, I	Percent error in I	EOQ	Percent error in EOQ
True rate = 0.10	—	True $EOQ = 3.16\sqrt{\dfrac{2DS}{C}}$	—
0.12	20	$2.89\sqrt{\dfrac{2DS}{C}}$	−8.5%
0.15	50	$2.58\sqrt{\dfrac{2DS}{C}}$	−18.4
0.20	100	$2.23\sqrt{\dfrac{2DS}{C}}$	−29.4

Sample calculation:

$$EOQ = \sqrt{\frac{2DS}{IC}} = \sqrt{\frac{1}{I}} \cdot \sqrt{\frac{2DS}{C}}$$

$$= \sqrt{\frac{1}{0.10}} \cdot \sqrt{\frac{2DS}{C}} = \sqrt{10} \cdot \sqrt{\frac{2DS}{C}}$$

$$= 3.16\sqrt{\frac{2DS}{C}}$$

Percent error in EOQ:

$$\frac{2.89 - 3.16}{3.16} = -8.5\%$$

from the minimum. Thus, in a practical sense EOQ may be thought of as a zone or range of lot sizes, not just the exact EOQ quantity.

The practicality of EOQ is also enhanced by the square-root relationship between the four data inputs and the EOQ result: A large error in a data input translates into less error—the square root of the error, to be exact—in computing the EOQ. Figure 5–4 shows this effect for the carrying-cost rate, *I*. (The effect is similar for *D*, *S*, and *C*.) For a 20 percent error in *I*, the EOQ error is only − 8.5 percent; for a 50 percent error in *I*, the EOQ error is − 18.4 percent; and for a 100 percent error in *I*, the EOQ error is − 29.4 percent. Thus, the data inputs need not be exact and the same cost inputs may often be used for various items.

Development of input data and use (and misuse) of basic EOQ are demonstrated in the following example of a small bookstore.

EXAMPLE 5–3 Economic order quantity, bookstore	B. K. Worm, manager of Surburban Books, is thinking of purchasing best-selling titles in economic order quantities. Worm has assembled the following data:

```
Inventory on hand:
    Estimated average last year  . . . . . . . . . . .      8,000 books
    Estimated average cost per book  . . . . . . .        $10
    Average inventory value  . . . . . . . . . . . . . .   $80,000 ┐
Annual holding cost:                                              │
    Rental, building and fixtures  . . . . . . . . . .     $7,000  │
    Estimated shrinkage losses  . . . . . . . . . . . .      700   │
    Insurance . . . . . . . . . . . . . . . . . . . . . . . . . .   300   │
    Total . . . . . . . . . . . . . . . . . . . . . . . . . . . . .  $8,000  │
Annual capital cost:                                              │
    Capital invested . . . . . . . . . . . . . . . . . . . . .  $80,000 ◄┘
    Interest rate  . . . . . . . . . . . . . . . . . . . . . . .     10%
    Total . . . . . . . . . . . . . . . . . . . . . . . . . . . . .  $ 8,000
Annual carrying cost (Annual holding
    cost + Annual capital cost):
    $8,000 + $8,000 . . . . . . . . . . . . . . . . . . . .   $16,000
Carrying-cost rate, I (Annual
    carrying cost ÷ Average
    inventory value):
    $16,000/$80,000 . . . . . . . . . . . . . . . . . . . .      0.20
Purchase order processing cost, S:
    Estimate for preparation and
        invoice handling  . . . . . . . . . . . . . . . . . .   $4 per order
```

Now Worm has the cost data to calculate EOQs. He selects his biggest seller as the first book to be ordered by EOQ. It is *Gone with the Wind*, which is enjoying a burst of renewed popularity in Worm's store. The book in paperback has recently been selling at a rate of 40 copies per month and wholesales for $3 per copy. Thus, for the EOQ equation,

$$C = \$3 \text{ per unit}$$
$$D = 40 \text{ units/mo.} \times 12 \text{ mo./yr.}$$
$$= 480 \text{ units/yr.}$$

Then,

$$EOQ = \sqrt{\frac{2DS}{IC}} = \sqrt{\frac{2(480)(4)}{0.2(3)}}$$
$$= \sqrt{6,400} = 80 \text{ copies/order}$$

The EOQ, 80 copies, is about two months' supply (80 copies/order ÷ 40 copies/month = 2 months/order); it is also $400 worth ($5/copy × 80 copies/order = $400 per order).[4]

Mr. Worm's assistant, M. B. Ainsworth, cannot resist pointing out to his boss a fallacy in this EOQ of 80 copies. M.B.A. puts it this way:

"Mr. Worm, I'm not so sure that *Gone with the Wind* is the right book to order by EOQ. The EOQ is based on last month's demand of 40. But demand might be 60 next month and 80 the month after. Also, the average carrying-cost rate, I, was based mostly on larger hardcover books, which cost more to store. Maybe we should use EOQ only on our stable sellers in hard cover. How about Webster's *New Collegiate Dictionary?*"

EOQ variations

By the above example, we can see that successful use of basic EOQ depends on certain conditions. Some of the conditions are:

1. The item being reordered is about average in regard to cost of holding; for example, it has no unusual temperature, humidity, security, or bulk characteristics.
2. Cost per unit is relatively fixed and known; quantity discounts are not provided for.
3. The whole quantity is delivered at one time; this is typical of purchased items, but it may not be true of made items.
4. Demand should be relatively stable and predictable, and without pronounced seasonality; for a new item it may be possible to estimate demand by referring to known demand for a similar existing item.

Variations on the basic EOQ model are available to offset each of these conditions. Four EOQ variations are considered next. The four are: carrying-cost variations, quantity discounts, economic manufacturing quantity, and probabilistic lot-size/reorder point.

Carrying-cost variations. Two variations on the basic EOQ treatment of carrying cost warrant some discussion. First is a variation in which annual carrying cost is based on maximum inventory rather than half of the maximum. Second is a variation in which capital cost and holding cost are treated separately rather than together.

In basic EOQ, annual carrying cost equals IC times $Q/2$; in a few situations it is more valid to use IC times Q. The former is proper when a large number

---

[4] The basic formula may be modified to directly yield an EOQ in months' supply or in dollars' worth:

$$EOQ \text{ (in months)} = \sqrt{\frac{288S}{ICD}}$$

$$EOQ \text{ (in dollars)} = \sqrt{\frac{2DCS}{I}}$$

of items share the same storage space. In that case the total storage space needed is *not* based on the sum of the maximum inventory quantities (Q's) for all the items, because it is unlikely that all the items will be at their maximums at one time. Instead some items will be low when others are high, and we may assume that space needs are equal to the sum of *half* the maximums ($Q/2$) for all items stored.

IC times Q is proper when only one item is to be stored in a given storage space. In that case there must be space enough to hold the whole order quantity, Q; since the cost of the space is not shared with other items, annual carrying cost for the given item must be based on maximum inventory, Q. Examples of items of this kind are:

Sides of beef in a walk-in freezer.

Autos in a parking lot.

Fuel in a storage tank.

For special items like this, EOQ is derived from annual carrying cost = ICQ; the result is

$$EOQ = \sqrt{\frac{DS}{IC}}$$

The second carrying-cost variation separates carrying cost into holding cost plus capital cost. Let H be equal to the cost of physically holding one unit in storage for one year. And let iC be equal to the capital cost per year, where

i = Interest rate (or discount rate or cost of capital)

C = Unit cost of the item

Then,

Annual carrying cost = ½ (Annual holding cost + Annual capital cost)
                     = ½ ($H + iC$)

And

$$EOQ = \sqrt{\frac{2DS}{H + iC}}$$

This version of EOQ is a bit more precise than basic EOQ for two reasons: First, it allows an inventory planner to separately estimate H according to how costly it is to store an item or items. For example, items that are bulky or that need special storage for reasons of security or temperature and humidity control would cost more to hold in storage; a higher estimate of H could be used in EOQ calculations for such items. Second, this EOQ version properly provides for item cost, C, to affect only the interest cost of tied-up capital. (The simpler, but cruder, basic EOQ multiplies C by I, which is a factor that includes holding cost as well as interest cost.)

EOQ with quantity discounts. In basic EOQ, periodic item cost is treated as constant and is·omitted. The item cost for purchased items may, however, be variable—in steps—via quantity discounts. Annual item cost then becomes a relevant cost—along with annual carrying cost and order-processing cost. The EOQ may be determined by trial and error. The method is iterative: Successively larger lot sizes are tried, and total annual cost is computed until the minimum cost is found. Another pass at the bookstore example will illustrate.

Example 5–4
EOQ with
quantity
discount,
bookstore

B. K. Worm, manager of Suburban Books, has applied basic EOQ to *Gone with the Wind.* But Worm didn't allow for quantity discounts. Popular Publications, Inc., offers the following price breaks for *GWTW:*

Quantity	Price per copy
1–48	$3.00
49–96	2.80
97 up	2.60

Other data, from Example 5–3 are:

$I = 0.20$
$S = \$4$ per order
$D = 480$ units/yr.

For a trial-and-error EOQ solution, Worm tries quantities of 12, 24, 36, 48, . . . 240; 49 and 97 are also tried since they are at the price breaks.

Figures 5–5 and 5–6 show some of the calculations and graphic results. Three trial lot sizes for the $3.00 unit cost result in a decreasing total cost pattern; the minimum cost of $1,494.40 is for a lot size of 48, the maximum quantity for that price. Three trial lot sizes for the $2.80 unit cost result in a falling, then rising, pattern; a minimum is shown in the vicinity of $Q = 72$, total cost = $1,390.83. Two trial lot sizes for the $2.60 unit cost result in an increasing pattern, and at $Q = 97$ we see the grand minimum cost of $1,292.22. That is the true economic order quantity.

Economic manufacturing quantity. Basic EOQ is well suited for purchased items—an economic *purchase* quantity—because the whole lot is usually delivered at one time; this simplifies determining average inventory and, therefore, EOQ. When an item is made instead of bought, the quantity ordered may sometimes be delivered in trickles as it comes off the production line. This complicates figuring average inventory, upon which annual carrying cost is based, and it results in a modified EOQ formula. The modification may be called an economic *manufacturing* quantity, EMQ, formula. (Note: Purchased items are sometimes delivered in trickles rather than all at once; if so, this EMQ modification would apply.)

The modified formula calls for one new term, the production rate, P. P is measured in the same units as D, the demand rate—typically in units per year. P must be greater than D in order for the demand to be covered. P —

FIGURE 5–5
EOQ calculations for alternative item costs

	C = $3.00			C = $2.80			C = $2.60	
Trial Q:	12	24	48	49	72	96	97	240
Annual order-processing cost: $\dfrac{D}{Q}(S) = \dfrac{480}{Q}(4) = \dfrac{1{,}920}{Q}$	$160.00	$80.00	$40.00	$39.20	$26.67	$20.00	$19.80	$8.00
Annual carrying cost: $IC\left(\dfrac{Q}{2}\right) = 0.2C\left(\dfrac{Q}{2}\right)$	$0.2(3)\left(\dfrac{Q}{2}\right) =$ $3.60		$6.00	$14.40	$0.2(2.80)\left(\dfrac{Q}{2}\right) =$ $13.72	$20.16	$26.88	$0.2(2.60)\left(\dfrac{Q}{2}\right) =$ $25.22	$62.40
Annual item cost: $DC = 480C$	$480(3) =$ $1,440.00 $1,440.00		$1,440.00	$480(2.80) =$ $1,344.00 $1,344.00		$1,344.00	$480(2.60) =$ $1,248.00 $1,248.00	
Total annual cost:	$1,603.60	$1,526.00	$1,494.40	$1,396.92	$1,390.83	$1,390.88	$1,292.22	$1,318.40

↑
EOQ

FIGURE 5-6
Annual cost
graph of lot sizes
with quantity
discounts

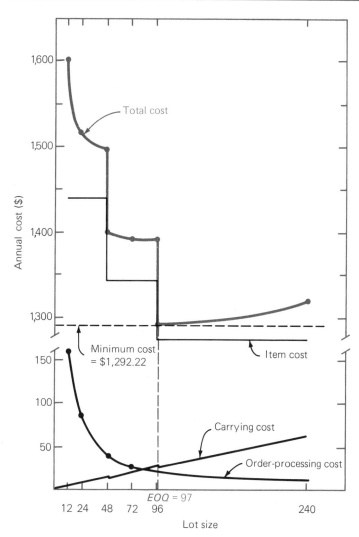

D is the rate of inventory buildup. That is, you produce at rate P and at the same time use at rate D; the difference equals the rate of increase in stock. If the lot is made in time, T, then

$$\text{Lot size} = Q = \text{Rate} \times \text{Time} = (P - D)\ (T)$$

Since Q is maximum planned inventory and $Q/2$ is average inventory,

$$\text{Average inventory} = \frac{Q}{2} = \frac{(P - D)(T)}{2}$$

The extra term, T, may be eliminated by substitution: The time needed to produce a lot, Q, is

$$T = \frac{\text{Quantity}}{\text{Rate}} = \frac{Q}{P}$$

By substitution,

$$\text{Average inventory} = \left(\frac{P-D}{2}\right)\left(\frac{Q}{P}\right) \text{ or } \left(\frac{P-D}{P}\right)\left(\frac{Q}{2}\right)$$

Now the EMQ equation may be derived in the same way that the basic EOQ equation was: by setting annual order-processing cost equal to annual carrying cost and solving for Q. The result is:

$$EMQ = \sqrt{\frac{2DS}{(IC)(1-D/P)}}$$

Differences between basic EOQ and EMQ may be shown graphically. Figure 5–7A shows the general pattern of usage and replenishment for basic EOQ. It looks like a ripsaw blade: The vertical line represents the increase in stock that occurs when the whole EOQ is received at one time (sometimes called *instantaneous replenishment*). The downward-sloping line is the average demand rate, D. Maximum inventory, $I_{max.}$, is equal to Q, and average inventory, $I_{ave.}$, is equal to $I_{max.}/2$.

Figure 5–7B shows the general inventory pattern for EMQ. It looks like a crosscut saw blade: The upward-sloping solid line represents the rate of inventory buildup, $P-D$; P, the production rate, is shown as a dashed line for reference purposes. The downward-sloping line is the average demand rate, D. Maximum inventory, $I_{max.}$, is not equal to Q; the stock level never reaches Q, because some of Q is being used up (delivered) as it is being produced. $I_{max.}$ is, instead, equal to $(P-D)(T)$ or $(P-D)\left(\dfrac{Q}{D}\right)$, as was shown earlier, and $I_{ave.}$ equals half of $I_{max.}$.

FIGURE 5–7
BASIC EOQ and EMQ replenishment patterns

A. Basic *EOQ* pattern of instantaneous replenishment

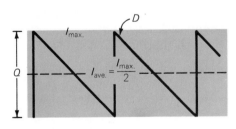

B. *EMQ* pattern of noninstantaneous replenishment

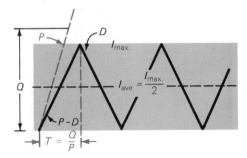

Note that for otherwise equal conditions, EMQ is larger than basic EOQ. Inspection of the EMQ formula shows this to be mathematically obvious, because the factor $1 - D/P$ in the denominator makes the denominator smaller and the EMQ larger. The logical reason is that with EMQ there is less stock to carry since stock level does not get up to Q; with less to carry, it is economical to produce a bit more per lot.

Comparison of lot-sizing methods

There are other, more elegant lot-sizing algorithms. There is neither the space nor the necessity to present all of them. The Wagner-Whitin algorithm,[5] for example, is theoretically important. (That is, it serves to expand the limits of our understanding of the reordering phenomenon.) Wagner-Whitin has been proven, on paper, to result in lower total inventory costs than a variety of other lot-sizing methods. But the costs are valid only if projections of demand in future time buckets are accurate. We have seen that forecasting accuracy drops as you go into the future; thus, an elaborate lot-sizing plan that depends on future projections will rarely achieve the economies predicted on paper.

This argument applies equally to other methods, including lot-for-lot, PPA, and EOQ. It is true that with computer power any of the methods can be run *dynamically*; that is, lot sizes can be recomputed every time demand projections change, which could be monthly, weekly, or even daily. The effect, however, is unstable planned lot sizes. That is, the lot size for a given planned order may be driven up and down by changing forecasting signals, which typically are not very reliable. The system becomes overly "nervous." For these reasons, many authorities feel that one lot-sizing method is about as good as another. In practice, simpler methods—for example, lot-for-lot, PPA, and EOQ—are usually preferred, because they are more easily understood by operating-level people.

Among the simpler methods, we have noted the advantage of lot-for-lot when demand is lumpy and dependent: Lumpiness is amplified in going from parent to component levels, and the smaller lot sizes derived from lot-for-lot hold this amplification down.

PPA and EOQ result in larger lot sizes, and this aggravates the problem of lumpy demand/uneven loads. But both methods save on order setup and processing costs. PPA has the advantage of looking ahead at planned net requirements. EOQ, on the other hand, is past-demand-oriented; but when EOQ is used in an MRP system, the replanning features of MRP allow the inventory planner to adjust the quantity upward and downward from the EOQ, as desired.

EOQ is frequently the partner of reorder point (ROP) in the independent-demand case. Independent demand is especially common in high-volume wholesale, retail, and other service industries: Large numbers of small demands tend to yield a rather stable demand rate (D in the EOQ formula), and zero-

---

[5] H. M. Wagner and T. M. Whitin, "Dynamic Version of the Economic Lot Size Model," *Management Science*, 5, no. 1 (October 1958), pp. 89–96.

demand time buckets are unlikely. Even if demand (or other) estimates are quite incorrect, the EOQ error may not be severe, because of the previously mentioned effect of the square root in the EOQ formula; it was also noted that EOQ can be considered as a zone rather than an inflexible point.

Variations in carrying-cost treatment in EOQ may be useful in special cases. The variations are not essential because of the aforementioned inherent margin of error attending EOQ.

Quantity discounts often dwarf other ingredients of inventory cost; this is certainly true in the bookstore example. Where quantity discounts are considerable, purchasing departments are unlikely to pay much attention to EOQ. For this reason it is not always necessary in practice to elaborate the EOQ model by including quantity-discount routines.

The EMQ variation can be helpful, but it is not critical—again because of the square-root effect. EMQ is most suitable when the production rate is not very much faster than the demand rate; the D/P factor then is large enough to make a difference in the lot size. When P is very large, however, EMQ approaches basic EOQ.

PROBABILISTIC LOT-SIZE/REORDER POINT

Most of the inventory models that we have considered are *deterministic;* that is, the input data estimates are treated as being invariable or nonprobabilistic. An exception is the statistical-service-level concept; it was discussed in the safety-stock section in the previous chapter. Other probabilistic (or stochastic) inventory models are also available. The probabilistic models generally apply to independent demand (e.g., wholesale, retail, and manufacturing service-part inventories). Generally, the objectives of the probabilistic models are:

1. To refine the safety-stock portion of reorder-point determination.
2. To obtain a combined optimal EOQ and ROP.

Advanced inventory models supporting these two objectives warrant brief discussion.

Lead-time variability

Lead time tends to be variable, though usually to a lesser extent than demand, and lead-time variability is somewhat easier to control than demand variability.[6] For example, lead time may be reduced via expediting actions. For these reasons, inventory models featuring probabilistic lead time will be only briefly mentioned here.

One model permits calculation of an optimal combination of order quantity and planned lead time. For example, if lead time has been varying between one and five days, the planner may release an order anywhere from one to five days prior to the time when delivery is needed; one of those five lead-

---

[6] In manufacturing, as much as ninety percent of lead time may be queue time. This is discussed further in Chapter 6.

time policies will result in minimum average (expected) annual inventory cost, where

$$\text{Total annual cost} = \text{Annual order processing cost}$$
$$+ \text{Annual cost of carrying half the EOQ}$$
$$+ \text{Annual cost of carrying excess}$$
$$\text{inventory to protect against stockout}$$

$$= (S + SO)\left(\frac{D}{Q_{LT}}\right) + (IC)\left(\frac{Q_{LT}}{2}\right) + CE$$

New terms are:

> SO, the expected stockout cost per cycle
> CE, the expected annual cost of carrying the excess
> Q_{LT}, the EOQ for the given lead-time policy

Q_{LT} is the same as basic EOQ except that order-processing cost includes expected stockout cost per order, SO, as well as S. Thus,

$$Q_{LT} = \sqrt{\frac{2D(S + SO)}{IC}}$$

The procedure for computing SO and CE values is based on the expected-value concept, and calculations can be tedious. Other calculations—of Q_{LT} and total annual cost—are straightforward.[7]

Combined demand and lead-time variability

Independently demanded items usually exhibit demand variability and lead-time variability, acting in concert. In basic EOQ and ROP models we ignore one or the other or both kinds of variability. As we have seen, high levels of numerical precision are usually not warranted in inventory management; simpler models usually suffice. Examining complex interactions between variable demand and variable lead times is usually not practical for day-to-day inventory management. It can, however, be useful for testing various inventory policies.

What we are talking about is Monte Carlo simulation of inventory behavior. Inventory simulation is similar to maintenance simulation, described in Chapter 13. Demands correspond to breakdowns (arrival rates, in general). But lead time is not quite like repair time (service time); lead time comes into play only when stock gets down to the ROP. Some possible objectives of Monte Carlo simulation of an inventory are:

1. Predict stockout frequency (or service level) and expected amount of the stockout, given any combination of EOQ and ROP.
2. Predict total annual inventory cost, given any combination of EOQ and ROP/service level.
3. Sensitivity analysis: To test the effects on service level or total annual

[7] Examples of the procedure may be found in James L. Riggs, *Production Systems: Planning, Analysis, and Control* (Wiley, 1976), pp. 454–56 (TS155.R45).

inventory cost of changes or inaccuracies in input data, such as demand and lead-time distributions and inventory costs.

Precise analysis to achieve these objectives is generally not possible with deterministic models, that is, models with single-valued data estimates. Monte Carlo processes are necessary to achieve precision because of the complex effects of interacting frequency distributions: Variable demand interacts with variable lead time, which leads to a demand during lead time (DLT) distribution; the DLT distribution, when matched against any given ROP, results in an expected probability of stockout during lead time (which follows the expected-value concept—discussed more fully in Chapter 13). An example follows:

EXAMPLE 5–5
Monte Carlo
simulation of a
stocked item

Historical data for a given item reveal the following demand and lead-time distributions:

Daily demand	Probability		Days of lead time	Probability
0	0.4		1	0.3
1	0.6		2	0.7
	1.0			1.0

With these distributions there are three possible demands during lead time: 2, 1, or 0. DLT of 2 can occur when lead time is two days (occurs seven times in ten), where demand is 1 on the first day of lead time (occurs six times in ten) and also is 1 on the second day of lead time (occurs six times in ten). Similarly, DLT of 1 occurs when lead time is one day and demand is 1 on the single day of lead time; and DLT of 0 occurs when lead time is one or two days and demand is 0.

These combinations are amenable to Monte Carlo simulation; Monte Carlo number ranges may be set up to represent the probabilities, and random numbers then may be drawn and fit to the number ranges, thereby yielding lead times, demands, and DLTs. (See maintenance simulation in Chapter 13.)

In the same simulation, each generated DLT value may be compared with a given ROP. When DLT is greater than ROP, a stockout results.

As an example, assume that ROP = 1, that in the first simulated cycle lead time is two days, and that the simulated demands are one unit on the first day and one on the second day. Then DLT is 2. Since DLT is one unit more than ROP, there is a stockout of 1 in that simulated cycle.

The expected stockout amount per cycle can be computed as an average over a number of simulated cycles. The frequency or average cost of stockout could be simulated, if that is the outcome of interest. Total annual inventory cost could be simulated by including a routine for keeping track of carrying cost and order-processing cost.[8]

It must be stressed that Monte Carlo simulation is costly and therefore not likely for day-to-day management purposes. Rather, it is a technique that

---

[8] Computer models for simulating total annual inventory costs are given in Claude McMillan and Richard F. Gonzalez, *Systems Analysis: A Computer Approach to Decision Models* (Irwin, 1973), ch. 6 (HD69.D4M235).

is suited for special design and sensitivity-analysis purposes—usually on a small number of representative items. MRP and simple ROP and EOQ models are more likely for day-to-day management of item inventories. And aggregate inventory analysis methods, covered next, are suitable for managing groups of inventory items and for planning overall inventory policies.

AGGREGATE INVENTORY PLANNING

Inventory in the aggregate is an element of adjustable capacity. That is, inventory on hand provides increased capacity to meet customer demands. Other aspects of adjustable-capacity planning were discussed in the capacity-planning chapter (Chapter 3). Aggregate inventory planning is discussed in this chapter, since the planning concerns lot sizing and safety stocks.

In most organizations, large and small, cash shortages are commonplace. What do you do if you are a financial manager and you see an impending cash shortage? You may look first at cutting inventories. Why pick on inventories? Because this *seems* fairly painless as compared, say, with labor layoffs, borrowing money, or slower paying of bills. Thus money tied up in inventories is a common target. A common financial ratio, inventory turnover, is one way to measure money tied up in inventories.

Two types of inventories may be cut. One is safety-stock inventories; the other is cycle-stock inventories, which result from the cycle of periodic replenishment. Safety-stock and cycle-stock inventories are considered in upcoming sections on aggregate safety-stock analysis and on the LIMIT technique for analyzing lot-size inventories. But first let us consider inventory turnover.

Inventory turnover

The inventory turnover ratio is:

$$\text{Inventory turnover} = \frac{\text{Cost of goods sold}}{\text{Average inventory in dollars}}$$

If last year's cost of goods sold was \$900,000 and average inventory was \$300,000, then

$$\text{Inventory turnover} = \frac{\$900,000}{\$300,000} = 3 \text{ times}$$

For, say, a manufacturer of industrial abrasives, a turnover of 3 would seem low. If average inventories were reduced by 20 percent, turnover would become a more respectable 3.75, and \$60,000 would become available for other purposes.

While lower inventories save money and make turnover ratios look good, they may hurt customer service. Less total inventory often means shortages of items customers want. If you are out of stock, the customer may go elsewhere. Thus there are competitive pressures to keep safety-stock inventories on hand.

Aggregate safety-stock analysis

Aggregate safety-stock analysis is aimed at showing how customer service drops off as average inventories are cut (and turnover is increased). The technique makes use of the statistical measure of customer service that was presented in Chapter 4. An example of aggregate safety-stock analysis follows. *Example of aggregate safety-stock analysis.*

EXAMPLE 5–6
Service versus aggregate safety-stock investment, W-X-Y-Z Distributors

As its name suggests, W-X-Y-Z Distributors distributes four major products named W, X, Y, and Z. Sales is at odds with Finance over size of inventory or inventory turnover. As an aid to resolving the controversy, an analysis of customer service versus aggregate safety-stock investment is performed. The given data for the analysis are:[9]

Product	Annual usage	Order quantity	Unit cost	MAD (per order cycle)
W	32,000	8,000	$1.50	180
X	80,000	5,000	1.00	1,100
Y	8,000	800	1.40	500
Z	45,000	3,000	0.80	150

FIGURE 5–8
Service/ investment calculations, W-X-Y-Z distributors

Sample calculations for a narrow range of service/investment options are given in Figure 5–8. The first column gives stockouts per year. This number is evenly divided among the four products.

The third column is simply annual usage divided by order quantity. That gives number of orders or number of exposures to stockout per year. That is, the product

(1) Stockout frequency	(2) Product	(3) Number exposures	(4) Service fraction	(5) Service level (%)	(6) MAD safety factor	(7) Safety stock	(8) Safety-Stock Investment ($)
Eight stockouts per year (two per item)	W	4	2/4	50.00%	0	0	$ 0
	X	16	14/16	87.50	1.45	1,595	1,595
	Y	10	8/10	80.00	1.05	525	735
	Z	15	13/15	86.67	1.40	210	168
							$ 2,498
One stockout per year (one every four years per item)	W	16	15/16	93.75%	1.92	346	$ 519
	X	64	63/64	98.44	2.67	2,937	2,937
	Y	40	39/40	97.50	2.45	1,225	1,715
	Z	60	59/60	98.33	2.66	399	319
							$ 5,490
"Never" (99.99%)	W	—	—	99.99%	5	900	$ 1,350
	X	—	—	99.99	5	5,500	5,500
	Y	—	—	99.99	5	2,500	3,500
	Z	—	—	99.99	5	750	600
							$10,950

[9] This example is conceptually similar to an example in G. W. Plossl and O. W. Wight, *Production and Inventory Control: Principles and Techniques* (Prentice-Hall, 1967), pp. 174–77 (HD55.P5).

is exposed to possible stockout at the end of each order cycle—when stock on hand is at its lowest. So, for product W, in the first case,

$$\text{Number of exposures} = \frac{32,000}{8,000} = 4.$$

The fourth and fifth columns are based on the first and third. For product W, in the second case, there are 16 exposures and 1 stockout every four years. Therefore, the product is in stock 15 of 16 times; the service fraction is 15/16, and the service level is the percentage equivalent, 93.75 percent.

The MAD safety factor may now be looked up in Table 4–1. The 93.75 percent service level falls between 93.32 and 94.00. By interpolation, the MAD safety factor (column 6) then becomes 1.92.

Safety stock, column 7, is merely the MAD times the MAD safety factor. For product W, in the third ("never") case, the MAD safety factor is the maximum value 5, from Table 4–1, and the MAD is 180. Therefore,

$$\text{Safety stock} = 180 \times 5 = 900.$$

Column 8 is the safety-stock inventory investment. It is found by multiplying unit cost times safety stock (column 7).

If these calculations are continued for intermediate service levels, the resulting total investment figures for each service option would be as shown in Figure 5–9.

FIGURE 5–9
Service/
investment
analysis results

Number of stockouts per year	Total investment in safety stock
Eight	$ 2,498
Four	3,684
Two	4,662
One	5,490
One half	6,285
One third	6,656
"Never"	10,950

These results show the financial consequences of improving customer service: In going from eight stockouts per year to "never," aggregate safety-stock investment increases from $2,498 to $10,950, a more than fourfold increase.

Uses and limitations of aggregate safety-stock analysis. Figure 5–9 is valuable mainly in that it provides a factual basis for deciding on aggregate investment in safety-stock inventory. It also helps promote the concept of statistical service levels. This concept can provide more uniform protection against stockouts than judgmental safety stock determinations can; at the same time aggregate investment may be reduced since excessive safety stocks would be discovered and reduced. (Where differing service levels are desired for different item groups, the aggregate safety-stock analysis method may be modified.)

Aggregate safety-stock analysis is useful where safety-stock inventories are necessary. Recently, however, experts have been challenging the old assumption that safety stocks of parts and raw materials are necessary. Some MRP-based production and inventory control systems do not provide for safety stocks—except for service parts or items purchased for resale.

Another limitation of aggregate safety-stock analysis concerns the statistical measure of service: It is based on a count of stockouts but not on their duration. An alternative measure of service level that accounts for stockout duration is the *percent service* measure, calculated by:

Percent service

$$= \frac{\text{Number of items out of stock} \times \text{Number of weeks out of stock}}{\text{Number of items carried} \times 52 \text{ weeks/year}}$$

Unfortunately the safety factors of Table 4–1 do not apply where percent service instead of stockout count is the measure of service level. Still, percent service is a useful concept for evaluating inventory policies.

A third limitation of aggregate safety-stock analysis is that it applies only to safety-stock inventories. Lot-size, or cycle-stock, inventories are usually a larger component of aggregate inventory. The LIMIT technique applies to the lot-size component.

LIMIT

We have seen that safety-stock inventory has direct effects on investment. In the case of lot-size inventory, the effect is not so direct. Size of the lot ordered (for replenishable items) is directly related to cost of carrying the goods, but it is inversely related to cost of processing the orders. As we have seen, there is a most economic lot size that minimizes the sum of the two kinds of costs. It is the economic order quantity (EOQ).

The EOQ seems to be a clear-cut approach to reducing lot-size inventory costs. But in the aggregate, EOQ savings sometimes do not come to pass. In real-life cases the savings may be limited—for reasons like the following:

1. A limit on the space available for storage.
2. A limit on the number of orders the clerical force can process.
3. A limit on the number of setups the labor force can make.
4. A limit on the time productive equipment can remain idle while it is being set up and still produce the total requirements.
5. A limit on the amount of money that can be invested in inventory.[10]

Over a period of a few years, perhaps these kinds of limitations on lot sizes can be overcome. They are real limits in the shorter run, however. The

---

[10] Plossl and Wight, *Production and Inventory Control: Principles and Techniques,* © 1967. Reprinted by permission of Prentice-Hall, Inc., Englewood Cliffs, New Jersey. p. 153.

LIMIT (*lot*-size *inventory management interpolation technique*) has been devised to show how to reduce inventory costs within the limitations.

LIMIT example. Variations of the LIMIT can show ways of saving on inventory costs for each limiting case. The following LIMIT example applies to the case of limited setups, items 3 and 4 in the above list.

EXAMPLE 5–7
Limit on setups,
Certainty Valve
Corporation

Certainty manufactures various kinds of valves from a large variety of parts. Some parts are purchased, and some are made. The present lot sizes were set judgmentally rather than calculated.

Certainty is considering EOQ for establishing lot sizes on parts that are made. Preliminary calculations show an adverse aggregate effect of using EOQ: Smaller average lots would result, meaning more frequent setups, which are disruptive to production. For the time being, Certainty prefers not to add setup workers and setup disruptions. Certainty managers would like to develop calculated lot sizes that are closer to the *economic* order quantity than present judgmental lot sizes, but without changing present setup patterns. LIMIT provides a calculation approach to suit this objective.

A trial use of LIMIT—for only three of Certainty's hundreds of parts—shows how LIMIT works. The given data for the three parts are:

Part number	Annual usage (units)	Unit cost	Setup hours per order	Setup cost per hour	Present lot size (units)
A	28,000	$5.00	3.0	$4.00	2,000
B	9,000	0.90	4.5	4.00	800
C	40,000	1.20	8.0	4.00	1,000

FIGURE 5–10
LIMIT
calculations,
Certainty Valve

LIMIT calculations for the three parts are given in Figure 5–10. In column 2 of the figure the present lot size, present average lot-size inventory investment, and EOQ lot size are given. Average lot-size investment is simply half the present lot size times cost per unit. The reason for halving the present lot size is that the average inventory is halfway between zero, the extreme low, and the lot size, the extreme

(1)	(2) Lot size			(3) Annual setup hours		(4) LIMIT		
Part number	Present	Present average $	EOQ	Present	EOQ-derived	Lot size	Annual setup hours	Average $
A	2,000	$5,000	220	42.0	381.9	363	231.4	$ 907
B	800	360	400	50.6	101.2	660	61.4	297
C	1,000	600	1,633	320.0	196.0	2,694	118.8	1,616
		$5,960		412.6	679.1		411.6	$2,820

Limit multiplier, $M = \dfrac{679.1}{412.6} = 1.65$

high. Present average lot-size inventory for part A is simply $(2,000/2)$ $(\$5.00) = \$5,000$. The total average investment for all three parts is $5,960.

The EOQ is calculated by the formula

$$EOQ = \sqrt{\frac{2DS}{IC}},$$

where

$D =$ Annual demand in units
$S =$ Cost per setup
$I =$ Inventory carrying cost, a decimal
$C =$ Unit cost

I is not a given and is not easy to determine accurately. As used in LIMIT, however, an accurate value for *I* is not required. $I = 0.20$ is used in this case. For part A, then,

$$EOQ = \sqrt{\frac{2(2,000)\,(3.0 \times \$4.00)}{(0.20)\,(\$5.00)}}$$

$$= \sqrt{\frac{48,000}{1}} = \sqrt{4,800} = 220$$

In column 3 the present setup hours are compared with the setup hours that would result from using EOQ. The present setup hours for part A equal the present setups per year times 3.0 hours per year. The present setups per year are found by dividing annual usage, 28,000, by present lot size, 2,000. This gives 14 setups per year, so there are $14 \times 3 = 42$ setup hours per year. EOQ-derived setup hours are based on the same 28,000 annual demand, but divided by the EOQ of 220. That equals 127.3 setups per year, so there are $127.3 \times 3 = 381.9$ setup hours per year. Total setup hours for the three parts are 412.6 at present; this would rise to 679.1 if EOQ-sized lots were ordered.

We have said that Certainty Valve Corporation does not want to add labor to its setup crew right now, so it wants to hold setup hours constant—at 412.6 in this case. That value, 412.6 hours, serves as a limit on lot-size changes. The limit is conveniently expressed as a ratio, the limit multiplier, *M*. *M* is equal to the EOQ-derived setup hours divided by present setup hours; *M*, then, equals $679.1/412.6 = 1.65$. *M* serves as a multiplier for calculating the LIMIT lot size by the formula LIMIT lot size $= M \times$ EOQ. For part A the result, in column 4 of Figure 5–10, is:

$$\text{LIMIT lot size} = 1.65 \times 220$$
$$= 363$$

Based on LIMIT lot sizes, LIMIT setup hours and LIMIT average lot-size investment may be calculated. For part A,

$$\text{LIMIT setup hours} = \frac{28,000}{363} \times 3$$
$$= 231.4$$

LIMIT average lot-size investment is $363/2$ times $5 = \$907$.

The two-headed arrows in Figure 5–10 link two key comparisons. The shorter arrow shows that the desired limit on setups was achieved: LIMIT setup hours are held equal (except for rounding effects) to the present 412.6 annual setup hours.

The longer arrow points to the large reduction in average lot-size inventory. It has been nearly halved, from the present $5,960 to a proposed LIMIT investment of $2,820.

What has happened? Noneconomic judgmental lot sizes have been adjusted closer to the economic order quantity. It is highly likely that savings (not always this large) in inventory investment will result if Certainty Valve Corporation applies this analysis technique to its whole line of parts. (It may be desirable to divide the parts into common family groups and to run LIMIT separately on each group.) Then, in future years, ways may be found to relax the limitation on setup hours and move still closer to EOQ lot sizes.

Uses and limitations of LIMIT. The above example shows that LIMIT offers the following benefits:

1. Helps "sell" EOQ.
2. Shows savings that are possible with EOQ.
3. Helps gradually adjust plant conditions to EOQ.
4. Assures that EOQ savings are captured (rather than "featherbedded").

LIMIT can also be applied where it is desirable to hold constant purchasing hours, storage space, or inventory investment. A variation called LIMIT-discount may be used to maximize quantity-discount savings while holding down the growth of lot-size inventories.[11]

Like aggregate safety-stock analysis, LIMIT works best for items purchased for resale. As was pointed out earlier, lot-for-lot, part-period, and other lot-sizing methods are often used instead of EOQ for planning fabricated parts in an MRP system.

SUMMARY

The size of orders—the lot size—is an issue related to the timing of orders. Several future orders for an item may be batched to save on setups and order-processing costs, but this increases inventory carrying costs (holding cost plus capital cost). Also larger batches of orders in the system tend to result in unbalanced workloads in producing work centers. Therefore lot-for-lot (no batching) ordering has some inherent advantages.

Some degree of batching is usually recommended, especially where setup cost is high. The part-period lot-sizing method is suitable for minimizing the sum of order-processing and carrying costs, given a planned future demand schedule (as in MRP).

The more traditional lot-sizing method is the economic order quantity (EOQ). EOQ is like part-period except that EOQ is based on past demand averages. Several EOQ variations are available to provide more precision in

---

[11] See Plossl and Wight, *Production and Inventory Control* pp. 163–69.

the treatment of carrying cost, quantity discounts, and delivery of the EOQ over time (rather than in one batch).

For both reorder point and EOQ—or their combination—demand and lead-time probability distributions may be used instead of single-valued extimates. Various ways of handling probabilistic inventory data are available, including Monte Carlo simulation. These advanced approaches allow for safety stocks to be refined and for various inventory planning policies to be tested. But highly precise models for planning item inventories are often unwarranted; simpler models used along with a system that has good replanning capability can often yield good results.

Inventory in the aggregate is affected by lot-sizing and safety-stock policies. High safety-stock inventories tend to provide high customer service levels; at the same time they mean lower inventory turnover and higher carrying cost. Aggregate safety-stock analysis helps to balance these conflicting objectives.

The lot-size inventory management interpolation technique (LIMIT) is a method of gaining EOQ benefits up to a limit, such as a limit on purchase orders.

REFERENCES

Books

Brown, Robert G. *Decision Rules for Inventory Management.* Holt, Rinehart and Winston, 1967 (HD55.B7).

Orlicky, Joseph. *Material Requirements Planning.* McGraw-Hill, 1975 (TS155.8.O74).

Plossl, G. W., and O. W. Wight. *Production and Inventory Control.* Prentice-Hall, 1967 (HD55.P5).

Prichard, James W., and Robert H. Eagle. *Modern Inventory Management.* Wiley, 1965 (HD55.P68).

Periodicals (societies)

Decision Sciences (American Institute for Decision Sciences).

Journal of Purchasing and Materials Management (National Association of Purchasing Management).

Production and Inventory Management (American Production and Inventory Control Society).

PROBLEMS

Note: Asterisked (*) problems require more than mimicry. They require judgment, and you should include discussion of reasons, assumptions, and outside sources of information.

PPA

1. Door handles that fit onto several different models of refrigerator are scheduled by MRP. It costs $40 to set up for a production run of door handles, and carrying cost is estimated at $0.20 to carry one door handle for one week. Net requirements for the next five weeks for the door handles are:

800   500   100   100   600

a. What is the economic part-period?
b. Calculate the first lot size, using PPA.
c. Carrying cost is often a rough estimate or an average that is figured for a variety of items. The estimate of $0.20 may not be accurate. Conduct a sensitivity analysis to see whether it makes much difference. That is, recalculate the PPA lot size by using a smaller and a larger carrying cost than $0.20 to see the effects on lot size.

2. In Example 5–2 a lot size of 70 is shown in week 4. Verify the correctness of that lot size by making the necessary PPA calculations.

EOQ

3. A chemical plant consumes sulfuric acid in a certain process at a uniform rate. Total annual consumption is 25,000 gallons. The plant produces its own sulfuric acid and can set up a production run for a cost of $4,000. The acid can be stored for $0.60 per gallon per year. This includes all carrying costs (cost of capital as well as cost to hold in storage). The production rate is so rapid that inventory buildup during production may be ignored.
a. What is the economic order quantity?
b. How many times per year should the acid be produced?

EOQ with quantity discount

4. A cannery buys knocked-down cardboard boxes from a box company. Demand is 40,000 boxes per year. The cannery's purchasing department estimates order-processing cost at $20. The box company prices the boxes as follows:

For a purchase of 100–3,999 boxes—$0.60 each (minimum order = 100).

For a purchase of 4,000 or more boxes—$0.50 each.

a. Determine the economic purchase quantity by trial and error. Set your own *reasonable* carrying-cost rate. Your trial-and-error solution need not be exact.
b. Express your EPQ in months' supply. In dollars' worth.

EMQ, EOQ, and ROP

5. A printshop manufacturers its own envelopes. Each production run costs $150 to set up and provides envelopes at a production rate of 2,000 per hour. Average usage of the envelopes is 10,000 per month. Envelopes cost $10 per thousand to produce. Inventory carrying cost is estimated at 15 percent of average inventory for this item. A working month averages 160 hours.
a. What is the economic manufacturing quantity for envelopes? How many months' supply is it?
b. The printshop is thinking of buying the envelopes instead of making them. If the order-processing cost is $150 (same as the setup cost), what would the EOQ be? Compare your answer with that in part *a*. Is the difference large or small? Explain why.
c. If the production lead time is two days, what is the reorder point?

Inventory costs and EOQ

6. A manufacturer of wooden furniture carries in its warehouse only one type of inventory: lumber. The following is a list of various costs that may or may not be associated with that inventory:

Rent on warehouse—$23,000/yr.
Wages and salaries, purchasing department—$80,000/yr.
Inventory taxes—$18,000/yr.
Cost of capital—14%
Value of average inventory on hand—$680,000
Insurance on warehouse contents—$3,500/yr.
Operating supplies, purchasing department—$1,400/yr.
Operating budget, production control department—$160,000/yr.
Expenditures on inventory—$3,400,000/yr.
Cost of a 12-foot 1″ × 4″ board—$1
Overhead, purchasing department—$25,000/yr.
Wages and salaries, warehouse—$48,000/yr.
Overhead, warehouse—$8,000/yr.
Miscellaneous expenditures, warehouse—$4,200/yr.

a. What is the inventory-carrying-cost rate, I (for the total inventory stored)?
b. What is the average cost of processing a purchase order, S? Assume that 3,000 purchase orders per year are processed.
c. What is the EOQ for 1″ × 4″ boards? Assume that 30,000 of these boards are used annually.
d. What is the annual cost of capital for the investment in 1″ × 4″ boards? (Ignore safety stock.)
e. What is the inventory turnover?

EOQ (EMQ) variations

7. An irrigation-system manufacturer makes its own pipes from coils of steel strip. Three sizes of pipe—three-inch, four-inch, and six-inch—are produced on a rotating schedule, on a single production line. Each size is used at a steady rate in assembly. The following are inventory data for the pipes:

Cost to set up for a new size of pipe—$130
Cost of capital—12%
Cost to store one pipe (any size)—$2/yr.
Manufactured cost of three-inch pipe—$20/section
Manufactured cost of four-inch pipe—$22/section
Production rate for pipes (all sizes)—120 sections/day
Usage (demand) rate, same for each size of pipe—90 sections/day

a. What is the economic manufacturing quantity for three-inch pipe? For four-inch pipe?
b. Assume that each of the three types of pipe is stored in a rack that is made to fit the pipe diameter. That is, a storage rack for one size of pipe may not hold another size. (This changes the method of calculating EMQ.) What is the EMQ for three-inch pipe? Explain why this answer is different from the answer in part a.

Probabilistic lot-size/ reorder point

8. A company that makes luggage buys locks from outside sources. If locks are not available, the luggage assembly line keeps running, but the lock insertion operation is postponed. This requires double handling. That is, when locks come in, the partly completed luggage has to be handled again to run it through lock insertion. The company estimates extra handling costs at $40 for each day that locks are out of stock—a stockout cost. The cost to carry a day's worth of locks is estimated at $30. Order-processing cost is $50, and lock demand is 50 per day, or 12,000 per year. Lead time for purchasing locks varies between four and seven days, as follows:

Lead time (days)	Probability
4	0.10
5	0.30
6	0.40
7	0.20

a. What combination of planned lead time and order quantity results in minimum total annual cost?

The following table provides the working figures needed to compute the EOQ for each lead-time option.

Lead time planned for	4 days 0.10	5 days 0.30	6 days 0.04	7 days 0.02	Expected cost Cost of carrying excess (CE)	Stockout cost (SO)
4 days	$ 0	$40	$80	$120	$ 0	$68
5 days	30	0	40	80	3	32
6 days	60	30	0	40	15	8
7 days	90	60	30	0	39	0

b. If demand were variable instead of a fixed 100 per day, how could stockout cost be calculated?

Aggregate inventory

9. For W-X-Y-Z Distributors, Example 5–6 in the chapter, further inventory calculations may be performed, using the given data. Sales and Finance agree that the following questions should be answered:

a. What is the total average inventory—including the average lot-size inventory—for each of the three stockout frequencies given in Figure 5–8?

b. If the cost of goods sold were $70,000, what inventory turnover ratios would result for each of the three stockout frequencies given in Figure 5–8?

Aggregate safety stock

10. Shamrock Shirt Company has a raw-materials inventory dilemma. To beat the competition, Shamrock must deliver quickly to apparel wholesalers, and large safety stocks of assorted rolled and cut fabrics are needed for fast response. But the cash tied up in safety stocks is also needed for new equipment. The following are some recent data bearing on the problem:

Cost of goods sold	$600,000
Raw materials:	
Average total inventory investment	120,000
Average safety-stock inventory investment	40,000

Dominant raw-material items to be analyzed:

Fabric	Annual usage	Order quantity	Unit cost	Mean absolute deviation
#201 white cotton, rolled	5,000	100	$40.00	40
#330 white cotton, cut	80,000	500	1.00	80
#865 striped cotton, cut	10,000	200	1.20	100

Present service level = 99.99%.

a. What is the present inventory turnover ratio at Shamrock?

b. For the three dominant fabrics, what total safety-stock investment is required for Shamrock's "perfect" service level of 99.99 percent?

CROSSWORD PUZZLE ON INVENTORY PLANNING (CHAPTERS 4 AND 5)

Across

1. Planning for independent-demand items. (Abbr.)
6. Batching tends to cause _____ demand at component levels.
8. $Q/2$ is often used as _____ inventory.
10. This plus demand during lead time equals reorder point. (Abbr.)
11. Expediters chase items on the _____ list.
13. The master production schedule is not for parts but for what? (Two words.)
15. Major element of holding cost.
16. Two-bin _____.
19. What type of lot sizing is recomputed whenever the demand projection changes?
20. If you buy the item, order-processing cost should include the cost of what?
23. Safety stock provides protection against stock _____.
24. An order accepted for a stockout item is a what?
26. The part-period algorithm. (Abbr.)
27. EOQ seeks to minimize period inventory _____.
28. Allowance sometimes included in planned-order-release quantity.
30. A hot-list item translates into what type of order besides a purchase order?
31. Type of list that exceptions appear on—in an ROP system.

Down

2. Inventory planners _____ orders out to shops and vendors. (A verb.)
3. In one lot-sizing algorithm, inventory is expressed in _____-periods.
4. Inventory controlled by ROP follows a continuous or a discrete _____ cycle.
5. Kind of stock that provides protection against running short.
6. Material may run out because of _____-time variability.
7. What a component part looks up to.
9. Where zero-level requirements are found. (Abbr.)
12. Another name for an order that is "active."
14. Safety stock (one way to compute) equals safety factor times what?
16. In the visual ROP system the stock clerk should "perpetually" _____ the bins.
17. What may be looked up in a table if you are given the service level? (Abbr.)
18. What kind of production schedule drives MRP?
20. MRP computes requirements for each component _____.
21. Inventory variability can be examined by using the Monte _____ technique.
22. Parent-item plus independent demand equals _____ requirements.
23. The planned-_____-release quantity must be at least as large as the net requirement.
24. Lot size is also called _____ size.
25. Planned orders are needed to _____ net requirements.
26. Net requirement equals gross requirement, _____ the sum of on-hand balance and scheduled receipts.
27. Outputs of MRP can serve as inputs to what? (Abbr.)
29. Another name for the least-total-cost method of lot sizing. (Abbr.)

  c. How do you account for the differences between Shamrock's (1) average total inventory investment, (2) average safety-stock inventory investment, and (3) total safety-stock investment for fabrics #201, #330, and #865?

  d. For the three dominant fabrics, what total safety-stock investment would be required for a service policy of one stockout per year for each item?

  e. How much cash would be freed for other uses if Shamrock adopted the policy in part *d?* What would be the effect on inventory turnover?

  *f. How can this analysis help Shamrock officers to converge on a decision concerning their safety stock-cash dilemma?

LIMIT

11. The inventory manager at Certainty Valve Corporation (Example 5–7 in the chapter) is skeptical about the use of 0.20 as the inventory-carrying-cost rate in LIMIT calculations. He has roughly estimated Certainty's average rate at 0.30. What changes in results would there be in LIMIT lot-size inventory if 0.30 were used instead of 0.20? Consider the *purpose* of LIMIT, and comment on the importance of accurate estimation of the carrying-cost rate.

12. Cotton's Candy Company has a one-person purchasing department. Economic order quantities are not used at present. But CCC is considering EOQs for sugar, cornstarch, and chocolate. Present typical order quantities are compared below with the EOQs that the purchaser has computed; other data are also shown:

Item	Present order quantity	EOQ	Annual usage (units)	Unit cost	Average cost to process an order
Sugar	500	300	3,600	$10	$20
Cornstarch	24	58	1,160	1	20
Chocolate	144	105	3,150	3	20

  Before the purchaser begins ordering by EOQs, Mr. Cotton asks for a LIMIT analysis, with annual orders as the limiting (constant) condition.

  a. Perform the LIMIT analysis.

  b. What does the LIMIT analysis suggest about ordering policies? What is the implication of there being only one purchaser?

IN-BASKET CASE*

Topic: EOQ—Seafood Restaurant

To:

From: Manager, Sea-and-Sand Restaurant

  Can we profitably use economic order quantities in our business? Prepare a thorough report on the question, carefully considering the nature of the key foodstuffs that we use in quantity.

---

* See instructions at end of problems section, Chapter 1.

chapter 6

OPERATIONS SCHEDULING AND CONTROL

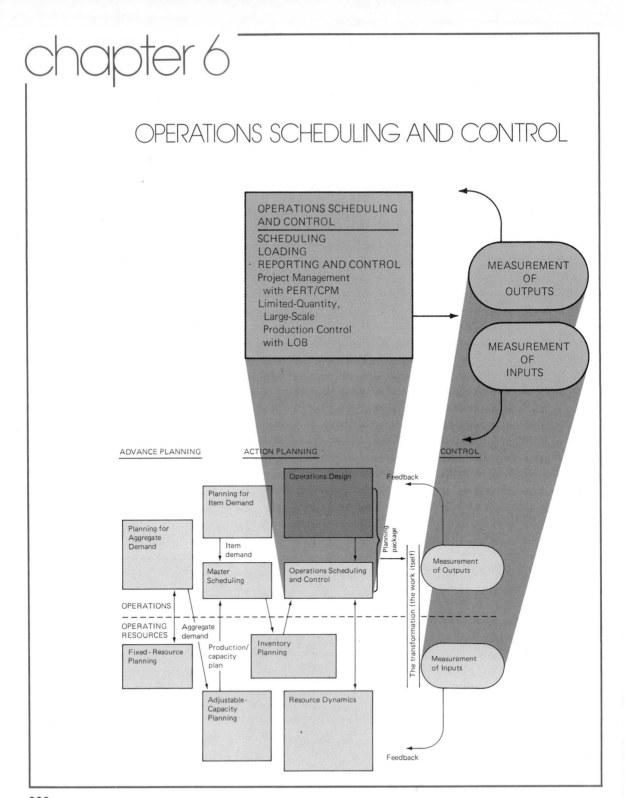

OPERATIONS SCHEDULING AND CONTROL

SCHEDULING
LOADING
REPORTING AND CONTROL
Project Management with PERT/CPM
Limited-Quantity, Large-Scale Production Control with LOB

MEASUREMENT OF OUTPUTS

MEASUREMENT OF INPUTS

ADVANCE PLANNING ACTION PLANNING CONTROL

Operations Design

Feedback

Planning for Item Demand

Planning for Aggregate Demand

Item demand

Planning package

Master Scheduling

Operations Scheduling and Control

Measurement of Outputs

OPERATIONS
OPERATING RESOURCES

Aggregate demand

The transformation (the work itself)

Fixed - Resource Planning

Production/ capacity plan

Inventory Planning

Measurement of Inputs

Adjustable - Capacity Planning

Resource Dynamics

Feedback

This is the first of two chapters on operations scheduling and control. This chapter pertains to repetitive, job, and job-lot operations. The next chapter deals with project and limited-quantity large-scale operations.

The chart on the chapter title page shows three inputs into the operations scheduling and control function. The downward arrow from operations design represents reference information. Included are methods and time standards data that are useful in scheduling operations. The two-headed arrow extending down to resource dynamics represents coordination: The schedule for operations should dovetail with the schedule for operating resources.

The arrow from inventory planning drives the scheduling function. That is, planned orders for parts are passed to the scheduler for scheduling shop orders to make parts, if necessary. In services, where there are no parts, inventory planning is bypassed: The master schedule of *services* drives the services scheduling or dispatching function.

The difference between scheduling and control for goods and for services

FIGURE 6-1
Differences in order scheduling and control for goods and services

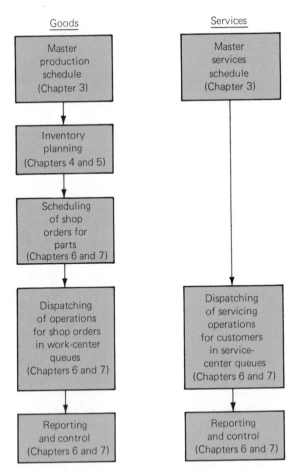

is shown more clearly in Figure 6–1. There is a master production schedule (MPS) for goods. For services by appointment there is an appointment book, which might be thought of as a master services schedule. End items on the MPS explode into component parts, which are planned (timing and quantities) and scheduled (shop orders). Services do not explode into parts, so for services there is no counterpart to inventory planning and order scheduling. Dispatching applies to both goods and services. For goods, production operations for shop orders in work-center queues (waiting lines) are dispatched; that is, the jobs in queue are arranged in some order of importance and passed along to the workers. For services, operations for customers in queue at service centers are dispatched (arranged for processing).

Reporting and control concepts are similar for goods and services. Both require measurement of outputs and resource inputs. Measurement information on outputs and inputs is fed back to the planners and schedulers for corrective action, if necessary. (See measurement and feedback in the chart on the chapter title page.)

Our discussion begins with scheduling repetitive production, which is followed by sections on job-lot and job-shop production control and scheduling. Work-center loading and shop-floor control are the next two chapter topics. The final two topics are reporting and feedback and control of managerial performance, and measurements and reports.

SCHEDULING REPETITIVE PRODUCTION

Repetitive production means long production runs that are carefully engineered. As much as is practical, stability is engineered in and variability is engineered out. Demand planning and capacity planning are important functions, and supervisory control of the transformation is also important. The functions most closely associated with production control—scheduling and dispatching—are largely designed into the process; therefore, there is little need for a large production-control staff.

Companies in repetitive production have "a good thing going," and much of management's job is to hold the unit cost of production down in order to keep it going. There are not many general techniques and tools for helping management in this effort, but there are some common concepts that we may consider in scheduling and flow control.

Scheduling flows

Large high-volume manufacturers are not necessarily repetitive producers. Most have to make a variety of sizes, colors, models, and so forth. It is common to run each of the various types intermittently, in rotation.

To be able to run mixtures of products down a production line requires a heavy investment in production engineering and materials management. In effect, such investments enable the manufacturer to run very small lot sizes economically. Small-lot economies apply not only to the final production line—

a changing mixture of end products—but also to the components supplied to the final production line. That is, fabricated parts and assemblies that feed the production line may be made in small lots, and purchased raw materials and parts that feed fabrication may be delivered in small lots, perhaps every day. The following example, for motorcycle manufacturing, contrasts the small mixed-lot way with the longer production run way.

EXAMPLE 6-1
Small lot sizes in motorcycle manufacturing

The plant manager in one U.S. motorcycle assembly plant explains its mixed production runs and very small lot sizes this way. First, parts ordering costs are kept low by use of long-term blanket orders with suppliers, which call for frequent deliveries. Setup costs for machines on feeder lines and on assembly lines are held down by engineering. For example, several dies for one machine tool were redesigned to be the same size, and a rotary conveyor was designed to keep the dies rotating around the machine, each ready to be fixed in place at short notice. Ideally, the process would not need to slow down at all for setup when a new die is required.

When mixtures are run on the production line, scheduling and inventory planning must be very exacting. The scheduled product mix must be matched with marketing projections weeks or months in advance, and the daily run sequence must be matched with latest very short-run shipping plans.

Figure 6–2 shows, in exaggerated form, some of the differences between mixed, small-lot production runs and larger-lot production of motorcycles. Part A shows an inventory-less process from receiving to fabrication, to subassembly, to assembly, to finish, to ship. The MPS for this system is shown at the lower right in Figure 6–2A. The MPS is a detailed sequence of motorcycle frame types to be run daily. A sample of the cost structure is also shown. There are high fixed costs and a normal carrying cost rate. But order-processing and setup costs are held down, and the result is lot sizes so small as to be unimportant. The general shape of the cost diagram applies to the whole motorcycle, to any subassembly, or to any component part.

Part B reflects the larger-lot approach. Since lots of each different model, size, and type are larger, inventories build between every process. The MPS is stated in weeks, not days, and it shows intermittent runs of different models of the given part. The cost diagram shows high inventory cost resulting from banks of inventory build-up between runs. (With MRP, the size of this build-up may be held down somewhat.) Period setup costs are shown to be high, because there are numerous job-lot setups for a new model, size, and type. An economic order quantity (EOQ) or lot size becomes relevant.

Flow control

As repetitive as motorcycle assembly seems to be, there are changes that need to be controlled. Variety of sizes and models was mentioned in the above example. Such discontinuities tend to result in occasional stalled orders; plans may need to be changed on short notice to run a different model or to temporarily bypass a bottleneck process.

Discontinuities are usually more severe if the firm is a fabricator as well as an assembler. Orders for fabricated parts to feed assembly lines have many opportunities to become stalled. The *flow-control* concept arose some years

FIGURE 6–2 Small-lot versus large-lot production, motorcycles

A. Long production runs: brief *MPS*; and low inventory costs

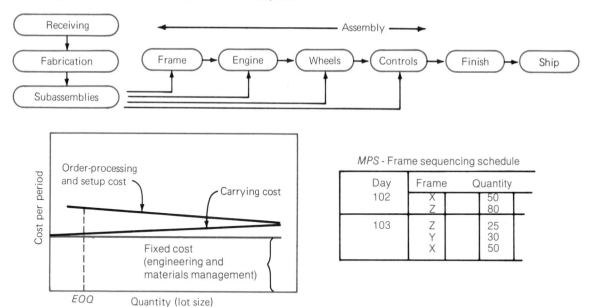

MPS - Frame sequencing schedule

Day	Frame	Quantity
102	X	50
	Z	80
103	Z	25
	Y	30
	X	50

B. Production in job lots; elaborate *MPS*; and high inventory costs

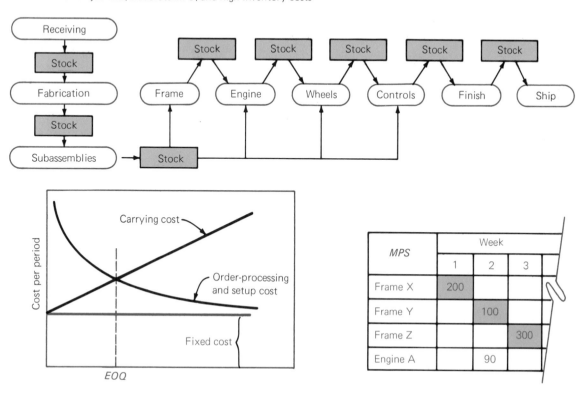

MPS	Week		
	1	2	3
Frame X	200		
Frame Y		100	
Frame Z			300
Engine A		90	

ago to help minimize problems of this kind. Features of flow control are as follows:[1]

1. Plan production rates based on key potential bottleneck processes and keep steady flows of parts and materials into those processes. If safety stocks are to be maintained at all, it is the bottleneck processes that deserve them most.
2. Label and date work-in-process (WIP) inventories.
3. Label (paint) *in* and *out* areas, and rigidly enforce proper placement of WIP inventories in designated areas; this may be referred to simply as "good housekeeping."
4. Keep track of jobs that are idled via a periodic idleness report. For example, the report may list idle jobs and number of days idled (a purpose of point 2).

JOB-LOT AND JOB-SHOP PRODUCTION CONTROL

In job-lot or job-shop production, which is probably more common than repetitive production, there is a changing mix of jobs produced in moderate or small quantities. In goods-producing job-lot/job-shop firms, production control departments tend to be increased in size so that they can provide greater assistance in controlling the job mix. A large PC staff is needed because orders for goods spawn orders for parts, often a great many parts.

In Chapter 4 we saw how material requirements planning can lead to correct planning for the parts. In the following sections we see how inventory plans are translated into scheduled manufacturing orders, how order priorities are kept current, and how progress data are collected and formatted for control purposes. The scheduling, progress reporting, and control of services are also considered.

Scheduling, priority control, and reporting in job-lot manufacturing are hard to understand. The difficult issues are not omitted in our discussion. Without examining the difficult issues, the reader would be hard put to see why production-control staffs are large, what the role of the computer is, why PC people are still needed even with extensive computerization, and why production control is a challenging career.

A main difficulty in understanding job-lot production control seems to be keeping straight the difference between a *job* and an *operation*, which are planned and controlled by the scheduler and the dispatcher. Definitions and an example at this point may make the upcoming discussion easier to understand. First the definitions:

Job: A job is the whole work activity that is required to produce a *component part*. In some firms a job is called a lot. The job or lot (or job lot) is also known

---

[1] G. W. Plossl and O. W. Wight, *Production and Inventory Control* (Prentice-Hall, 1967), pp. 293–96 (HD55.P5).

as an order, job order, or lot order. A document about the job may be known as a shop order, manufacturing order, work order, or job order.

Operation: An operation is one step or task in a job. But more important, each operation requires a new *setup*. Usually the new setup is at a different work center. There are good reasons to separately plan, schedule, and control each operation. One reason is that a special setup crew may need to be on hand. A second reason is that material handlers and handling devices may need to be on hand. A third reason is that an inventory can build before each operation. The final and most important reason is that there is usually a choice of operations for different jobs queued up at a given work center. A document showing priority-order operations for a work center is known as a dispatch list or priority report.

We shall see that the scheduler schedules both jobs and operations. The dispatcher tries to meet the operation due dates. Dispatchers' actions may include arranging for setups and handling, arranging for jobs to be run in priority order, counting units, and reporting when operations are completed. An example of jobs and operations follows:

EXAMPLE 6–2
Distinction between jobs and operations, bookcase shelf

In bookcase manufacturing the bookcase appears on the master schedule and is exploded into component parts. One part is a shelf. Making a quantity of the shelf involves planning and controlling one job and several operations. Figure 6–3 shows a job consisting of ten bookcase shelves. The shelf part number is 777, and the shop order is shown as a five-operation job. Next, the figure shows each of the five operations and the inventory conditions between them. First, boards are withdrawn from the stockroom. Second, boards are sawed. Third, sawed boards are planed. Fourth, planed boards are sanded. Fifth, sanded boards are finished. The result is ten finished shelves. These are component parts that go into the next-higher-level item on the bill of materials for the bookshelf order.

It is noteworthy that each operation requires a separate setup and that after each operation WIP inventories form and may sit idle for a time. The separate setups and the WIP inventory stages call for managerial attention. We shall see that a *dispatcher* is often the management specialist in charge of scheduling and controlling the operations. Scheduling concepts are explained next.

JOB-LOT AND JOB-SHOP SCHEDULING

In production-control jargon, master scheduling pertains to end items (or services), but *scheduling* pertains to parts orders (or service tasks) that come before the end item (or service) due date. Three questions have to be answered in scheduling for a given job (or task):

1. When can the job be completed?—based on standard times.
2. When should the job be completed?—based on date of customer or parent-item need.
3. When will the job be completed?—based on realities in production work centers.

FIGURE 6–3
Job and
operations for
ten bookcase
shelves

Job: Make 10 shelves,
part number 777

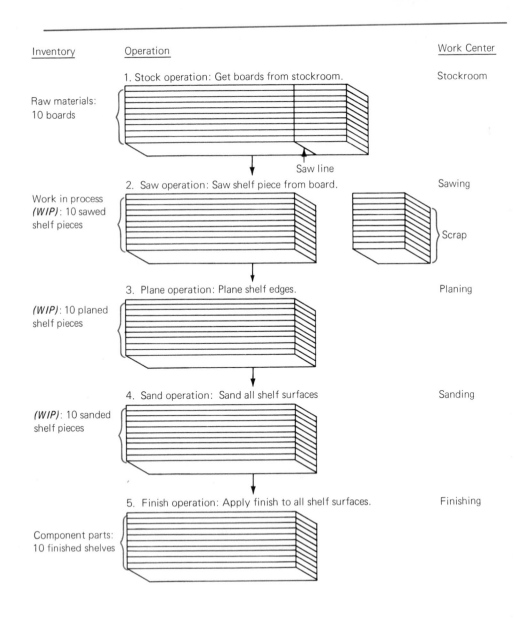

Shop order
1. Stock
2. Saw
3. Plane
4. Sand
5. Finish

Inventory   Operation   Work Center

1. Stock operation: Get boards from stockroom.   Stockroom

Raw materials:
10 boards

Saw line

2. Saw operation: Saw shelf piece from board.   Sawing

Work in process
(WIP): 10 sawed
shelf pieces

Scrap

3. Plane operation: Plane shelf edges.   Planing

(WIP): 10 planed
shelf pieces

4. Sand operation: Sand all shelf surfaces   Sanding

(WIP): 10 sanded
shelf pieces

5. Finish operation: Apply finish to all shelf surfaces.   Finishing

Component parts:
10 finished shelves

Ideally, all three questions have the same answer. For example, let us say that a patient is undergoing a complete physical examination. An early step is withdrawing specimens of various body fluids. The physician may want the results of laboratory analysis of a certain specimen to be ready at the end of the exam, say 30 minutes later; that is the answer to question 2. Perhaps the standard time, adjusted for efficiency and utilization, is also 30 minutes; that answers question 1. Suppose the lab has no higher-priority jobs that would interfere with this lab test; then the job can be expected to be completed in 30 minutes, which answers question 3. Since all three questions have the same answer, it is clear that the lab test should be scheduled to start upon withdrawal of the body fluids and to be completed 30 minutes later.

Actually, it is not very likely that a lab can complete its testing as soon as the physician would desire the results. A lab is a job shop, and in job shops queues of job orders form and jostle for priority. In repetitive production, by contrast, jobs generally do not compete for the same resources and schedules may be set based largely on standard times.

Production lead-time elements

In job and job-lot production, realities in production work centers result in inflated production lead times—inflated, that is, beyond standard times and often beyond customer and parent-item needs. According to Orlicky,[2] the elements of production lead time for a given part are as follows, in descending order of significance.

Queue time
Run time
Setup time
Wait (for transportation) time
Inspection time
Move time
Other

Orlicky and others maintain that in machine shops, queue time, the first element, normally accounts for about 90 percent of total lead time. Standard time—to run and perhaps to set up, inspect, and move—therefore accounts for less than 10 percent of lead time. Obviously, realistic schedules for manufactured parts must be based on total lead time and not simply on standard times.

While standard times may be developed with precision (as is discussed in Chapter 8), lead-time precision is elusive. Accurate lead-time estimates, and therefore accurate schedules, are likely only when work centers are uncongested, because only then may the typical job be able to sail through without long and variable queue times at each work center. It is the scheduler's job

---

[2] Joseph Orlicky, *Material Requirements Planning* (McGraw-Hill, 1975), p. 83 (TS155.8.O74).

to keep things uncongested, that is, without an unnecessary amount of work in process (WIP).

Work in process

In recent years much attention has been given to the WIP problem. Today good manufacturing managers recognize the benefits of keeping WIP low:

1. *Service.* Low WIP means less queue time and faster response to customer orders; also, with less queue time, there is less uncertainty in the schedule and customers may be given better status information.
2. *Forecasts.* We know that forecasts are more accurate for shorter periods into the future, that is, for the shorter lead times that result from smaller amounts of WIP.
3. *Production-control work force.* Less WIP means less congestion and less need for shop-floor control by expediters and dispatchers.
4. Floor-space and inventory costs. These are lower when fewer jobs are in process.

There are practical limits to WIP reductions. There should be enough work to keep work centers busy. As was noted in Chapter 3, the operations required to produce certain parts do not spread evenly over all the work centers. They tend to cluster, overloading some work centers and perhaps underloading. others. As the job mix changes, and it often changes quite fast, the pattern of over- and underloading changes. There is pressure on the scheduler to overload on the average in order to hold down the number of underloaded work centers. Production supervisors get nervous about cost variances (explained later) when workloads get low.

Lead-time accuracy

The scheduler seems caught in a bind: Scheduling a workload sufficient to keep work centers busy means that queue times will grow and make schedules less realistic. It is difficult to predict average queue time, because the average changes with the changing job mix. It is even more difficult to predict queue time for a given job, because the job may queue up at several work centers as it completes its routing. Therefore, it is not uncommon to include a fixed number of days for queue time in the schedule or simply to omit queue time.

For example, lead time may be set equal to run time plus inspection and move time (engineered or estimated); a queue-time allowance may or may not be added on. If time standards (or estimates) are poor or nonexistent, an even simpler approach may be used, such as:

$$LT = 2N + 6,$$

where

N = Number of operations in the job
LT = Lead time in days

This formula allows two days for each operation plus six days for queue time and other delays.

A *dynamic queue-time* approach is another possibility. In the dynamic approach, queue time includes an extra-time allowance for current or projected shop congestion. A simple measure might be number of open job orders, which the computer could find in the open-order files. Another measure of shop congestion is number of operations in all open orders (which would require computer search of the open-order file and then the routing file).

In an MRP system accurate lead times are not vital for job and priority control. If a simple but inaccurate static approach is used, lead-time errors may be adjusted for. Changing the due date for a part that is on order is one type of adjustment. Advice about the need to change due dates is in the form of *rescheduling notices* from the weekly MRP run. While planned order releases from an MRP run trigger inventory planning (ordering) actions, rescheduling notices trigger scheduling actions. Together, these two MRP outputs provide comprehensive support for component parts planning and control. A second type of adjustment may be made each day (between weekly MRP runs): A daily dispatch list from the computer tells the dispatcher of the need to change the priorities of work in process in order to meet due dates. (Dispatch lists are discussed later.)

Inaccurate lead times have a more severe effect on capacity control. Capacity requirements planning (CRP) is a computer-based extension of MRP in which future work-center loads are computed. Accuracy of computed loads may be improved by including some kind of queue-time allowance in lead-time estimates; allowances based on shop congestion—the dynamic scheduling idea mentioned above—would be helpful. With more accurate load projections, work-center capacity may be more accurately planned so that there is less need for last-minute capacity control measures.

Backward and forward scheduling

For services offered on demand, the usual customer need date is "as soon as possible." (ASAP is a well-known abbreviation.) The customer order is scheduled forward from the current date or from the date on which resources are expected to be available.

For services provided by appointment, backward scheduling may be used. An example is deliveries of checks and deposit slips from a small bank to a larger bank's computer service center. The service center may require that the delivery be made by 9:00 P.M. each day. If so, schedules for each delivery stop are backward-scheduled. That is, operation lead times (time between stops) are successively subtracted from 9:00 P.M. The resulting schedule might appear as shown in the accompanying illustration.

Backward and forward scheduling may be used in tandem. A scheduler might be asked to estimate the earliest date on which a job can be completed, which calls for forward scheduling. The date of need might be beyond the calculated earliest completion date; backward scheduling might then be used to determine the scheduled start date.

Goods producers also use both forward and backward scheduling. Generally, manufacturing inventories that are replenished by reorder point (ROP) are

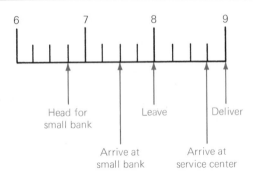

forward-scheduled. But MRP yields planned order releases that are backward-scheduled from the date of the net requirement. Actually, in most MRP systems the planned-order-release date is not the scheduled start *day*. The scheduler is advised by the computer of the (backward-scheduled) start *week*, and the scheduler then determines the start *day*. The following is an example of the scheduler's procedure.

EXAMPLE 6–3 Scheduling a shop order, QUIDCO, Inc.	The weekly MRP run at QUIDCO, Inc., shows a planned order in the current time bucket for Part no. 1005CX. The part is due on Monday of time bucket (week) 3, which is shop calendar date 105. (See Figure 6–4A.)

The inventory planner validates the need for the order and the order quantity and timing. The planner decides that it should be a make rather than a buy order and therefore requests a shop order.

The scheduler finds the part number in the routing file, and the routing and time standards for each operation are displayed on a CRT screen. A shop order is prepared, using data from the routing file. (See Figure 6–4B.) Backward scheduling is used, along with the following "rules" for computing operation lead times.[3]

1. Allow eight standard hours per day; round upward to even days.
2. Allow one day between operations.
3. Allow two days to inspect.
4. Release shop order to the stockroom five days before the job is to be started into production.
5. All dates are treated as end of the eight-hour day.

Backward scheduling begins with the due date, 105, in the lower right corner. (A shop calendar of consecutively numbered work days, omitting weekends and holidays, is common among manufacturing firms, because it facilitates computation.) That is the finish date for the last operation, inspect. Inspect, two days, and one day between operations are subtracted, which makes 102 the due date for the finish operation. Finish takes 9.4 standard hours ($0.4 + 0.18 \times 50$ pieces), which rounds upward to two days. Subtracting that two, plus one day between operations, equals 99 as the due

---

[3] Adapted from Oliver W. Wight, *Production and Inventory Management in the Computer Age* (Cahners, 1974), pp. 81–82 (TS155.W533). Note that operation lead times are detailed, whereas job-order lead times, discussed earlier (for computing planned order releases), are gross.

FIGURE 6–4
Generating shop
order from
current planned
order listing

A.   Computer listing of planned orders due for scheduling

> *Week of 90*
> *orders planned for*
> *release this week*
> *QUIDO Inc.*

Part no.	*Due date*
0052X	110
0077AX	115
≀	≀
1005CX	105
≀	≀

B.   Shop order, backward-scheduled

Shop order no. 9925
Part no. 1005CX   *Quantity: 50*   *Release date: 92*

Operation	*Description*	*Work center*	*Setup*	*Cycle time*	*Standard hours*	*Finish date*
190	Bend rod	16	4.2	0.05	6.7	99
008	Finish rod	85	0.4	0.18	9.0	102
092	Inspect rod	52				105

	Due date: 105

date for the bend operation. Finally, one day (6.7 hours rounded upward) for bend, five days for stockroom actions, and one day for move are subtracted, which makes day 92 the release date. Shop order 9925 is therefore held in the scheduler's *hold-for-release* file on Monday and Tuesday (days 90 and 91) and released on Wednesday (day 92).

A week goes by. The inventory planner notifies the scheduler that part no. 1005CX has a new need date: the week of 110 instead of 105. (The latest MRP run informed the inventory planner of the later date.) The scheduler recomputes operation due dates as follows:

```
Job due date = Inspect due date = Day   110
    Less inspect time              =       2   days
                              Day   108
    Less move time                 =       1   day
Finish due date                = Day   107
    Less finish time               =       2   days
                              Day   105
    Less move time                 =       1   day
Bend due date                  = Day   104
```

The scheduler enters the three new operation due dates into the computer. The computer uses the new dates in printing out a daily dispatch list. The daily dispatch list informs the three work centers about the changes in operation due dates.

In this type of computer-based system there is no need for the scheduler to issue paperwork giving initial due dates and revised due dates. The daily dispatch list serves as the notification of operation due dates. The scheduler does need to assemble a planning package that may include job tickets, inspection tickets, and forms on which to record such things as material usage, scrap, and labor changes.

In a manual system there may not be a daily dispatch list. In that case the scheduler will need to put due dates on job tickets or other planning-package paperwork. Rescheduling notices may be issued manually, but keeping the paperwork flowing properly becomes a problem.

In the QUIDCO example the backward scheduling is done by a human scheduler. The computer could be programmed to perform the back-scheduling calculations for a scheduler at an on-line terminal. The rules may be expressed as algorithms, and the algorithms expressed as computer code.

In future years perhaps it will become common for MRP systems to plan in days rather than weeks. Then the scheduler would probably be planning in hours instead of days. This is highly desirable because it cuts WIP inventory further and shortens lead times, which makes the firm stronger financially and competitively. Later in the chapter, we discuss shop-floor recorders, which provide the scheduler with faster feedback on how jobs are doing so that schedule changes can be more responsive.

Scheduling operating resources

We have been talking about the scheduling of jobs and job operations. It is just as valid to schedule in terms of operating resources. In the chart on the chapter title page, there is a two-headed arrow between scheduling and resource dynamics. The intent is to stress the need for the ends (operations) to be scheduled to match the means (resources).

In an earlier era, the tendency was to schedule jobs and operations with little regard for availability of resources. This was the case in manufacturing for two main reasons:

1. Labor resources were largely unskilled, and labor laws were weak. Labor could therefore be readily adjusted up or down, on short notice, as job schedules required.
2. Material resources, that is, purchased and made parts, were planned by reorder point, because there was insufficient data-processing power to *schedule* these resources based on future net requirements—today's MRP process. The same was true of reusable resources such as tools, gauges, fixtures, dies, machines, and space.

Today labor-hours, machine-hours, and aggregate inventories may be scheduled roughly to meet aggregate demand via the production planning and rough-cut capacity-planning techniques presented in Chapter 3. Component parts may be precisely scheduled via MRP.

Requirements planning is gradually being extended to include such operating resources as labor, machines, gauges, dies, and tools. The bill of materials is exploded in MRP to yield parts requirements. Similarly, for the same end item, a bill of labor may be exploded to yield skill-category requirements, a bill of tools may be exploded into tool requirements, and so on. In each case the master production schedule is the driver, the bills serve as reference files, and item master files provide the on-hand balances of each resource. Data-processing power is available to do this, and some firms, especially those that use a large variety of specialized resources, are beginning to do it.[4]

Gantt scheduling charts

Henry Gantt's name is attached to a type of chart that is widely used for displaying a schedule. The basic form of the Gantt chart is to have time divisions on the horizontal axis (usually) and to have rows represent the jobs or resources to be scheduled. Lines, bars, brackets, shading, and other such devices mark the start, duration, and end of a scheduled entity. Schedules for a variety of operating resources may be displayed on Gantt charts. The purpose of the charts, like that of any visual aid, is to clarify and so to improve one's own understanding and to serve as a focus for discussion. Some common and perhaps familiar examples are shown in Figure 6–5.

The examples shown are for scheduling three different resource types: equipment, space, and workers. Each also identifies the jobs to be performed by the resources. Notice also that each is a services example. While Gantt's original chart was for the control of repetitive manufacturing, Gantt charts today, in simpler forms, are more widely used in services, where routings are short and queues have few chances to form.[5]

In goods production, Gantt charts may be usable if:

1. *There are not many work centers.* With many work centers a carefully developed Gantt display of schedules tends to be a piece of gross fiction, because queuing effects (discussed earlier) make lead time unpredictable. Keeping the chart up to date under such conditions would be time-consuming and pointless.

2. *Cycle times are long—days or weeks rather than hours.* An example is a construction project. Drywallers, painters, cement crews, roofers, and so on, may each spend several days or even weeks at a worksite. (The use of Gantt charts in project management is discussed further in Chapter 7.)

3. *Job routings are short.* In parts manufacturing, routings can be extensive; a single job may pass through 5, 10, or even 15 work centers, incurring unpredictable queue time at each stop. In maintenance work, routings tend to be short and Gantt charts can be helpful. But maintenance is often thought of more as a service than a goods-oriented activity, even though it is goods that are being maintained. As a service, maintenance may be expected to benefit

---

[4] One such firm is a Bendix Corporation plant in Kansas City. See W. G. Hoppen, "Automated Scheduling of Manufacturing Resources," *Production and Inventory Management*, 2d quarter 1976, pp. 73–87.

[5] The original purpose was to display variances from planned production rates in repetitive production. Today the Gantt chart is used almost exclusively for displaying schedules in nonrepetitive work.

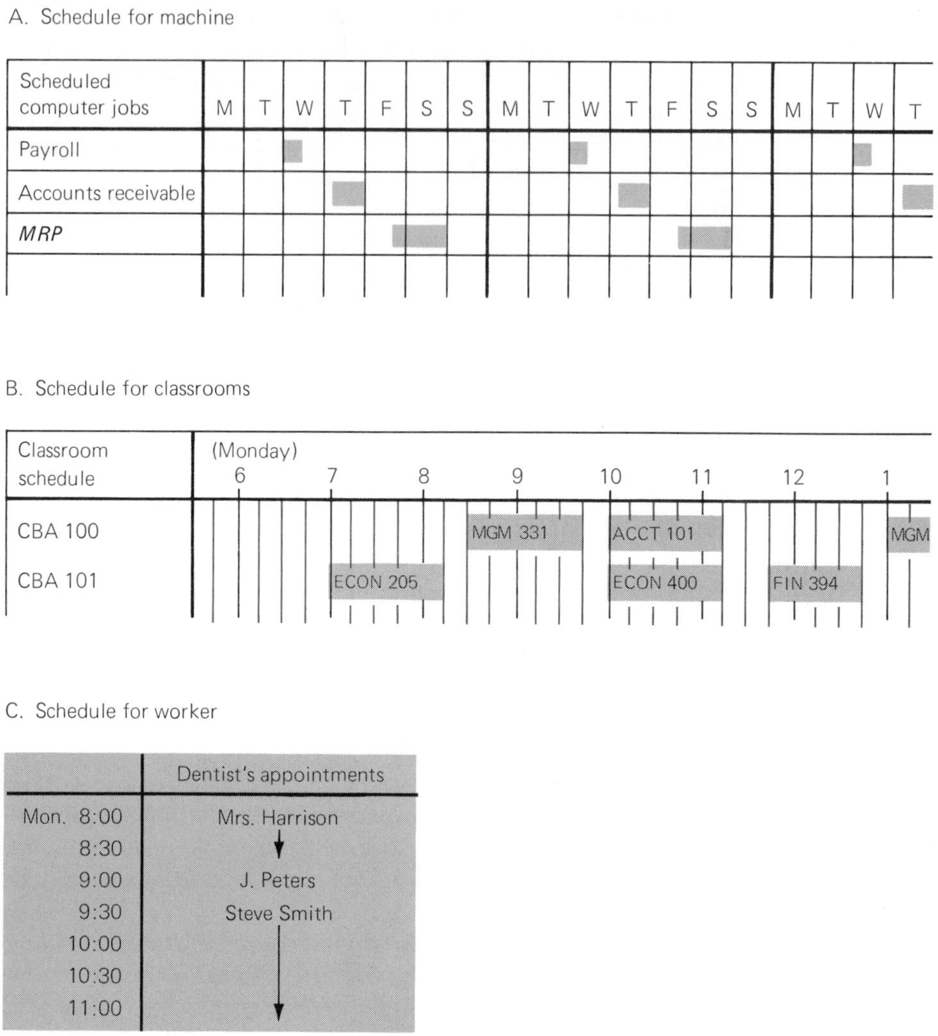

FIGURE 6–5
Common forms
of the Gantt
chart

A. Schedule for machine

Scheduled computer jobs	M	T	W	T	F	S	S	M	T	W	T	F	S	S	M	T	W	T
Payroll			▪							▪							▪	
Accounts receivable				▪							▪							▪
MRP					▪							▪						

B. Schedule for classrooms

Classroom schedule	(Monday) 6	7	8	9	10	11	12	1
CBA 100				MGM 331	ACCT 101			MGM
CBA 101		ECON 205			ECON 400	FIN 394		

C. Schedule for worker

	Dentist's appointments
Mon. 8:00	Mrs. Harrison
8:30	↓
9:00	J. Peters
9:30	Steve Smith
10:00	
10:30	↓
11:00	

from Gantt-charted schedules, just as other services do. Later in the chapter the use of Gantt charts in controlling maintenance jobs is presented.

WORK-CENTER LOADING AND CAPACITY CONTROL

Keeping the work centers loaded with work—but assuring that loads do not exceed work-center capacity—is a day-to-day management problem. The problem exists for work centers of all kinds: The typing pool in an office is a work center; so is the X-ray area in a clinic or hospital; and in a factory a machine or a group of machines with similar functions is a work center. Staff analysts' reports constitute workload for a typing pool; hospital patients generate workload for an X-ray work center; and component-parts orders in support of an MPS generate workloads for machine centers.

Load is short for workload, and *loading* refers to workloads that are imposed on work centers. As was explained in the chapter on capacity planning (Chapter 3), capacity control at the work-center level can be properly discussed only after the chapters on inventory planning. It is orders for inventory components that create workload in the work centers.

In job-lot production, loads are likely to be distributed very unevenly. For a given work center, loads will vary from week to week. And some work centers will be overloaded, some underloaded. This loading unevenness may call for short-term capacity adjustments.

The traditional approach is to make short-term capacity adjustments "at the last minute," because of lack of good information about loadings in future periods. In this older approach work-center loads are calculated for upcoming weeks based only on open orders. (An open order is a component-parts order that has been released by production control to the work centers.) No planned (future) orders are included; the traditional planning system is simply not future-oriented. Therefore work-center load reports are incomplete for future time buckets, which means that capacity adjustments cannot be planned very far in advance. Attention is on the current week. Production control's tendency is to overload each work center for the current week, to have expediters "pull" the high-priority jobs through, and to use overtime or similar last-minute adjustments when all else fails.

Backlog tracking

Load reports, even incomplete ones, may be useful in projecting past loading trends into the future. The method is as follows: Each week the current load and all future loads (from open orders) are totaled. The total may be referred to as the work center's backlog. The backlog may be plotted, or tracked, week by week on a graph. Trends in plotted points may suggest a need for short-term capacity (or other) adjustments. An example is given in Figure 6–6.

Part A of the figure is a machine-oriented work center (extrusion). The load or backlog is expressed in machine-hours, and it is rising. The rising trend tells production control that more machine capacity will be needed soon. Otherwise, lead times will lengthen and service to customers will deteriorate.

Part B is labor-oriented work center (welding). The backlog is in labor-hours, and it is falling. Production control may recommend layoffs or a similar capacity adjustment, unless marketing can generate more orders that include welding work.

Capacity requirements planning

Capacity requirements planning (CRP) is a modern computer-based method of revealing work-center loads. A CRP run on the computer requires two inputs. One input is planned order releases for component parts. Planned order releases are calculated by the computer in an MRP run (see Chapter 4). The other input is routing data that tells what work centers each component-parts order goes through and how long it takes in each. The routing file must

FIGURE 6–6
Work-center load
(backlog) trends

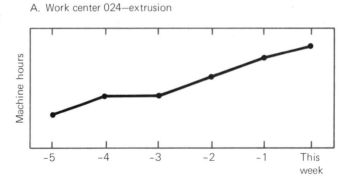

A. Work center 024—extrusion

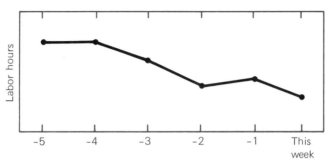

B. Work center 016—welding

be computerized in order to run CRP. (Many firms that adopt MRP do not add CRP for several years—because of the trouble and cost of creating a computer file of valid routing and operation-timing data.)

CRP reports project loads in work centers that have been having difficulty in keeping up with planned output. Projections show deficient capacity in each critical work center far enough in advance to do something about it; two or three months of future projections are often sufficient. (There is no sense in asking the computer to run CRP projections for all work centers and for 52 weeks into the future, because the problems are more immediate and selective.) Common actions to be taken are training new workers, shifting labor to new jobs, layoffs, subcontracts, and so on. With CRP's potential to alert managers so as to keep work-center capacities reasonably close to planned loads, the usual chaotic atmosphere on the shop floor may give way to reasonable order and tranquillity. The differences between traditional and CRP load projections are examined further below.

Loading to infinite versus finite capacity

In repetitive production, balanced assembly lines may be designed. The capacities of work centers are then in balance (as near as is practical) with one another and with the rate of product flow. The work centers are said to be loaded to finite capacity.

In job-lot production a variable mix of orders loads unevenly on work centers, as was explained earlier. *Planning* a balanced load, that is, loading to finite capacity, is quite possible. However, *completing* work-center operations in the planned amount of time is seldom achieved, and when the timing is upset, a carefully developed finite-capacity loading plan would fall apart. Therefore most firms do not attempt finite-capacity loading. Loading to infinite capacity can be made to work fairly well.

Loading to infinite capacity means scheduling job orders without regard for resulting work-center loads. That is, the scheduler tries to set job-order due dates based on planned dates when parts are needed; there is no attempt to smooth out lumpy groups of operations so as to ease overloads in particular work centers. In effect, the scheduler seems to be assuming infinite capacity in the work centers. The rationale for scheduling without regard for loading is that production-control people may be relied on to see that more important jobs get run first in overloaded work centers.

Infinite-capacity loading is normal in manufacturing firms that rely on complete computer-produced load reports via MRP-CRP as well as in firms that make do with incomplete load reports based only on open orders. Figure 6–7 shows a major difference in how a visual loading report might look for each type of firm. Figure 6–7A shows the usual falling-off load projected for a work center in a firm relying on incomplete data. The load falls off because it is based only on open orders for parts that are low in the warehouse. The week 0 load is a backlog of parts orders already in the work center; the remaining loads are for parts orders due into this work center after passing through upstream work centers. The backlog and the week 1 load are shown to be more than double the work center's capacity. This is not a great problem. Only a few of the orders are essential for current production, and they will appear on a shortage list. Expediters will see that they are run first. Other orders are for stock replenishment (fill warehouse supplies) and may safely be delayed.

Figure 6–7B shows the up-and-down loading pattern common for work centers in firms that use computer-calculated inventory planning and loading (CRP). The dashed line divides open orders—those already released by the scheduler to the shops—from planned orders calculated by the computer to meet future needs. Overloads are shown in weeks 2, 3, and 8. Daily dispatching of more urgent jobs in those weeks can deal effectively with most of the overload problem.

When overloads are severe, a few end-item batches may be moved on the MPS. Moving end-item batches to an earlier or later time bucket also moves the dates of need for component parts that go into the end items. A good deal of study (or computer processing) may be necessary to establish the linkage from overloaded work center to job orders causing the overload, to parts, to end items. Once the linkage has been established, the master scheduler may move an end-item batch and thereby move all the other links in the chain down to the level of the overloaded work center.

FIGURE 6–7
Infinite-capacity
loading

A. Manually calculated loads

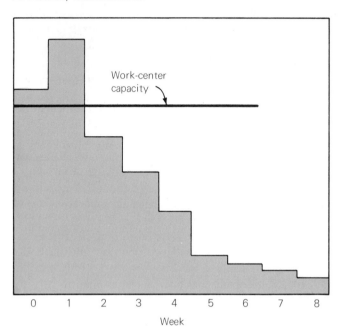

B. Computer-calculated *(CRP)* loads

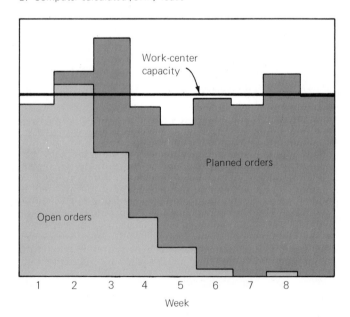

SHOP-FLOOR CONTROL

The workplace or shop floor is out of control if it is choked with partly completed jobs. This is true for a restaurant, clinic, or bank as well as for a goods producer. In Chapter 3 we studied rough-cut capacity planning and master scheduling, which help to keep an overall balance between workload and capacity, and in the last section we considered work-center loading concepts. In this section we consider ways for the scheduler or dispatcher to deal with work-center loading problems. These include *input control* of work releases to gateway or bottleneck work centers (scheduling), *input/output control* over work-center loads, *priority control* of operations in work centers (dispatching), and *expediting* of urgent jobs when all else fails.

Input control

The first half of the scheduler's job is to determine due dates for each operation and a release date for the whole job. The second half is to judiciously release orders so as not to overload the work centers; this is often referred to as input control. Two techniques of input control are discussed below.

Input load leveling via firm planned orders. The scheduler's hold-for-release file will typically contain a mixture of priorities. There will be some shop orders due for release in the next few days, some orders due for release today, and often some new rush orders. There may also be orders that were due for release on a previous day but were withheld so as not to overload certain work centers.

The purpose of input load leveling is as the words suggest: to release or input a level load. A level load is a mix of shop orders that neither overloads nor underloads a work center. Input load leveling works well only for work centers at the input end of the operation sequence. The input end refers to "gateway" work centers. The foundry or certain work centers in the machine shop are common gateways. (The scheduler could work up an elaborate schedule to level not only gateway but also downstream work centers. It might be possible to devise such a schedule with computer help. But because of variable queue times at later work centers, it is unlikely that the later operations would follow the schedule. Later operations are attended to via input/output control and via dispatching in each work center—covered later.)

The *firm planned order* is an MRP tool that may be used to overrule the automatic rescheduling feature of MRP. This can be helpful in load leveling, because the scheduler may schedule a firm planned order earlier than the actual need in order to get the order into a gateway work center in a slack (underloaded) week. Figure 6–8 illustrates this use of the firm planned order. To invoke the firm planned order the scheduler instructs the computer to flag a particular planned order and move it to a given time bucket. In the example, planned order 688 is chosen to be moved from week 3, its calculated date of need, to week 2, which helps level the load imbalance in weeks 2 and 3. The next MRP run will not reschedule the flagged job back to its need date (but will issue a reschedule message, which may be ignored).

FIGURE 6–8
Firm planned
order for load
leveling in
gateway work
center

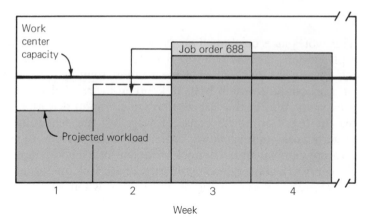

Action taken: Job order 688 is scheduled as a firm planned order in week 2 instead of week 3, its MRP-generated date of need.

Load balancing in non-MRP firms. In ROP-oriented manufacturing firms, work-center workload projections are based only on open orders, which means shop orders generated to replenish parts that are below their reorder points. There can be no workload projections based on planned orders, because the ROP system does not plan in advance. Without planned orders, load projections are understated, and increasingly so as you go further into future weeks. Load leveling for a given work center by moving an order to another time bucket is therefore not applicable. But another technique, this one for rough *load balancing among bottleneck work centers,* can be helpful.

The goal is to release (schedule into the shops) a mixture of shop orders that have high priorities and also a balanced impact on bottleneck work centers. The bottleneck work centers may or may not be gateways; it doesn't matter. An example follows:

EXAMPLE 6–4
Load
balancing,
Flickertail
Looms, Inc.

Every Monday morning the scheduler at Flickertail Looms, Inc., releases shop orders from his hold-for-release file. The file is organized with higher-priority orders on top; all orders in the file are below their ROPs; and the higher-priority orders are those which are expected to stockout the soonest.[6] Besides basing the current week's releases on priority, the scheduler bases them on their impact on three bottleneck work centers: a special loom, a stretching machine and a large-capacity dyeing vat.

The seven highest-priority jobs in the hold-for-release file are currently being analyzed to see their loading effects on those three work centers. The analysis yields the loading data shown in Figure 6–9A. The run times for the seven orders total 38.8 hours, which is 8.8 hours above the average weekly capacity, for the loom. (Capacity varies about the average because of variable job setup times and downtime for mainte-

---

[6] A method of ranking ROP orders by priority is given in Plossl and Wight, *Production and Inventory Control.* See especially fig. 9–3, p. 245.

FIGURE 6-9
Load balancing
among
bottleneck work
centers

A. Run times

Run times (hours) for bottleneck work centers

Orders in hold-for-release file, priority order	Loom: Average capacity = 30 hrs./wk.	Stretcher: Average capacity = 36 hrs./wk.	Vat: Average capacity = 20 hrs./wk.
208x	—	4.5	5.3
200x	4.8	2.8	1.7
195z	9.3	—	2.8
211x	2.1	12.9	2.0
197w	10.9	8.0	4.6
205x	6.5	10.2	7.3
199z	5.2	—	1.5
Totals	38.8	38.4	25.2

B. Alternative schedules

Workloads (hours)

Schedule A: Orders 208x, 200x, 195z, 211x, and 197w	27.1	28.2	16.4
Schedule B: Orders 208x, 200x, 195z, 211x, 205x, and 199z	27.9	30.4	20.6

nance.) The 38.4 hours of run time for the stretcher slightly exceeds the average capacity of 36 hours per week. And the 25.2 hours of vat time exceeds by 5.2 hours its average weekly capacity. To avert the overloads, fewer than seven orders should be scheduled.

Two alternative schedules are shown in Figure 6–9B. Schedule A is made up of the top five orders in the priority list, and it is within capacity limits—30, 36, and 20 hours per week, respectively—for all three bottleneck work centers; adding the sixth order would overload all three work centers. Schedule B seems better because it yields loads that are closer to capacities, especially for the vat.

The scheduler is satisfied with schedule B, which includes all but order 197w. Next week 197w will probably appear at the top of the priority list and will get scheduled first.

A weakness in the load-balancing technique is its failure to consider timing (e.g., *when* a given order will arrive at the loom, the stretcher, and the vat). For example, the five orders in schedule A in Figure 6–9A are to be released in the coming week. But some of these orders might be routed to other (non-bottleneck) work centers first and not get to loom, stretcher, or vat until next week or the week after. Still, load balancing is helpful because it results in loads that over several weeks should be equal to bottleneck capacities *on the average.* If too many orders pile up at a bottleneck facility one week, the excess orders may be delayed until the next week, which may well be underloaded. Expediters with hot lists can see to it that the less urgent orders get delayed and that the more urgent are done on time.

Input/output control

The input control techniques just discussed concern only the gateway and bottleneck work centers. The input/output control technique concerns loads on any work center. Input/output control helps control capacity by revealing where work-center outputs are inadequate and where inputs are inadequate or excessive. An input/output control report provides the necessary information. Figure 6–10 is an example.

The report is for work center 111, and it shows work-center performance against plan for the last three weeks. As is explained in the footnote below the report, the planned input is the average of CRP loads. Raw, unaveraged loads are not usable, because work is not likely to arrive at the same erratic rate that is projected in the CRP computer run; too many things can happen in prior work centers for CRP loads to be valid except as averages.

The botton half of the report in Figure 6–10 shows a drop in actual output. Planned output is not getting done. The result will be a buildup of WIP and a negative cost variance (explained later) in work center 111, and later work centers will be delayed because of the inadequate output in work center 111.

The top half of the report shows that the output problems are not all the fault of work center 111. There is a growing deficiency of work coming in. Previous work centers would seem to be bottlenecks for work center 111.

Examination of input/output control reports for all work centers can reveal where the severe bottlenecks are. Foremen will be encouraged to improve performance in those work centers. Foremen may motivate extra effort or resort to overtime. If actual output is not brought up to planned output, or if actual inputs are chronically low, the master production schedule may need to be changed.

Data needed to produce the bottom half of the report may be readily available in non-MRP as well as MRP firms. Actual output is simply a count of work produced, in standard hours. Planned output is the same as planned

FIGURE 6–10
Input/output
control report

Work center 111	Date: Week ending 94			
Week ending	80	87	94	101
Planned input*	720	720	720	720
Actual input	700	690	710	
Cumulative deviation	−20	−50	−60	
Planned output	720	720	720	720
Actual output	725	704	698	
Cumulative deviation	+5	−11	−33	

* Calculated by averaging the loads that result from capacity requirements planning for many weeks into the future:

CRP loads | 685 | 730 | 690 | 730

Average = 720

input in the example of Figure 6–10. But sometimes planned output is set at a higher level than planned input; a reason might be to work off a backlog.

The output part of the report is beneficial with or without the input part. But the input information helps to show causes of output deviation and thus may be worthwhile. Getting actual input data requires that the firm keep track of work moved to next work centers, which in many firms are data not normally collected. Thus, new procedures for collecting data on moves between work centers might be necessary.

Priority control (dispatching)

While the input/output control report is concerned with work-center capacity control, dispatching is concerned with work-center priority control. In job-lot production, priority control is essential, because a given work center typically has a queue of jobs waiting to have an operation performed at the work center. Priority control means selecting (dispatching) jobs in order of the latest information as to the urgency of the operation. If a job is delayed at one work center, it deserves higher-priority dispatching at the next work center, and vice versa. The following discussion treats the concept of priority, the daily priority report, shop recorders, and centralized versus decentralized dispatching.

Priority. At retail, the priority system is simply first come, first served. Customers are considered homogeneous; one is not more important than another. First come, first served is encouraged by the retailer because it runs itself. The retailer need not pay a dispatcher to pick and choose among customers.

The wholesaler and the factory are not blessed with such simplicity. Their orders are *not* homogeneous. Some orders are more urgent than others—or more profitable, or for more important customers, or fit better with the present plant-capacity situation. Therefore, scheduling shipments or scheduling end-item manufacturing (i.e., the MPS) should involve priority trade-offs among:

Customer importance.
Order urgency.
Order profitability.
Impact on capacity utilization.

For example, customer orders for items held within the Department of Defense supply system are scheduled to be filled based on a priority composed of two factors. One is urgency. The other, called the force activity designator, is importance of the customer. A combat unit deployed in a combat zone is treated as a most important customer. If such a unit requisitions bullets, these can probably justify a high-urgency factor. The combination of customer importance and urgency yields a priority number calculated by the computer, probably priority 1 in this case. The supply system has procedures for very fast delivery, say 24 hours, for priority 1 requisitions; orders with very low priority call for delivery to take a certain number of weeks or months. Note that priority decisions are simplified here because profitability is not a factor. Capacity utilization is also not a factor (though it affects the supply system's delivery performance).

Scheduling *parts* for end items involves simpler priority decisions than does scheduling the end-items themselves. At the component-parts level, orders for the same part are often batched. Customer identification is lost in batching orders, and so it would be hard to schedule the orders based on end-item profits or customer importance. It is even more difficult to make these connections (i.e., profit or customer importance) for orders queued up at a given work center, awaiting dispatching decisions. Therefore, dispatching priorities (for dependent-demand parts) should generally be based on order urgency and impact on capacity utilization, not on profitability or customer importance.

Various priority rules have been proposed to aid in dispatching. Some are given in Figure 6–11 and discussed below. Those based on the whole job (right column) are more typical of dispatching without the aid of a computer; those based on the current operation (left column) require more data processing but are better able to adapt to current conditions.[7]

Note that the priority rules in Figure 6–11 that are based on the whole job may also be used in scheduling (as opposed to dispatching). For example, the scheduler could follow one of the rules in deciding on the order of releasing job orders from a hold-for-release file.

First come, first served. This rule was discussed above. It may simply be noted here that there are two ways to apply it as a dispatching rule. One is to select jobs for the current operation in their order of arrival at the work center. Another (less likely) is to select jobs at the work center by the order in which they entered the work stream upon release by the scheduler.

Shortest processing time. When this rule is applied to the current operation at the current work center, processing time means setup time plus run time. If applied to the whole job, it means all setups and runs for the job as it moves from work center to work center, plus move times and other times. Earlier in the chapter, in the QUIDCO, Inc., example (Figure 6–4), the *job* processing time for shop order number 1005CX was shown to be 13 days (day 105 minus day 92); the *operation* processing time for the bend operation (operation 190) at work center 16 was shown as 6.7 standard hours, of which 4.2 hours was setup time.

Shortest *operation* processing time is noteworthy, because the rule has been shown to be superior to several other rules in computer simulations. The simulations show more on-time completions when the rule is used. Even so, few firms have seen fit to adopt the rule. Instead, more advanced manufacturers usually base priority decisions on some measure of relative lateness, such as earliest due date, slack time, or critical ratio.

---

[7] *Global* and *local* are terms that have been used occasionally to refer to job- and operation-level priorities. That is, a global priority applies to the whole job, and a local priority applies to an operation.

FIGURE 6-11
Some work-center dispatching rules

Priority based on just the current operation— determined at every setup	Priority based on characteristics of the whole job order—determined only when job is scheduled/ rescheduled*
Timing-based rules	
First come, first served	First come, first served
Shortest operation processing time	Shortest job processing time
Longest operation processing time	Longest job processing time
Earliest operation due date	Earliest job due date
Earliest operation start date	Earliest job start date
Least operation slack	Least job slack
Critical ratio	Hot list

Other rules

Profitability rules
Cost rules
Preferred customer rules
Work-center capacity rules

* These may be used in scheduling the whole job order as well as in dispatching at each work center.

Longest processing time. This rule is the opposite of the preceding rule. Neither simulation studies nor actual practice support its use.

Earliest due date. Unlike the above rules, this one is based on *need* date. This may be the due date for the whole *job;* in the QUIDCO example (Figure 6–4) the job due date was day 105. The rule may be based instead on *operation* due dates, which are more precise. For example, the due date for the bend operation in the QUIDCO illustration was day 99.

A simple (static) approach is for the scheduler to compute due dates (for job or for operation) just once. Then dispatching priorities at every work center are based on the earliest due date among jobs in queue.

A dynamic approach is for due dates to be recomputed to keep up with changing conditions. *Job* due dates could be updated by the scheduler weekly, based on MRP output stating that the need date for a part has changed. *Operation* due dates could be updated every day via computer generation of a daily dispatch list for each work center. The dispatch list keeps operation due dates (or start dates) current to reflect delays or early completions as the order travels through its planned routing.

Earliest start date. Earliest *operation* start date is recommended by at least one prominent MRP authority.[8] It is simple, and it has the advantage of corresponding to the order in which jobs *should* arrive at a given work center. That logic does not apply to earliest *job* start date.

---

[8] Wight, *Production and Inventory Management in the Computer Age,* p. 126; see. fig. 24.

Least slack. Earliest due date and earliest start date have a slight flaw: If an eight-hour operation and an eight-day operation each have the same operation due date (or start date), their priorities are equal, when actually the eight-day operation should begin seven days sooner (or end seven days later). Least slack is more precise (though more complicated). Slack is computed as follows:

Operation slack
$$= (\text{Planned start day}) - (\text{Present day}) - (\text{Operation processing time})$$

The computation is similar for job slack. Operation slack (but not job slack) is popular among advanced MRP-using companies.

Critical ratio. Dates and operation times may also be formulated as a critical ratio. There are several versions of critical ratio, which is loosely defined as supply time divided by demand time. One formula is:

$$CR = \frac{\text{Job due date} - \text{Today's date}}{\text{Remaining planned lead time on unstarted operations}}$$

For example, if QUIDCO's shop order No. 1005CX (see Figure 6–4) were moved from the stockroom to work center 16 on day 100, the critical ratio applicable to day 101 is:

$$CR = \frac{105 - 100}{105 - 98} = \frac{5}{7} = 0.71$$

The numerator is self-explanatory. The denominator is the shop order due date, 105, minus the planned start date for operation 190, which is day 98 (92 plus 5 days to pull materials from the stockroom and a day to move).

The CR of 0.71 means that only 71/100 of the planned lead time remains; thus the shop order is behind schedule. It deserves high-priority dispatching. A CR equal to 1.0 means that the order is right on schedule, and a CR greater than 1.0 means that the order is ahead of schedule.

The critical ratio was developed originally for reorder-point parts replenishment. The result is interpreted in the same way, but the formula is different:

$$CR_{ROP} = \frac{\text{Ratio A}}{\text{Ratio B}},$$

where

$$\text{Ratio A} = \frac{\text{Stock on hand}}{\text{Reorder point}}$$

$$\text{Ratio B} = \frac{\text{Remaining planned lead time}}{\text{Total planned lead time}}$$

Hot list and other rules. The hot list was partly explained in Chapter 4 in connection with the ROP/shortage-list way of planning parts inventories. Hot-listed jobs receive priority dispatching at each work center. The other rules listed in Figure 6–11 are based on profitability, cost, preferred customer, and work-center capacity. These are generally more complex than the timing-based rules (and they should normally be used in conjuction with timing-based rules); elaboration on these kinds of rules is reserved for an advanced course.

Daily priority report. The means of setting priorities is less important than the dispatching procedure. The recommended procedure, especially for MRP-using firms, is the daily priority report, often called a dispatch list, issued by work center. Non-MRP firms could produce the report as easily as MRP firms, but without a weekly MRP run to show changes in part need dates, operation priorities on the dispatch list become out of date. Still, some non-MRP firms may find benefits in the dispatch list.

Figure 6–12 is an example of the daily priority report. The example is an extension of the QUIDCO, Inc., shop-order example of Figure 6–4, but the priority report is drawn up one work center at a time. This example is for work center 16, which is a metal-bending machine (or machine group). With this daily report the foreman merely sees that jobs are run in order, starting with the one at the top of the list.

In this example the top three jobs are late by five, four, and two days, respectively, which is indicated by the negative slack. The slack of −4 for job 9925 (from Figure 6–4) is computed following the operation-slack formula given earlier:

$$\text{Operation slack} = \text{Planned start} - \text{Today} - \text{Processing time}$$
$$= 98 - 101 - 1 = -4$$

The critical ratio for the same job and the same present day was computed earlier as 0.71. Critical ratios could be used in the daily dispatch list instead of slack. Or the earliest operation due date may be the basis for the report. The key feature of the priority report is its recomputation every day.

Centralized versus decentralized dispatching. Activities on the shop floor are usually controlled from the shop floor. Typically, production control department representatives—called dispatchers or shop schedulers—are assigned to work in foremen's offices. One job of the dispatcher is to make sure that higher-priority jobs are run ahead of lower-priority jobs. Dispatchers also handle such documents as blueprints, route sheets, shop orders, job tickets, move tickets,

FIGURE 6–12
Daily priority report by least operation slack

Work center 16—Metal bending			Day 101	
Job number	*Part number*	*Operation description*	*Run time (Standard hours)*	*Operation slack*
9932	0092CX	Bend bar	0.3	−5
9925	1005CX	Bend rod	6.7	−4
9938	0181A	Bend bar	5.8	−2
9918	1125C	Bend sheet	1.4	0
9916	1002B	Bend sheet	0.8	+1

inspection forms, tool orders, material issue forms, and completion forms. These documents get jobs started and account for their completion at each stage of their routing. Dispatchers are on the scene and can therefore react quickly to delays. One reaction is to assign higher priority to the delayed job at the next work center; another is to reroute upstream jobs around serious sources of delay, such as a machine breakdown. Still others are to split a job or to interrupt a job already in process in order to set up an urgent one. The job of the shop-floor dispatcher is quite like that of a dispatcher in a railroad yard.

An occasional company sees fit to set up a central dispatching group, physically located away from shop-floor action. Why centralize? Consider this analogy. In an airport, decentralized air traffic control would amount to putting one air traffic controller on each runway. They would try to communicate with one another via walkie-talkies. But the results would surely be suboptimal: The peak number of planes handled per hour would be small, or else there would be frequent disasters. Thus, air traffic controllers—aircraft dispatchers—are centralized. That way they can coordinate tight scheduling and high peak volumes.

So it is with centralized dispatching in manufacturing companies. The major reason appears to be a need for high-volume production and tight scheduling with little margin for error. Automobile assembly, shoe manufacturing, and small appliance manufacturing may be among the better candidates for centralized dispatching.

Centralized dispatching does not mean that production control no longer has shop-floor representatives. There may be a need to have PC people on the floor to report activities by phone or other electronic media so that central dispatching can make realistic, up-to-date priority-control decisions.

Expediting

Launch orders by ROP, and have expediters pull through those that become hot: This describes the standard shop-floor control system of an earlier age. The production control department was large, and expediters were a sizable proportion of its staff. Under MRP, expediting is less common and can usually be managed by foremen instead of full-time expediters.

A production control chief who was guest-lecturing to one operations management class expressed his philosophy of production control: "The whole world is out there trying to stop my job, but I ain't gonna let 'em." His firm relied heavily on expediting, which is a defensive, fire-fighting approach.

The expediting procedure often involves hurried searches for parts needed for a hot subassembly, and for this reason the expediter is sometimes called a parts chaser. Finding the parts can involve preparing shop orders and purchase orders, hand-carrying paperwork, special trips to freight terminals to meet incoming orders, Teletype messages and phone calls to search for parts orders in transit, and so forth. Expediting is disruptive, expensive, and not always successful. It is a mode of operation that many modern firms have been happy to leave behind.

REPORTING AND FEEDBACK CONTROL OF MANAGERIAL PERFORMANCE

The best-laid plans of mice and men
Oft go awry.[9]

If plans did not go awry, there would be no need for reporting and feedback controls and mangerial intervention. But plans do go awry, and there are two reasons why. First, best-laid plans are based on conditions at a given time and always suffer somewhat from the lack of complete information at that time. Changed conditions and unforeseen events render the original plan out of step with reality. Second, those who carry out the plans are not perfect robots but are imperfect and sometimes irrational. We cannot count on them to follow the plans exactly.

In spite of all this, the best control is still a well-laid plan properly fed forward. The plan or piece of the plan that goes awry should be the exception, to be dealt with through management controls based on feedback information.

The previous section was about control, but a very short-range variety. Shop-floor control decisions are highly task-related; they are made by workers and foremen in small organizations and by production-control specialists only in larger organizations. In this chapter we turn to feedback control based on periodic historical reports which are able to show the larger control picture. By this means, operations management policies can be tested and supervisory and managerial performance can be assessed. The basic control cycle provides a framework for discussion.

The control cycle

Control is a cyclic process. Control is characterized by plans (or standards) being fed forward and measured results being fed back. Feedback information is analyzed, and new plans (or standards or policies) may be developed and fed forward. An option is for supervisors to motivate compliance with plans—that is, get back on track—instead of developing new plans. The basic control loop, with the motivational option, is shown in Figure 6–13.

The chart on the chapter title page shows the control loop (minus the motivational option) as applied to operations planning and control. The chart also refers to the transformation, that is, the transformation of resource inputs into goods and services. There is no reason to discuss the transformation, or the work per se. It is appropriate, however, to discuss control over the transformation. In the first part of this section problems in controlling the transformation are discussed. Control tools, including secondary controls such as labor, material, and cost variances, are examined, in addition to primary controls over schedules. (Another type of primary control—over quality—is the topic of Chapter 9, Quality Assurance.)

---

[9] A popular adaptation of lines from the poem *To a Mouse*, 1789, by the Scottish poet Robert Burns. The original lines are:

The best-laid schemes o'mice an' men
Gang aft a-gley.

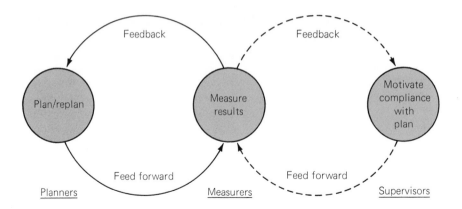

FIGURE 6–13
Basic control loop

Control responsibilities

The first-line supervisor has first-line responsibility for control over the transformation of resources into outputs. The scope of control can be quite comprehensive. In advanced operations control systems, the results of the transformation are formally measured and reported on. Production control departments perform the measurements and provide the reports on which supervisory performance is judged. Furthermore, since production has advisory (staff) authority for planning operations and operating resources, the periodic reports also serve to show how well production control's planning advice has served the supervisory group.

The chart on the chapter title page shows two types of measurements that production control is concerned with. First and foremost is *output* measurement, on the upper right side. Secondarily, below that, is *input* (resource-utilization) measurement. Direct control over operations is based on measurement of output *quality* and output *performance against schedules*. Over a period of time actual costs of resources (inputs used in producing the outputs) may be compared with standard costs; this type of report relates outputs to inputs and results in a comprehensive *cost-variance report*. Finally, more detailed reports on *utilization* and *efficient use* of various resources (inputs) may help show causes of cost variance and poor output performance. The nature of these three types of measurements and reports—on outputs, costs, and utilization/efficiency—is considered next.

MEASUREMENTS AND REPORTS

Our discussion of measurement and periodic reporting begins with cost-variance reporting, because this type of report is the bottom line, so to speak. We then consider resource-usage reports, which provide detailed information on resource utilization and efficiency. Finally, we examine ways to measure and report on outputs.

Cost-variance reporting

In considering the rationale for cost-variance reports, it is necessary to show why more detailed reports on specific operating resources are not sufficient. Operating managers should be held responsible for labor and machine efficiency and for controlled usage of materials, tools, and space. If there are reports that cover the resources over which operating managers have direct control, it may seem unnecessary to also judge operating managers' performance by cost-variance reports. That is, if the operating resources are controlled, then the costs of those resources may also be under control (not counting purchasing's responsibility to get good prices and finance's responsibility to get good financing rates). Nevertheless, cost-variance reports are necessary—more so than detailed resource-utilization reports. The reason has to do with economy of control.

Economy of control. Economy of control has become a popular idea in regard to national policy. The deregulation movement is partly based on it. The idea is that a regulated organization should be held accountable for overall results but that it should be free to apply its own managerial talents and innovativeness to figuring out means of achieving those results. At the national level economy of control sometimes conflicts with traditions, long-standing policies, and so on. Within the firm there is little that conflicts with the economy-of-control idea. In fact, it may be viewed as a principle of good management. Cost-variance reporting is to the operating manager what profitability reporting is to the chief executive officer.

Trade-offs. The beauty of cost variance as a primary control tool is that it allows operating managers room to make the trade-offs that are necessary to hold costs down. For example, the manager may elect to spend more on equipment maintenance to avoid costly labor idleness from equipment failure; more on training to avoid costly rework; more on employee selection to avoid costly turnover; and so on. Without cost-variance reports, there could still be reports on labor idleness, equipment failure, training time, rework, turnover, and so forth. But those factors are often in conflict, and management of individual resources based on individual resource reports is likely to be frustrating and to produce suboptimal results.

Therefore, as the organization grows large enough to be able to afford systematic reports, cost-variance reports should be among the first. Supporting detailed reports on labor idleness, equipment failure, and so forth, may come later.

Cost-variance measurement. Methods of developing cost-variance reports are beyond the scope of this book,[10] but types of cost-variance reports deserve brief comment. The two primary types of cost-variance reports are variance from budget and variance from standard cost.

It is the variance-from-standard-cost report that is most relevant for opera-

---

[10] But see, for example, Charles T. Horngren, *Cost Accounting: A Managerial Emphasis,* 4th ed. (Prentice-Hall, 1977) (HF5686.C8H).

tions management. Standard cost may be established for any product or service. Standard cost includes standard labor and standard material, which are obvious direct costs. It could include the direct costs of utilities, tools, and even equipment and space. But usually it is hard to associate such costs with a given product or service; therefore, the costs may be totaled over, say, a month's time and allocated to individual products based on simple ratios or more complex formulas.

The resulting standard costs are imprecise. Over time, however, overestimates tend to offset underestimates. Accumulated standard costs for all products produced over a month's time may be compared with actual accumulated costs for labor, materials, and utilities, and with some sort of estimates for tool, equipment, and space consumption (or absorption). The difference between standard and actual is the cost variance. Operating managers generally have the chance to explain negative variances. Other detailed reports on resource usage can point to specific areas needing improvement.

Actual resource-usage data is needed in order to compute resource costs and cost-variance reports. Labor, material, and tool usage data may be furnished by production control; other costs, for example, maintenance, supplies, utilities, equipment, and space costs, may be based on bills paid and on allocation formulas determined by cost accounting.

Resource-usage reporting

Resource-usage data are also collected in order to produce resource-utilization and efficiency reports. Resource utilization means, simply, "busyness." Utilization rates are often measured in percentages, but there are various other measures as well. A gross measure is intensity of use of total plant or company capacity, generally expressed as a percentage. This measure was discussed in Chapter 3. More specific measures are considered here.

Utilization rate. Sometimes measurement of resource utilization is automated, especially in the case of expensive *equipment*. For example, computers often have executive software that enables them to measure and report on their own utilization. Industrial and commercial vehicles often have time- and mileage-recording meters; time-of-use readings may be taken so that utilization reports may be prepared. Automated assembly lines and expensive industrial machines also sometimes have time-recording meters.

Space is another resource that may be partially controlled via utilization-rate reporting. Large organizations commonly develop space-utilization reports that express space in use as a percentage of total space. Such reports are often broken down by type of space or type of use. (Colleges and universities generally report based on several room-use categories, as specified in guidelines published by the Department of Education.)

Labor-utilization rates are best measured by work sampling. Random observations of whether or not workers are busy are taken by an outside observer using the procedure described in Chapter 8. Sampling is necessary because continuous observation is prohibitively costly, and self-reporting of busyness cannot be depended on as being accurate or truthful. Work sampling may also be used to measure equipment utilization; time-recording meters are preferable for this purpose, but these are not always available.

Equipment-, space-, and labor-utilization rates are usually computed by the formula

$$\text{Utilization rate} = \frac{\text{Time in use}}{\text{Time available}},$$

expressed as a percentage. Idleness rate is 100 percent minus utilization rate.

Even information resources may be controlled based on utilization rates. The measure is usually frequency of use, as compared to some standard, rather than percentage of time in use. For example, records and files may be archived based on a certain standard of use or nonuse, and records and files may be disposed of completely in the next phase of records/file control. (*Migration* is a common term for moving information from active storage to archives to disposal.) These are common techniques of records management in organizations as a whole, and for file management in computer centers.

There are many other detailed kinds of measures of resource utilization. For example, for the labor resource it is common to keep track of absences resulting from illness, jury duty, military duty, labor-union activities, tardiness, and so forth—all of which eat into productive time. Measures of materials utilization might include scrap, theft, deterioration, obsolescence, and misplacement—all of which eat into productive use of materials. Some of the same kinds of measures may be applied to tools, equipment, space, and information.

Resource utilization in perspective. Reports about resources tend to proliferate as organizations grow. Greater revenue absorbs (or amortizes) more reporting costs. Close control of expensive resources is easiest to justify. But such controls can be, and often are, overdone.

It is staff organizations, such as purchasing, personnel, maintenance, and inventory control, that generate resource-utilization reports. These are operating-resources organizations. They are below the dashed line in the chart on the title page of the chapter, and they exist only for purposes of above-the-line operations. But preservation, growth, and power instincts conflict with the mandate to serve operations. Such instincts tend to result in resource management and reports beyond what is good for the whole organization. When large organizations fall on hard times, cutting staff employees and many of their reports is a common prescription for regaining economic health.

Another tendency to guard against is indiscriminate use of resource-utilization. One government agency, for example, followed a rigid policy for allocating forklifts among its departments and shops. The policy required that a request for a forklift be based on a projected utilization rate exceeding (let us say) 60 percent. A shop could have its forklift removed if the time meter showed utilization falling below that figure. One result of this policy was that none of the agency's hundreds of industrial shops could justify the purchase of low-cost nonpowered "pallet movers." These are simple hand trucks with elevatable forks, selling for a few hundred dollars up to below $2,000. Instead, whenever a shop needed to have a pallet moved a few feet, a large vehicular forklift costing $10,000–$30,000 had to be dispatched from a central location. Meters on the central forklifts showed a high utilization rate, but mostly from driving, not lifting. Assigning a hand truck to each of the various shops might have been less expensive as well as quicker and more convenient.

It should also be noted that 100 percent utilization is not necessarily ideal. For example, no computer center wants its computer to be 100 percent utilized. With such high use there are sure to be long backlogs, interminable delays in getting a job run, and many customers who balk at the long backlogs and do without the service. The waiting-line simulation and queuing sections of Chapter 13 include a more complete discussion of trade-offs between facility (server) utilization and waiting lines.

Finally, utilization rate is a surrogate rather than a true measure of efficiency. Busyness fails to take output into consideration. Therefore, a good control system for operations/operating resources management should also include efficiency reporting.

Efficiency reporting. Labor is the only resource that is measurable in efficiency terms. Machines, tools, space, and materials have no will and cannot work at any pace other than normal. Labor efficiency is measured by the following formulas (further explained in Chapter 8).:

$$\text{Efficiency} = \frac{\text{Actual output}}{\text{Standard output}} \text{ or } \frac{\text{Standard time}}{\text{Actual time}}$$

Labor *utilization* requires a special work-sampling study, which makes it too expensive for regular weekly, biweekly, or monthly reporting. Labor *efficiency,* however, is a natural by-product of data collection on outputs, which will certainly be measured, along with time standards data.

The first version of the efficiency formula given above is in terms of output, actual divided by standard. It is nevertheless an input measure, because it is a measure of actual speed or pace or effort against standard or normal speed or pace or effort. A similar measure of output would compare actual output to *scheduled* (rather than standard) output. The difference is that scheduled output should already allow for expected levels of efficiency (or pace), and for utilization as well.

Output reporting

The immediate goal of the first-line supervisor is on-time completions. The way to measure on-time completions depends on type of operations, as is shown in Figure 6–14.

Measures. In repetitive or limited-quantity large-scale production, measuring output is simple. As Figure 6–14 shows, output is measured by *counting units* produced that meet minimum quality standards. In factories it is parts that are counted. In other organizations miles of highway, square yards of concrete, clients visited, patients seen, and so forth, are suitable measures.

FIGURE 6–14
Output measures
by type of
operations

Type of operations	Output measures
Repetitive or limited-quantity large-scale	Unit count
Job or job-lot	Unit count (work center)
	Due dates met (job orders)
	Percent of completion
Project	Percent of completion
	Milestones completed on time
	Events completed on time

The count is in units per day, per week, or per some other time unit. Automatic counters or scales are sometimes available to perform the measurement. Periodic reports may show variances from scheduled output. A variance might be expressed as a deficiency of actual output as compared with scheduled output per day; or it might be expressed in hours or days late, or in need for overtime.

In job-lot production, output measurement can be difficult or expensive. A parts order may be routed through multiple work centers, with output measurement taking place at each of them. As is shown in Figure 6–14, the measurement may include a *unit count* of parts successfully produced (not scrapped); time of completion is also reported, so that priorities may be recomputed for upcoming work centers. Periodically, perhaps every two weeks, a report may summarize parts moved out (after successful completion) as compared with raw materials moved into each work center; and another report may show job-order *due dates met*, which is a measure of success for all the work centers put together. Due dates met is also a suitable output measure in simpler job-shop work involving perhaps only one unit and one work center. Examples are repairing a pair of shoes, papering the walls of a room, performing a lab test, and cooking a meal. *Percent of completion* is a suitable measure in job shops in which processing time at a given work center is long—days or weeks—and the output is not readily countable. Examples are major overhauls and renovations.

Three kinds of output measures for project operations are listed in Figure 6–14. These are discussed in connection with project management and the PERT/CPM technique in Chapter 7.

Gantt control chart. The Gantt chart as a visual aid for scheduling services was discussed earlier, and examples of Gantt charts were given in Figure 6–5. It was stated that Gantt charts are no longer used for repetitive manufacturing control. But Gantt *control* charts are useful in certain job-shop work. Renovation, major maintenance, and extensive overhaul work are examples.

Figure 6–15 shows a Gantt control chart for renovation work. The Gantt chart in Figure 6–15A, is an initial schedule for three crews. Note that an arrow at the top of each chart designates the current day.

FIGURE 6–15
Gantt control
chart, renovation
work

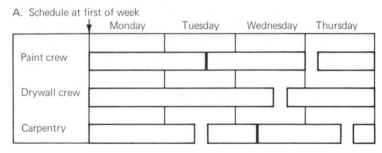

A. Schedule at first of week

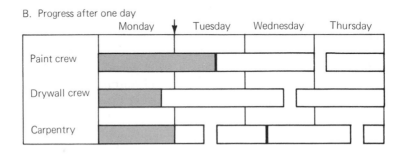

B. Progress after one day

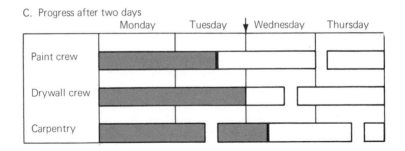

C. Progress after two days

Figure 6–15B shows the progress that has been made after one day. The shading indicates amount of work done, which is probably estimated by the crew chief, in percent of completion. The paint crew has 100 percent of its first job done, whereas only two thirds of that job was scheduled for Monday. While the paint crew is one-half day ahead of schedule, drywall is one-quarter day behind. Carpentry did Monday's scheduled work on Monday and is therefore on schedule.

Figure 6–15C shows painting falling behind, drywall on schedule, and carpentry ahead.

There are several commercially available schedule boards that use felt or magnetic strips, pegs, plastic inserts, and the like to block out schedules and to show progress. Such boards are most commonly found in construction offices, project managers' headquarters, and maintenance departments. But Gantt control charts are largely unsuitable for parts fabrication, because parts schedules and work-center priorities change too fast to make plotting on a schedule board worthwhile.

Shop recorders. Some years ago, large numbers of shop recorders were sold to manufacturing companies. The recorders were placed in shops for recording both output and input data, which usually included charging labor and material to a given job and recording quantities of parts successfully produced. Foremen or workers could enter the data, thus reducing the need for production-control data-collection people. The data could be entered into the computer each day or more often, and the computer could then develop new schedules and priorities.

It seems that in most companies the recorders were a failure. Why? Because it was too easy to enter false data. If the operation calls for machining 90 widgets and the operator scraps 15, the operator should enter 75 as the number produced. But the operator may "fudge" a bit and enter 80 or even 90. In a few days, after the parts have passed through several remaining operations, the job order is closed and a shortage is discovered. The operator who fudged may claim that the shortage occurred before he received the order—or after. Or the operator may simply say that he miskeyed the "damn recording machine." Many of the recorders ended up on a shelf someplace.

In recent years shop recorders have been enjoying healthy sales once again. This time they are working. The difference is that the recorders are so-called smart terminals, or they link up to smart terminals, and the terminals in turn link up to a mainframe computer to form a distributed computer network. A smart terminal has some memory and computing power. The terminal can be programmed to perform simple data checks. One effective check is to compare the produced quantity that is entered by one operator with the quantity entered by the operator in the preceding work center. If an operator claims to have produced 90, but the preceding operator forwarded only 75, the discrepancy is caught right away. The smart terminal may prompt the second operator to try again.

With smart on-line shop recorders, some firms have been able to cut priority-update time from a day or two to virtually instant updating. The daily priority report gives way to continuous recomputation of priorities. The effect is less WIP inventory, shorter lead times, and more responsive service to customers.

SUMMARY

The execution of inventory plans or service plans involves scheduling, dispatching, reporting and control. Schedules for repetitive operations are largely designed into the production process, because design costs may be spread over long production runs. The flow-control concept for controlling repetitive runs is simple, involving little more than orderly material movements.

Job-lot production control is more challenging. The scheduler's job is to determine when to release a job order for component parts, so that the order will arrive when the inventory planner says the parts are needed. Production lead time is a key uncertainty, because parts orders tend to spend time in queues at each work center in the process flow. Queue time should be held in check, which also reduces work-in-process inventory investment. The scheduler can help by regulating the flow of work to the shops. Lead-time estimates used in scheduling can be made more accurate, and thus better for capacity planning, if some measure of shop congestion is included. Scheduling may include matching scheduled jobs and operations with schedules for operating resources—labor, equipment, tools, and so on. In services, it is often helpful to display schedules on a visual aid known as a Gantt chart, but the use of Gantt charts is limited in scheduling goods production.

Having enough capacity at individual work centers to handle the parts orders routed through them is an old problem. Work-center loads that are computed manually are somewhat valid for the near future and can also be used to track the size of the backlog of open orders. But a fully valid load report must add planned orders to open orders. This can be done by computer, using capacity requirements planning (CRP), an extension of MRP. CRP load reports allow for work-center capacity control with plenty of lead time.

The scheduler can contribute to improved shop-floor control, that is, the control of jobs at the work centers. For example, the scheduler can make use of the firm-planned-order feature of MRP, which can be used in connection with load leveling in gateway work centers. In ROP-using firms the scheduler may exercise judgment in releasing balanced loads to a few designated bottleneck work centers. Another device, the input/output control report shows which work centers are failing to meet planned outputs and whether the preceding work centers are at fault for forwarding less-than-planned inputs to the next work centers.

The queuing of jobs at each work center affords the opportunity for selecting the next job, based on priority. This is the dispatching function, and it is a way to get delayed jobs back on schedule. Some method of computing the latest priorities provides the basis for the selection. Priority rules based on timing of the whole job were common in an earlier era; rules based on timing of the current operation are more common in modern computer-based dispatching. First come, first served is almost universal for dispatching in retailing, but timing—meeting schedules—is more important as a priority factor within the firm. The shop-floor dispatcher (or foreman) follows a daily priority report in assigning work and handling shop documents. Dispatchers sometimes work in a centralized office instead of on the shop floor, especially where operations must be tightly coordinated. When all else fails, expediting may be used to pull a late job through.

A variety of historical reports are useful in assessing overall production and production-control performance. A periodic cost-variance report is a foundation report showing weaknesses, and resource-utilization and efficiency reports provide details on the causes of problems. Even more basic are reports on output, that is, on-time completions. Outputs are measured variously, depending on type of operations. The Gantt control chart is one way of displaying progress against due dates, but it is useful only for such applications as renovation and overhaul work, where tasks extend over more than a day.

A modern approach is to place recording devices in shops. They may be connected on-line to computers, which can quickly verify the reasonableness of claimed production data and can reschedule jobs as necessary.

REFERENCES

Books

Fuchs, Jerome H. *Computerized Cost Control Systems.* Prentice-Hall, 1976 (HD47.5.F8).

O'Brian, James S., ed. *Scheduling Handbook.* McGraw-Hill, 1969 (TS157.O2).

Plossl, G. W., and O. W. Wight. *Production and Inventory Control: Principles and Techniques.* Prentice-Hall, 1967 (HD55.P5).

Wight, Oliver W. *Production and Inventory Management in the Computer Age.* Cahners, 1974 (TS155.W533).

Periodicals (societies)

Decision Sciences (American Institute for Decision Sciences), an academic journal.

Production and Inventory Management (American Production and Inventory Control Society).

Operations Management Journal (American Production and Inventory Control Society and American Institute for Decision Sciences), an academic journal.

PROBLEMS

Note: Asterisked (*) problems require more than mimicry. They require judgment, and you should include discussion of reasons, assumptions, and outside sources of information.

Production control

1. A manufacturer of stereo speakers produces five main types of high-quality speakers. The company considers itself a job-lot producer: The single production line produces job lots of each type of speaker on a rotating schedule. Price competition has been severe, and the company's profits have eroded. A conglomerate is buying the stereo manufacturer, and it intends to invest a considerable amount of cash to improve production control and cut production costs.
    a. What should the money be invested in if the decision is made to continue as a job-lot producer?
    b. What should the money be invested in if the decision is made to convert to small lots?
2. A scheduler at QUIDCO, Inc., is working up a schedule for making 20 of Part no. 0077AX. The inventory planner advises that the order should be released

this week, week 90, and that the order is due on the week of 115, when it will be needed to go into a parent item.

a. How would the inventory planner have determined the week due and the week of release? If the inventory planner has determined these dates, doesn't that constitute rescheduling and eliminate the need for the scheduler to do anything? Discuss.

b. The A in the part number signifies a costly item. For A items the following rules are followed for computing operation lead times:

(1) Allow eight standard hours per day; round upward to even (eight-hour) days.

(2) Allow *no time* between operations. A items receive priority material handling.

(3) Allow one day to inspect.

(4) Release the job to the stockroom four days before it is to be started into production.

(5) All dates are treated as of the end of the eight-hour day.

Schedule a shop order for the item, assuming that the part goes through three operations, plus inspection. You make up the setup times and operation times such that the schedule will fit between weeks 90 and 115. Explain.

c. Compare the operation lead-time rules for Part no. 0077AX with the rules in Example 6–3 for Part no. 1005CX. Why should a more expensive item have different lead-time rules? (Hint: WIP has something to do with it.)

d. A week passes. Inventory planning notifies scheduling that Part no. 0077AX is now due (to go into a parent item) in week 120 instead of 115. The shop order, along with a planning package (blueprints, job tickets, etc.), has already been released. There is no need to issue new paperwork, because QUIDCO has a computer-produced daily dispatch list for each work center. Least operation slack is the dispatching rule. The scheduler merely gets on a terminal and inputs updated scheduling information. Explain how that information would be used in generating dispatch lists. Also explain how the dispatch lists serve the purpose of adjusting for the new due date.

Loading and expediting

3. Open Air Furniture Co. makes patio furniture. There are just three work centers: rough saw, finish saw, and assemble.

Production control uses loading charts for short-term scheduling and capacity management. Each week's component-parts orders are translated into machine-hours in rough saw and finish saw and into labor-hours in assemble. Current machine-hour and labor-hour loads are given below:

	Rough saw	Finish saw	Assemble
Current week	270	470	410
Week 2	40	110	100
Week 3	—	40	50
Week 4	—	30	15
Weekly capacity ..	150	225	190

a. Discuss probable reasons for the load pattern given for each work center.

b. Is this the type of firm that is likely to rely heavily on expediting? Explain.

4. Part of a daily open-order file and part of a routing file are shown below.

Daily open-order file   Date: 93

Part no.	Shop-order no.	Quan-tity	Work centers and dates in routing sequence (current location signified by X)					
00112	836	10	11–91	X18–94	40–96	22–100	42–103	. . .
00810	796	48	11–84	X21–88	18–93	38–95	. . .	
00901	816	6	X16–88	26–91	12–98	18–100	40–103	. . .
00904	821	20	21–90	12–92	X18–95	28–98	. . .	
00977	801	30	21–83	51–86	28–90	X40–94	18–96	16–99 . . .
00989	806	18	09–84	40–88	X18–98	13–102	. . .	
01016	844	4	X12–94	41–98	29–102	18–104	23–107	. . .

Routing file (only selected part numbers are included)

Part no.	Work center	Setup time	Cycle time
00112	11	—	0.8
	18	2.2	0.2
	09	0.6	1.2
	31	1.1	0.1
	14	5.0	0.7
00810	18	0.5	0.1
00901	18	1.0	2.0
00904	18	3.0	0.6
00977	18	1.5	0.3
00989	18	5.0	1.0
01016	18	1.2	3.1

Note: The complete routing is given only for the first part number.

a. Using the information in the files, compute the load on work center 18 (WC18) for the weeks beginning on days 94, 99, 104 and 109. Plot the computed totals for each week on a load chart similar to Figure 6–7A and the open-orders part of Figure 6–7B.

b. What is the total backlog for WC18 as of week 94? Backlogs in the recent past were:

As of week	Backlog
79	96 hours
84	97 hours
89	91 hours

What concerns should the foreman over WC18 have in view of the backlog pattern?

c. Why is it necessary to state "rules" for computing operation lead times for scheduling purposes but not for loading purposes?

d. Explain how your load chart (from part a) could be augmented to include planned orders.

5. The chart below shows projected loads for one work center.
    a. What may the scheduler do to help correct the imbalance between load and capacity in some weeks? Discuss, including any limitations or difficulties in correcting the imbalance.
    b. How would the load report be produced?
    c. Assume that the foreman has set work-center output (via planned staffing) at 590 per week for these five weeks. A report after five weeks shows actual output in the five weeks as:

    585   590   575   590   585

    What may be concluded about the five-week results?
    d. A second part of the five-week report shows actual inputs of:

    565   650   650   570   600

    What should be listed as planned inputs for the period? Now what may be concluded about the five-week results? Discuss fully.

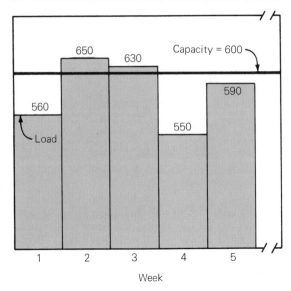

Week

6. Two bottleneck work centers in a manufacturing company are mixing and blow molding. Mixing capacity is 70 hours per week, and blow-molding capacity is 110 hours per week. On Monday morning the scheduler goes through his hold-for-release file. He finds six job orders that pass through either or both of the bottleneck work centers. The six job orders and their run times at the two work centers are given below in order of arrival in scheduling:

Order of arrival	Mixing hours	Blow-molding hours
1	16	17
2	10	18
3	25	14
4	7	21
5	17	41
6	12	18

a. If first come, first served is used as a rough priority rule in releasing job orders from scheduling, what orders would you recommend for release this week? Explain.

b. If shortest job processing time is used as a rough priority rule in releasing job orders from scheduling, what orders would you recommend for release this week? Explain.

c. Which of the above priority rules is preferable in this case? Explain.

Dispatching

7. An antenna manufacturer produces in job lots. Part of the daily dispatch list on day 314 is shown below for the chrome-plating work center.

Shop order	Part	Setup time (standard hours)	Operation time (standard hours)	Operation slack
910	AS65	0.5	3.5	−3
914	AS41	2.0	12.0	0
.				
.				
.				
885	AL88	4.5	10.0	+6

a. If shop order 885 is as shown below, what is the critical ratio of the plating operation on day 314 (a Friday)?

Shop order 885	Part no. AL88	Quantity: 5 loads	
Operation	Setup hours	Run hours	Finish
Cut	1.0	6.0	320
Move			321
Chrome plate	4.5	10.0	323
Trim		8.0	324

b. What rules for computing operation lead times can be detected from shop order 885?

c. On day 315 (Monday morning) inventory planning notifies scheduling that the due date for Part no. AL88 is now day 319 instead of 324. The chrome-plating operation has not yet been done for the part. What is the new operation slack in the chrome-plating work center? What is the new critical ratio? Is shop order 885 now urgent?

d. On day 315, where are shop orders 910 and 914 likely to be? Base your answer only on the above information.

e. Assume that on day 316 the (partial) daily dispatch list is as follows:

Shop order	Part number	Setup time (standard hours)	Operation time (standard time)	Operation slack
898	AL26	1.5	4.0	−4
914	AS41	2.0	12.0	−1
885	AL88	4.5	10.0	−1
.				
.				
.				

Explain what has happened to yield this dispatch list.

f. Will shop order 885 also appear on the daily dispatch list for the trim work center? Explain.

      g. Is this company likely to use centralized or decentralized dispatching? Explain.

      h. Would on-line shop recorders make sense for this firm? Explain.

Feedback controls

8. An aggressive new chief of production control has developed full computer-based MRP and CRP plus a wide assortment of feedback reports. The feedback reports include the following, in order of importance according to the PC chief:

    Input/output control report

    Efficiency report

    Report of percent of job orders completed on time

    Quality-control report of defectives

    Scrap report

    Report of stockroom parts-shortage rate

    Various other minor reports and special audits

One effect of these reports is that foremen complain about all the paperwork and about the continual need to defend their performance as indicated in the reports. What is missing in the reporting system? Explain?

*9. In chapter discussion the cost-variance report was stated to be a cornerstone of an effective feedback control system. Is the grade that a student gets in a course similar as a performance indicator to the cost-variance report in manufacturing? Fully discuss this analogy.

Measurement

*10. The following is a list of the ways in which the results in a given organization or program are measured.

Agency, firm, or program	Measurement of results
Library	Books circulated per full-time employee
Highway safety program	Expenditures on safety advertising
Tax service	Cost per tax return prepared
Computer center	Minutes of downtime
Personnel department	Expenditures versus budget
Sales department	Number of clients visited
Hospital	Average length of stay
School lunch program	Average pounds of uneaten food from plates
Antismoking program	Number of antismoking clinics established
School	Student credit hours per full-time equivalent instructor
Maintenance department	Percent of repair orders completed on time
Welding shop	Tons of scrap produced

    a. The above list includes (1) output measures, (2) input efficiency measures, (3) input utilization measures, (4) input cost measures, and (5) other less precise input measures. Which of the five types of measures applies to each item on the list? Explain each answer briefly.

    b. Suggest an improved (but similar) type of output measure for each item on the list. Explain.

Gantt chart

11. Four jobs are on the desk of the scheduler for the minor construction department in a firm. Each of the four jobs begins with masonry and is followed by carpentry and wiring. Work-order data are given below:

Work order	Estimated task time, masonry	Estimated task time, carpentry	Estimated task time, wiring
58	2 weeks	3 weeks	1½ weeks
59	1 week	1½ weeks	1 week
60	3 weeks	2 weeks	3 weeks
61	5 weeks	½ week	1½ weeks

a. Prepare a Gantt chart scheduling the four jobs through the three crafts (crafts are rows on the chart). Use first come, first served as the priority rule for scheduling (first *job* first—the *whole* job). Assume that a craft cannot divide its time between two work orders. How many weeks do the four jobs take?

b. Repeat part *a*, but use the shortest-job-processing-time rule instead of first come, first served. Now how many weeks are required?

c. Three weeks pass. The following progress is reported to the scheduler:

Masonry completed on WO 58.

Masonry not started on WO 59, 60, or 61.

Carpentry half completed on WO 58.

Show the progress on a Gantt control chart.

d. In this problem situation each shop is fully loaded as the jobs are sequenced and scheduled. It is finite-capacity loading. What is there about minor construction work of this kind that makes scheduling and loading so uncomplicated (as compared with job-lot parts fabrication)?

IN-BASKET CASE*

Topic: Scheduling—Clinic

To:

From: The clinic physicians

Some of our patients have complained about long waits even when they have appointments. What kinds of scheduling techniques are there that allow for the flexibility that we need in this business? Discuss fully in your report.

*See instructions at end of problems section, Chapter 1.

CASE

Western Electric

The Carterfone ruling, made by the Federal Communications Commission in 1968, allowed "foreign" phone equipment to be interconnected with equipment of a host phone company. This milestone ruling and other rulings resulted in increased competition in the U.S. communications industry.

One firm that has felt the effects of greater competition is Western Electric. One sizable Western Electric factory has had to cease making telephone sets and now produces transmission equipment and enclosures. Jack Sampson (not his real name), who has been chief of production control for 20 years, has assembled a dedicated team who pride themselves on avoiding parts shortages. For example, it is not uncommon for one of Mr. Sampson's people to be on hand at the airport or the company receiving dock at night or on weekends to meet an important incoming parts order and to hand-process the order to get it to the production line fast. This is not to say that production control is all manual. Computers are used for several production-control and inventory purposes, as follows:

Computer applications in production control	*Computer applications in inventory control*
Production simulation (what-if?)	Multilevel explosion
Order entry	Component ordering/expediting
Product file and history	Receiving
Shop loading/scheduling	Storage control
Order tracking/shop status	Select sheets and hot lists
Delivery-ticket generation	Perpetual inventory routines

What is your assessment of production control at Western Electric? Has the effect of competition reached the production control department yet? Is the department modern and up to date?

chapter 7

PERT/CPM AND LOB SYSTEMS

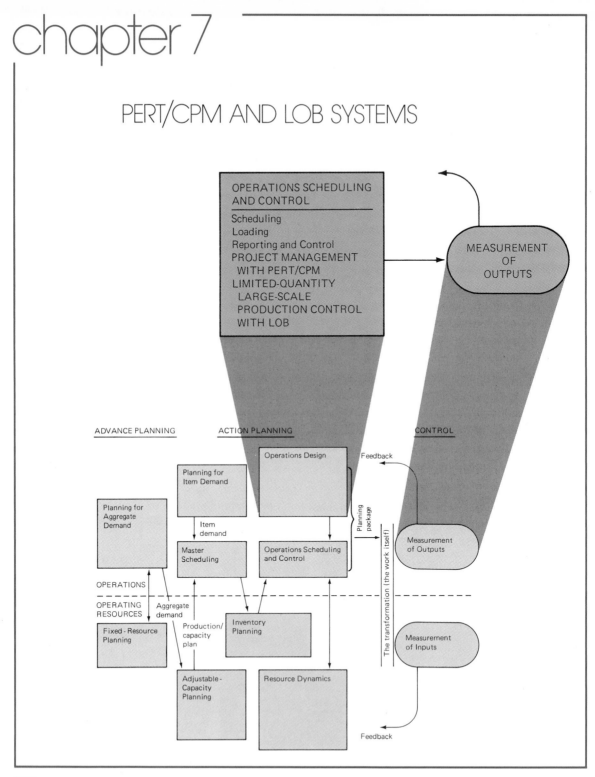

OPERATIONS SCHEDULING
AND CONTROL

Scheduling
Loading
Reporting and Control
PROJECT MANAGEMENT
 WITH PERT/CPM
LIMITED-QUANTITY
 LARGE-SCALE
 PRODUCTION CONTROL
 WITH LOB

MEASUREMENT
OF
OUTPUTS

ADVANCE PLANNING   ACTION PLANNING   CONTROL

Operations Design   Feedback

Planning for
Item Demand

Planning for
Aggregate
Demand

Item
demand

Master
Scheduling

Operations Scheduling
and Control

Planning
package

Measurement
of Outputs

OPERATIONS

OPERATING
RESOURCES   Aggregate
demand

Fixed - Resource
Planning

Production/
capacity
plan

Inventory
Planning

The transformation (the work itself)

Measurement
of Inputs

Adjustable -
Capacity
Planning

Resource Dynamics

Feedback

PERT/CPM
    Networks
    Project phases and PERT/CPM subsystems
PROJECT PLANNING AND SEQUENCING SUBSYSTEM
    Work breakdown structure
    Task lists, network segments, and whole networks
    Networking conventions
    Alternative forms of networks
TIME-ESTIMATING AND PATH-ANALYSIS SUBSYSTEM
    Activity times
    Path analysis
    Activity slack
    Negative slack
    Slack-sort computer listing
    Network simulation
PROJECT SCHEDULING SUBSYSTEM
    "Crashing" the network
    Time-cost trade-off analysis
    Event scheduling
REPORTING AND UPDATING SUBSYSTEM
    Reporting
    Updating
USES AND MISUSES OF PERT/CPM
    PERT/Cost
    PERT/CPM environment
LINE-OF-BALANCE ANALYSIS
    LOB example
    LOB advantages
SUMMARY
REFERENCES
PROBLEMS
IN-BASKET CASE: GERT—AERO-SPACE PRODUCTS
CASE: ABM SITE
SUPPLEMENT—PERT THREE-TIME-ESTIMATING PROCEDURE
    Expected time and variance
    Probability statements

This chapter is a continuation of the previous one on operations scheduling and control. The last chapter concerned concepts and techniques that apply to repetitive, job-lot, and job-shop operations. The two techniques singled out for separate treatment in this chapter apply to the two remaining types of operations: Project operations may be planned and controlled with the aid of the program evaluation and review technique (PERT) or the critical path method (CPM). Limited-quantity large-scale production, a hybrid of repetitive and project operations, may be controlled with the aid of the line-of-balance (LOB) technqiue.

PERT/CPM

The critical path method was developed by Catalytic Construction Company in 1957. Catalytic developed CPM as a method for improving planning and control over a project to construct a plant for Du Pont Corporation. CPM was credited with having saved time and money on that project, and today CPM is well known and widely used in the construction industry.

The program evaluation and review technique was developed in 1958 by Booz, Allen, and Hamilton, a large consulting firm, along with the U.S. Navy Special Projects Office. PERT was developed to facilitate more intensive management of the Polaris missile project. Polaris was one of the largest research and development projects ever undertaken. Nevertheless, Polaris was completed in record time—about four years. PERT received much of the credit, and it was rapidly adopted as a tool for intensive project management throughout the R&D industry.

Networks

Both CPM and PERT are based on a task sequence chart known as a network (also called a PERT chart or arrow diagram); see Figure 7–1 for an abbreviated sample of a network. A few early differences between CPM and PERT have mostly disappeared, and it is convenient to think of PERT and CPM as being one and the same, referred to by the combined term PERT/CPM. The con-

FIGURE 7–1
A PERT/CPM
network

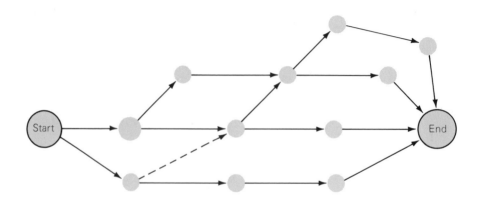

struction industry still calls it CPM, and the R&D people still usually call it PERT; a few other terminological differences are mentioned later.

Project phases and PERT/CPM subsystems

PERT/CPM is among the more interesting and written-about contemporary management techniques. Actually PERT/CPM may be more than a technique. Perhaps it is, or can be, a management system.

A system has subsystems, and our discussion of PERT/CPM will identify four subsystems. We shall see that most projects are not complex enough to justify the expense of implementing all four. But managing grand projects may call for a full computer-based PERT/CPM system, which, throughout the project, can help cope with sequence and time-management problems and also aid in resource allocation and cost control. The four subsystems that would be found in a full computer-based system are:

Project planning and sequencing. This is about the same as the product design and process planning/routing activities in repetitive and job-lot operations.

Time estimating and path analysis. Time estimating for projects is like time estimating in a job shop, but path analysis is unique to project operations.

A *project scheduling subsystem.* Scheduling projects has some elements of both repetitive and job-lot scheduling. But treating a project network as a self-contained unit of work gives rise to special ways of analyzing scheduling options.

Reporting and updating. Treating the network as a self-contained unit permits intensive project control using the management-by-exception principle.

PROJECT PLANNING AND SEQUENCING SUBSYSTEM

The initial PERT/CPM subsystem is to develop the network. In planning job-lot operations, we begin with a bill of materials (BOM); in planning project operations, the same is true, but it is labeled a work breakdown structure (WBS) rather than a BOM. The WBS defines major project modules, secondary components, and so on. As in job-lot manufacturing, production of a bottom-level component part requires a routing through several different work centers. Thus, for each bottom-level part of the project, task lists are prepared. The sequencing or routing of the tasks forms the PERT/CPM network.

In job-lot production the sequence of tasks to produce a part is merely listed on a route sheet, but in projects sequences of tasks for parts are linked together to form a network. Why the need for so elaborate a sequence display? Because projects, by common definition, are relatively complex, with multiple tasks in progress at any given time; and projects tend to be large, sometimes involving tens or hundreds of thousands of tasks. The PERT/CPM network was developed in response to the need to know how these tasks fit together.

Work breakdown structure

An example of a work breakdown structure (WBS) for building a house is presented next. Actually building houses is so routine and standardized that it approximates repetitive rather than project production. But since house building is a familiar example, it will serve to illustrate the WBS concept.

EXAMPLE 7–1
Work breakdown structure, house construction

A WBS for building a house is shown in Figure 7–2. Figure 7–2A is a preferred way to construct a WBS; the project is broken down into tangible products at levels 2 and 3. Figure 7–2B is a process-oriented way to draw it—not recommended. The process-oriented chart does not provide tangible products whose completion may be assigned to a single manager. Carpentry, for example, results in several tangible products or parts: forms for footings, the frame of the house, finished cabinets, and so forth. Painting, landscaping, and masonry are similarly interspersed throughout the project and result in several outputs. When the project is delayed or resources are idled, it may be convenient for painters to blame carpenters, and so forth. If managers are appointed to "honcho" given parts of the project—instead of having foremen only for each craft or process—the managers may work to secure cooperation from the various crafts; this may save time and cut the costs of idle resources.

FIGURE 7–2
Work breakdown structures for house-building project

A. Product-oriented *WBS*

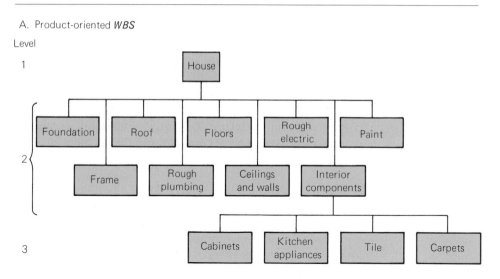

B. Process-oriented *WBS*

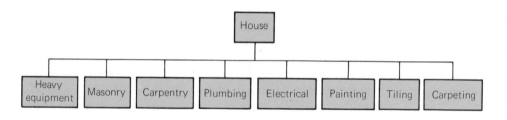

Task lists, network segments, and whole networks

Once the project has been broken down into products as in Figure 7–2A, task lists for each product may be identified. Finally the tasks are arranged into a PERT/CPM network. The following example demonstrates the networking technique.

EXAMPLE 7–2
Networking, house construction

Figure 7–3 shows how a WBS evolves into network segments, which combine into networks. The figure is a continuation of the simple example of a WBS for house building. The lowest level in the WBS is for three parts: cabinets, kitchen appliances, and tile. Task lists for each part are identified in Figure 7–3A.

FIGURE 7–3
Translating task lists into network segments

A. Task lists for project parts

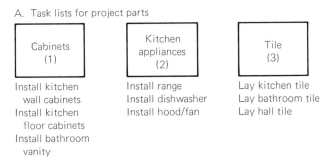

B. Network segments

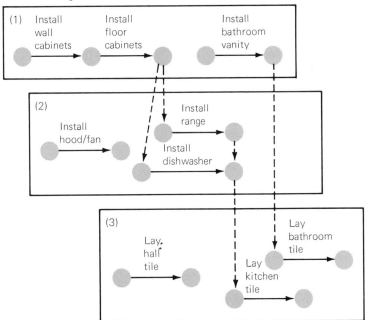

Source: Adapted from Fred Luthans, *Introduction to Management: A Contingency Approach* (Richard J. Schonberger, contributing author) (McGraw-Hill, 1976) (HD31.L86), p. 375. Used with permission.

Without the task lists for all of the other parts of the house, it is not possible to properly sequence all of the tasks into networks. But Figure 7–3B demonstrates the kind of sequencing logic that must occur. Kitchen wall cabinets go first since they are easier to install if the lower cabinets are not in the way. Floor cabinets are installed with gaps for the range and dishwasher, which are installed next. Kitchen tile is installed after the kitchen cabinets and appliances have been installed; if it were installed sooner, it might not butt closely against the cabinets and appliances and it might also get marred. Bathroom tile follows the bathroom vanity for the same sort of reason. Since there appears to be no reason why the hood/fan and the hall tile should come either before or after the other tasks shown, they are drawn unlinked to the other tasks (but they would link to tasks not shown when the full network is constructed).

The rectangles, numbered (1), (2), and (3) in Figure 7–3B, are not essential. They merely show craft groupings. Later, when schedules are developed, each craft may develop Gantt charts to show when its project responsibilities occur. Note that it would serve no purpose to group all kitchen activities together, all bathroom activities together, and so forth; the kitchen is a room, but it is neither a product to be separately managed nor the responsibility of a separate craft.

FIGURE 7–4
Network for house construction

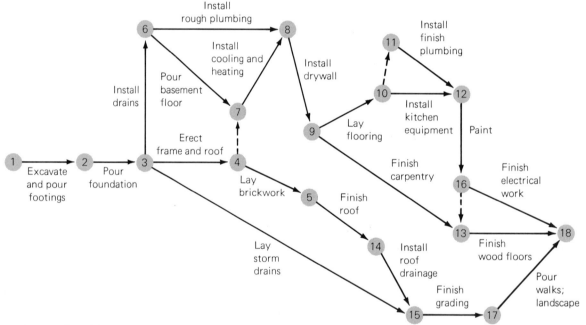

Source: Adapted from Jerome D. Wiest and Ferdinand K. Levy, *A Management Guide to PERT/CPM,* © 1969, p. 16. Reprinted by permission of Prentice-Hall, Inc., Englewood Cliffs, New Jersey.

Task lists and network segments are combined to form a whole-project network. Figure 7–4 is an example of a whole-project network. It is a continuation of the house-building example, but further simplified; for example, this house has no tile, carpets, or bathroom vanity.

Networking conventions

A few rules and conventions of networking may be mentioned:

1. *One destination.* A PERT/CPM network (except segments) has only one start event and one end event. (In Figure 7–4 these are numbered 1 and 18.) To bring this about, all arrows must progress toward the end, and there can be no doubling back, no loops, and no either-or options.[1] Figure 7–5 shows these three no-no's. In large networks it is not uncommon to make a few such errors inadvertently; for example, an arrowhead may be carelessly placed at the wrong end of a line. This results in entering event numbers into wrong data fields on computer records—if the network plan is computerized. Most PERT/CPM computer packages will detect such errors and print error messages.

2. *Event completion.* A network event (or node) signifies the completion of all activities (or arrows) leading into it. Furthermore, in PERT/CPM logic no activity may begin at an event until *all* activities leading into that event

FIGURE 7–5
Networking errors

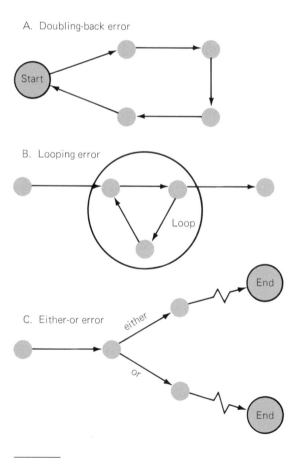

A. Doubling-back error

B. Looping error

C. Either-or error

---

[1] But these and other options *are* allowed in a PERT/CPM variation called GERT (*graphical evaluation and review technique*).

have been completed. For example, consider event 8 in Figure 7–4. If rough plumbing is installed and *inside* cooling and heating work is completed, it should be all right to install drywall, which is strictly inside work. But the network logic says no. An outside cooling compressor would be a part of activity 7–8, so event 8 includes it. The network must be drawn differently and the activities labeled differently if we prefer that drywall not depend on the completion of all cooling work.

3. *Dummy activity.* A dummy activity is a dashed arrow; it takes no time, and it consumes no resources. Four of the five dummies in Figure 7–3 merely connect subnetworks. They are not essential, and may be left out when the full network is drawn.

In Figure 7–4 two of the dummies are necessary for project logic. These are activities 4–7 and 16–13. Activity 4–7 is there in order to assure that both 3–4 and 6–7 precede 7–8 but that only 3–4 precedes 4–5. The logic is thus: You want cooling and heating to be installed on top of a basement floor (6–7) and through holes drilled in the frame (3–4). You want brickwork to go up against the frame (3–4), but it need not wait for a basement floor (6–7) to be poured. The dummy, 4–7, decouples the two merging and the two bursting activities to correctly show the logic. There is no other way to show it. Dummy activity 16–13 has the same sort of purpose.

Dummy activity 10–11 is there only to avoid confusing the computer—if the network is computerized. The problem is that two different activities occur between events 10 and 12. Most PERT/CPM computer packages identify activities and their direction by predecessor and successor event numbers. For example, the dummy activity 10–11 goes *from* 10 *to* 11. The computer knows this because the 10 is punched (or otherwise input) into a predecessor field and the 11 into a successor field in a record for that activity. (Each activity gets a separate record.) In Figure 7–4 an extra event, 11, and the resulting dummy activity, 10–11, assure that finish plumbing and kitchen equipment are uniquely numbered. Three equivalent ways to do this are shown in the accompanying illustration.

4. *Level of detail.* Every activity in Figure 12–4 could be divided into several subactivities. In fact, the activities could be subdivided all the way down to therbligs (basic hand and body motions), which would result in tens of thousands

of activities instead of the 24 shown. Besides the burden that more activities impose, there is no need to plan for a level of detail beyond what a manager would want to exercise control over. On the other hand, there should be enough detail to show when a given activity should precede another activity. The above explanation of dummies points out reasons of sequential logic for the level of detail shown in the example.

5. *Plan versus actual.* The network is only a plan. It is unlikely to be followed exactly. Maybe, for example, walks and landscapes will get poured (17–18 in Figure 7–4) *before* finished grading (15–17). Or maybe money will run out and finished grading will be cut from the project. Thus, the network is not an imperative, and it is not "violated" when it is not followed. The network is merely your best estimate of how you expect to do the project. Your best estimate is far better than no plan at all.

Alternative forms of networks

The original and most common form of the PERT/CPM network shows activities as arrows. Figure 7–3B and Figure 7–4 are of this type. The rationale is that an activity takes time, and a line or arrow tends to imply the passage of time. The circle before and after each arrow signifies an instant in time: the start or end of an activity. Alternative ways to draw and label networks follow:

1. *Activity-oriented networks.* The activity-on-node (AON) network is popular in some quarters. AON is a reversal of the usual activity-on-arrow (AOA) form. Figures 7–6A and 7–6B contrast AOA and AON. The advantage of AON is that it eliminates the need for dummy activities: Dummy 4–7 in Figure 7–6A does not appear in Figure 7–6B.

A disadvantage of AON is that it requires more computer inputs: The nine punched-card inputs shown in Figure 7–6B exceed the seven shown in Figure 7–6A. The reason is the need to show predecessor activities; each of the three merge activities—07, 08, and 10 in Figure 7–6B—has two predecessors, and therefore each takes two punched cards. The burden of extra computer inputs makes the AON form uneconomical in computerized PERT/CPM. But AON is convenient for learning purposes.

A final comment regarding Figure 7–6: The reader may discern that the computer keeps track of sequence by the fields that event numbers are punched into. For example, the computer will know that the dummy, 04–07, follows "Erect frame and roof," 03–04, because the 04 is punched in the second field on the latter card but in the first field on the former. Most PERT/CPM software therefore does not require that event numbers go from smaller to larger.

2. *Event-oriented networks.* Operating-level people are interested in actions, which we refer to as activities. Upper managers are more interested in completions, which we refer to as events. The event-oriented network is created from an activity-oriented network, and its purpose is to provide upper managers with a basis for reviewing project completions. Figure 7–7 shows two forms of event-oriented networks. Figure 7–7A is a portion of the construc-

tion project example expressed as an event-oriented network. Nodes are drawn large to hold event descriptions. Descriptions use present-tense verb forms in activity-oriented networks, but they use past-tense forms in event-oriented networks. For example, "Pour basement floor" in Figure 7–6 becomes "Basement floor poured" in Figure 7–7A. At merge points (nodes where two or more activities converge), the event description can get lengthy and cumber-

FIGURE 7–6
Activities and computer inputs

A. Activity-on-arrow network segment and computer inputs

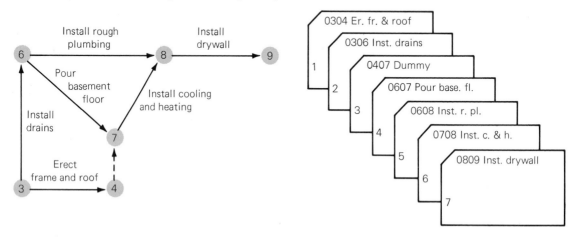

B. Activity-on-node network segment and computer inputs

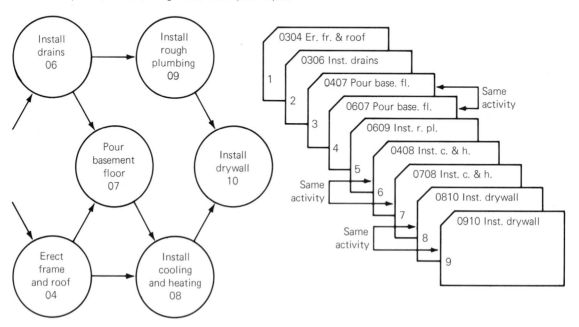

some. For example, the description at event 8 is "Rough plumbing, cooling, and heating installed."

Networks for larger projects may include tens or even hundreds of thousands of events. Upper-level managers surely do not care to review the project event by event. It is common instead to create a summary network for upper-management use. The summary network may be limited to certain key events, which may be called *milestones*. The large arrows from Figure 7–7A to Figure

FIGURE 7–7
Events and milestones

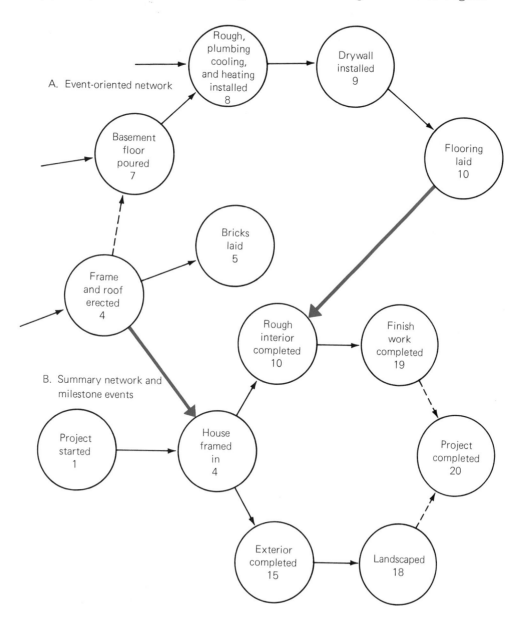

A. Event-oriented network

B. Summary network and milestone events

7–7B show how five events (4, 7, 8, 9, and 10) are condensed into two milestone events. Milestones are usually events that signify the end of major project stages. In house construction, the completion of framing and the completion of rough interior work tend to be recognized as major stages; these are milestones 4 and 10 in Figure 7–7B.

A certain amount of sequential accuracy is lost in condensing a network. For example, milestone event 4 subsumes events 2 and 3 (from Figure 7–4). But in cutting out event 3, two "branches" of the "tree" at that point—branches 3–6 and 3–15—are unceremoniously chopped off, as is shown in the accompanying illustration. From an upper-management perspective, however, the inaccuracy is of little concern.

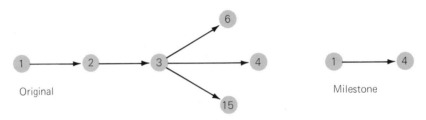

Original   Milestone

TIME-ESTIMATING AND PATH-ANALYSIS SUBSYSTEM

The time-estimating and path-analysis subsystem begins with estimates of the time required to complete each activity in the network. By adding time estimates from the beginning to the end of the network, the estimated project duration is determined. There are multiple paths through a given network, and each path may have a different total time.

Activity times

Accurate time estimating is more difficult for projects than for repetitive and job-shop operations because of project uncertainty and task variability. Engineered time standards are unlikely for project activities, except for activities that tend to recur from project to project. It is common for the project manager to obtain technical estimates from the managers and professionals who are in charge of given project activities. (A technical estimate is a type of historical, and nonengineered, time standard; see Chapter 8.)

The person who does the estimating tends to "pad" the estimate, because an overestimate is easier to achieve. In construction projects, usually enough prior experience and historical data are available to prevent estimators from getting away with gross padding of estimates.

Not so with research and development projects. In R&D a good many of the activities concern an advanced state of the art; historical benchmark data are scarce. Because of this, PERT, the R&D-oriented half of PERT/CPM, was originally outfitted with a special statistically based time-estimating procedure. PERT project managers asked not for one activity time estimate but for three: a most likely estimate, an optimistic estimate, and a pessimistic estimate. The chapter supplement explains the statistical method for *(a)* converting sets of three time estimates into most likely times and variances and *(b)* calculating the probability of completing any given event by a given date.

The apparent rationality of the statistical procedure has been confounded in practice by human behavioral problems. First of all, for an activity never done before, it is hard to pry one time estimate out of people, much less three. A request for three estimates may result in drawn-out discussion of the definitions of most likely, optimistic, and pessimistic. Second, many of the people who are called upon to give estimates for R&D activities are scientists, engineers, and other professionals; they tend to be strong-willed, and unafraid to withhold their cooperation. When ordered to provide three estimates, they may provide arbitrary and meaningless estimates like 5–10–15 or 8–10–12.

For these reasons, the PERT three-time-estimating procedure has apparently fallen into disuse. Today in both PERT and CPM a single best estimate is the norm, and best estimate is simply defined as how long the activity is expected to take under normal conditions and with normal resources.

In view of the practical problems with three time estimates, the main value of studying the chapter supplement may be that it can promote a better understanding of the R&D environment of uncertainty.

Path analysis

The path (or paths) that takes the most time is the *critical path*. That path is *time*-critical because a delay in completing any of its activities delays the whole project. A continuation of the house-construction example, as follows, serves to demonstrate path analysis.

EXAMPLE 7–3
Path analysis, house construction

The house-construction network of Figure 7–4 is reproduced in Figure 7–8. Time estimates, shown on each activity, have been added. Path durations are given below the network. Although this network is very small—for illustrative purposes—there are still 15 paths to add up. Computers are efficient at adding path times, and path-analysis subroutines are usually included in PERT/CPM software, which is widely available.

In the figure, path 12 is critical, at 34 days. It is shown by colored lines in the network. Several other paths—6, 7, 8, 9, 10, 11, 13, 14, and 15—are nearly critical, at 31 to 33 days. The critical-path and nearly-critical-path activities deserve close managerial attention. Other activities have *slack* or *float* time and need not be managed so closely. The more slack, the more flexibility there is for managers to schedule the activities.

Activity slack

Slack time may be explained by a continuation of the example, as follows.

EXAMPLE 7–4
Slack time, house construction

In Figure 7–8, paths 7, 11, and 14 take 33 days, or 1 day less than the critical path. This means that relative to the critical path, paths 7, 11, and 14 contain a day of slack (in PERT lingo) or float (in CPM lingo). The day of slack does not apply to the whole path, but rather to one or more path activities. Which ones? Consider path 7 first.

FIGURE 7-8: Path analysis

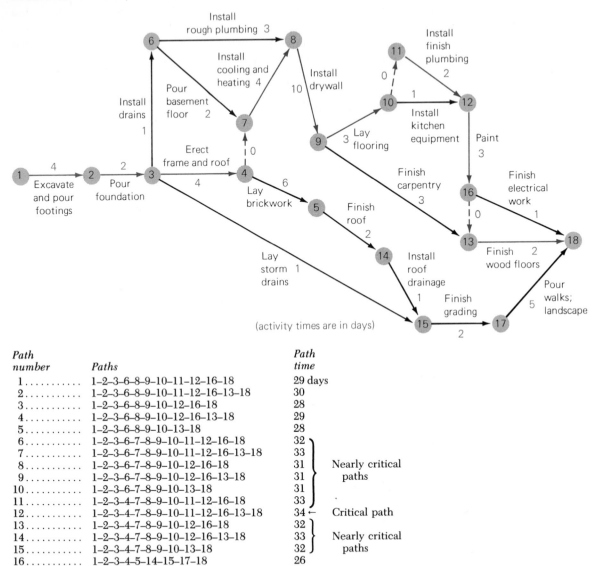

(activity times are in days)

Path number	Paths	Path time	
1	1–2–3–6–8–9–10–11–12–16–18	29 days	
2	1–2–3–6–8–9–10–11–12–16–13–18	30	
3	1–2–3–6–8–9–10–12–16–18	28	
4	1–2–3–6–8–9–10–12–16–13–18	29	
5	1–2–3–6–8–9–10–13–18	28	
6	1–2–3–6–7–8–9–10–11–12–16–18	32	Nearly critical paths
7	1–2–3–6–7–8–9–10–11–12–16–13–18	33	
8	1–2–3–6–7–8–9–10–12–16–18	31	
9	1–2–3–6–7–8–9–10–12–16–13–18	31	
10	1–2–3–6–7–8–9–10–13–18	31	
11	1–2–3–4–7–8–9–10–11–12–16–18	33	
12	1–2–3–4–7–8–9–10–11–12–16–13–18	34 ← Critical path	
13	1–2–3–4–7–8–9–10–12–16–18	32	Nearly critical paths
14	1–2–3–4–7–8–9–10–12–16–13–18	33	
15	1–2–3–4–7–8–9–10–13–18	32	
16	1–2–3–4–5–14–15–17–18	26	
17	1–2–3–15–17–18	14	

Path 7 is identical to critical path 12 except in the segment from event 3 to event 7. The critical-path segment from 3 to 4 to 7 takes four days; the slack-path segment from 3 to 6 to 7 takes three days. Activities 3–6 and 6–7 are said to have one day of slack. This means that 3–6 *or* 6–7 (but not both) could be delayed by one day without affecting the planned project duration. By similar reasoning, activity 16–18 on path 11 has a day of slack and activity 10–12 on path 14 has a day of slack.

Slack analysis is complicated when an activity is on more than one slack-path segment. Activity 3–6, for example, is on slack-path segments 3–6–7 and 3–6–8. Slack segment 3–6–8 takes four days, which compares with eight days for the critical-path segment 3–4–7–8. Thus it may seem that activities 3–6 and 6–8 have four days of slack and that either could be delayed four days without affecting the planned project duration. But we learned above that activity 3–6, on slack segment 3–6–7, may be delayed no more than one day. Slack on 3–6 is therefore one day, not four days; the larger value is rejected. Activity 6–8, however, does have four days of slack.

The logic of calculating slack by comparing slack-path segments with critical-path segments is relatively simple. It becomes tedious, however, for larger networks. An algorithm has been developed to avoid much of the tedium. The algorithm is demonstrated in Figure 7–9 for a portion of the house-construction example. The three-step calculation procedure is explained below for the positive-slack example of Figure 7–9A.

1. *Earliest start.* Beginning with the first event, earliest activity start times are determined in a *forward pass* through the network. In the figure, the project start time (event 1) is set equal to zero, and the earliest start (ES) for activity 1–2 is also zero. ES for each successive activity equals the previous ES plus the previous activity time, t. For activity 2–3, then, $ES = 0 + 4 = 4$; for activity 3–4, $ES = 4 + 2 = 6$; and so forth.

2. *Latest start.* Beginning with the final event, the latest activity start times are determined in a *backward pass* through the network. In the figure, the project due date at event 8 is set equal to 14, the critical-path time. The latest start (LS) for each preceding activity equals the last LS minus the preceding activity time, t. For activity 4–7, then, $LS = 10 - 0 = 10$; for activity 3–4, $LS = 10 - 4 = 6$; and so forth.

3. *Slack.* Slack for each activity simply equals LS − ES. In Figure 7–9A slack is 4 for activity 6–8, 1 for activities 6–7 and 3–6, and 0 for each of the critical-path activities.[2]

Negative slack

If LS is less than ES, negative slack results. Negative slack means that the activity is late. Not only is this possible, but it is almost the norm—at least for critical-path activities. It is rare enough for projects to be on time that *The Wall Street Journal* published a front-page story some years ago with headlines proclaiming that a certain large construction project was completed on time. (The project was the domed stadium in Pontiac, Michigan, which also met targeted costs!)

Figure 7–9B illustrates negative slack. What produces the negative slack is an earlier due date, day 11 instead of day 14. For activity 7–8, $LS = 11 - 4 = 7$; slack $= LS - ES = 7 - 10 = -3$. Each of the other critical-path activities also has a slack of −3, which means that the project is three days late while still in the planning stage. The network plan could be changed to make the

---

[2] *Event* slack may be computed by a similar procedure. Instead of using ES and LS for each activity, event slack is based on T_E and T_L for each event. T_E stands for time earliest (to complete the event) and T_L stands for time latest. Event slack $= T_L - T_E$.

FIGURE 7–9
Calculating
activity slack

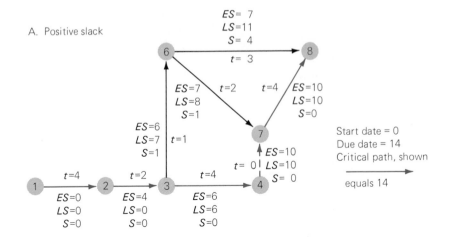

A. Positive slack

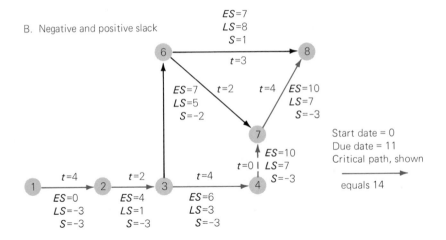

B. Negative and positive slack

planned completion time equal the due date, or the project could start out three days late in the hope of catching up.

Slack-sort computer listing

Computer assistance is important in the path-analysis stage of PERT/CPM. The most common computer output is a slack-sorted list of all project activities. An example follows.

EXAMPLE 7–5
Slack-sort
computer
listing, house
construction

Figure 7–10 is an abbreviated example of a slack-sort computer listing. Least-slack activities are listed first in sequential order. Critical-path activities have the least slack and therefore appear first; next-most-critical activities, usually from more than one path, appear next; and so on. In the figure a space separates each group of activities having common slack times. Bottommost activities are least critical; the last one, activity 3–15, has +17 days of slack, which means that it may be delayed by 17 days without affecting the project due date.

FIGURE 7–10
Computer listing
for path analysis

Slack-Sorted Activity Report

Activity number	Description	Time	Earliest start	Latest start	Activity slack
1–2	Excavate, pour footings	4	0	−3	−3
2–3	Pour foundation	2	4	1	−3
3–4	Erect frame and roof	4	6	3	−3
4–7	Dummy	0	10	7	−3
.	.	.	.	.	.
.	.	.	.	.	.
.	.	.	.	.	.
13–18	Lay flooring	2	32	29	−3
3–6	Install drains	1	6	4	−2
6–7	Pour basement floor	2	7	5	−2
10–12	Install kitchen equipment	1	27	25	−2
16–18	Finish electrical work	1	32	30	−2
10–13	Finish carpentry	3	27	26	−1
.	.	.	.	.	.
.	.	.	.	.	.
.	.	.	.	.	.
15–17	Finish grading	2	19	24	+5
17–18	Pour walks and landscape	5	21	26	+5
3–15	Lay storm drains	1	6	23	+17

(Activities 1–2 through 13–18 bracketed as) Critical path

The slack-sorted computer listing is more convenient for managerial use than a network. Indeed, most managers rely on this type of listing[3] and never need to see a network.

Network simulation

As we have seen, the critical path is easily computed by successive path-time addition. Unfortunately the procedure considers each path as if it were independent of all other paths. It fails to allow for probabilistic time variation and its cascading effects on multiple paths and the project duration. It is easy to prove by Monte Carlo simulation that the deterministic critical-path time understates the likely project duration.[4] Figure 7–11 illustrates.

The figure presents the simplest possible project network: two activities occurring together. (A single activity is a job; multiple simultaneous activities seem to be a key distinguishing feature of a project.) In Figure 7–11A both

---

[3] Often the listing is event- rather than activity-oriented; for example, instead of earliest- and latest-start activity times (ES and LS) there will be time-earliest and time-latest event times (T_E and T_L).

[4] An explanation is given in A. R. Klingel, Jr., "Bias in PERT Project Completion Time Calculations for a Real Network," *Management Science*, vol. 13, no. 4 (December 1966), pp. B–194–201.

FIGURE 7-11
Effects of
variable activity
times on project
duration

A. 5-day project

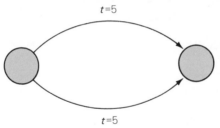

B. 5.4-day project

$t=4$, 5, or 6; equal (1/3) probabilities

$t=4$, 5, or 6; equal (1/3) probabilities

Possible time combinations

	Top path	*Bottom path*	*Project duration*
1	4	4	4
2	4	5	5
3	5	4	5
4	5	5	5
5	4	6	6
6	5	6	6
7	6	6	6
8	6	5	6
9	6	4	6

Mean = 5.4 days

paths are critical at five days, so it is a five-day project. In Figure 7–11B the mean or expected task time on each path is still five days. Yet, as the table shows, the simulated mean project duration is 5.4 days. In the Figure 7–11 table the variability—three, four, and five days—is simulated by considering all time combinations and allowing equal chances for each time value on each path. For each combination the higher path time is the project duration, which pushes the expected (mean) project duration up to 5.4 days.

If more variability is added, the expected project duration increases further. For example, if path time is 3, 4, 5, 6, or 7, each equally probable, expected duration is 5.8 days. If more paths are added, expected project duration also goes up. As a general rule, then, the fatter the network and the more variable the activity times, the greater the project duration is in excess of the deterministic critical-path time. This provides a mathematical explanation of why projects tend to be late.

Since the critical path understates reality, why is is widely used? The key reason is that path addition is simple and inexpensive, whereas Monte Carlo simulation is costly. A second reason is that Monte Carlo simulation is more difficult to understand. A third reason is that activity time estimates are rough anyway, and there are diminishing returns from applying increased analytical rigor to rough data. A fourth reason is that it is difficult to know what to do with simulated network data. Do you add a percentage to each estimated activity time? If so, then perhaps those new times should be inputs to another round of simulation. Where would these rounds of simulation end?

The question will be left unanswered. The point to be made here is that project managers should be aware that the critical path understates reality.

PROJECT SCHEDULING SUBSYSTEM

Path analysis reveals how long the project is expected to take using normal resources. But forward scheduling may yield a project completion date that is too late. Upper management may elect to spend more on resources to cut the expected project duration. Numerous combinations of cost and time are possible. A time-cost trade-off procedure for analyzing these combinations is discussed in this section. After the time-cost issue is settled, activities may be scheduled; project and work-center scheduling are also considered in this section.

"Crashing" the network

Expected project duration may be reduced by spending more on resources. The extra expenditures for resources must be applied to critical-path activities if project duration is to be reduced or "crashed." As time is cut on the critical path, new critical paths may emerge. The cost to cut more time from the project may then involve extra resource costs to reduce activity times on multiple paths. The analysis can get complicated.

If resource costs are inconvenient to collect, the choice of which critical-path activity to crash is not clear-cut. Crashing an early activity on the critical path may seem wise, because the reduction will apply to other paths that could become critical later; but money spent early is gone. The opposite wait-and-see approach seems wise for another reason: Perhaps some critical-path activities will be completed earlier than expected, thus averting the need to crash at all; but if that does not happen, late options for crashing may be few and costly.

Time-cost trade-off analysis

When it is convenient to collect resource costs, a technique known as time-cost trade-off analysis may be used. The technique is explained in an example, as follows.

EXAMPLE 7–6
Time-cost
trade-off
analysis

A small network and related time and cost data are shown in Figure 7–12. The critical path is B–D–E, eight days long. The cost for that eight-day project is shown to be $390. This plan need not be accepted. There is the possibility of spending more money—for extra shifts, airfreight, and so on—to reduce the time required to complete various tasks. For example, activity A costs $50 to do in three days (normal), $75 to do in two days (paying for overtime perhaps), and $100 to do in one day (paying still more, perhaps for extra shifts).[5] The linear assumption—$25 for each day reduced—may be somewhat erroneous, but it is generally accurate enough for planning purposes.

FIGURE 7–12
Network and
time-cost data

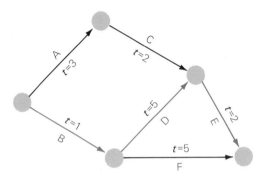

(critical path ⟶ is B-D-E at 8 days)

	Normal		Crash		
Activity	Time	Cost	Time	Cost	Cost per day
A.	3	$ 50	1	$100	$25
B.	1	40	1	40	—
C.	2	40	1	80	40
D	5	100	3	160	30
E.	2	70	1	160	90
F	5	90	2	300	70
		$390			

Source: Adapted from Fred Luthans, *Introduction to Management: A Contingency Approach* (Richard J. Schonberger, contributing author) (McGraw-Hill, 1976) (HD31.L86), p. 378. Used with permission.

The method of calculating average cost per day may be expressed as a formula:

$$\text{Cost per day} = \frac{\text{Crash cost} - \text{Normal cost}}{\text{Normal time} - \text{Crash time}}$$

For activity A, the calculation is:

$$\frac{\$100 - \$50}{3 \text{ days} - 1 \text{ day}} = \frac{\$50}{2 \text{ days}} = \$25 \text{ per day}$$

---

[5] The normal and crash costs are often engineering estimates or managers' estimates based on current known standard costs; a careful cost accounting estimate may not be necessary. Also, the cost estimates may be incremental costs rather than full costs.

Cost per day for each of the other activities is calculated the same way. Activity B cannot be crashed and thus does not have a cost-per-day entry.

The question is, If it costs $390 to do the project in eight days, what would it cost to do it in seven? If you pick the lowest total in the cost-per-day column, $25 for A, you are wrong. Spending $25 more on A would reduce A from three days to two days. But it would not affect the eight-day projection duration. A critical-path activity—B, D, or E—must be selected. B is out because its crash time is no better than its normal time. The choice between D and E favors D—at an extra cost of $30, as opposed to $90 for E. Thus, doing the project in seven days requires $30 more, for a total cost of $420.

The next step is to try two days' reduction. But the above reduction of D to four days results in two critical paths, B–D–E and A–C–E, both seven days long. Reducing the project duration to six days is possible by crashing A and D together at a cost of $55, D and C together at $70, or E alone at $90. The first option is cheapest, and it is selected, bringing the total project cost up to $475.

Next try three days' reduction. After the above step, all paths are critical at six days. The only choice (since B and D are already crashed to their minimum times) is to crash E and F by one day. The added cost is $160, with a total project cost of $635. No further reductions in times are possible since the B–D–E path is fully crashed.

If this were a construction project with a penalty of $100 for every day beyond a six-day project duration, then alternative 3 below would be most desirable in terms of total project costs:

Alternative	Time	Construction cost	Penalty cost	Total cost	
1	8 days	$390	$200	$590	
2	7	420	100	520	
3	6	475	0	475	← Minimum
4	5	635	0	635	

Time-cost trade-off analysis was developed as a part of CPM in the construction-project setting. It remains more suitable for construction projects than for R&D projects. One reason is that construction costs and perhaps times tend to be more accurately estimated than R&D costs and times. The cost per day to crash is thus more meaningful in construction projects. The practice of using late penalties in construction contracts is further reason why time-cost trade-off analysis tends to be associated with construction and CPM.

Event scheduling

The final step after a time-cost alternative has been selected is to put dates on each event in the final network. Dating is based on the final activity times, allowing appropriate time off for holidays and weekends. Dating, as well as the trade-off analysis itself, may be done by a computer. Most computer vendors offer software to compute workdays from calendar days; such event-dating subroutines are usually available in PERT/CPM programs. A card identifying the planned date of the first event is input, and the program computes the rest. The resulting computer listing will usually show time-earliest (T_E) and time-latest (T_L) to complete each event, and event slack $(T_L - T_E)$ will be listed in another column.

FIGURE 7-13
Decomposition
of network
activities into
work-center
schedules

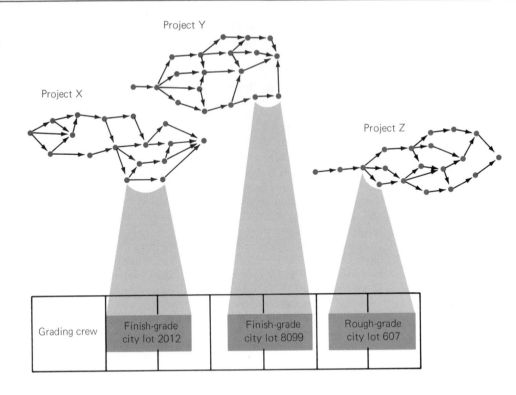

Each subcontractor, department, or work center that is involved in a given project is also likely to be involved in other projects, jobs, and perhaps repetitive operations. The focus of attention is on how their activities in multiple projects fit together.

Figure 7–13 graphically illustrates this concern. The work center, a grading crew, has developed a Gantt chart showing three upcoming activities that are on the PERT/CPM networks for three different projects. The figure helps make the point that the goals of project managers and work-center managers sometimes conflict. The work-center manager strives for high utilization of capacity, but this may conflict with the timing of work-center activities on project managers' networks. The project manager strives to get work crews to the job according to PERT/CPM schedules, but work crews are frequently wanted by more than one project manager at the same time. These conflicts are resolved mostly by compromise, although some multiproject-scheduling computer software exists. In most cases tasks can be scheduled earlier or later within available slack-time limits. This meets the needs of the project manager and also helps spread the work more evenly on the work-center manager's Gantt chart. The tasks that appear on a critical path do not have flexibility for rescheduling and thus are most apt to cause conflict.

REPORTING AND UPDATING SUBSYSTEM

PERT/CPM management may be applied in the project control phase as well as in project planning. PERT/CPM control centers on periodic reports. The reporting periods are generally every two weeks or once a month.

Reporting

Figure 7–14 shows a typical reporting scheme. The partial network at the top of the figure divides into monthly reporting periods. At the end of each reporting period event-completion data are forwarded to the project management office, where they are prepared for entry into the computer. In Figure 7–14, the current month is February and February-planned events 1, 2, 3, 5, and 6 have been completed. A card is punched for each; on the first card, for example, an 01 is punched in the event field and the completion date—020482, for February 4, 1982—is punched in another field.

Event 4 was scheduled for February, but no notice of completion has been received. Instead, an activity reestimate notice is received; the first activity reestimate card has the activity 03–04 punched in the key field, and 21 (days) is the new time estimate punched in another field. That reestimate pertains to why event 4 has not been completed: Event 3, completed on February 12, plus 21 days for activity 3–4, pushes the planned completion date for event 4 into March. Future activities may also be reestimated, as 08–10 has been in Figure 7–14.

Updating

With event completions and activity reestimates as inputs, the PERT/CPM network is updated by the computer. A new slack-sort report is produced. It shows the new slack status of each activity. The report is like the report shown in Figure 7–10, but it is more likely to be event- and date-oriented; it may be used to inform all parties what the new project schedule is for all events. Other reports may be printed—for example, a report listing activities by work center (or department or subcontractor); various resource, budget, and cost reports; and summary (milestone) reports for upper managers. Some of the reports get wide distribution, and in some firms those responsible for activities completed late are called upon to explain why.

Replanning is inherent to control. It is possible to redo the time-cost trade-off analysis each month after the network has been updated, using event-completion data and activity reestimates. Without this analysis, the computer will replan (reschedule) all events anyway, but without considering the possibility of using more or less resources on given activities.

Another major type of replanning is altering the network. Activities may be added or subtracted, and sequence may be changed. All that is required is adding, removing, or repunching a few cards. The ease of making such changes is a key asset of PERT/CPM, because project uncertainty demands planning flexibility.

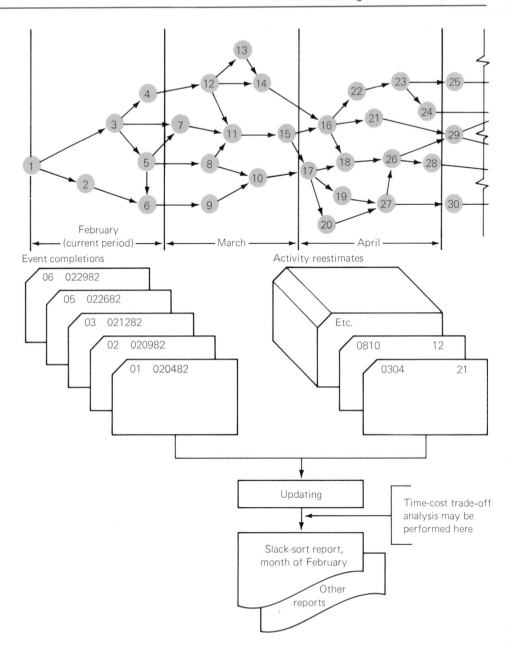

FIGURE 7-14
PERT/CPM
periodic
reporting

USES AND MISUSES OF PERT/CPM

PERT/CPM is, like many management techniques, expensive. Fully computerized PERT/CPM may eat up an additional 1 or 2 or 3 percent of the total project cost, because it is not a replacement for conventional management. Conventional forecasting, scheduling, inventory control, quality control, budgeting, and so forth, are still performed in each functional area (e.g., department or work center). A project management group and PERT/CPM systems hardware and software expenses are additional. PERT/Cost, considered next, is even more expensive than ordinary PERT/CPM. Following the discussion of PERT/Cost is a section on the PERT/CPM environment and suitable reaction to it.

PERT/Cost

In the early 1960s a PERT extension known as PERT/Cost was tried in the Department of Defense (DoD) and the National Aeronautics and Space Administration (NASA). In PERT/Cost, cost as well as time estimates are made for each activity; actual cost and time data are collected as project activities are done, and cost as well as time variances are reported. But the cost side of PERT/Cost generally proved to be unacceptably expensive to administer, because it required a new and additional bookkeeping system. PERT/Cost may yet be resurrected—if the bookkeeping burden can be eased somehow. But the DoD and NASA abandoned PERT/Cost long ago, and probably few other organizations use it today, except in diluted forms.[6]

PERT/CPM environment

Some organizations have tried out and abandoned ordinary PERT/CPM as well, because it seemed not to pay for itself. In some such cases the problem is trying to apply full computerized PERT/CPM to small-scale projects. Figure 7–15 reemphasizes a point partially made early in the chapter: that PERT/CPM consists of several distinct and separable subsystems. The figure further suggests that only projects that are grand in scope warrant the full PERT/CPM treatment. At the other extreme, projects of modest scope seem to justify the expense of only the first subsystem.

Project scope is expressed in Figure 7–15 in terms of four characteristics: size, uncertainty, urgency, and complexity. Size and urgency are self-explanatory. Project uncertainty is of two types:

Task uncertainty—doubts about what is to be done.

Time uncertainty—doubts about activity time estimates.

Similarly, complexity may be thought of in two ways:

Organizational complexity—numerous organizations involved in the project.

Activity complexity—numerous activities in progress at the same time.

To illustrate the model in the figure, consider the kinds of construction projects managed by a typical Army Corps of Engineers district: dams, man-made lakes, dredging, channel straightening, levees, bridges, and riverbank

---

[6] PERT/Cost should not be confused with time-cost trade-off analysis. In the latter, costs are estimated for scheduling purposes only. But PERT/Cost includes a full range of accounting: budgeting, cost accounting, and cost-variance reporting.

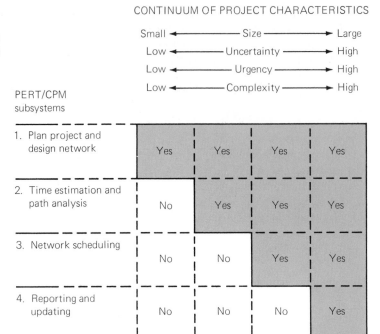

FIGURE 7–15
Matching PERT/
CPM subsystems
to project scope

CONTINUUM OF PROJECT CHARACTERISTICS

Small ◄─────── Size ────────► Large
Low ◄─────── Uncertainty ───────► High
Low ◄─────── Urgency ───────► High
Low ◄─────── Complexity ───────► High

PERT/CPM
subsystems

1. Plan project and design network	Yes	Yes	Yes	Yes
2. Time estimation and path analysis	No	Yes	Yes	Yes
3. Network scheduling	No	No	Yes	Yes
4. Reporting and updating	No	No	No	Yes

stabilization, to name a few. Perhaps 100 projects are in progress at a given time.

A project like a major dam may be only moderately urgent and uncertain, but it is likely to be very large and complex. In sum, the project characteristics seem to be far enough to the right in Figure 12–15 to warrant full computer-based PERT/CPM, including all four subsystems (four yeses in the figure). Without computer-based scheduling, reporting, and control, coordinating the many concurrent activities of the numerous participating organizations might be chaotic.

Most bridge-construction jobs are much smaller and less complex. For such intermediate-scope projects the project engineer should probably design networks, conduct path analysis, and perhaps use the computer to schedule project events, which may include time-cost trade-off analysis (two or three yeses). But subsystem 4, reporting and updating, may not be warranted. It is the most expensive subsystem to administer—it probably costs a lot more than subsystems 1, 2, and 3 combined; a typical bridge is not so urgent as to require the tight time controls of subsystem 4.

Channeling and riverbank stabilization projects are still less urgent, and they are not often large, complex, or uncertain. The project engineer may expend a small amount of time, effort, and cost to accomplish subsystem 1, designing PERT/CPM networks (one yes, left column of the figure). The benefits—seeing who has to do what and in what order—are large for the modest cost. There seems to be little reason to perform path analysis and the other subsystems.

In R&D projects the model seems equally valid. Designing a major aircraft, such as a Boeing 747, is a project of massive scope—and urgency as well, in view of the capital that it ties up. Full PERT/CPM is easily justified. Redesign of a wing for an existing aircraft is a modest project; subsystem 1 may be sufficient.

The good sense of this situational approach to employing PERT/CPM subsystems may be clear. Nevertheless, there are organizations that have viewed PERT/CPM in only one way: as a single, indivisible system to be used for every project. Disappointment is likely.

LINE-OF-BALANCE ANALYSIS

Line-of-balance (LOB) analysis is useful in controlling

> repetitive production of a
> limited quantity of a
> large-scale item.

A project does not qualify, for a project involves production of only one unit of a large-scale item. Neither does repetitive production qualify, because in LOB analysis the quantity is limited. Limited quantity is in the range of, say, 25 to 400 units. If the quantity were smaller, the production run might be over before the LOB reporting system were fully operational. If the quantity were in excess of 400, production control would normally settle into a standardized routine, as in mass production.

It is the intermediate-quantity realm that may benefit from the special management control that LOB can exert over large-scale items. Good examples are aircraft, missiles, ships, large boats, tanks, earth-moving equipment, large dynamos, and large generators. Delivery schedules for such items are generally time-phased over a period of months.

There are four steps in LOB analysis:

1. *Objective.* A graphic time-phased cumulative delivery schedule constitutes the objective.
2. *Process plan.* The second step, the process plan, shows the total sequence (for a single unit) in the form of control points on a lead-time chart.
3. *Progress.* The third step, which is performed each reporting period, is plotting progress on a bar chart for each control point and against the objective.
4. *Line of balance.* The line of balance, which is calculated each reporting period, shows the cumulative quantities required to date to meet the objective (schedule) in the future. The "line" indicates the "balance" quantity. The line (or line of balance) is plotted on top of the bars on the progress chart, and discrepancies are studied to determine how to catch up.

LOB example

The example below explains the LOB method.

EXAMPLE 7-7
Line-of-balance analysis, solar power generators

Solesource, Inc., has been awarded a federal energy agency contract for 50 of a new type of solar power generator. The contract calls for deliveries over five months, as shown in Figure 7–16A. The cumulative delivery schedule is curved: The increasing rate allows for increased production efficiency as the contract moves forward (the learning-curve idea).

The process plan for producing one solar generator is shown in Figure 7–16B. There are nine *control points*, that is, completion points, to be monitored. The process plan is based on the manufacturing engineers' best estimates. The total process time for one unit is 24 working days. The first activity, "Fabricate gyro," takes 10 days—from 24 days (at control point 1) to 14 days (at control point 5) prior to shipment. (Lead time for acquiring gyro parts is not included in the lead-time chart; material deliveries are assumed to be no problem.) Each of the other activity times is also defined as the time between control points.

Figure 7–16C shows the status of the nine control points as of June 30. Such a status report is developed each month, beginning with April 30. The only conclusion that may be safely drawn from the bar chart alone is whether the final control point, 9, is on schedule. The bar for point 9 is at 16 units; a check on the cumulative delivery schedule, Figure 7–16A, reveals that 15 are due, so shipments are slightly ahead of schedule.

This is not a complete picture. Shipments may be slightly ahead, yet other control points may be far ahead or far behind. The final step, laying down the line of balance, is necessary to show the status of the other control points.

Figure 7–17 shows the LOB laid on top of the bars. The LOB height is determined graphically. The graphic method is demonstrated in the figure for control points 6 and 7. Both have nine days' lead time (see Figure 7–16B). Therefore, June 30 performance for those control points has its impact on the delivery schedule nine workdays into July. The vertical arrow in Figure 7–17 intersects the cumulative delivery schedule as of the ninth July workday. The point of intersection, 20 units, is the quantity that should be done today, June 30, at control points 6 and 7 in order to have 20 ready for shipment on the ninth workday of July. That amount, 20, is the proper height of the line of balance at points 6 and 7.

Each of the other LOB heights is calculated in the same way. (If the delivery schedule were a straight line, the LOB could be calculated by an easy algebraic procedure instead of graphically.)

Each month the officers at Solesource review progress on the solar-generator contract. The LOB chart is displayed at the monthly review meeting, and it serves as the focal point for discussion.

At the July 1 meeting the LOB of Figure 7–17 is displayed. The contract administrator points out the following to the officers:

1. Shipments, control point 9, are slightly ahead of schedule.
2. The solar subassembly, control points 1, 2, 5, and 6, is on or ahead of schedule.
3. Casting of the housing, control points 3 and 4, is ahead of schedule, but machining of the castings, control point 7, is behind.
4. Final assembly, control point 8, is a bit behind schedule. In fact, there are the same number of final assemblies completed (16) as there are shipments, even though four days of testing are required between final assembly and shipment.

FIGURE 7–16
Delivery
schedule and
lead-time chart,
solar power
generator

A. Cumulative delivery schedule

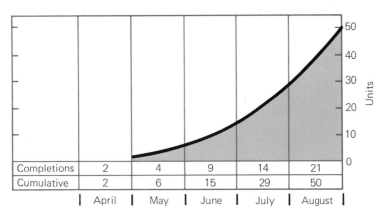

Completions	2	4	9	14	21
Cumulative	2	6	15	29	50

April   May   June   July   August

B. Process plan

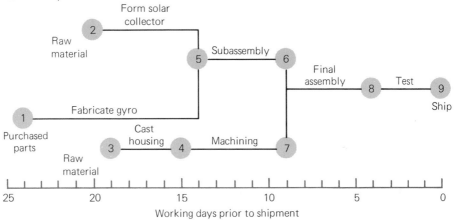

Form solar
collector

Raw
material

2

Subassembly

5   6

Final
assembly

8   Test   9

Ship

1   Fabricate gyro

Purchased
parts

Raw
material

Cast
housing

3   4   Machining   7

Working days prior to shipment

25   20   15   10   5   0

C. Progress as of June 30

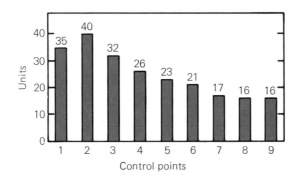

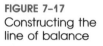

FIGURE 7–17
Constructing the line of balance

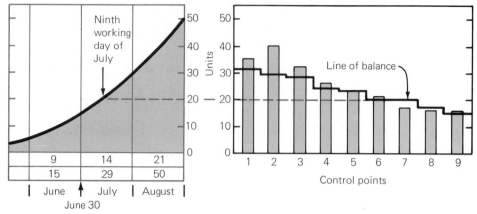

Cumulative delivery schedule

Progress and line of balance as of June 30

It is clear to the officers that a potentially serious problem has arisen in machining. Castings are ahead of schedule, but the castings are not being machined on time. Furthermore, it appears that lack of machined castings is the reason why final assemblies have fallen behind schedule.

Two actions are needed to deal with the problem. One is investigation to find out the cause of the machining delay. The second action, which depends on what is learned in the investigation, is to get machining and final assembly back on schedule. Overtime, hiring, expediting, or other actions may be taken. A more extreme measure is to change the process plan to provide more lead time for machining.

LOB advantages

In the LOB technique there are usually more control points than in the above simplified example. With more control points the periodic review pinpoints problem areas more precisely. Two special advantages of LOB analysis are suggested by the example:

1. *LOB is simple and inexpensive.* The graphic simplicity makes LOB effective for management review meetings. Little effort and cost are needed to update the bar charts and construct the line of balance each month.

2. *LOB is future-oriented* (unlike most periodic reporting methods). A discrepancy between the LOB and the bar for a given control point is not a problem today; instead, it points to upcoming contract delivery problems if action is not taken now to get the earlier activity back on schedule. LOB analysis is aimed at forestalling future contract delivery failures.

SUMMARY

The program evaluation and review technique (PERT) and the critical path method (CPM) are useful in planning and controlling projects. Both are based on a type of sequence chart called a network.

PERT/CPM consists of four subsystems: designing the network, path analysis, scheduling, and reporting and updating. Designing the network begins with planning project goals; the project plan may be displayed as a work breakdown structure (WBS). Task lists are then drawn up and arranged into networks. Networks may be activity-oriented for lower managerial use or event-oriented for high-level managers.

Time estimates may be collected for each network activity. Activity times for each of the various paths through the network may be added up, and the sum for the most time-consuming path—called the *critical path*—is the estimated project duration. Path analysis also includes determining slack for each activity. Slack is the amount that an activity may be delayed without making the whole project late. Negative slack is possible, and in fact is common, especially on the critical path.

The project scheduling subsystem is aimed at determining due dates for each network event. If forward scheduling yields a late project completion time, certain activities may be "crashed." Crashing (cutting activity time) is done by spending more for resources, for example, overtime. Combinations of project times and costs may be produced via time-cost trade-off analysis. One time-cost alternative is selected, and the selected times are the basis for scheduling network events. Finally, organizations having a role in various projects must fit the scheduled project due dates so that their capacities are not overloaded.

The reporting and updating subsystem may come into play after the work begins. Reports are usually monthly or every two weeks. A basic report displays slack time for each activity, and the report is arranged to list most critical activities first, then next-most-critical activities, and so forth. The reports are valuable for replanning and rescheduling.

The four PERT/CPM subsystems are increasingly costly. All four should be used only if project size, uncertainty, urgency, and complexity are sufficient to justify the cost.

Line-of-balance (LOB) analysis applies only to limited-quantity large-scale production, for example, a contract for 80 ballistic missiles. LOB analysis begins with a cumulative delivery schedule and a process plan in the form of a lead-time chart. Then, as the project progresses, line-of-balance charts are produced at periodic intervals, often monthly. A bar chart showing units completed for each control point on the process plan is developed, and the line of balance is laid on top of the bars. The line of balance, for a given control point, equals the cumulative deliveries that the contract calls for, LT (lead time for that control point) days into the future. Thus, the LOB shows future contract impacts of present progress. Discrepancies between the height of the LOB and the bars suggest the need for investigation and corrective action.

REFERENCES

Books

Harris, Robert B. *Precedence and Arrow Networking Techniques for Construction.* Wiley, 1978 (TH438.H37).

Moder, Joseph J., and Cecil R. Phillips. *Project Management with CPM and PERT.* 2d ed. Van Nostrand Reinhold, 1970 (T56.8.M63).

O'Brien, James Jerome. *CPM in Construction Management: Project Management with CPM.* 2d ed. McGraw-Hill, 1971 (HD9715.A202).

Wiest, Jerome D., and Ferdinand K. Levy. *A Management Guide to PERT/CPM.* Prentice-Hall, 1969 (T57.85.W5).

Periodicals (societies)

Project Management Quarterly (Project Management Institute); sometimes cataloged as a monograph series (HD69.P75p76) instead of a periodical.

PROBLEMS

Note: **Asterisked (*) problems require more than mimicry. They require judgment, and you should include discussion of reasons, assumptions, and outside sources of information.**

Work breakdown structure

*1. Develop a product-oriented work breakdown structure for a nonconstruction project of your own choice. (Examples are a market research project, a political campaign, a disaster-relief project, a research and development project, and a large-scale computer-based information system development.) You may need to speculate about the nature of your chosen project—since most of us have little actual experience in large projects. In addition to drawing the WBS, explain the nature of your project. Show part of at least three levels on your WBS.

WBS, task lists, and network

2. The R&D group of Home Products Company (HOPROCO) is developing a prototype for a new gasoline-powered lawn mower. The project is to be managed using PERT/CPM. Project activities include all design, manufacturing, and testing

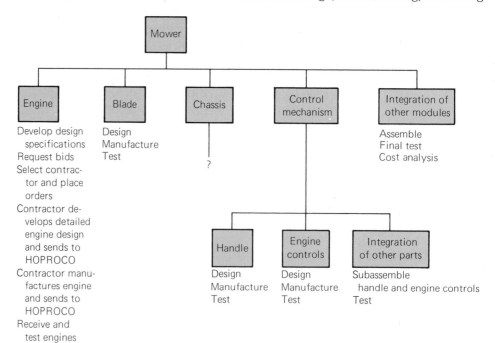

for the single prototype mower. The mower engine is to be designed and made by another firm, an engine manufacturer. All other major modules are to be designed and made by HOPROCO's own employees.

a. A partial WBS and task lists are shown for the mower. One module, the chassis, has not been broken down into major parts and task lists. Your first assignment is to do this. You must decide, as best you can, what major parts the chassis would need to include. Then decide on tasks for each major part. Notice that the WBS is product-oriented, except for an integration activity whenever there is a need to combine other modules or parts.

b. Some of the beginning and ending activities for the mower project are shown as a partial PERT/CPM network in the accompanying illustration. Network activities are taken from the task lists in the WBS. Your second assignment is to complete the network. (Note: Engine-design data are needed before certain HOPROCO tasks can begin. You must reason where this is the case and draw the network that way.)

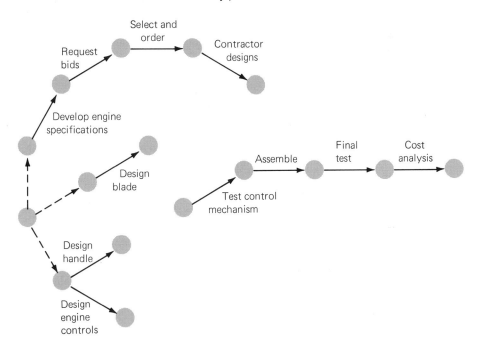

c. Some of the dummy activities in your network are not needed. Redraw portions of the network to show the elimination of all unnecessary dummy activities.

Dummy activity

3. Explain the purpose of activity 16–13 in Figure 7–4.

Networks

4. You and several others have been appointed as a planning committee by the president of your social organization. It has been decided that in order to obtain

additional funds for operating expenses you will produce a play (or a variety show). You have been asked to submit a plan for the next meeting. This plan is to include all of the activities or tasks that will have to be accomplished up to the opening of the play. Publicity, tickets, the printed program, and so on, as well as the staging for the production, should be part of the plan. It has already been decided that the scenery will be constructed in a member's garage and that the costumes will be rented.

To facilitate presentation of the plan, a network diagram of about 30 activities is to be drawn. Brief descriptions of the activities should appear on the network diagram.

AON and AOA network forms

5. A manufacturer of tape and record players buys turntables from outside contractors. A new contract is to be awarded for a new style of turntable. The company has developed an activity-on-node network for the turntable project. The accompanying network includes an initial contract for turntable development and a second contract (assuming that the turntable tests are OK) for production.

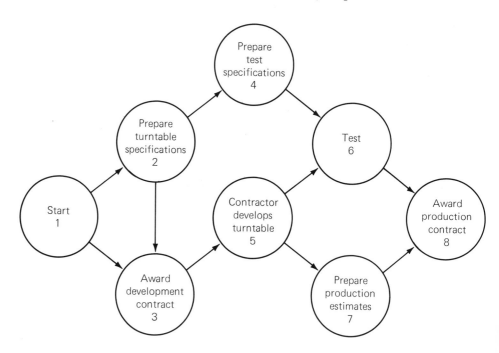

   a. Redraw the network in the activity-on-arrow form.
   b. List the activity numbers for every punch card needed for each network form. What are the total numbers of punch cards for each of the forms?

Networks and path analysis

6. The manager for a project to develop a special antenna system is preparing a PERT-based project plan. Data for the plan are given below:

		Expected time (days)
Activity number	*Description*	
1–2	Design frame	4
1–3	Procure mechanism	5
2–4	Procure parts	1
3–4	Dummy	
3–7	Determine repair requirements	4
4–6	Assemble	2
4–7	Hire maintenance crew	
6–7	Test	1

    a. Draw the network.

    b. Enter your own *reasonable* expected times in the two empty spaces (for activities 3–4 and 4–7). Compute and indicate the critical path.

    c. Compute slack times for all activities, assuming that the project is scheduled for completion in the number of days on the critical path.

    d. Five working days have passed, and status data have been received, as follows:

        (1) Activity 1–2 was completed in five days.

        (2) Activity 1–3 was completed in four days.

        (3) Activity 4–6 has been reestimated at four days.

        Based on the data, recompute the critical path and slack on all of the remaining project activities.

Paths, milestones, and periodic reporting

7. Aeropa, Inc., has a contract to develop a guided missile. A PERT/CPM network and activity times are given in the accompanying illustration. Times are in weeks.

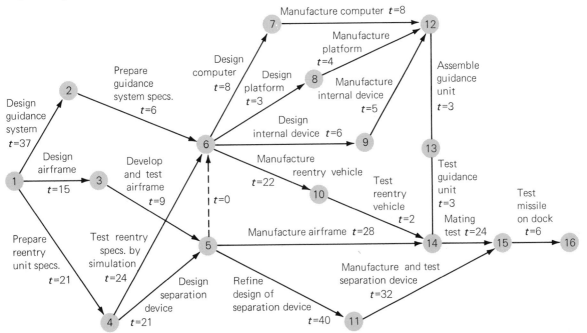

a. Compute ES, LS, and S for each activity. Assume that slack = 0 on the critical path. Identify the critical-path activities and the critical-path duration.

b. Draw a condensed event-oriented network with only six milestone events in it. The six events should be designated: 1. Start. 5. Shell specs completed. 6. Guidance specs completed. 13. Guidance manufactured. 14. Modules completed. 16. Missile tested.

Put activity times on the arrows between your events. Compute ES, LS, and S for each activity. Verify that the critical-path duration is the same as in part *a* above. What activity time goes on the arrow 1–6? Explain the difficulty in deciding on a time for this activity.

c. Assume the following project status at the end of week 50:

Activity	Actual duration
1–2	39
1–3	17
1–4	20
2–6	7
3–5	9
4–5	28
4–6	20

No other activites have been completed.

Develop a slack-sorted activity report similar to Figure 7–10 for the project as of the end of week 50. What is the new projected project duration?

d. (*Optional:* Feature explained in the supplement.) Make up optimistic and pessimistic activity times for all activities preceding event 6. What is the probability of completing event 6 within 50 days? Within 40 days?

Network simulation

8. Figure 7–11 shows a simulation of a simple network with equally possible activity times of 4, 5, or 6. In discussion of the figure it was stated that expected project duration increases to 5.8 for the five equally probable activity times—3, 4, 5, 6, and 7. Verify the figure 5.8.

Networks, times, paths, and time-cost trade-offs

9. The following data have been collected for a certain project:

Activity		Normal		Crash	
Predecessor event	Successor event	Time (days)	Cost ($)	Time (days)	Cost ($)
1	2	6	250	5	360
2	3	2	300	1	480
2	4	1	100	1	100
2	5	7	270	6	470
3	4		120	1	200
4	5		200	1	440

a. Draw the network.

b. Enter your own *reasonable* normal times (greater than one day) in the two empty spaces (for activities 3–4 and 4–5); compute and indicate the critical path and the normal project cost.

c. Compute the slack time for each activity in the network, using 12 days as the project due date.

    d. Perform time-cost trade-off analysis, crashing down to the minimum possible project duration. Display each of the time-cost alternatives.

Time-cost trade-off analysis

10. Normal and crash data are given below for the accompanying network. Compute all time-cost options. Which is best if there is a $40 per day penalty for every day beyond a seven-day project duration?[7]

	Normal		*Crash*	
Activity	*Days*	*Cost*	*Days*	*Cost*
A	3	$ 50	2	$ 100
B	6	140	4	260
C	2	25	1	50
D	5	100	3	180
E	2	80	2	80
F	7	115	5	175
G	4	100	2	240
		$610		$1,085

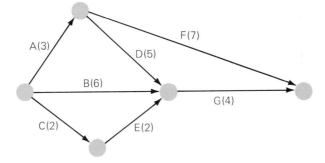

PERT/CPM subsystems

11. A number of kinds of projects are listed below. The projects range from small and simple to grand. As is indicated in Figure 7–15, modest projects warrant only the first PERT/CPM subsystem, whereas grand projects warrant all four subsystems; in-between projects warrant subsystems 1 and 2 or subsystems 1, 2, and 3. Decide which subsystems should apply for each of the listed projects. Explain each.

    Computer selection and installation for company of 200 employees.

    Moving the computer facility for a large bank to a new building in a major city.

    Moving the computer facility (same size as bank's) to a new building at a major university.

    Community project to attract new industry in three large abandoned factory buildings (town of 10,000 people).

    Five-year overhaul of a nuclear submarine.

    Implementing MRP in a manufacturing company of 1,000 employees.

---

[7] Adapted from J. S. Sayer, J. E. Kelly, Jr., and M. R. Walker, "Critical Path Scheduling," *Factory* (July 1960).

New product development and testing (including market research) for a major
food company.

Moving an army division from one closed-down post to a new one in another
state.

Planning an NCAA-sponsored national sports championship event.

Building a 500-room hotel in Lincoln, Nebraska.

Building a 500-room hotel in Manhattan.

Line-of-balance

12. On February 1, 1981, Global Associates, Inc., was awarded a contract to produce
130 Doppler search units. The contract calls for completion by the end of December 1982. Lead-time information was developed by company engineers. It is shown
in the accompanying lead-time chart.

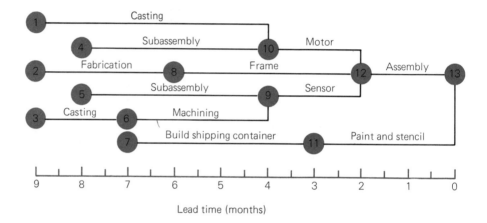

Lead time (months)

The following delivery schedule has been agreed upon:

Month (1982)	Deliveries	Month (1982)	Deliveries
January	2	July	12
February	4	August	14
March	5	September	16
April	7	October	18
May	9	November	17
June	11	December	15

a. It is now one year later (February 1982). The following status information
has just been received:

Control point	Completions	Control point	Completions
1	90	8	64
2	80	9	18
3	72	10	20
4	100	11	15
5	80	12	8
6	72	13	0
7	64		

Use graph paper to plot the delivery schedule, plot the status information in the form of a bar chart, and lay down the line of balance.

b. What areas need corrective action, and why?

13. A contract calls for delivery of five swamp buggies per week for 30 weeks. The process plan is shown below. (Note: Deliveries begin in week 9 since there is a nine-week lead time. Therefore the total contract covers 39 weeks.)

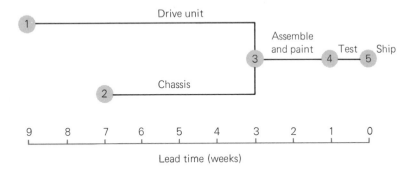

a. Calculate the line-of-balance quantity for each of the five control points as of the end of the 19th week (in the 39-week contract period). If a completion report shows that 50 swamp buggies have been assembled and painted after 19 weeks, what is your assessment of the assemble and paint operation?

b. The delivery schedule makes it easy to calculate line-of-balance quantities. Is this form of delivery schedule realistic? Discuss briefly.

IN-BASKET CASE*

Topic: GERT—Aero-Space Products

To:

From: Coordinator, Project Management Group, Aero-Space Products Corp.

GERT is a variation of PERT/CPM which I don't believe is widely used. But its advocates claim it has several advantages over regular PERT. I'd like you to investigate to see how applicable GERT might be for our space-related projects. Be sure to consider the pros and cons and compare it with PERT.

* See instructions at end of problems section, Chapter 1.

CASE

ABM site

In 1967 contractors were at work around the country developing a multibillion-dollar antiballistic missile (ABM) system. One contractor had developmental responsibility for the first ABM site, to be constructed near Grand Forks,

North Dakota. A team of consultants had been called in to help the contractor design a PERT system.

The consultant's first step was to develop a work breakdown structure, which consisted of such major project modules as site acquisition, hiring and training, and logistics planning. Then each consultant was assigned to work with a military liaison representative on one of the WBS modules.

After one week of consulting with scores of contractor people and the military representatives, the consultants had the subnetworks about done. On Friday evening several members of the team were relaxing over a beer and reflecting on their week of drawing networks. One topic of conversation was the upcoming weeks of activity time estimating and path analysis.

John Abbott, the consultant for the logistics planning subnetwork and his military liaison, Master Sergeant Delvin Martin, speculated on whether the critical path would include logistics planning activities. The logistics plan, some 400 activities, involved developing technical manuals and so forth for supply and maintenance of the ABM site. John remarked that activating the ABM site and staffing it were urgent and really needed to be fully completed when the antiballistic missile was scheduled for delivery to the site (another contractor had the ABM contract), but he wasn't so sure about the logistics plan. John turned to Sergeant Martin and asked, "Delvin, what would happen if they delivered the ABM to the site, but the log plan wasn't done?" Delvin, who had had years of experience in missile logistics, thought for a moment and replied, "Continue to march, I guess."

What did Sergeant Martin mean? What is different about the types of activities in a logistics plan as compared with those in, say, site selection?

supplement to chapter 7

PERT THREE-TIME-ESTIMATING PROCEDURE

In this supplement the PERT three-time-estimating procedure is presented. The discussion includes two topics:

1. Expected time and variance.
2. Probability statements.

Expected time and variance

The three-time-estimating procedure calls for the following three time estimates for every network activity:

Optimistic time, a—assumes that all goes well in completing the activity.
Most likely time, m—assumes normal conditions as the activity is in progress.
Pessimistic time, b—assumes misfortune in completing the activity.

The three estimates collapse into a single *expected time*, t_e, by

$$t_e = \frac{a + 4m + b}{6}$$

It is this weighted average, t_e, that is used in path analysis.

The a and b estimates have a second use. The estimated range of variability is $b - a$. There is a statistical method for converting a range of variability into an estimated variance. The formula for estimated variance, V_t, of any activity is:

$$V_t = \left(\frac{b - a}{6}\right)^2$$

Calculations

Activity	t_e	V_t
1–2	$\dfrac{4 + 4(4) + 10}{6} = 5$	$\left(\dfrac{10 - 4}{6}\right)^2 = 1.0$
1–3	$\dfrac{9 + 4(9) + 9}{6} = 9$	$\left(\dfrac{9 - 9}{6}\right)^2 = 0.0$
2–3	$\dfrac{6 + 4(8) + 16}{6} = 9$	$\left(\dfrac{16 - 6}{6}\right)^2 = 2.8$

Figure S7–1 shows a small network with t_e and V_t calculations for each activity. For activity 1–2 in the figure $a = 4$, $m = 4$, and $b = 10$. The calculated

FIGURE S7-1
Expected times
and variances

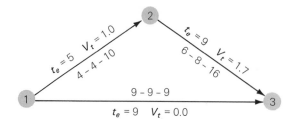

t_e is 5, and the calculated V_t is 1.0. Activity 1–3 has the same value, 9, for a, m, and b. Therefore the range is $9 - 9 = 0$, which is zero variance. Activity 2–3 has the largest range and therefore the greatest variance, V_t.

Probability statements

With variance estimates for each activity, it becomes possible to make various predictions. For example, one may predict the probability of event 2 in Figure S7–1 being completed within four days. Two steps are required to compute the probability:

1. Calculate the number of standard deviations between four days and the ES for event 2. (ES means earliest start, and it is equal to 5, the t_e, in this case.) The usual assumption is that event-completion times are normally distributed. Therefore, a statistical formula for the normal distribution is used to find number of standard deviations, Z:

$$Z = \frac{X - \mu}{\sigma_t},$$

where

$X =$ Given event-completion time—4 in this case
$\mu =$ Mean completion time—ES, or 5 in this case
$\sigma_t =$ Standard deviation of preceding activity times, which equals $\sqrt{V_t}$ for activity 1–2, or $\sqrt{1}$ in this case

By substitution,

$$Z = \frac{4 - 5}{\sqrt{1.0}} = \frac{4 - 5}{1} = -1.0$$

2. Go to a normal probability distribution table. See Table S7–1. Find $Z = 1.0$, and read off the probability. It is 0.3413. For negative Z-values it is necessary to subtract from 0.5 (the probability of meeting the mean completion time, ES). The result is

$$0.5 - 0.3413 = 0.1587$$

This means that there is about a 16 percent chance of completing event 2 within four days.

TABLE S7-1
Areas under the
standard normal
probability
distribution

A value in the table is the proportion of area under
the normal curve that is between the mean (where
$Z = 0$) and a positive value of Z.

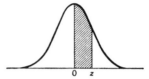

z	.00	.01	.02	.03	.04	.05	.06	.07	.08	.09
0.0	.0000	.0040	.0080	.0120	.0160	.0199	.0239	.0279	.0319	.0359
0.1	.0398	.0438	.0478	.0517	.0557	.0596	.0636	.0675	.0714	.0753
0.2	.0793	.0832	.0871	.0910	.0948	.0987	.1026	.1064	.1103	.1141
0.3	.1179	.1217	.1255	.1293	.1331	.1368	.1406	.1443	.1480	.1517
0.4	.1554	.1591	.1628	.1664	.1700	.1736	.1772	.1808	.1844	.1879
0.5	.1915	.1950	.1985	.2019	.2054	.2088	.2123	.2157	.2190	.2224
0.6	.2257	.2291	.2324	.2357	.2389	.2422	.2454	.2486	.2517	.2549
0.7	.2580	.2611	.2642	.2673	.2703	.2734	.2764	.2794	.2823	.2852
0.8	.2881	.2910	.2939	.2967	.2995	.3023	.3051	.3078	.3106	.3133
0.9	.3159	.3186	.3212	.3238	.3264	.3289	.3315	.3340	.3365	.3389
1.0	.3413	.3438	.3461	.3485	.3508	.3531	.3554	.3577	.3599	.3621
1.1	.3643	.3665	.3686	.3708	.3729	.3749	.3770	.3790	.3810	.3830
1.2	.3849	.3869	.3888	.3907	.3925	.3944	.3962	.3980	.3997	.4015
1.3	.4032	.4049	.4066	.4082	.4099	.4115	.4131	.4147	.4162	.4177
1.4	.4192	.4207	.4222	.4236	.4251	.4265	.4279	.4292	.4306	.4319
1.5	.4332	.4345	.4357	.4370	.4382	.4394	.4406	.4418	.4429	.4441
1.6	.4452	.4463	.4474	.4484	.4495	.4505	.4515	.4525	.4535	.4545
1.7	.4554	.4564	.4573	.4582	.4591	.4599	.4608	.4616	.4625	.4633
1.8	.4641	.4649	.4656	.4664	.4671	.4678	.4686	.4693	.4699	.4706
1.9	.4713	.4719	.4726	.4732	.4738	.4744	.4750	.4756	.4761	.4767
2.0	.4772	.4778	.4783	.4788	.4793	.4798	.4803	.4808	.4812	.4817
2.1	.4821	.4826	.4830	.4834	.4838	.4842	.4846	4850	.4854	.4857
2.2	.4861	.4864	.4868	.4871	.4875	.4878	.4881	.4884	.4887	.4890
2.3	.4893	.4896	.4898	.4901	.4904	.4906	.4909	.4911	.4913	.4916
2.4	.4918	.4920	.4922	.4925	.4927	.4929	.4931	.4932	.4934	.4936
2.5	.4938	4940	.4941	.4943	.4945	.4946	.4948	.4949	.4951	.4952
2.6	.4953	.4955	.4956	.4957	.4959	.4960	.4961	.4962	.4963	.4964
2.7	.4965	.4966	.4967	.4968	.4969	.4970	.4971	.4972	.4973	.4974
2.8	.4974	.4975	.4976	.4977	.4977	.4978	.4979	.4979	.4980	.4981
2.9	.4981	.4982	.4982	.4983	.4984	.4984	.4985	.4985	.4986	.4986
3.0	.4987	.4987	.4987	.4988	.4988	.4989	.4989	.4989	.4990	.4990

Source: Paul G. Hoel, *Elementary Statistics* (New York: John Wiley & Sons, 1960), p. 240.

The method may be applied to any event including the final event. For the network in Figure S7–1, the probability of completing event 3 in, say, fifteen days is computed as follows:

$$Z = \frac{15 - 14}{1.0 + 2.8} = \frac{1}{1.95} = 0.51$$

Note that only critical-path activities, 1–2 and 2–3 in this case, are included in the calculation. From Table S7–1, the probability value for $Z = 0.51$ is 0.1950. For positive Z-values the probability is added to 0.5:

$$0.5 + 0.1950 = 0.695$$

This means that there is about a 70 percent chance of completing the whole project within fifteen days.

PART THREE

Operations design and quality assurance

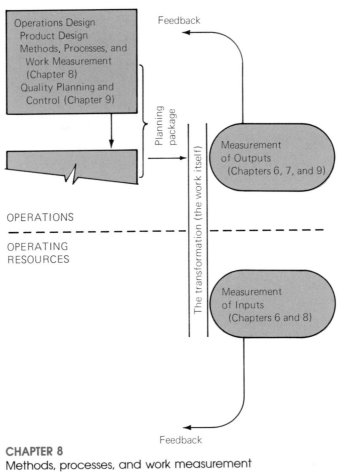

CHAPTER 8
Methods, processes, and work measurement
CHAPTER 9
Quality assurance

As is shown in the chart on the opposite page for Part Three, the full operations design function includes product design; methods, processes, and work measurement; and quality planning and control. Product design is mostly an engineering activity and is discussed rather little. (Chapter 10 on product planning is concerned with developing the product line; that discussion touches on product design in a small way.)

The part of Chapter 8 on methods and processes concerns how to produce the product or provide the service. The next question taken up in the chapter is how long it is likely to take to produce or provide, which is what is meant by work measurement. Time standards from work measurement serve several planning purposes. Time standards may also be compared with feedback on labor performance (see the lower feedback arrow in the chart on the opposite page).

Chapter 9 is on quality planning and control. The chapter concerns quality assurance, including quality standards, inspection procedures, and ways of measuring quality. Feedback on quality (see the upper feedback arrow in the chart) is compared with quality standards or norms in the quality-control process.

Operations design information—such as blueprints, process sheets, and inspection plans—and operations schedules form a planning package. The planning package directs the work activities, and measurement of outputs and inputs may be fed back to the planners, who may need to revise plans. The arrow pointing downward from operations design in the chart on the opposite page is intended to show the importance of operations design data in scheduling. That is, methods data and time standards provide a sound basis for scheduling.

chapter 8

METHODS, PROCESSES, AND WORK MEASUREMENT

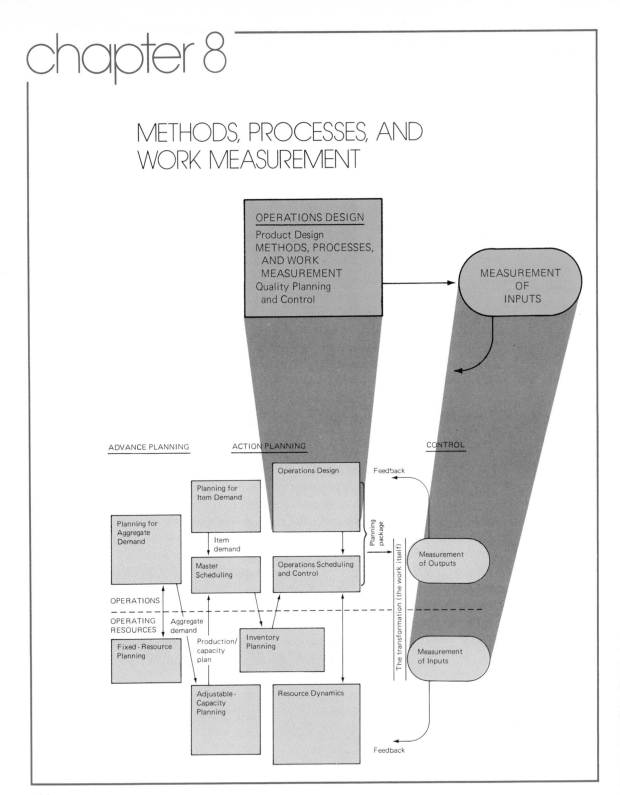

Methods, processes, and work measurement were basic interests of the pioneers of scientific management, especially Frederick W. Taylor and Frank Gilbreth. At the turn of the century these men developed ways to standardize the labor element of production. Their focus was on standard methods, processes, and times; their techniques were methods study and work measurement. (In some countries, it is called work study.)

The scientific management movement may be thought of as a final phase of the industrial revolution. Earlier phases were concerned with invention, mechanization, standardization of parts, division of labor, and the factory system. Machines and parts were standardized, and labor was divided into narrow specialties, but worker performance was controlled more by supervisors' skill than by design. Taylor's and Gilbreth's techniques for methods study (or motion study) and time study extended science into the realm of the worker, and U.S. Supreme Court Justice Louis Brandeis coined the term *scientific management* as a name for the approach.

Since scientific management is native to the United States, its benefits accrued earlier to the United States than to other industrial countries. Methods and standards programs spread rapidly in U.S. manufacturing firms between 1900 and 1950, and this may help to explain the phenomenal growth rate of industrial output in the United States in the first half of the century.

More recently, methods and standards applications have expanded beyond the manufacturing sector, especially in human-service delivery—for example, hospitals, food service, hotels, and transportation. So carefully industrially engineered is the McDonald's hamburger that Levitt calls it "the technocratic hamburger."[1] It is becoming increasingly hard to compete in these industries without attention to methods design and standards of labor performance.

Scientific management is not without critics. Labor unions have often resisted time standards, and there are humanistic arguments that under work measurement people become cogs in the machine. Job enrichment and nonlinear assembly are ideas that respond to some of the criticisms about work measurement. The final section of this chapter is devoted to the issue of how the workplace may be designed to gain in efficiency without serious losses in humanity. It is preceded by three sections on concepts and techniques. The first section provides an overview of organization for methods. Techniques of methods study and of time standards or estimates are the topics of the second and third sections.

ORGANIZATION FOR METHODS AND STANDARDS

Methods study deals with how a task is done; time standards refer to how long it takes. These questions of how and how long may be left up to the

---

[1] Theodore Levitt, "Production-Line Approach to Service," *Harvard Business Review*, September–October 1972, pp. 41–52. Also see Richard J. Schonberger, "Taylorism Up-to-Date: The Inevitablility of Worker Boredom," *Business and Society*, Spring 1974, pp. 12–17.

worker or the worker's boss, or they may be "staffed off," that is, assigned to staff specialists such as industrial engineers. In larger organizations methods and standards work goes on at several organizational levels, and there may be extensive formal programs to oversee these efforts.

Organizational elements

Figure 8–1 illustrates a comprehensive methods and standards program. Each box on the chart contributes. Employees and supervisors are always involved; the other contributors are staff units rather than line units, and these may not exist in some organizations. Each is discussed below.

Employees and supervisors. Employees make choices about details of methods and timing and sometimes perform analysis using work simplification. Supervisors—for example, foremen—give directions on methods and timing and assist in on-the-job training (OJT).

FIGURE 8–1
Methods and time-standards activities throughout the organization

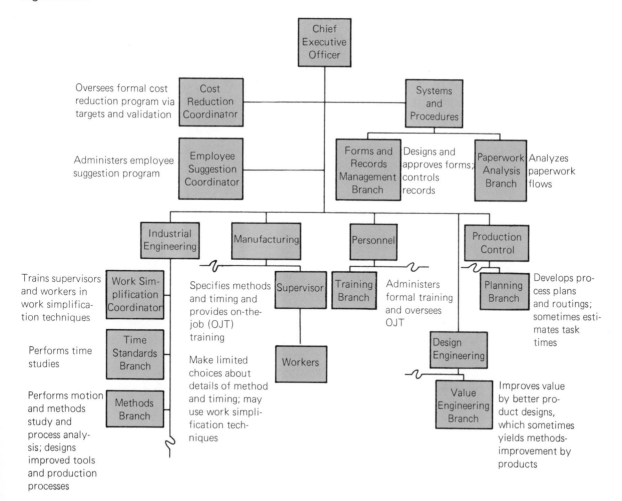

Personnel. The training branch in personnel departments relieves supervisors of some of the training burden. The training branch develops training procedures, materials, and facilities; and training may oversee the OJT process, including the development of standards for judging when an employee is sufficiently trained.

Production control. Production control (PC) departments assist manufacturing in the planning and control of work. PC help is especially valuable for work that moves through several work centers. Production control prepares the routing plan (route sheets) for such work. In the absence of formal industrially engineered time standards, PC planners also estimate labor-hours and machine-hours.

Industrial engineering. Industrial engineering (IE) specializes in engineered methods and time standards. Many imaginative people contributed to the development of the industrial engineering field (née scientific management), but the techniques of methods and time standards analysis are easy to learn. Often, graduate IEs are in charge of the work-measurement program, but nongraduate IE technicians carry out the analyses. This allows the graduate IE to focus more on operations research analyses.

Industrial engineering may also set up and coordinate a work-simplification program, in which workers and supervisors are trained to perform their own work studies. Work simplification was developed partly in response to problems that IEs were having in imposing their ideas upon those directly responsible for task performance. Work-simplification programs were widely installed in the 1940s and 1950s, but they are not common today.

Forms, records, and paperwork. Office applications of scientific management have grown steadily in government over the years and have grown in spurts in business offices. Methods and standards programs grew rapidly among insurance companies in the 1950s and in banks in the 1950s and 1960s.[2] Part of the reason was a paperwork explosion, in which there were cases of 10- and even 15-copy forms. Paperwork flowcharts became useful for tracking the flows of copies, and these flowcharts sometimes papered the four walls of a good-sized room.

The Systems and Procedures Society of America (SPSA) was founded in 1947 for specialists in paperwork management, and a "management analyst" specialty was established by the U.S. Civil Service for the same purposes: forms design, reports control, records management, standard (office) operating procedures, and paperwork flow analysis. Commercial computers were able to internalize many paper-processing steps, thus simplifying paper flows. (In 1957 SPSA became the Association for Systems Management, which focuses on computer systems analysis as well as traditional paperwork systems and procedures.)

---

[2] Donald L. Caruth cites 60 articles written about commercial—mostly banking—uses of work measurement; nearly all were published in the late 1950s and into the 1960s. *Work Measurement in Commercial Banks* (Bankers Publishing, 1971), pp. 219–22 (GH1720.W63C36).

Value engineering. Value engineering (VE) is mainly directed toward improving product designs. However, in improving product designs, ideas for better method and process designs often emerge.

Employee suggestions. Many larger organizations have formal programs for encouraging employees to suggest better ideas. Most suggestions concern methods and processes, including tools, equipment, and other productive resources. Typically suggestion forms are in wall boxes in each work area; employees write their ideas on the forms and forward the forms to the program coordinator. The coordinator gets an expert to review the ideas. Cash payments are usually made to the suggesters of ideas judged to be worthy.

Cost reduction. In some organizations a cost-reduction program is set up to monitor the whole methods-improvement effort. Annual cost-reduction goals are set for the whole oreganization (much like contribution targets in charitable organizations such as the United Way). A program coordinator monitors accomplishments. The coordinator may also cost out or validate claimed savings from improved methods. Formal cost-reduction programs are common in federal government agencies and also in some large industries that do considerable federal government business—such as the aerospace, shipbuilding, and automotive industries.

Assembling the planning package

The chart on the title page of the chapter shows the components that make up a *planning package,* which consists of directions to the workers. The planning package is a formal set of documents in larger organizations, especially goods producers.

A characteristic flow pattern and set of planning-package documents are shown in Figure 8–2. Design engineering is the first step. The engineer's product design is conveyed forward as a set of blueprints, bills of materials, and product specifications.

Methods and times come next. In the less formal version, the flow is directly to the process planner in the production control (PC) department. This version is more likely for nonrepetitive tasks, especially in the job-shop operating environment. The process planner is often an employee who began in the shop and whose background enables him to plan the operations and estimate operation times. These are entered on what is often called a *route sheet.*

More repetitive tasks may be planned in a more specialized way. A methods analyst in the industrial engineering (IE) department may formally analyze ways to produce the product in the engineer's blueprints. The methods analyst often uses flowcharts as an aid. A new method may be displayed as a flowchart of operations; new workplace layouts, tool designs, and so on, may accompany the flowchart. Copies of documents on the new method are filed. The training branch in the personnel department may use the methods documents to create training materials, and the documents are also an input to time-standards development.

The time-standards analyst in the IE department develops a standard time

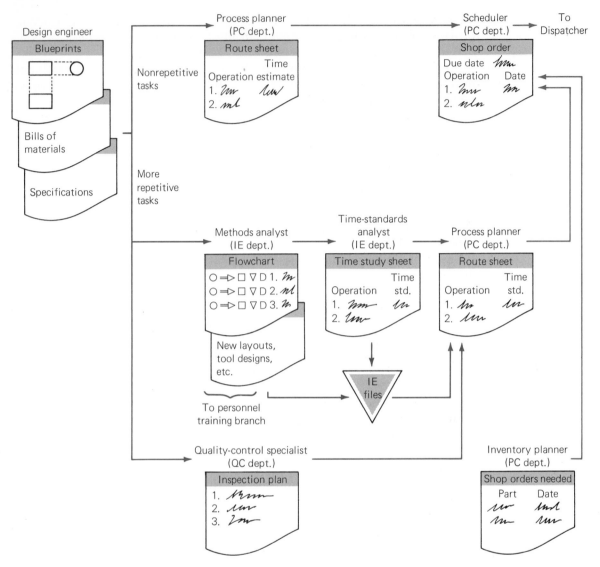

FIGURE 8–2
Characteristic
flow in
assembling
planning
package

for each operation. Standard times may be developed on some sort of time-study form, and the results are kept on file.

In this more formal flow the process planner develops the route sheet from routings (sequences of operations) and standard times on file. Quality-control inspection procedures may be inserted in the proper places on the route sheet.

The planning package is completed by an inventory planner, who notes the need for a parts order, and by a production control scheduler, who prepares a shop order for the parts. The scheduler computes operation due dates based on work-center lead times and enters them on the shop order. The shop order is entered into the job stream, and dispatchers steer it through to completion.

The flow patterns described are generalized—not precise as to details, because details vary from firm to firm.

The methods and time-standards inputs to the planning package are explained in detail in the next two sections. Quality-control and inventory inputs are discussed in other chapters.

METHODS STUDY

Formal methods-study techniques are based on the scientific method, a generalized method of inquiry. The steps in the scientific method (one version of it) are:

1. Define problem.
2. Collect data.
3. Generate alternatives.
4. Evalute alternatives and choose.
5. Implement.

Now let us see how Taylor, Gilbreth, and other pioneers of scientific management translated the scientific method into a procedure for methods study. Figure 8–3 illustrates, and explanation follows.

FIGURE 8–3
Methods study and scientific method

Scientific method	Methods study
1. Define problem.	Select a present task for methods improvement (or a new task for methods development).
2. Collect data.	Flow-chart present method (the *before* chart), or synthesize a flowchart for a new task.
3. Generate alternatives.	Apply questioning attitude, principles of motion economy, etc., to arrive at alternative method(s) and flow-chart the method(s) (the *after* chart).
4. Evaluate alternatives and choose.	Evaluate new method(s) via savings in: Cost. Time. Effort. Storages. Delays. Transportations. Transportation distances. Choose best method.
5. Implement.	Implement—in training workers and in job planning.

Methods-study procedures

Methods study begins with task selection. The candidate task may be a present task that seems inefficient or that has never been studied before, or it may be a new task in need of methods development.

Steps 2 and 3 often feature *before* and *after* comparison. Data is collected in the form of a flowchart showing the present method—the "before" condition. Then an alternative or alternatives are generated in the form of an "after" flowchart (or flowcharts).

In arriving at alternative method(s), the questioning attitude may be applied. Methods analysis, like newspaper reporting, embraces Kipling's six honest serving men:

> I keep six honest serving men
> (They taught me all I knew);
> Their names are what and why and when
> and how and where and who.
>
> Rudyard Kipling
> *The Elephant's Child*

The methods analyst may also employ principles of methods improvement. Frank and Lillian Gilbreth were early developers of such principles.[3] Ralph Barnes elaborated on the Gilbreths' work in developing "principles of motion economy." Further refinements have been offered more recently; for example, Mundel provides a list of "general principles," which attempt to incorporate the current emphasis on the human factor among industrial engineers. (Study of the human factor is a subfield of industrial engineering known as ergonomics.) Mundel's list is given in Figure 8–4.[4]

These general principles are grouped under four headings: elimination, combination, rearrangement, and simplification. Notice that some of the items emphasize the human factor. For example, A4 concerns more normal body motions; A5 concerns better posture; A8 concerns danger; B1 suggests natural, sweeping motions as opposed to choppy, irregular ones; C2 suggests use of the eyes as a substitute for use of the hands; and most of D concerns the physiology of effort. This emphasis on the human factor stems from the realization that much of the potential for productivity gain is found at the labor-machine interface and that this calls for attention to human comfort and emotions as well as physical efficiency.

Step 4 in Figure 10–3 is evaluating new method(s) according to cost or other criteria. Cost analysis is often itself costly, and cost estimates for methods not yet tried can be inaccurate. Therefore, other criteria are often used as

---

[3] F. B. Gilbreth and L. M. Gilbreth, *Fatigue Study* (Sturgis and Walton, 1916). The book was written by Lillian Gilbreth.

[4] Marvin E. Mundel, *Motion and Time Study: Improving Productivity*, 5th ed. (Prentice-Hall, 1978), pp. 172–73 (T60.7.M86).

surrogates for cost: time, effort, storages, delays, transportations, and transportation distances. Quality is usually *not* one of the criteria, because in a methods study a minimum level of quality is usually treated as a given.

The chosen method is implemented (Step 5) for worker-training and job-planning purposes. In some organizations the industrial engineer's chosen method must be "signed off" by the foreman and perhaps also by quality control, safety, production control, personnel, and a labor-union steward.

FIGURE 8–4
General principles of methods improvement

A. *Elimination*
1. Eliminate all possible jobs, steps, or motions. (This applies to body, leg, arm, hand, or eye.)
2. Eliminate irregularities in a job so as to facilitate automaticity. Provide fixed places for things.
3. Eliminate the use of the hand as a holding device.
4. Eliminate awkward or abnormal motions.
5. Eliminate the use of muscles to maintain a fixed posture.
6. Eliminate muscular force by using power tools, power feeds, etc.
7. Eliminate the overcoming of momentum.
8. Eliminate danger.
9. Eliminate idle time unless needed for rest.

B. *Combination*
1. Replace with one continuous curved motion short motions which are connected with sudden changes in direction.
2. With fixed machine cycles, make a maximum of work internal to the machine cycle.
3. Combine tools.
4. Combine controls.
5. Combine motions.

C. *Rearrangement*
1. Distribute the work evenly between the two hands. A simultaneous symmetrical motion pattern is most effective. (This frequently involves working on two parts at the same time.) With crew work, distribute the work evenly among members of the crew.
2. Shift work from the hands to the eyes.
3. Arrange for a straightforward order of work.

D. *Simplification*
1. Use the smallest muscle group capable of doing the work, providing for intermittent use of muscle groups as needed.
2. Reduce eye travel and the number of fixations.
3. Keep work in the normal work area, the area reached without moving the body.
4. Shorten motions.
5. Adapt handles, levers, pedals, buttons, and so on, to human dimensions and musculatures.
6. Use momentum to build up energy in place of the intense application of muscular force.
7. Use the simplest possible combination of motions.
8. Reduce the complexity of each motion, particularly the motions performed at one location (as contrasted with motions that change the location of things).

Source: Marvin E. Mundel, *Motion and Time Study: Improving Productivity* (Prentice-Hall, 1978), p. 173 (T60.7.M86). Used with permission.

FIGURE 8–5
Four levels of
methods study

Type	Application	Flowchart
Motion study	Manual task at workbench or desk	Right-and-left-hand chart
Worker-machine analysis	Machine tending at workplace	Worker-machine chart
Worker analysis	Task involving mobile worker	Flow process chart (worker-oriented)
Product analysis	Product flow	Flow process chart (product-oriented)

The five steps in methods study may be applied to small, medium, or large units of work. In fact, the history of methods study began with motion study of workers confined to the workbench and gradually grew to encompass larger work stations and work that crossed work-center and departmental boundaries. There are variations on the five-step process that apply to various levels of work-unit analysis.

Figure 8–5 presents four such levels: The names of the four types in the figure are not standard, but these types serve to differentiate the levels. The four applications exhibit growth—from workbench to machine to work area to whole plant; the focus shifts from hand motions to worker and machine to mobile worker to product flow. Each type of flowchart listed in the figure is suited for one type of application, as is discussed next.

Motion study

Frank Gilbreth is the father of motion study, initially a laboratory approach to analyzing basic hand and body motions. In fact, basic motions such as reach and grasp are known as "therbligs," which is Gilbreth spelled backward (except for the *th*). It is natural that the early efforts in motion study were placed on the highly repetitive short-cycle manual motions that are common in work performed at the workbench. Rather small gains can yield large benefits, and the analysis is not complicated by concerns about costly machines, worker travel, and irregular activities.

The left-and-right-hand chart is suitable for before-and-after analysis. An objective is to keep both hands busy, because an idle hand is like half an idle worker. An example follows.

EXAMPLE 8–1
Left-and-right-hand chart, bolt-washer-nut assembly

One repetitive task in a certain firm is to assemble a washer and a nut onto a bolt. The present method seems inefficient, and it is undergoing study using the left-and-right-hand charting method.

Figure 8–6 charts the present method for the assembly operation. In this variation of the left-and-right-hand chart the operation is described in symbols as well as words. The meanings of the symbols are:

○ Operation
⇒ Move
▽ Hold
D Delay

FIGURE 8–6
Left-and-right-hand chart for bolt-washer-nut assembly, present method

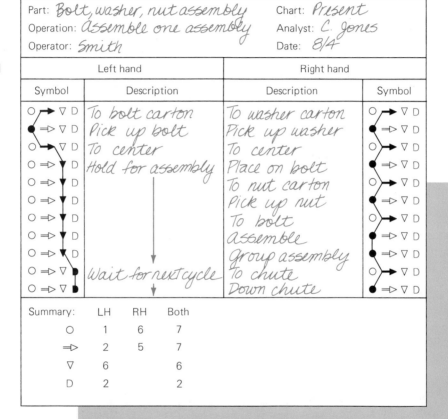

Part: *Bolt, washer, nut assembly*		Chart: *Present*	
Operation: *Assemble one assembly*		Analyst: *C. Jones*	
Operator: *Smith*		Date: *8/4*	

Left hand		Right hand	
Symbol	Description	Description	Symbol
○➤▽ D	*To bolt carton*	*To washer carton*	○➤▽ D
●⇒▽ D	*Pick up bolt*	*Pick up washer*	●⇒▽ D
○➤▽ D	*To center*	*To center*	○➤▽ D
○⇒▼ D	*Hold for assembly*	*Place on bolt*	●⇒▽ D
○⇒▼ D		*To nut carton*	○➤▽ D
○⇒▼ D		*Pick up nut*	●⇒▽ D
○⇒▼ D		*To bolt*	○➤▽ D
○⇒▼ D		*assemble*	●⇒▽ D
○⇒▼ D		*Group assembly*	●⇒▽ D
○⇒▽●	*Wait for next cycle*	*To chute*	○➤▽ D
○⇒▽●		*Down chute*	●⇒▽ D

Summary:	LH	RH	Both
○	1	6	7
⇒	2	5	7
▽	6		6
D	2		2

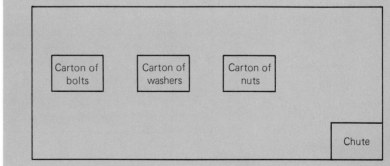

Carton of bolts   Carton of washers   Carton of nuts

Chute

FIGURE 8–7
Left-and-right-hand chart for bolt-washer-nut assembly, proposed method

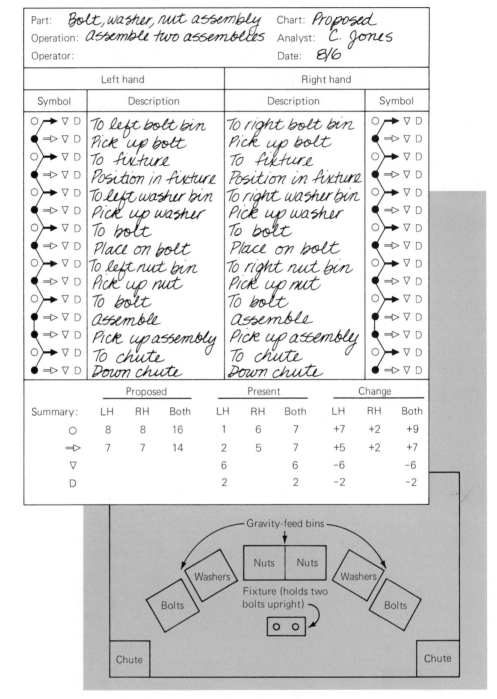

Part: *Bolt, washer, nut assembly*   Chart: *Proposed*
Operation: *Assemble two assemblies*   Analyst: *C. Jones*
Operator: Date: *8/6*

Left hand		Right hand	
Symbol	Description	Description	Symbol
○⟋▶ ▽ D	To left bolt bin	To right bolt bin	○⟋▶ ▽ D
●⟹ ▽ D	Pick up bolt	Pick up bolt	●⟹ ▽ D
○⟋▶ ▽ D	To fixture	To fixture	○⟋▶ ▽ D
●⟹ ▽ D	Position in fixture	Position in fixture	●⟹ ▽ D
○⟋▶ ▽ D	To left washer bin	To right washer bin	○⟋▶ ▽ D
●⟹ ▽ D	Pick up washer	Pick up washer	●⟹ ▽ D
○⟋▶ ▽ D	To bolt	To bolt	○⟋▶ ▽ D
●⟹ ▽ D	Place on bolt	Place on bolt	●⟹ ▽ D
○⟋▶ ▽ D	To left nut bin	To right nut bin	○⟋▶ ▽ D
●⟹ ▽ D	Pick up nut	Pick up nut	●⟹ ▽ D
○⟋▶ ▽ D	To bolt	To bolt	○⟋▶ ▽ D
●⟹ ▽ D	Assemble	Assemble	●⟹ ▽ D
●⟹ ▽ D	Pick up assembly	Pick up assembly	●⟹ ▽ D
○⟋▶ ▽ D	To chute	To chute	○⟋▶ ▽ D
●⟹ ▽ D	Down chute	Down chute	●⟹ ▽ D

	Proposed			Present			Change		
Summary:	LH	RH	Both	LH	RH	Both	LH	RH	Both
○	8	8	16	1	6	7	+7	+2	+9
⟹	7	7	14	2	5	7	+5	+2	+7
▽				6		6	−6		−6
D				2		2	−2		−2

Gravity-feed bins

Nuts Nuts
Washers   Washers
Bolts   Bolts

Fixture (holds two bolts upright)

Chute   Chute

FIGURE 8–8
Left-and-right-
hand chart with
timed elements,
bolt-washer-nut
assembly

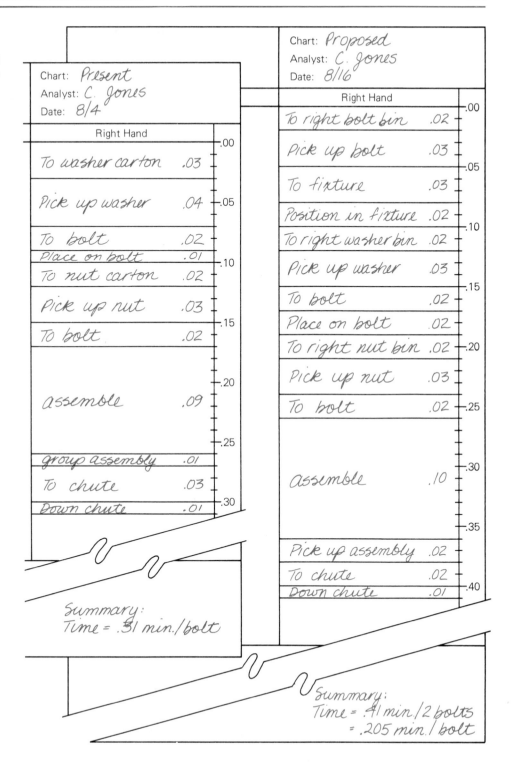

Chart: *Present*
Analyst: *C. Jones*
Date: *8/4*

Right Hand		
		.00
To washer carton	.03	
Pick up washer	.04	.05
To bolt	.02	
Place on bolt	.01	
To nut carton	.02	.10
Pick up nut	.03	
To bolt	.02	.15
assemble	.09	.20
		.25
group assembly	.01	
To chute	.03	
Down chute	.01	.30

Summary:
Time = .31 min./bolt

Chart: *Proposed*
Analyst: *C. Jones*
Date: *8/16*

Right Hand		
		.00
To right bolt bin	.02	
Pick up bolt	.03	.05
To fixture	.03	
Position in fixture	.02	.10
To right washer bin	.02	
Pick up washer	.03	
To bolt	.02	.15
Place on bolt	.02	
To right nut bin	.02	.20
Pick up nut	.03	
To bolt	.02	.25
assemble	.10	.30
		.35
Pick up assembly	.02	
To chute	.02	
Down chute	.01	.40

Summary:
Time = .41 min./2 bolts
= .205 min./bolt

Operations are productive, moves and holds less so, and delays not at all. The summary at the bottom of the flowchart shows a preponderance of low-productive and nonproductive elements. A workbench sketch commonly goes with the left-and-right-hand chart, because a poor workbench design would impede productivity.

Figure 8–7 charts a proposed method, which is based on improved design of the workbench. The new workbench design and method follow some of the principles of methods improvement given in Figure 8–4. For example, the proposed method "eliminates the use of the hand as a holding device" (principle A3) and it "distributes the work evenly between the two hands" (C1).

The summary in Figure 8–7 shows elimination of holds and delays. There are more moves, but the proposed method results in two assemblies every cycle versus one assembly per cycle under the present method. The proposed method clearly increases productivity. Furthermore, it appears to provide for smoother, more natural motions and shorter hand-travel distances; the proposed method may therefore be less tiring.

Figure 8–8 shows segments of an alternative form of the left-and-right-hand chart. The operation—assembly of bolt, washer, and nut—is the same, but vertical time graduations replace the preprinted flowchart symbols. The summary is in time units instead of in counts of each type of element. Time provides better proof of productivity improvement, but having to time the elements complicates the analysis. If the results of the motion study appear likely to be disputed, it may be worthwhile to take the extra effort to measure elements in time units. Also, having the results in minutes permits conversion into dollars, so that operating savings may be compared with the costs of new-methods development and implementation.

Worker-machine analysis

When the worker is a machine tender instead of a tool user, the productivity of the machine as well as the worker is of interest, since a machine is a costly resource. A worker-machine-time chart may be used to record present (before) and proposed (after) methods for work involving one or more workers and machines. For example, a two-person crew might sort, wash, dry, and iron sheets in a hospital laundry. The worker-machine-time chart could be set up as in Figure 8–9. There are five columns for recording activities and durations, one column for the first crew member, one for the second crew member, one for the washer, one for the dryer, and one for the ironing machine. A workplace layout normally accompanies the chart. As with the right-and-left-hand chart, time saving is the criterion for comparing the new method with the old.

Worker analysis

The activities of a mobile worker may be studied by the flow process chart, another contribution of Gilbreth. A simple version of the flow process chart for worker analysis is given in the following example.

EXAMPLE 8–2
Flow-process chart for worker analysis in meter reading

A gas company is engaged in the first phase of a complete methods-improvement program—recording present methods. One task being studied is meter reading. Results of a study of the present meter-reading method are shown in Figure 8–10

The flow process chart is used because the task involves a mobile worker. The gas company plans to file this (before) chart in a book of standard operating procedures

(SOP) and to update it with an improved (after) chart after methods improvement has been performed. New workers may study the pages of the SOP book that pertain to their jobs.

In the version of the flow process chart shown in Figure 8–10, the data are recorded on a blank piece of paper rather than a preprinted form. Four symbols are used. The circle, the arrow, and the large *D* were discussed earlier; the fourth symbol, a square, stands for inspection. The inverted triangle, representing storage, is not used in worker analysis because you do not store a person (at least not until the very end).

FIGURE 8–9
Worker-machine-time chart and workplace layout

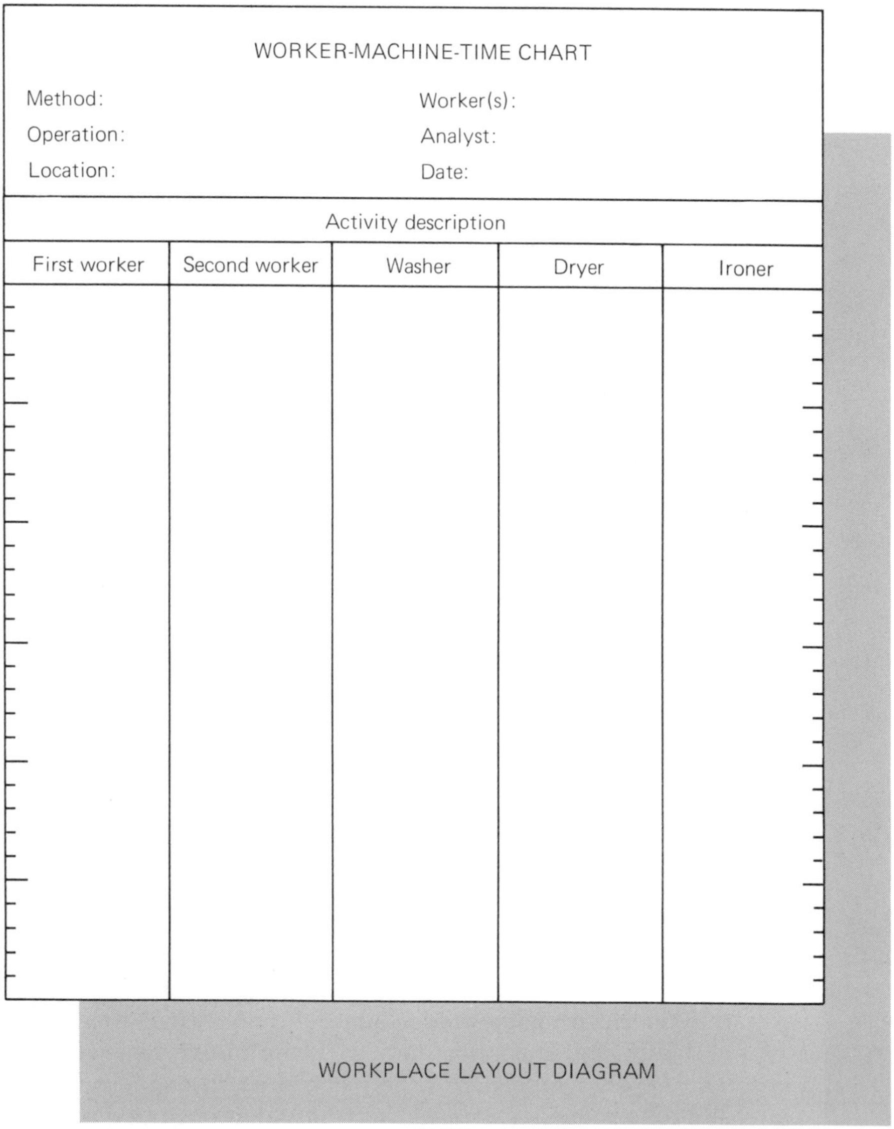

WORKER-MACHINE-TIME CHART

Method: Worker(s):
Operation: Analyst:
Location: Date:

Activity description

First worker	Second worker	Washer	Dryer	Ironer

WORKPLACE LAYOUT DIAGRAM

FIGURE 8-10
Flow process
chart, worker
analysis, meter
reading

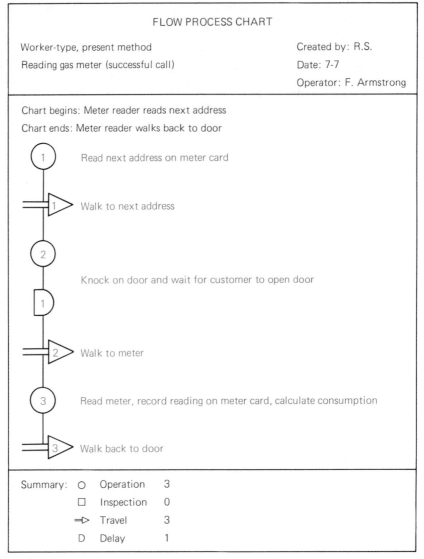

FLOW PROCESS CHART

Worker-type, present method   Created by: R.S.

Reading gas meter (successful call)   Date: 7-7

                                        Operator: F. Armstrong

Chart begins: Meter reader reads next address

Chart ends: Meter reader walks back to door

①   Read next address on meter card

▷1   Walk to next address

②   Knock on door and wait for customer to open door

▢1

▷2   Walk to meter

③   Read meter, record reading on meter card, calculate consumption

▷3   Walk back to door

Summary:	○	Operation	3
	□	Inspection	0
	⇒	Travel	3
	D	Delay	1

Source: Adapted from Alan Fields, *Methods Study* (Cassell, London, 1969), p. 50 (T60.F5).

**Product
analysis**

    The flow process chart is also used to chart the flow of products. For product flows, five charting symbols are used: the four used in worker analysis, plus the inverted triangle, for storage. These five symbols were standardized by the American Society of Mechanical Engineers (ASME), which provided considerable aid and encouragement in the formative years of scientific management. The ASME symbols are widely accepted throughout the world. The symbols and the product analysis flowchart are demonstrated in the following example.

EXAMPLE 8-3
Flow process chart for product analysis in sack filling

One operation in a continuous-flow-oriented firm is filling, weighing, and stenciling sacks. The operation is a candidate for methods improvement. The analyst has completed the data-collection step. Results are shown on the flow process chart of Figure 8–11.

The summary at the upper right shows that there are no delays but that there are six moves and two storages. The methods analyst's attention will be focused on the moves and storages. The proposed new method will be recorded on the same type of standard form.

In Figure 8–11 there is one case of a double symbol, the weighing operation. Weighing is an operation, but it is also an inspection for a quality variable, weight. Thus, both the square symbol and the circle symbol are used. (On a nonpreprinted charting document, the circle should be drawn inside the square.) A similar case occurs when a boss signs a letter or form. The signing is an operation, and the examination leading up to the signature is an inspection.

FIGURE 8–11
Flow process chart, product analysis, sack filling

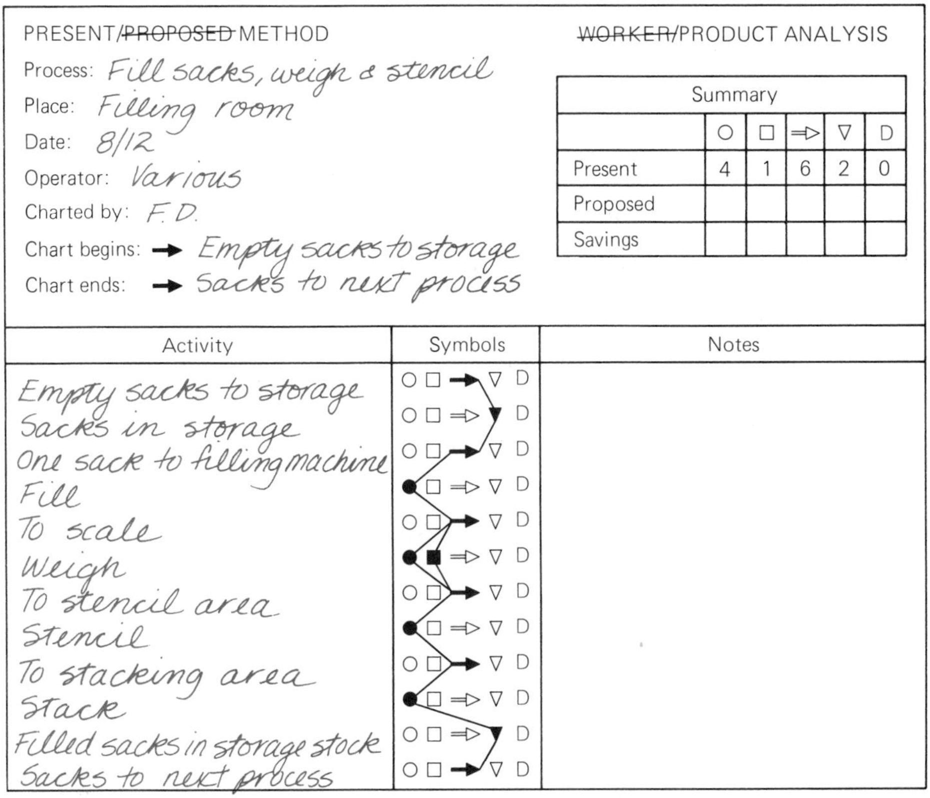

PRESENT/~~PROPOSED~~ METHOD   ~~WORKER~~/PRODUCT ANALYSIS

Process: *Fill sacks, weigh & stencil*
Place: *Filling room*
Date: *8/12*
Operator: *Various*
Charted by: *F. D.*
Chart begins: → *Empty sacks to storage*
Chart ends: → *Sacks to next process*

Summary					
	O	□	⇒	▽	D
Present	4	1	6	2	0
Proposed					
Savings					

Activity	Symbols	Notes
Empty sacks to storage	O □ → ▽ D	
Sacks in storage	O □ ⇒ ▽ D	
One sack to filling machine	O □ → ▽ D	
Fill	● □ ⇒ ▽ D	
To scale	O □ → ▽ D	
Weigh	● ■ ⇒ ▽ D	
To stencil area	O □ → ▽ D	
Stencil	● □ ⇒ ▽ D	
To stacking area	O □ → ▽ D	
Stack	● □ ⇒ ▽ D	
Filled sacks in storage stock	O □ ⇒ ▽ D	
Sacks to next process	O □ → ▽ D	

Adapted from Stanley Johnson and Grant Ogilvie, *Work Analysis* (Butterworths, London, 1972), p. 33 (T60.J63).

Other methods analysis tools

Design and improvement of methods and processes are closely associated with the preceding bedrock flow-charting techniques. A number of other tools of analysis are also related, more or less, to methods analysis. Systems flow charting and program flow charting are similar tools in the computer industry. Material handling and plant/office layout, discussed in Chapter 12, are special-purpose process analysis techniques. The capital budgeting/engineering economy techniques of Chapter 11 are used mainly to evaluate facilities proposals, but they are also used to compare manual methods with automated facilities. Linear programming, queuing, simulation, and other models of management science are discussed in several chapters, and their application is often in analysis of alternative processes.

One bedrock analysis tool quite different from the flow-charting tools is work sampling. Work sampling is a tool for both process analysis and time-standards analysis and will thus be discussed twice in this chapter.

Work-sampling analysis. Work sampling is like the *before* flowchart. It shows what is happening at present. The work-sampling study yields data on percentage of idle or delay time.[5] More than that, the study can be designed with idleness broken down into various categories, thereby showing process bottlenecks. An example follows.

EXAMPLE 8–4
Work sampling (ratio delay), pathology lab

The director of Midtown Pathological Labs is concerned. Costs are going up rapidly; the staff has plenty to do, yet it frequently seems to be idled by assorted problems. The director decides to probe the various sources of delay by conducting a one-week work-sampling study. Of special interest are lab equipment failures, shortages of supplies, delays waiting for instructions, excessive coffee breaks, and lab technicians out of the work area. A work-sampling data sheet is constructed to include those five categories of delay (plus an "other" category), and a schedule of 100 sample observations (20 per day) is developed by the director.

The schedule of random observation times and the completed work-sampling form are shown in Figure 8–12. The results—the staff not working 35 percent of the time—confirm the director's impression of serious delay problems. The breakdown into categories of delay yields valuable insight into causes.

The management system can be blamed for the first 18 percent of nonworking time. Equipment failure (3 percent), supplies shortage (6 percent), and wait for instructions (9 percent) are failures to provide technicians with resources to keep busy.

The 13 percent of delay for coffee breaks is an employee problem. Authorized coffee breaks are a 15-minute morning break and a 15-minute afternoon break. This amounts to 30 minutes or, in percent of an eight-hour day,

$$\frac{30 \text{ min.}}{8 \text{ hr.} \times 60 \text{ min./hr.}} = 0.0625 \approx 6\%$$

---

[5] In fact, work sampling used to be known as *ratio delay*, a term proposed by R. L. Morrow, an early U.S. user of the technique. (L. H. C. Tippett developed the method in England in the 1920s.) Later the editor of *Factory* magazine, recognizing its usefulness in time-standards analysis as well as delay analysis, proposed the more general term *work sampling.* Ralph M. Barnes, *Work Sampling* (Wiley, 1957), pp. 8–10 (T60.T5B3).

The coffee-break abuses may be dealt with immediately. The data on resource shortages do not suggest a solution, but they do tip off the director as to where to look.

Work-sampling concerns. Work sampling yields delay statistics. It also yields the complement, utilization statistics. Utilization rate (65 percent in the example) means "busyness," that is, hours busy divided by hours available. But most of us are very busy at times and not so busy at other times. This means that, to avoid bias, the analyst conducting work sampling must be careful to select a representative period of time in which to conduct the study (representative of average conditions if that is the goal of the study; representative of very busy conditions if peak conditions are being examined; etc.).

There are other types of bias to guard against. Some guidelines are:

Conduct the study over a number of days or weeks—so that results are not biased by a single unusual day.

FIGURE 8–12
Work-sampling data sheets, Midtown Pathological Labs

SCHEDULE OF OBSERVATION TIMES

	Mon.	Tues.	Wed.	Thurs.	Fri.

Mon.
8:01
8:13
9:47
9:59
10:12
10:59
11:16
11:32
1:00
1:15
1:19
2:52
2:55
2:56
2:57
3:02
3:29
3:37
4:07
4:32

WORK-SAMPLING FORM

Category of Activity	Observations (tallies)	Percentages
Working	‖‖‖ ... (65)	65%
Not working:		
• Equipment failure	⦙⦙ (3)	3%
• Supplies shortage	‖‖ ⦙ (6)	6%
• Wait for instructions	‖‖ ⦙⦙⦙⦙ (9)	9%
• Coffee break	‖‖ ‖‖ ⦙⦙⦙ (13)	13%
• Out of area	⦙⦙ (2)	2%
• Other	⦙⦙ (2)	2%
Total	100	100%

Make "instantaneous" observations—instead of observing the worker over a period of time that might include changing activities.

Vary the route of travel if the study comprises several work areas—to guard against having workers in one area alert workers in the next area to the observer's impending arrival.

Observe at random intervals—so that workers may not come consciously or unconsciously to expect and "prepare for" the observer's arrival at set intervals.

Tell the workers what you are doing, and emphasize the goal of improving resource support—to prevent an atmosphere of hostility and deliberate attempts to invalidate the study.

When in doubt, ask the worker what the observed activity is—to avoid judgmental bias.

Take a large enough sample to yield convincing results.

The last item—size of sample—may be statistically determined. In view of the many other sources of bias, concern about the statistically correct sample size can be overdone. The statistical formula does tell us, however, that if you are interested in an activity that occurs *often* or *seldom,* you can get by with a relatively small sample, in order to be confident about the percentage of occurrence that results from the study. You need a larger sample when your interest is in activities that occur close to 50 percent of the time. The statistical formula is:

$$N = \frac{Z^2(p)(1-p)}{S^2},$$

where

N = Sample size
Z = Number of standard errors (note: $Z \approx 2$ for a 95% confidence level)
p = Percentage of occurrence of the activity of interest
S^2 = Desired accuracy (e.g., use 0.05 if ±5% accuracy is desired)

It should be noted that utilization is not the same as efficiency. That is, one who works (is utilized) 100 percent of the time may or may not also be efficient. Efficiency is a measure of the speed at which work is turned out (output), and that is best determined with standard time as the basis. Standard time and related matters are considered next.

TIME STANDARDS OR ESTIMATES

Methods study comes first; time study comes next. Why? Because you prefer not to set a time standard on a poor method.

Actually, as we shall see, the ideal sequence of method first, time standard second, is not always practiced. Time standards tend to be more important—at least in the short run—than improved methods. In launching a new methods and standards program, some firms may therefore reverse the process: first cover all tasks with time standards—perhaps "quick and dirty" ones; later turn attention to methods studies; and finally refine time standards based on the improved methods. Let us see why time standards are thought to be so important.

Uses of time standards/ estimates

Work is simply a form of exertion. But a *work unit* (e.g., a job, task, project, or other unit) tends to imply a finite *time to do work*. Our thoughts about work time may not need to go beyond that notion of an implied time. But sometimes, perhaps to motivate ourselves or others, we are more specific about work time: We estimate it in advance. Time estimating—in advance—becomes more essential when more than one person is involved. If one person is waiting for another person's job to be finished, that person wants an estimate of how

FIGURE 8–13
Uses of time estimates or standards

Coordinational uses

    Scheduling. The time to perform a scheduled task is as shown below:

$$|\!\longleftarrow\!\text{Time standard—with efficiency and utilization adjustments}\longrightarrow\!|$$

Start   Finish
of   of
task   task

Analytical uses

    Staffing, budgeting, and estimating/bidding.

        Example: Forecast of × Standard time = Staff needed
                 work units   per unit   (e.g., in labor-hours)

    Evaluating alternative methods/equipment. The labor-cost element of a method/equipment alternative might include:

        Operating cost—based on standard time per unit of output.
        Maintenance cost—based on standard time to repair equipment.

Motivational uses

    Efficiency evaluation and incentive wages. Labor efficiency may be evaluated by:

$$\text{Efficiency} = \frac{\text{Standard time/unit}}{\text{Actual time/unit}} \text{ or } \frac{\text{Actual units/day}}{\text{Standard units/day}}$$

    Targets for personal motivation. Knowing what is expected of you provides self-motivation.

long the job will take. An explicit time estimate is also useful in analyzing labor needs and labor costs.

These different uses of time estimates or standards suggest three sorts of purposes: One is motivational, another is coordinational, and the third is analytical. The three types are listed in more detail in Figure 8–13.

Coordination. Under coordinational uses in the figure is *scheduling*. This may be the primary use of a time standard. It could be argued that, by definition, a schedule is a time standard, with adjustments for efficiency and utilization. That is, the time between the scheduled start and the scheduled finish of a task equals:

Standard time—the time that it should take under normal assumptions.

Adjusted downward for a fast worker or upward for a slow worker.

Adjusted downward for less than 100 percent labor utilization (i.e., for expected idleness).

Mathematically, scheduled output per eight-hour day is:

$$\text{Daily output} = \frac{8 \text{ hours/day}}{\text{Standard time/unit}} \times \text{Efficiency} \times \text{Utilization},$$

where

Efficiency = Speed or pace, expressed as a percentage of normal (100%) pace

Utilization = Percent of the day spent working (or available time minus idle time, expressed as a percent of available time)

A useful inversion of the formula is:

$$\text{Scheduled task time} = \frac{\text{Standard time/unit}}{\text{Efficiency} \times \text{Utilization}}$$

Many firms use a single combined efficiency-utilization rate instead of two separate rates. This might be called a productivity rate. Then,

$$\text{Scheduled task time} = \frac{\text{Standard time/unit}}{\text{Productivity rate}}$$

A benefit of this rate is that it permits productivity to be measured from recent historical data (e.g., standard output divided by actual output). But the historical data do not show how much of the productivity is efficiency and how much is utilization.

Using separate rates for efficiency and utilization adds precision. Efficiency is fairly stable over a few months. But utilization is controllable by management: Utilization goes up when workers are kept busy and provided with proper tools, etc.; it goes down when workers are not kept busy. Management may make adjustments when utilization is poor and then estimate a better rate for upcoming scheduling purposes. An example follows.

EXAMPLE 8–5
Translation of time standard into schedule, tire installation

Gate City Tire Company sells and installs tires, some by appointment, the rest to drop-in customers. Appointments are carefully scheduled so that (1) the customer may be told when the car will be ready and (2) installers are kept busy. The manager has determined that under normal conditions a four-tire installation should take 20 minutes. The time varies, depending on the speed of the installer and the delays encountered.

Current schedules are based on current speed and delay (i.e., efficiency and utilization) estimates. A recent study shows efficiency to be 90 percent (where normal efficiency or speed is 100 percent); it is low because the present crew is rather inexperienced. Utilization is predicted to be 80 percent (it would be 100 percent for a crew that is busy every minute of the eight-hour day). Delays arise mainly from tool breakdowns, parts shortages, special customer requests, and two authorized 15-minute coffee breaks; these, plus miscellaneous delays, account for the 20 percent nonutilization time.

The current scheduled daily output is:

$$\frac{8 \text{ hrs.} \times 60 \text{ min./hr.}}{20 \text{ min./installation}} \times 90\% \text{ efficiency}$$
$$\times 80\% \text{ utilization}$$
$$= 17.28 \text{ installations/day}$$

Seventeen installations per day is the expected output, but each of the 17 or so jobs in a day may be separately scheduled. For example, let us assume that the third job of the day, a phoned appointment, is assigned to Jeff, who has been only 80 percent efficient; but the manager expects no delays for lack of materials, tool breakdowns, or other problems, and it is not near to coffee-break time. So utilization is expected to be 100 percent. The scheduled installation time is:

$$\frac{20 \text{ min./installation}}{80\% \times 100\%} = 25 \text{ minutes}$$

Where coordinational demands are light, work units may not be formally scheduled. But we nearly always have at least a vague time plan for starting and finishing an upcoming task. That vague time plan is an implied schedule, and it is surely based on an implied time standard, with adjustments for expected pace and utilization. The time standard is pervasive indeed.

Analysis. One of the analytical uses listed in Figure 8–13 is staffing, budgeting, and estimating/bidding. As the figure suggests, staffing needs are the product of demand forecast and standard time. An analytically developed budget for staff goes one step further: staff needed times wage rate equals staff budget.

The staff component of an estimate or bid is computed in the same way as the staff component of a budget. Needless to say, accurate bidding is a key factor of success in contract-oriented businesses, for example, construction. Accurate cost estimating is important in job-shop work, because pricing is based on estimated cost plus profit margin. Physicians, attorneys, and consultants also often operate in this way.

The following example shows how a time standard is translated into the staff component of a budget/estimate/bid.

EXAMPLE 8-6
Bidding based on time standards, Teen Labor Services

An enterprising group of teenagers needing work have organized themselves into Teen Labor Services. Teen Labor bids on a variety of common-labor jobs. Teen Labor is currently preparing a bid that it will present to a nearby farmer who has two acres of nearly ripe cucumbers. One member of the group is experienced, and he says that three bushels per hour is standard for one worker. The farmer estimates that the field will yield 80 bushels per acre.

The bid is based on an estimate that the inexperienced crew will work at 85 percent efficiency. With breaks, plus delays caused by waiting for more baskets, waiting for the pickup truck, and so forth, it is estimated that utilization will be 80 percent. The group bids at a labor rate of $4 per hour. The bid is calculated as follows:

$$\text{Scheduled output per hour} = 3 \text{ bushels/hr.} \times 85\% \text{ efficiency} \times 80\% \text{ utilization}$$
$$= 2.04 \text{ bushels/hr.}$$

$$\text{Total bushels} = 2 \text{ acres} \times 80 \text{ bushels/acre}$$
$$= 160 \text{ bushels}$$

$$\text{Scheduled hours} = \frac{160 \text{ bushels}}{2.04 \text{ bushels/hr.}}$$
$$= 78.43 \text{ hrs.}$$

$$\text{Labor component of bid} = 78.43 \text{ hrs.} \times \$4/\text{hr.}$$
$$= \$313.72$$

For this job Teen Labor foresees no expenses for supplies, tools, materials, utilities, and so on, and Teen Labor never adds an overhead charge or a profit margin. Therefore, the bid consists entirely of the labor cost, $313.72.

The other analytical use of time standards is evaluating alternative methods/equipment. Most such alternatives involve some labor costs. The labor component of operating cost is based on standard time per unit of output, with adjustments for efficiency and utilization. This component is based on standard time per unit of output, with adjustments for efficiency and utilization. The labor component of maintenance cost is based on standard time to repair, with adjustments.

Motivation. Motivational uses of time standards are control uses rather than planning uses. The time standard serves as a target for the control of labor output.

The control may be external—efficiency evaluation and incentive wages in Figure 8–13. A typical efficiency evaluation provides a periodic report of efficiency by worker, work center, and/or department. Efficiency is determined in one of two ways:

1. For nonrepetitive operations:

$$\text{Efficiency} = \frac{\text{Standard labor hours scheduled in reporting period}}{\text{Actual clock time in reporting period}}$$

$$\text{or, simply,} \frac{\text{Standard hours}}{\text{Actual hours}}$$

2. For repetitive operations:

$$\text{Efficiency} = \frac{\text{Actual units produced in reporting period}}{\text{Standard units scheduled in reporting period}}$$

$$\text{or, simply, } \frac{\text{Actual output}}{\text{Standard output}}$$

Notice that the two versions are mathematically equivalent, and, in fact, the formula for nonrepetitive operations would also work for repetitive operations (but not the other way around). For example, if 440 actual units are produced in a 40-hour week, and 400 is the standard output per week,

$$\text{Efficiency (by formula 2)} = \frac{\text{Actual units/week}}{\text{Standard units/week}}$$

$$= \frac{440 \text{ units/week}}{400 \text{ units/week}}$$

$$= 1.10, \text{ or } 110\%$$

and

$$\text{Efficiency (by formula 1)} = \frac{\text{Standard min./unit}}{\text{Actual min./unit}}$$

$$= \frac{\dfrac{40 \text{ hrs./wk.} \times 60 \text{ min./hr.}}{400 \text{ units/wk.}}}{\dfrac{40 \text{ hrs./wk.} \times 60 \text{ min./hr.}}{440 \text{ units/wk.}}}$$

$$= \frac{\dfrac{2{,}400 \text{ min./wk.}}{400 \text{ units/wk.}}}{\dfrac{2{,}400 \text{ min./wk.}}{440 \text{ units/wk.}}}$$

$$= \frac{6 \text{ min./unit}}{5.45 \text{ min./unit}}$$

$$= 1.10, \text{ or } 110\%$$

Sometimes incentive wages are paid. There are many ways to set up an incentive-wage system.[6] A pure incentive is simply a piece rate; for example, a berry picker's piece rate might be $1 per bucket. But wage-and-hour laws require that piece-rate earnings may not fall below the minimum wage, based on hours worked.

Incentive wages may also be based on standard times. In some plans incentive wages are paid for increments of output above an acceptable productivity

---

[6] See, for example, John A. Patton, C. L. Littlefield, and Stanley Allen Self, *Job Evaluation* (Irwin, 1964).

level (APL). The APL equals standard output or some agreed-upon percentage of it.

A more typical system is measured daywork (MDW), which is only nominally an incentive-wage system. In MDW, standard output serves as a target that methods engineers, trainers, and supervisors help the worker attain. If the worker cannot attain it, he is helped into another position or advised to seek work elsewhere.

The final item in Figure 8–13 is the time standard as a target for personal motivation. An open-ended assignment invites delay. An explicit statement of how long the task should take serves as self-motivation to the worker. Some research suggests that self-motivation is greater if the worker also plots his own output on a graph.

Time standards techniques

There are common abuses (to be discussed later) as well as common uses of time standards. Some uses and abuses pertain to the techniques by which time standards are developed. The common techniques may be grouped into two levels of precision: engineered and nonengineered. These are described in Figure 8–14.

Engineered and nonengineered time standards. Four techniques may result in engineered time standards. The engineered standard is prepared at

FIGURE 8–14
Techniques for setting time standards

Technique	Source of times	Timing role of analyst
Engineered		
1. Time study	Stopwatch (or film)	Direct observation: record times for several cycles of the task; judge and record pace.
2. Work sampling	Percent of study period busy at given task divided by number of units produced	Direct observation: randomly check worker status; keep tallies of worker activities and pace; obtain production count.
3. Predetermined	Table look-up	Define task in basic body motions; look up time values in basic motion tables.
4. Standard data	Table look-up	Define task in small common elements (e.g., pound nail); look up time value in standard-data tables.
Nonengineered		
5. Historical (statistical)	Past records on actual task times	Determine arithmetic mean and/or other useful statistics.
6. Technical estimate ("guesstimate")	Experienced judgment	Experienced person estimates times, preferably after breaking task into operations.

some expense, generally following the scientific methods of the industrial engineering profession. Two of the engineered techniques require direct observation. These are stopwatch time study, a well-known approach, and work sampling, which was presented earlier as a process analysis technique. The other two engineered techniques, predetermined and standard data, do not require direct observation; instead, the analyst building a standard uses tables of time values. Since a real worker is not involved, these standards are sometimes referred to as synthetic time standards.

Two techniques are listed as nonengineered. The first is historical or statistical. It is based on past records rather than on controlled study. The second is the technical estimate or "guesstimate."[7] It is developed from subjective instead of statistical (recorded) experience.

Requisites of an engineered standard. The expense of an engineered time standard is worthwhile if a precise time estimate is needed: for example, in highly repetitive processes where gains in unit output accrue with each unit produced. Precision may be gained by including the following steps in the time-standards study.

1. Clearly specify the method.
2. Obtain time values via a proper sampling procedure or from validated tables.
3. Adjust for worker pace.
4. Include allowances for personal, rest, and delay.

Each step adds precision. A precise time standard is associated with a known standard method (ideally an improved or engineered method). Precise time values may be obtained by a proper sampling procedure in which a direct observation technique is used; sampling is avoided by using a synthetic technique that relies on validated tables of time values. The time value should be adjusted for worker pace where a direct observation technique is used; but validated tables for synthetic standards have built-in pace adjustments. Finally, the pace-adjusted time is further adjusted by adding reasonable allowances for workers' personal and rest time and for unavoidable delay.

The nonengineered techniques control for none of the four above factors of precision. Indeed, the four techniques listed as engineered in Figure 8–14 are not engineered by definition or by title; they are worthy of the term *engineered* only if they are precisely developed, following the four steps. In the following discussions of each technique, we see how the steps apply in each case. Time study is discussed first and in some detail; the other techniques include many of the same steps.

Time study

The most direct approach to time standards is direct timing of a worker performing the task. Times are usually taken by stopwatch, but motion-picture

---

[7] It is also known as a WAG or a SWAG, common abbreviations for slightly salty terms that some readers may be familiar with.

film also works.[8] Time study is best for shorter-cycle tasks. The expense of having an analyst physically present at the worksite and timing a proper number of cycles of the task tends to rule out time study for longer-cycle tasks. The four time-study steps and an example are explained below.

Task selection and method definition. Time study begins with selection of a task to study. There are choices to be made here. For example, packing and crating a large refrigeration unit might consist of packing the unit into a carton, placing the carton on a pallet, building a wooden crate around the carton and pallet, stenciling, and steel-strapping. A single time study of the whole series of operations is one possibility. Or separate time studies could be done for each major operation—packing, placing, and so forth. But each of these operations involves lesser operations, which could be separately time-studied. The pounding of a single nail into a crate could be the task chosen for study.

Once the task has been chosen, the analyst defines the method. This involves dividing the task into elements that are easy to recognize and to time. The definition must clearly specify the actions that constitute the start and the end of each element; this is how the analyst knows when to take each stopwatch reading.

Cycle time. Tools of the time-study analyst include a clipboard, a preprinted time-study data sheet, and a stopwatch. The watch is usually mounted on the clipboard. Without timing, the analyst observes the task a few times in order to be sure that the worker is following the prescribed method.

In the timing phase a stopwatch reading is taken and recorded for each element. Several cycles of the task should be timed so that effects of early or late readings can be averaged out. Multiple cycles also provide a better basis for judging pace and for observing unavoidable delays and irregular activities. A "remarks" section on the data sheet may be used for comments on irregularities.

The number of cycles to time could be calculated based on the statistical dispersion of individual element readings. However, most firms pay more attention to the cost of multiple cycles than to the statistical dispersion of element readings. For example, General Electric has established a table as a guide to the number of cycles.[9] The table calls for timing only three cycles if the cycle time is 40 minutes or more. But it calls for timing 200 cycles if the cycle time is as short as 0.1 minute. Since 200 cycles at 0.1 minute adds up to only 20 minutes of total observer time, the 200-cycle study may cost less to do than the 3-cycle study of a 40-minute task.

The result of timing is an average *cycle time (CT)*.

---

[8] Use of film analysis seems to have peaked in the World War II era. Any idea that might help with the war effort had a good chance of being funded at that time, and industrial film labs seemed to have the potential to help increase productivity. Today few firms use film techniques.

[9] Benjamin W. Niebel, *Motion and Time Study,* 6th ed. (Irwin, 1976), p. 325; also see a more elaborate table from Westinghouse on p. 278 (T56.N48).

Pace rating. If the analyst times a slow worker, the average cycle time will be excessive—*loose* is the term usually used; if a faster worker is timed, the CT will be tight. To avoid loose or tight standards, the analyst judges the worker's pace during the study. The pace rating is then used mathematically to adjust CT so that the result is a normal time. This is called *normalizing* or *leveling*. The normal pace is 100 percent; a 125 percent pace is 25 percent faster; and so on.

Pace rating is the most judgmental part of setting time standards. But it need not be pure guesswork. Films are available from the American Management Association and other sources for training in pace rating. A variety of factory and office tasks are shown in the films. The same task is shown at different speeds, and the viewer writes down what the pace appears to be for each speed. The projector is shut off, and the viewer's ratings are compared with an "answer key." The correct answers were decided upon by experts or measured by film speed.

Expert opinion has been channeled to some extent by reference to two widely accepted benchmarks of normal (100 percent) pace. One benchmark, for hand motions, is dealing 52 cards into four equal piles (bridge hands) in 30 seconds. The other benchmark is walking on a smooth, level surface, without load, at three miles per hour. These concepts of normal may be extrapolated to a wide variety of other manual activities.

Most people can become good enough at pace rating to be able to come within ±5 percent of the correct ratings on training films. It is generally easier to rate a worker who is close to normal than one who is very slow or fast. Because of this, it is a good idea for the analyst to try to find a rather normal worker to observe in doing a time study (or a work-sampling study). Sometimes pace rating is "omitted" by preselecting a worker who is performing at normal; the omission of pace rating is illusory, since the rating is done in the worker-selection step.

Personal, rest, and delay (PR&D). The normalized time per unit is not usable as a standard time. It is unfair to expect a worker to produce at that normal rate hour after hour without stopping. Personal time (drinking fountain, rest room, etc.) must be allowed for. Rest time, such as coffee breaks, must also be allowed for. And there may be unavoidable delays that should be included in the time standard.

Personal and rest time may be a matter of company policy or union contract. The rest (fatigue) allowance may be a strictly coffee-break allowance. This is common with clerical employees. The rest or fatigue allowance may be job dependent in industrial shops. For example, tasks performed in a cold-storage freezer or near a blast furnace sometimes entail fatigue allowances as high as 50 percent.

Unavoidable delay could be set by contract or policy. More often, it is task dependent. Unavoidable delays may result from difficulty in meeting tight tolerances, from material irregularities, and from machine inbalances when a worker operates more than one machine. Interruptions by foreman, dispatcher, material handler, and so on, may also qualify. Strictly speaking, an unavoidable delay is one inherent in the method. Some delays caused by foremen or other staff may be like material or tool shortages and machine breakdowns: They may be avoided by better management of resources. Unavoidable delays are sometimes determined by a work-sampling study in which occurrences of various types of delay are tallied.

The allowances are usually combined as a percentage, referred to as the *PR&D* or *PF&D allowance*. The combined allowance is then added to the normalized time. The result is the *standard time*.

Time-study example. The steps in a time study are best understood by seeing how they are treated on the time-study data sheet. An example follows.

EXAMPLE 8–7 Time study of bolt-washer- nut assembly	The proposed bolt-washer-nut assembly method (see Figure 8–7) was approved, and a time-study analyst was assigned to develop a time standard for the task. The analyst has, after observation, reduced the task to 4 timeable elements (as opposed to 15 elements that were defined for purposes of detailed methods study). Six cycles are timed[10] by the continuous stopwatch method, and each element is pace-rated.

The time-study data sheet is shown in Figure 8–15. The stopwatch is read in hundredths of a minute; decimal points are not inserted by the analyst until after the last computation. The stopwatch begins at zero and runs continuously for 7.55 minutes. Continuous readings are entered below the diagonal line, and elemental times are then computed by successive subtraction. (The subtraction step could be avoided by using the snap-back method instead of continuous timing; that is, snap the sweep hand back to zero after each reading by pushing the button on top of the stopwatch.)

Average cycle time (CT) is computed by summing elemental times and dividing by 6; for element 2, CT is divided by 5 because one irregular elemental time was thrown out. The averge is below the diagonal line in the CT column. Pace ratings are in the rating factor (RF) column, with decimal points not included. Normalized time (NT) equals CT times RF. The total of the NT column is 110, or 1.10 minutes per cycle.

The firm has a PR&D allowance negotiated with the labor union. The current allowance provides 3 percent personal time (e.g., blow nose), two 15-minute rest (coffee) breaks, and 2 percent unavoidable delay allowance. (These are minimum allowances; the contract allows rest time to be set higher for highly fatiguing work, and the delay allowance may be set higher for tasks involving abnormal delays.)

The two 15-minutes breaks are converted to percentages of an eight-hour or 480-minute day by:

$$\frac{30 \text{ min.}}{480 \text{ min.}} = 0.0625, \text{ or } 6.25\%$$

$$\text{Total PR\&D allowance} = 3\% + 6.25\% + 2\%$$
$$= 11.25\%.$$

---

[10] For a short-cycle task like bolt-washer-nut assembly, it would take less than an hour to time, say 30 cycles, and this would improve reliability. The six-cycle example is thus less than ideal.

Element	Cycles						CT	RF	NT	Remarks
	1	2	3	4	5	6				
1. Get bolts and place in fixture	12	10	13	11	16	10	72	110	13.2	
	12	116	240	349	468	656	12			
2. Get washers and place on bolts	14	16	15	14	93	14	73	100	14.6	5th cycle: Blew nose
	26	132	255	363	561	670	14.6			
3. Get nuts and assemble onto bolts	75	86	77	82	79	78	477	95	75.5	
	101	218	332	445	640	748	79.5			
4. Drop assemblies down chutes	05	09	06	07	06	07	40	100	6.7	
	106	227	338	452	646	755	6.7			

Total normalized time 110.0
PR&D allowance + 100% 111.25%
Standard time.................. 122.375, or 1.22 min./cycle

Note: CT is sometimes called the select time (ST); NT is sometimes called the leveled time (LT) or rated time (RT).

FIGURE 8–15
Time-study data sheet, bolt-washer-nut assembly

The final computation is multiplying the total normalized time by the PR&D allowance of 11.25 percent plus 100 percent (which is mathematically the same as adding 11.25 percent to the total normalized time). The result is the standard time of 1.22 minutes per cycle.

Work-sampling standards

Work sampling was discussed earlier as a technique for determining labor-utilization and -delay rates. To extend the use of work sampling into time-standards setting requires one extra piece of data: a production count, that is, a count of units produced or customers served during the study period. Cycle time (CT), then, is:

$$\text{Cycle time} = \frac{\% \text{ utilization} \times \text{Total minutes in study period}}{\text{Production count}}$$

Cycle time is transformed into standard time by normalizing for worker pace and adding PR&D allowance—the same as for time study. An example follows.

EXAMPLE 8–8
Work sampling for setting time standards, pathology lab

The director of Midtown Pathological Labs has conducted a one-week work-sampling study of the lab staff. The results, in Figure 8–12, were that the staff was working 65 percent of the time. The director also tallied, on a separate data sheet, the type of work task observed. The lab performs two major types of analysis and a host of miscellaneous analyses, and the director found that the 65 percent work time was divided as follows:

Serum-blood tests (standard tests) in chemistry lab 30%
Whole-blood tests (complete blood count) in hematology lab 25
Miscellaneous tests in either lab 10
    Total work time 65%

There are two lab technicians in the chemistry lab and one in hematology.

At the end of the study the director found that 48 serum tests and 32 whole-blood tests had been performed in the lab. The director's estimates of worker pace are 90 percent for serum tests and 105 percent for whole-blood tests. Midtown allows a PR&D allowance of 13 percent.

Based on the data, it is possible to set a time standard for both the serum test and the whole-blood test.

Serum test:

$$\text{Cycle time} = \frac{0.30 \times 5 \text{ days} \times 480 \text{ min./day/technician} \times 2 \text{ technicians}}{48 \text{ tests}}$$

$$= \frac{1{,}440 \text{ min.}}{48 \text{ tests}}$$

$$= 30 \text{ min. per test}$$

$$\begin{aligned}\text{Standard time} &= CT \times RF \times (100\% + \text{PR\&D})\\ &= 30 \times 90\% \times 113\%\\ &= 30.51 \text{ min. per test (per technician)}\end{aligned}$$

Whole-blood test:

$$\text{Cycle time} = \frac{0.25 \times 5 \text{ days} \times 480 \text{ min./day/technician}}{32 \text{ tests}}$$

$$= \frac{600 \text{ min.}}{32 \text{ tests}}$$

$$= 18.75 \text{ min.}$$

$$\begin{aligned}\text{Standard time} &= CT \times RF \times (100\% + \text{PR\&D})\\ &= 18.75 \times 105\% \times 113\%\\ &= 22.25 \text{ min. per test}\end{aligned}$$

Are these precise (engineered) time standards? The technicians in the chemistry lab do not think so. They point out to the director that their method is to run the serum tests in batches and as a two-person team. There could be one or many samples in a batch, but the time to run a batch does not directly depend on the number of samples in a batch. The time standard for serum testing is imprecise, indeed invalid, because the work-sampling study was not precise as to method.

The hematology technician has a milder objection: A mere 25 observations of the whole-blood testing were extrapolated into an assumed 600 minutes of testing time during the week. While the sample size seems rather small, the technician and the director decide that the standard time of 22.25 minutes per test is usable for the critical purpose of planning adjustments in short-term capacity. These include scheduling overtime, using part-time help, and subcontracting to other labs.

For example, on a given day perhaps 30 blood samples will arrive at the lab and require testing in hematology. At 22.25 minutes per test, the workload is 22.25 × 30 = 667.5 minutes of testing. Since an eight-hour day is only 480 minutes, the director had better tell the technician to plan on some overtime that evening. Or part-time help or subcontracting could be arranged.

Predetermined standards

Predetermined time standards are really partway predetermined. The predetermined part is the tables of time values for basic motions. The other part is properly selecting basic-motion time values in order to build a time standard for a larger task.

Basic-motion tables were Gilbreth's idea. But it took some 35 years of effort by a variety of researchers to develop the tables. The best-known tables are those of the MTM (Methods-Time Measurement) Association.[11] Others include the Work-Factor, Brief Work-Factor, and Basic Motion Timestudy (BMT) systems. Our limited discussion focuses on MTM.

MTM and other synthetic techniques have several advantages:

1. No need to time; the data are in tables.
2. No need to observe; the standard may be set before the job is ever performed and without disrupting the worker.
3. No need to rate pace; the time data in the table were normalized when the tables were created.

A disadvantage of MTM is the great amount of detail involved in building a standard from the tables. Basic MTM motions are tiny; times are measured in time measurement units (TMU's), and one TMU is only 0.0006 minute. The bolt-nut-washer assembly with a time standard of 1.22 minutes per cycle by time study (see Figure 8–15) is equal to 2,033 TMU's. Basic MTM motions usually take 10 to 20 TMU's. Therefore the bolt-nut-washer assembly would be described in something like 100 or 200 basic MTM motions. The MTM analyst needs considerable training to be able to specify tasks in that amount of detail. Still, MTM is perceived as being a fair approach to time standards, and it has become widely used.

The MTM Association has developed tables for the following types of basic motions: reach; move; turn and apply pressure; grasp; position; release; disengage; eye travel and eye focus; body, leg, and foot motions; and simultaneous motions. Most of the tables were developed by film analysis.

One of the tables, the reach table, is shown in Figure 8–16. From the table we see, for example, that reaching 16 inches to an "object jumbled with other

---

[11] The tables were originally developed by H. B. Maynard and associates. See Harold B. Maynard, G. J. Stegemerten, and John L. Schwab, *Methods-Time Measurement* (McGraw-Hill, 1948) (T60.T5M3).

FIGURE 8–16
Reach table for
MTM analysis

Length of reach in inches	Time in TMU's*				Hand in motion (TMU)		Case and description
	Case A	Case B	Case C or D	Case E	A	B	
¾ or less ..	2.0	2.0	2.0	2.0	1.6	1.6	A—Reach to object in a fixed
1	2.5	2.5	3.6	2.4	2.3	2.3	location or to object in
2	4.0	4.0	5.9	3.8	3.5	2.7	other hand or on which the
3	5.3	5.3	7.3	5.3	4.5	3.6	other hand rests
4	6.1	6.4	8.4	6.8	4.9	4.3	B—Reach to single object in
5	6.5	7.8	9.4	7.4	5.3	5.0	location which may vary
6	7.0	8.6	10.1	8.0	5.7	5.7	slightly from cycle to cycle
7	7.4	9.3	10.8	8.7	6.1	6.5	
8	7.9	10.1	11.5	9.3	6.5	7.2	C—Reach to object jumbled
9	8.3	10.8	12.2	9.9	6.9	7.9	with other objects in a
10	8.7	11.5	12.9	10.5	7.3	8.6	group so that search and select occur
12	9.6	12.9	14.2	11.8	8.1	10.1	
14	10.5	14.4	15.6	13.0	8.9	11.5	D—Reach to a very small
16	11.4	15.8	17.0	14.2	9.7	12.9	object or where accurate
18	12.3	17.2	18.4	15.5	10.5	14.4	grasp is required
20	13.1	18.6	19.8	16.7	11.3	15.8	E—Reach to indefinite
22	14.0	20.1	21.2	18.0	12.1	17.3	position to get hand in
24	14.9	21.5	22.5	19.2	12.9	18.8	position for body balance,
26	15.8	22.9	23.9	20.4	13.7	20.2	next motion, or out
28	16.7	24.4	25.3	21.7	14.5	21.7	of way
30	17.5	25.8	26.7	22.9	15.3	23.2	

* One time measurement unit (TMU) represents 0.00001 hour.
Source: MTM Association for Standards and Research. Copyrighted by the MTM Association for Standards and Research. No reprint permission without written consent from the MTM Association, 16–01 Broadway, Fair Lawn, New Jersey   07410.

objects in a group so that search and select occur" takes 17 TMU's. That motion, abbreviated as an *RC16* motion, is equal to about 0.01 minute, or less than a second.

If this were the first motion of the left hand as part of an MTM study, it would be entered at the top of a left-and-right-hand chart (or a simultaneous motion—SIMO—chart) serving as a data sheet. Right-hand motions would be entered on the right side, with nonhand motions fitted in. TMU's are totaled at the bottom, and converted to minutes. The total is the rated (leveled) time, not the cycle time, because 100 percent pace is built into the tables. The addition of a PR&D allowance yields the standard time.

Standard data

Standard-data standards, like predetermined (e.g., MTM) standards, are synthetically produced from tables. But standard-data tables are for larger units of work. The best-known example is the flat-rate manuals used in the auto-repair industry.[12] Flat-rate tables list repair times for a wide variety of repair tasks, such as "Replace points" and "Change oil."

If the standard-data tables are developed by using precise time study, work sampling, or MTM, then standard times extracted from the tables could be considered to be engineered. It is normal for a firm to keep time standards on file, and it is just one more step to pull standards out of the files and assemble them into standard-data tables. The next step is to assemble standard data for a whole trade or industry. This has been done in auto repair and many other trades, notably machining and various maintenance trades.[13]

Variable working conditions and lack of common methods from firm to firm compromise somewhat the precision built into standard data. Still, standard data are a powerful tool in that they bring time standards down to the level of the planner, the supervisor, and the operator. Experts create the tables, but laymen can use them.

Historical standards and technical estimates

It seems safe to say that nonengineered techniques—historical and technical estimates—are far more widely used than engineered techniques. And rightly so. Most of the work (or play) that most of us do is variable, and the cost to measure it with precision is prohibitive. Still, explicit time estimates or standards are needed because they help to improve management, and nonengineered techniques serve the purpose.

Historical standards and technical estimates are simple to develop and need not be explained further. As all six standards-setting techniques have been treated, discussion turns to questions of humanity and fairness.

HUMANITY AND FAIRNESS IN SCIENTIFIC MANAGEMENT

Scientific management is a two-edged sword. It cuts waste (improves productivity), but it alienates people. Under the rigorous applications of scientific management, we see fewer jobs that are made interesting by task variety and opportunity to exercise judgment. Jobs with these characteristics tend to be broken apart into narrow and invariable jobs. Unskilled workers may be hired at less pay to perform these narrow and highly engineered jobs. The payoff is cheaper goods and services of more uniform quality.

But the unskilled worker lacks the pride and commitment of the craftsman.

---

[12] Auto manufacturers produce such tables for repairs on new cars. Flat-rate manuals for older cars, which take more time to repair, are available from various independent companies. Best known are the Chilton manuals, which are available to the general public through bookstores and libraries.

[13] It should be noted that there are various levels of standard data. Some would consider basic motions (e.g., MTM) to be standard data at the most detailed level. Next come combinations of basic data (e.g., the MTM Association's general-purpose data), such as a joint time for reach–grasp–release. Then come elemental standard data for common elements like gauging and marking. Standard data for still larger units of work are at the level of whole tasks, such as the tasks of auto-repair mechanics or electricians.

Visible immediate gains in productivity may be eroded by longer-term losses in motivation and by the growth of alienation.

One solution is to automate the boring jobs out of existence. This has been the promise of automation. But automation requires massive capital expenditure. The need for humans persists.[14]

Another solution is not to break jobs down into narrow tasks but instead to apply methods improvement and time standards to more variable jobs. Let us examine this possibility further.

Task variety and job design

Use of the step-by-step analytical approach to methods improvement leads inevitably to decreased task variety for the jobholder. Avoiding that kind of foregone conclusion calls for a different approach. *Job design,* as opposed to task analysis, is emerging in response to that need. (Note: A worker holds a job and performs tasks. Job design has more to do with labor-resource planning; task design has more to do with operations planning.)

Job design is still more a concept or idea than a formal step-by-step technique. It is easier to point to examples of results of job design than to talk about how to do it. Prime examples of the job-design approach are the efforts in many firms to enlarge and enrich jobs through job-enrichment programs. IBM's early efforts to enlarge jobs in its manufacturing areas have been well publicized. Other notable examples are found in the insurance, appliance, and textile industries.

In the late 1960s and early 1970s a few manufacturers began experimenting with *nonlinear assembly.* When this approach is used, assembly lines are replaced by assembly areas and assembly-line workers become assembly-area team members who are no longer isolated at spots along an assembly line. Team members are cross-trained, and the team has a daily or weekly production quota or standard to meet. Sometimes teams are leaderless and do their own interviewing to fill vacancies. Usually the team has responsibility for the quality or operability of the end product (and even packaging, shipping, and office work in the case of one General Foods pet food plant in Topeka).

Nonlinear assembly is aimed at restoring task variety, social interaction, commitment, and motivation. But nonlinear assembly has not caught the fancy of many manufacturers. Part of the reason may be high training costs and greater variability (less dependability) of output. Training costs are high because methods are less well defined and jobs less specialized. Variability of

---

[14] The point is elaborated upon in the following quotation:

> In the automotive industry . . . many of the component-producing departments are highly automated, while there is no essential difference in assembly methods today from those used in making the Model T. As the machining departments are automated, workers are laid off or transferred to the assembly lines where the work is still manual. . . . [Assembly] is the last frontier of manufacturing automation.

Theodore O. Prenting and Nicholas T. Thomopoulas, *Humanism and Technology in Assembly Line Systems* (Spartan Books, 1974), p. 5 (TS178.4.P73).

output can lead to factory coordination problems, because group quotas are loose (perhaps nonengineered) as compared with the tight task time standards in assembly-line jobs. In short, some of the traditional advantages of methods and standards are lost in nonlinear assembly.

Responses to variability

Work measurement seems best suited for repetitive tasks. It may seem poorly suited to variable tasks, for example, job-shop tasks. A better way of putting it is that work measurement should be applied differently to variable tasks. Four key differences between work measurement for variable tasks and repetitive tasks are:

1. *For variable tasks, nonengineered time standards are often more suitable.* Engineered standards are likely to be too expensive, and for a job just received and about to begin there is not enough time to develop more than a technical estimate. (But variable jobs are sometimes assembled from tasks which have been done before and for which engineered standards exist, e.g., as standard data.)

2. *For variable tasks, evaluation against standards should be less frequent.* Nonengineered standards will sometimes be unfairly high and sometimes low. High and low estimates may cancel each other out over a suitable reporting period; that allows efficiency reporting to be used fairly—but only if times for many jobs are aggregated over the reporting period.

Example: The U.S. Air Force Logistics Command, which operates very large job shops for aircraft repair, compares accumulated standard times against accumulated clock hours for most of its repair-shop crews. The reporting period is two weeks, a period long enough to include perhaps hundreds of task time standards, most of which are technical estimates.

3. *When a task covered by a time standard includes variable operations, the standard should not be a basis for comparing employees, unless all employees encounter the same mix of operations.*

Example: Many college libraries use computers to produce catalog cards for newly acquired books. A cataloging aide with book in hand enters data about a newly acquired book at a remote terminal, and the data are transmitted across the country to a central library cataloging service center. The service center's computer data base is searched to find a Library of Congress catalog number for the book. For the search to be successful, the cataloging aide must enter the right data. This can be difficult, for example, for foreign-language books, musical compositions, and government documents.

One college library set a monthly standard rate (historical) of 300 books per cataloging aide. The standard rate was deeply resented, because some aides arrived early in the morning in order to fill their carts with easy books, which allowed them to easily exceed 300 books per month. Some of the aides who were challenged by the tough books actually looked worse when the monthly statistics were compiled. The solution: Distribute books to cataloging aides at random each morning. That way, each receives about the same variety of types of books over a period of months.

4. *For variable tasks, time standards uses may be limited.* For example, in one effort to set time standards on lawyers' tasks the sole purpose was to straighten out a staffing mess. The lawyers worked in 36 program offices of U.S. Department of the Interior, and it was difficult to assign the proper number of lawyers to each office.

A consultant was hired to help define work units and set standards.[15] The basic work unit was a *matter* (not a case, because matters often did not result in cases). Fifty-nine varieties of matters were defined, and secretaries kept records on the time spent by lawyers on each matter. The results were fairly consistent throughout the United States, and the average times served as historical (nonengineered) standards for use in staffing decisions. That is, in a given office each matter could be forecasted (by trend projection, etc.) and multiplied by standard time to yield labor-hours, which converted into staff needs.

Professional work like that of a lawyer is not only variable but is often perceived as something of an art and as resistant to standardization. The lawyers in this example cooperated because the limited purpose—better staffing—was made clear. It seems likely that there would have been no cooperation had the purpose been to judge efficiency or even to schedule lawyers' tasks or matters.

The element of judgment

The engineered time standard purports to be scientific. And it is to a degree, but elements of judgment are always present. Bertram Gottlieb, an industrial engineer for the AFL–CIO, makes that point in his monograph *The Art of Time Study: An Exercise of Personal Judgement.*[16] Gottlieb is able to cite court opinions supporting the general view that company standards are not always so scientific that they are exempt from collective bargaining.

Besides collective bargaining, there is in some firms a good deal of informal negotiation ("horse trading") over time standards. The analyst may produce a standard that follows engineered procedures to the letter and then be talked into loosening up the standard. The analyst's principles are compromised, but such compromising makes life a bit easier for the analyst in future visits to the work center.

Fair pay

The idea of tying pay directly to output or efficiency is an appealing one. Nevertheless, direct wage incentives are rather uncommon. Differing concepts of fair pay may be part of the reason why. The notion that *fair* pay is pay according to output is a limited view. Figure 8–17 helps put the concept of fair pay into perspective.

One concept of fair pay is that everyone should be paid the same, and minimum-wage laws are a means of bringing that about. Pay by time worked is a second concept of fair pay, and a popular one. Pay by job content also seems fair, especially in large organizations where unequal pay for the same

---

[15] Part of the consultant's story is told in Mundel, *Motion and Time Study,* pp. 485–94.

[16] Center for Labor and Management, College of Business Administration, University of Iowa, October 1966 (T60.T5G65).

FIGURE 8–17
Concepts of fair
pay

What is fair pay?	Who subscribes to this?
1. *Everyone paid the same* Rationale: We are all created equal; we are all products of our environments and partners in society. Means: High minimum wages applied equally to all.	Organized labor Socialists
2. *Pay by the hour (or week, month, year)* Rationale: Though we are products of our environment, society's work must be done, and work is most easily measured in time units. Means: Have workers punch time clocks, and reprimand them for tardiness.	Supervisors (easy to figure out pay) Organized labor (workers like to "put in their time"—or their time and a half)
3. *Pay according to job content* Rationale: It is not the person who should be paid but the position; "heavy" positions should be paid heavily, "light" positions lightly. Means: Job evaluation, using job ranking/classification, point plan, factor comparison	Personnel managers (requires a large pay-and-classification staff) Bureaucrats (seems rational and impersonal; fits concept of rank or hierarchy)
4. *Pay according to output* Rationale: Though we are products of our environment, society's work should be done, and work should be measured in output (not merely time on the job). Output efficiency is based on a count of actual units produced as compared to a standard. Means: Piecework, incentive pay, profit sharing.	Industrial engineers Economists
5. *Pay according to supply and demand* Rationale: Society's messiest jobs must be done too, and greater pay for less desirable jobs is necessary to attract workers. Means: Let the labor market function (or list jobs needing to be done, and set pay according to willingness to do each job—the Walden II method)	Some economists (e.g., those advocating below-minimum wages for teenagers) B. F. Skinner (see his book *Walden II*)

work would be a visible problem; evaluating job content is an important function in larger personnel departments. A fourth concept of fair pay is pay based on output against standards, which has appealing productivity advantages. The last concept in Figure 8–17 (not necessarily a complete list) is pay by supply and demand; this seems fair to society in that it provides greater rewards for people willing to do society's messiest jobs.

What Figure 8–17 suggests is that time standards (also minimum wages, time clocks, job evaluation, and free-market labor pricing) are not the whole answer to fair pay and should therefore be used with discretion.

SUMMARY

Scientific management emerged at the turn of the century as a final phase of the industrial revolution. Its main ingredients are methods and process design and time standards.

Methods and process design may involve many parties: employees, supervisors, personnel training branch, production control planners, industrial engineers and IE technicians, paperwork specialists, computer systems analysts, and programmers. Work-simplification, employee-suggestion and cost-reduction programs are aimed at the coordination of methods-improvement efforts.

Methods and time standards are central in the assembly of a planning package, which goes to workers and involved staff. Engineers develop the product design; methods analysts develop methods and processes, often in the form of a route sheet; standard times or estimates are entered on the route sheet; and finally the scheduler determines due dates.

Formal methods study follows the scientific method. A task is selected; data about it are collected; the data are analyzed, leading to alternative methods; the alternatives are evaluated; and the chosen alternative is implemented. It is common to use flowcharts to gather data (on a "before" flowchart), analyze data, and generate and evaluate alternatives (on an "after" flowchart). Another tool, work sampling, can yield data on employee or facilities utilization, or "busyness," and it can show percentages of work time in various delay categories of the resource-delivery system.

Time standards improve coordination by providing a sound basis for scheduling; are useful for analyzing the labor component in staff needs, for budgeting and estimating/bidding, and for evaluating operating and maintenance costs; and are also valuable for self-motivation and for external motivation derived from efficiency reporting, including incentive wages.

There are six basic techniques for setting time standards: stopwatch time study, work sampling, predetermined standards, standard-data time standards, historical standards, and technical estimates. Engineered (high-precision) standards require controls on methods, time measurement, worker pace, and allowances for personal, rest, and delay (PR&D) time.

Scientific management has contributed considerably to increasing industrial output and is rapidly being extended into the services sector, but it has some negative effects on workers. Job enrichment and nonlinear assembly help combat tendencies to mold workers into mindless cogs in the machine. While time standards may be applied in variable-task environments, their application requires careful thought to avoid variability biases.

REFERENCES

Books

Caruth, Donald L. *Work Measurement in Commercial Banks.* Bankers Publishing, 1971 (HG1720.W63C36).

Kazarian, Edward A. *Work Analysis and Design for Hotels, Restaurants, and Institutions.* AVI Publications, 1969 (TX911.K36).

Krick, Edward V. *Methods Engineering: Design and Measurement of Work Methods.* Wiley, 1962 (T56.K7).

Maynard, Harold B., editor in chief. *Industrial Engineering Handbook.* 3rd ed. McGraw-Hill, 1971 (T56.M38).

Maynard, Harold B., G. T. Stegemerten, and John L. Schwab. *Methods-Time Measurement.* McGraw-Hill, 1948 (T60.T5M3).

Mundel, Marvin E.　*Motion and Time Study: Improving Productivity.* 5th ed. Prentice-Hall, 1978 (T60.7.M86).

Periodicals (societies)

Industrial Engineering (American Institute of Industrial Engineering).

Industrial Engineering Transactions (American Institute of Industrial Engineering), an academic journal.

Journal of Systems Management (Association for Systems Management), paperwork management and systems analysis.

PROBLEMS

Note:　Asterisked (*) problems require more than mimicry. They require judgment, and you should include discussion of reasons, assumptions, and outside sources of information.

Organization for methods and standards

*1.　You are the president of a company that is in serious financial trouble. Your production costs are higher than the production costs of all your competitors. You realize that these costs must be cut drastically, and that the measures used must include layoffs of nonessential people. Part of your company's organization chart is shown in Figure 8–1. Do you see any nonessentials that could be cut on this chart? Think about this carefully, since production cost is your problem, and many of these functions purport to reduce costs. On the other hand, you should reflect on the meaning of the word *essential.*

Planning package

*2.　Refer to Figure 8–2, which shows the characteristic flow in assembling a planning package. One route generally applies to nonrepetitive tasks, and the other generally applies to more repetitive tasks.

　　a.　A small printing plant would probably not have staff specialists to do such things as prepare route sheets, determine time estimates or standards, and prepare shop orders. Who would perform these and other functions associated with the planning package? Or would some of the functions be unnecessary in a small printing plant? Explain.

　　b.　The parts-fabrication department for a machine-tool manufacturer follows the flow pattern for more repetitive tasks. The process planner sometimes finds operation and time data in IE files and must sometimes wait for IE analysts to do a special study to provide operation and time data. Explain why there should be two sources of process and time data. Also, at some times the planner must assemble the route sheet; at other times the planner finds a *standard route sheet* (or *standard routing*) in the IE files. Explain this distinction.

　　c.　What are the differences between the route sheet, the shop-orders-needed listing, and the shop order.

Methods study and scientific method

3.　Figure 8–3 lists a number of ways to evaluate new methods: cost, time, effort, storages, delays, transportations, transportation distances. Explain how each of these types of evaluation data may be determined from flowcharts. Refer to one or more of the types of flowcharts in the chapter in your explanations.

Principles of methods improvement

4. Mundel's *general principles of methods improvement* (Figure 8–4) are newer but less well known than the *principles of motion economy* developed by Barnes. Find Barnes's principles in your library. Compare Barnes's principles with Mundel's principles. Discuss. (Barnes's principles may be found in many industrial engineering and production/operations management books, including Barnes's own work: R. M. Barnes, *Motion and Time Study,* Wiley, 1937.)

Left-and-right-hand chart

5. Find a screw-together type of ball-point pen. Take it apart and set the pieces before you. Imagine that you are an assembler in a factory making this type of pen. Develop a left-and-right-hand chart for your method of assembly. Now develop an "after" flowchart for an improved method—which may use a special workbench, feed trays, chutes, fixtures, and so on. You may wish to include a workbench sketch. Evaluate the extent of improvement.

Flow process chart

6. The present method of reading gas meters (on a successful call) is shown below (reproduced from Figure 8–10).

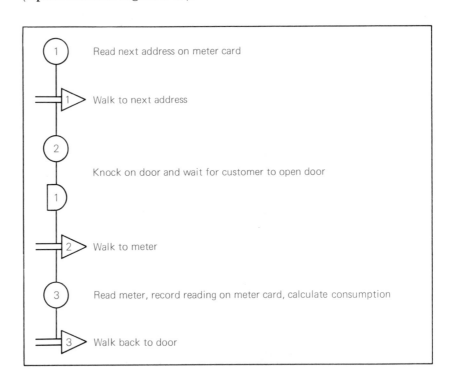

a. The gas company is considering a requirement that all gas meters be located outside or be visible through a window. Draw a new flow process chart for meter reading for the proposed new meter locations. Develop a summary of the improvements.

*b. What other improvements are there that are not shown on the summary? What are the disadvantages of the new method?

Activity	○ □ ⇨ ▽ D
Empty sacks to storage	○ □ → ▽ D
Sacks in storage	○ □ ⇨ ▼ D
One sack to filling machine	○ □ ⟋ ▽ D
Fill	● □ ⇨ ▽ D
To scale	○ □ ⟋ ▽ D
Weigh	● ■ ⇨ ▽ D
To stencil area	○ □ → ▽ D
Stencil	● □ ⇨ ▽ D
To stacking area	○ □ → ▽ D
Stack	● □ ⇨ ▽ D
Filled sacks in storage stock	○ □ ⇨ ▼ D
Sacks to next process	○ □ → ▽ D

7. The present method of billing, weighing, and stenciling sacks is shown in the accompanying illustration (reproduced from Figure 8–11).

    Develop a flow process chart for a proposed new, improved method. Include a summary of the improvements.

Work sampling

8. The accompanying chart shows five days of actual on-the-job activities of a seamstress who sews decorator pillows together. (Ten minutes is used as the smallest time increment so that time values can be read off the chart easily.) You are to conduct a 50-observation work-sampling study, taking your observations from the chart instead of from on-site observation.

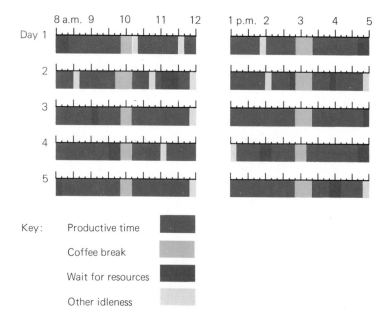

Key: Productive time
     Coffee break
     Wait for resources
     Other idleness

    a. As a first step in conducting the study, you will need a schedule of 50 random observation times. You will find a list of two-digit random numbers in Table S13–1 (in the supplement to Chapter 13). Select 50 of those numbers, and devise a method of translating them into 50 clock times between 8:00 A.M. and 12:00 P.M. and between 1:00 and 5 P.M. for a five-day study period. Show your 50 random numbers and 50 times.

    b. Develop a tally sheet and conduct the work-sampling study. The desired end result is percentages of time in four activity areas: productive time and coffee break, wait for resources, and other idleness.

    c. The unavoidable-delay component of the PR&D allowance is to be based on the wait-for-resources element of the work-sampling study in part *b.* The rest component is set at two 15-minute coffee breaks per day. And personal time is set by company policy at 5 percent. What is the total PR&D allowance?

    d. Explain the difference between the time allowed for coffee breaks and the time taken, as revealed by the work-sampling data.

    e. During the five-day study period the seamstress completed 760 pillows. You, the analyst, judged her pace during the study period. State what your pace rating is (make up a figure), and calculate the standard time. Also, express the standard in pieces per day (standard production rate).

    f. Discuss possible weaknesses or sources of bias in the work-sampling study. Is the time standard engineered?

    g. What should be the primary uses of this time standard? Explain.

Uses of Time Standard

9. A salesman has an order for 1,000 candles in the shape of an athletic team's mascot. Production control assembles the following data from the candlemaking shop, to be used in setting a price (direct cost and overhead + markup):

Cycle time . . . . 20,000 TMU's
Allowance for personal time
   and unavoidable delay 9%
Authorized break time . . . . 20 minutes per day

Recent candlemaking statistics:

Total clock hours for candlemakers . . . . 350 hours
Standard hours' worth of candles produced . . . . 380 hours

    a. What standard time should be used in computing direct cost?

    b. If there are two employees in candlemaking, how many hours should be scheduled for them to complete the order for the 1,000 special candles?

    c. Assume that the candle order has been finished. It took 190 hours to complete. What rate of efficiency did the crew attain?

10. The director of a social agency is preparing next year's budget. The agency's case load averaged 42 clients per day last year, but it has been increasing at an annual rate of 15 percent. The caseworkers and directors agree that it takes 3.5 hours to handle each client properly.

    a. How many caseworkers should be requested as the staff component of next year's budget, assuming the 15 percent increase in case load. Assume that caseworkers work an average 250 days per year (which allows for vacation days, sick days, etc.).

> *b.* What kind of time standard is used by the agency? Is there any way to improve the time standard?
>
> *c.* What other reasonable uses are there for the time standard?

Work-sampling time standard

11. A supervisor has done a work-sampling study of a subordinate, a clerk-typist. The purpose of the study was to set time standards for typing letters and retrieving letters on file. Therefore, those two tasks were tallied on the work-sampling tally sheet, along with a miscellaneous category for all other activities of the clerk-typist. The complete tally sheet is given below (except for pace ratings).

Subject: Typist

Tasks: Typing letters and retrieving letters on file

Dates: November 29–December 10

Analyst: Clerical supervisor

Activities sampled	Tallies	Total	Per- centage	Work count	Pace rating
1. Type letters	ⵊN ⵊN ⵊN ⵊN ⵊN ⵊN ⵊN ⵊN ⵊN ⵊN ⵊN ⵊN ⵊN ⵊN ⵊN ⵊN	80	40%	60	
2. Retrieve letters	ⵊN ⵊN ⵊN ⵊN ⵊN ⵊN	30	15	150	
3. Miscellaneous	ⵊN ⵊN ⵊN ⵊN ⵊN ⵊN ⵊN ⵊN ⵊN ⵊN ⵊN ⵊN ⵊN ⵊN ⵊN ⵊN ⵊN ⵊN	90	45	—	—
	Totals	200	100%		

> *a.* Make up your own pace ratings for the two tasks (*not* 100 percent). PR&D allowance is 12 percent. Compute cycle time, rated time, and standard time for each of the tasks.
>
> *b.* Discuss the possible uses of these time standards.
>
> *c.* Comment on the fairness and/or validity of these time standards. Are they engineered?

Time study and task variability

12. An insurance company mail room prepares all of the company's premiums and letters for mailing. A time study has been done on the job of enclosing premium statements in envelopes. Continuous stopwatch data are given below (except for cycles 6 and 7). The readings are in hundredths of minutes.

Job elements	Cycle							Performance rating
	1	2	3	4	5	6	7	
Get two envelopes......	11		55		105			105
Get and fold premium	22	41	65	83	116			115
Enclose in envelope and seal	29	48	73	97	123			95

Irregular element: At every 25th envelope, 25 envelopes are wrapped with a rubber band and placed in a box. This element was timed once, and the elemental time was 15 with a performance rating of 90.

    a. Develop a time standard, providing 15 percent for allowances, based on the continuous stopwatch data—but make up your own realistic data for cycles 6 and 7.

    b. Assume that the premiums and letters are of various sizes and shapes. The get-and-fold element takes much longer if the item is large and requires several more folds than are needed if the item is small. Therefore, the time standard could be unfair to some of the employees it covers. Suggest some situations in which the standard would be unfair. Suggest some options for making it fair.

Time-standards techniques

13. The following is a list of tasks on which time standards/estimates may be set. Suggest a suitable technique or techniques for setting a time standard for each of the tasks, and explain your choice.

    Mowing grass.

    Soldering connections in small electronic components.

    Drafting (design drawing).

    Typing and filing.

    Overhauling or adjusting carburetors.

    Cooking in fast-food restaurant.

    Computer programming.

    Installing auto bumpers on car assembly line.

IN-BASKET CASE*

Topic: Time-Standards Techniques—Packing and Crating

To:

From: Foreman, Packing and Crating Department

    As you know, the president wants all shops, including ours, covered by time standards. We may ask our own company industrial engineers to do the necessary studies, or we may hire an outside consulting firm. Before I make that decision, I'd like you to do a preliminary study to see how reasonable time standards could be set for our shop. Everything we pack is of a different size; it seems that there is no standard product, so how can we have standard times? In your report, include discussion of which technique for setting time standards would be best.

* See instructions at end of problems section, Chapter 1.

CASE

Sir Galahad County

    In 1975 the county commissioners of Sir Galahad County hired a prominent consulting firm to conduct a "staffing study" of all wage-earning county employees. The consulting team used standard efficiency and labor-utilization techniques in making the study.

The team's recommendations had minor effects on clerical employees but major effects on maintenance and food-service people. Janitorial staffs were cut considerably. Some reductions in janitorial duties were recommended, such as emptying wastebaskets every other day instead of every day. Several outspoken janitors wrote letters of protest in the "letters" column of the county employees' paper.

The number of food-service employees was also cut. One cafeteria director was quite upset. Her feeling was that the employee cuts were made without consideration of customer service. That is, she felt that cafeteria lines would grow longer and customers would be lost because there were fewer employees to staff the lines. She stated, "One of the consultants came right out and told me that the consulting firm pays so much a head for each employee that can be cut."

Have the consultants been fair and professional?

chapter 9

QUALITY ASSURANCE

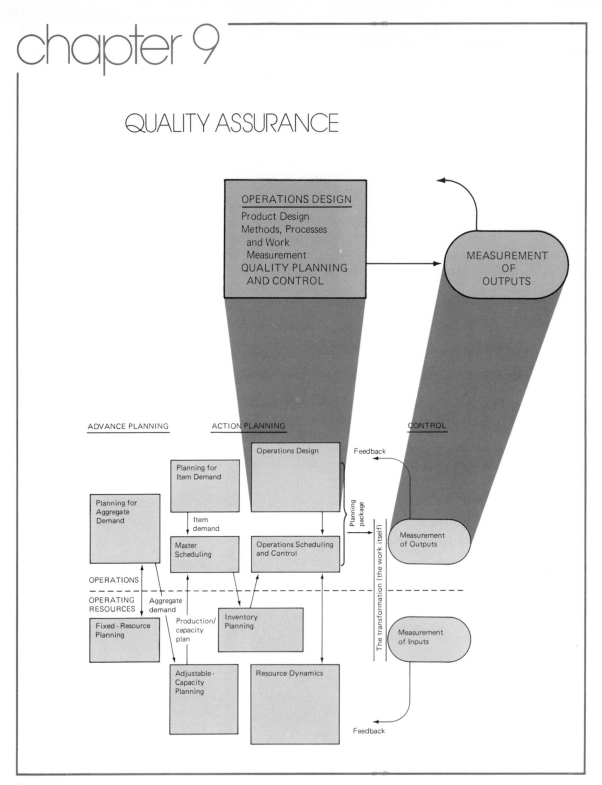

Planning and control of quality is a broad-based function. There may be a quality-control department with central responsibility, but other groups scattered about the organization chart also have important roles in quality management. The following is a list of contributors to the quality function in a goods-producing organization. The idea of quality as a broad-based function also applies to service organizations, but the list of contributing departments would vary, depending on the type of service provided.

1. Customers show a willingness to pay for a certain level of quality.
2. Marketing interprets customer requirements for quality.
3. Design engineering translates quality requirements into design specifications.
4. Purchasing procures materials of the desired quality.
5. Production engineering develops processes to produce goods of the desired quality.
6. Manufacturing produces to meet specified quality levels.
7. Inspection (quality control) inspects for the desired quality.
8. Packing and shipping act to preserve the produced quality.
9. Service departments correct quality defects and service goods to prolong quality.

The combined efforts of these parties to achieve optimum levels of quality may be called *quality assurance* (QA); the older term *quality control* (QC) will also do. Optimum quality means not too much as well as not too little quality. Since quality planning begins with customers' "willingness to pay," number 1 on the above list, the cost of too much quality is a factor to consider. Marketing interprets customers' requirement (number 2) and passes them on to design engineering (3). Engineering's material specifications are a standard for procurement (4), and engineering's product specifications are a standard for production engineering (5). Manufacturing, number 6, tries to meet design specifications using processes designed by production engineering, and quality control (7) inspects. Packing and shipping (8) preserve and protect the product, and service departments (9) handle customer complaints about quality.

In this chapter the focus is mostly on number 7: inspection. The inspection techniques discussed are mostly based on statistical sampling, which aids both in holding down inspection costs and in aiming at the right level of quality—not too much, not too little.

THE QUALITY-ASSURANCE FUNCTION

Before the industrial revolution quality assurance was in the hands of the craftsman. The industrial revolution brought about the factory system and labor specialization, which serve to increase output and decrease cost, but usually with losses in quality. The factory worker (office "factories" included) loses touch with the quality of the end product or service.

An early solution was to inspect after the product was made or the service provided. Inspection became a specialty. Inspectors identify defective products, which may sometimes be removed before shipment to the customer. As important or more important are the data yielded by inspection. Inspection data show achieved quality levels, which can be compared with desired quality levels. Quality variances may call for investigation and corrective action: better design, better purchasing, better production engineering, need for rework, and so on.

In this section we consider some of the major issues that impact on the quality-assurance function: organization for quality control, consumerism, measures aimed at the prevention of defects, and the nature of inspection.

Organization for quality control

While quality assurance as a whole involves people scattered about the organization chart, the coordinators, planners, and inspectors for quality are often clustered in a single staff department. In some firms or agencies it is the quality-assurance department; more commonly it is called quality control.

Sizes of QA or QC departments are highly variable. The departments are generally small for consumer-goods manufacturers, larger for producers of precision parts and instruments, and very large for some federally regulated companies. One maker of medical syringes has over 100 people in QC in a plant of 700 employees. Much of QC's work in that plant is directed toward meeting quality standards imposed by the Food and Drug Administration.

Location of the QC department on the organization chart also varies a good deal from organization to organization. Along with size, vertical location on the chart indicates the power and importance of QC in the organization. QC deserves to be high on the chart, perhaps at the vice-presidential level, when product defects can result in loss of life. Drug, food, and aerospace firms are prime examples. Auto, electrical, and chemical manufacturers are also likely to have highly placed QC departments.

When QC is highly placed, QC advice to line departments carries more weight. Assume, for example, that QC inspectors in a small appliance plant find cases of hazardous wiring in electric coffee makers. QC's advice is to stop production until the cause can be corrected, but production is reluctant to stop because of pressures to meet scheduled output levels. If the QC director is a vice president, the director may carry the dispute to the president, and the president can order compliance with QC's advice. The effect of this option of going to the president is that QC advice often tends to be taken as law much of the time.

In most companies, defects are not life threatening and QC departments are therefore placed lower on the organization chart. It is not uncommon to find the QC manager under the plant superintendent or the production manager. In such a location the power of QC is indeed weak. Production managers may choose to ignore QC advice and push for production rather than quality. QC inspectors may even become cowed into not reporting some of what they see, because QC reports of poor quality carry the implication that QC's bosses, the production managers, are not doing a good job in meeting quality targets.

On the surface it seems a bit unethical for a production manager to sweep bad inspection reports under the rug. However, the production manager may rationalize that QC's advice is erroneous. The advice is usually based on sampling inspections, and there is some risk of error in sampling. Also, human inspectors are known to make judgmental mistakes.[1] (However, the mistakes tend to be vigilance errors, which usually means *less* detection of defects.)

Furthermore, there is the argument that a production manager should have the authority to make trade-offs among conflicting goals. (See the section on trade-offs in Chapter 6.) The quality goal is always in conflict with cost and output goals, and the production manager is judged on how well these conflicts are resolved in the longer run. In a company making nails, inspectors may report that too many nails have weak heads or dull points. The production manager may not want to slow down to correct the problem, because there may seem to be longer-run advantages in maintaining production rates. Getting back to the original point about organization, it does not seem to make sense to place QC in a nail-making firm at a powerful vice-presidential level. Placement under the production department may be high enough. In recent years, however, consumers may have had some indirect influence on the degree of organizational importance assigned to QA/QC.

Consumerism   The years from the mid-1960s through much of the 1970s represent a period of elevated public interest in product quality and safety. Contributing to that interest were Ralph Nader, the Consumer Federation of American and its affiliates, action-line columns in the newspapers, and investigative TV and newspaper journalists. In 1965 the American Law Institute issued its "Restatement of the Law of Torts," which defined the emergent legal philosophy of *strict liability:* making manufacturers legally liable for product defects even without proof of negligence. In 1972 the U.S. Congress passed the Consumer Product Safety Act, which aims at preventing hazardous or defective products from reaching the consumer. Extended warranties and massive product recalls became commonplace during this period. The period also seems to have spawned in affluent nations of the world large numbers of a new and demanding type of consumer: the consumer of average means who prefers to do without rather than pay for second best. Neglected crafts like handweaving, the stone-grinding of flour, and the creation of stained-glass windows have resurged as consumers have sought the quality of the earlier age of the craftsman.

With higher premiums on quality, the producer's QA functions grow in importance. Demand grows for QA managers, for statisticians to develop statistical inspection plans, and for legal counsel to assist with warranties, compliance, and litigation on quality and safety matters. Some consumer-products

---

[1] There is a whole book devoted to the subject: C. G. Drury and J. G. Fox, eds., *Human Reliability in Quality Control* (Taylor and Francis, 1975) (TS156.2.I57).

manufacturers have given new powers to QA. Gillette, for example, has a vice president for product integrity who has broad powers to pull products off the market if his staff notes quality defects, safety problems, or unrealizable advertising claims. And some companies have encouraged an expanded view of quality assurance: not just inspection but also attention to preventing defects in the first place.

Prevention
A report in 1970 stated that 5 percent of the products that the Department of Defense procured in a year was rejected for quality reasons.[2] If that reject rate, 5 percent, is applied to consumer products, as measured by recent U.S. gross national product figures, it amounts to $100 billion yearly in rejects. The alternative to detecting and fixing or disposing of all these rejects is prevention. The arguments for preventive medicine and preventive maintenance also apply to quality assurance.

Preventing product defects is largely a matter of providing the right operating resources: high-quality purchased materials, a well-trained work force, a well-designed and well-maintained plant, and good tools. These are emphasized in Part Five, Resource Dynamics.

Prevention is also a matter of attitude. If the attitude of the work force is that a certain number of defects is normal and expected, that attitude and expectation tend to be fulfilled. Two ways of discouraging such attitudes may be noted. The traditional way is to set tough quality goals, measure produced quality, and report on variances from the quality goals. This tried-and-true approach is a foundation of good management—of budgets, costs, profits, sales, output, efficiency, and resource utilization, as well as quality. In the well-managed firm, variance reports constitute an important basis for judging the worth of a manager. (See related discussion in the last sections of Chapter 6.) The manager who is under pressure to meet, say, a target of decreasing product rejects by 10 percent is likely to act to improve operating resources and also to forcefully convey the quality message to his work force. This is how reports of past results translate into prevention of future errors.

A second way of dealing with casual attitudes toward quality is an attitude-change program directed right at the work force. In the early 1960s Martin Marietta Corporation developed such a program, calling it a *zero-defects* (ZD) program. The success of Martin Marietta's ZD program was publicized, and in a few years many firms launched their own ZD programs.

Most ZD programs begin with plantwide kickoff rallies. Banners, announcements, speakers, and publicity drum the message that errors are abnormal, not normal, and that each worker should expect to produce zero defects. Pledge cards are passed out for employees to sign, ZD committees are formed, data on employee achievements are collected, and ZD performance is publicly recognized. Error-cause-removal forms are placed in convenient locations, and

---

[2] Elwood G. Kirkpatrick, *Quality Control for Managers and Engineers* (Wiley, 1970), p. 2 (TS156.K49).

employees may use them to make note of any resource problems that prevent attainment of zero defects.[3]

Martin Marietta's ZD program was developed at plants in Florida that were producing Pershing missiles. This was the era of the missile gap, and there was a good deal of national resolve to close the gap between the United States and the Soviet Union. It was a good time to convince missile workers of the need for zero defects. ZD was later adopted by many of the firms involved in the manned space program, and the results were surely good for those firms as well. Successful manned space missions were a matter of national prestige.

Manufacturing consumer products is not nearly as glamorous as closing a missile gap or sending man into space. ZD in consumer products can hardly be linked to national prestige and patriotism. Still, many consumer-products firms have implemented ZD. It is difficult to know what success they have had. It seems safe to conclude only that such firms would have to work harder for success.

A newer approach to worker involvement in quality is the quality-circle concept, which was conceived in Japan.[4] Like zero defects, quality circles stress pride of workmanship. But while zero defects is aimed at individuals, the quality circle features group study.

The quality circle is a voluntary group of workers who have a shared area of responsibility. They meet together, usually weekly, to discuss, analyze, and propose solutions to quality, waste, and productivity problems. Each circle includes a leader, such as a foreman, but the circles rely on democratic processes. Members are trained in various analysis techniques by a quality-circle coordinator (often referred to as a facilitator), who serves the whole plant.

The quality-circle approach in Japan grew from just an idea in the early 1960s to involve over 5 million workers registered by a national society in 1977. Phenomenal results have been attributed to quality circles in Japan. Industrialists in other countries have been very interested. Reluctance to try this approach stems from the common view that quality circles may conflict with the cultures and traditions of the countries outside Japan. Cultural attributes that seem to favor quality circles in Japan include traditions of lifetime employment and a strong commitment to cooperative decision making. More recently in scattered Western companies, people have challenged the view that quality circles are ill-suited to Western cultures and have established their own quality circles. Lockheed was the first to do so in the United States. It is too early to tell what the prospects for success are for quality circles outside Japan. Perhaps the concept will be modified to suit the more individualistic temperaments common among Western workers.

---

[3] ZD is thoroughly discussed in James F. Halpin, *Zero Defects: A New Dimension in Quality Assurance* (McGraw-Hill, 1966) (TS156.Q3H28).

[4] J. M. Juran, "The QC Circle Phenomenon," *Industrial Quality Control*, January 1967, pp. 335–41.

Like any management technique, ZD and quality-circle programs cost money to implement, and they compete with other management techniques and programs based on return on investment. One of the programs that ZD and quality circles compete with is inspection, the more traditional after-the-fact approach to QA/QC.

Inspection

Inspection is well established as a specialty. Inspectors are often former production workers, though some engineers or technicians with expert knowledge of chemical and physical properties are also hired to inspect products. Engineers, statisticians, and holders of business degrees commonly design sampling plans and manage QC units.

Where and how to inspect. Inspection is performed on receiving docks, on the shop floor, in testing labs, and in parts and finished-goods warehouses. Inspectors rely heavily on eyes and hands. They may also make use of a variety of aids such as gauges, micrometers, scales, bending and crushing gear, centrifuges, spectrometers, X-ray equipment, ammeters, oscilloscopes, and control charts. Those who devise inspection plans work closely with the customer, marketing, legal counsel, engineering, purchasing, and manufacturing in order to determine what to inspect for and where. Sampling tables are a key tool to show how many items to inspect.

Inspection, like the work itself, is a candidate for automation. A certain amount of automated inspection is found on most automated production lines. Typical advantages are fewer delays, lower cost, and more reliable inspection. Also, automated inspection is generally a 100 percent inspection rather than a sampling inspection. An exception is automated sampling of fluids, gases, and other products that pour (continuous-flow operations). And, of course, destructive testing, whether automated or manual, must be done by sampling.

Humans are best for many inspection tasks. Formal sampling plans, the subject of most of the remainder of the chapter, are aimed at holding down the cost of human inspection. Besides having cost advantages, sampling is sometimes better than 100 percent inspection at detecting errors: Inspector vigilance wanes and detection errors increase during a prolonged inspection period.

Attribute and variables inspection. The simplest inspection is the yes-no inspection: Yes, the product is good, or no, it is defective. In QC parlance, this is *attribute* testing. That is, you inspect a given attribute—color, performance, finish, bonding, and so forth—and it is either good (yes) or not good (no). For example, in an attribute inspection of a light bulb, the bulb is good if it goes on, not good—and rejected—if it will not light. Vacuum-tube testers in drugstores usually test for attributes that are unknown to the layman. We simply set the dials, insert the tube, press the button, and observe whether the pointer advances to the green zone (good) or stays in the red zone (defective).

The electronics technician conducts a more sophisticated test. Instead of having just a green and a red zone, his tester has a graduated scale for measuring *how* good or bad a tube is. Taking measurements—instead of yes-no readings—is known as *variables* inspection. A variable can take on a range of values, and it is necessary to measure to find out how much of the variable is present in the product. Common variables to inspect for include length, weight, voltage, footcandles, rotations per minute and temperature. However, if the measuring scale used for inspecting is covered up by a red zone and a green zone, the process becomes attribute inspection rather than variables inspection.

Statistical sampling. The random statistical sample has become a widely used tool for efficiency in data collection. Efficiency is gained by its use because far less data need be collected when samples are inspected than when 100 percent of products are inspected. Statistics are used in sampling to show how many of the total population of products need be inspected to provide the desired level of confidence in the results. The desired level of confidence is stated in advance, and statistical formulas (or tables) show how many products to inspect. The statistically correct sample size enhances efficiency, because it provides for collecting enough data to ensure confidence but not more data than are necessary.

Statistical sampling as applied to data collection on product quality dates back to the work of Walter Shewhart in 1924. Shewhart, of Bell Laboratories, is the developer of statistical quality control (SQC). A few years later H. F. Dodge and H. G. Romig, also of Bell Labs, began developing tables for lot-acceptance sampling. Demand for massive amounts of war-related products during World War II resulted in rapid growth in the use of these and other statistical inspection aids.

Formal statistical sampling for quality is suitable for large- but not small-volume production and for goods but generally not services. Small-volume (job-shop) production is not a suitable application because the population of identical goods is too small. Furthermore, it would be costly to devise a separate sampling plan for each job order. Also, in job shops the skill level of workers tends to be higher than in repetitive production, and there is less division of labor. Therefore, job-shop workers, including service and professional people, are likely to assume a good deal of responsibility for the quality of their efforts. When sampling inspection is performed in the job shop, the sample size is likely to be judgmental rather than statistical.

Formal statistical sampling plans are generally not suitable for services, even for large populations, because of problems in getting unbiased random samples from human consumers of the services. Consider, for example, a rest area alongside a major highway. The highway department may place questionnaires in the rest area to solicit opinions about the quality of rest rooms, tourist brochures, state roads, state patrol, and so on. Travelers' opinions may be measured in numbers, perhaps on a scale of one to seven, just as a micrometer might measure diameters from one to seven centimeters. But there is little way of knowing whether you have a representative sample of travelers.

A good deal of admirable work has gone into sampling surveys of consumer or public opinion on the quality of intangible services. Our point here is simply that formal sampling plans—following SQC or lot-acceptance sampling concepts—are generally not a basis suitable for such surveys. Goods do not have the will to resist being sampled, but humans certainly do, and there's the rub.

STATISTICAL QUALITY CONTROL

Statistical quality control (SQC) means controlling the quality of the production process by statistical sampling inspections. Since it is the production process that is controlled, the sampling may not wait until products accumulate. SQC inspection goes on during production. Results are immediately plotted as points on a control chart. When points are outside control-chart limits, it is a sign that the quality has probably gone out of control. Investigation is needed to find the cause. Process quality is controlled in that the process may be stopped and corrected when control charts show that quality has strayed too far from the norm.

Control charts are designed so that only samples of very high or low quality will fall outside control limits. The area between control limits is the area of so-called *natural variability* in quality. Normal variations in materials, machine performance, and operator performance lead to quality differences from product to product, and quality samples of products usually fall within the area of natural variability. The inspector is alert for the sample that falls outside the limits of that area, which suggests that a dominant event has changed the product quality.

There are three common types of SQC. First is SQC using variables inspection, which employs two types of control chart. Second is SQC for attribute inspection in which defects are expressed as a percentage, and another type of control chart is used. Third is SQC for attribute inspection in which defects are expressed as a number per surface area or per group, and still another type of control chart is used.

An inspection procedure using any of the three types of SQC may be divided into the following steps:

A. *Design.* Design control chart.
 1. Choose quality variable or attribute.
 2. Choose sample size and number, and sampling frequency.
 3. Collect data by sampling.
 4. Calculate trial control limits.
 5. Discard any samples that fall outside control limits, and recalculate limits.
 6. Assess economic feasibility of control limits. If unsatisfactory, production process and control charts may require revision.
B. *Inspection.* Perform routine sampling and special investigations.
 1. Inspector plots quality of sample on control chart.

2. A copy of the control chart is put on display in order to provide feedback to the operator and possibly to motivate efforts to keep quality high.
3. Investigate for assignable cause when control chart suggests that process is out of control, that is, out of control for the worse or for the better.

C. *Action.* After investigation, take corrective action.
1. If assignable cause if found and it is bad, try to correct it.
2. If assignable cause is found and it is good, try to adopt it as a permanent part of the process.
3. Design new control chart if process quality has changed and the change is accepted.

Along with data-collection efficiencies from the use of statistically correct sample sizes, SQC promotes labor efficiencies through its use of control charts: Usually a well-paid SQC analyst designs the control charts and investigates for assignable cause, but lower-paid up-from-the-shops people are normally assigned to perform the inspections. Higher-paid analysts and managers need not be bothered except when charts show an out-of-control condition (the management-by-exception principle, which some readers will be familiar with).

The steps in the SQC inspection procedure are explained further in the following discussions of each type of control chart.

SQC for variables

Two control charts are used in SQC for variables. The first, the $\bar{x}$ chart, is used to plot the mean measurement for each sample. That is, each unit in the sample is measured, and the mean or average measurement is plotted as a point on the $\bar{x}$ (called "x-bar") chart. A very high or low mean measurement suggests that the process is out of control. A coffee machine, for example, may historically fill cups to within one-half inch of the top. If you sample five cups over the course of a day and the average (mean) is 1½ inches from the top (or perhaps the average is an overflow!), then you might safely conclude that the process is out of control.

The second chart, the R chart, is used to plot the range of each sample. The range, R, is simply the highest measured value minus the lowest. The range of the sample serves as a simple check on process consistency. Sometimes the process is normal on the average but very inconsistent or variable around that average. Your coffee machine may have filled your five cups to within a reasonable one-half inch of the top on the average. But perhaps one overflowed and one was only one third full. The range of variation within your sample is unacceptable; the process is out of control because of inconsistency.

When you find that the coffee machine is out of control, you may take some sort of corrective action. Perhaps you will call the vendor, who may investigate to find the cause. Or you might just kick the machine.

Design of $\bar{x}$ and R charts is a way of describing normal quality. For the coffee-cup example, a normal fill—perhaps one-half inch from the top—would be $\bar{x}$. The normal range of variation, R, was not stated for the coffee cup, but would be in formal SQC.

Note that normal quality is not necessarily ideal quality. Normal is simply the way it is, based on recent history. Assume, for example, that the aforementioned coffee machine had been overfilling cups—say, to one-eighth inch of the top on the average $(\bar{x})$—ever since the machine was installed. Machine patrons would then consider overfilling to be normal. But it is not ideal, because overfilled cups spill coffee, thus burning fingers, making a mess, and wasting the product. If the process goes out of control to a new mean of one-half inch from the top, everyone is happy. There may still be an investigation to find the cause, but probably in order to preserve the new norm rather than to revert to the old one.

The following example demonstrates the steps in SQC for variables more formally. Statistical proofs, derivations, and explanations are minimized.

EXAMPLE 9–1
SQC for variables inspection, tablet testing

The QA department of a company producing medicines has devised a small machine to be used in controlling its tableting operation. The variable to be tested is the cohesiveness of the tablet (pill). A few tablets are to be put into the machine, and the machine tumbles the tablets, producing dust, which is extracted. Several such dust extractions make up a sample; each pile of dust in the sample is to be weighed, and the weight data are to be plotted on $\bar{x}$ and R charts. The charts have not yet been designed.

Design of control charts for variables inspection. The first step in chart design has been completed: Cohesiveness is the variable chosen for inspection. Step 2 is choosing the sample size, number, and frequency. For variables, the sample size, n, is generally from 4 to 10, and the number of samples, m, is often 20. The SQC analyst decides to use four units (piles of tablet dust) per sample and to take 20 samples over a four-day period. Step 3 is collecting the data by sampling inspections. Figure 9–1 is a summary of the data collected.

Measurements are in grams of tablet dust collected. The mean, $\bar{x}$, is the simple average of the four units in each sample. Thus, for sample 1,

$$\bar{x}_1 = \frac{\Sigma x}{n} = \frac{7 + 10 + 6 + 6}{4} = \frac{29}{4} = 7.25$$

The range, R, is the highest minus the lowest of the four units in each sample. For sample 1, the highest is x_2, at 10; the lowest is x_3 or x_4, at 6. So,

$$R_1 = 10 - 6 = 4$$

Step 4 is calculating trial control limits. It is common in SQC to set control limits at three standard deviations (3σ) above and below the mean. (The Greek letter sigma, σ, is the symbol for standard deviation.) The confidence interval between control limits at $\pm 3\sigma$ is 99.7 percent. What this means is that 99.7 percent of the sample means are expected to fall within the control limits and that only 0.3 percent, or 3 out of 1,000, are expected to fall outside the limits—if the process quality has not changed. With such wide control limits, if a sample plots outside them, the suspicion is very strong that the process has changed.

FIGURE 9–1
Inspection data
for designing
SQC variables
charts

Sample number	Date	Time	Measurements (grams) x_1	x_2	x_3	x_4	Mean $(\bar{x})$	Range (R)
1	10/10	8:22	7	10	6	6	7.25	4
2		9:15	5	8	9	8	7.50	4
3		11:05	11	8	5	9	8.25	6
4		2:10	6	5	7	7	6.25	2
5		4:02	8	3	7	6	6.00	5
6	10/11	10:10	9	6	6	7	7.00	3
7		11:21	10	8	7	10	8.75	3
8		2:06	6	8	10	5	7.25	5
9		3:06	7	6	6	6	6.25	1
10		4:31	6	10	11	7	8.50	5
11	10/12	8:59	7	9	5	6	6.75	4
12		9:45	7	12	4	4	6.75	8
13		10:12	8	9	6	6	7.25	3
14		11:49	10	12	8	11	10.25	4
15		3:08	7	5	6	9	6.75	4
16	10/13	9:19	5	6	11	8	7.50	6
17		9:58	6	9	11	6	8.00	5
18		1:10	16	8	5	8	9.25	11
19		3:19	6	6	9	9	7.50	3
20		4:27	7	6	11	5	7.25	6
						Totals	150.25	92

Determining control limits requires calculating 3σ, with the aid of a value from a table. The means, $\bar{x}$, of sample measurements of a wide variety of phenomena are known to be normally distributed (they describe a bell-shaped frequency distribution). We mention this because the reader may wonder where the tables come from that are used in calculating the 3σ limits. The tables were derived from the underlying mathematics of the normal distribution. For the $\bar{x}$ chart the calculation of 3σ is simplified by use of a table, the "A" table.[5] A factor from the A table times the average range, $\bar{R}$, serves as an estimate of 3σ. Symbolically,

$$A\bar{R} = 3\sigma,$$

where

$A =$ A factor from the A table that is related to sample size, n
$\bar{R} =$ Average (mean) range for the samples
$\sigma =$ Sigma, the Greek letter commonly used to represent standard deviation

---

[5] The reader who is familiar with the standard deviation for normal distributions may wonder why we do not use the familiar square-root formula,

$$\text{SD} = \sqrt{\frac{\Sigma(x - \bar{x})^2}{n - 1}},$$

along with the T-distribution to adjust for small sample size. The square-root formula is more accurate since it accounts for deviation from the mean $(x - \bar{x})$ for all units in the sample. The range is a rougher measure of deviation, but R times A yields results thought to be good enough for SQC, and a good deal of calculation is saved.

From the data in Figure 9–1, the sum of the ranges for the 20 samples is 92. Therefore, the average range is

$$\bar{R} = \frac{\Sigma R}{m} = \frac{92}{20} = 4.60 \text{ grams}$$

The A table is included in Table 9–1. From the table the A-factor for a sample size, n, of 4 is 0.729. Therefore, our estimate of 3σ is:

$$A\bar{R} = (0.729)(4.60) = 3.35 \text{ grams}$$

TABLE 9–1
Factors for computing 3σ control limits

Number of observations in sample, n	A-factors for control limits about the mean	B-factors for UCL for range	C-factors for LCL for range
4	0.729	2.282	0
5	0.577	2.115	0
6	0.483	2.004	0
7	0.419	1.924	0.076
8	0.373	1.864	0.136
9	0.337	1.816	0.184
10	0.308	1.777	0.223

One more piece of data, the mean or chart center line, is needed to design the trial $\bar{x}$ chart. The mean of the sample data is the sum of the sample means, 150.25 (from Figure 13–1), divided by the number of means, m, where $m = 20$:

$$\bar{\bar{x}} = \frac{\Sigma \bar{x}}{m} = \frac{150.25}{20} = 7.51 \text{ grams}[6]$$

Trial control limits for the $\bar{x}$ chart are:

$$\text{Upper control limit } (UCL_{\bar{x}}) = \bar{\bar{x}} + A\bar{R}$$
$$\text{Lower control limit } (LCL_{\bar{x}}) = \bar{\bar{x}} - A\bar{R}$$

Since $\bar{\bar{x}} = 7.51$ and $A\bar{R} = 3.35$,

$$UCL_{\bar{x}} = 7.51 + 3.35 = 10.86$$
$$LCL_{\bar{x}} = 7.51 - 3.35 = 4.16$$

The trial R chart is calculated next. The center line of the R chart is $\bar{R}$, which has been computed as 4.60. The control limits, at $\pm 3\sigma$, are easily computed using a B table and a C table. The upper and lower control limits are:

$$UCL_R = B\bar{R}$$
$$LCL_R = C\bar{R}$$

---

[6] The double bar over the x indicates that this is the grand mean, or the mean of the 20 sample means. A simpler way to calculate the mean of the entire group of 80 measurements is to total them and divide the total by 80; a slightly different answer results from this method. Why do it the hard way? The reason is the central limit theorem, which the reader may have encountered in statistics studies. The theorem says that, regardless of how data in the population are distributed, the grand mean of sample means from that population will be normally distributed. The SQC tables (e.g., the A table) used to compute estimates of 3σ are based on an assumed normal distribution, and $\bar{\bar{x}}$ is used in order to assure a normal distribution.

For n = 4 the B and C tables in Table 9–1 indicate that $B = 2.282$ and $C = 0$. Since $\bar{R} = 4.60$,

$$UCL_R = (2.282)(4.60) = 10.50$$
$$LCL_R = (0)(4.60) = 0$$

The trial $\bar{x}$ and R charts are now drawn as shown in Figure 9–2. The 20 sample means and the 20 sample ranges have been plotted on the charts. Putting the data back on the charts permits inspection to see whether the charts need to be revised (step 5).

In this case they do. One of the data items, the range value for sample 18, falls outside its control limits. As stated earlier, 3σ control limits are so wide that we can expect only 3 of 1,000 data samples to fall outside the limits. Since 1 out of the 20 samples has fallen outside the limits, that one value, range sample 18, is highly abnormal and must be discarded.

We can trace range sample 18 back to the basic data in Figure 9–1. The cause is clear: The first unit in the sample is 16 grams, 4 grams more than the next highest of the 80 units. Perhaps the measurement was incorrect, or perhaps the tablets that were tumbled in the machine for that sample were really abnormally "crumbly." In any case, we don't want our control charts to reflect so abnormal a value.

Step 5 includes revising the charts, if necessary—as it is in this case. In revision, all calculations are redone using 19 of the 20 samples, since the 18th sample was discarded. The new calculations are:

$$\bar{R} = \frac{\Sigma R}{m} = \frac{81}{19} = 4.26$$

$$\bar{\bar{x}} = \frac{\Sigma \bar{x}}{m} = \frac{141.00}{19} = 7.42 \text{ grams}$$

Revised control limits for the $\bar{x}$ chart are:

$$UCL_{\bar{x}} = \bar{\bar{x}} + A\bar{R} = 7.42 + (0.729)(4.26)$$
$$= 7.42 + 3.10 = 10.52$$
$$LCL_{\bar{x}} = \bar{\bar{x}} - A\bar{R} = 7.42 - 3.10 = 4.32$$

Revised control limits for the R chart are:

$$UCL_R = B\bar{R} = (2.282)(4.26) = 9.72$$
$$LCL_R = C\bar{R} = (0)(4.26) = 0$$

The revised charts are displayed in Figure 9–3. The 19 sample ranges are plotted on the charts. All are within the limits, so the charts are assumed to be representative of the data.

The sixth step in chart design is to assess the economic feasibility of the control limits. The key question usually is: Can a product with those quality levels be marketed for a price that will bring an adequate return? This kind of question should have been thoroughly addressed during the design of the product when the product design team determines product specifications and tolerances. (Tolerance means how much above or below desired quality level is considered to be acceptable.) All that remains for the SQC chart designer to do is compare the chart control limits with design tolerances to see whether the production process quality is what it is supposed to be. The SQC analyst in our example finds that the charts in Figure 9–3 are within tolerances.

FIGURE 9-2
Trial control
charts for
variables
inspection

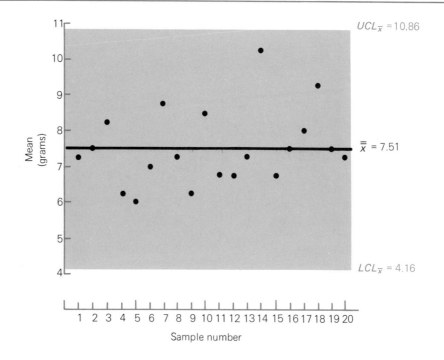

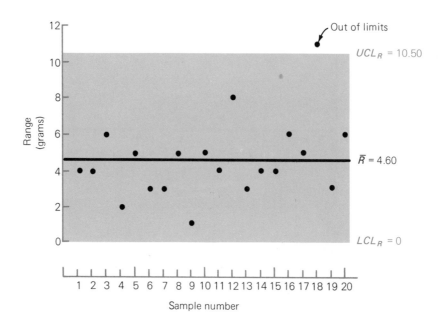

FIGURE 9-3
Revised control charts for variables inspection

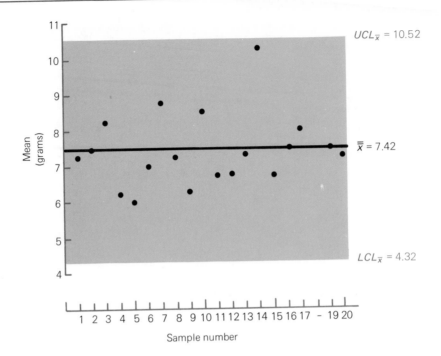

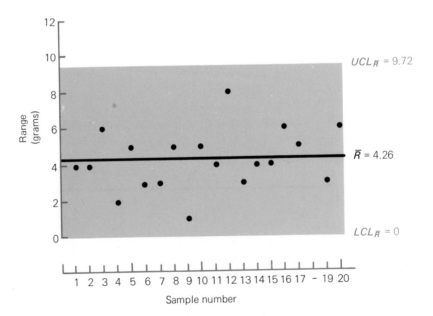

Inspection using SQC charts for variables. The revised $\bar{x}$ and R charts are copied onto standard forms, which the inspector uses in the course of sampling tablets from the production line. The inspector samples at random intervals when the tableting machines are in operation. (The tablets are produced in lots intermittently.) The sample size is again four units of tablet dust, from which $\bar{x}$ and R are calculated and plotted.[7]

The inspector need not report except when there is evidence that the process is out of control, as signaled by:

1. An $\bar{x}$ plotted above the UCL or below the LCL on the $\bar{x}$ chart or an R plotted above the UCL on the R chart. (In this example a point may not be plotted below the LCL on the R chart, since LCL $= 0$; a negative range is impossible.)

2. A run of eight successive samples plotted on the same side of the centerline. (The number 8 is arbitrarily chosen by the SQC analyst.) Such a run strongly suggests that process quality has changed.

Each day the inspector enters the day's $\bar{x}$ and R results on a copy of the control charts posted on a bulletin board in the tableting department. After about three weeks the inspector plots a sample below the LCL on the $\bar{x}$ chart. The samples had seemed to be trending downward before that. The suggestion was strong that tablet cohesiveness was improving. Figure 9–4 shows the pattern of plotted points.

The SQC analyst investigates when informed of the out-of-limits sample. The analyst finds an assignable cause: The tableting machine operator admits to adjusting the liquid intake valves twice as often as was done before the SQC inspections began. Greater vigilance has improved the quality.

Actions taken based on investigation in SQC for variables. Process quality has changed for the better at no increase in cost. Consumer acceptance of the product may improve somewhat over time, and the firm's reputation for quality may increase in a small way. The action taken by QA is to design new $\bar{x}$ and R charts. The major change is that the center line, $\bar{\bar{x}}$, is lower on the new $\bar{x}$ charts. Process consistency is

FIGURE 9–4
Samples plotted on $\bar{x}$ chart over three-week period

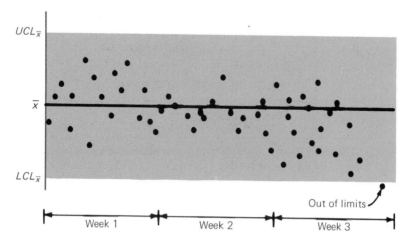

---

[7] A point of terminology: The charts have $\bar{\bar{x}}$ and $\bar{R}$ as their center lines, yet they are not called the $\bar{\bar{x}}$ and $\bar{R}$ charts. They are named for the inspection results that are plotted on the charts, namely $\bar{x}$ and R for each sample.

still about the same, so the upper and lower control limits are about the same distance from the centerline as before. The R chart changes very little.

The effect is that normal quality is now at a new improved level, and the process is now inspected based on the improved-quality norm.

SQC for attributes— The p chart

A single control chart is used in SQC for attributes. The percent-defective, or p, chart is used when quality is measured by the percentage in the sample that does not possess the attribute. A very high or low percent defective suggests that the production process is out of control. For example, the headwaiter at a restaurant may conduct an informal attribute inspection of table settings just before the dinner crowd arrives. He would judge a table setting to be defective if anything—fork, napkins, candle, saltshaker, and so on were missing or misplaced. The attribute is the table setting, and it is judged good if no defects are found and not good if any defect is found.

In this example a variables inspection is not possible because defects in table settings are not measurable. They are simply present or absent. Attribute inspection is the only way. Attribute inspection is also useful when measurements are possible but are not made because of time, cost, or need. The diameter of a ball bearing is a variable and can be measured. But if thousands of ball bearings are produced per hour, it is fast, cheap, and easy to inspect them for a size attribute. What comes to mind is rolling the bearings across a hole-filled surface, and those bearings falling through are defective for being too small. No measurement is recorded; the holes serve instead as a go no-go gauge.

The p chart is not appropriate for either of the above examples. The headwaiter certainly would not bother with formal control charts for the few table settings per day that must be inspected. Control charts are not suitable in the bearing example, because the hole-filled surface would serve to inspect 100 percent of the bearings; control charts are only for sampling.

The following example describes a case in which the production volume is large enough for sampling and in which sampling is used in order to save on the labor costs of inspection.

EXAMPLE 9–2 SQC for attribute inspection using the p chart, light bulbs

There are many operations in the manufacture of a light bulb. There may be hundreds of quality variables that could be inspected for. It might be economical to formally inspect for some of them: Perhaps the width of filament-wire samples could be measured, and perhaps the strength of glass-bulb samples could be tested by applying measured degrees of force to the glass surfaces. But a likely final test of samples of completed bulbs is a simple attribute inspection: Apply current, and reject those that do not light. This attribute inspection has been selected, and p-chart design is under way.

Design of p chart for attribute inspection. The first step in chart design has been completed: The whole light bulb has been chosen for attribute inspection, and the light bulb is judged defective if it does not light–and also if it is cracked, improperly mounted, and so on.

FIGURE 9–5
Attribute inspection data for designing p chart

Sample number	Number of defective lights	Fraction defective
1	4	0.020
2	1	0.005
3	6	0.030
4	3	0.015
5	8	0.040
6	10	0.050
7	7	0.035
8	3	0.015
9	2	0.010
10	2	0.010
11	6	0.030
12	12	0.060
13	7	0.035
14	9	0.045
15	9	0.045
16	6	0.030
17	2	0.010
18	4	0.020
19	5	0.025
20	1	0.005
Total	107	

Step 2 is choosing sample size, number, and frequency. Sampling frequency is not very important, but there should be 20 or more samples or lots. Sample size is usually somewhere between 50 and a few hundred, depending on how good the product quality is judged to be. If the product seems to be running about 1 percent defectives, then a sample size of 50 would be too small, because so many samples would have zero defectives in them. If the defectives are, say, more than 10 percent, then 50 would be all right. The SQC analyst believes that the light bulbs will test out at much better than 10 percent defectives, and he chooses a sample size, n, of 200; the samples will be taken once a day for 20 days ($m = 20$).

Step 3 is collecting data. Figure 9–5 is a summary of the data collected.

Step 4 is calculating trial control limits. The p chart, like the $\bar{x}$ and R charts, normally has control limits at $\pm 3\sigma$ from the centerline. The p chart is based on the binomial statistical distribution (instead of the normal distribution). *Bi-nomial* means two numbers, which is fitting since an attribute has only two degrees of quality: good or defective. The formula for σ in the binomial distribution is:

$$\sigma = \sqrt{\frac{\bar{p}(1 - \bar{p})}{n}} \, ,$$

where

$\bar{p} =$ Average (mean) fraction defective (or percent defective)
$n =$ Number in each sample

Therefore the control limits, at 3σ from the centerline, $\bar{p}$, are:

$$UCL = \bar{p} + 3\sqrt{\frac{\bar{p}(1-\bar{p})}{n}}$$

$$LCL = \bar{p} - 3\sqrt{\frac{\bar{p}(1-\bar{p})}{n}}$$

The average fraction defective, $\bar{p}$, is obtained by dividing total defectives by total items inspected, where total items inspected equals number of samples, m, times sample size, n:

$$\bar{p} = \frac{\text{Total defectives found}}{mn}$$

Since 107 defectives were found (from Figure 9–5),

$$\bar{p} = \frac{107}{(20)(200)} = \frac{107}{4,000} = 0.027$$

The control limits are:

$$UCL = \bar{p} + 3\sqrt{\frac{\bar{p}(1-\bar{p})}{n}}$$

$$= 0.027 + 3\sqrt{\frac{(0.027)(1-0.027)}{200}}$$

$$= 0.027 + 3\sqrt{\frac{0.0263}{200}}$$

$$= 0.027 + 3\sqrt{0.00013}$$

$$= 0.027 + 0.034 = 0.061$$

$$LCL = 0.027 - 0.034 = -0.007 \text{ or } 0.0$$

(The control limit may not be negative.)

FIGURE 9–6
Trial and final p chart for attribute inspection

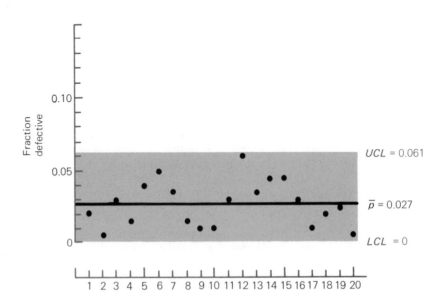

Step 5 in control-chart design is discarding any samples that fall outside the limits, and recalculating if necessary. Figure 9–6 shows the trial p chart. All 20 samples are within the control limits, so the limits are considered representative of the process quality.

Step 6 is assessing the economic feasibility of the limits. The limits are judged to be all right, and the chart is placed on standard forms for regular sampling inspections.

Inspection and corrective action using p charts for attributes. The light-bulb example need not be carried further. Inspection using the p chart is much like inspection using the $\bar{x}$ and R charts, as described in Example 9–1.

Investigation is required only when the fraction defective in a sample is above the UCL or when there is a run of several samples on the same side of the centerline. (The sample quality cannot plot below the LCL since the LCL is at zero.) Investigation may not reveal much. Sampling data from attribute inspections provide the investigator with few clues as to assignable cause. Data are available on the percent defective but not on the severity of the defects or on the consistency of the process; in the light-bulb example you would not even know what the defects were, since not only failure to light but also cracked glass, poor mounting, and so on, counted as defects. In view of these limitations on p-chart data, some firms collect further data about out-of-control processes by variables sampling. That is, if the percentage of defectives is on the increase, inspectors may be assigned to conduct more detailed sampling inspections of several product variables to find out which variables seem to be leading to defective products. Once the problem has been isolated and corrected, the variables inspections may be dropped to save money. Even though sample sizes are only 4 to 10 in variables inspection, as opposed to 50 or more for p charts, the variables inspection tends to be more time-consuming and more expensive overall.

SQC for attributes— The c chart

A single control chart, the c chart, is used in SQC when inspection consists of counting the number of defects found on a surface area or unit. The attribute is the surface or unit being inspected, and c is the number of defects found on it. There are far fewer applications for c charts than for $\bar{x}$ and R or p charts. The best applications of c charts seem to be in industries that produce sheets of a basic product: glass, steel, plastics, paper, and fabric. Some products in a more finished state may also be suitable for c charts: a keg of nails, the wing of an aircraft, or the hull of a ship. Scratches, bubbles, and breaks per sheet, per surface, or per ten lineal yards are examples of ways in which defects might be counted for such products.

The basis for the c chart is the Poisson statistical distribution rather than the normal or binomial distribution. In the Poisson distribution the formula for standard deviation, σ, is very simple:

$$\sigma = \sqrt{\bar{c}},$$

where

$\bar{c}$ = Average (mean) number of defects per surface area. Thus, the control limits, at 3σ, are:

$$UCL = \bar{c} + 3\sqrt{\bar{c}}$$
$$LCL = \bar{c} - 3\sqrt{\bar{c}}$$

The centerline, $\bar{c}$, is the sum of the defects found on the sampled surface areas (or units) divided by the number of samples, m (m should be at least 25):

$$\bar{c} = \frac{\Sigma c}{m}$$

Design, inspection, and corrective action for c charts follow the same general steps as for $\bar{x}$ and R charts and for p charts.

LOT-ACCEPTANCE SAMPLING

Lot-acceptance inspection takes place after production and therefore is not used for control. As the term implies, it is lots, literally, that are to be inspected—and accepted if they are of acceptable quality. A lot is generally large, perhaps hundreds or thousands of units. The lot to be inspected may be an incoming shipment of raw materials, a completed production order for parts or end items, or an impending shipment of finished goods. In each case the purpose is to allow good lots to proceed but to stop bad lots.

Sampling is advantageous in lot-acceptance inspection for the same reasons as in SQC: It saves inspection time, and it is nearly as effective as (and sometimes more effective than) 100 percent inspection. Lot-acceptance sampling (or acceptance sampling, for short) is also like SQC in that a professional commonly designs the sampling plan and a lower-paid inspector commonly carries it out.

In designing an acceptance-sampling plan, some thought must be given to the method of drawing a *random* sample. The inspector may have to select from the back, middle, front, top, and bottom of the pile to assure randomness (and not just select from a part of the lot that the producer might prefer the sample to be drawn from).

The effects of a bad sample are somewhat different in acceptance sampling than in SQC: In SQC the whole production process may be brought to a halt; in acceptance sampling the whole lot may be returned to the producer. The rejected lot may then be 100 percent inspected and rectified; that is, defectives found in the lot may be reworked or replaced with good items. This is often called the 100 percent rectifying inspection. If the item is cheap, the rejected lot may be discarded, melted down and reprocessed, or sold for scrap.

Like SQC, acceptance sampling may be for variables or attributes, but acceptance sampling is far more popular for attributes than for variables. Perhaps the reason has something to do with the similarity between making a yes-no (attribute) assessment of each unit inspected and the goal of a yes-no decision on the lot as a whole.

Acceptance sampling for attributes

There are four options in designing an acceptance-sampling plan for attributes:

1. Single sampling (or single-lot sampling)—the decision to accept or reject the lot is based on the quality found in a single sample.
2. Double sampling—the decision to accept or reject is based on one or two smaller samples; the second sample is drawn only if the first leaves doubts about the quality.
3. Multiple sampling—the decision to accept or reject is based on some specified maximum number of still smaller samples (such as three, four, or five); more samples are drawn until doubts about the quality are removed.
4. Sequential sampling—the decision to accept or reject is based on as many very small samples as it takes to remove doubts about the quality.

All four options have the same goal: to determine the quality of the lot. Numbers to be sampled and bases for accepting or rejecting the lot may be looked up in books containing standard acceptance-sampling tables. No preliminary sampling need be done as in SQC chart design. To look up the details of a sampling plan in tables requires only that decisions be made on how discriminating the sampling plan is to be. *Discrimination* refers to how good the sampling plan is at detecting the true quality of the lot. The degree of discrimination may be defined in numbers, which are inputs into statistical formulas. Calculations based on those formulas lead to the sampling plan, but those calculations have been worked out for a variety of discrimination parameters and constitute the tables. Thus, we are spared the need to calculate. Instead, we need to examine how to specify the level of discrimination of a sampling plan. The single-sampling plan is examined first.

Single sampling

The single-sampling plan consists of at least three characteristics:

N = Lot size
n = Sample size
c = Acceptance number, i.e., the acceptable number of defective units in the sample

The most discriminating sampling plan is that in which $n = N$, that is, the sample size is 100 percent—the whole lot. This is the only sample size for which planned statistical sampling errors are zero, because you are really not sampling. When you actually sample, that is, inspect less than the whole lot, there is some risk of error. Possible acceptance-sampling errors are of two types: (1) Rejecting a lot that is actually good is often called the producer's risk and is labeled α (alpha). (2) Accepting a lot that is actually bad is often called the consumer's risk and is labeled β (beta).

The risk of α and β errors, for any sampling plan, may be calculated as a probability or percent chance. Or, better yet, the level of risk may be specified in advance, and a statistical sampling plan (as opposed to an informal plan) to achieve that level may be calculated or looked up in tables. The reader should clearly understand that we refer only to *planned* risk of sampling error. Planned risk does not account for additional errors in inspector judgment. Although the planned risk of error is zero for a 100 percent inspection, judgment errors are likely. (Recall the point made earlier that inspector vigilance wanes in prolonged inspection sessions; sampling offers more variety and is less fatiguing and thus may result in fewer errors in judging lots than does 100 percent inspection.)

In determining the statistical sampling plan, two more parameters must be given besides the risk of each type of error: the acceptable quality level (AQL) and the unacceptable quality level, commonly called the lot tolerance percent defective (LTPD). Between the AQL and the LTPD is a zone of decreasing acceptability (or indifference), and the LTPD is at the limit of one's tolerance for defectives in the lot. A nickname for the LTPD is the "buyer's rebellion point."

The idea behind the AQL and the LTPD is that the standard of quality cannot be perfection; if perfection were the basis for accepting or rejecting lots, then nearly all lots would be rejected. Furthermore, it is a bit silly to say that below a fixed level of defectives a lot is good and above it the lot is bad. Who can specify good and bad so precisely? Instead of a single defectives level, the AQL and LTPD may be specified. Good is less defectives than the AQL; bad is more defectives than the LTPD; and indifference is the zone in between.

AQL and LTPD, as well as α and β risks, may be specified in advance, sometimes by contract. For example, a large contract to buy transistors may specify the four parameters, so that producer and buyer are in agreement about transistor quality. Then the producer's QC people can devise a sampling plan that neither overinspects nor underinspects. This is in the interest of both parties, because overinspecting is a cost that ultimately raises the price and underinspecting results in customer dissatisfaction and costly returns of orders that the customer will not accept.

When the parameters are not in a contract, the producer may make an educated guess about the quality level wanted by customers. Quality control is not in the best position to make such a guess; a joint decision with marketing and production is preferable. Frequently the producer will adopt a single set of quality parameters for a whole line of products.

Displaying the sampling plan—The OC curve. The statistical sampling plan may be visualized by plotting its characteristics on a graph. The visual representation is called an operating-characteristics curve (OC curve). We may review the characteristics of the sampling plan that would be represented by the OC curve.

Inputs:

α = Alpha error, the sampling risk of rejecting a lot that is actually good

β = Beta error, the sampling risk of accepting a lot that is actually bad

AQL = Acceptable quality level

$LTPD$ = Lot tolerance percent defective (buyer's rebellion point)

N = Lot size

Outputs:

n = Sample size

c = Acceptance number

P_a = Probability of accepting the lot for any given percent defective in the lot

The output P_a was not previously discussed because it serves only as extra information; the inspector needs to know only n and c.

Figure 9–7 is an example of a typical OC curve. The AQL is 2 percent, which means that a lot with up to 2 percent defectives is considered good. The LTPD of 8 percent means that more than 8 percent defectives in the lot is considered bad. The actual percent defective is not known. Inspectors sample from the lot and draw inferences about its quality, but sampling carries risk of error: In the figure the producer's risk, α, is set at 0.05, which means that, based on sampling, the producer is willing to reject a good lot 5 percent of the time; the consumer's risk, β, of 0.10 means that the sampling plan incurs the risk of sending bad lots to the consumer 10 percent of the time.

FIGURE 9–7
Typical OC curve

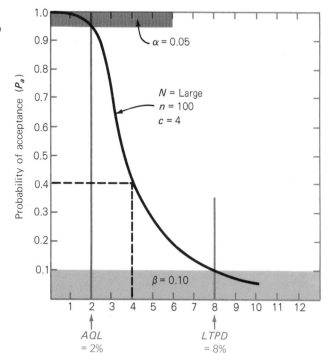

For a large lot size, N (N need not be specified), and the four inputs AQL, LTPD, α, and β, the inspection parameters may be calculated. The calculations in the case of Figure 9–7 would yield a sample size, n, of 100 and an acceptance number, c, of 4.

To carry out the sampling plan, inspectors randomly select 100 units from each lot and inspect those 100. If zero, one, two, three, or four defectives are in the sample, the lot is accepted. If there are five or more defectives, the lot is rejected (and usually subjected to 100 percent rectifying inspection).

The probability of accepting (P_a) a lot of some given quality may be read from the curve. In the figure the dotted line illustrates: A lot with 4 percent defectives has a 0.4 or 40 percent chance of being accepted based on the sample.

The OC curve itself is not of any importance to the inspector, since the inspector simply needs to know n and c, which are parameters that cannot

FIGURE 9–8
OC curve shapes

A. Effect of sample size on *OC* curves

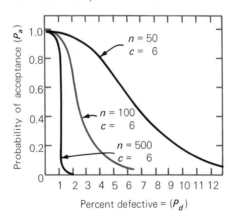

Percent defective = (P_d)

B. Effect of acceptance number on *OC* curves

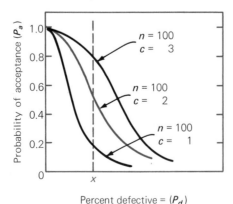

Percent defective = (P_d)

even be read from the curve. OC curves are, more correctly, a tool for under-standing the nature of acceptance sampling. Let us take a closer look.

Comparison of OC curves. Figure 9–8 shows several OC curves which demonstrate how the shape of the curve relates to sample size and acceptance number. Figure 9–8A shows the effect of varying sample sizes, n, on the shape of the OC curve. The acceptance number, c, is held constant at 6. When the sample size is as small as 50, the OC curve stretches out (is skewed) lazily to the right. For any given percent defective in the lot, the probability of accepting (P_a) the lot is rather high. Even with 10 percent defectives, P_a is about 20 percent. The obvious conclusion is that such a sampling plan is not very good at detecting bad lots: It is not very discriminating.

When the sample size is 100 (medium-sized), the sampling plan is better at discriminating between bad and good lots. Lots are rejected more often than not if there are 3 percent or more defectives; they are usually accepted if there are 2 percent or fewer defectives.

When the sample size is 500 (large), the sampling is nearly perfect at discriminating bad lots from good ones. The curve is almost a perpendicular Z, in which any P_d to the left of the perpendicular is nearly certain to be accepted and any P_d to the right of the perpendicular is nearly certain to be rejected.

Figure 9–8B shows the effect of varying acceptance numbers, c, on the OC curve. The sample size, n, is held constant at 100. The dashed line at $P_d = X$ percent defectives shows the effects of different c values. The chances of accepting the lot are about 80 percent for $c = 3$, about 50 percent for $c = 2$, and about 20 percent for $c = 1$. The sampling plan gets tougher or more discriminating (and the curve gets closer to a perpendicular Z) with smaller acceptance numbers.

The OC curve for any set of AQL, LTPD, α, and β can be drawn through calculated points. The calculation method is presented in the supplement at the end of the chapter.

OC curves and average outgoing quality. A sampling plan based on a set of AQL, LTPD, α, and β is efficient: It meets the input targets with just the right sample size and acceptance number. But what about effectiveness? That is, will the sampling plan be effective in preventing bad lots from being released to the customer? The average-outgoing-quality (AOQ) curve helps answer the question.

The average outgoing quality is measured in percent defective in the outgoing lot—after inspection has removed some of the defectives in the produced lot. The AOQ for any given level of defectives in the produced lot may be calculated by:[8]

---

[8] This is a simplified version of the more precise formula

$$AOQ = \frac{P_a \times P_d (N - n)}{N}$$

Frequently N (the lot size) is very large compared with n (the sample size); then

$$\frac{(N - n)}{N} \approx 1 \text{ and } AOQ = P_a \times P_d$$

$$AOQ = P_a \times P_d,$$

where

P_a = Probability of accepting the lot
P_d = Percent defective in the lot

Since P_a and P_d are the y and x axes on the OC curve, the formula provides for transforming an OC curve into an AOQ curve. An example follows.

EXAMPLE 9–3
Transforming
an OC curve
into an AOQ
curve

The acceptance-sampling plan for certain raw materials is $n = 60$ and $c = 3$. Ten points on the OC curve for the plan have been computed (see method in chapter supplement). The points are organized into a table, columns 1 and 2 of Figure 9–9A.

Column 3 of Figure 9–9A contains calculated values of AOQ for each of the ten sets of P_d and P_a values. As the figure shows, each AOQ is calculated by $AOQ = P_d \times P_a$.

Figure 9–9B displays the average outgoing quality curve that forms by plotting AOQ against P_d.

The AOQ curve shows that for this sampling plan the planned average outgoing quality never gets worse than about 3.24, the high point on the hill-shaped curve. The high point is known as the average-outgoing-quality limit (AOQL). The AOQL could serve as a quality specification in a contract. If so, one could work backward to get a sampling plan that meets the specified AOQL. The AOQL in this example occurs at a P_d of 5 percent, which means that if you are producing lots that have 5 percent defectives, then on the average the outgoing quality is 3.24 percent defectives. Of course, that is only an average, so it includes outgoing (from inspection to the consumer) lots of better and worse quality.

FIGURE 9–9
Calculating and
graphing the
AOQ curve

From the above example, it can be seen that average outgoing quality is always better than average incoming quality, that is, the P_d of lots coming into inspection. This stands to reason because lots that are accepted and passed

A. Calculation of AOQ values

(1)		(2)		(3)
P_d		P_a		AOQ
1%	×	0.997	=	1.00%
2		0.966		1.99
3		0.891		2.67
4		0.779		3.12
5		0.647		3.24
6		0.515		3.09
7		0.395		2.76
8		0.294		2.35
9		0.213		1.92
10		0.151		1.51

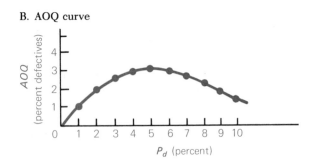

B. AOQ curve

Fig. 9-9, msp. 631

along to the consumer are purged of any defectives found in the inspected sample.

Notice also that average outgoing quality beyond the AOQL improves—even though P_d, the incoming or produced quality of lots, gets worse. This is no mistake. The explanation is that when produced lots contain many defectives, the sample will also usually contain many defectives. If so, the lot is rejected and subjected to 100 percent rectifying inspection. Bad items are removed and replaced with good ones, and the outgoing lot is perfect (except for judgmental errors, which are not a part of planned AOQ). When a lot has 8 percent defectives, for example, we see from Figure 9–9 that there is only a 0.294 probability of acceptance. Most of the time the sample from a lot this bad will also be bad enough to be rejected (more than 3 defectives in the sample of 60), and the lot will be rectified. Sometimes, however, the sample will paint a false picture of good quality, and the poor ($P_d = 8\%$) lot will be accepted, purged only of the defectives found in the sample. In the example, the mix of accepted and rejected lots that start into inspection with 8 percent defectives ends with an average outgoing quality of 2.35 percent defectives.

Double, multiple, and sequential sampling

If you bought a shipment of tennis balls, opened the first can, and found that the balls would hardly bounce, you would strongly suspect that the whole shipment was of unacceptable quality. And you would be right to suspect this. The statistical chance that a lot is good when the first group you inspect is bad is quite small.

The concept of double, multiple, and sequential sampling is based on that idea—that a bad *small* sample is reason enough to reject the whole lot. In double, multiple, and sequential sampling a smaller sample is inspected than in single sampling, and you can be as statistically certain about the correctness of lot rejection as you can with single sampling. The catch is that if the small sample is not bad, you sample again. In double sampling two samples are the maximum; in multiple sampling the maximum is three, four, or maybe more samples; and in sequential sampling there can be numerous small samples from the same lot before the statistical evidence is conclusive enough to decide whether to accept or reject.

A double-sampling plan is shown in Figure 9–10A. The plan is for a first sample, n_1, of 80 and a second sample, n_2, if necessary, of 60 more. The acceptance number, c_1, for the first sample is 2, which means that the lot is accepted if there are zero, one, or two defectives in the first 80. If there are three, four, or five defectives, you need more evidence. A second sample of 60 is inspected, and the accept-reject decision is based on the defectives in the combined sample of 140. The acceptance number, c_2, is 5, which means that the lot is rejected if there are six or more defectives in either the first 80 or the total of 140.

Frequently n_1 and n_2 will be the same size instead of unequal (80 and 60), as in this example. In every case n_1 is less than n would be in a comparable

FIGURE 9–10
Double- and sequential-sampling plans

A. Double-sampling plan

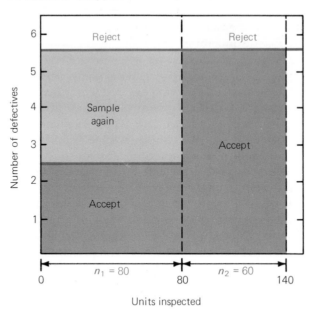

Sampling plan:
$n_1 = 80$
$c_1 = 2$
$n_2 = 60$
$c_2 = 5$

B. Sequential-sampling plan

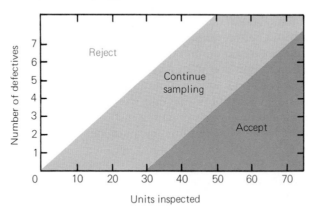

Sampling plan:
$n = 1,2,3,...$

single-sampling plan; however $n_1 + n_2$ are always greater than n would be. To illustrate, a double-sampling plan and an equivalent single-sampling plan might be as follows:

Double	*Single*
$n_1 = 50$, $c_1 = 1$	$n = 80$
$n_2 = 50$, $c_2 = 4$	$c = 3$

The sample size is 80 every time in the single-sampling plan, but the sample size would average less than 80 in the long run in the double-sampling plan. Since the plans are equally discriminating, the double-sampling plan is less expensive. The disadvantage of double sampling is the difficulties it presents in scheduling and controlling the time of the inspectors. If there were a string of medium-quality lots (with two or three defectives), the inspector would need to sample 100 units $(n_1 + n_2)$ every time. A string of very good or very bad lots would call for only 50 units (n_1). Single sampling always calls for the same lot size and thus is more predictable for scheduling.

Multiple sampling is like double sampling except that the maximum number of samples is set at three, four, or possibly more. Average long-run number of units inspected (for equal discrimination) is smaller than in double sampling, but the scheduling of inspector time is less predictable.

A sequential-sampling plan is shown in Figure 9–10B. Sequential sampling is multiple sampling carried to the extreme that sample size is as low as one unit. The figure shows that if the first sample is defective, the whole lot is rejected (as in the tennis ball example mentioned earlier); if the first sample is good, another is taken, and if one out of two samples is bad, the lot is rejected; if the first two samples are good, then a third is taken; and so on. The lot is accepted if the first 30 samples are good, or if there is only one defect in the first 40 samples, two in the first 50, and so on. The average long-run number of units inspected (for equal discrimination) is lower for sequential sampling than for multiple sampling.

One weakness of sequential sampling is uncertainty about how long an inspection will take. Uncertainty on the high side can be reduced somewhat by angling the diagonal accept and reject lines so that they converge. That way, the "continue sampling" zone comes to an end after some number of units have been inspected. Another weakness of sequential sampling is that no minimum number is inspected for the purpose of building a history of product quality. Where such history is important, the plan can be modified to assure a minimum sample.

Sampling plans for double, multiple, and sequential sampling may be calculated based on the same input paramaters as for single sampling: AQL, α, LTPD, and β. The method is not included in this book, but it is similar to the calculation method for single samples, as discussed in the chapter supplement. OC curves may also be developed for double, multiple, and sequential sampling.[9] As an alternative to calculation, the sampling plans may be found in sampling tables, discussed next.

Sampling tables[10]

Sample sizes and acceptance numbers for given levels of discrimination can be found in sampling tables. The most popular set of tables is the Military

---

[9] Calculation of each type of sampling plan and OC curve is explained in Richard C. Vaughn, *Quality Control* (Iowa State University Press, 1974) (TS156.V365).

[10] A handy reference that includes the tables discussed in this section is J. M. Juran, Frank M. Gryna, Jr., and R. S. Bingham, Jr., eds., *Quality Control Handbook*, 3d ed. (McGraw-Hill, 1974) (TS156.Q3J8).

Standard Sampling Procedures and Tables for Inspection by Attribute, which is better known as MIL-STD-105D. It includes attribute-sampling tables for single, double, and multiple sampling. An excerpt for single sampling is examined in the chapter supplement. Though MIL-STD-105D was devised for military procurement, it has become the standard for attribute inspection for all industry. (It is known internationally as ABC-STD-105D or International Standard ISO/DIS2859.)

Most of the tables in MIL-STD-105D do not allow the quality analyst to specify both (AQL, α) and (LTPD, β). Most require that the acceptable quality level, AQL, and the lot size, N, be given; the producer's risk, α, is fixed in the tables at about 1 or 2 percent for normal inspection. The lot tolerance percent defective, LTPD, and the consumer's risk, β, are allowed to float. This emphasis on (AQL, α) makes these tables most suitable for sampling a continuing series of lots of the same product. In such cases a fairly consistent level of quality is usually achieved, and there is not much worry about the consumer's risk, β (risk of accepting bad lots). The focus is on inspection costs. If quality begins to turn sour, the plan calls for shifting to a tightened plan with larger samples; if quality improves, there is a shift to reduced inspection.

As was explained in a previous section, lot size does not have much to do with the level of discrimination of the sampling plan. But when the lot is larger, it is sensible to want to be more careful with evidence about lot quality. For that reason, sample size rises with lot size in the tables.

For isolated lots for which there is no recent pattern of known quality, the LTPD and β, the consumer's risk, become more important. There are two special tables in MIL-STD-105D that allow LTPD and β to be specified. (But LTPD is referred to as LQ, limiting quality.) As an alternative, the Dodge-Romig tables could be used. The Dodge-Romig tables, for single or double sampling only, call for (LTPD, β) but not (AQL, α) to be specified. (Instead, some of the Dodge-Romig and MIL-STD-105D tables call for average-outgoing-quality limit, AOQL, to be specified.)

For sampling lots by variables inspection, MIL-STD-414 may be used. Variables sampling is not often used. Its best application is in destructive testing. The advantage of variables inspection is that much more is found out about the product when a variable is measured than when a simple yes-no decision is made about an attribute, and with more information fewer samples need be destroyed in the testing. (The normal statistical distribution, which is used for variables sampling, results in smaller sample sizes than do the Poisson or hypergeometric statistical distributions, which are used for attribute sampling.)

SUMMARY

Quality assurance (QA) or quality control (QC) in the broad sense concerns a quality level that meets customers' quality/price needs. Where product safety is a concern, QA departments tend to be large and high on the organization chart. Consumerism and product-safety regulations serve to increase the importance and power of QA.

Inspection is one of the tasks involved in QA. Inspection tends to be informal for services and small jobs. Larger lots may justify the use of statistical sampling, which provides for sampling the optimum number of units. Besides inspection, QA may involve preventive measures. Zero-defects and quality-circle programs are preventive measures that aim at motivating the work force to strive for zero errors and innovative solutions to quality problems.

Inspection may occur at receiving and shipping, in warehouses, and on the production floor. The simplest type of inspection is inspection for attributes, in which a product attribute such as color is determined to be either good or defective. The other type of inspection is the variables inspection, which requires a measurement. Some inspection is automated. Where human inspectors are used, statistical sampling may help to hold down inspection costs. Two types of sampling are statistical quality control (SQC) and acceptance sampling.

In SQC small samples are frequently taken from an ongoing production process. The average quality of each sample is plotted on a control chart, and if the sample plots outside the control limits (set at $\pm 3\sigma$), the suggestion is strong that the process is out of control. An investigation is needed as to the cause. The cause of the process change may be corrected, sometimes after stopping the production process; if correction is not desirable, new control charts may be designed to reflect the new quality norms.

Design of control charts is different for variables than for attribute plans. Two control charts apply for variables sampling: an $\bar{x}$ chart for the mean measurement of each sample and an R chart for the range of variability of each sample. A single control chart applies for attribute sampling: a p chart when the attribute is measured in percent defective in the sample or a c chart when the attribute is measured in defects per surface area.

While the purpose of SQC is control of the production process, the purpose of acceptance sampling is acceptance or rejection of a lot that has already been produced. Attribute acceptance sampling is very popular, but variables acceptance sampling is uncommon, being most suitable for destructive sampling when you wish to get by with the smaller sample sizes that arise from the statistics governing variables.

Attribute acceptance sampling is of four types: single, double, multiple, and sequential sampling. Double, multiple, and sequential sampling rely on more than one sample if the initial sample or samples are not clearly good or bad. These sampling plans require progressively fewer average units to be inspected per lot but entail progressively less certain total hours of inspector time.

Any of the four types of acceptance-sampling plans may be calculated. The calculations require that four inputs be specified: acceptable quality level (AQL) and lot tolerance percent defective (LTPD), both of which are expressed as percent defectives in the lot, and producer's risk (α) and consumer's risk (β), which are two types of sampling error. The outputs of the calculations are sample sizes, acceptance numbers, rejection numbers (for sequential sampling), and probabilities of accepting the lot for any percent of defectives in the lot. These inputs and outputs may be expressed as a graph, called an operating-characteristics (OC) curve.

Single-, double-, and multiple-sampling characteristics may be looked up in tables instead of being calculated. MIL-STD-105D is a set of sampling tables that are used throughout industry for this purpose.

REFERENCES

Books

Besterfield, Dale H. *Quality Control.* Prentice-Hall, 1979 (TS156.B47).

Drury, C. G., and J. G. Fox, eds. *Human Reliability in Quality Control.* Taylor and Francis, 1975 (TS156.2.I57).

Juran, J. M., Frank M. Gryna, Jr., and R. S. Bingham, Jr., eds. *Quality Control Handbook.* 3d ed. McGraw-Hill, 1974 (TS156.Q3J8).

Vaughn, Richard C. *Quality Control.* Iowa State University Press, 1974 (TS156.V365).

Periodicals (societies)

Journal of Quality Technology (American Society for Quality Control).

Quality Assurance.

Quality Progress (American Society for Quality Control).

PROBLEMS

Note: Asterisked (*) problems require more than mimicry. They require judgment, and you should include discussion of reasons, assumptions, and outside sources of information.

Quality assurance

*1. Some years ago the Bon Vivant Company went bankrupt. There were quality problems in its line of canned soups (e.g., Bon Vivant Vichyssoise). Find recorded accounts of the bankruptcy in your library. What went wrong? Suggest quality-assurance steps that Bon Vivant might have taken to avert the bankruptcy.

*2. What sorts of quality-assurance programs are used by the more successful fast-food franchisors?

QA/QC organization

*3. Contact three goods-producing firms in your area, and obtain information about where their quality-assurance/quality-control functions are located on their organization charts. For each of the three firms, explain whether the organizational location is "correct," considering the kinds of products made.

Inspection

4. Two columns of products/services are shown below. Select two from each column, and do the following:
   a. For each of your four selections decide on two attributes and/or variables that you think are most suitable for inspection. Explain your reasoning.

b. Discuss whether a formal statistical sampling method or an informal inspection method is sensible for each of your four selections.

Column 1	Column 2
Telephone	Auto tire mounting
Ball-point pen	Bookbinding
Pocket calculator	Keypunching
Dice	Proofreading
Space heater	Wallpaper hanging
Electric switch	Library reference
Glue	services
Bottle of Coke	Nursing care
Watch	Food catering
Handgun	Cleanliness of dishes
Light bulb	Bank teller service
	Roadside rest stop

SQC

5. Orville's Ready-Pop Popcorn is packaged in jars. The jars are supposed to contain a certain quantity of popcorn, and Quality Control inspects for quality using statistical quality control. Which of the three SQC methods—$\bar{x}$, R; p; and c charts—could or could not be used for SQC inspection of this product? Explain.

6. Explain why each of the three SQC inspection techniques—$\bar{x}$, R; p; and c—could be used in inspecting tabletops.

SQC using p chart

7. Determine the trial control limits for a p chart using the data from the table below. If there are any out-of-control points, take the necessary action to revise the chart. Graph the control chart or charts.

Sample number	Number inspected	Number defective
1	400	6
2	400	2
3	400	8
4	400	9
5	400	4
6	400	10
7	400	3
8	400	3
9	400	11
10	400	8
11	400	7
12	400	3
13	400	6
14	400	2
15	400	9

8. A manufacturer of coat hangers has decided on what constitutes a defective hanger. Samples of 200 hangers have been inspected on each of the last 20 days. The numbers of defectives found are given below, except for samples 18, 19, and 20. Make up *realistic* numbers defective for those three days. (No two students should use the same numbers.) Now construct a p chart for the data, and revise the chart if necessary.

Day	Number defective	Day	Number defective
1	22	11	21
2	17	12	21
3	14	13	20
4	18	14	13
5	25	15	19
6	16	16	24
7	12	17	14
8	11	18	
9	6	19	
10	16	20	

SQC for variables

9. Sixteen-ounce chunks of longhorn cheese are packaged by a cheese processor. Quality control has designed $\bar{x}$ and R charts: $\bar{x}$ is at 16.09 ounces, with $UCL_{\bar{x}} = 16.25$ and $LCL_{\bar{x}} = 15.93$; R is at 0.376, with $UCL_R = 0.723$ and $LCL_R = 0$.

   a. What sample size, n, would have been used? (It may be calculated.)

   b. Although the cheese packages are labeled as 16-ounce chunks, $\bar{x} = 16.09$. What is a reasonable explanation of the difference? (Note: The SQC plan *has* been approved and is in use.)

10. Hypodermic needles are subjected to a bend test, and the results, in grams, are to be plotted on $\bar{x}$ and R charts. A suitable number of samples have been inspected. The resulting $\bar{\bar{x}}$ is 26.1, and the resulting $\bar{R}$ is 5.0.

    a. For $n = 8$, calculate the control limits for the SQC charts.

    b. What should be done with the data calculated in part a?

    c. Assume that SQC charts have been developed for the data given above and that inspectors have been using the charts regularly. For one sample of hypodermics, $\bar{x} = 26.08$ and $R = 0.03$. Should there be an investigation for an assignable cause? Explain.

11. Random samples, each with a sample size of six, are periodically taken from a production line that manufactures one-half-volt batteries. The batteries sampled are tested on a voltmeter. The production line has just been modified, and a new quality-control plan must be designed. For that purpose, ten random samples (of six each) have been taken over a suitable period of time; the test results are given below:

Sample no.	Tested voltages					
	V_1	V_2	V_3	V_4	V_5	V_6
1	0.498	0.492	0.510	0.505	0.504	0.487
2	0.482	0.491	0.502	0.481	0.496	0.492
3	0.501	0.512	0.503	0.499	0.498	0.511
4	0.498	0.486	0.502	0.503	0.510	0.501
5	0.500	0.507	0.509	0.498	0.512	0.518
6	0.476	0.492	0.496	0.521	0.505	0.490
7	0.511	0.522	0.513	0.518	0.520	0.516
8	0.488	0.512	0.501	0.498	0.492	0.498
9						
10						

a. Samples 9 and 10 are left blank. Part of your assignment is to fill in the blanks with *realistic* data.

b. Compute and draw the appropriate SQC chart(s) for the data, using control limits at three standard deviations.

c. What else should be done to complete the SQC plan? Discuss and/or make appropriate calculations.

Single-sampling plan

12. Marketing, Manufacturing, and Quality Control have agreed upon average-outgoing-quality limits for three products. Quality Control has devised a single-sampling plan, and P_d values corresponding to the agreed upon AOQLs are as follows:

Product	P_d	AOQL
A	4.2%	3.6%
B	10.0	7.0
C	3.5	3.4

For each product, what is the probability of accepting the lot?

Average outgoing quality

13. A single-sampling plan has been devised for inspecting lots of fish-tank bubblers. The sample size is 90, and the acceptance number is 2. Based on that plan, the following OC-curve points have been calculated.

Lot percent defective (P_d)	Probability of lot acceptance (P_a)
1.0	0.94
2.0	0.73
3.0	0.49
5.0	0.18
7.0	0.06
9.0	0.01

a. Calculate the average outgoing quality for each of the lot-percent-defective values. What is the average-outgoing-quality limit?

b. Plot the P_a and AOQ curves on the same chart. Referring to your data from part a, explain what happens (and why) to AOQ when the probability of lot acceptance gets very low.

Single and double lot sampling

14. A QA analyst has calculated *equivalently discriminating* single- and double-sampling plans for five products. The five products and the single- and double-sampling plans are listed below.

Product	Single sampling	Double sampling
1	$n = 400$ $c = 16$	$n_1 = 450, c_1 = 18$ $n_2 = 450, c_2 = 25$
2	$n = 50$ $c = 2$	$n_1 = 5, c_1 = 1$ $n_2 = 70, c_2 = 3$
3	$n = 80$ $c = 1$	$n_1 = 60, c_1 = 0$ $n_2 = 50, c_2 = 3$
4	$n = 70$ $c = 5$	$n_1 = 35, c_1 = 3$ $n_2 = 35, c_2 = 8$
5	$n = 120$ $c = 10$	$n_1 = 40, c_1 = 6$ $n_2 = 60, c_2 = 9$

The analyst made some errors in calculating one or more of the sampling plans. Examine the pairs of plans for each of the five products, and look for inconsistencies that point to errors. Explain your findings.

Single-sampling plan (supplement)

15. A company makes low-cost home scissors (for cutting paper, etc.). A single-sampling plan is being devised, with $AQL = 1\%$, $LTPD = 8\%$, $\alpha = 0.03$ and $\beta = 0.20$. The lot size, N, is 6,000.

   a. What is the sampling plan? Use the search procedure in the chapter supplement.

   b. What do the α and β values tell you about the company's views about product quality?

   c. Now determine the sampling plan, using MIL-STD-105D and general inspection level II. Which plan do you think the company ought to use, the plan from part a or this one? Explain.

MIL-STD-105D (supplement)

16. A machine shop has a contract to supply pistons to an engine manufacturer. The pistons are made in lots of 1,200, and the contract stipulates that MIL-STD-105D, general inspection level II, will be used in single-sampling inspection of the lots. AQL is set at 2.5 percent.

   a. Use the sampling tables for MIL-STD-105D to arrive at a sampling plan for the pistons.

   b. Now consult the tables to see what the sampling plans would be if general inspection level I were used. Is the level I plan tighter (more discriminating) or looser than the level II plan.

   c. If the lot size were 1,201, the sampling plan would change. Explain how it would change and why lot size should make a difference.

IN-BASKET CASE*

Topic: Quality Control—Brick Mfg.

To:

From: Production Manager of Grand View Brick Works

Our customers demand large quantities of high-quality product. This requires that our machines and operators adhere closely to the specifications. We don't have the facilities to check every brick that is produced, so how can we insure quality control? I'd like you to make an investigation of this question and write a report of your findings and recommendations.

---

* See instructions at end of problems section, Chapter 1.

supplement to chapter 9

SINGLE-SAMPLING PLANS–CALCULATIONS AND TABLES

This supplement is in three parts:

1. Calculation of a single-sampling plan using Poisson tables.
2. Calculation of probability of acceptance (P_a) and average outgoing quality (AOQ), given a single-sampling plan.
3. Determination of a single-sampling plan using MIL-STD-105D.

Single-sampling plan using Poisson tables

A single-sampling plan consists of a sample size, n, and an acceptance number, c. There are various ways to arrive at the plan, given the AQL, LTPD, α, and β. Trial and error is a well-known but cumbersome method. A search method using Poisson statistical tables is discussed here.[1] A rule of thumb is that the Poisson distribution reasonably approximates the actual distribution of sample quality when the lot size, N, is at least ten times the sample size, n. (The true distribution is not Poisson but hypergeometric.)[2]

In the search procedure the producer's risk, α, and the consumer's risk, β, are treated as upper limits. The search involves starting with a small acceptance number, c, and increasing it until α and β are closely approached.

The steps are as follows (recall that P_d is the actual percent defective in the lot):

1. Set $c = 0$ (or a bit higher if a higher starting c seems unlikely to result in α and β being exceeded).
2. In a table of cumulative Poisson probabilities, find the largest np value for which the Poisson probability $\geq (1 - \alpha)$. Divide that np by AOQ, giving n_L, which is the largest n that keeps the plan within α limits.
3. In the same table, find the smallest np value for which the Poisson probability $\leq \beta$. Divide that np by $LTPD$, giving n_S, which is the smallest n that keeps the plan within β limits.

---

[1] Richard C. Vaughn, *Quality Control* (Iowa State University Press, 1974), pp. 116–17 (TS156.V365).

[2] Binomial distribution was stated in the chapter as being suitable for attributes in SQC. But binomial is based on infinite populations (e.g., a production line) and constant probabilities. In lot-acceptance sampling the lot is finite and the percent defective changes every time a unit is removed for inspection. Hypergeometric, which is cumbersome, is the distribution that fits. But for large lots, binomial and, by extension, the related Poisson distribution are acceptable approximations of hypergeometric.

4. If $n_S \leq n_L$, then the sampling plan, n_S and c, is used.
5. If $n_S > n_L$, increase c by one and repeat steps 2 through 5.

The search procedure is followed below for the OC-curve data from Figure 9–7, in which $AQL = 2\%$, $LTPD = 8\%$, $\alpha = 0.05$, and $\beta = 0.10$. Figure 9–7 states that $n = 100$ and $c = 4$ for those inputs. We shall see how close the search procedure comes to $n = 100$ and $c = 4$.

EXAMPLE S9–1
Search for n and c

Problem:

Given $AQL = 2\%$, $LTPD = 8\%$, $\alpha = 0.05$, and $\beta = 0.10$, find n and c.

Solution:

1. Let $c = 0$.
2. Refer to Table S9–1, which is an abbreviated Poisson table. Follow the $c = 0$ column down to the probability nearest to 0.95, since $1 - \alpha = 1 - 0.05 = 0.95$. The probability is 0.961 in the row where $np = 0.04$. Then,

$$n_L = \frac{np}{AQL} = \frac{0.04}{0.02} = 2$$

3. Follow the $c = 0$ column in Table S9–1 down to the probability nearest to but below 0.10, since $\beta = 0.10$. The probability is 0.091 in the row where $np = 2.4$. Then

$$n_S = \frac{np}{LTPD} = \frac{2.4}{0.08} = 30$$

4. Since n_S at 30 is not less than or equal to n_L at 2, proceed.
5. Since n_S is greater than n_L, increase c by 1 and return to step 2.

TABLE S9–1
The Poisson distribution—Cumulative probabilities

np	c										
	0	*1*	*2*	*3*	*4*	*5*	*6*	*7*	*8*	*9*	*10*
0.02	0.980	1.000									
0.04	0.961	0.999	1.000								
0.06	0.942	0.998	1.000								
0.08	0.923	0.997	1.000								
0.10	0.905	0.995	1.000								
0.15	0.861	0.990	0.999	1.000							
0.20	0.819	0.982	0.999	1.000							
0.25	0.779	0.974	0.998	1.000							
0.30	0.741	0.963	0.996	1.000							
0.35	0.705	0.951	0.994	1.000							
0.40	0.670	0.938	0.992	0.999	1.000						
0.45	0.638	0.925	0.989	0.999	1.000						
0.50	0.607	0.910	0.986	0.998	1.000						

TABLE S9-1 *(continued)*

np	c										
	0	1	2	3	4	5	6	7	8	9	10
0.55	0.577	0.894	0.982	0.998	1.000						
0.60	0.549	0.878	0.977	0.997	1.000						
0.65	0.522	0.861	0.972	0.996	0.999	1.000					
0.70	0.497	0.844	0.966	0.994	0.999	1.000					
0.75	0.472	0.827	0.959	0.993	0.999	1.000					
0.80	0.449	0.809	0.953	0.991	0.999	1.000					
0.85	0.427	0.791	0.945	0.989	0.998	1.000					
0.90	0.407	0.772	0.937	0.987	0.998	1.000					
0.95	0.387	0.754	0.929	0.984	0.997	1.000					
1.00	0.368	0.736	0.920	0.981	0.996	0.999	1.000				
1.1	0.333	0.699	0.900	0.974	0.995	0.999	1.000				
1.2	0.301	0.663	0.879	0.966	0.992	0.998	1.000				
1.3	0.273	0.627	0.857	0.957	0.989	0.998	1.000				
1.4	0.247	0.592	0.833	0.946	0.986	0.997	0.999	1.000			
1.5	0.223	0.558	0.809	0.934	0.981	0.996	0.999	1.000			
1.6	0.202	0.525	0.783	0.921	0.976	0.994	0.999	1.000			
1.7	0.183	0.493	0.757	0.907	0.970	0.992	0.998	1.000			
1.8	0.165	0.463	0.731	0.891	0.964	0.990	0.997	0.999	1.000		
1.9	0.150	0.434	0.704	0.875	0.956	0.987	0.997	0.999	1.000		
2.0	0.135	0.406	0.677	0.857	0.947	0.983	0.995	0.999	1.000		
2.2	0.111	0.355	0.623	0.819	0.928	0.975	0.993	0.998	1.000		
2.4	0.091	0.308	0.570	0.779	0.904	0.964	0.988	0.997	0.999	1.000	
2.6	0.074	0.267	0.518	0.736	0.877	0.951	0.983	0.995	0.999	1.000	
2.8	0.061	0.231	0.469	0.692	0.848	0.935	0.976	0.992	0.998	0.999	1.000
3.0	0.050	0.199	0.423	0.647	0.815	0.916	0.966	0.988	0.996	0.999	1.000
3.2	0.041	0.171	0.380	0.603	0.781	0.895	0.955	0.983	0.994	0.998	1.000
3.4	0.033	0.147	0.340	0.558	0.744	0.871	0.942	0.977	0.992	0.997	0.999
3.6	0.027	0.126	0.303	0.515	0.706	0.844	0.927	0.969	0.988	0.996	0.999
3.8	0.022	0.107	0.269	0.473	0.668	0.816	0.909	0.960	0.984	0.994	0.998
4.0	0.018	0.092	0.238	0.433	0.629	0.785	0.889	0.949	0.979	0.992	0.997
4.2	0.015	0.078	0.210	0.395	0.590	0.753	0.867	0.936	0.972	0.989	0.996
4.4	0.012	0.066	0.185	0.359	0.551	0.720	0.844	0.921	0.964	0.985	0.994
4.6	0.010	0.056	0.163	0.326	0.513	0.686	0.818	0.905	0.955	0.980	0.992
4.8	0.008	0.048	0.143	0.294	0.476	0.651	0.791	0.887	0.944	0.975	0.990
5.0	0.007	0.040	0.125	0.265	0.440	0.616	0.762	0.867	0.932	0.968	0.986
5.2	0.006	0.034	0.109	0.238	0.406	0.581	0.732	0.845	0.918	0.960	0.982
5.4	0.005	0.029	0.095	0.213	0.373	0.546	0.702	0.822	0.903	0.951	0.977
5.6	0.004	0.024	0.082	0.191	0.342	0.512	0.670	0.797	0.886	0.941	0.972
5.8	0.003	0.021	0.072	0.170	0.313	0.478	0.638	0.771	0.867	0.929	0.965
6.0	0.002	0.017	0.062	0.151	0.285	0.446	0.606	0.744	0.847	0.916	0.957
6.2	0.002	0.015	0.054	0.134	0.259	0.414	0.574	0.716	0.826	0.902	0.949
6.4	0.002	0.012	0.046	0.119	0.235	0.384	0.542	0.687	0.803	0.886	0.939
6.6	0.001	0.010	0.040	0.105	0.213	0.355	0.511	0.658	0.780	0.869	0.927
6.8	0.001	0.009	0.034	0.093	0.192	0.327	0.480	0.628	0.755	0.850	0.915
7.0	0.001	0.007	0.030	0.082	0.173	0.301	0.450	0.599	0.729	0.830	0.901
8.0	0.000	0.003	0.014	0.043	0.100	0.192	0.314	0.454	0.594	0.718	0.817
9.0	0.000	0.001	0.006	0.021	0.055	0.116	0.207	0.324	0.456	0.588	0.707
10.0	0.000	0.000	0.002	0.009	0.028	0.066	0.129	0.219	0.332	0.457	0.582

The steps repeat for $c = 1, 2, 3, 4,$ and 5. The results for each are:

For $c = 1$, $n_L = 17.5$ and $n_S = 50$.

For $c = 2$, $n_L = 40$ and $n_S = 67.5$.

For $c = 3$, $n_L = 65$ and $n_S = 85$.

For $c = 4$, $n_L = 95$ and $n_S = 100$.

For $c = 5$, $n_L = 130$ and $n_S = 19$.

The result for $c = 5$ is explained below:

1. Let $c = 5$.
2. Follow the $c = 5$ column down to the probability nearest to 0.95. The probability is 0.951 in the row where $np = 2.6$. Then $n_L = \dfrac{2.6}{0.02} = 130$.
3. Follow the $c = 5$ column down to the probability nearest to but below 0.10. The probability is 0.066 in the row where $np = 10.0$. Then $n_S = \dfrac{10.0}{0.10} = 100$.
4. Since n_S at 100 is less than n_L at 130, the sampling plan is:

$$n = n_S = 100$$
$$c = 5$$

We see that the computed sampling plan and the plan of Figure 9–7 have the same sample size ($n = 100$) but that the acceptance numbers differ—$c = 5$ versus $c = 4$. It could be shown that $c = 4$ comes a bit closer to the target of $\beta = 0.10$; we arrived at $c = 5$ because the search procedure calls for seeking a probability *below* β. Either $c = 5$ or $c = 4$ is probably suitable.

Calculation of P_a and AOQ, given n and c

For any given sampling plan (n and c) an OC curve and an average-outgoing-quality (AOQ) curve may be constructed. The probabilities of acceptance (P_a) on the vertical axis of the OC curve are needed in order to calculate AOQ values. AOQ values are sometimes useful (or required) for assessing the effectiveness of a sampling plan. The example below demonstrates how P_a and AOQ may be determined. The sampling plan of Figure 9–9 ($n = 60$, $c = 3$) is used in the example.

**EXAMPLE S8–2
Calculation of P_a and AOQ**

Problem:

Given $n = 60$ and $c = 3$, find P_a and AOQ for various levels of lot quality, measured in percent defective (P_d).

Solution:

When N is at least ten times n, the Poisson distribution may be used to approximate the quality of attribute samples. For any P_d, then, the P_a may be found by Poisson calculations or by reference to Poisson tables. (See Table S9–1.)

Figure S9–1 shows how Poisson tables are used to calculate P_a. Column 1 lists possible levels of actual produced quality, P_d, for a lot to be inspected. Column 2 is the sample size, $n = 60$, times each P_d value. Column 3 is the probability of lot acceptance, P_a,

FIGURE S9–1
P_a and AOQ for sampling plan $n = 60$ and $c = 3$

(1) Lot percent defective (P_d)	(2) Sample size times P_d ($n\,P_d$)	(3) Probability of lot acceptance* (P_a)	(4) Average outgoing quality (AOQ) (1) × (3)
1%	0.6	0.997	1.00%
2	1.2	0.966	1.99
3	1.8	0.891	2.67
4	2.4	0.779	3.12
5	3.0	0.647	3.24
6	3.6	0.515	3.09
7	4.2	0.395	2.76
8	4.8	0.294	2.35
9	5.4	0.213	1.92
10	6.0	0.151	1.51

* P_a values are found in cumulative Poisson tables using $c = 3$ and $np = nP_d$.

for each P_d value. The P_a values may be found in Table S9–1 in the column, $c = 3$, and in the rows, np, which correspond to nP_a. Column 4, the AOQ for each P_d, is found by multiplying P_d by P_a.

The results in Figure S9–1 are the same as those in Figure 9–9.

FIGURE S9–2
Sample-size code letters, MIL-STD-105D

Lot or batch size		Special inspection levels				General inspection levels		
		S–1	S–2	S–3	S–4	I	II	III
2 to	8	A	A	A	A	A	A	B
9 to	15	A	A	A	A	A	B	C
16 to	25	A	A	B	B	B	C	D
26 to	50	A	B	B	C	C	D	E
51 to	90	B	B	C	C	C	E	F
91 to	150	B	B	C	D	D	F	G
151 to	280	B	C	D	E	E	G	H
281 to	500	B	C	D	E	F	H	J
501 to	1,200	C	C	E	F	G	J	K
1,201 to	3,200	C	D	E	G	H	K	L
3,201 to	10,000	C	D	F	G	J	L	M
10,001 to	35,000	C	D	F	H	K	M	N
35,001 to	150,000	D	E	G	J	L	N	P
150,001 to	500,000	D	E	G	J	M	P	Q
500,001 and over		D	E	H	K	N	Q	R

Source: Acheson J. Duncan, *Quality Control and Individual Statistics*, 4th ed. (Homewood, Ill.: Richard D. Irwin, 1974), p. 223. © 1974 by Richard D. Irwin, Inc.

FIGURE S9-3
Master table for single-sampling plans (normal inspection), MIL-STD-105D

Acceptable Quality Levels (normal inspection). Each cell shows **Ac Re** (Ac = Acceptance number, Re = Rejection number). ↓ = Use first sampling plan below arrow. ↑ = Use first sampling plan above arrow.

Sample size code letter	Sample size	0.010	0.015	0.025	0.040	0.065	0.10	0.15	0.25	0.40	0.65	1.0	1.5	2.5	4.0	6.5	10	15	25	40	65	100	150	250	400	650	1000
A	2	↓	↓	↓	↓	↓	↓	↓	↓	↓	↓	↓	↓	↓	↓	↓	↓	0 1	1 2	2 3	3 4	5 6	7 8	10 11	14 15	21 22	30 31
B	3	↓	↓	↓	↓	↓	↓	↓	↓	↓	↓	↓	↓	↓	↓	↓	0 1	1 2	2 3	3 4	5 6	7 8	10 11	14 15	21 22	30 31	44 45
C	5	↓	↓	↓	↓	↓	↓	↓	↓	↓	↓	↓	↓	↓	↓	0 1	1 2	2 3	3 4	5 6	7 8	10 11	14 15	21 22	30 31	44 45	↑
D	8	↓	↓	↓	↓	↓	↓	↓	↓	↓	↓	↓	↓	↓	0 1	1 2	2 3	3 4	5 6	7 8	10 11	14 15	21 22	30 31	44 45	↑	↑
E	13	↓	↓	↓	↓	↓	↓	↓	↓	↓	↓	↓	↓	0 1	1 2	2 3	3 4	5 6	7 8	10 11	14 15	21 22	30 31	44 45	↑	↑	↑
F	20	↓	↓	↓	↓	↓	↓	↓	↓	↓	↓	↓	0 1	1 2	2 3	3 4	5 6	7 8	10 11	14 15	21 22	↑	↑	↑	↑	↑	↑
G	32	↓	↓	↓	↓	↓	↓	↓	↓	↓	↓	0 1	1 2	2 3	3 4	5 6	7 8	10 11	14 15	21 22	↑	↑	↑	↑	↑	↑	↑
H	50	↓	↓	↓	↓	↓	↓	↓	↓	↓	0 1	1 2	2 3	3 4	5 6	7 8	10 11	14 15	21 22	↑	↑	↑	↑	↑	↑	↑	↑
J	80	↓	↓	↓	↓	↓	↓	↓	↓	0 1	1 2	2 3	3 4	5 6	7 8	10 11	14 15	21 22	↑	↑	↑	↑	↑	↑	↑	↑	↑
K	125	↓	↓	↓	↓	↓	↓	↓	0 1	1 2	2 3	3 4	5 6	7 8	10 11	14 15	21 22	↑	↑	↑	↑	↑	↑	↑	↑	↑	↑
L	200	↓	↓	↓	↓	↓	↓	0 1	1 2	2 3	3 4	5 6	7 8	10 11	14 15	21 22	↑	↑	↑	↑	↑	↑	↑	↑	↑	↑	↑
M	315	↓	↓	↓	↓	↓	0 1	1 2	2 3	3 4	5 6	7 8	10 11	14 15	21 22	↑	↑	↑	↑	↑	↑	↑	↑	↑	↑	↑	↑
N	500	↓	↓	↓	↓	0 1	1 2	2 3	3 4	5 6	7 8	10 11	14 15	21 22	↑	↑	↑	↑	↑	↑	↑	↑	↑	↑	↑	↑	↑
P	800	↓	↓	↓	0 1	1 2	2 3	3 4	5 6	7 8	10 11	14 15	21 22	↑	↑	↑	↑	↑	↑	↑	↑	↑	↑	↑	↑	↑	↑
Q	1250	↓	↓	0 1	1 2	2 3	3 4	5 6	7 8	10 11	14 15	21 22	↑	↑	↑	↑	↑	↑	↑	↑	↑	↑	↑	↑	↑	↑	↑
R	2000	↓	0 1	1 2	2 3	3 4	5 6	7 8	10 11	14 15	21 22	↑	↑	↑	↑	↑	↑	↑	↑	↑	↑	↑	↑	↑	↑	↑	↑

⇩ = Use first sampling plan below arrow. If sample size equals, or exceeds, lot or batch size, do 100 percent inspection.

⇧ = Use first sampling plan above arrow.

Ac = Acceptance number.

Re = Rejection number.

Single-sampling plan using MIL-STD-105D

MIL-STD-105D provides different sampling plans for 7 possible levels of inspection and 15 possible lot-size ranges. Figure S9–2 displays sample-size code letters for the combinations of levels of inspection and lot sizes.

After finding the code letter, the QA analyst refers to a second "master table" to find the lot size, n, and the acceptance number, c. The master table is shown as Figure S9–3.

The master table is used by specifying the sample-size code letter (from Figure S9–2) and the desired AQL. AQL may be specified in either of two ways: (1) AQLs less than or equal to 10.0 may be expressed in defects per 100 units (where more than one defect per unit may be counted) or in percent defective. (2) AQLs greater than 10.0 are expressed only in percent defective.

The following example demonstrates the use of the two tables.

EXAMPLE S9–3 MIL-STD-105D for single sampling

Problem:

Reeds are produced in lots of 2,000 for the replacement market of owners of clarinets and other reed instruments. Samples of reeds are visually inspected for cracks, chips, and so on. MIL-STD-105D is used to find the single-sampling plan for general inspection level II. (General inspection level II is for "normal" inspection and is suitable much of the time.) The acceptable quality level (AQL) for the reeds is set at 1.5 percent. What is the sampling plan?

Solution:

Go to Figure S9–2 to find the sample-size code letter. The lot size of 2,000 is in the row 1,201 to 3,200. For that row and general inspection level II the code letter is K.

Find code letter K in Figure S9–3. The sample size for code letter K is 125. For an AQL of 1.5 percent, or 0.015, and code letter K, an arrow points downward to an acceptance number (Ac) of zero. (The rejection number, Re, of 1 is also given.)

The sampling plan is $n = 125$ and $c = 0$. Thus, if as much as one defective reed is found in a sample of 125, the whole lot of 2,000 is rejected.

PART FOUR

Strategic planning: The product line and fixed resources

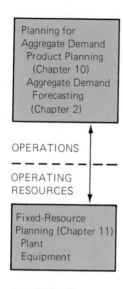

Planning for
Aggregate Demand
Product Planning
(Chapter 10)
Aggregate Demand
Forecasting
(Chapter 2)

OPERATIONS

OPERATING
RESOURCES

Fixed-Resource
Planning (Chapter 11)
Plant
Equipment

CHAPTER 10
Product planning

CHAPTER 11
Facilities acquisition and replacement

Part Four is on strategic planning of the product line and fixed resources. Strategic means long-range. That is, strategic plans for product line and for fixed resources have long-range effects. Once a line of goods and services is set and a plant is equipped, the organization is committed, perhaps for years to come.

High-level operating managers and their staffs, along with counterparts in marketing, engineering, and finance, are likely to be involved in planning the line of goods and services. Operations managers are interested in assuring that proposed products are of the right type and quantity (aggregate demand) to keep existing capacity utilized, that production targets (to break even or make a profit) are attainable, and that demands for operating resources do not require capacity committed to other products. The last factor, commitment of capacity, is often the dominant concern in strategic planning since the capital investment for capacity is of an order that can bankrupt a firm. The discussion of product planning in Chapter 10 is oriented toward managing the search for a mix of products that will not strain capacity but will utilize existing capacity, thereby keeping the organization in financial health. (Aggregate demand adequacy is covered in Part Two along with item forecasting.)

It is scarcely possible to discuss plans for product line without also discussing fixed resources. Product planning and fixed-resource planning are natural partners. The two functions are separated by a dashed line in the chart on the title page for Part Four. As is true throughout the book, the intended meaning is that the function to the north of the line is the master and that the function to the south of the line is the servant. In this case, the product line provides strategic operating ends (master) and the fixed resources provide strategic means (servant).

chapter 10

PRODUCT PLANNING

PLANNING FOR AGGREGATE DEMAND

PRODUCT PLANNING
○ PLANNING PRODUCTS AND SERVICES
○ DEVELOPING PRODUCTS AND SERVICES
Aggregate Demand Forecasting

ADVANCE PLANNING   ACTION PLANNING   CONTROL

Planning for Aggregate Demand

Planning for Item Demand

Operations Design

Feedback

Item demand

Master Scheduling

Operations Scheduling and Control

Planning package

Measurement of Outputs

OPERATIONS
- -
OPERATING RESOURCES

Aggregate demand

Fixed - Resource Planning

Production/ capacity plan

Inventory Planning

Measurement of Inputs

The transformation (the work itself)

Adjustable - Capacity Planning

Resource Dynamics

Feedback

Planning the line of products and services is half of planning for aggregate demand. The other half is aggregate demand forecasting, covered in Chapter 2. The combination is the plan for what and how many to produce. This plan for aggregate demand is an important input to two other functions, as is shown by the chart on the chapter title page. The arrow pointing south on the chart indicates the need for planned aggregate demand to influence fixed-resource planning. The diagonal arrow labeled *aggregate demand* represents input into adjustable-capacity planning, which is medium-range planning for levels of labor, inventory, and tools.

Planning products and services involves high-risk decisions. These are the most basic strategic decisions in the operations management function. They set in motion plans for fixed resources—plans that can be set aside only at great expense. Because fixed resources are so expensive to change, they influence the planning of the product line; that is why the arrow on the chart also goes from fixed-resource planning to planning for aggregate demand.

Two types of planning are considered in this chapter. The first, *innovation*, provides ideas and development for a product line. The second, *feasibility*, establishes whether the innovations are beneficial and fit in well with present products and with existing capability/capacity to make them. After a brief section on factors involved in planning the product line, these topics, innovation and feasibility, are taken up in the remainder of the chapter.

THE LINE

Figure 10–1 shows that the plan for an organization's products and services depends on market forces and technological forces. An innovative *design* for a proposed product or service must be matched with a customer *need* for it. Then, given a design and a need for it, it must be *feasible* to provide the item at a price customers will be *willing* to pay.

FIGURE 10–1
Forces affecting planning of products and services

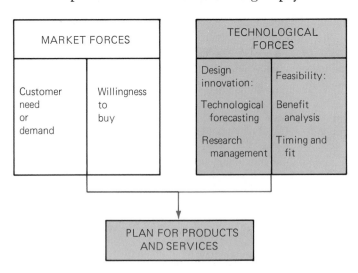

This applies just as well to, say, a government service as to a privately produced product or service, but the words would be a bit different. An innovative design might be to promote exports of U.S. peanuts, provided that U.S. peanut farmers could see a need for this service. Moreover, it must be feasible for some government agency to promote peanut exports at a reasonable cost. Otherwise, Congress, the executive, and the taxpayer will not be willing to "buy" the idea.

Customer need and willingness to buy (market research and pricing) are not discussed in this book. These market forces are more properly studied in marketing courses and textbooks. Our emphasis is on technological forces, which are the direct concern of operations managers and operating resource managers. Thus the technological-forces block is highlighted in Figure 10–1.

Design innovation, presented first, begins with long-range projection, that is, with *technological forecasting*. This provides at least fuzzy target areas for research. *Research management* is then directed toward those targets.

Feasibility is the second aspect of managing technological forces. The term *feasibility* has different meanings to different people in management. The focus here is on practicability. That is, will the product or service produce net benefits to the organization, and does it fit in? Thus we consider *benefit analysis* on the one hand and *timing* and *fit* of the product/service on the other.

INNOVATION

The concern here is neither with basic scientific breakthroughs nor with applied research itself. Those are the purview of the scientist and the engineer. Our interest is in *planning for* scientific or technical advances and then *managing* the research effort. Planning for scientific and technical advances is discussed first.

Technological forecasting

Technological forecasting can be thought of as systematic crystal ball gazing. It predates but fits in with the new field of study known as futurology.[1] Some colleges now offer courses and even degrees in futurology.

Most of the emphasis in futures studies concerns broad socioeconomic matters: food and energy supplies, automation, leisure, lifestyles, population, and so forth. Technological forecasting, however, is generally directed toward specific organizations or industries.

Techniques of technological forecasting are discussed in the following order:

Predictive techniques
  Trend extrapolation
  Enveloping
  "Involvement" (or gaming) techniques

---

[1] A World Futures Society was formed in 1966.

> Normative (advocacy) techniques
> Morphological analysis
> Relevance trees

Many of these techniques have been developed in so-called think tanks. These include RAND Corporation, the Hudson Institute, and the more recent Institute for the Future. Contributions have also been made by a few consulting and research groups, including Battelle Memorial Institute, Stanford Research

FIGURE 10–2
Examples of
trend
extrapolations

A. Output of coal mine drilling equipment

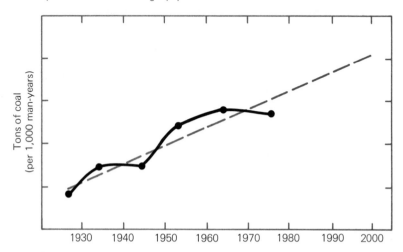

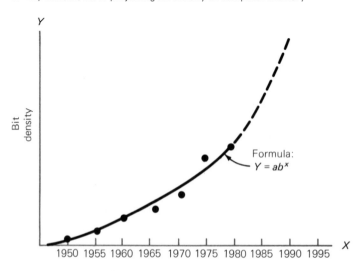

B. Exponential curve projecting bit density in computer memory

Institute, and Arthur D. Little. The Department of Defense, NASA, and the aerospace and electronics industries have provided much of the backing.

The predictive techniques are best known. These include trend extrapolation methods as well as various methods of active involvement, such as role playing, scenario writing, brainstorming, and Delphi.

Trend extrapolation. Everyone who is old enough or is knowledgeable enough about history tries his hand at trend extrapolation. Some are doomsayers and see trends leading to flood, famine, and war. Others extrapolate hopeful trends and forecast peace, plenty, and happiness.

Scientific extrapolation aims at avoiding optimism or pessimism. It involves plotting points on graph paper, fitting curves to the points, and projecting into the future.

One step in graphic trend extrapolation is to establish the past rate of technological improvement in some technological area, for example, coal-mining output per miner or the density of information bits in computer memory. The rate of improvement may then be projected any number of years into the future. The projected improvement may show when present items in the product line are likely to become obsolete. The projection may also show where new products need to be introduced. For example, a company making coal-drilling equipment may project when its current line of drills will be obsolescent. This projection enables it to put a research and development team to work at the right time to have an advanced type of drill developed when it will be needed.

Figure 10–2 shows examples of graphic projection. Figure 10–2A plots hypothetical outputs of mine-drilling equipment. A curve is drawn through the plotted points and extended by "eyeball" into the future. The projection may be analyzed for product development opportunities, as was discussed above.

Figure 10–2B plots hypothetical densities of information bits in computer memory. In this case the plotted points are fitted to a curve that follows a particular mathematical formula. In the example the general formula $Y = ab^x$ is shown—for illustrative purposes only. (The parameters, a and b, would have to be determined to actually plot or describe the curve.) $Y = ab^x$ happens to be the general form of what is known as an exponential curve. Some experts feel that technological advances of many kinds have tended to follow an exponential pattern.[2]

There are statistical curve-fitting techniques for finding out the type of mathematical formula (such as exponential or straight line) and the formula parameters that best fit a group of plotted points. The techniques are beyond the scope of this book but are widely available in statistics and operations research books.

---

[2] But other experts are not so sure. A logarithmic curve plots as a straight line on a special type of graph paper known as semilog paper, and Lenz charges "semilogarithmic paper with . . . occult powers which distort data and extort false forecasts." Ralph C. Lenz, Jr., "Forecasts of Exploding Technologies by Trend Extrapolation," in *Technological Forecasting for Industry and Government*, ed. James R. Bright (Prentice-Hall, 1968), p. 58 (T174.T4).

The advantages of finding a mathematical formula are like those mentioned in Chapter 2 in connection with item forecasting. The main advantage is that this permits turning over to a computer much of the work of projecting technological advances. Extrapolating technological advances by computer is worthwhile if there are a good many extrapolations to perform.

Enveloping. Trend extrapolation may be improved by the construction of "envelopes." Real trends do not often follow a clear mathematically projectable pattern such as those shown in Figure 10–2. Instead, there is often a series of curves, each curve representing a technological forward leap. Such a series may be plotted on a graph—usually over a very long period so as to include several major technological changes. Then the small curves may be connected by a larger curve, which may be projected into the future. Connecting up the smaller curves is called enveloping. The verb *envelop* means to wrap or surround, which, in a way, is what is done in connecting the smaller curves.

Since enveloping must usually cover a long period, it is not suitable for products as narrow and recent as coal-drilling equipment or computer memory. Instead, enveloping is applied to broad *classes* of devices—such as cooking devices. (But a particular device like a waffle iron would be too recent, and a class of devices like appliances would not be specific enough to measure.)

Figure 10–3 is an example of an enveloping projection. It shows that the trend in vehicle velocity yields an envelope that extrapolates toward the speed

FIGURE 10–3
Velocity trends

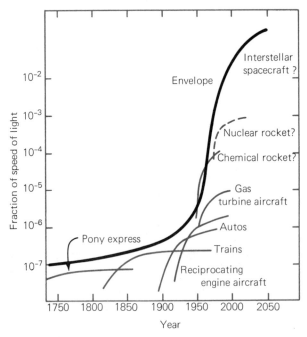

Source: D. G. Samaras, USAF, as cited by Robert U. Ayres, *Technological Forecasting and Long-Range Planning* (McGraw-Hill, 1969), p. 21 (T174.A9). Used with permission.

of light. The curve suggests that a vehicle for interstellar travel will be developed. In the enveloping method there is no suggestion as to *how*. Predicting how is a possible aim in other methods of technological forecasting.

Involvement (or gaming) methods. Involvement methods are governed more by principles (heuristics) or trial and error than by mathematics and graphs. These methods involve people in a gaming mode. (Gaming refers to a type of training or education in which participants make decisions or interact in a simulated situation.) Role playing is a gaming technique that has been used mainly in human relations training; a trainee acts out an assigned role to gain insights into the role. This approach has been extended to generating possible futures, including futures in which technological changes have taken place. For example, two teams could be formed, one representing the firm and the other representing a major competitor. The teams could then interact in role-playing sessions to generate scenarios of plausible future actions and reactions.

In the dictionary a scenario is an outline of a dramatic performance. As used here, the term *scenario* refers to an outline of an imagined set of future conditions: possible outcomes of battles, political campaigns, and in our case, product development.

Besides being used in role playing, scenario writing is a gaming technique in itself. The environmental impact statement is a special type of scenario used for forecasting. For example, an environmental impact statement on the consequences of building a power plant in Western coalfields (filed for approval with the Environmental Protection Agency) might forecast a scenario in which strip-mined lands are restored to bloom with native grasses.

Another involvement technique is brainstorming. In brainstorming a group is assembled to generate ideas, perhaps on new products or future predictions. Uninhibited thinking is encouraged. A wild idea may trigger a good idea. A brainstorming session at one company is described as follows: "The staff bats around ideas, and scrawls them down on scraps of paper, which are tossed into a huge fishbowl. . . . Any idea goes in if it has aroused even a glimmer of response from the group. Later on, a two-man team—always one engineer and one industrial designer—cull out the most promising candidates."[3]

Still another involvement technique is the Delphi process. This technique is named after the Greek oracle at Delphi. The technique obtains a consensus among experts through an anonymous process. Delphi avoids some of the shortcomings of typical face-to-face committees, such as dominance by a vigorous member, majority pressures, and pressures to be done and adjourn.

The Delphi process is led by a coordinator, who sends written questions to a selected group of experts who may be unaware of one another's participation. The experts' written predictions are pooled statistically, and such data as the mean prediction, the interquartile range, and pertinent supporting comments are sent out again to the same group. Each participant learns what

---

[3] *Business Week,* July 2, 1966, p. 54.

the others are predicting and why, and then the participants submit new, perhaps modified, predictions. These steps are repeated, usually for two to four rounds, with some degree of consensus the usual end result.[4]

Delphi is frequently used to project a date for a particular technological event. For example, a maker of cough medicines might conduct a Delphi poll to determine in what year the protein interferon will be in widespread use for killing the viruses that cause the common cold. The panel of experts might include molecular biologists engaged in basic interferon research, developmental biochemists, research managers, and public health specialists. First-round replies to the question "What year?" might range from "Never" to "Well into the 21st century." The coordinator might express the replies as a mean and as an interquartile range. (The interquartile range is the highest year minus the lowest year, but only for the middle 50 percent of the predictions.) If an expert has a good argument for saying "Never" or "The year 2030," the coordinator summarizes the argument and passes it on to the panel for the second round. When the polling ceases, the consensus should be valuable in indicating to the manufacturer how urgent it is, if at all, to move out of the cough-medicine business.

Normative techniques. Normative techniques try to determine what the future should be and then to make this happen. These are searching techniques; they involve looking for technological gaps that might be exploited.

Morphological analysis is one such technique. Morphology is a commonly used term in such sciences as biology, physical geography, and linguistics. It means the study of forms and structures. When morphological analysis is applied to technological forecasting, diagrams, lists, tables, and so forth, are used to show the structures of given technology areas.

For example, a morphological analysis of feasible kinds of components to propel an auto could be structured as in Figure 10–4. The next step is to inspect the morphology and develop a list of possible combinations of propulsion components. First on the list is a three-wheeler with one powered wheel, no transmission, and one internal-combustion hydrocarbon-fueled engine. There are numerous possible combinations of auto propulsion components besides the four shown, but many of these combinations would make no sense and would not be considered. Among those that are feasible, there might be ideas that no one has given adequate thought to and that might lead to a technological breakthrough.

Relevance-tree analysis is also a type of morphological approach. The form and structure (morphology) of a productive objective are expressed as a "tree" that looks somewhat like an organization chart (it also resembles a work breakdown structure, which is discussed in the PERT/CPM section of Chapter 7). The first "branches" are major modules that are necessary to achieve the productive objective, which is usually to provide a good or a service. Second

---

[4] Teachers sometimes try out Delphi on their students for instructional purposes. This is really just opinion polling, not Delphi—unless the topic is one on which the students are truly experts.

FIGURE 10-4
Morphological
Analysis of Auto
Propulsion

Components	*Feasible alternatives*			
	Set 1	*Set 2*	*Set 3*	*Set 4* . . .
Number of wheels	3	4	3	4
Number of driven wheels	1	2	3	4
Number of engines	1	1	1	2
Number/type of transmissions	0	Mechanical	Fluid	0
Type of engine	Internal combustion	External combustion	Turbine	Electric
Power source	Hydrocarbon fuel	Primary battery	Secondary battery	Fuel cell

Source: Adapted from Joseph P. Martino, *Technological Forecasting for Decision Making* (American Elsevier, 1972), p. 305. Used with permission.

branches drop from the first ones, third branches from the second, and so forth, until an entire structure of the relevant parts of the objective has been displayed—as a relevance tree.

The relevance tree aids in planning a complex future set of events. For example, a relevance tree might be helpful in planning a governmental program. A governmental manpower program, for example, might be displayed in a relevance tree like the one in Figure 10–5. The tree shows what is relevant in planning for the program. The whole program should provide for the high school dropout, the illiterate, the physically handicapped, the technologically displaced, and the returnee to the labor market. Training the high school dropout is shown broken down into a third level of relevant needs, which break down into fourth-level needs, and so on.

There is no more to relevance-tree analysis than constructing the tree. The relevance tree does nothing more than show—*clearly*—what factors are relevant in planning for future events. But this information can be valuable. The tree in Figure 10–5 shows areas into which governmental agencies might expand their line of services, and it sets the stage for further analysis of demand, capacity needs, costs, feasibility, and so forth.

The auto propulsion example, shown earlier as a morphological analysis, could also be constructed as a relevance tree. There are various ways in which the tree could be designed to show alternative propulsion *methods,* propulsion *problems,* or breakdowns of *components.*

Focusing on propulsion methods helps to show propulsion design possibilities that may have been overlooked. Focusing on propulsion problems may lead to research and development that can overcome a critical impediment (e.g., heat loss) to a design breakthrough. And focusing on components serves to suggest new combinations, as in the morphological example of Figure 10–4.

FIGURE 10–5
Relevance tree

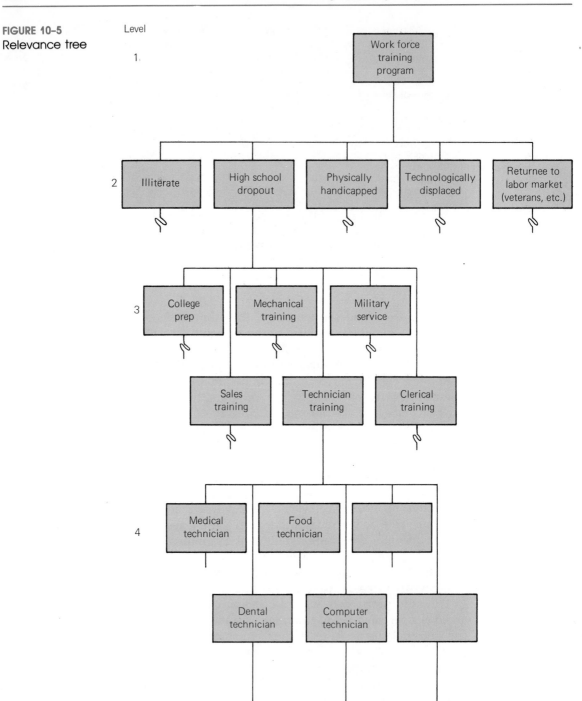

Source: Adapted from Fred Luthans, *Introduction to Management: A Contingency Approach* (Richard J. Schonberger, contributing author) (McGraw-Hill, 1976), p. 88 (HD31.L86). Used with permission.

As can be seen, morphological analysis and relevance-tree analysis suggest some technological futures. But research and development are necessary to take advantage of those suggestions.

Research management

Technological forecasting sets the stage for research into the gaps and opportunities disclosed. The decision to proceed with the research is based on its projected impact on operations, marketing, profits, and other functions. It also involves timing and product life cycles. Once the go-ahead has been given, the task becomes one of research management. Research management is discussed in terms of:

Research strategies.

Project management.

Research strategies have to do with the extent of research, the type of research, and the source of research expertise. Research efforts are often designated as projects, which call for project management.

Research strategies. Commitment to product research ranges from massive for a corporation like Du Pont to meager for, say, the cemetery business. The proper degree of commitment depends more on the dynamics and competition in the industry than on the size of the organization. It also depends on the character and image of the given organization.

Surveys have been done to show the relative amounts of money spent on research among various organizations. More data are available for manufacturing industries than for service industries. Table 10–1 gives the results of a survey of R&D expenditures as a percentage of sales in 200 of the largest manufacturing firms plus 200 smaller ones. As might be expected, food processors, at 1.25 percent, are at the bottom of the list (though they might be near the top in a survey of *market* research expenditures). As might also be expected, electrical equipment, which includes electronic equipment, and

TABLE 10–1
Percentage of sales spent on company-financed R&D

Industry	Percent of annual sales spent on company-financed R&D
Electrical equipment	4.17%
Chemicals (including pharmaceuticals)	3.80
Instruments	3.40
Machinery (including computers)	3.40
Transportation (other than aircraft)	3.29
Aircraft	2.25
Food	1.25

Source: Adapted from Arthur Gerstenfeld, *Effective Management of Research and Development,* © 1970, Addison-Wesley Publishing Company, Inc., chapter 2, page 17, table 2.1, "Percentage of Sales on Company-Financed R&D" Reprinted with permission.

FIGURE 10–6
Research
strategies for
coping with
uncertainties

Case	Uncertainties			Research strategies
	Can we design it?	Can we make it?*	Can we sell it?†	
1	Easily	Easily	Easily	Little research except for pilot testing and trial marketing
2	Easily	Easily	Uncertain	Intensive market research
3	Easily	Uncertain	Uncertain	Market research and process/plant studies
4	Easily	Uncertain	Easily	Intensive production process and plant design study
5	Uncertain	Easily	Easily	Intensive product design research using parallel approaches
6	Uncertain	Easily	Uncertain	Product design research and market research
7	Uncertain	Uncertain	Easily	Product design research and process study
8	Uncertain	Uncertain	Uncertain	Exploratory product design, process, and market research

* Uncertainty about "making it" calls for process research; see process planning in Chapter 8.
† Uncertainty about "selling it" calls for marketing research, which is not discussed in this book.
Source: Reprinted from *Innovation: The Management Connection* by Robert O. Burns (Lexington, Mass.: Lexington Books, D. C. Heath and Company, Copyright 1975, D. C. Heath and Company).

chemicals (including pharmaceuticals) rank highest. Firms in these industries spend more than triple the percentage that food processors spend.

In both manufacturing and services, research expenditures wax and wane. Much of this change is reaction to competitive pressures. A prominent example is the U.S. government's reaction to the missile crisis of the 1960s. Congress was prompted to appropriate huge amounts of research money to close the Soviet-U.S. missile gap. Later, having closed it, Congress saw fit to cut way back on research support.[5]

Commitment to research should depend primarily on conditions. Figure 10–6 shows how the organization's research strategy might be roughly related to various uncertainty conditions. The question in column 1—Can we design it?—is the one most germane to this discussion. But that question is best viewed

[5] "From 1961 to 1967 government-funded R&D increased 5.6% a year. . . . But from 1967 to 1975 the government R&D shrank 3% a year." Reported in "The Silent Crisis in R&D," *Business Week*, March 8, 1976, p. 90.

in context with these equally important questions: Can we make it? Can we sell it? Yeses to all three questions are needed before the product or service is added to the line. Where the answer is uncertain, research may be called for. Thus, product design research is called for in the last four cases, where there is uncertainty about designing the product or service. That research should be intensive if it is already believed that the product can easily be made and marketed (case 5). The research should be exploratory where uncertainty surrounds all three questions (case 8).

Commitment to research is secondarily a matter of organizational character. There is room for both leaders and followers in most industries. The leaders may adopt aggressive or *offensive* product design strategies; the followers may adopt *defensive* strategies; and those in between may make moderate commitments by *contracting* research or by *licensing* other people's product designs as necessary.

The offensive strategy is to commit a lot of money to building a research team. The objective of such a strategy is to design and market products while competition is light or nonexistent. An organization may also assume an offensive strategy for a short-run reason, such as product diversification. Large firms are better able to afford the risks of an offensive strategy, but many small firms have grown large by taking such risks. Xerox, Polaroid, and Texas Instruments are examples. In some industries—the aerospace and electronics industries, for example—nearly every firm sees the need for an offensive strategy. Other industries, such as railroads, seem to have a defensive research strategy.

The defensive strategy carries little risk of loss—or gain either. But for firms that have their niche in the market and are successful low-cost producers and marketers, this strategy may produce high profits. Note that the defensive strategy is not one of no research but one of minimal research, mainly as a safeguard against surprise. It also tends toward the highly practical rather than the basic or innovative.

Contracting for research is the norm in the federal government. The U.S. Government Printing Office publishes *Commerce Business Daily,* which lists new research solicitations that are open to all who would bid. These requests for proposals (RFPs) once dealt mainly with defense research but now span all of the social and physical sciences.

Contracting is used increasingly as a research strategy for private firms. Research contracts often stipulate that the researchers are to share heavily in any successes. Some firms are willing to share research success with others, because they feel that research is not what they do best. Therefore, they feel that they should focus their energies on what they do best, namely, producing—or marketing; then contract out other functions, like research (and perhaps janitorial service, food service, etc.), instead of dabbling in them.

Less messy than the research contract is the license agreement. The growth of product licensing is related to the growth in the number of independent labs, research institutes, and academic researchers that bid on research contracts. These frequently develop product design ideas that are marketable under license agreements. Companies following offensive strategies are also often in the product licensing business. Some, such as Eastman Kodak, Polaroid, and Du Pont, license from others as well as licensing to others. Du Pont, for example, has marketed the following products under licensing agreements with another product developer: viscose rayon, tetraethyl lead, cellophane, synthetic ammonia, acetate rayon, Freon, titanium pigments, Lucite, polyethylene, and titanium metal.[6]

After the source of research expertise has been determined, research projects are formulated. Project management, discussed next, refers to the planning and control of research efforts.

Project management. In the first 50 years of management as a recognized field of study (about 1900–1950) project management was mostly ignored. The emphasis was on managing routine jobs and repetitive production. One reason is that large projects were rare. The Manhattan Project, which developed the atom bomb in the 1940s, signaled the start of a new era of large research projects. The largest were found in the Department of Defense (DoD). Managing them was a slow, bureaucratic process. The process was especially slow when many agencies and private contractors and subcontractors were involved, as was common. Coordination problems were severe.

In 1961 the DoD did something about it. It expanded on the concept of the project engineer, which had come into common use for coordinating construction projects. It borrowed some of the reasoning that Procter and Gamble followed when, some 50 years ago, that company originated the concept of brand managers. The result was the R&D *project manager.* A 1961 DoD directive required that each of the services establish a project manager[7] for every R&D effort costing over $25 million (or for a few reasons other than cost, such as national urgency). All smaller or less urgent R&D efforts would be managed in one of the more traditional slow, bureaucratic ways.

Three unique features of DoD project management are:

1. *Authority.* The project manager receives a charter signed by a high authority, sometimes the secretary of defense. The charter states project objectives and gives authority to "order" certain agencies to do project work.
2. *Money.* The project budget goes to the project manager. This gives the project manager the "power of the purse." The budgeted funds pay for services from other agencies and for contracting with private firms.
3. *Staffing.* Normal federal hiring restrictions are modified to permit handpicking the project manager, who in turn handpicks a staff. The project management staff is chartered to do the project planning and monitoring, including scheduling and contracting, but not to do the research itself. (If the project manager has the research staff too, then it is not project management any more; it is a complete new agency.)

---

[6] W. F. Mueller, "Origins of Du Pont's Major Innovations, 1930–50," in *Research, Development, and Technological Innovations,* ed. James R. Bright (Irwin, 1964) (HD45.B68).

[7] The U.S. Air Force uses the term *system program officer* instead of project manager.

These features of project management, in combination, comprise what may best be thought of as a new organizational form. It is shown as an organization chart in Figure 10–7. This type of chart is often called a *matrix* organization chart. The regular functional organization, bureaucratically organized, is in the rectangular boxes. Superimposed on it (forming a matrix) is the project management structure in the circular boxes. People in the middle end up having two bosses, their permanent bosses and their temporary project bosses. This creates conflict but speeds up the project research.

Unlike the regular manager the project manager is supposed to end the assignment by getting the project done. The first DoD project managers were enormously successful in doing this. For example, five massive DoD projects undertaken in the late 1950s served somewhat as pilot tests of the project management idea. These were Polaris, Atlas, Minuteman, BMEWS (Ballistic Missile Early Warning System), and Titan. Each was completed in 4–6 years as compared with 10–15 years of R&D for many far less complex weapon systems prior to the use of project management.[8]

By 1968 the number of DoD project managers had grown to about 170. That seemed to be too many. A study team found that the system was overloaded with project managers who were asking for preferential treatment from other agencies and contractors.[9] The lesson seems to be that project management is a concept that works best when it is used least.

Project management is by no means restricted to the Department of Defense. It is common practice, for example, in the highly research-oriented aerospace and electronics industries. The project manager's authority is not always as great as in the DoD's "pure" form of project management. In both the private and public sectors project management forms range from the pure form to the form in which the project coordinator has no money, staff, or authority.

Project management as a career is for those with a venturesome spirit. The large project that a project manager is responsible for is perhaps no more subject to cancellation than one of the many small jobs that a functional manager is responsible for. The difference is that project cancellation puts the project manager out of work. Thus, project managers tend to lead a rather uncertain, nomadic existence. Their employers sometimes provide for some security by setting forth guarantees of a new project or the right to go back to a job in the functional organization. Whatever the degree of uncertainty, some people like project management because of the challenge and the high degree of responsibility involved. Whole volumes have been written about the special attributes of project managers and their engineering and scientific

---

[8] Gerstenfeld reports average R&D project times of 3.3 years for a sample of *Fortune's* largest 500 firms and 2.1 years for a sample of other firms, but DoD projects tend to be much larger, more complex, and more time-consuming. Arthur Gerstenfeld, *Effective Management of Research and Development* (Addison-Wesley, 1970), p. 27 (T175.5.G47).

[9] *AMC Project Management: An Assessment of Seven Years' Field Testing of the Concept,* U.S. Army Management Engineering Training Agency, Rock Island, Illinois, July 15, 1969.

FIGURE 10-7
Project
management
organization
structure

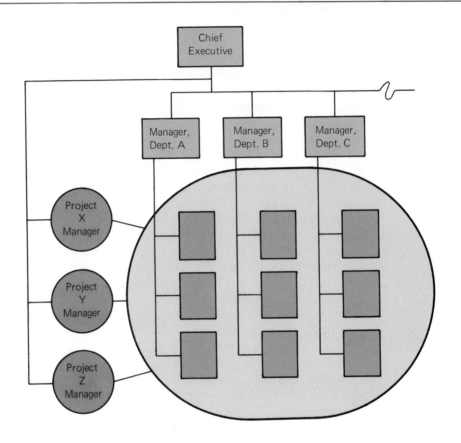

counterparts. It is an area of study full of issues for both the behavioral scientist and the management scientist.

FEASIBILITY

In parallel with planning and managing innovation the feasibility of innovation is periodically assessed. Preliminary feasibility study is undertaken before project management begins. Project management may then include one or more rounds of more detailed feasibility study. Given the riskiness of research, a project that passes preliminary feasibility tests might well be shown to be infeasible after more data come in. This would signal the end of the project. One article on that topic has the descriptive title "Effective Project Costing and Killing Techniques."[10] Methods and concepts of feasibility that will be discussed in this section are:

---

[10] John Chapman, "Effective Project Costing and Killing Techniques," in *Information Systems Administration*, ed. F. Warren McFarlan, Richard L. Nolan, and David P. Norton (Holt, Rinehart and Winston, 1973), pp. 391–400 (HF5548.2.M217). This happens to concern computer projects but the message applies equally to any kind of project. (To a "computernik" the term *project management* is likely to be thought to refer to a computer project.)

Benefit-cost analysis.
Profit-volume (P-V) ratio analysis.
Contribution ratio.
P-V analysis with fixed costs.
Product mix by simplex linear programming.

This section does not include a discussion of *technical feasibility*. The assumption is that technicians, engineers, or scientists would have had to demonstrate that the project was technically feasible before the above kinds of management-oriented analysis would be undertaken.

Benefit-cost analysis

It is more common to hear this referred to as cost-benefit analysis than as benefit-cost analysis. The term *benefit-cost analysis* may be more precise, however, since the end product of the analysis is a benefit-cost ratio, namely

$$B\text{-}C\text{ ratio} = \frac{\text{Dollars of benefit}}{\text{Dollars of cost}}$$

This test of feasibility is met if the B-C ratio is greater than 1.0. For example, a B-C ratio of 1.5 means that there is $1.50 in benefits for every $1.00 in cost.

There are complications in B-C analysis. For one thing the dollars of benefit and the dollars of cost must be "common-time" dollars. You cannot, for example, add an initial project cost of $20,000 to a $1,000 per year operating cost and call it $21,000. You cannot even add $20,000 initial cost to $1,000 per year for ten years and call it $30,000. The reason is that money today is more valuable than money in the future. So future streams of money must be discounted before adding them to present money—or present money must be "annualized" before adding it to other annual costs. Methods of converting all dollars to common-time dollars are explained fully in Chapter 11.

Let us consider two examples of benefit-cost analysis. First a simple example:

EXAMPLE 10-1
Benefit-cost analysis for Environmental Preservation League

The Plains City chapter of the Environmental Preservation League, a nonprofit group, has been asked to sponsor research on the environmental impact of not catching grass clippings in lawn mowing. The cost of the research is estimated at $50,000. The projected benefits of doing the research are based on similar research done in other locales having different soil and climate conditions. These benefits include:

Savings on fertilizer	$40,000/yr
Savings on garbage pickup	10,000/yr.
Savings on disposable plastic bags (nonbiodegradable)	2,000/yr.
	$52,000/yr.
Less the effects of losses of income to sellers of the above	$42,000/yr.
Net projected benefits for Plains City	$10,000/yr.

The projected benefit-cost ratio is calculated for a 15-year period (the "expected life" of the current lawn-mowing technology) and an 8 percent interest rate as follows:

$$B\text{-}C\text{ratio} = \frac{\$10,000 \times 8.559}{\$50,000} = \frac{\$85,590}{\$50,000} = 1.71,$$

where 8.559 is the interest factor for 15 years and 8 percent. (That interest factor is variously known as the capital-recovery factor, the P/A factor, and the present-value annuity factor. Explanation and interest tables are found in the supplements to Chapter 11.) This is a favorable benefit-cost ratio, a $1.71 return for every $1.00 spent.

The league is not quite satisfied. It questions the use of 8 percent since most consumers and businesses borrow at higher interest rates. Recalculating for a 12 percent rate, the ratio is:

$$B\text{-}C\text{ratio} = \frac{\$10,000 \times 6.811}{\$50,000} = \frac{\$68,110}{\$50,000} = 1.36,$$

where 6.811 is the present-value annuity factor for 15 years and 12 percent. The benefit-cost ratio is still favorable. The research project appears to be worthy based on this test of economic feasibility—if the benefit and cost estimates can be relied on.

In this example the annual costs in the numerator were converted to a present value (PV). That way, both the numerator and the denominator are in common-time dollars so that the ratio may be calculated.

A second example is a benefit-cost analysis of a proposal to dam the Platte River in central Nebraska—the Mid-State Project, an actual case. In this example the common-time dollars in the numerator and the denominator are in terms of equivalent annual costs (EAC), also called annuities. (The B-C ratio comes out the same whether PV or EAC is used.)

EXAMPLE 10–2
Benefit-cost analysis for the Mid-State Project

Figure 10–8 shows 16 benefit-cost ratios for the Mid-State Project. These are based on different estimates of benefits, project life, and interest rates. The project was opposed by the author of the article referred to in Figure 10–8. He was trying to show that the project had a favorable B-C ratio only if you accepted the estimates used in the first column, 3.125 percent and a 100-year project life and that even then the B-C ratio was unfavorable if the annual benefits were reestimated downward to $2,879,000 by one set of assumptions or to $2,296,500 by another set. The proper way to estimate benefits is not at issue here. But the example is excellent for showing several things:

1. *EAC method.* The example shows a second way to do B-C ratios. In the previous example present values were used. In this one the common-time dollars are in equivalent annual costs (or annuities). Annual benefits are divided by equivalent annual cost to give the B-C ratio.

2. *Cost estimates.* In such projects cost estimates are usually not very controversial; no one is arguing about them in this case. These are mostly estimates of construction and operation costs, and estimators are experienced at making such estimates. If their estimates are very wrong, this is usually because of unpredictables like excess inflation, strikes, or catastrophes.

3. *Benefits estimates.* In projects of this kind benefits are hard to estimate. Benefits have been estimated for years in the water resources field. But in a world suddenly

FIGURE 10–8
Benefit-cost summary for the Mid-State Project

		Discount rates and equivalent annual costs:			
		3.125%*	5.375%†	7%†	10%†
		$4,543,000	$6,487,000	$9,002,800	$12,193,000
Costs:					
Construction cost:	$112,000,000				
Operating costs:	$863,000/year				
	Total per year	**Benefit-cost ratios:**			
Benefits:					
1967 bureau estimates:					
New lands (direct)	$2,471,000				
New lands (secondary)	499,000				
Land acquisition/withdrawal	−295,000				
Supplemental water	1,096,000				
Groundwater stabilization	772,000				
Flood control	518,000				
Recreation	175,500				
Fish and wildlife	425,000	$5,661,500	1.24	0.87	0.63	0.46
Reduced multipurpose benefits:					
Fish and wildlife	−347,000				
Flood control	341,500	4,713,000	1.03	0.72	0.52	0.38
Reduced new-lands benefits (direct and secondary):					
Using adjusted normalized prices					
Direct	1,136,500				
Secondary	0	2,879,000	0.63	0.44	0.31	0.23
Using Brandow's prices					
Direct	553,500				
Secondary	0	2,296,500	0.50	0.35	0.25	0.18

* 100-year life assumed.
† 50-year life assumed.
Sample calculation: At 7 percent and 50 years the proper interest factor is 0.07246. Therefore, the initial cost of the project, $112,000,000, has an equivalent annual cost of ($112,000,000)(0.07246) = $8,137,000. Then,

$$B\text{-}C \text{ ratio} = \frac{\$5,661,500}{\$8,137,000 + \$863,000} = 0.63$$

Source: Adapted from Steve H. Hanke, "Adjusted Benefit-Cost Ratios for the Mid-State Reclamation Project," *Nebraska Journal of Economics and Business*, Spring 1975, p. 8. Used with permission.

concerned about water, energy, and the environment, new things to measure and new ways of measuring crop up.

4. *Life.* How long the project earns the benefits (the project life) is sometimes a matter for dispute. The first column of B-C ratios is based on the Bureau of Reclamation's 100-year life assumption. The writer of the article argues for a 50-year life, which is used in the rest of the table. Actually this is a moot point. When you project that many years into the future, project life makes little difference. For example, converting the $112 million initial project cost to EAC requires multiplying it by a "capital-recovery factor." (This is the same as dividing by an annuity factor). The factor for, say, 7 percent interest is 0.07246 if a 50-year life is assumed and 0.07008 if a 100-year life is assumed. (These factors are in Table S11–1 of Supplement A in Chapter 11.) This is a very small difference. The difference is large if the dispute is over short lives, for example, five years versus ten.

5. *Interest rate.* The results are highly *sensitive* to the choice of interest rate. Examine the top row of B-C ratios in Figure 10–8. You benefit 87 cents for each dollar of cost at 5.375 percent. You benefit only 46 cents per dollar of cost at 10 percent interest. The choice of interest rate in the private sector is not highly debatable. It *is* in the public sector. The subject has frequently been debated by Congress, the Bureau of the Budget, the Council of Economic Advisers, and so forth. More is said of this in Chapter 11. Our purpose here is just to show its importance.

Benefit-cost analysis dates back to the 1930s, when Agg of Iowa introduced the concept for evaluating public works projects.[11] Since that time benefit-cost analysis has become standard operating procedure in public works. This is especially true of water resources projects undertaken by the Department of the Interior and the Army Corps of Engineers. The concept is now being widely used by governmental agencies in the social services and education.

Recently benefit-cost analysis has come into use in private firms and the term *benefit-cost* or *cost-benefit* has come into general use. For instance, it is common to be asked something like, "Is it cost-beneficial?" Here the questioner is probably not really asking for the results of a careful benefit-cost ratio analysis in which all money is in common-time dollars. Thus, we must be careful to realize when the term is being used precisely and when it is being used in just a general way.

A matter that must be reserved for later discussion is the differences between benefit-cost analysis, rate-of-return analysis, and cost-effectiveness analysis. Suffice it to say here that benefit-cost is best suited to situations in which there are diverse kinds of benefits (as in government) and that rate-of-return is best suited to situations in which profit on sales is the dominant benefit (as in private firms). Cost-effectiveness is most suitable for the public sector, but it is more useful for evaluating *what way* to do something than for determining *whether* to do it. In this section on feasibility the concern is over whether to pursue new product or service projects. Formal benefit-cost analysis

---

[11] Cited in J. Morley Engish, ed., *Cost-Effectiveness: The Economic Evaluation of Engineered Systems,* (Wiley, 1968), p. 2 (TA183.C63).

and the general concept of benefits versus cost are helpful in answering such questions.

Profit-volume (P-V) ratio

Benefit-cost analysis assesses whether a proposed *project* will pay its way. P-V analysis, by contrast, assesses whether *repetitively* produced items will pay their way. P-V analysis is one form of break-even or indifference analysis; other forms are discussed later in the book. The following example demonstrates P-V analysis:

EXAMPLE 10–3
P-V analysis, Copy-Boy, Inc.

Copy-Boy, Inc., is a commercial firm offering duplicating and copying services. It is doing P-V analysis of its line of services, which consists of offset printing, mimeographing, and xerography. The following data are based on the past year's performance:

Service	Profit	Fixed cost	Sales volume	Average price per copy
Offset.....................................	20,000	40,000	150,000	$0.05
Mimeograph	24,000	4,000	140,000	0.02
Xerography	30,000	20,000	100,000	0.08

Fixed costs represent costs that are incurred whether or not you operate, for example, plant and equipment costs. Not directly shown above are variable costs; these costs (e.g., labor, materials, and utilities costs) are incurred by operating.

The P-V ratio is determined by

$$P\text{-}V\,\text{ratio} = \frac{\text{Profit} + \text{Fixed cost}}{\text{Sales volume}}$$

Thus, for Copy-Boy,

$$\text{P-V ratio for offset services} = \frac{\$20,000 + \$40,000}{\$150,000} = \frac{\$60,000}{\$150,000} = 0.40$$

$$\text{P-V ratio for mimeograph services} = \frac{\$24,000 + \$4,000}{\$140,000} = \frac{\$28,000}{\$140,000} = 0.20$$

$$\text{P-V ratio for xerography services} = \frac{\$30,000 + \$20,000}{\$100,000} = \frac{\$50,000}{\$100,000} = 0.50$$

It can be seen from the above that the term *profit-volume ratio* is a bit of a misnomer. The ratio is really between *profit and fixed cost* and sales volume. It is useful to compare Copy-Boy's P-V ratios, just calculated, with simple profit-to-sales ratios:

	P-V ratio (including fixed cost)	Profit-to-sales ratio
Offset	0.40	0.13
Mimeograph	0.20	0.17
Xerography	0.50	0.30

Xerography is the top performer by either measure. Mimeograph is second best in simple profit-to-sales ratios but is a distant third in P-V ratios.

FIGURE 10-9
P-V charts, Copy-
Boy, Inc.

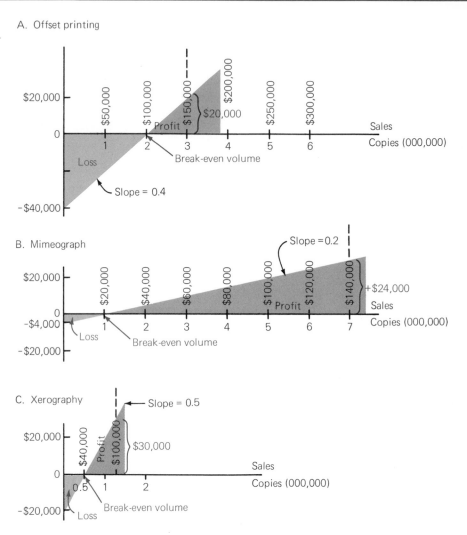

A. Offset printing

B. Mimeograph

C. Xerography

The meaning of these differences in P-V ratios is clearer when the differences are viewed graphically. Figure 10–9 is a P-V chart of Copy-Boy's three kinds of service. The slopes of the constructed lines are equal to the P-V ratios. Break-even volumes, the sales volumes at which revenues are great enough to recover fixed costs, are determined by:

$$\text{Break-even volume (\$)} = \frac{\text{Fixed cost}}{\text{P-V ratio}}$$

Or,

$$\text{B-E volume (in units)} = \frac{\text{Fixed cost}}{\text{P-V ratio} \times \text{Price per copy}}$$

Thus, for Copy-Boy,

$$B\text{-}E \text{ volume for offset services} = \frac{\$40,000}{0.40} = \$100,000 \text{ per yr.}$$
$$\text{(or 2,000,000 copies/yr.)}$$

$$B\text{-}E \text{ volume for mimeograph services} = \frac{\$4,000}{0.20} = \$20,000 \text{ per yr.}$$
$$\text{(or 1,000,000 copies/yr.)}$$

$$B\text{-}E \text{ volume for xerography services} = \frac{\$20,000}{0.50} = \$40,000 \text{ per yr.}$$
$$\text{(or 500,000 copies/yr.)}$$

The P-V charts show the mimeograph services (Figure 10–9B) to have the least potential for profit increases. The P-V slope of Figure 10–9B is gentle, meaning that a large sales increase is needed for much profit improvement. In fact, even though mimeograph sales are 6 million copies beyond the break-even point, profit is only $24,000. By contrast, the offset (Figure 10–9A) and xerography (Figure 10–9C) slopes are steep. With sales of only about 1 million copies beyond their break-even points, offset and xerography achieve the same range of profits as is achieved by mimeograph with sales of 6 million copies beyond its break-even point. On the other side of the coin, offset and xerography are susceptible to high losses, but mimeograph losses cannot exceed the $4,000 fixed cost per year.

Having completed the P-V analysis, Copy-Boy has a useful information base for making decisions about its line of services. The many possible decisions depend on demand forecasting, which is the topic of Chapter 2. Two possible decisions are:

1. *For a forecast of no change or significant sales increase: Drop the mimeograph service.* The $24,000 profit would be lost. But if a small portion of the 7 million mimeograph copies could be recovered as offset or xerography copies, that $24,000 would be quickly made back. Existing talent, space, and other resources are better used for producing services with high P-V ratios when times are good. *Caution:* Mimeograph service may be needed for a reason other than direct profits. It may be that Copy-Boy would not be perceived as a full-fledged copy-service firm if it did not offer such a basic kind of copy service. Just as banks see value in being known as full-service banks, a copier may see value in being known as a full-service copier.

2. *For a forecast of decreasing sales: Drop offset.* By so doing, you lose the offset profits, if any. You also lose $40,000 in fixed costs! The hope would be to shift some of the lost 3 million offset copies to the highly profitable xerography line. (There may be an equally strong argument for dropping xerography and hoping for a shift to offset copying.)[12]

Contribution ratio

The P-V ratio is the same as the *contribution ratio.* Contribution means the contribution of the sales dollar toward payment of fixed costs and toward any profit above fixed costs. While P-V ratio and contribution ratio give you the same result, contribution ratio, CR, is likely to be calculated based on unit costs and prices rather than annual figures:

$$CR = \frac{\text{Unit price} - \text{Variable cost per unit}}{\text{Unit price}}$$

---

[12] This P-V analysis also suggests various marketing tactics such as price changes and advertising changes. Discussion of such subjects is beyond the scope of this book.

For Copy-Boy's offset service, unit price is $0.05. Variable cost per unit was not given, but it may be figured from the given data.

Since

$$\text{Sales volume} = \text{Variable cost} + \text{Fixed cost} + \text{Profit},$$

$$\begin{aligned} \text{Variable cost} &= \text{Sales volume} - \text{Fixed cost} - \text{Profit} \\ &= \$150,000 - \$40,000 - \$20,000 \\ &= \$90,000 \end{aligned}$$

Then, since $150,000 sales are at $0.05 per unit,

$$\text{Sales volume} = \frac{\$150,000}{\$0.05} = 3,000,000 \text{ units.}$$

Finally, $90,000 variable cost for 3,000,000 units yields:

$$\text{Variable cost per unit} = \frac{\$90,000}{3,000,000} = \$0.03 \text{ per copy}$$

Thus,

$$CR \text{ for offset} = \frac{\$0.05 - \$0.03}{\$0.05} = 0.40,$$

which is the same as the P-V ratio calculated earlier.

P-V analysis with common fixed costs

The P-V chart tells a less ambiguous story where the line of products/services shares common costs. Let us consider the case of Kopy-Kat, Inc., a competitor of Copy-Boy.

Example 10–4
P-V analysis with common fixed costs, Kopy-Kat, Inc.

Kopy-Kat has only an offset capability. The offset provides two kinds of service, plain black-and-white copy and four-color copy. Historical records for last year show:

Service	Profit	Fixed cost*	Sales volume	Average price per copy	P-V ratio	Profit-to-sales ratio
B&W	$15,000	$12,000	$ 80,000	$0.04	0.34	0.19
4-color	5,000	18,000	120,000	0.42	0.19	0.04

* Total offset fixed costs—for plant and equipment—are $30,000 for the year. Accounting allocates the cost to the B&W and the four-color service lines in the ratio of their sales volumes, that is, 4/10 for B&W and 6/10 for four-color.
  P-V ratio calculations:

$$\text{P-V ratio for B\&W} = \frac{\$15,000 + \$12,000}{\$80,000} = \frac{\$27,000}{\$80,000} = 0.34$$

$$\text{P-V ratio for four-color} = \frac{\$5,000 + \$18,000}{\$120,000} = \frac{\$23,000}{\$120,000} = 0.19$$

Four-color copying is the poorer performer by a large margin as measured by P-V ratio or by profit-to-sales ratio. The P-V chart in Figure 10–10 shows what would happen if four-color copying service were dropped. The P-V chart begins with a negative $30,000 combined fixed cost, the sum of $12,000 and $18,000. An inflection point is calculated in addition to a break even point. (An inflection point is a point where two lines of different slopes come together.)

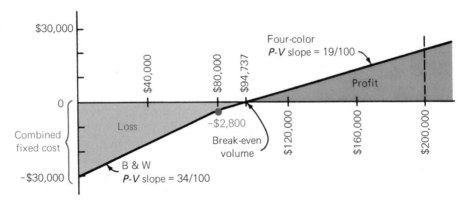

FIGURE 10-10
P-V chart, Kopy-
Kat, Inc.

The inflection point is known to be at \$80,000 on the horizontal scale since sales are \$80,000 for the first service, B&W copying. The vertical component of the inflection point is determined algebraically using the P-V slope, $^{34}/_{100}$, and the \$80,000:

$$\frac{34}{100} = \frac{y}{\$80,000}$$
$$100y = 34 \times \$80,000 = \$2,720,000$$
$$y = \$27,200$$

This \$27,200 is the contribution made by the B&W copying sales revenue toward combined fixed cost of \$30,000. That means that the inflection point is at −\$2,800 on the vertical (−\$30,000 + \$27,200 = −\$2,800).

The B-E volume is determined next. Rising from −\$2,800 at a slope of $^{19}/_{100}$ for four-color processing, the distance to the B-E point is:

$$\frac{19}{100} = \frac{\$2,800}{x}$$
$$19x = \$280,000$$
$$x = \$14,737$$

Now add the \$14,737 to the sales for B&W copying, \$80,000, and the result is:

$$B\text{-}E \text{ point} = \$80,000 + \$14,737 = \$94,737$$

It is clear from Figure 10–9 that four-color copying should not be dropped from the line of services even though it is not very profitable. The reason is that dropping it would mean loss of sales income of \$120,000; but there would be no reduction in fixed costs, because fixed costs for the two services are inseparable.

It could be shown that four-color copying should not be dropped *even if it lost*, *say, \$5,000 per year!*[13] This will not be demonstrated here. Instead it is an exercise at the end of the chapter.

---

[13] But something could perhaps be done to make four-color copying more profitable, for example, raise the price or cut variable costs.

The P-V chart has been shown to be especially useful for the case of products/services sharing the same fixed costs. For this case P-V ratios or contribution ratios alone would not show the true effects of changing the line of products/services.

Product mix by simplex linear programming

Linear programming (LP) is the mathematical tool most closely associated with the operations research (OR) field. (See brief discussion of OR in Chapter 1.) LP enthusiasts tend to see the world and all of its subsystems through LP-tinted glasses. There is some merit in that. The world of humanity is one of too many demands for too few resources. In fact, that is not a bad description of "the management problem." Linear programming and its variants are ways to solve any problem of multiple demands for limited resources.

The objective in LP problems is to maximize gain or minimize loss. A term that means either maximize gain or minimize loss is *optimize.*

It is not hard to see that planning the line of products/services may be set up as an LP problem: too many products or services that might be profitable and too few resources to produce or offer them all. So you want to offer the optimal mix of these products/services. Operations researchers call this the *product-mix problem.*

The *simplex method* is an approach to solving an LP problem. An example of a product-mix problem is used to explain simplex LP in the chapter supplement.

SUMMARY

Planning products and services is partly a marketing task: that is, what can be sold? But operations managers are concerned with what it is *possible* to do. This means managing design innovation and assuring feasibility.

The prudent manager of innovation begins with technological forecasting. Techniques include trend extrapolation, gaming, morphological analysis, and relevance trees.

If there are technological opportunities and if the marketing, financial, and timing outlooks are good, research management begins. First, the research strategy is set. There are such questions as amount of money to be spent and whether to do internal research or deal with outside researchers. Second, organization of the project management task is called for. The project manager's authority may range from mere coordination to the total management of planning, budgeting, contracting, and controlling.

Feasibility studies are often a part of project management. Benefit-cost analysis is one test of economic feasibility. It is most useful in messy nonprofit situations involving nonrepetitive operations.

Profit-volume analysis and the related contribution analysis are more useful in assessing economic feasibility for repetitively produced products or services. Profit-volume and contribution ratios show the relative importance of products/services that do not share fixed costs. A profit-volume chart helps show importance where fixed costs are shared.

The feasibility question gradually shifts from what is possible to what is reasonable. One test for reasonability is the test for optimality. A powerful tool for optimizing the mix of products/services is the simplex method of linear programming. The simplex technique ends by showing what ought to be in the line and in what quantities, given their profits (or costs) and the limits on resources.

Chapter 10 has concerned itself with the long-range or strategic side of the aggregate-planning function. That is, it has focused on planning the line of products and services. Once the line has been set, there is a shift to aggregate demand forecasting for those products and services, which was examined in Chapter 2.

REFERENCES

Books

Ayres, Robert U. *Technological Forecasting and Long-Range Planning.* McGraw-Hill, 1969 (T174.A9).

Bright, James R., ed. *Research, Development, and Technological Innovations.* Irwin, 1964 (HD45.B68).

————, ed. *Technological Forecasting for Industry and Government.* Prentice-Hall, 1968 (T174.T4).

Burns, Robert O. *Innovation: The Management Connection.* Heath, 1975 (HD20.R564).

Cetron, Marvin J., and Joel D. Goldhar, eds. *The Science of Managing Organized Technology.* Gordon and Breach, 1970 (T175.5.C47).

Gerstenfeld, Arthur. *Effective Management of Research and Development.* Addison-Wesley, 1970 (T175.5.T94).

Heyal, Carl, ed. *Handbook of Industrial Research Management.* 2d ed. Reinhold, 1968 (T175.5.H4).

Martino, Joseph P. *Technological Forecasting for Decision Making.* American Elsevier, 1972.

Periodicals (societies)

The Futurist (World Futures Society).

IEEE Transactions on Engineering Management (Institute of Electrical and Electronics Engineers).

Long Range Planning—British.

R&D Management—British.

R&D Management—digest.

Research Management—international.

Research Policy—international.

Technological Forecasting and Social Change—international.

PROBLEMS

Note: Asterisked (*) problems require more than mimicry. They require judgment, and you should include discussion of reasons, assumptions, and outside sources of information.

Enveloping

*1. Assume that you are an analyst for Kitchen Technology, Inc. Develop an enveloping projection for predicting technological advances in the cooking of food. Technological developments in the past would range from cooking on an open fire to cooking in microwave ovens. Your task is to fill in with intervening developments and to project into the future. You will need to select a suitable unit of measure as the vertical scale on the graph.

Morphological analysis

2. Develop a morphological analysis table for the Figure 10–5 example of a work force training program.

Relevance tree

3. Develop a relevance tree for the auto propulsion example of Figure 10–4.

Research strategies

*4. See whether you can find out something about the research in your community. Some questions are:

 a. What percent of annual sales is spent on company-financed R&D in the average firm (or a sample of firms) in your community? See Table 10–1 in the chapter for comparison.

 b. Are there prominent examples of government-funded R&D in your community?

 c. Are there companies in your community that hire outside firms to do their product development work instead of using an internal R&D staff?

 d. Is there a strong market for project management expertise in your community?

Project management

*5. In what way (or ways) do you think the Procter-and-Gamble type of brand manager is different from the DoD type of project manager?

*6. Figure 10–7 in the chapter shows that personnel at the intersections in matrix or project organizations have more than one boss, but the advantage of such organizations is faster project completion. What do you think makes it faster? In your answer try to compare project management with ordinary management of a project.

Benefit-cost analysis

*7. In recent years one of the more controversial U.S. public works projects, from a benefit-cost standpoint, has been the Tennessee-Tombigbee Waterway project. (It was at one time near the top of President Carter's "hit list.") Do a brief library search on the project to try to discover the roots of the controversy. Are there arguments about benefit-cost ratio? About choice of discount rate? About estimated cost? About estimated benefits? About estimated project life?

8. Mt. Luck Observatory has been one of the world's major centers for discoveries in astronomy. But in recent years lights from a nearby city have drastically cut the viewing power at Mt. Luck, causing speculation that it will close. Astronomers have requested that the city adopt an ordinance requiring all new outdoor lights to wear some kind of hat to keep them from shining skyward. A city analyst has collected the following data (admittedly rough) on the benefits and costs of such an ordinance.

Benefits: Preserving an educational resource for the community, very conservatively estimated to be equal to the Mt. Luck payroll, for Mt. Luck's projected technological life of 20 years = $100,000/yr.

Costs: Annual cost of "hats" in community = $20,000/yr. This year cost of hats (special large city project with a 20-year life) = $180,000.

The city uses a discount rate of 10 percent.

Compute the benefit-cost ratio, using the present-value method or the equivalent annual cost method.

Profit-volume and contribution

9. Plastico, Inc., has three manufacturing processes: molded polyolefin, extruded polyurethane, and sprayed fiberglass. The following summarizes last year's performance for the three processes (which are housed in three separate facilities with separate labor crews):

Process	Sales volume	Fixed cost	Variable cost	Profit	Units sold
Molded	$400,000	$300,000	$50,000	$50,000	5,000
Extruded......	200,000	170,000	20,000	10,000	2,000
Sprayed	100,000	20,000	40,000	40,000	500

a. Compute P-V ratios and break-even volumes for the three processes.
b. Plot the data on P-V charts.
c. What does the P-V analysis suggest to us about Plastico's product line? Are the same conclusions shown by simple profit-to-sales ratios?
d. Compute contribution ratios (based on dollars per unit) for the three processes. How do the contribution ratios compare with the PV ratios from part *a?*

P-V, common fixed costs

*10. In Example 10–4 in the chapter, Kopy-Kat, Inc., four-color copying sales were shown to be a valuable contributor toward fixed costs. The statement at the end of the example is that "four-color copying should not be dropped *even if it lost, say, $5,000 per year.*" Perform calculations to verify this statement.

LP product-mix analysis

11. Aguas Purificados, S.A., is expanding operations northward into the United States and Canada. A line of one, two, or three of the following bottled products has been proposed for sale: pure water, plain ("sin gas"); pure water, sparkling ("con gas"); and pure water, flavored. Demand has been forecasted for a test market. Projected demand for plain is 30,000 bottles per week; for sparkling, 40,000 bottles per week; and for flavored, 18,000 bottles per week. The products go through two limited-capacity facilities, mixing and bottling, but they go through at different rates, as follows:

	Mixing	Bottling
Plain	—	14,400/wk.
Sparkling ...	8,000/wk.	12,000/wk.
Flavored	4,000/wk.	9,600/wk.

The mixing facility will have a capacity of 9,000 per week, and the bottling capacity will be 21,000 per week. If plain earns a contribution of $0.03 per bottle, sparkling $0.02 per bottle, and flavored $0.015 per bottle, what should the product line consist of? Why? Use simplex LP as an aid in your analysis.

(Put the problem on the computer if suitable computer facilities and software are available to you.)

12. Aguas Purificados, S.A., has reestimated the contributions on its three bottled products, based on an alternative pricing scheme. The new contributions are $0.02 per bottle for plain, $0.03 for sparkling, and $0.025 for flavored. Follow all of the instructions for problem 11, but use these new contribution figures.

IN-BASKET CASE*

Topic: Product line—Toy Mfg.

To:

From: Plant Superintendent, Alpha Toys

We [Alpha Toys] are continually adding new items to our product line. The new president says we do this on an "irrational" basis. What good methods are there for evaluating the product line regarding possible additions and deletions? Note: Please treat the subject in terms familiar to a production manager rather than in strictly marketing terms.

---

* See instructions at end of problem section, Chapter 1.

supplement to chapter 10

LINEAR PROGRAMMING, SIMPLEX METHOD

This supplement examines the simplex method of linear programming (LP). Simplex is the most general and powerful of the various methods of solving LP problems. The discussion of simplex includes the following topics, which are explained via an example of a product-mix problem:

1. Product-mix problem data.
2. Objective function and constraints.
3. Initial matrix.
4. Recycle or stop.
5. Other simplex considerations.

Product-mix problem data

High-Rider, Inc., can make motorcycles and waterborne "rocket skis." Each product is processed through three work centers: fabrication, assembly, and test. Relevant data are given below:

	Hours required per unit		*Work-center*
	Motorcycles	*Rocket skis*	*capacity per week (hours)*
Fabrication	10	3	90
Assembly	6	2	120
Test	5	6	40
Contribution per unit	$100	$50	

Objective function and constraints

In simplex the goal is to optimize an objective function. For High-Rider, the objective function, based on the $100 and $50 contributions per unit, is to maximize $Z = 100M + 50R$, where

M = Units produced of motorcycles
R = Units produced of rocket skis
Z = Total contribution (i.e., contribution toward fixed cost and profit)

The limited capacities in the three work centers put a limit on the total contribution Z. The three limits may be expressed as inequations:

Fabrication:	$10M + 3R \leq 90$
Assembly:	$6M + 2R \leq 120$
Test:	$5M + 6R \leq 40$

Thus, in fabrication 10 hours times each unit of M plus 3 hours times each unit of R should be less than or equal to the 80-hour-per-week capacity. Assembly and test are interpreted similarly.

Simplex requires converting all inequations to equations. This is done by simply adding slack variables to each constraint and making it an equality, as follows:

$$\begin{aligned} \text{Fabrication:} && 10M + 3R + 1S_1 &= 90 \\ \text{Assembly:} && 6M + 2R + 1S_2 &= 120 \\ \text{Test:} && 5M + 6R + 1S_2 &= 40 \end{aligned}$$

Now the slack variables, S_1, S_2, and S_3, take up whatever capacity is not used to produce M or R. In other words slack represents unused capacity.

The objective function may now be modified to account for the three slack variables (even though their rate of contribution is $0 per unit):

$$Z = 100M + 50R + (0)S_1 + (0)S_2 + (0)S_3$$

All data are now in a form suitable for entry into the initial simplex matrix. The initial matrix is shown in Figure S10–1. In the matrix the three constraint equations have been slightly expanded so that each equation has the same size variables: M, R, S_1, S_2, and S_3. The expanded equations, below, are really not changed, because the two new variables have zero coefficients:

$$\begin{aligned} \text{Fabrication:} && 10M + 3R + 1S_1 + (0)S_2 + (0)S_3 &= 90 \\ \text{Assembly:} && 6M + 2R + (0)S_1 + 1S_2 + (0)S_3 &= 120 \\ \text{Test:} && 5M + 6R + (0)S_1 + (0)S_2 + 1S_3 &= 40 \end{aligned}$$

FIGURE S10–1
Initial simplex matrix

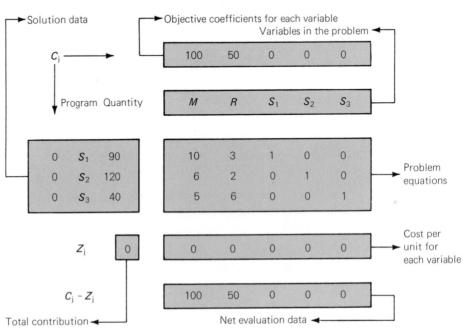

Initial matrix

Each simplex matrix displays variable data on the right and solution data on the left. The initial simplex matrix for a maximization problem is always set up as the worst possible solution at the origin; then later revisions move toward the best or optimum solution. For High-Rider the initial solution, or program, includes only slack variables. Eighty units of S_1 remain in fabrication; that is, all 80 units of fabrication capacity are idle. The contribution per unit, C_j, is zero. S_2 and S_3 are similarly interpreted for assembly and test.

The total contribution of the initial solution is zero, the Z_j value under the quantity column. It is computed as follows:

$$\text{For } S_1, \$0 \text{ per unit} \times 90 \text{ units} = \$0$$
$$\text{For } S_2, \$0 \text{ per unit} \times 120 \text{ units} = \$0$$
$$\text{For } S_3, \$0 \text{ per unit} \times 40 \text{ units} = \$0$$

The Z_j values for the five variables or products represent the cost per unit for producing each product. Since no motorcycles or rocket skis are in the initial solution, their Z_j values are zero; since it costs nothing to produce slack, the Z_j values for the slack variables are also zero.

Optimality test

The net evaluation row is simply the C_j values in the top row minus the Z_j values in the bottom row. The net evaluation row provides data for an optimality test: If any of the $C_j - Z_j$ values is positive, the solution is not optimal. The two positive values, 100 and 50, in Figure S10–1 represent the opportunity costs of not having one unit of M and R, respectively, in the solution. They represent the potential per unit improvement to the total contribution when M and R are entered into the solution. The nonoptimal solution begs revision.

Revised solution

Revision begins with identification of the most beneficial product and the most limiting resource. These are called the key column and the key row, and their intersection is a key number, useful in further calculations.

1. *Key column.* The M column is the key column because it contributes the most toward profit. The rule is;

The key column is the one with the greatest $C_j - Z_j$ value.

2. *Key row.* The key row is the resource (work center) that most severely limits the contribution of the key column product. The capacity constraint on the key column must therefore be assessed. Dividing work-center hours available by hours required per unit of the product chosen in the key column provides the limiting quantity:

Fabrication: $90 \div 10 = 9$ units per week
Assembly: $120 \div 6 = 20$ units per week
Test: $40 \div 5 = 8$ units per week ← *Key row*

The most limiting of the three is *test* at 8 units per week. Therefore, *test*, the S_3 row in Figure S10–1, is the *key row*.

3. *Key number.* At the intersection of the key column and the key row is

FIGURE S10–2
Key column, key row, and key number

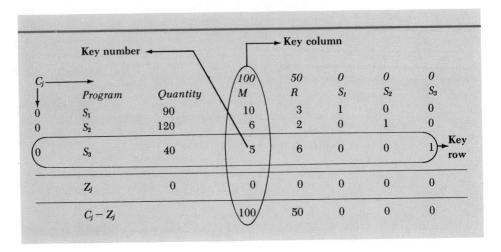

the key number, which is 5. Figure S10–2 shows the key factors that have been identified.

4. *Transforming the key row.* Since the product in the key column is the most profitable, it should be made in maximum quantity. The maximum quantity is 8, since it has been shown that eight units per week is, in *test,* the most limiting resource or key row. Therefore, the revised solution uses up all of the test resource and the key row S_3 falls out of the solution. It is replaced by M as a new row in the solution. The C_j of 100 for motorcycles joins M in the new row. All other values in the row are calculated by this *key row transformation rule:*

Divide all values in the key row by the key number. The results go into the new transformed row.

Following the rule, the key row values—40, 5, 6, 0, 0, and 1—are divided by 5; the results in the new row are:

$$100 \quad M \quad 8 \quad 1 \quad \tfrac{6}{5} \quad 0 \quad 0 \quad \tfrac{1}{5}$$

5. *Transforming nonkey rows.* The new product in the solution uses up some of the resources in the nonkey rows, S_1 and S_2 in this case. Nonkey row values must be revised to reflect the correct amount of resource usage. The *nonkey row transformation rule* is:

Subtract from the old row value (in each column) the product of that row's key column value and the corresponding new key row value.

Following the rule the nonkey row values are computed below. For S_1 the key column value is 10, and

Quantity	M	R	S_1	S_2	S_3
$80 - (10 \times 8)$	$10 - (10 \times 1)$	$3 - (10 \times \tfrac{6}{5})$	$1 - (10 \times 0)$	$0 - (10 \times 0)$	$0 - (10 \times \tfrac{1}{5})$
$= 0$	$= 0$	$= -9$	$= 1$	$= 0$	$= -2$

For S_2 the key column value is 7, and

$$
\begin{array}{llllll}
120 - (7 \times 8) & 7 - (7 \times 1) & 2 - (7 \times \%) & 0 - (7 \times 0) & 1 - (7 \times 0) & 0 - (7 \times \frac{1}{8}) \\
= 64 & = 0 & = -32\% & = 0 & = 1 & = -\frac{7}{8}
\end{array}
$$

The revised matrix is shown in Figure S10–3; Z_j and $C_j - Z_j$ values in the figure are discussed below.

6. *New Z_j values.* New Z_j values are computed based on new row values. The Z_j *computation* rule is:

Multiply by the C_j value at the left of each row, and sum up the products by columns.

Following the rule, we have

	Quantity	M	R	S_1	S_2	S_3
Row products $\left\{\begin{array}{c} \\ \\ \\ \end{array}\right.$	0	0	0	0	0	0
	0	0	0	0	0	0
	800	100	120	0	0	20
Z_j = Column sums =	800	100	120	0	0	20

7. *New $C_j - Z_j$ values.* The new $C_j - Z_j$ values are computed by subtracting the new Z_j values for the variable columns from the corresponding C_j values. The results are given in Figure S10–3.

Recycle or stop

At this point the revised solution is subjected to the optimality test described earlier. Inspection of Figure S10–3 reveals an optimal solution since there are no positive $C_j - Z_j$ values. If there were positive $C_j - Z_j$ values, the seven steps toward revised solution would be repeated, beginning with identification of the new key column.

The optimal solution is to produce eight motorcycles per week for a net contribution of $800 per week. Rocket skis do not appear in the solution and therefore would not be produced.

FIGURE S10–3
First revision and optimal solution

$C_j \rightarrow$			100	50	0	0	0
$\downarrow$	Program	Quantity	M	R	S_1	S_2	S_3
0	S_1	0	0	−9	1	0	−2
0	S_2	64	0	−32\%	0	1	−\frac{7}{8}
100	M	8	1	\frac{6}{8}	0	0	\frac{1}{8}
	Z_j	800	100	120	0	0	20
	$C_j - Z_j$		0	−70	0	0	−20

The solution also shows a quantity of 0 units of S_1 and 64 of S_2. These values are the unused portions of fabricating and assembly capacities, respectively.

Other simplex considerations

There are numerous other simplex considerations beyond the scope of this book. Some examples are:

1. Tie for key column.
2. Tie for key row (degeneracy).
3. Mixed constraints, for example, "greater than or equal to" or "exactly equal to," in addition to the usual "less than or equal to."
4. Nonpositive quantities.
5. Cost minimization, instead of contribution maximization.
6. Multiple feasible solutions.
7. No feasible solution.
8. Unbounded problem.
9. The *dual* formulation of simplex (where rows and columns are reversed, for reasons of computational efficiency).
10. Shadow prices.
11. Sensitivity analysis.

Discussion of these and other topics is readily available in a variety of books on linear programming, management science, and operations research.

chapter 11

FACILITIES ACQUISITION AND REPLACEMENT

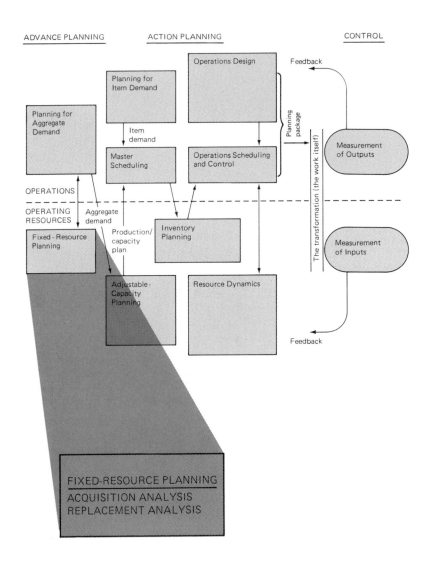

ADVANCE PLANNING   ACTION PLANNING   CONTROL

Operations Design — Feedback

Planning for
Item Demand

Planning for
Aggregate
Demand

Item
demand

Master
Scheduling

Operations Scheduling
and Control

Planning
package

Measurement
of Outputs

OPERATIONS

OPERATING
RESOURCES

Aggregate
demand

Fixed - Resource
Planning

Production/
capacity
plan

Inventory
Planning

Measurement
of Inputs

Adjustable-
Capacity
Planning

Resource Dynamics

The transformation (the work itself)

Feedback

FIXED-RESOURCE PLANNING

ACQUISITION ANALYSIS
REPLACEMENT ANALYSIS

Facilities is a term that means plant and equipment. Facilities are the fixed resources of the organization. Planning for facilities acquisition and replacement, the subject of this chapter, is strategic because the costs of such decisions are so high and their effects are so lasting. In large measure, facilities in place set the character of the organization for years to come.

In fact, as is suggested by the upward-pointing arrow in the chart on the chapter title page, plans for fixed resources can influence plans for aggregate demand. (The operating resources or means influence the operations or ends.) That is, existing facilities have the capability to turn out a limited variety of goods and services. Planning for changes in the product line is partly limited by those existing capabilities. Also, existing facilities have a maximum productive capacity that planners of product line and aggregate demand must try to utilize. Since fixed resources can be very expensive, capacity utilization, that is, keeping facilities busy, is vital to the organization's financial solvency.

The downward-pointing arrow on the title-page chart is a key concern in this chapter. The arrow represents information on the need for new or updated facilities. Some techniques for analyzing facilities proposals are cost-oriented and seem not to consider need for the facility (or benefits). Chapter discussion of how facilities proposals are reviewed makes it clear, however, that need is established either before cost analysis begins or in the final decision after cost analysis has been completed. A proposal-review process is divided into three levels of analysis, which are three sections of the chapter: preliminary analysis, detailed analysis, and final analysis. A concluding section deals with the special issues involved in the replacement of existing facilities.

While the chapter focuses on *facilities* proposals, the concepts and techniques presented are quite applicable to other high-cost pursuits. For example, investment in consulting, market research, product design, or computer software can call for large expenditures. Also, management techniques themselves are an expensive investment—in the talents and time required to implement them. Hundreds of management techniques are presented in this and other books. All of them may be good techniques, but only in the proper place, and a given organizational unit cannot afford to use many of them. In the final analysis the benefits and costs of a proposed management technique or program should compete for funding right along with proposals for buying a drill press or remodeling a wing of the plant or office.

PROPOSAL REVIEW

Careful review of proposals to acquire or upgrade facilities is particularly important in capital-intensive organizations. In purely service-oriented organizations, there may be little plant and equipment to be concerned about. Most services, however, require at least an owned or leased building. In some cases (e.g., fast foods), plans for the building can be critical to success. In manufacturing, both building and equipment planning are critical. It is in manufacturing that planning for facilities tends to be done most carefully.

FIGURE 11–1
Proposal-review
process

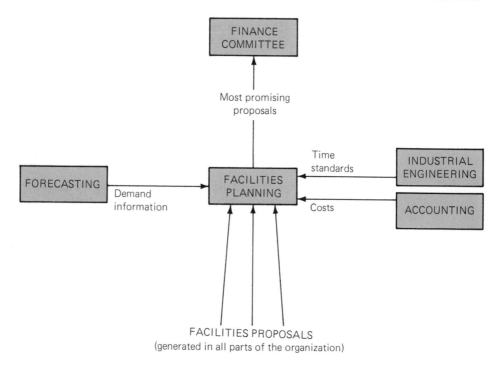

FACILITIES PROPOSALS
(generated in all parts of the organization)

Many larger manufacturers have a separate department for coordinating facilities planning. (In other firms facilities planning may be assigned to industrial engineering, to accounting, or simply to each using department.) The facilities planning department becomes the focal point for data collection and analysis of facilities proposals. Figure 11–1 displays facilities planning and other units having a role in the total proposal-review process.

Facilities proposals may arise anywhere in the organization: A mechanic suggests that a tool crib be installed nearer to the workplace; a foreman asks that an old drill press be replaced with a new one; an inventory manager recommends that additional warehouse space be obtained; or an engineer develops a proposal for a backup power generator. As Figure 11–1 shows, such proposals may be directed to the facilities planning department.

To evaluate proposals properly, costs must be determined. Industrial engineering may be asked to supply labor and productivity estimates. Accounting may furnish cost data, such as labor rates, overhead rates, tax rates, and cost-of-capital rates.

The need for a proposed facility is not based simply on the fact that someone asked for it. The proposal should be supported by a forecast of sufficient demand for the product or service that would be produced by the proposed facility. In some cases the demand forecast may be translated into revenues or savings generated. Then the revenues or savings may be compared with costs. The importance of the demand forecast, covered in an earlier chapter, should be clear. The analysis is wrong if the forecast is wrong. A multimillion-dollar plant with no demand for its production is the kind of mistake that can be made.

Proposals approved by facilities planning may have one more hurdle: a finance committee composed of high-level executives. The finance committee normally puts proposals into rank order and creates a cutoff line: Those above the cutoff get funded; those below may be rejected or deferred for a year or more. While facilities planning does its work piecemeal, the finance committee considers the big picture—how well the mix of projects fits into overall plans and policies and money-market conditions.

At different stages in the review of a facilities proposal different analysis methods may be used. In business colleges such methods are generally referred to as *capital-budgeting* techniques. (Industrial engineers prefer the term *engineering economy*.) Eight proposal-review techniques are discussed under three headings:

Preliminary analysis
    Break-even (indifference) analysis
    Payback period
    Simple rate-of-return
    Average annual cost
Detailed analysis
    Equivalent annual cost
    Present value of cost
    Cost-effectiveness
Final analysis
    Time-adjusted rate-of-return
    Net present value
    Benefit-cost

Each of these techniques is considered in the following sections. The preliminary-analysis methods are most easily understood and used by line operations managers and therefore are explained thoroughly. The detailed-analysis methods are used more often by staff specialists who serve the line managers. An example is a facilities planning or plant engineering department. This concern is with facilities as operating resources or capacity. Problem examples of detailed-analysis methods are included in the body of the chapter. The final-analysis *methods* are closely associated with money management, and problem examples of those methods are reserved for a chapter supplement. The final-analysis *stage* of proposal review is explained rather fully in the chapter, since higher-level operating resource people are among the final decision makers.

PRELIMINARY ANALYSIS

As will be shown, the preliminary-analysis methods omit time-value-of-money considerations and are therefore not entirely valid. Yet they are simple, and for this reason they are widely used. This is especially true in smaller firms that lack analysts capable of doing deeper analysis. In larger firms it may be customary for preliminary analysis to be done by the proposing departments; then facilities planning could do detailed analysis for proposals it receives from these departments.

Break-even

The idea of a break-even point is easy to understand, even for the layman; break-even is a term that is used without explanation in the nation's newspapers. Break-even *point* usually means break-even *volume,* that is, sales volume or production volume. It is the amount of sales or production that just allows you to break even: that is, to earn enough revenue to cover costs. Break-even analysis belongs to a more general family of *indifference analysis* techniques. At break-even volume there is no profit and no loss, so the asset in question makes no difference; thus, the break-even point is also the point of indifference.

One type of indifference analysis was discussed in Chapter 10: profit-volume analysis in decisions about product line. In this chapter two more kinds of indifference analysis are considered as an aid in facilities planning:

1. *A single facilities proposal.* Is the proposal worthy? To find out, it is helpful to determine how much sales or savings would be needed to pay for it, that is, what the break-even point is.

2. *Two or more competing proposals for doing the same thing.* A fancy but accurate term for this is *mutually exclusive alternatives:* Selection of the best alternative excludes the others. Such alternatives may be analyzed by searching for the indifference point, the production volumes at which the costs of one alternative are exactly the same as the costs for another. Here the problem is simplified because revenue is ignored. It is proper to ignore revenue because the decision to do one or the other has already been made; it remains to find out which alternative is least costly—for various production volumes.

Single proposals—Complete-recovery method. Examples of this type of question are whether or not to invest in a building addition, a new utility system (power, water, disposal, communications), or a new machine or other equipment. One way of analyzing is to find the sales volume needed to completely recover the costs of the equipment. This is the *complete-recovery* approach to break-even.

EXAMPLE 11–1
Break-even by complete-recovery approach, treespade proposal

Capitol Landscape Co. is considering the purchase of an industrial treespade, a piece of vehicular equipment that can dig up and move whole trees. The question is, Could anticipated revenue pay for the cost? Business volume is hard to estimate. It therefore makes sense to construct a break-even chart to see how much volume is needed to completely recover the costs.

Given data:

Delivered price of treespade, 44-inch: $9,000.

Estimated cost to operate and maintain: $10 per hour of use.

(Sales representative says $8 per hour; Capitol uses $10 to be on the safe side.)

"Going rate" for treespade service: $20 per hour of use.

Solution: These symbols may be used to solve for the break-even point:

B = Break-even point, the unknown
FC = Fixed cost = $9,000
V = Variable cost rate = $10 per hour
P = Price = $20 per hour

The break-even point *(B)* is the point at which total revenue *(TR)* equals total cost *(TC)*. Total revenue is price times volume, so total revenue at the break-even point is *(P)(B)*. Total cost is fixed cost plus variable cost, so total cost at the break-even point is *FC+ (V)(B)*. Therefore,

$$TR = TC$$
$$(P)(B) = FC + (V)(B)$$
$$(P)(B) = (V)(B) = FC$$
$$B(P - V) = FC$$
$$B = \frac{FC}{P - V}$$

For the given data,

$$B = \frac{9,000}{20 - 10} = \frac{9,000}{10} = 900 \text{ hours}$$

This means that Capitol would have to operate the proposed treespade 900 hours before it could recover its fixed and continuing costs.

FIGURE 11–2
Break-even graph for proposed treespade— Complete-recovery approach

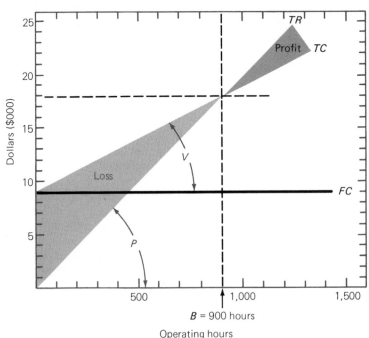

Operating hours

More detailed information is offered by graphing the data. Figure 11–2 is a graph of this break-even problem. By referring to the graph, the amount of profit or loss for any given volume may be seen. For example, it appears that for 500 hours of treespade operation, the loss would be $4,000: $10,000 revenue minus $14,000 cost. For 1,000 hours of operation the profit is $1,000: $20,000 revenue minus $19,000 cost.

How does this help Capitol decide whether or not to buy the treespade? The reasoning might be something like this: If the treespade were only operated two hours a day, it would take about 450 days (900/2) to break even. That is less than two years, which seems to be a fairly fast recovery of costs.

Sensitivity analysis may offer further insights. Sensitivity analysis means reevaluating the solution result by questioning the data inputs. The object is to see whether different assumptions about data inputs lead to large changes in the solution result; that is, you want to see whether the result is *sensitive* to the inputs.

For example, the analyst could see what would happen to the break-even point if there were an increase in operating costs. This might happen if the price of fuel increased significantly or if the operators' union won a large wage increase. It might also be of interest to see how sensitive the break-even point is to a price decrease: The going rate for treespade services could be driven down by the entry of more competitors.

If preliminary analysis by the break-even method is favorable, the next step might be a more precise analysis using time-value-of-money methods. These are considered later.

Single proposals—Annual-volume method. An alternative break-even method is the *annual-volume* approach: the result obtained from this approach is break-even volume *per year*. The annual-volume approach is as simple as the complete-recovery approach, except that input data are in a form that corresponds more closely to profit-and-loss accounting conventions. This complicates the analysis in that the proposing department may need to go through the added step of requesting cost data from the accounting department. But it results in break-even and profit information based on the legal meaning of profit. This is more valid than the general idea of a profit zone beyond a complete-recovery point. On the other hand, the approach does not show how many years the break-even volume per year applies to. In sum, the simpler complete-recovery approach lends itself better to decisions about proposed facilities. Nevertheless, the annual-volume approach is widely used. (Bear in mind that, either way, break-even is a rough, preliminary-analysis method.) Here is how Capitol Landscape Co. might do a break-even analysis by the annual-volume approach.

EXAMPLE 11–2
Break-even by annual-volume approach, treespade proposal

The problem for Capitol Landscape Co. is the same as in Example 11–1. But the fixed cost is different.

Given data:

Fixed cost per year for 44-inch treespade *(FC):* $1,000/yr. (Provided by accounting department; includes annual depreciation charges.)

FIGURE 11–3
Break-even
graph for
proposed
treespade—
Annual-volume
approach

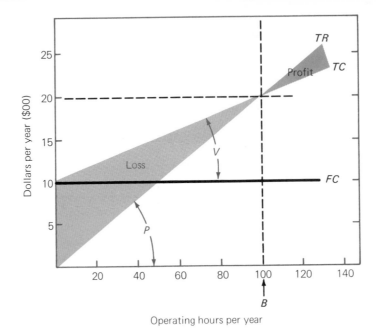

Variable cost to operate and maintain *(V):* $10/hr.

Price for treespade service *(P):* $20/hr.

Again the break-even point *(B)* is the point at which total revenue *(TR)* equals total cost *(TC).* And *B = FC/(P− V).* So,

$$B=\frac{1,000}{20-10}=\frac{1,000}{10}=100 \text{ hours/yr.}$$

This is shown graphically in Figure 11–3. Figure 11–3 is not very different in appearance from Figure 11–2. But as has been explained, two figures are interpreted quite differently, since Figure 11–3 gives all results on a per year basis.

It would be prudent to see whether the break-even point is sensitive to changed assumptions about input data. As was discussed in Example 11–1, sensitivity to a fuel or wage hike could be tested by increasing *V.* A lower market price, *P,* could also be tested. And Accounting's estimate of $1,000 per year fixed cost is a prime target for sensitivity analysis, since accounting costs are often based on averages and simple cost allocation methods rather than actual cash flow.

Competing (mutually exclusive) proposals. At the risk of overdoing it, we shall stick with the treespade case for another example. This one is break-even or indifference analysis for competing proposals. Let us say that Capitol Landscape Co. has decided to buy a treespade. But it isn't sure whether to buy a cheap Acme or an expensive Ajax treespade. Indifference analysis is applied.

EXAMPLE 11–3
Indifference
analysis for
competing
treespade
proposals

Given data:

	(1) Acme	(2) Ajax
Fixed cost *(FC):* Delivered price	$7,000	$11,000
Variable cost rate per hour of operation *(V):*		
Fuel consumption.............................	$2.50/hr.	$1.75/hr.
Repair and maintenance	0.50/hr.	0.25/hr.
Total variable cost	3.00/hr.	2.00/hr.

Two pieces of data are conspicuously absent, but for good reason: (1) Operators' wages and overhead costs are omitted because they are equal for the two brands and thus cannot affect the outcome. (2) Revenue is also omitted—for the same reason: It is the same for either brand.

The break-even point *(B)* may be computed based on costs alone. It is the production volume (sales volume is not at issue) for which the total costs of Acme equal the total costs of Ajax. So,

$$TC_1 = TC_2$$
$$FC_1 + (V_1)(B) = FC_2 + (V_2)(B)$$
$$(V_1)(B) - (V_2)(B) = FC_2 - FC_1$$
$$B(V_1 - V_2) = FC_2 - FC_1$$
$$B = \frac{FC_2 - FC_1}{V_1 - V_2}$$

For the given data,

$$B = \frac{\$11,000 - \$7,000}{\$3 - \$2}$$
$$= \frac{\$4,000}{\$1} = 4,000 \text{ hr.}$$

Interpretation: For 4,000 hours of operation Capitol is indifferent between Acme and Ajax. But 4,000 is a lot of hours. It seems doubtful that the operating economies of Ajax ($1 per hour cheaper) would justify its $4,000 higher price; it would take too many years (even considering a large inflation in fuel costs) to recover the higher price through operating economies.

Again a graph is helpful; see Figure 11–4. It shows the $4,000 advantage for Acme at zero operating hours; Acme maintains its total cost advantage up to the point of indifference, 4,000 hours. Beyond that, Ajax becomes cheaper.

Payback period

The object of payback analysis is to find out how long it will take to pay off the initial cost of a facility: the payback period. A firm that does not do detailed analysis but relies on payback may set a maximum payback period of, say, three years. Then any proposal with a payback period shorter than three years would be judged worthy; longer ones would be judged unworthy.

This is a rather rough way to judge proposals. It is often best to limit payback to preliminary screening. The proposing department could, for example, drop any of its proposals that fail to pay back the investment in, say, six years.

FIGURE 11–4
Indifference
analysis for
competing
proposals—
Treespades

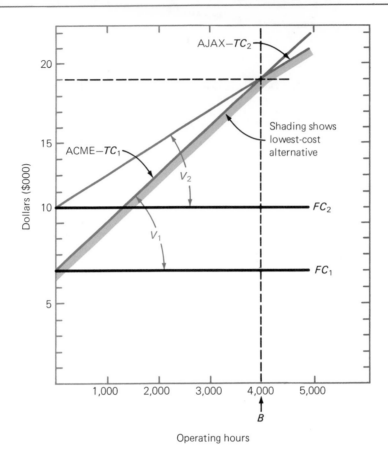

Proposals with shorter payback periods could be forwarded to facilities planning for more precise analysis. Two ways of doing payback are discussed, along with weaknesses in the method, in the following sections.

Payback with uniform cash inflow. Payback is simple if cash inflows— profit or savings—are the same every year. The payback period is simply:

$$P = \frac{I}{A},$$

where

P = Payback period
I = Investment
A = Annual savings or profit

The following example will illustrate.

EXAMPLE 11–4
Payback
period for
uniform cash
inflow case—
Office collator

MidAm Gas and Electric Company is considering the purchase of an office collator. The collator costs $6,000. The savings in clerical costs that it will effect are estimated at $1,250 per year. What is the payback period?

Solution:

$$P = \frac{I}{A} = \frac{\$6,000}{\$1,250/\mathrm{yr.}} = 4.8 \text{ yr.}$$

Since 2.4 years is fairly slow payback, MidAm may elect not to fund the proposal or to advance it for detailed analysis.

Payback with non-uniform cash inflow. Savings or profits are often not uniform from year to year. In that case the payback formula does not apply. Instead, the payback period is determined by adding each year's cash inflow until it equals the investment, as in the following example.

EXAMPLE 11–5
Payback
period for
nonuniform
cash inflow
case—Kiln

As a source of income, Marblecone Abbey is considering the purchase of a kiln to manufacture salable pottery. The kiln costs $2,000. Profits are expected to rise slowly as sales increase and experience is gained. Profit estimates are shown below, with the rightmost column showing progress toward payback:

Year	Profit	Investment less profit
0	—	$2,000
1	$ 200	1,800
2	500	1,300
3	1,000	300
4	1,000	—

As is shown, it takes a bit more than three years to pay back the $2,000 cost of the kiln.

Strengths and weaknesses of payback. Payback is enormously popular. One reason is its simplicity. Another is its adaptability: Payback works the same way for any type of organization, public or private, and for any size or type of investment. Still another reason is its independence of other data: Payback can be calculated without the trouble of finding out about cost of capital, minimum attractive rate-of-return, capital supply, and other attractive capital expenditure proposals.

There is a notable weakness in payback analysis: It is concerned only with the years until the investment is paid back. But what of profits or savings after that? Figure 11–5 shows two contrasting cash inflow patterns, each for a proposed facility costing $10,000.

The falling cash inflow pattern (dark line) is $5,000 the first year, then

FIGURE 11-5
Contrasting cash
inflows and
paybacks for
equivalent
investments

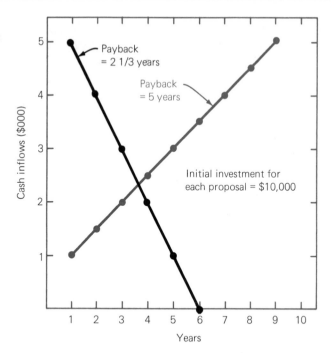

FIGURE 11-5
Contrasting cash inflows and paybacks for equivalent investments

$4,000, $3,000, and so forth; payback of the $10,000, then, is one third of the way—equal to $1,000—into year 3: $5,000 + $4,000 + $1,000. Cash inflow continues to decline, reaching zero in year 6. The rising pattern (light line) starts small, so that it takes five years to pay back the $10,000 investment: $1,000 + $1,500 + $2,000 + $2,500 + $3,000. But after that the rise continues, year after year. Clearly the proposal with the rising pattern is preferred. Yet its payback period is nearly four times as long as the payback period for the other proposal.

Another weakness of the payback method is that it does not consider compound interest on the investment and on cash inflows. In the above case, interest charges (opportunity costs) on the two investments of $10,000 would presumably be the same and would therefore be of no concern. But interest earnings on the cash inflows are quite different for the two investments. Actually, since the falling pattern has higher early cash inflows, its inflows would earn considerably more interest in the early years than the rising pattern would. This offsets some of the long-run advantage of the rising-pattern proposal. Just how much this amounts to must be determined by time-value-of-money methods, covered later in this chapter.

Simple rate-of-return

Simple rate-of-return is the reciprocal of the payback period. That is,

$$\text{Payback } (P) = \frac{\text{Investment } (I)}{\text{Annual savings or profit } (A)},$$

and

$$\text{Simple rate-of-return } (R) = \frac{A}{I}$$

For the office collator of Example 4–4,

$I = \$6,000$
$A = \$1,250/\text{yr.,}$

and

$$R = \frac{\$1,250/\text{yr.}}{\$6,000} = 0.208, \text{ or } 20.8\% \text{ per year}$$

A rate-of-return on investment of 20.8 percent seems excellent—compared to borrowing rates of 8 percent to 15 percent. But the comparison is faulty in two ways: (1) Borrowing rates are always based on compound interest, whereas the computed 20.8 percent does not include year-to-year compound effects. (2) More important, the number of years of cash inflow is left out; therefore the 20.8 percent figure may be quite different from the time-adjusted rate-of-return—to be discussed later. In sum, simple rate-of-return has the same weaknesses as its reciprocal, payback. It is best used for preliminary screening.

Average annual cost

The average annual cost (AAC) method is limited to mutually exclusive proposals. The reason is that *cost* alone is analyzed, not revenue. It is reasonable to do this where the need for *a* facility has been agreed upon but the particular make or model must still be chosen: You choose the one that costs least.

While the AAC method does not allow for interest, it at least considers all life-cycle costs. Therefore, in validity (if not in scope) AAC is superior to break-even, payback, and simple rate-of-return.

The following example illustrates AAC and, for good measure, combines it with break-even analysis.

EXAMPLE 11–6
Average annual cost method, alternative elevator motors

Two ten-horsepower motors are being considered for an elevator that is to be installed in a new state office building. Motor 1 costs $450 and has operating costs of $0.16 per hour. Motor 2 costs $350 and has operating costs of $0.18 per hour. After five years, motor 1 is expected to have a salvage value of $270, motor 2 a salvage value of $175.

It is difficult to estimate annual hours of operation. Therefore, it has been decided to find the number of hours per year for which average annual costs of the motors are equal: a break-even point.

Solution:

At the break-even point, B, the total costs per year, TC, are equal. So,

$$TC_1 = TC_2$$

Since

$$TC = FC + V(B),$$
$$FC_1 + V_1(B) = FC_2 + V_2(B)$$

Fixed cost FC_1 is the average annual capital cost of motor 1: The capital paid out, $450, minus the $270 received for salvage is divided by the five years. Variable cost is the annual operating cost; for motor 1 and at the break-even hours per year it is: 0.16(B). Motor 2 is interpreted similarly. Substituting in the equation, we have:

$$\frac{\$450 - \$270}{5} + \$0.16B = \frac{\$350 - \$175}{5} + \$0.18B$$

$$\frac{\$180}{5} + \$0.16B = \frac{\$175}{5} + \$0.18B$$

$$\$36 + \$0.16B = \$35 + \$0.18B$$
$$\$0.02B = \$1$$
$$B = 50 \text{ hours per year}$$

Interpretation: The cheaper motor 2 is preferred if it is operated less than 50 hours per year. Above 50 hours per year, the operating economies of motor 1 are sufficient to justify its higher price.

PROPOSAL-REVIEW STAGES

Before going on to detailed and final analysis, it is desirable to take a closer look at proposal review. There are several paths that a proposal might take through the proposal-review stages. The choice of a path hinges on what decision is needed.

Three types of decisions are shown in Figure 11–6. Type 1 is the preliminary decision (usually by the using department) on the question, Is the facility needed? This really means: Is there a function that must be performed and a facility that can perform it to economic advantage? As we have seen, the question may be partly answered by break-even, payback, and simple rate-of-return analysis. As we shall see, it may be answered more carefully, in final analysis, by time-adjusted rate-of-return, net present value, and benefit-cost analysis.

Decision type 2 is directed to the question, Which facility can perform the function less expensively? The need for the function has already been determined. Therefore, benefit analysis is not relevant; the decision is based simply on minimizing costs. Preliminary analysis may be done by the average annual cost (AAC) method; detailed analysis is done by the equivalent annual cost (EAC), present-value (PV) of cost, and cost-effectiveness (C-E) methods.

Decision type 3 concerns the question, When should the facility be traded for a newer (identical) facility?[1] This is the kind of decision that most of us

---

[1] There is also a type 4 question: Determining when to trade for an identical facility, given a finite instead of an infinite time horizon. Because of added complications, discussion of this case is beyond the scope of this book.

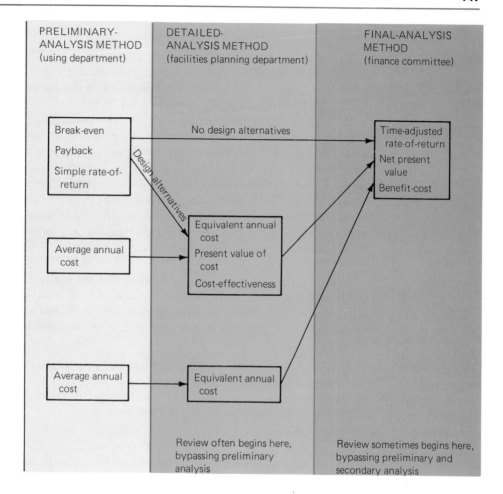

FIGURE 11–6
Facilities proposal-review stages

face with our personal automobiles. AAC and EAC are the preferred methods. The computation is more complicated than that required in the other types of decisions. But whether to trade (replace) is a question that operating managers must raise over and over again for the same piece of equipment. The importance of the decision to operating managers makes it worthwhile to consider type 3 analysis quite thoroughly. The topic is given emphasis in a separate section, the last in the chapter.

Type 2 and type 3 proposals may be passed on to the finance committee for a final analysis. Final analysis would normally include rank-ordering all proposals—type 1, type 2, and type 3—according to time-adjusted rate-of-return, net present value, or benefit-cost ratio. These techniques require additional data on revenue or savings generated by a given proposal.

Type 2 questions *(which* facility) are considered in the next section from the standpoint of detailed analysis.

DETAILED ANALYSIS

This discussion of detailed analysis is in four parts. The equivalent annual cost (EAC) method is considered first. The present value of cost (PV) method is the next topic. Commentary on the users of the proposed facility is third. And cost-effectiveness analysis is the final topic.

EAC and PV analysis involve interest calculations, which some readers are familiar with. Review of the concept of interest—the time-value of money—with EAC and PV examples, may be found in Chapter Supplement A. EAC and PV examples presented in the following section are solved using six interest tables. Some readers will be familiar with methods that use only two interest tables. The two-table methods, which are commonly presented in finance and managerial accounting courses, produce the same answers as the six-table methods. The two tables (present-value tables) are provided in Supplement B for those who prefer that approach.

Equivalent annual cost

As is noted in Supplement A, EAC is the annualized (or annuitized) sum of all relevant costs. It is like the amount of an installment-loan payment. Some examples of EAC can indicate its strengths and weaknesses. The first example demonstrates EAC for proposals with unequal lives.

EXAMPLE 11-7
Equivalent annual cost method, alternative roofing materials

A popular material for roofing a building has an estimated life of eight years and an initial cost of $2,500. A heavier grade of roof costs $825 more but has an estimated life of 12 years. The installed cost for either roof is $1,200. If the interest rate is 10 percent, which roof has the lower equivalent annual cost?

Solution:

The popular roof has a total initial cost of $2,500 + $1,200 = $3,700. That is a present amount, symbolically a P. Since we want to know A and are given P, the "A, given P" or A/P column in the 10 percent interest table is found. That value, for $N = 8$, is found in Table S11–1 (in Supplement A):

$$A/P^8_{10\%} = 0.1874$$
$$EAC = (A/P^8_{10\%})(P)$$
$$= 0.1874(\$3,700)$$
$$= \$693.38/\text{yr}.$$

The heavier grade has a total P of $2,500 + $825 + $1,200 = $4,525. This time A/P for 12 years and 10 percent is looked up.

$$EAC = (A/P^{12}_{10\%})(P)$$
$$= (0.1468)(\$4,525)$$
$$= \$664.27/\text{yr}.$$

The heavier grade at $644.27 per year is cheaper than the lighter grade at $693.38 per year.

Comment on unequal lives. It makes no difference that the EAC of the heavier grade is computed over 12 years as opposed to only 8 years for the popular roof. The reason is that the same equivalent annual costs—$693 versus $664—would apply as well for purchasing the roof for a second 8 or 12 years, and a third, and a fourth, and so on indefinitely. (Possible cost increases are ignored since there is no reason to believe that both roofing grades would not go up in cost by the same proportional amount.) This characteristic of EAC makes it a preferred method for comparing proposals having *unequal lives*. The next example uses EAC for proposals with equal lives.

EXAMPLE 11-8
Equivalent annual cost method, generating plant

A hospital is considering two options for backup power generation:
1. Lease a portable generator at an annual cost of $5,000. The lease cost includes repair and maintenance.
2. Purchase a generator. The vendor's installed cost is quoted as $25,000. The generator's useful life is estimated at 25 years with no salvage value. Major maintenance is expected as follows: $500 cost after 5 years, $1,200 after 10 years, $2,500 after 15 years, and $4,000 after 20 years. Labor costs for operation plus routine maintenance costs (O&M costs) are estimated at $1,000 per year. Which alternative has the most favorable EAC if interest is 12 percent?

The accompanying diagrams show the cash flows for the two generator alternatives.

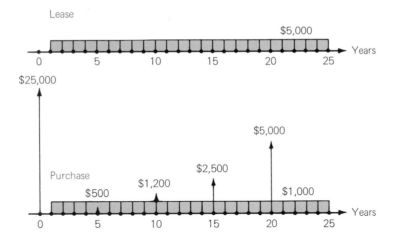

Solution:

Option 1 has an EAC of $5,000, which is the lease cost.

Option 2 must be evaluated in steps based on the following givens and relevant interest table factors (Table S11–1 in Supplement A):

$$
\begin{aligned}
P &= \$25,000 & (A/P)^{25}_{12\%} &= 0.1275 \\
F_5 &= \$500 & (P/F)^{5}_{12\%} &= 0.5674 \\
F_{10} &= \$1,200 & (P/F)^{10}_{12\%} &= 0.3220 \\
F_{15} &= \$2,500 & (P/F)^{15}_{12\%} &= 0.1827 \\
F_{20} &= \$4,000 & (P/F)^{20}_{12\%} &= 0.1037 \\
A &= \$1,000
\end{aligned}
\right\}
\quad (A/P)^{25}_{12\%} = 0.1275
$$

The purchase cost, \$25,000, can be translated to EAC in one step, while the O&M cost, \$1,000, is already EAC. The four major maintenances require two steps: First, each is converted to present value; then each present value (or the sum of the present values) is converted from present value to EAC. It would be incorrect to try to convert directly from F to A, because each F occurs at a different point in the future. Therefore,

$$
\begin{aligned}
EAC = &[\$25,000 + \$500\,(0.5674) \\
&+ \$1,200(0.3220) + \$2,500(0.1827) \\
&+ \$4,000(0.1037)][0.1275] + \$1,000 \\
= &(\$25,000 + \$284 + \$386 + \$457 + \$415)(0.1275) + \$1,000 \\
= &(\$26,542)(0.1275) + \$1,000 \\
= &\$3,384 + \$1,000 = \$4,384
\end{aligned}
$$

Purchase at \$4,384 per year is favored over leasing at \$5,000 per year.

Comment on equal lives. It makes no difference that the EAC of the purchase option is computed over 25 years as opposed to an unstated number of years for the lease option. The reason is that the lease option, at \$5,000 per year, may be assumed to apply for a full 25 years. That period, 25 years, is the common-time horizon for both proposals.

EAC holds no advantage over PV in this problem. It is just as valid to translate all costs for each option into present values (PV). Also, it takes about the same number of computations. The four major maintenance costs must first be translated into PV in the EAC method anyway; the purchase price, \$25,000, and the O&M cost, \$1,000, could also be translated into PV so that a total PV could be summed up for each option.

The principle is that where lives are equal (a 25-year common-time horizon in this problem), either EAC or PV is suitable.

Present value of cost

As noted in Supplement A, PV of cost is the present (discounted) equivalent sum of all relevant costs. An example of its use follows.

EXAMPLE 11-9
Present-value method, NC equipment

A firm purchased a numerically controlled (NC) jig-boring machine one year ago for \$100,000. The machine was expected to last ten years and to have no salvage value at the end of that time. The machine is operated by a highly skilled machinist at an annual labor cost of \$14,000. It has now been discovered that a reputable specialty shop will contract to do the work for \$15,000 per year. Investigation reveals that, because of design quirks, the jig-boring equipment would bring only \$20,000 today on the used equipment market. If the firm figures that its money is worth 10 percent, what is the best alternative based on present-value analysis?

The accompanying diagrams show the cash flows for the two alternatives.

Solution:

The first alternative is to continue jig-boring "in house." The given data and the relevant interest factor (from Table S11-1) are:

$A = \$14,000$ per year for labor

$n = 9$ years (since one year of the ten-year life of the NC equipment has passed)

$i = 10\%$

$P/A^9_{10\%} = 5.759$

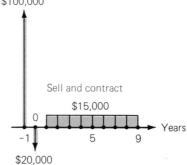

The total present value of cost is:

$$P = \$14,000 \ (5.759)$$
$$= \$80,626$$

The second alternative is to contract to have the work done and to sell the NC equipment. Given data and relevant interest factor are:

$A = \$15,000$ per year contract cost

$P = -\$20,000$ proceeds on sale of equipment

$n = 9$ years

$i = 10\%$

$P/A^9_{10\%} = 5.759$

The total present value of cost is:

$$P = \$15,000 \ (5.759) - \$20,000$$
$$= \$86,385 - \$20,000$$
$$= \$66,385$$

Comparison: Contracting is cheaper by $14,241 (\$80,626 - \$66,385).

What of the equipment cost, $100,000, paid out a year ago? It must be ignored. It is a *sunk cost*—incurred in a prior period and thus not a relevant cost for the decision at hand. (But its influence on taxes *is* still relevant.)

The users   The examples show that while computations are quite different between EAC and PV, the resulting decisions are the same. The choice of method should therefore be based on computational efficiency and user understanding. The main conclusion regarding efficiency is that EAC is preferred when proposals have unequal lives. PV is sometimes a bit more efficient when proposals have nonuniform cash flows: a number of major maintenances, for example.

User understanding is a special concern at the level of detailed analysis. While the analysis may be done by a facilities planning group, the group would usually confer a good deal with the using department. Any user should be able to comprehend EAC; it is the same idea as installment loan payments. On the other hand, some users—up-from-the-ranks foremen, for example— may have difficulty in assimilating the concept of a present value. This may have somethig to do with the tendency of industrial engineers to gravitate toward EAC—since IEs usually work closely with foremen. Accountants, on the other hand, are more likely to work with peers in accounting and with people like the vice president of finance, who can appreciate the present-value idea of a single lump sum that could be used to pay off all future obligations.

Tax considerations are sometimes omitted at the level of detailed analysis. Ignoring taxes simplifies computations and makes it easier to explain results to users. Taxes may not be omitted in final analysis, because final analysis involves money management in which all inflows and outflows, including taxes, must be allowed for. In detailed analysis the objective is narrower: Just to decide which alternative facility is least costly. While tax is a cost, the tax cost *tends* to affect each alternative similarly. This is less true if there are special tax write-offs. It is probably safer to always include tax considerations.

Cost-effectiveness

Cost-effectiveness analysis is far different from EAC and PV analysis. EAC and PV provide a single (unidimensional) measure of merit; C-E provides a whole matrix or table of values (multidimensional) for comparing alternatives. Also, time-value-of-money computations are central in EAC and PV analysis but incidental in C-E analysis.

Multidimensional results are desirable in the complex case. Examples are: selecting a computer system from among several competing vendors; selecting a missile from among several alternative designs; and selecting a contractor for, say, bridge construction from among several bidders.

In these cases there are many effectiveness criteria, each with a different unit of measure. Effectiveness criteria for a missile, for example, might include speed, range, accuracy, payload, launch reliability, and so forth. Cost criteria include design cost, development cost, manufacturing cost per missile, and maintenance cost.

Selection of C-E evaluation criteria is an early step in C-E analysis; it is done by a knowledgeable group of analysts and decision makers. In Kazanowski's "standardized" C-E analysis approach,[2] the C-E criteria are chosen and

---

[2] A. D. Kazanowski, "A Standardized Approach to Cost-Effectiveness Evaluations," in *Cost-Effectiveness: The Economic Evaluation of Engineered Systems*, ed. J. Morley English (Wiley, 1968), pp. 151–65 (TA183.C63).

FIGURE 11–7
C-E matrix,
alternative
conveyor
systems

	Criteria of cost and effectiveness*					
	(1)	(2) Time	(3)	(4)	(5)	(6) Floor
Alternative vendors	Bid price	until delivery	O&M cost/year	Conveyor speed	Estimated life	space required
Roll-A-Matic	50K	65 wk.	12K	15 FPS	20 yr.	400 sq. ft.
Automaterial	87	48	10	22	16	500
Rapid-Flow	45	60	12	25	18	360

* These criteria have been arranged in order of importance, left to right.

then arranged in rank order, most to least important. Measurement and cost estimation follows, and results are displayed in the C-E matrix. Figure 11–7 is a simplified example.

Figure 11–7 displays the costs and effectiveness criteria for a proposed conveyor system. Three vendors have bid on it. High-level decision makers—call them an evaluation group—have judged that bid price is the most important of the six criteria and that floor space required is the least important.

Criteria 1 and 3 in Figure 11–7 could have been reduced to a single column by using time-value-of-money conversion. The single cost column would then be either total equivalent annual cost or total present value of cost. A composite effectiveness-over-cost criterion that could have been listed is life per dollar bid. For Roll-A-Matic the amount would be 20/50K, or 0.4 year per K dollars. (K is the systems analyst's symbol for thousand.)

It is possible to weight the C-E criteria, normalize the measurement values, and multiply them so that the matrix is reduced to a single measure of merit. While this is possible, it may not be desirable. Reducing to single values from a large array of diverse units of measure is a large step, and important detail may be lost from view in this way. Kazanowski recommends instead that data reduction go only as far as translation into a rank-ordered matrix.[3] Figure 11–8 is an example.

In Figure 11–8 the raw cardinal numbers from Figure 11–7 are simply converted to ordinal numbers. (Ordinal means first, second, third, etc.) Figure 11–8 is a summary, for talking purposes, that is to be placed on display along with the raw values of Figure 11–7. The evaluation group might tentatively conclude, based on scrutiny of Figures 11–7 and 11–8, that the Rapid-Flow conveyor is best. Rapid-Flow seems to be ranked first on more criteria, including the most important one, bid price; and it is ranked third the fewest times. The group should delve into the question of risk and confidence in input data before making a decision. For example, if Rapid-Flow were a new company, it might be rejected as being too risky or because its input data estimates are not based on sufficient experience.

---

[3] Ibid.

FIGURE 11–8
Rank-ordered
C-E matrix,
alternative
conveyor
systems

	Criteria of cost and effectiveness					
Alternative vendors	(1) Bid price	(2) Time until delivery	(3) O&M cost/year	(4) Conveyor speed	(5) Estimated life	(6) Floor space required
Roll-A-Matic	2	3	2,3	3	1	2
Automaterial	3	1	1	2	3	3
Rapid-Flow	1	2	2,3	1	2	1

Formal cost-effectiveness analysis was developed in the public sector and has been used most extensively by the Department of Defense. While it has rarely been used in business firms, perhaps this will change as firms become more involved with environmental impact statements and other complex socio-economic issues. Today in private firms the term *cost-effectiveness* is apt to be used loosely instead of in reference to the formal C-E analysis method presented above.

FINAL ANALYSIS

Facilities proposals of modest cost may be decided on by middle managers. High-cost proposals will surely go to a high-level finance committee (or its equivalent) for a decision. The high-level group will want to decide based not only on cost but also on benefits (e.g., revenue and/or intangible gain). Cost data from the detailed-analysis stage must be combined with benefits data. Methods of doing this include time-adjusted rate-of-return (TAR), net present value (NPV), and in the nonprofit sector, benefit-cost analysis.

TAR and NPV are important analysis tools for money managers (e.g., financial analysts and accountants). Benefit-cost is an important tool of the planner in nonprofit organizations. Operating managers do not often commission proposal-review analysis using TAR, NPV, and benefit-cost, because revenues and intangible benefits come to the whole organization, not to the manager using the facility. But operating managers are among the decision makers who sit on finance committees to evaluate the results of TAR, NPV, or benefit-cost analysis. TAR, NPV, and benefit-cost are briefly examined below.

TAR, NPV, and B-C analysis

Time-adjusted rate-of-return (TAR) is also known as internal rate-of-return. TAR takes timing of cash flows into consideration, whereas simple rate-of-return does not. In the TAR method the interest rate, i, is the unknown. It is the compound interest rate at which cash inflows exactly equal cash outflows. Computing the TAR is a trial-and-error procedure (except in simple cases) that may be found in basic finance and managerial accounting textbooks.

Net present value (NPV) is the *net* of present value of inflows minus present value of outflows. The method is the same as that presented earlier for present value of cost, except that the procedure is also applied to cash inflows.

Benefit-cost analysis is a preferred method in more complex cases. For example, governments and public utilities tend to have more complex benefits to consider because they serve so many diverse interests.

Data computations in benefit-cost analysis are the same as in time-adjusted rate-of-return and net present value analysis. That is, all benefits or inflows and all costs or outflows are expressed as either equivalent annual cost (annuity) or present value. It might seem that the only difference among the techniques is in what is done with those subtotals—that is, they are translated into a rate (TAR), an amount (NPV), or a ratio (B-C ratio). Not so. There is a major difference, and it is in the way that qualitative factors are treated.

In TAR and NPV analysis qualitative factors tend to be called *intangibles.* The private firm has profit, in dollars, as the dominant measure of worth. A few factors, such as employee morale, do not readily translate into dollars. So they are withheld from the TAR or NPV computations; they may be interjected into final decisions as intangible judgment elements.

In public projects, where profit in dollars is not the measure of worth, nearly all the benefits are of the so-called intangible variety. The quest for a more objective or scientific process of public decision making has led to dissatisfaction with a method in which the benefits are intangibles, presented in prose rather than numbers. Hence, B-C analysis was developed. In B-C analysis, as was explained in Chapter 10, *all* benefits, intangible or not, are expressed in dollars (EAC or PV dollars). This is a highly uncertain, speculative, and often controversial process. But dollars seem to be the logical measure of worth, because costs are likely to be expressed that way. A B-C *ratio* results when the dollar sign in the numerator is canceled out by the dollar sign in the denominator (see example in Chapter 10).

Ranking proposals

Final analysis ends with comparison of proposals and selection of the best ones for funding. Selection is easier when proposals are ranked. A useful approach is ranking by TAR and by amount of investment. Consider, for example, the following proposals:

Proposal	Description	TAR	Investment
A	Treespade	14%	$ 7,000
B	Building	20	70,000
C	Research project	35	50,000
D	Computer project	10	30,000
E	Collator	16	6,000
F	Replace truck	9	14,000
G	Kiln	31	2,000

Putting these seven proposals into rank order by time-adjusted rate-of-return yields the following table, with cumulative investment added:

Proposal	TAR	Investment	Cumulative investment
C	35%	$50,000	$ 50,000
G	31	2,000	52,000
B	20	70,000	122,000
E	16	6,000	128,000
A	14	7,000	135,000
D	10	30,000	165,000
F	9	14,000	179,000

Now selection may be made based on TAR. For example, if the firm's minimum attractive rate of return is 12 percent, then proposals C, G, B, E, and A could be funded; D and F, the computer project and the truck, are below the cutoff rate and thus would be dropped.

A bar graph is helpful in showing rankings. In Figure 11–9 the height of the bars stands for TAR; the width stands for amount of investment. Superimposed is a dashed line drawn at the 12 percent level, which is the minimum attractive rate-of-return. Proposals that extend above the line—C, G, B, E, and A—are worth funding. Those below the line—D and F—do not return enough to pay for their investments.

In addition to the horizontal cutoff line, a vertical cutoff may be appropriate. A vertical line would signify a limit in the amount of capital that the firm could readily generate. The firm would like to generate $135,000 to fund the five proposals that have attractive rates-of-return. But if, say, only $100,000 could be readily generated (at the 12 percent rate), then that $100,000 would have to be budgeted among the five attractive projects. The term for this process is *capital budgeting,* and, as was mentioned earlier, a high-level finance committee is often given final responsibility in the capital-budgeting process.

For firms using NPV analysis instead of TAR, ranking is by NPV from most to least. Public agencies using B-C analysis rank projects by B-C ratio from most to least. But the rank-ordering should not be final. Since B-C ratios are

FIGURE 11-9
Proposals ranked by time-adjusted rate-of-return (TAR)

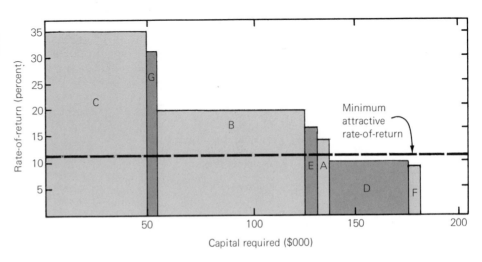

quite speculative, sensitivity and risk analysis should be injected to see whether some of the projects with high B-C ratios are especially dependent on a given set of assumptions or on uncertain data.

REPLACEMENT OF EXISTING FACILITIES

The term *replacement* suggests replacing a facility with another facility of the same type—sometimes a direct trade-in. If you are upgrading to a radically different type, then replacement would probably not be the term used. It is important to keep this in mind, because the replacement method discussed below applies only to the case of replacing a facility with another facility of the same kind—with all of the same life-cycle costs. Assuming the same costs simplifies the calculation process.[4]

The replacement calculations are based purely on costs. A facility is already owned and assumed to be worthwhile; therefore the amount of benefit or revenue it generates is not the immediate question. As was shown in Figure 11–6, replacement/trade-in analysis follows the average annual cost (AAC) and equivalent annual cost (EAC) methods. Both methods are treated in the following example.

EXAMPLE 11–10
Replacement analysis by ACC and EAC methods, forklift truck

A 3,000-pound forklift truck on a loading dock cost $5,000 new. It gets high use, and it is therefore generally traded in for a new one every one, two, or three years. Given the following operation and maintenance (O&M) cost and trade-in (salvage) value data, what is the most economical number of years until trade-in? Assume a 10 percent discount rate.

Year	O&M cost*	End-of-year trade-in-value
1.............	$ 500	$3,600
2.............	800	2,800
3.............	1,000	1,800

* As always in capital budgeting problems, O&M costs are assumed to be incurred at the end of the given year.

Diagrams of the cash flows for the three trade-in alternatives are shown in Figure 11–10.

ACC solution:

The average annual cost (ACC) is computed by adding all costs, subtracting trade-in value, and dividing the result by number of years in the trade-in period. So,

---

[4] Replacement models in operations research are usually associated with *component* replacement. Chapter 13, Maintenance Management, includes discussion of component replacement. Replacement of *facilities*, the present subject, is a quite different problem—a capital expenditure problem since large amounts of capital are involved.

$$ACC \text{ for trading after one year} = \$5,000 + \$500 - \$3,600 = \$1,900 \text{ per year}$$

$$ACC \text{ for trading after two years} = \frac{\$5,000 + \$500 + \$800 - \$2,800}{2} = \frac{\$3,500}{2}$$

$$= \$1,750 \text{ per year}$$

$$ACC \text{ for trading after three years} = \frac{\$5,000 + \$500 + \$800 + \$1,000 - \$1,800}{3}$$

$$= \frac{\$5,500}{3} = \$1,833 \text{ per year}$$

These computations suggest that it is best to trade after two years, at an average annual cost of $1,750 per year. But, of course, interest has been ignored, and the conclusion may not be valid. Detailed analysis by the EAC method, below, will confirm or deny the conclusion. Discussion follows.

FIGURE 11-10
Cash flow diagrams, forklift truck replacement proposals

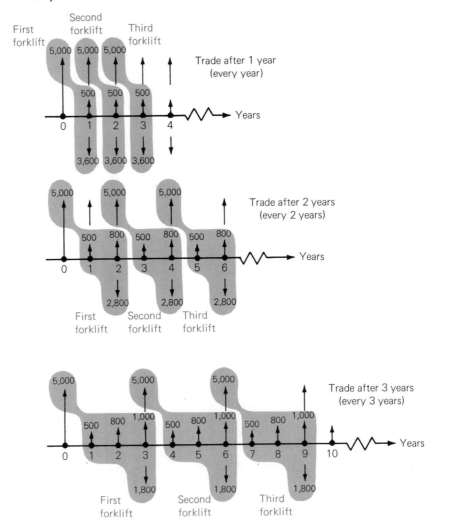

EAC solution:

Option 1. Trade after one year.

$$EAC = [\text{Price} + (\text{First-year O\&M}) \ (P/F^1_{10\%})$$
$$- (\text{First-year trade-in}) \ (P/F^1_{10\%})] \ [A/P^1_{10\%}]$$
$$= [\$5,000 + \$500 \ (0.9091) - \$3,600 \ (0.9091)] \ [1.100]$$
$$= (\$5,000 + \$455 - \$3,273) \ (1.100)$$
$$= (\$2,182)(1.100) = \$2,400 \text{ per year}$$

Option 2. Trade after two years.

$$EAC = [\text{Price} + (\text{First-year O\&M}) \ (P/F^1_{10\%})$$
$$+ (\text{Second-year O\&M}) \ (P/F^2_{10\%})$$
$$- (\text{Second-year trade-in}) \ (P/F^2_{10\%})] \ [A/P^2_{10\%}]$$
$$= [\$5,000 + \$500 \ (0.9091) + \$800 \ (0.8264)$$
$$- \$2,800 \ (0.8264)] \ [0.57619]$$
$$= (\$5,000 + \$455 + \$661 - \$2,314)(0.57619)$$
$$= (\$3,802)(0.57619) = \$2,191 \text{ per year}$$

Option 3. Trade after three years.

$$EAC = [\text{Price} + (\text{First-year O\&M}) \ (P/F^1_{10\%})$$
$$+ (\text{Second-year O\&M}) \ (P/F^2_{10\%})$$
$$+ (\text{Third-year O\&M}) \ (P/F^3_{10\%})$$
$$- (\text{Third-year trade-in}) \ (P/F^3_{10\%})] \ [A/P^3_{10\%}]$$
$$= [\$5,000 + \$500 \ (0.9091) + \$800 \ (0.8264)$$
$$+ \$1,000 \ (0.7513) - \$1,800 \ (0.7513)] \ [0.40211]$$
$$= (\$5,000 + \$455 + \$661 + \$751 - \$1,350)(0.40211)$$
$$= (\$5,517)(0.40211) = \$2,220 \text{ per year}$$

Solution aid: The computations in the replacement method may be simplified by organizing the data and the computed results into tables. The tables may be of uniform format, easily printed as computer output. Figure 11–11 is such a table; it presents the data of the EAC solution to the forklift truck problem. Each line is a replacement alternative, and all relevant costs, factors, and subtotals, as well as the final computed EAC, are given on that line. Columns 5, 8, and 9 are subtotals, and column 11 is the final EAC.

FIGURE 11–11
Tabular format
for replacement
calculations

Discussion:

O&M and trade-in values are being incurred at the ends of various years, with price incurred at time zero. These figures may be combined only after they have been

(1)	(2)	(3)	(4)	(5)	(6)	(7)	(8)	(9)	(10)	(11)
				(3) × (4)			(4) × (7)	(2) + (5) − (8)		(9) × (10)
Replacement age	Price (PV)	O&M cost	10 percent p/f	PV of O&M	Cumulative PV of O&M	Trade-in value	PV of trade-in	Total PV	10 percent a/p	Total EAC
1	$5,000	$ 500	0.9091	$455	$ 455	$3,600	$3,273	$2,182	1.100	$2,400
2	5,000	800	0.8264	661	1,116	2,800	2,314	3,802	0.57619	2,191 ←
3	5,000	1,000	0.7513	751	1,867	1,800	1,350	5,517	0.40211	2,220

* Arrow (←) shows optimal result.

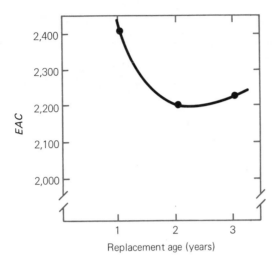

converted to common-time dollars—present value in this case. Hence O&M and trade-in value are first converted to present values and then combined with price, giving total present value. The total PV is then converted to EAC or annuity.

As was explained earlier in the chapter, EAC or annuity is time-independent. Thus, the result for trading in after one year is validly comparable with the result for trading in after two years, three years, and so forth.

Trading in after two years, at $2,191 per year, yields results that are preferable to the one-year EAC of $2,400 per year and the three-year EAC of $2,220 per year.

It is helpful to view the results in the form of a graph, as is done in Figure 11–12. As the figure shows, the minimum on the EAC curve is in the middle, trading in after two years. In replacement problems, the computations continue until the bottom of the curve, which is normally U-shaped, is found. (Luckily, in the forklift problem the minimum was found among the first three options; there were no cost data for continuing computations beyond that.)

As it happens, the EAC results confirm the ACC conclusion that it is best to trade in after two years. The two methods, EAC and ACC, are more likely to produce the same conclusions in short-life cases like this one than in cases where analysis extends for several years until trade-in. For example, if the forklift truck received lighter use, there would be smaller projected O&M costs and better trade-in values; this would probably create the need to extend the analysis to trading every four years, every five years, every six years, and so on.

Replacement tends to be an operating-level decision: It concerns existing facilities that are assigned to operating-level managers, such as foremen and other first-line supervisors. By contrast, new facilities tend to be proposed by engineers, middle managers, and planners; the concern of such personnel is more with modernization strategies than with day-to-day operating problems such as breakdowns and repairs of existing facilities.

Replacement decisions tend to occur often, whereas new-facilities decisions are less frequent. With computers readily available in most organizations, it makes good sense to set forth systematic procedures to review and project O&M costs and salvage values and to compute when to replace by EAC methods.

SUMMARY

A key strategic decision is planning for facilities: buildings and equipment. Such decisions are not frequent, but they involve large amounts of capital. It makes good sense to develop a systematic process for generating, screening, and reviewing facilities proposals.

A complete proposal-review system provides for (1) preliminary screening of proposals generated throughout the organization, (2) detailed analysis by facilities planning specialists, and (3) final analysis and decision by a high-level finance committee. Preliminary screening may be associated with rather simple analysis methods, such as break-even, payback, simple rate-of-return, and average annual cost. Detailed analysis injects compound interest and is limited to cost comparisons; the analysis techniques used are equivalent annual cost, present value of cost, and cost-effectiveness. Final analysis is also based on compound interest, but for revenue (or savings) as well as cost; the analysis techniques used are time-adjusted rate-of-return, net present value, and benefit-cost. Results of any of these three analysis techniques are easily presented as a rank-ordered list of proposed demands on capital investment; a rank-ordered list simplifies the finance committee's job of capital budgeting.

REFERENCES

Books

English, J. Morley, ed. *Cost-Effectiveness: The Economic Evaluation of Engineered Systems.* Wiley, 1968 (TA183.C63).

Horngren, Charles T. *Cost Accounting: A Managerial Approach.* 4th ed. Prentice-Hall, 1974 (HF5686.C8H59).

Riggs, James L. *Engineering Economics.* McGraw-Hill, 1977 (TA177.4.R53).

Weston, J. F., and E. F. Brigham. *Essentials of Managerial Finance.* 3d ed. Dryden Press, 1974 (HG4011.W42).

Periodicals

The Engineering Economist.

Financial Management.

Management Accounting.

PROBLEMS

Note: Asterisked (*) problems require more than mimicry. They require judgment, and you should include discussion of reasons, assumptions, and outside sources of information.

Break-even   1. National Aeronautics Corp. is evaluating a proposal to build an entire new factory for full production of a new supersonic aircraft. The factory is expected to cost $50 million; aircraft production costs (not including the factory and related fixed assets) are estimated at $200,000 per aircraft, and each aircraft is to be priced at $300,000. What is the break-even volume? Graph your results. How are the results interpreted, and why should this calculation be considered *preliminary* analysis?

*2. Capital Landscape Co. has evaluated a proposal to purchase an industrial tree-spade. Analysis is based on a delivered price of $9,000, O&M cost of $10 per hour of use, and $20 revenue per hour of use. The complete recovery break-even (B-E) point, then, is 900 hours of use (see Example 11–1). You are to carry the analysis further, using sensitivity analysis.
   a. Perform calculations to see how sensitive the B-E point is to the O&M cost estimate. Hint: Increase the O&M cost (or the price for the service) by some percentage; calculate the revised B-E point; and determine the percentage change in the B-E value. Decrease by a percentage, and follow the same steps. Compare percentage changes in input data with percentage changes in B-E result; draw your conclusions about sensitivity.
   b. What are some possible causes of inaccurate estimates—or sudden changes— in O&M cost or price for the service? How likely are those variations in input data? Discuss.

3. Suburban Hospital is considering the purchase of a CAT (computerized axial to-mography) scanner for its radiology department. The amortized fixed costs for the scanner and related facilities are projected at $10,000 per year. The cost to operate and maintain the CAT system are estimated to average $180 per scan, and the hospital plans to charge an average of $200 per scan.
   a. What is the break-even volume? Plot the results on a B-E graph. How are the results interpreted? Why should the B-E data be considered *preliminary* analysis?
   *b. Stories about the costs, benefits, and criteria for acquisition of CAT scanners have appeared in many newspapers. The criteria of the Department of Health, Education, and Welfare are based on the population to be served by a scanner. Obtain what information you can about CAT scanners in your area, including more information about the HEW criteria. (For example, are the HEW criteria based on any sort of break-even analysis?)

4. Two college students are starting up a lawn-care service. Two types of rider-mower are being considered for purchase. Data on each type are given below:

	Mower X	Mower Y
Fixed cost (delivered price)	$1,000	$1,600
Variable costs per 1,000 square feet mowed:		
Repair and maintenance	$0.10	$0.07
Labor	1.00	0.78

   a. How much grass would the students need to cut to justify the more expensive Mower Y? Graph your results, and discuss them briefly. Recommend a decision based on the data if you can; or explain why you cannot decide.

b. If the students had a single lawn-care contract to care for a 10,000-square-foot plot—and sought no other work—break-even analysis would no longer be the logical method of analysis. Explain why, and work the problem by a more logical method.

Payback and simple rate-of-return

5. Central Plumbing Supply Co. is considering the purchase of an $8,100 microcomputer system. The system would cut the costs of inventory posting, invoicing, billing, and financial reporting. The firm selling the microcomputer system estimates these clerical savings at $3,600 per year, based on a brief benefit-cost analysis.

 a. Based on payback analysis, does the investment appear to be worthwhile?
 b. What is the simple rate-of-return? Is that an impressive rate-of-return?
 c. What are some weaknesses of the payback and simple rate-of-return analyses?
 d. The son of Central Plumbing's owner, a major in business administration, disputes the vendor's savings estimate. The son's analysis is based on the assumption of an increasing cash flow from benefits and decreasing costs to program and debug. The resulting savings projection is:

Year	Net savings
1.........	−$4,000
2.........	− 1,000
3.........	+ 3,000
4.........	+ 5,000
5.........	+ 5,000
6.........	+ 5,000
⋮	⋮

What is the payback? Is further (secondary) analysis desirable, or should the project be killed?

AAC and EAC

6. Able-Baker Distributors uses mainly its own fleet of single-axle trucks for regional pickups and deliveries. For larger long-haul loads, a double-axle semitrailer tractor is rented. The rental charges are $350 per week, plus 10 cents per mile, with renters providing their own fuel. The truck was rented 20 weeks last year, and the weekly trips averaged 2,000 miles. Able-Baker management is now considering having the company purchase its own semi, which may be cheaper than renting in the long run. The following data on having the company own its own rig have been assembled for analysis of the rent-versus-buy alternatives:

Price of a double-axle tractor	$50,000
Useful life	8 years
Resale value after eight years	$4,000
Maintenance cost	$0.08 per mile

Fuel and driver wages are presumed to be the same for either alternative.
 a. Which alternative is preferred, based on an average annual cost analysis?
 b. Which alternative is preferred, based on an equivalent annual cost analysis using an 8 percent interest rate? What are some important nonquantifiable factors that might bear on the decision?

7. Snow removal from the walkways of City College Campus can be hand-loaded or machine-loaded. For an average snowfall, hand loading requires 50 men at

$32 per day each. The annual cost of shovels, including storage, is $1,500. Machine loading requires snow removal equipment costing $60,000. The equipment would last ten years and have a salvage value of $2,000. Twelve operators are needed to operate the equipment; their wage rate is $44 per day. Fuel, oil, and repairs would amount to $250 per snow day. Storage cost would be $400 per year. City College uses 10 percent as its cost of capital.

a. Assuming that there are five days of snow removal per year, how do the two alternatives compare—based on calculations of average annual cost and equivalent annual cost? Which alternative should be selected? Explain.

b. If an analysis of your snow removal records produced this information, would your decision change?

Days of snow removal per year	4	5	6	7	8
Probability	0.05	0.40	0.35	0.15	0.05

EAC and PV of cost

8. Chompin' Chicken is a national franchisor in the fast-food business. A decision is to be made on the type of chair that will be installed in new franchised outlets as the highly successful business expands. Chair A costs $25 and has a projected useful life of five years with a salvage value of $5. Chair B costs $40 and has a projected useful life of eight years with a salvage value of $10. Chompin' Chicken uses an interest rate of 12 percent in its investment calculations.

a. Which chair is preferred? Base your answer on EAC analysis.

b. Explain the calculation procedure that would be required using PV-of-cost analysis. Draw cash flow diagrams as part of your explanation.

9. A new performing arts center will have either tile or stone floors in the lobby and main floor hallways. The choice will be made based on a cost analysis using an 8 percent interest rate and the following data:

Tile: Installed cost per square foot is $15. The tile will last 20 years, and it will require annual upkeep cost (for waxing, etc.) of $1 per square foot.

Stone: Installed cost per square foot is $50. The tile will last 60 years. Upkeep costs are negligible. (Both tile and stone require dusting and mopping, but only tile requires waxing.)

a. Which tile is preferred, based on equivalent annual costs?

b. Repeat the analysis, but this time use PV of cost.

10. Two types of coal-car wheel are under consideration by a railroad. One type is a conventional wheel, which lasts eight years and is refurbished (cleaned, reground, and pressed onto a new axle) at year 3 and year 6. Initial cost is $250, and salvage value is $40. The first refurbishment costs $80, and the second costs $125. The other wheel type is made of specially treated metal alloys. These special wheels will last four years, but they cannot be refurbished economically. Initial cost is $350, and salvage value is $60.

a. If the interest rate is 8 percent, which wheel is preferable? Use either EAC or PV analysis. Draw cash flow diagrams in support of your analysis.

b. Which method, EAC or PV, is the most efficient for this analysis (i.e., the method requiring the fewest interest calculations)?

    c. Railroad executives want to be sure that lower-level supervisors understand the economics in selecting one wheel over the other. How may the calculations be best explained so that those supervisors will understand?

Cost-effectiveness

11. A vocational-technical college has three models of microcomputers under consideration for its computer training program. The director and the department head have established, in order of importance, the following criteria of cost-effectiveness to be used in ranking the three models:

    (1) Similarity to machines used by firms that hire our graduates.
    (2) High-level programming languages supported.
    (3) Initial cost.
    (4) Reliability.
    (5) Availability of compatible peripherals.

Relevant data on the three models are as follows:

AF80. Price is $1,600. A computer magazine has surveyed owners, who report an average breakdown frequency of once per 18 months. The AF80 is the leader among all microcomputers in sales to businesses. Furthermore, the AF80 incorporates the 9090 microprocessor unit, which is the most widely used among microcomputer manufacturers. The AF80 supports integer and floating-point BASIC plus FORTRAN programming languages. At present, five manufacturers sell printers that are compatible with the AF80 and three manufacturers sell compatible floppy disk units.

Critter. The Critter sells for $1,900. The Critter is 18th among microcomputers in sales. But there is a large backlog of customers who have been attracted by the Critter's high reliability and variety of languages: integer and floating-point BASIC, FORTRAN, COBOL, and PASCAL. The Critter is one of the few micros that uses the AA12 microprocessor unit. Three manufacturers' printers and four manufacturers' floppy disks are compatible with the Critter.

Banana. The Banana sells for $1,450. It is the most popular personal (home) microcomputer, and it is the third most popular microcomputer among business users. The Banana is compatible with printers made by two manufacturers and with floppy disks made by three manufacturers. No information is available about the machine's reliability, but Banana Corp.'s widely available service centers have a good reputation. Banana Corp. claims to have a superior advanced BASIC programming capability (both floating-point and integer), but the Banana microcomputer does not support other languages.

    a. Do a cost-effectiveness analysis comparing the three machines. Display the results in a C-E matrix. Which machine do you recommend, and why?
    b. Is C-E analysis suitable in this situation? What about other analysis methods, such as benefit-cost and equivalent annual cost?

Facilities replacement

12. Paramount Linen Service has a large industrial washer. The washer has been experiencing considerable breakdown time, and the general manager wonders whether it should be replaced. The washer is four years old, and it has the following history and projected future pattern of maintenance costs and resale (or trade-in) values:

	Year	Maintenance cost	Resale
	1	$ 300	$45,000
	2	570	32,000
	3	990	23,000
Current year →	4	2,025	15,000
	5	4,500	9,000
	6	7,830	4,000
	7	11,050	3,000
	8	16,040	2,000

If that type of washer costs $60,000 new, is it time to replace? If not, when? Assume a 12 percent interest rate. Suggestion: Set the problem up in a tabular format similar to that of Figure 4–8.

IN-BASKET CASE*

Topic: MAPI Replacement Technique—Motor Pool

To:

From: Motor Pool Manager, Apex Co.

In order to improve our procedures for replacing aging vehicles (trucks, forklifts, mobile cranes, bulldozers), I'm investigating a few techniques. The one I'd like you to investigate is the MAPI technique, which I heard about some years ago. (It is a technique developed by the Machine and Allied Products Institute; hence the name.) In your investigation, be sure to consider the nature of our company.

*See instructions at end of problems section, Chapter 1.

CASE

Carpentry shop, U.S. Naval Supply Depot

The U.S. Naval Base at Guantánamo Bay, Cuba, has several major tenants, two of which are a supply depot (SD) and a public works department (PWD). Each has its own carpentry shop. The carpentry shop at PWD serves the whole base, including housing. The carpentry shop at SD exists to build crates and shelves, and to perform minor construction and remodeling. The shop is part of the Packing Department at SD.

In a cost-cutting drive the SD commander has assigned an analyst to study the carpentry shop. A segment of the analyst's study report follows:

The Packing Department has a complete carpentry shop in the west end of Building 401. The shop has 11 large pieces of power equipment, which is about as much as the PWD carpentry shop has. For crating operations in the Packing Department, only three large power saws (at the most) are required; the remainder of the equipment is currently used for miscellaneous carpentry jobs assigned to the Packing Department in the slack winter months.

Since providing carpentry and woodworking services to all base tenants is part of the mission of PWD, the Packing Section has no reason for being in the carpentry business except to construct required shipping crates. All skills and equipment in excess of those needed for crate construction are an unnecessary duplication of the PWD effort. Disposal action should be taken on this equipment, which is listed below.

Name of equipment	Original price
Planer	$2,260
Jointer-planer	2,725
Radial-arm saw	552
Radial-arm saw	n.a.
Band saw	n.a.
Jointer-planer	n.a.
Sander	n.a.
Drill press	n.a.

The analyst's report went to the commander, who presented it at a staff meeting. The chief of the Packing Department, who had played a role in acquiring the equipment 20–30 years earlier, objected, as did a few other old-timers. The analyst's recommendation for disposal ended up being "shelved." When the analyst heard about the result, his wry comment was,

> The noble art of losing face
> May someday save the human race.

What did the analyst mean? Assess the analyst's study and its outcome.

supplement A to chapter 11

TIME-VALUE OF MONEY

In Supplement A time-value-of-money concepts and techniques are examined. The topics considered are:

1. Interest and interest tables.
2. Solution procedure.
3. Payment patterns.

Interest and interest tables

"A bird in the hand is worth two in the bush." Similarly $1 in hand is worth $2 five years from now. That is a true statement—if the interest rate for a savings account is 15 percent. Here is the proof (the final figure is a penny too high because of rounding error):

1st year: $1.00 at 15 percent interest equals $1.15 at year-end.
2d year: $1.15 at 15 percent interest equals $1.32 at year-end.
3d year: $1.32 at 15 percent interest equals $1.52 at year-end.
4th year: $1.52 at 15 percent interest equals $1.75 at year-end.
5th year: $1.75 at 15 percent interest equals $2.01 at year-end.

There is a much faster way to find what money today is worth in the future: Multiply (or divide) today's amount by the appropriate compound interest factor for the given interest rate and number of years. The interest factor may be found in interest tables, which are widely available in banks and finance companies; in the facilities planning and accounting departments of firms; and in appendices of textbooks in business administration and industrial engineering.

Finance and management accounting textbooks generally include two interest tables. Industrial engineering (engineering economy) textbooks[1] include the same two, plus four (or sometimes five) more, which are mathematical transpositons of the first two. Operations management textbooks tend to spend time in both camps, and thus may include either the two tables or the six tables. In this textbook the six-table approach is demonstrated, since most students are exposed to the two-table approach in other courses.

The six-table approach provides interest factors (Table S11–1, end of Supplement A) for

1. Finding the *future* value of a *present* sum, abbreviated as F/P_i^n, where

---

[1] The first major work on time-value-of-money analysis was probably J. C. L. Fish, *Engineering Economics* (McGraw-Hill, 1923).

F/P means "F, given P," or "Find the *future* sum, given the present
sum." Note that the slash (/) stands for the word *given.*
n stands for *n*umber of years.
i stands for *i*nterest rate.

2. Finding the *p*resent value of a *f*uture sum, abbreviated P/F_i^n.
3. Finding the equivalent *a*nnual cost (or annuity) of a *f*uture sum, abbreviated A/F_i^n.
4. Finding the equivalent *a*nnual cost of a *p*resent sum, abbreviated A/P_i^n.
5. Finding the *f*uture value of a uniform *a*nnual amount (or an equivalent annual cost, or an annuity), abbreviated F/A_i^n.
6. Finding the *p*resent value of a uniform *a*nnual amount, abbreviated P/A_i^n.

Numbers 1 and 4 above are simply the reciprocals of all the interest factors in 2 and 6, respectively. That is, P/F is the reciprocal of F/P, and A/P is the reciprocal of P/A.

Number 5 above is useful only in special situations, but number 3, the A/F interest factor, is often useful. A typical situation is this: You want to find the equivalent annual cost of a proposed machine costing X dollars, having Y dollars per year operation and maintenance (O&M) cost, and returning Z dollars salvage value at the end of its useful life. To work the problem you must combine the three costs, but only after translating them into common-time-dollars—in this case equivalent annual cost (EAC).

Initial cost X is translated into EAC:

$$EAC = X(A/P)_i^n$$

O&M cost Y is already annual and uniform from year to year, so:

$$EAC = Y$$

Salvage value Z may be translated into EAC:

$$EAC = -Z(A/F)_i^n$$

Then add the three EAC components.

The salvage value step may be interpreted thus: (1) Salvage value is a receipt or negative cost and therefore bears a minus sign. (2) The equivalent annual cost of salvage value is like a prepayment plan—or a sinking fund. (3) The A/F factor allows you to "annualize" salvage value in one step (whereas this would take two steps using the two-table method).

Solution procedure

It may seem that time-value-of-money methods make detailed analysis rather difficult. A few tips can help the learner cope with these difficulties:

1. Begin by labeling the given data. In the six-table method this means labeling each item of numeric data as being P, A, F, i, or n; these, of course, are the five labels found in the interest tables, Table S11–1. Recall that:

P stands for *present* amount, or *principal*, or *present* value, or *present* worth—any sum that occurs at time *zero*, the time that the decision on the proposal is to be made.

A stands for uniform *annual* amount, or equivalent *annual* cost, or *annualized equivalent of a present or future sum with interest included (like* installment loan payments)—it must occur every year of the life of the proposal, and it is always assumed to occur at year-end.

F stands for *future* amount that occurs at the end of some given year—typically a trade-in or salvage value at the end of a proposal's life or an overhaul in one or more intermediate years.

i stands for *interest* rate, or discount rate, or cost of capital, or minimum attractive rate of return, or time-adjusted rate-of-return, or internal rate-of-return, or opportunity cost rate.

n stands for *number* of years—for which a uniform annual amount is paid or received, or until a future sum occurs, or the life of the proposal.

2. Decide what the unknown is—the numeric value that is to be solved for; generally it is P, A, F, i, or n. This numeric solution is used in some way to help decide on the merits of the proposed facility. Often there is a choice of unknowns to solve for. For example, results may sometimes be expressed in terms of present value (P), equivalent annual cost (A), or time-adjusted rate-of-return (i). Each usually results in the same decision about the proposal. The choice of unknown, then, may be based on which form is most familiar to the analyst or decision maker or which form is easiest to compute.

3. Use appropriate interest tables to compute the unknown. This may be easy and quite mechanical, because you simply choose the proper interest table and column and row by referring to the desired unknown and the given data. For example, suppose that you are given a future amount (F) and that the desired unknown is present value (P). For short, you want *"P, given A."* Therefore, you go to the P/A column—on the page for the given interest rate (i) and down the page to the given number of years (n).

Payment patterns

In facilities proposals there will often be a cost of operating that is about the same in each year of use. For example, it may cost $500 per year—for wages and power—to operate a proposed copying machine. If the machine is expected to last ten years, the present value equivalent, at 10 percent, is (using the appropriate P/A factor):

$$\text{Present value} = (\$500)(6.145) = \$3,072.50$$

Wages would probably be paid out in weekly increments, and power in monthly increments. It is convenient, however, to treat all such costs as if they were paid for in a lump sum at the end of the year; this is standard practice among accounting, financial, and engineering analysts. The resulting inaccuracy is slight.

TABLE S11-1
Six interest tables
1%

	To find F, given P: $(1 + i)^n$	To find P, given F: $\dfrac{1}{(1 + i)^n}$	To find A, given F: $\dfrac{i}{(1 + i)^n - 1}$	To find A, given P: $\dfrac{i(1 + i)^n}{(1 + i)^n - 1}$	To find F, given A: $\dfrac{(1 + i)^n - 1}{i}$	To find P, given A: $\dfrac{(1 + i)^n - 1}{i(1 + i)^n}$	
n	$(f/p)_n^1$	$(p/f)_n^1$	$(a/f)_n^1$	$(a/p)_n^1$	$(f/a)_n^1$	$(p/a)_n^1$	n
1	1.010	0.9901	1.00000	1.01000	1.000	0.990	1
2	1.020	0.9803	0.49751	0.50751	2.010	1.970	2
3	1.030	0.9706	0.33002	0.34002	3.030	2.941	3
4	1.041	0.9610	0.24628	0.25628	4.060	3.902	4
5	1.051	0.9515	0.19604	0.20604	5.101	4.853	5
6	1.062	0.9420	0.16255	0.17255	6.152	5.795	6
7	1.072	0.9327	0.13863	0.14863	7.214	6.728	7
8	1.083	0.9235	0.12069	0.13069	8.286	7.652	8
9	1.094	0.9143	0.10674	0.11674	9.369	8.566	9
10	1.105	0.9053	0.09558	0.10558	10.462	9.471	10
11	1.116	0.8963	0.08645	0.09645	11.567	10.368	11
12	1.127	0.8874	0.07885	0.08885	12.683	11.255	12
13	1.138	0.8787	0.07241	0.08241	13.809	12.134	13
14	1.149	0.8700	0.06690	0.07690	14.947	13.004	14
15	1.161	0.8613	0.06212	0.07212	16.097	13.865	15
16	1.173	0.8528	0.05794	0.06794	17.258	14.718	16
17	1.184	0.8444	0.05426	0.06426	18.430	15.562	17
18	1.196	0.8360	0.05098	0.06098	19.615	16.398	18
19	1.208	0.8277	0.04805	0.05805	20.811	17.226	19
20	1.220	0.8195	0.04542	0.05542	22.019	18.046	20
21	1.232	0.8114	0.04303	0.05303	23.239	18.857	21
22	1.245	0.8034	0.04086	0.05086	24.472	19.660	22
23	1.257	0.7954	0.03889	0.04889	25.716	20.456	23
24	1.270	0.7876	0.03707	0.04707	26.973	21.243	24
25	1.282	0.7798	0.03541	0.04541	28.243	22.023	25
26	1.295	0.7720	0.03387	0.04387	29.526	22.795	26
27	1.308	0.7644	0.03245	0.04245	30.821	23.560	27
28	1.321	0.7568	0.03112	0.04112	32.129	24.316	28
29	1.335	0.7493	0.02990	0.03990	33.450	25.066	29
30	1.348	0.7419	0.02875	0.03875	34.785	25.808	30
31	1.361	0.7346	0.02768	0.03768	36.133	26.542	31
32	1.375	0.7273	0.02667	0.03667	37.494	27.270	32
33	1.391	0.7201	0.02573	0.03573	38.869	27.990	33
34	1.403	0.7130	0.02484	0.03484	40.258	28.703	34
35	1.417	0.7059	0.02400	0.03400	41.660	29.409	35
40	1.489	0.6717	0.02046	0.03046	48.886	32.835	40
45	1.565	0.6391	0.01771	0.02771	56.481	36.095	45
50	1.645	0.6080	0.01551	0.02551	64.463	39.196	50
55	1.729	0.5785	0.01373	0.02373	72.852	42.147	55
60	1.817	0.5504	0.01224	0.02224	81.670	44.955	60
65	1.909	0.5237	0.01100	0.02100	90.937	47.627	65
70	2.007	0.4983	0.00993	0.01993	100.676	50.169	70
75	2.109	0.4741	0.00902	0.01902	110.913	52.587	75
80	2.217	0.4511	0.00822	0.01822	121.672	54.888	80
85	2.330	0.4292	0.00752	0.01752	132.979	57.078	85
90	2.449	0.4084	0.00690	0.01690	144.863	59.161	90
95	2.574	0.3886	0.00636	0.01636	157.354	61.143	95
100	2.705	0.3697	0.00587	0.01587	170.481	63.029	100

	To find F, given P:	To find P, given F:	To find A, given F: [*]	To find A, given P:	To find F, given A:	To find P, given A:	
	$(1 + i)^n$	$\dfrac{1}{(1 + i)^n}$	$\dfrac{i}{(1 + i)^n - 1}$	$\dfrac{i(1 + i)^n}{(1 + i)^n - 1}$	$\dfrac{(1 + i)^n - 1}{i}$	$\dfrac{(1 + i)^n - 1}{i(1 + i)^n}$	
n	$(f/p)^2_n$	$(p/f)^2_n$	$(a/f)^2_n$	$(a/p)^2_n$	$(f/a)^2_n$	$(p/a)^2_n$	n
1	1.020	0.9804	1.00000	1.02000	1.000	0.980	1
2	1.040	0.9612	0.49505	0.51505	2.020	1.942	2
3	1.061	0.9423	0.32675	0.34675	3.060	2.884	3
4	1.082	0.9238	0.24262	0.26262	4.122	3.808	4
5	1.104	0.9057	0.19216	0.21216	5.204	4.713	5
6	1.126	0.8880	0.15853	0.17853	6.308	5.601	6
7	1.149	0.8706	0.13451	0.15451	7.434	6.472	7
8	1.172	0.8535	0.11651	0.13651	8.583	7.325	8
9	1.195	0.8368	0.10252	0.12252	9.755	8.162	9
10	1.219	0.8203	0.09133	0.11133	10.950	8.983	10
11	1.243	0.8043	0.08216	0.10218	12.169	9.787	11
12	1.268	0.7885	0.07456	0.09456	13.412	10.575	12
13	1.294	0.7730	0.06812	0.08812	14.680	11.348	13
14	1.319	0.7579	0.06260	0.08260	15.974	12.106	14
15	1.346	0.7430	0.05783	0.07783	17.293	12.849	15
16	1.373	0.7284	0.05365	0.07365	18.639	13.578	16
17	1.400	0.7142	0.04997	0.06997	20.012	14.292	17
18	1.428	0.7002	0.04670	0.06670	21.412	14.992	18
19	1.457	0.6864	0.04378	0.06378	22.841	15.678	19
20	1.486	0.6730	0.04116	0.06116	24.297	16.351	20
21	1.516	0.6598	0.03878	0.05878	25.783	17.011	21
22	1.546	0.6468	0.03663	0.05663	27.299	17.658	22
23	1.577	0.6342	0.03467	0.05467	28.845	18.292	23
24	1.608	0.6217	0.03287	0.05287	30.422	18.914	24
25	1.641	0.6095	0.03122	0.05122	32.030	19.523	25
26	1.673	0.5976	0.02970	0.04970	33.671	20.121	26
27	1.707	0.5859	0.02829	0.04829	35.344	20.707	27
28	1.741	0.5744	0.02699	0.04699	37.051	21.281	28
29	1.776	0.5631	0.02578	0.04578	38.792	21.844	29
30	1.811	0.5521	0.02465	0.04465	40.568	22.396	30
31	1.848	0.5412	0.02360	0.04360	42.379	22.938	31
32	1.885	0.5306	0.02261	0.04261	44.227	23.468	32
33	1.922	0.5202	0.02169	0.04169	46.112	23.989	33
34	1.961	0.5100	0.02082	0.04082	48.034	24.499	34
35	2.000	0.5000	0.02000	0.04000	49.994	24.999	35
40	2.208	0.4529	0.01656	0.03656	60.402	27.355	40
45	2.438	0.4102	0.01391	0.03391	71.893	29.490	45
50	2.692	0.3715	0.01182	0.03182	84.579	31.424	50
55	2.972	0.3365	0.01014	0.03014	98.587	33.175	55
60	3.281	0.3048	0.00877	0.02877	114.052	34.761	60
65	3.623	0.2761	0.00763	0.02763	131.126	36.197	65
70	4.000	0.2500	0.00667	0.02667	149.978	37.499	70
75	4.416	0.2265	0.00586	0.02586	170.792	38.677	75
80	4.875	0.2051	0.00516	0.02516	193.772	39.745	80
85	5.383	0.1858	0.00456	0.02456	219.144	40.711	85
90	5.943	0.1683	0.00405	0.02405	247.157	41.587	90
95	6.562	0.1524	0.00360	0.02360	278.085	42.380	95
100	7.245	0.1380	0.00320	0.02320	312.232	43.098	100

	To find F, given P: $(1 + i)^n$	To find P, given F: $\dfrac{1}{(1 + i)^n}$	To find A, given F: $\dfrac{i}{(1 + i)^n - 1}$	To find A, given P: $\dfrac{i(1 + i)^n}{(1 + i)^n - 1}$	To find F, given A: $\dfrac{(1 + i)^n - 1}{i}$	To find P, given A: $\dfrac{(1 + i)^n - 1}{i(1 + i)^n}$	
n	$(f/p)_n^3$	$(p/f)_n^3$	$(a/f)_n^3$	$(a/p)_n^3$	$(f/a)_n^3$	$(p/a)_n^3$	n
1	1.030	0.9709	1.00000	1.03000	1.000	0.971	1
2	1.061	0.9426	0.49261	0.52261	2.030	1.913	2
3	1.093	0.9151	0.32353	0.35353	3.091	2.829	3
4	1.126	0.8885	0.23903	0.26903	4.184	3.717	4
5	1.159	0.8626	0.18835	0.21835	5.309	4.580	5
6	1.194	0.8375	0.15460	0.18460	6.468	5.417	6
7	1.230	0.8131	0.13051	0.16051	7.662	6.230	7
8	1.267	0.7894	0.11246	0.14246	8.892	7.020	8
9	1.305	0.7664	0.09843	0.12843	10.159	7.786	9
10	1.344	0.7441	0.08723	0.11723	11.464	8.530	10
11	1.384	0.7224	0.07808	0.10808	12.808	9.253	11
12	1.426	0.7014	0.07046	0.10046	14.192	9.954	12
13	1.469	0.6810	0.06403	0.09403	15.618	10.635	13
14	1.513	0.6611	0.05853	0.08853	17.086	11.296	14
15	1.558	0.6419	0.05377	0.08377	18.599	11.938	15
16	1.605	0.6232	0.04961	0.07961	20.157	12.561	16
17	1.653	0.6050	0.04595	0.07595	21.762	13.166	17
18	1.702	0.5874	0.04271	0.07271	23.414	13.754	18
19	1.754	0.5703	0.03981	0.06981	25.117	14.324	19
20	1.806	0.5537	0.03722	0.06722	26.870	14.877	20
21	1.860	0.5375	0.03487	0.06487	28.676	15.415	21
22	1.916	0.5219	0.03275	0.06275	30.537	15.937	22
23	1.974	0.5067	0.03081	0.06081	32.453	16.444	23
24	2.033	0.4919	0.02905	0.05905	34.426	16.936	24
25	2.094	0.4776	0.02743	0.05743	36.459	17.413	25
26	2.157	0.4637	0.02594	0.05594	38.553	17.877	26
27	2.221	0.4502	0.02456	0.05456	40.710	18.327	27
28	2.288	0.4371	0.02329	0.05329	42.931	18.764	28
29	2.357	0.4243	0.02211	0.05211	45.219	19.188	29
30	2.427	0.4120	0.02102	0.05102	47.575	19.600	30
31	2.500	0.4000	0.02000	0.05000	50.003	20.000	31
32	2.575	0.3883	0.01905	0.04905	52.503	20.389	32
33	2.652	0.3770	0.01816	0.04816	55.078	20.766	33
34	2.732	0.3660	0.01732	0.04732	57.730	21.132	34
35	2.814	0.3554	0.01654	0.04654	60.462	21.487	35
40	3.262	0.3066	0.01326	0.04326	75.401	23.115	40
45	3.782	0.2644	0.01079	0.04079	92.720	24.519	45
50	4.384	0.2281	0.00887	0.03887	112.797	25.730	50
55	5.082	0.1968	0.00735	0.03735	136.072	26.774	55
60	5.892	0.1697	0.00613	0.03613	163.053	27.676	60
65	6.830	0.1464	0.00515	0.03515	194.333	28.453	65
70	7.918	0.1263	0.00434	0.03434	230.594	29.123	70
75	9.179	0.1089	0.00367	0.03367	272.631	29.702	75
80	10.641	0.0940	0.00311	0.03311	321.363	30.201	80
85	12.336	0.0811	0.00265	0.03265	377.857	30.631	85
90	14.300	0.0699	0.00226	0.03226	443.349	31.002	90
95	16.578	0.0603	0.00193	0.03193	519.272	31.323	95
100	19.219	0.0520	0.00165	0.03165	607.288	31.599	100

	To find F, given P: $(1 + i)^n$	To find P, given F: $\dfrac{1}{(1 + i)^n}$	To find A, given F: $\dfrac{i}{(1 + i)^n - 1}$	To find A, given P: $\dfrac{i(1 + i)^n}{(1 + i)^n - 1}$	To find F, given A: $\dfrac{(1 + i)^n - 1}{i}$	To find P, given A: $\dfrac{(1 + i)^n - 1}{i(1 + i)^n}$	
n	$(f/p)_n^5$	$(p/f)_n^5$	$(a/f)_n^5$	$(a/p)_n^5$	$(f/a)_n^5$	$(p/a)_n^5$	n
1	1.050	0.9524	1.00000	1.05000	1.000	0.952	1
2	1.103	0.9070	0.48780	0.53780	2.050	1.859	2
3	1.158	0.8638	0.31721	0.36721	3.153	2.723	3
4	1.216	0.8227	0.23201	0.28201	4.310	3.546	4
5	1.276	0.7835	0.18097	0.23097	5.526	4.329	5
6	1.340	0.7462	0.14702	0.19702	6.802	5.076	6
7	1.407	0.7107	0.12282	0.17282	8.142	5.786	7
8	1.477	0.6768	0.10472	0.15472	9.549	6.463	8
9	1.551	0.6446	0.09069	0.14069	11.027	7.108	9
10	1.629	0.6139	0.07950	0.12950	12.578	7.722	10
11	1.710	0.5847	0.07039	0.12039	14.207	8.306	11
12	1.796	0.5568	0.06283	0.11283	15.917	8.863	12
13	1.886	0.5303	0.05646	0.10646	17.713	9.394	13
14	1.980	0.5051	0.05102	0.10102	19.599	9.899	14
15	2.079	0.4810	0.04634	0.09634	21.579	10.380	15
16	2.183	0.4581	0.04227	0.09227	23.657	10.838	16
17	2.292	0.4363	0.03870	0.08870	25.840	11.274	17
18	2.407	0.4155	0.03555	0.08555	28.132	11.690	18
19	2.527	0.3957	0.03275	0.08275	30.539	12.085	19
20	2.653	0.3769	0.03024	0.08024	33.066	12.462	20
21	2.786	0.3589	0.02800	0.07800	35.719	12.821	21
22	2.925	0.3418	0.02597	0.07597	38.505	13.163	22
23	3.072	0.3256	0.02414	0.07414	41.430	13.489	23
24	3.225	0.3101	0.02247	0.07247	44.502	13.799	24
25	3.386	0.2953	0.02095	0.07095	47.727	14.094	25
26	3.556	0.2812	0.01956	0.06956	51.113	14.375	26
27	3.733	0.2678	0.01829	0.06829	54.669	14.643	27
28	3.920	0.2551	0.01712	0.06712	58.403	14.898	28
29	4.116	0.2429	0.01605	0.06605	62.323	15.141	29
30	4.322	0.2314	0.01505	0.06505	66.439	15.372	30
31	4.538	0.2204	0.01413	0.06413	70.761	15.593	31
32	4.765	0.2099	0.01328	0.06328	75.299	15.803	32
33	5.003	0.1999	0.01249	0.06249	80.064	16.003	33
34	5.253	0.1904	0.01176	0.06176	85.067	16.193	34
35	5.516	0.1813	0.01107	0.06107	90.320	16.374	35
40	7.040	0.1420	0.00828	0.05828	120.800	17.159	40
45	8.985	0.1113	0.00626	0.05626	159.700	17.774	45
50	11.467	0.0872	0.00478	0.05478	209.348	18.256	50
55	14.636	0.0683	0.00367	0.05367	272.713	18.633	55
60	18.679	0.0535	0.00283	0.05283	353.584	18.929	60
65	23.840	0.0419	0.00219	0.05219	456.798	19.161	65
70	30.426	0.0329	0.00170	0.05170	588.529	19.343	70
75	38.833	0.0258	0.00132	0.05132	756.654	19.485	75
80	49.561	0.0202	0.00103	0.05103	971.229	19.596	80
85	63.254	0.0158	0.00080	0.05080	1245.087	19.684	85
90	80.730	0.0124	0.00063	0.05063	1594.607	19.752	90
95	103.035	0.0097	0.00049	0.05049	2040.694	19.806	95
100	131.501	0.0076	0.00038	0.05038	2610.025	19.848	100

	To find F, given P: $(1+i)^n$	To find P, given F: $\dfrac{1}{(1+i)^n}$	To find A, given F: $\dfrac{i}{(1+i)^n-1}$	To find A, given P: $\dfrac{i(1+i)^n}{(1+i)^n-1}$	To find F, given A: $\dfrac{(1+i)^n-1}{i}$	To find P, given A: $\dfrac{(1+i)^n-1}{i(1+i)^n}$	
n	$(f/p)_n^7$	$(p/f)_n^7$	$(a/f)_n^7$	$(a/p)_n^7$	$(f/a)_n^7$	$(p/a)_n^7$	n
1	1.070	0.9346	1.00000	1.07000	1.000	0.935	1
2	1.145	0.8734	0.48309	0.55309	2.070	1.808	2
3	1.225	0.8163	0.31105	0.38105	3.215	2.624	3
4	1.311	0.7629	0.22523	0.29523	4.440	3.387	4
5	1.403	0.7130	0.17389	0.24389	5.751	4.100	5
6	1.501	0.6663	0.13980	0.20980	7.153	4.767	6
7	1.606	0.6227	0.11555	0.18555	8.654	5.389	7
8	1.718	0.5820	0.09747	0.16747	10.260	5.971	8
9	1.838	0.5439	0.08349	0.15349	11.978	6.515	9
10	1.967	0.5083	0.07238	0.14238	13.816	7.024	10
11	2.105	0.4751	0.06336	0.13336	15.784	7.499	11
12	2.252	0.4440	0.05590	0.12590	17.888	7.943	12
13	2.410	0.4150	0.04965	0.11965	20.141	8.358	13
14	2.579	0.3878	0.04434	0.11434	22.550	8.745	14
15	2.759	0.3624	0.03979	0.10979	25.129	9.108	15
16	2.952	0.3387	0.03586	0.10586	27.888	9.447	16
17	3.159	0.3166	0.03243	0.10243	30.840	9.763	17
18	3.380	0.2959	0.02941	0.09941	33.999	10.059	18
19	3.617	0.2765	0.02675	0.09675	37.379	10.363	19
20	3.870	0.2584	0.02439	0.09439	40.995	10.594	20
21	4.141	0.2415	0.02229	0.09229	44.865	10.836	21
22	4.430	0.2257	0.02041	0.09041	49.006	11.061	22
23	4.741	0.2109	0.01871	0.08871	53.436	11.272	23
24	5.072	0.1971	0.01719	0.08719	58.177	11.469	24
25	5.427	0.1842	0.01581	0.08581	63.249	11.654	25
26	5.807	0.1722	0.01456	0.08456	68.676	11.826	26
27	6.214	0.1609	0.01343	0.08343	74.484	11.987	27
28	6.649	0.1504	0.01239	0.08239	80.698	12.137	28
29	7.114	0.1406	0.01145	0.08145	87.347	12.278	29
30	7.612	0.1314	0.01059	0.08059	94.461	12.409	30
31	8.145	0.1228	0.00980	0.07980	102.073	12.532	31
32	8.715	0.1147	0.00907	0.07907	110.218	12.647	32
33	9.325	0.1072	0.00841	0.07841	118.923	12.754	33
34	9.978	0.1002	0.00780	0.07780	128.259	12.854	34
35	10.677	0.0937	0.00723	0.07723	138.237	12.948	35
40	14.974	0.0668	0.00501	0.07501	199.635	13.332	40
45	21.002	0.0476	0.00350	0.07350	285.749	13.606	45
50	29.457	0.0339	0.00246	0.07246	406.529	13.801	50
55	41.315	0.0242	0.00174	0.07174	575.929	13.940	55
60	57.946	0.0173	0.00123	0.07123	813.520	14.039	60
65	81.273	0.0123	0.00087	0.07087	1146.755	14.110	65
70	113.989	0.0088	0.00062	0.07062	1614.134	14.160	70
75	159.876	0.0063	0.00044	0.07044	2269.657	14.196	75
80	224.234	0.0045	0.00031	0.07031	3189.063	14.222	80
85	314.500	0.0032	0.00022	0.07022	4478.576	14.240	85
90	441.103	0.0023	0.00016	0.07016	6287.185	14.253	90
95	618.670	0.0016	0.00011	0.07011	8823.854	14.263	95
100	867.716	0.0012	0.00008	0.07008	12381.662	14.269	100

	To find F, given P: $(1 + i)^n$	To find P, given F: $\dfrac{1}{(1 + i)^n}$	To find A, given F: $\dfrac{i}{(1 + i)^n - 1}$	To find A, given P: $\dfrac{i(1 + i)^n}{(1 + i)^n - 1}$	To find F, given A: $\dfrac{(1 + i)^n - 1}{i}$	To find P, given A: $\dfrac{(1 + i)^n - 1}{i(1 + i)^n}$	
n	$(f/p)_n^{10}$	$(p/f)_n^{10}$	$(a/f)_n^{10}$	$(a/p)_n^{10}$	$(f/a)_n^{10}$	$(p/a)_n^{10}$	n
1	1.100	0.9091	1.00000	1.10000	1.000	0.909	1
2	1.210	0.8264	0.47619	0.57619	2.100	1.736	2
3	1.331	0.7513	0.30211	0.40211	3.310	2.487	3
4	1.464	0.6830	0.21547	0.31547	4.641	3.170	4
5	1.611	0.6209	0.16380	0.26380	6.105	3.791	5
6	1.772	0.5645	0.12961	0.22961	7.716	4.355	6
7	1.949	0.5132	0.10541	0.20541	9.487	4.868	7
8	2.144	0.4665	0.08744	0.18744	11.436	5.335	8
9	2.358	0.4241	0.07364	0.17364	13.579	5.759	9
10	2.594	0.3855	0.06275	0.16275	15.937	6.144	10
11	2.853	0.3505	0.05396	0.15396	18.531	6.495	11
12	3.138	0.3186	0.04676	0.14676	21.384	6.814	12
13	3.452	0.2897	0.04078	0.14078	24.523	7.103	13
14	3.797	0.2633	0.03575	0.13575	27.975	7.367	14
15	4.177	0.2394	0.03147	0.13147	31.772	7.606	15
16	4.595	0.2176	0.02782	0.12782	35.950	7.824	16
17	5.054	0.1978	0.02466	0.12466	40.545	8.022	17
18	5.560	0.1799	0.02193	0.12193	45.599	8.201	18
19	6.116	0.1635	0.01955	0.11955	51.159	8.363	19
20	6.727	0.1486	0.01746	0.11746	57.275	8.514	20
21	7.400	0.1351	0.01562	0.11562	64.002	8.649	21
22	8.140	0.1228	0.01401	0.11401	71.403	8.772	22
23	8.954	0.1117	0.01257	0.11257	79.543	8.883	23
24	9.850	0.1015	0.01130	0.11130	88.497	8.985	24
25	10.835	0.0923	0.01017	0.11017	98.347	9.077	25
26	11.918	0.0839	0.00916	0.10916	109.182	9.161	26
27	13.110	0.0763	0.00826	0.10826	121.100	9.237	27
28	14.421	0.0693	0.00745	0.10745	134.210	9.307	28
29	15.863	0.0630	0.00673	0.10673	148.631	9.370	29
30	17.449	0.0573	0.00608	0.10608	164.494	9.427	30
31	19.194	0.0521	0.00550	0.10550	181.943	9.479	31
32	21.114	0.0474	0.00497	0.10497	201.138	9.526	32
33	23.225	0.0431	0.00450	0.10450	222.252	9.569	33
34	25.548	0.0391	0.00407	0.10407	245.477	9.609	34
35	28.102	0.0356	0.00369	0.10369	271.024	9.644	35
40	45.259	0.0221	0.00226	0.10226	442.593	9.779	40
45	72.890	0.0137	0.00139	0.10139	718.905	9.863	45
50	117.391	0.0085	0.00086	0.10086	1163.909	9.915	50
55	189.059	0.0053	0.00053	0.10053	1880.591	9.947	55
60	304.482	0.0033	0.00033	0.10033	3034.816	9.967	60
65	490.371	0.0020	0.00020	0.10020	4893.707	9.980	65
70	789.747	0.0013	0.00013	0.10013	7887.470	9.987	70
75	1271.895	0.0008	0.00008	0.10008	12708.954	9.992	75
80	2048.400	0.0005	0.00005	0.10005	20474.002	9.995	80
85	3298.969	0.0003	0.00003	0.10003	32979.690	9.997	85
90	5313.023	0.0002	0.00002	0.10002	53120.226	9.998	90
95	8556.676	0.0001	0.00001	0.10001	85556.760	9.999	95
100	13780.612	0.0001	0.00001	0.10001	137796.123	9.999	100

TABLE S11-1
(continued)
12%

n	To find F, given P: $(1 + i)^n$ $(f/p)_n^{12}$	To find P, given F: $\dfrac{1}{(1 + i)^n}$ $(p/f)_n^{12}$	To find A, given F: $\dfrac{i}{(1 + i)^n - 1}$ $(a/f)_n^{12}$	To find A, given P: $\dfrac{i(1 + i)^n}{(1 + i)^n - 1}$ $(a/p)_n^{12}$	To find F, given A: $\dfrac{(1 + i)^n - 1}{i}$ $(f/a)_n^{12}$	To find P, given A: $\dfrac{(1 + i)^n - 1}{i(1 + i)^n}$ $(p/a)_n^{12}$	n
1	1.120	0.8929	1.00000	1.12000	1.000	0.893	1
2	1.254	0.7972	0.47170	0.59170	2.120	1.690	2
3	1.405	0.7118	0.29635	0.41635	3.374	2.402	3
4	1.574	0.6355	0.20923	0.32923	4.779	3.037	4
5	1.762	0.5674	0.15741	0.27741	6.353	3.605	5
6	1.974	0.5066	0.12323	0.24323	8.115	4.111	6
7	2.211	0.4523	0.09912	0.21912	10.089	4.564	7
8	2.476	0.4039	0.08130	0.20130	12.300	4.968	8
9	2.773	0.3606	0.06768	0.18768	14.776	5.328	9
10	3.106	0.3220	0.05698	0.17698	17.549	5.650	10
11	3.479	0.2875	0.04842	0.16842	20.655	5.938	11
12	3.896	0.2567	0.04144	0.16144	24.133	6.194	12
13	4.363	0.2292	0.03568	0.15568	28.029	6.424	13
14	4.887	0.2046	0.03087	0.15087	32.393	6.628	14
15	5.474	0.1827	0.02682	0.14682	37.280	6.811	15
16	6.130	0.1631	0.02339	0.14339	42.753	6.974	16
17	6.866	0.1456	0.02046	0.14046	48.884	7.120	17
18	7.690	0.1300	0.01794	0.13794	55.750	7.250	18
19	8.613	0.1161	0.01576	0.13576	63.440	7.366	19
20	9.646	0.1037	0.01388	0.13388	72.052	7.469	20
21	10.804	0.0926	0.01224	0.13224	81.699	7.562	21
22	12.100	0.0826	0.01081	0.13081	92.503	7.645	22
23	13.552	0.0738	0.00956	0.12956	104.603	7.718	23
24	15.179	0.0659	0.00846	0.12846	118.155	7.784	24
25	17.000	0.0588	0.00750	0.12750	133.334	7.843	25
26	19.040	0.0525	0.00665	0.12665	150.334	7.896	26
27	21.325	0.0469	0.00590	0.12590	169.374	7.943	27
28	23.884	0.0419	0.00524	0.12524	190.699	7.984	28
29	26.750	0.0374	0.00466	0.12466	214.582	8.022	29
30	29.960	0.0334	0.00414	0.12414	241.333	8.055	30
31	33.555	0.0298	0.00369	0.12369	271.292	8.085	31
32	37.582	0.0266	0.00328	0.12328	304.847	8.112	32
33	42.091	0.0238	0.00292	0.12292	342.429	8.135	33
34	47.142	0.0212	0.00260	0.12260	384.520	8.157	34
35	52.800	0.0189	0.00232	0.12232	431.663	8.176	35
40	93.051	0.0107	0.00130	0.12130	767.091	8.244	40
45	163.988	0.0061	0.00074	0.12074	1358.230	8.283	45
50	289.002	0.0035	0.00042	0.12042	2400.018	8.305	50

TABLE S11–1
(continued)
15%

	To find F, given P: $(1 + i)^n$	To find P, given F: $\dfrac{1}{(1 + i)^n}$	To find A, given F: $\dfrac{i}{(1 + i)^n - 1}$	To find A, given P: $\dfrac{i(1 + i)^n}{(1 + i)^n - 1}$	To find F, given A: $\dfrac{(1 + i)^n - 1}{i}$	To find P, given A: $\dfrac{(1 + i)^n - 1}{i(1 + i)^n}$	
n	$(f/p)_n^{15}$	$(p/f)_n^{15}$	$(a/f)_n^{15}$	$(a/p)_n^{15}$	$(f/a)_n^{15}$	$(p/a)_n^{15}$	n
1	1.150	0.8696	1.00000	1.15000	1.000	0.870	1
2	1.322	0.7561	0.46512	0.61512	2.150	1.626	2
3	1.521	0.6575	0.28798	0.43798	3.472	2.283	3
4	1.749	0.5718	0.20027	0.35027	4.993	2.855	4
5	2.011	0.4972	0.14832	0.29832	6.742	3.352	5
6	2.313	0.4323	0.11424	0.26424	8.754	3.784	6
7	2.660	0.3759	0.09036	0.24036	11.067	4.160	7
8	3.059	0.3269	0.07285	0.22285	13.727	4.487	8
9	3.518	0.2843	0.05957	0.20957	16.786	4.772	9
10	4.046	0.2472	0.04925	0.19925	20.304	5.019	10
11	4.652	0.2149	0.04107	0.19107	24.349	5.234	11
12	5.350	0.1869	0.03448	0.18448	29.002	5.421	12
13	6.153	0.1625	0.02911	0.17911	34.352	5.583	13
14	7.076	0.1413	0.02469	0.17469	40.505	5.724	14
15	8.137	0.1229	0.02102	0.17102	47.580	5.847	15
16	9.358	0.1069	0.01795	0.16795	55.717	5.954	16
17	10.761	0.0929	0.01537	0.16537	65.075	6.047	17
18	12.375	0.0808	0.01319	0.16319	75.836	6.128	18
19	14.232	0.0703	0.01134	0.16134	88.212	6.198	19
20	16.367	0.0611	0.00976	0.15976	102.444	6.259	20
21	18.821	0.0531	0.00842	0.15842	118.810	6.312	21
22	21.645	0.0462	0.00727	0.15727	137.631	6.359	22
23	24.891	0.0402	0.00628	0.15628	159.276	6.399	23
24	28.625	0.0349	0.00543	0.15543	184.168	6.434	24
25	32.919	0.0304	0.00470	0.15470	212.793	6.464	25
26	37.857	0.0264	0.00407	0.15407	245.711	6.491	26
27	43.535	0.0230	0.00353	0.15353	283.569	6.514	27
28	50.066	0.0200	0.00306	0.15306	327.104	6.534	28
29	57.575	0.0174	0.00265	0.15265	377.170	6.551	29
30	66.212	0.0151	0.00230	0.15230	434.745	6.566	30
31	76.143	0.0131	0.00200	0.15200	500.956	6.579	31
32	87.565	0.0114	0.00173	0.15173	577.099	6.591	32
33	100.700	0.0099	0.00150	0.15150	664.664	6.600	33
34	115.805	0.0086	0.00131	0.15131	765.364	6.609	34
35	133.176	0.0075	0.00113	0.15113	881.170	6.617	35
40	267.863	0.0037	0.00056	0.15056	1779.090	6.642	40
45	538.769	0.0019	0.00028	0.15028	3585.128	6.654	45
50	1083.657	0.0009	0.00014	0.15014	7217.716	6.661	50

TABLE S11-1
(concluded)
20%

	To find F, given P: $(1 + i)^n$	To find P, given F: $\dfrac{1}{(1 + i)^n}$	To find A, given F: $\dfrac{i}{(1 + i)^n - 1}$	To find A, given P: $\dfrac{i(1 + i)^n}{(1 + i)^n - 1}$	To find F, given A: $\dfrac{(1 + i)^n - 1}{i}$	To find P, given A: $\dfrac{(1 + i)^n - 1}{i(1 + i)^n}$	
n	$(f/p)_n^{20}$	$(p/f)_n^{20}$	$(a/f)_n^{20}$	$(a/p)_n^{20}$	$(f/a)_n^{20}$	$(p/a)_n^{20}$	n
1	1.200	0.8333	1.00000	1.20000	1.000	0.833	1
2	1.440	0.6944	0.45455	0.65455	2.200	1.528	2
3	1.728	0.5787	0.27473	0.47473	3.640	2.106	3
4	2.074	0.4823	0.18629	0.38629	5.368	2.598	4
5	2.488	0.4019	0.13438	0.33438	7.442	2.991	5
6	2.986	0.3349	0.10071	0.30071	9.930	3.326	6
7	3.583	0.2791	0.07742	0.27742	12.916	3.605	7
8	4.300	0.2326	0.06061	0.26061	16.499	3.837	8
9	5.160	0.1938	0.04808	0.24808	20.799	4.031	9
10	6.192	0.1615	0.03852	0.23852	25.959	4.192	10
11	7.430	0.1346	0.03110	0.23110	32.150	4.327	11
12	8.916	0.1122	0.02526	0.22526	39.581	4.439	12
13	10.699	0.0935 *	0.02062	0.22062	48.497	4.533	13
14	12.839	0.0779 ·	0.01689	0.21689	59.196	4.611	14
15	15.407	0.0649	0.01388	0.21388	72.035	4.675	15
16	18.488	0.0541	0.01144	0.21144	87.442	4.730	16
17	22.186	0.0451	0.00944	0.20944	105.931	4.775	17
18	26.623	0.0376	0.00781	0.20781	128.117	4.812	18
19	31.948	0.0313	0.00646	0.20646	154.740	4.843	19
20	38.338	0.0261	0.00536	0.20536	186.688	4.870	20
21	46.005	0.0217	0.00444	0.20444	225.025	4.891	21
22	55.206	0.0181	0.00369	0.20369	271.031	4.909	22
23	66.247	0.0151	0.00307	0.20307	326.237	4.925	23
24	79.497	0.0126	0.00255	0.20255	392.484	4.937	24
25	95.396	0.0105	0.00212	0.20212	471.981	4.948	25
26	114.475	0.0087	0.00176	0.20176	567.377	4.956	26
27	137.371	0.0073	· 0.00147	0.20147	681.853	4.964	27
28	164.845	0.0061	0.00122	0.20122	819.223	4.970	28
29	197.813	0.0051	0.00102	0.20102	984.068	4.975	29
30	237.376	0.0042	0.00085	0.20085	1181.881	4.979	30
31	284.851	0.0035	0.00070	0.20070	1419.257	4.982	31
32	341.822	0.0029	0.00059	0.20059	1704.108	4.985	32
33	410.186	0.0024	0.00049	0.20049	2045.930	4.988	33
34	492.223	0.0020	0.00041	0.20041	2456.116	4.990	34
35	590.668	0.0017	0.00034	0.20034	2948.339	4.992	35
40	1469.772	0.0007	0.00014	0.20014	7343.858	4.997	40
45	3657.258	0.0003	0.00005	0.20005	18281.331	4.999	45
50	9100.427	0.0001	0.00002	0.20002	45497.191	4.999	50

Source: Paul G. Hoel, *Elementary Statistics*, 4th ed. Copyright © 1976 by John Wiley & Sons, Inc. Reprinted by permission.

supplement B to chapter 11

PRESENT-VALUE TABLES

The two interest tables in this supplement are the types commonly found in finance and managerial accounting books. They are:

Table S11–2: Present value of a sum (which is the same as the *P/F* column in Table S11–1).

Table S11–3: Present value of an annuity (which is the same as the *P/A* column in Table S11–1).

TABLE S11-2
Present value of
a sum

Year	1%	2%	3%	4%	5%	6%	7%	8%	9%	10%	12%	14%	15%
1	.990	.980	.971	.962	.952	.943	.935	.926	.917	.909	.893	.877	.870
2	.980	.961	.943	.925	.907	.890	.873	.857	.842	.826	.797	.769	.756
3	.971	.942	.915	.889	.864	.840	.816	.794	.772	.751	.712	.675	.658
4	.961	.924	.889	.855	.823	.792	.763	.735	.708	.683	.636	.592	.572
5	.951	.906	.863	.822	.784	.747	.713	.681	.650	.621	.567	.519	.497
6	.942	.888	.838	.790	.746	.705	.666	.630	.596	.564	.507	.456	.432
7	.933	.871	.813	.760	.711	.665	.623	.583	.547	.513	.452	.400	.376
8	.923	.853	.789	.731	.677	.627	.582	.540	.502	.467	.404	.351	.327
9	.914	.837	.766	.703	.645	.592	.544	.500	.460	.424	.361	.308	.284
10	.905	.820	.744	.676	.614	.558	.508	.463	.422	.386	.322	.270	.247
11	.896	.804	.722	.650	.585	.527	.475	.429	.388	.350	.287	.237	.215
12	.887	.788	.701	.625	.557	.497	.444	.397	.356	.319	.257	.208	.187
13	.879	.773	.681	.601	.530	.469	.415	.368	.326	.290	.229	.182	.163
14	.870	.758	.661	.577	.505	.442	.388	.340	.299	.263	.205	.160	.141
15	.861	.743	.642	.555	.481	.417	362	.315	.275	.239	.183	.140	.123
16	.853	.728	.623	.534	.458	.394	.339	.292	.252	.218	.163	.123	.107
17	.844	.714	.605	.513	.436	.371	.317	.270	.231	.198	.146	.108	.093
18	.836	.700	.587	.494	.416	.350	.296	.250	.212	.180	.130	.095	.081
19	.828	.686	.570	.475	.396	.331	.276	.232	.194	.164	.116	.083	.070
20	.820	.673	.554	.456	.377	.312	.258	.215	.178	.149	.104	.073	.061
25	.780	.610	.478	.375	.295	.233	.184	.146	.116	.092	.059	.038	.030
30	.742	.552	.412	.308	.231	.174	.131	.099	.075	.057	.033	.020	.015

Year	16%	18%	20%	24%	28%	32%	36%	40%	50%	60%	70%	80%	90%
1	.862	.847	.833	.806	.781	.758	.735	.714	.667	.625	.588	.556	.526
2	.743	.718	.694	.650	.610	.574	.541	.510	.444	.391	.346	.309	.277
3	.641	.609	.579	.524	.477	.435	.398	.364	.296	.244	.204	.171	.146
4	.552	.516	.482	.423	.373	.329	.292	.260	.198	.153	.120	.095	.077
5	.476	.437	.402	.341	.291	.250	.215	.186	.132	.095	.070	.053	.040
6	.410	.370	.335	.275	.227	.189	.158	.133	.088	.060	.041	.029	.021
7	.354	.314	.279	.222	.178	.143	.116	.095	.059	.037	.024	.016	.011
8	.305	.266	.233	.179	.139	.108	.085	.068	.039	.023	.014	.009	.006
9	.263	.226	.194	.144	.108	.082	.063	.048	.026	.015	.008	.005	.003
10	.227	.191	.162	.116	.085	.062	.046	.035	.017	.009	.005	.003	.002
11	.195	.162	.135	.094	.066	.047	.034	.025	.012	.006	.003	.002	.001
12	.168	.137	.112	.076	.052	.036	.025	.018	.008	.004	.002	.001	.001
13	.145	.116	.093	.061	.040	.027	.018	.013	.005	.002	.001	.001	.000
14	.125	.099	.078	.049	.032	.021	.014	.009	.003	.001	.001	.000	.000
15	.108	.084	.065	.040	.025	.016	.010	.006	.002	.001	.000	.000	.000
16	.093	.071	.054	.032	.019	.012	.007	.005	.002	.001	.000	.000	
17	.080	.030	.045	.026	.015	.009	.005	.003	.001	.000	.000		
18	.089	.051	.038	.021	.012	.007	.004	.002	.001	.000	.000		
19	.030	.043	.031	.017	.009	.005	.003	.002	.000	.000			
20	.051	.037	.026	.014	.007	.004	.002	.001	.000	.000			
25	.024	.016	.010	.005	.002	.001	.000	.000					
30	.012	.007	.004	.002	.001	.000	.000						

Source: Richard B. Chase and Nicholas J. Aquilano, *Production and Operations Management,*
rev. ed. (Homewood, Ill.: Richard D. Irwin, 1977), p. 151. © 1977 by Richard D. Irwin, Inc.

TABLE S11–3
Present value of an annuity

Year	1%	2%	3%	4%	5%	6%	7%	8%	9%	10%
1	0.990	0.980	0.971	0.962	0.952	0.943	0.935	0.926	0.917	0.909
2	1.970	1.942	1.913	1.886	1.859	1.833	1.808	1.783	1.759	1.736
3	2.941	2.884	2.829	2.775	2.723	2.673	2.624	2.577	2.531	2.487
4	3.902	3.808	3.717	3.630	3.546	3.465	3.387	3.312	3.240	3.170
5	4.853	4.713	4.580	4.452	4.329	4.212	4.100	3.993	3.890	3.791
6	5.795	5.601	5.417	5.242	5.076	4.917	4.766	4.623	4.486	4.355
7	6.728	6.472	6.230	6.002	5.786	5.582	5.389	5.206	5.033	4.868
8	7.652	7.325	7.020	6.733	6.463	6.210	6.971	5.747	5.535	5.335
9	8.566	8.162	7.786	7.435	7.108	6.802	6.515	6.247	5.985	5.759
10	9.471	8.983	8.530	8.111	7.722	7.360	7.024	6.710	6.418	6.145
11	10.368	9.787	9.253	8.760	8.306	7.887	7.499	7.139	6.805	6.495
12	11.255	10.575	9.954	9.385	8.863	8.384	7.943	7.536	7.161	6.814
13	12.134	11.348	10.635	9.986	9.394	8.853	8.358	7.904	7.487	7.103
14	13.004	12.106	11.296	10.563	9.899	9.295	8.745	8.244	7.786	7.367
15	13.865	12.849	11.938	11.118	10.380	9.712	9.108	8.559	8.060	7.606
16	14.718	13.578	12.561	11.652	10.838	10.106	9.447	8.851	8.312	7.824
17	15.562	14.292	13.166	12.166	11.274	10.477	9.763	9.122	8.544	8.022
18	16.398	14.992	13.754	12.659	11.690	10.828	10.059	9.372	8.756	8.201
19	17.226	15.678	14.324	13.134	12.085	11.158	10.336	9.604	8.950	8.365
20	18.046	16.351	14.877	13.590	12.462	11.470	10.594	9.818	9.128	8.514
25	22.023	19.523	17.413	15.622	14.094	12.783	11.654	10.675	9.823	9.077
30	25.808	22.397	19.600	17.292	15.373	13.765	12.409	11.258	10.274	9.427

Year	12%	14%	16%	18%	20%	24%	28%	32%	36%
1	0.893	0.877	0.862	0.847	0.833	0.806	0.781	0.758	0.735
2	1.690	1.647	1.605	1.566	1.528	1.457	1.392	1.332	1.276
3	2.402	2.322	2.246	2.174	2.106	1.981	1.868	1.766	1.674
4	3.037	2.914	2.798	2.690	2.589	2.404	2.241	2.096	1.966
5	3.605	3.433	3.274	3.127	2.991	2.745	2.532	2.345	2.181
6	4.111	3.889	3.685	3.498	3.326	3.020	2.759	2.534	2.339
7	4.564	4.288	4.039	3.812	3.605	3.242	2.937	2.678	2.455
8	4.968	4.639	4.344	4.078	3.837	3.421	3.076	2.786	2.540
9	5.328	4.946	4.607	4.303	4.031	3.566	3.184	2.868	2.603
10	5.650	5.216	4.833	4.494	4.193	3.682	3.269	2.930	2.650
11	5.988	5.453	5.029	4.656	4.327	3.776	3.335	2.978	2.683
12	6.194	5.660	5.197	4.793	4.439	3.851	3.387	3.013	2.708
13	6.424	5.842	5.342	4.910	4.533	3.912	3.427	3.040	2.727
14	6.628	6.002	5.468	5.008	4.611	3.962	3.459	3.061	2.740
15	6.811	6.142	5.575	5.092	4.675	4.001	3.483	3.076	2.750
16	6.974	6.265	5.669	5.162	4.730	4.033	3.503	3.088	2.758
17	7.120	5.373	5.749	4.222	4.775	4.059	3.518	3.097	2.763
18	7.250	6.467	5.818	5.273	4.812	4.080	3.529	3.104	2.767
19	7.366	6.550	5.877	5.316	4.844	4.097	3.539	3.109	2.770
20	7.469	6.623	5.929	5.353	4.870	4.110	3.546	3.113	2.772
25	7.843	6.873	6.097	5.467	4.948	4.147	3.564	3.122	2.776
30	8.055	7.003	6.177	5.517	4.979	4.160	3.569	3.124	2.778

Source: Richard B. Chase and Nicholas J. Aquilano, *Production and Operations Management,* rev. ed. (Homewood, Ill.: Richard D. Irwin, 1977), p. 152. © 1977 by Richard D. Irwin, Inc.

Resource dynamics

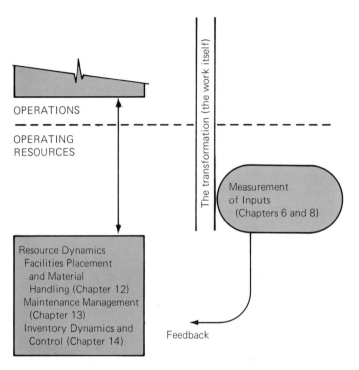

OPERATIONS

OPERATING
RESOURCES

The transformation (the work itself)

Measurement
of Inputs
(Chapters 6 and 8)

Resource Dynamics
  Facilities Placement
    and Material
    Handling (Chapter 12)
  Maintenance Management
    (Chapter 13)
  Inventory Dynamics and
    Control (Chapter 14)

Feedback

CHAPTER 12
Facilities placement and material handling
CHAPTER 13
Maintenance management
CHAPTER 14
Inventory dynamics and control

Part Five, Resource Dynamics, concerns operating resources as they enter the organization, are cared for, and leave. These actions are resource dynamics, as opposed to resource plans. Resource dynamics may be thought of as a life cycle in four stages, as follows:

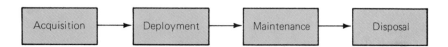

Acquisition includes contracting for plant and equipment, purchasing materials and tools, and hiring people. Chapter 14 includes contracting and purchasing; hiring is a topic more suitable for a personnel management book.

Deployment includes locating plants, positioning operating and handling equipment within plants (plant and office layout), and handling resource movements (mostly materials). Each of these topics is examined in Chapter 12.

Maintenance means keeping operating resources in good working order. Maintenance management of plant and equipment is covered in Chapter 13. Physical care and storage of materials is a form of maintenance examined in Chapter 14.

Disposal is getting rid of excess resources. Chapter 14 considers disposal of excess inventories.

As is shown in the sketch on the opposite page for Part Five, resource dynamics is closely related to the operations scheduling and control function. Schedules for operations depend on availability of operating resources, and operating resource dynamics, in turn, follows operations scheduling.

The sketch also shows feedback information returning to the resource-dynamics block. Feedback information regarding inventories is particularly important, because paperwork accompanies the large volume of inventory transactions, and the paperwork may be summarized into useful performance data.

chapter 12

FACILITIES PLACEMENT AND MATERIAL HANDLING

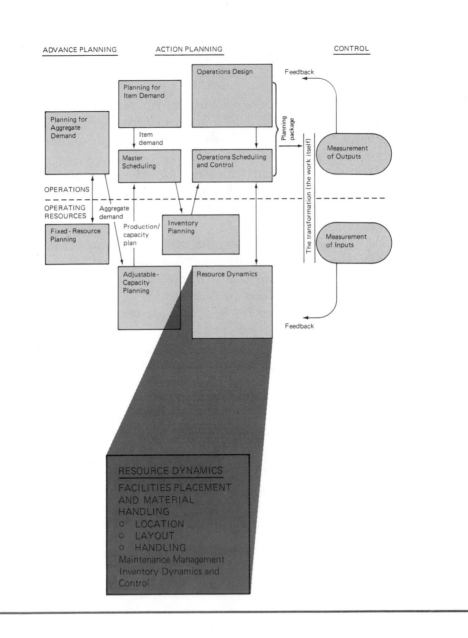

ADVANCE PLANNING   ACTION PLANNING   CONTROL

Operations Design

Planning for Item Demand

Planning for Aggregate Demand

Item demand

Master Scheduling

Operations Scheduling and Control

Feedback

Planning package

Measurement of Outputs

OPERATIONS

OPERATING RESOURCES

Aggregate demand

Fixed - Resource Planning

Production/ capacity plan

Inventory Planning

The transformation (the work itself)

Measurement of Inputs

Adjustable - Capacity Planning

Resource Dynamics

Feedback

RESOURCE DYNAMICS

FACILITIES PLACEMENT AND MATERIAL HANDLING
○ LOCATION
○ LAYOUT
○ HANDLING
Maintenance Management
Inventory Dynamics and Control

The subject of this chapter is deployment of facilities and materials. Facilities include plant and equipment; materials handling is treated broadly to allow for the handling of other resources (such as tools and people) besides materials.

Deployment is the second of the four life-cycle stages for operating resources which are referred to as resource dynamics, as is shown below:

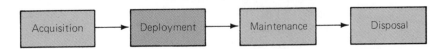

Deciding on where to locate geographically is the initial deployment question. Geographic *location* decisions apply to plants, offices, and wholesale/retail outlets. Location of equipment within plants, offices, and wholesale/retail outlets is a second type of location decision; the usual term for this is *layout* (of equipment).

Shorter-range deployment decisions concern adjustable capacity: work force, materials, and tools. In this chapter the focus is on physically *handling* these resources—moving them from one location to another. In goods-producing firms, handling materials is the dominant resource-handling problem. But well-designed handling systems integrate material handling with the transportation of work force (where necessary) and tools. Furthermore, the handling system should be designed along with plant and office layout, as the goals of layout and handling overlap considerably.

LOCATION

Location of plants, offices, and wholesale/retail outlets is a broad topic. In fact, location theory is treated as a separate branch of economic theory. In this book there is room to treat the topic in only a small way. We focus mainly on how location decisions are affected by handling distances and costs.

It should be noted, however, that operations/operating resources factors are seldom dominant influences on location decisions. The casual student of history and current events is probably aware of a variety of reasons why organizations locate or relocate. Some move to escape labor unions—for example, movement of the textile industry to the South. Some locate near scientific centers—for example, the clustering of semiconductor manufacturers in "Silicon Valley" near San Francisco. Nuclear power plants locate where water for cooling is plentiful; aluminum producers desire to locate where electric power is cheap.

Retailers tend to cluster in shopping centers, partly for marketing reasons and partly because of zoning (legal) restrictions. Manufacturers and wholesalers often locate in urban industrial parks because the municipality and private developers have aggressively induced companies to locate there.

The meat-packing industry has, in recent years, undergone extensive relocation. Packing plants have moved out of the cities and into rural stock-raising and -feeding locales. In many cities hospitals and clinics cluster into health-care encalves. The major location factor in both of these cases seems to be movement/handling of resources: livestock on the one hand and medical personnel, supplies, and patients on the other. Analysis of handling costs in such cases is sometimes simple and straightforward. If there are multiple sources and destinations for resource movement, the resulting problem complexity may be addressed by using the transportation method of linear programming, considered next.

Transportation-cost analysis

The simplex method of linear programming was introduced in Chapter 10, and a simplex example for determining optimal product mix is contained in the supplement to Chapter 10. Simplex may also be used in analysis of transportation costs, but the simplex approach is cumbersome. The transportation method was developed as a simpler alternative. Some limitations of the transportation method, in contrast with simplex, should be noted:

Transportation method—limited to problems involving a single homogeneous resource (which must be moved in quantity from multiple sources to multiple destinations).

Simplex method—suitable for a single homogeneous resource or a variety of unlike resources (e.g., various resource inputs transformed into various resource outputs or products, as in the supplement to Chapter 10).

The transportation method is in two steps. First, an initial feasible transportation routing is developed—a routing pattern that satisfies demand and supply (capacity) constraints. Second, the initial solution is improved until the optimum is reached. There are alternative techniques for developing initial and optimal solutions:

Initial-solution techniques:
1. Northwest-corner rule.
2. Vogel's approximation method (VAM).

Optimal-solution techniques:
1. Stepping-stone method.
2. Modified distribution method (MODI).

Our discussion shall be limited to northwest-corner and stepping-stone—and VAM in the chapter supplement. MODI, not discussed, generates the same result as stepping-stone but by a different procedure. NW-corner is a quick way to get started. VAM is a slower way to begin, but it approximates (*approaches* is a better word) the optimum. If VAM is used for the initial solution, fewer steps are likely to be required in developing the optimum.

Transportation-method example

The following example of the transportation method shows its usefulness in location decisions. The example demonstrates another use of the method as well: determining optimum transportation routings once geographic locations of sources and destinations have been set. The example is long, and it is divided into parts.

EXAMPLE 12–1
Transportation
method for
locating a
printing plant in
the Hawaiian
Islands

Basic problem. The *Island Explorer,* a newspaper serving the Hawaiian Islands, is at present printed in two plants. One plant is in Honolulu on the island of Oahu, and the other is in Hana on the island of Maui. The two printing plants serve readers in the six major islands: Oahu, Maui, Hawaii, Kauai, Molokai, and Lanai.

Printing capacity has become insufficient at Honolulu and Hana. Honolulu's capacity is 300 pallets of newspapers per week, and Hana's capacity is 100 pallets per week. Demands are: Oahu, 275 per week; Maui, 60 per week; Hawaii, 60 per week; Kauai, 50 per week; Molokai, 30 per week; and Lanai, 20 per week. Total demand, 495, exceeds capacity, 400, by 95 pallets per week, which are lost sales.

The publisher has decided to locate a third printing plant either at Hilo on Hawaii or at Lihue on Kauai.[1] A transportation-cost analysis is needed to support the location decision.

Additional problem data—Hilo location. Figure 12–1 is a map of the island region. The arrows between islands in Figure 12–1A show all possible routes—and air-transportation costs—from printing plants to destinations if the new plant is located at Hilo. No arrows lead into Oahu, Maui, and Hawaii, because the Honolulu, Hana, and Hilo plants can provide newspapers to readers on their own islands at zero air-transportation cost.

For analyzing a plant location at Lihue instead of Hilo, Figure 12–1B applies. It shows three arrows leading into Hawaii instead of into Kauai.

Transportation matrix—Hilo location. In the transportation method routes and costs are organized as a transportation matrix. Quantities to be transported from each source to each destination are also shown on the matrix. Figure 12–2 is the matrix for the Hilo plant-location option. Transportation costs are shown above the slash (/) in each cell of the matrix. The upper left or "northwest"-corner cell, for example, represents the route from Honolulu to the island of Lanai, with a transportation cost of $7 per pallet. Demands for the three destinations are shown at the bottom of the three destination columns: 20, 30, and 50. Supply of the three sources, at the right in the three source rows, is the net transportable capacity of each. Net capacities, computed below, are based on the logic that each printing plant services its own island:

$$\text{Honolulu net capacity} = \text{Honolulu gross capacity minus Oahu demand}$$
$$= 300 - 275 = 25$$

$$\text{Hana net capacity} = \text{Hana gross capacity minus Maui demand}$$
$$= 100 - 60 = 40$$

$$\text{Hilo net capacity} = \text{Capacity shortage minus Hawaii demand}$$
$$= 95 - 60 = 35$$

The above calculation for Hilo is based on a plan for the Hilo plant to have a capacity just sufficient to meet the capacity shortage, 95, that was mentioned at the outset.

---

[1] A note on pronunciation to those unfamiliar with the lingual heritage of the 50th state: Pronounce every letter of a Hawaiian word. Thus, Kauai is pronounced Kah-oo-ah-ee.

FIGURE 12-1
Map showing
transportation
routes and costs

A. New plant at Hilo

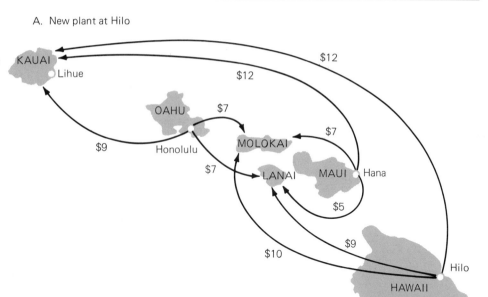

B. New plant at Lihue

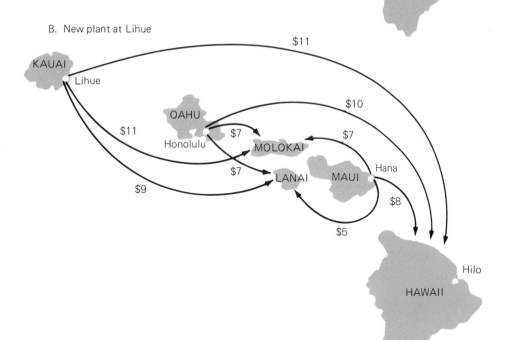

Note: Transportation costs are per pallet of newspapers.

FIGURE 12-2
Transportation matrix, Hilo location

Sources	Destinations: Lanai	Molokai	Kauai	Supply
Honolulu	7 / 20	7 / 5	9	25
Hana	5	7 / 25	12 / 15	40
Hilo	9	10	12 / 35	35
Demand	20	30	50	100 / 100

Supply and demand are totaled in the lower right corner of Figure 12–2. Both equal 100 pallets per week.

Initial solution—Hilo location. A feasible solution following the NW-corner rule is developed in Figure 12–3. A beginning allocation is made to the NW-corner cell, Honolulu-Lanai. The most that can be allocated is 20, which is Lanai's entire require-

FIGURE 12–3
NW-corner initial solution, Hilo location

Sources	Destinations: Lanai	Molokai	Kauai	Supply
Honolulu	7 / 20 →	7 / 5 ↓	9	25
Hana	5	7 / 25 →	12 / 15 ↓	40
Hilo	9	10	12 / 35	35
Demand	20	30	50	100 / 100

ment; this leaves 5 more units available from Honolulu, which goes into the adjacent cell to the right, Honolulu-Molokai. Molokai needs 25 more units, which it gets from the adjacent cell below, Hana-Molokai. This leaves 15 more available from Hana, which goes into the adjacent cell to the right, Hana-Kauai. Kauai needs 35 units more, which it gets from the adjacent cell below, Hilo-Kauai. All rim requirements are now met; the solution is feasible. (An equally simple initial solution could be developed from the SW, NE, or SE corners; the NW corner has no particular significance.)

The total weekly transportation cost for the NW-corner solution is $950 per week, as calculated below:

Honolulu-Lanai:	$ 7 × 20 = $140 per week
Honolulu-Molokai:	7 × 5 = 35 per week
Hana-Molokai:	7 × 25 = 175 per week
Hana-Kauai:	12 × 15 = 180 per week
Hilo-Kauai:	12 × 35 = 420 per week
	Total $950 per week

The NW-corner solution may usually be improved. (See the VAM solution in the chapter supplement as an improved alternative to this NW-corner solution.) Improvements would aim, for example, at avoiding the $12 cells (to Kauai from Hana and from Hilo) in favor of low-cost cells, like the $5 Hana-to-Lanai cell, which was not used in the NW-corner solution. Improvements may be developed by trial and error or by the stepping-stone or MODI methods, which may be computerized.

Optimal solution—Hilo location. After all improvements have been taken, an optimal solution is achieved. The optimum for the Hilo location is given in Figure 12–4. The total weekly transportation cost for the optimal solution is calculated below:

Honolulu-Kauai:	$ 9 × 25 = $225 per week
Hana-Lanai:	5 × 20 = 100 per week
Hana-Molokai:	7 × 20 = 140 per week
Hilo-Molokai:	10 × 10 = 100 per week
Hilo-Kauai:	12 × 25 = 300 per week
	Total $865 per week

The improved solution, at $865 per week, is $85 per week less than the NW-corner solution, at $950 per week. If the plant is to be built at Hilo, the optimal solution should constitute the transportation routing plan. But first we must see whether it is more economical to build at Lihue.

Additional problem data—Lihue location. The publisher of the *Island Explorer* has decided that if the plant is built in Lihue, it will have five pallets per week of excess capacity. The reason is projected expansion of the market to the small island of Niihau near to Kauai. But projected transportation costs that would apply to Niihau are not included in the current transportation-cost analysis.

Transportation matrix—Lihue location. The excess capacity at Lihue results in an unbalanced transportation problem: Supply exceeds current demand by five pallets per week. The transportation method still works, but only after demand is artificially adjusted upward to equal supply. The necessary adjustment is the addition of a dummy column with a dummy demand of 5 in the transportation matrix. (In the reverse situation, demand greater than supply, a dummy row with the required extra supply is added to the matrix.)

Figure 12–5 shows the adjusted matrix. The demands, including the dummy demand of 5, total 115 pallets per week. The supply (capacity) for Lihue is set at 50 in order

FIGURE 12-4
Optimal
transportation
solution, Hilo
location

FIGURE 12-4
Optimal transportation solution, Hilo location

that supply be equal to demand. The dummy's transportation costs are set at zero, because it costs nothing to ship to a dummy destination.

Initial solution—Lihue location. An initial feasible solution using the NW-corner rule is shown in Figure 12–6. The total weekly transportation cost for the NW-corner solution is $965, as calculated below:

Honolulu-Lanai:	$ 7 × 20 = $140	per week
Honolulu-Molokai:	7 × 5 = 35	per week
Hana-Molokai:	7 × 25 = 175	per week
Hana-Hawaii:	8 × 15 = 120	per week
Lihue-Hawaii:	11 × 45 = 495	per week
Lihue-Dummy:	0 × 5 = 0	per week
	Total $965	per week

As we noted in developing the Hilo solution, NW-corner is subject to improvement. For the Lihue analysis, we shall manually improve the NW-corner solution using the stepping-stone method. While computers usually perform these calculations, there are insights to be gained from manual calculations.

Optimal solution—Lihue location. Stepping-stone begins with a degeneracy test. The solution is degenerate if the number of cells in the solution ("filled" cells, that is) is not equal to one less than the number of sources (S) plus destinations (D), or $S + D - 1$. In this case there are six filled cells resulting from the NW-corner method, and $S + D - 1 = 3 + 4 - 1 = 6$. The number of filled cells equals $S + D - 1$, so the initial solution is not degenerate. If it were degenerate, the solution would have to be modified slightly in order to proceed with the stepping-stone method.

Next, empty cells are tested. The test determines whether the solution can be improved—that is, whether the total transportation cost can be reduced—by transferring some units into an empty cell. But supply-and-demand restrictions ("rim conditions") must be maintained.

FIGURE 12–5
Transportation matrix with dummy destination, Lihue location

Sources \ Destinations	Lanai	Molokai	Hawaii	Dummy	Supply
Honolulu	7	7	10	0	25
Hana	5	7	8	0	40
Lihue	9	11	11	0	50
Demand	20	30	60	5	115 / 115

The first empty cell to test is Honolulu-Hawaii. Suppose that one pallet-load is transferred to that cell. That added unit creates an imbalance, which requires a series of corrections, as shown in Figure 12–7A. The pallet-load can be transferred from Hana in the same column; this keeps the total in the column at 60, but it drops the total in the Hana row from 40 to 39. The correction is to add one unit to the Hana-Molokai

FIGURE 12–6
NW-corner initial solution, Lihue location

Sources \ Destinations	Lanai	Molokai	Hawaii	Dummy	Supply
Honolulu	7 — 20	7 → 5	10	0	25
Hana	5	7 — 25 → 15	8	0	40
Lihue	9	11	11 — 45 → 5	0	50
Demand	20	30	60	5	115 / 115

A. Testing the Honolulu-Hawaii cell

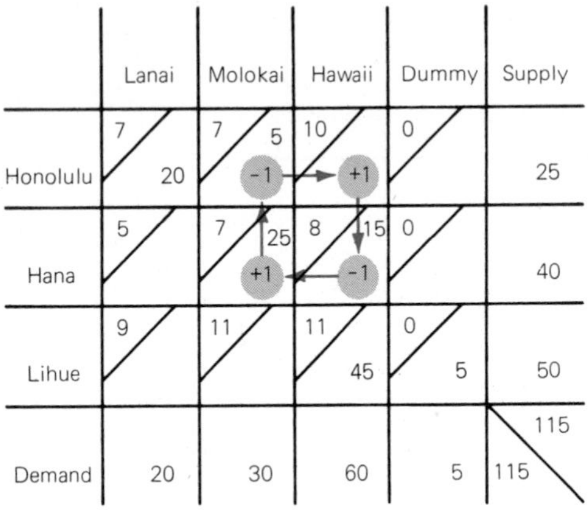

Cell	Units		Rate		Cost change
Honolulu-Hawaii	+1	x	$10	=	+$10 per week
Hana-Hawaii	−1	x	$8	=	−$8 per week
Hana-Molokai	+1	x	$7	=	+$7 per week
Honolulu-Molokai	−1	x	$7	=	−$7 per week
Net change				=	+$2 per week

B. Testing the Honolulu-dummy cell

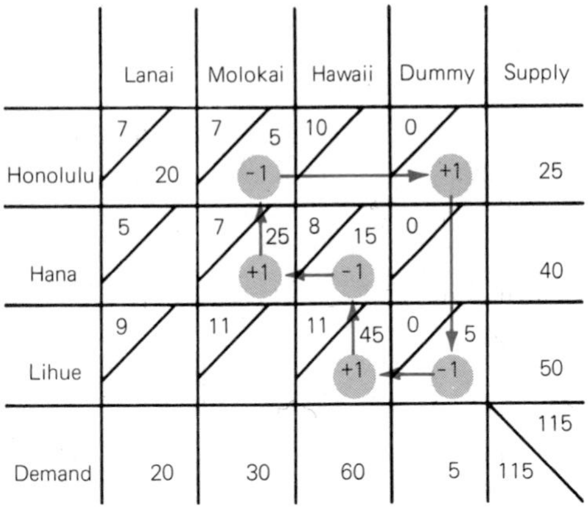

Cell	Units		Rate		Cost change
Honolulu-Dummy	+1	x	$0	=	$0 per week
Lihue-Dummy	−1	x	$0	=	$0 per week
Lihue-Hawaii	+1	x	$11	=	+$11 per week
Hana-Hawaii	−1	x	$8	=	−$8 per week
Hana-Molokai	+1	x	$7	=	+$7 per week
Honolulu-Molokai	−1	x	$7	=	−$7 per week
Net change				=	+$3 per week

FIGURE 12–7
Stepping-stone revisions, Lihue location

cell, which brings the Hana row back up to 40 but also raises the Molokai column total from 30 to 31. The correction is to subtract one unit from the Honolulu-Molokai cell; this brings Molokai back to 30 and also drops the Honolulu row total back to 25 (recall that one unit was added to Honolulu-Hawaii in the first step, which raised the Honolulu row total to 26). In Figure 12–7A the four steps—adding one, subtracting one, adding one, and subtracting one—are shown connected by arrows. The rectangular circuit of pluses balanced by minuses in affected rows and columns preserves rim values.

The effect on transportation cost is calculated at the right-hand side of Figure 12–7A. Adding one unit in the Honolulu-Hawaii cell increases transportation cost by $10

C. Testing the Hana-Lanai cell

	Lanai	Molokai	Hawaii	Dummy	Supply
Honolulu	7 / 20 / -1	7 / 5 / +1	10	0	25
Hana	5 / +1	7 / 25 / -1	8 / 15	0	40
Lihue	9	11	11 / 45	0 / 5	50
					115
Demand	20	30	60	5	115

Cell	Units		Rate		Cost change
Hana-Lanai	+1	x	$5	=	+$5 per week
Honolulu-Lanai	-1	x	$7	=	-$7 per week
Honolulu-Molokai	+1	x	$7	=	+$7 per week
Hana-Molokai	-1	x	$7	=	-$7 per week
Net change				=	-$2 per week

D. Improved transportation solution

	Lanai	Molokai	Hawaii	Dummy	Supply
Honolulu	7	7 / 25	10	0	25
Hana	5 / 20	7 / 5	8 / 15	0	40
Lihue	9	11	11 / 45	0 / 5	50
					115
Demand	20	30	60	5	115

			New cost		
Honolulu-Molokai:	$7	x	25	=	$175 per week
Hana-Lanai:	$5	x	20	=	$100 per week
Hana-Molokai:	$7	x	5	=	$35 per week
Hana-Hawaii:	$8	x	15	=	$120 per week
Lihue-Hawaii:	$11	x	45	=	$495 per week
Lihue-Dummy:	$0	x	5	=	$0 per week
					$925 per week

FIGURE 12-7
(continued)

per week; Hana-Hawaii decreases cost by $8 per week; and so forth. The net change is +$2 per week. This is a higher cost, so the test fails. Honolulu-Hawaii should remain an empty cell; no newspapers should be sent via that route.

The next empty cell is Honolulu-Dummy. The test is shown in Figure 12-7B. This test requires pluses and minuses in six rather than four cells: a minus offsetting every plus in three rows and three columns. There is no other way to preserve rim values and thus satisfy both supply and demand.

The test starts by adding one unit to the Honolulu-Dummy cell. Next, one unit must be subtracted from Lihue-Dummy and one unit added to Lihue-Hawaii. Why not add to Lanai or Molokai instead of to Hawaii? A simple reason is that we want to test only one empty cell at a time, and adding Lihue-Lanai or Lihue-Molokai, which are empty, would confound our test of the empty Honolulu-Dummy cell. To

E. Testing the Hana-dummy cell

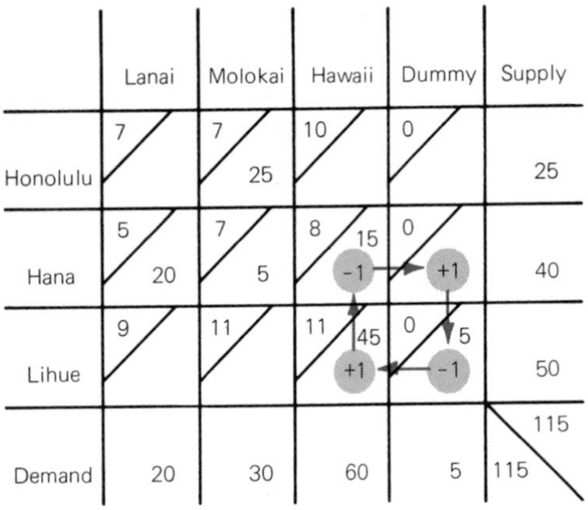

Cell	Units		Rate		Cost change
Hana-Dummy	+1	×	$0	=	$0 per week
Lihue-Dummy	−1	×	$0	=	$0 per week
Lihue-Hawaii	+1	×	$11	=	+$11 per week
Hana-Hawaii	−1	×	$8	=	−$8 per week
Net change				=	+$3 per week

F. Testing the Lihue-Lanai cell

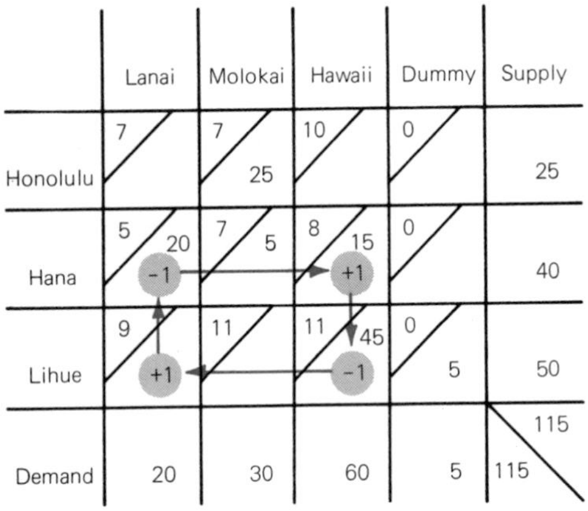

Cell	Units		Rate		Cost change
Lihue-Lanai	+1	×	$9	=	+$9 per week
Hana-Lanai	−1	×	$5	=	−$5 per week
Hana-Hawaii	+1	×	$8	=	+$8 per week
Lihue-Hawaii	−1	×	$11	=	−$11 per week
Net change				=	+$1 per week

FIGURE 12–7
(continued)

conduct a pure test of only one cell at a time requires that all other cells involved in the test be already filled.[2]

After adding one unit to the Lihue-Hawaii cell, one unit is subtracted from Hana-Hawaii, one unit is added to Hana-Molokai, and one unit is subtracted from Honolulu-

---

[2] Lee offers a picturesque explanation of the rule that only filled cells be used to support the test of an empty cell:

> When we walk into a Japanese garden, we often see a beautiful pond. There are water lilies, goldfish, frogs and dragonflies. Then, no doubt, we will notice a set of stepping-stones going across the pond. We can go across the pond if we carefully step on these stones. [In] the stepping-stone method . . . we evaluate all the empty cells by carefully stepping on the occupied cells. We should always remember that if we step on an empty cell, we shall be in the water, screaming, "help!"

Sang M. Lee, *Linear Optimization for Management* (Petrocelli-Charter, 1976), p. 261 (HD20.5.L39).

G. Testing the Lihue-Molokai cell

	Lanai	Molokai	Hawaii	Dummy	Supply
Honolulu	7	7 / 25	10	0	25
Hana	5 / 20	7 / 5 / −1 → +1	8 / 15 / +1	0	40
Lihue	9	11 / +1	11 / 45 / −1	0 / 5	50
					115
Demand	20	30	60	5	115

Cell	Units		Rate		Cost change
Lihue-Molokai	+1	x	$11	=	+$11 per week
Hana-Molokai	−1	x	$7	=	−$7 per week
Hana-Hawaii	+1	x	$8	=	+$8 per week
Lihue-Hawaii	−1	x	$11	=	−$11 per week
Net change				=	+$1 per week

FIGURE 12–7
(concluded)

Molokai. These steps keep the Lihue row at 50, the Hawaii column at 60, the Hana row at 40, the Molokai column at 30, and the Honolulu row at 25. The net change, calculated at the right-hand side of Figure 12–7B, is +$3 per week; therefore the test fails.

The Hana-Lanai cell is tested as shown in Figure 12–7C. Adding a unit to the cell saves $2 per week, so the test passes. If moving one unit into the Hana-Lanai cell saves $2, then moving three units would save $6, moving seven units would save $14, and so forth. (Costs are linearly related to quantities in linear programming.) When an empty-cell test saves any money, you want to move maximum units into that cell to save maximum dollars. The maximum here is 20 units, because 20 is the limit that may be subtracted from the "minus" cells without going negative. It is the Honolulu-Lanai cell that so limits the quantity moved: Honolulu-Lanai is at 20 in Figure 12–7C, and it is reduced to zero (emptied) in the improved solution of Figure 12–7D. Each of the other cells tested in Figure 12–7C was also changed by 20 units (up or down).

To the right in Figure 12–7D are cost calculations for the new solution. The new cost is $925 per week. That is $40 less than the NW-corner initial cost of $965—which is to be expected, since 20 units were moved at a savings of $2 each.

Whenever units are moved within a matrix, cell testing begins all over again. Conditions have changed, and cells previously tested might test out differently.

Thus, we turn again to the first cell, Honolulu-Lanai. The cell need not be retested, since it was emptied for good reason in the test in Figure 12–7C. The Honolulu-Hawaii and Honolulu-Dummy cells need not be retested either, because inspection shows that testing them would include exactly the same cells and transportation costs that were involved in the earlier tests of those cells.

Hana-Dummy is the next cell to be tested. The test result, in Figure 12–7E, is a net change in cost of +$3 per week; the test fails.

The last two tests are Lihue-Lanai and Lihue-Molokai. Both result in $1 greater cost and therefore fail; see Figure 12–7F and 12–7G.

There are no more empty cells to be tested. The solution in Figure 12–7D, costing $925 per week, is optimal. If the *Island Explorer* builds at Lihue, $925 is the expected transportation cost.

Assessment. The Hilo location has an optimal transportation cost of $865 per week. For the Lihue location the optimal transportation cost is $925 per week; that is $80 or 9.2 percent more. We would expect the Lihue solution to cost more, because Hawaii's demand of 60 in the Lihue solution is 10 units more than Kauai's demand of 50 in the Hilo solution. Therefore, the total to be shipped from the three sources to the three destinations is 110 (not counting the dummy demand) if the plant is at Lihue, but it is 100 if the plant is at Hilo.

The Hilo location has the advantage in transportation costs. The costs of such other items as labor, taxes, utilities, plant construction, and raw materials would also bear on the decision and indeed may be more significant than transportation cost. (We have focused on the transportation method, because it is a useful model for sorting out complex transportation routing options, not because transportation costs dominate.) Less tangible factors, such as labor availability and future expansion, may also be important in the final location decision.

Transportation method— Other factors

If a nonoptimal solution is degenerate, there are not enough filled cells to be able to test all of the empty ones. The correction is to place a very small quantity into one or more empty cells to eliminate the degeneracy. The small quantity is generally designated ϵ (the Greek letter *epsilon*). The transportation cost for the cell, times the quantity, ϵ, equals zero because ϵ is so small; therefore ϵ does not alter the cost structure but only facilitates solution. There is no good rule for selecting the proper empty cell in which to place ϵ. You can try a spot and see whether it works out; if not, try another.

The use of ϵ was actually devised for computer-based solutions. Putting ϵ into a degenerate matrix allows the computer to proceed with the normal transportation algorithm. (The computer treats ϵ as equaling the lowest character in the computer's collating sequence; in COBOL that character is called LOW-VALUES.)

Sometimes there is reason to exclude certain transportation routes. For example, fishermen between Maui and Lanai may object to the noise of a predawn airplane transporting newspapers from Hana. Perhaps one hotheaded fisherman may decide to shoot at the plane. The newspaper may avoid the risk of being hit by excluding Hana as the source of newspapers to Lanai. In the transportation method it is simple to assure that the Hana-Lanai cell ends up empty: Use the value ∞ (symbol for infinity) as the transportation cost in that cell (the symbol M, for *m*aximum cost, is sometimes used).

LAYOUT

Once a plant has been located and built, plant facilities must be arranged. Arranging facilities is referred to as layout planning. Layout planning is performed under two conditions: New layout planning is required for new facilities. Relayout is periodically undertaken for existing facilities.

In our discussion of layout we consider four major layout-planning environments. One is the environment of the mechanized assembly line, in which layout tends to have a high level of permanence. The second is the labor-intensive assembly line, which is not so permanently built in but is expensive to keep in good balance. The third environment is job-lot production, which involves complex relayout trade-offs. The fourth environment is that of people-intensive services, in which interpersonal relationships are key factors.

Our discussion also considers three distinct layout types. These are the product-oriented layout, the process-oriented layout, and the fixed-position layout.

Layout-planning environments

In manufacturing, layout planning can have important long-range effects, because it is costly to reposition large machinery and related facilities. In a petrochemical plant, for example, the layout of tanks, chambers, valves, pipes, and other equipment is so much a part of the plant itself that major relayout may never be feasible. In steel manufacturing the expense of major relayout is also enormous, and steel plants may close rather than retool and relayout to improve efficiency, meet pollution control regulations, and so on. Mechanized assembly lines are also expensive to relayout. Retooling of auto assembly lines is undertaken every few years for marketing reasons (design changes). But the *layout* of retooled machines changes infrequently. In each of these examples—petrochemicals, steel, autos—the initial choice of layout in a plant greatly restricts the firm's ability to respond to major changes in product line or technology for years to come.

Labor-intensive assembly lines and job-lot production facilities are less fixed, and therefore initial layout planning is less critical for these. The focus is on relayout. In the labor-intensive assembly line, relayout itself is not prohibitively costly because people and their tools are mobile. There may, however, be significant costs of planning; line balancing; retraining; and rearranging benches, storage facilities, material handling aids, and any larger pieces of equipment.

Job-lot production often involves large machines and storage and handling aids. Relayout may be affordable, however, because the equipment used tends to be general-purpose, loosely coupled, and built to move; conveyors may even be on wheels. Also, with shorter production runs, there is a need for flexibility and movability. The need for relayout tends to grow over time. Symptoms of the need include production bottlenecks, backtracking, overcrowding, poor utilization of capacity (including space), poor housekeeping, too much temporary storage, a growing ratio of handling time to productive time, and missed due dates.

Labor-intensive services tend to undergo frequent relayouts. It is not uncommon for office workers to "wonder where my desk will be" on Monday morning. The desk may be across town in newly rented office space. There are few physical impediments to moving; most offices could move overnight if telephone hookups could be arranged. With few physical problems, office relayout tends to focus on interpersonal relationships and a productive atmosphere.

Layout types

Process-oriented layout (process layout, for short) means arranging facilities into process groups. There are symbiotic benefits of putting like facilities together. These benefits include mutual support, learning from one another, cross-training, talent development, and flexibility. Job-shop production of goods or services is generally process-oriented.

Product-oriented layout (product layout, for short) means laying out the facilities along product-flow lines. It is reasonable to let product flow dictate the layout if the product is made in volume, that is, repetitive production. The high cost of the product layout may be amortized over the large volume. The main benefits are faster product throughput with lower unit costs of handling and less work-in-process inventory.[3]

In the fixed-position layout (fixed layout, for short), the product itself is fixed and the facilities must come to it. Construction is a good example. Another good example is the manufacture of oversized vehicles and heavy equipment— items too large to be moved easily.

Mixed layouts. Mixed layouts—two or more layout types in a single facility—are common, if not the norm. An apt example is a restaurant that sets up a buffet brunch line on Sunday mornings. The patron has the choice of going through the buffet line or sitting down and ordering from a menu. A patron entering the restaurant may be thought of as raw materials; a patron leaving is finished goods. The production process transforms an empty patron into a full one.

The two types of patrons are processed through two types of facilities layouts. The buffet customer goes through a product layout, very much like an assembly line. The menu customer is processed in a fixed-position layout: Menu, waiter, food, drinks, and check come to the fixed position.

Figure 12–8 is a sketch of such a restaurant. The sketch identifies the product layout and the fixed layout, and it shows that the restaurant also includes a process layout. The process layout is found in the kitchen. There foods, not patrons, are the products that are being transformed. The process areas in the kitchen layout include grill, salad area, range, desert area, ovens, freezer, and pantry.

As compared with a single-layout facility, a mixed-layout facility is more difficult to plan, more costly to equip, and more troublesome to maintain. Marketing and facility-utilization advantages may offset these disadvantages.

Distinguishing features. A few of the common distinguishing features among the three primary layout types are given in Figure 12–9. The figure lists eight operating resource factors and the ways in which each factor is commonly treated in the three layout types.

The first factor, facilities arrangement, serves to define the three layout types. The definitions were discussed earlier.

Type of production is the second factor. Process layout is dominant in the

---

[3] A movement centered in Great Britain is promoting a concept known as group technology (GT). GT features a *group layout* in which a process layout is altered to gain some of the advantages of the product layout. The idea is to group machines by common families of products. See John L. Burbidge, *The Introduction of Group Technology* (Wiley/Halstead Press, 1975) (TS155.B787).

FIGURE 12-8
Mixed layout in
a restaurant

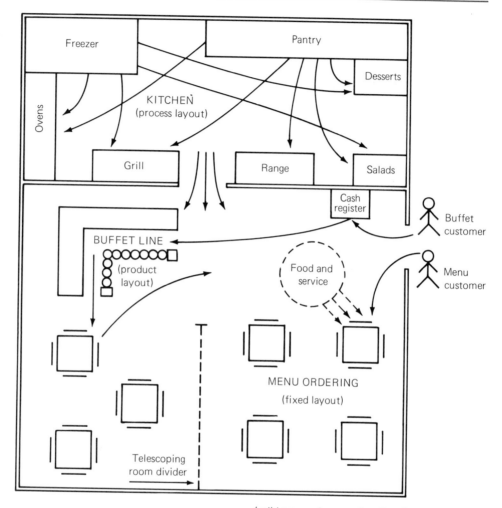

(solid arrows show product flows)

job shop and common in job-lot production. Product layout is typical of repetitive production and sometimes of the production of larger lots in the job-lot environment. Fixed layout is common in construction and industrial projects (as opposed to research and development projects) and in limited-quantity large-scale production (e.g., missiles and dynamos). Fixed layout is also found where special human services are provided: surgery, grooming, feeding, and so forth.

Cost of layout/relayout is third. Process layout involves groupings of work centers that need not be closely coupled by elaborate handling devices; thus process layout is generally not costly. As was explained earlier, the cost of a product layout is very high if the production line is mechanized, but the cost may be moderate if it is labor-intensive. Fixed layout of a construction site

FIGURE 12–9
Common characteristics of operating resources for each layout type

Operating resource factors	Types of layout		
	Process-oriented	Product-oriented	Fixed-position
1. Facilities arrangement	Facilities grouped by specialty	Facilities placed along product-flow lines	Facilities arranged for ease of movement to fixed product
2. Type of production	Job-lot and job-shop	Repetitive and job-lot	Construction and industrial projects; medium-quantity large-scale production; special human services
3. Cost of layout/relayout	Moderate to low	Moderate to very high	Moderate to low
4. Relayout frequency	Moderately often to often	Seldom	Moderately often
5. Facility utilization	Usually low	High	Moderate
6. Type of production facilities	General-purpose	Special-purpose	Mostly general-purpose
7. Handling equipment	Variable-path	Fixed-path	Variable-path
8. Worker skill level	Skilled	Unskilled	Unskilled to skilled

involves arranging for temporary parking and storage of operating resources, a low-cost function. Fixed layout for goods production and for special human services may involve more permanence; examples are well-equipped bays for assembling a missile or for wheel alignment and the well-equipped operating room. The layout cost can be low if the facilities are mainly general-purpose hand tools, but it can be moderate if special lighting, holding fixtures, work pits, and so forth, are involved.

The fourth factor is relayout frequency. Process relayouts tend to be frequent or moderately frequent since cost is not a major impediment. Product layouts are seldom redone because they are designed for long-term volume production and because relayout costs may be high. Fixed layouts are not often redone because they are geared to a certain unique type of project, product, or service—for a medium or long time period.

Fifth is facility utilization. The facilities in process layouts tend toward low utilization. This is not desirable, but it is typical, because the job mix is typically changing and different jobs use different facilities. Very high facility utilization—little idleness—is a goal of the product layout. Good line balancing helps achieve the goal. With fixed layouts the tendency is toward moderate facility utilization because the product mix is not very diverse.

The sixth factor is type of production facilities. Process layouts usually involve standard general-purpose machines, hand tools, handling aids, and so forth. Special-purpose machines, handling aids, and other facilities are worth spending money on if the product volume is large, as it normally is where there are product layouts. In fixed layouts the focus on special products permits the use of some special-purpose facilities, such as an overhead crane or a mounting fixture, but most of the facilities are likely to be general-purpose since production volume is not high.

Seventh is handling equipment. Variable-path equipment—carryable or on wheels—provides needed handling flexibility in process layouts. Fixed-path handling equipment—conveyors, elevators, chutes, and so on—helps cut handling time in product layouts. Variable-path handling equipment is common in fixed layouts because low production volume usually does not require fixed-path devices.

The eighth factor is worker skill level. Workers in process layouts tend to be skilled. Stenographers, machinists, plumbers, computer operators, nurses, and accountants fit the category. In industry such workers were historically organized by craft in the American Federation of Labor. If the skill is based on higher education or apprenticeship, the pay tends to be high; if it is based on vocational training, the pay tends to be moderate or low. Workers along product layouts tend to be unskilled. Such workers may become adept at installing rivets or molding or soldering connections. But they are classed as unskilled because they are easily replaced from a labor market of the unskilled. Historically, they are the type of assembly-line workers that were organized into the Congress of Industrial Organizations (CIO). Their pay may be minimum wage in smaller nonunion shops, although under Walter Reuther's presidency CIO members gained respectable pay levels. In fixed layouts skilled craftsmen, such as carpenters or welders, often work alongside unskilled laborers, such as shovelers or riveters.

While there are many more operating-resource factors that could be discussed, these eight are perhaps enough to demonstrate the basic nature of each layout type. Figure 12–9 is not intended as an if-then analysis device. One would not try to conclude, for example, that if there are skilled workers, low facility utilization, and so on, a process layout should be developed.

A better basis for determining proper type of layout is number of products and quantity of product units flowing between work areas. Muther[4] proposes the product-quantity (P-Q) chart as a simple tool for indicating layout type. An example of the P-Q chart is shown in Figure 12–10. The chart is intended to show the P-Q combination that leads to a product layout, a process layout, or a mixed layout: A small number of products produced in large quantities suggests a product layout; a moderate number produced in variable quantities suggests a mixed layout; and a large number produced in small quanti-

---

[4] Richard R. Muther, *Systematic Layout Planning* (Cahners, 1973), pp. 3–1 through 3–8 (TS178.M87).

FIGURE 12–10
P-Q chart
indicating type
of layout

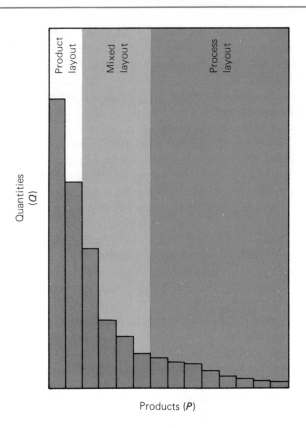

Products (*P*)

ties suggests a process layout. But P-Q analysis is only preliminary. Much more complete analysis is needed to produce the layout plans.

Layout-planning methodology

In a complex layout situation hundreds or thousands of small jobs and medium lots may be in progress at any given time. Repetitive, job, and project work may be included, with products and resources delivered to work centers via many routings.

When routes are so diverse, does it matter how work areas are arranged in a building? Yes, it does. Dominant flow patterns are likely to be discernible among the apparent jumble of routings. Layout analysis may be directed toward finding those patterns. One layout principle or heuristic is to arrange work areas in the order of dominant flows. A goal is to get production or resources into, through, and out of each work center in minimum time at reasonable cost. The less time products/resources spend in the flow pattern, the less chance they have to collect labor and overhead charges.

Other factors besides flows may be important in a given layout situation. If so, the factors should be identified and combined with flow data. The combined data may be assessed in order to develop an ideal arrangement of work areas. Then space requirements for the arrangement are determined. The last step in layout planning is to fit the arrangement into the available space, that is, a building. Several optional layout plans may be developed for managers to choose from. These steps in layout planning are reviewed below, along with useful layout-planning tools.

Steps	*Possible tools*
1. Analyze product (resource) flows.	Flow diagram From–to chart
2. Identify and incorporate nonflow factors, where significant.	Activity-relationship (REL) chart Combined REL chart
3. Assess data and arrange work areas.	Activity-arrangement diagram
4. Determine space-arrangement plan.	Space-relationship diagram.
5. Fit space arrangement into available space.	Floor plan Detailed layout models

Layout-planning example

The following multipart example demonstrates the above layout-planning steps. The method and some of the tools were developed by Muther, who calls the approach *systematic layout planning* (SLP).[5] SLP is a practical approach that is widely referenced and extensively used.

EXAMPLE 12–2
Layout planning, Globe County Offices[6]

The main contact that Globe County citizens have with county offices is in registering and licensing vehicles. Many complain because the three county offices involved have not consolidated their services. On busy days there are waiting lines at all three offices, and many vehicle owners must visit all three.

Recently elected heads of the three offices have decided to jointly undertake consolidation. A consultant has been hired to conduct layout analysis using SLP.

The consultant's preliminary investigation shows that there are 16 activities to be located in the available space. The 16 activities and their space requirements are listed in Figure 12–11. Significant product/resource flows are found among four of the activities, which are starred in the figure. Three of these are the service counters that patrons visit; patrons constitute the "product" flow. The fourth is the copier, which employees from two of the service-counter areas must visit rather often; employees carrying documents to be copied constitute the resource flow. There is negligible product/resource flow between the three county offices.

Product (resource)-flow analysis. The four work areas in which there are heavy flows are studied in more detail. Counts of numbers of people traveling between each pair of activities are taken. The results are sometimes summarized on a simple device called a from–to chart. (It is much like the distance chart found on many road maps.) The from–to chart provides a measure of volume of flow *from* one work area *to* another. Volume may be measured in natural units like pounds, pallets, gallons, or people. Sometimes it is important to account for distance and transportability as well as volume of flow. (Composite measures of these flow factors have been developed but are not discussed.)

The from–to chart for the county offices is given in Figure 12–12. The greatest

---

[5] *Ibid.*

[6] This is an adaptation of a real case. Thanks go to Ross Greathouse of Greathouse-Flanders Associates, Lincoln, Nebraska, for providing original case data.

FIGURE 12–11
Major work
areas, county
offices

Activity	Space requirements (square feet)
County assessor's office	
1. Management	600 sq. ft.
*2. Motor vehicle—counter	300
3. Motor vehicle—clerical	240
4. Real estate—counter	480
5. Real estate—clerical	480
6. Assessors	960
County clerk's office	
7. Management	840
8. Recording and filing—counter	240
9. Recording and filing—clerical	960
*10. Motor vehicle—counter-clerical	960
County treasurer's office	
11. Management	420
*12. Motor vehicle—counter-clerical	1,600
13. Real estate, etc.—counter	480
14. Real estate, etc.—clerical	960
Support areas	
*15. Mail and copier	240
16. Conference room	160
Total	9,920 sq. ft.

* Significant flows.

FIGURE 12–12
From–to-chart,
county offices

From \ To	Clerk 1	Assessor 2	Treasurer 3	Copier 4	Totals
Motor-vehicle counter —clerk 1		A 100	B 250	D 30	380
Motor-vehicle counter —assessor 2	C 20		A 100	D 10	130
Motor-vehicle counter —treasurer 3	C 40				40
Copier 4	D 30	D 10			40
Totals	90	110	350	40	590

Flow volume in people per day.

Types of product flow:

A Patrons licensing newly purchased vehicles.
B Patrons licensing same-owner vehicles.
C Patrons to wrong office—backtrack to correct office.
D Round trips to copier.

flow, an average of 250 people per day, is from the motor-vehicle counter in the county clerk's office to the motor-vehicle counter in the county treasurer's office. These are patrons relicensing their vehicle(s). They may skip the assessor's office since the assessment is mailed to them. The next largest flow is for licensing of newly purchased vehicles, which requires a visit to all three county offices; 100 per day is the average flow. Other flows are smaller: backtracking by patrons who are in the wrong office (backtracking is generally indicated by entries below the diagonal dashed line on the from-to chart); and round trips to the office copier by counter employees of the county clerk and the county assesor.

The next step is to simplify the volume-of-flow numbers. The SLP approach is to convert to a rating value designated by one of the five vowels:

A for *a*bnormally high flow.

E for *e*specially high flow.

I for *i*mportant flow.

O for *o*rdinary flow.

U for *u*nimportant moves of negligible flow volume.

Figure 12–13 displays the conversion. Each activity pair or route is entered in the left column. Pairs are listed in descending order of flow volume based on examination of the from–to chart data. Flow volume for each pair is plotted as a horizontal bar. Bars are then divided at logical breakpoints to form a zone for each vowel. Breakpoints are a matter of judgment, but the "vital few" normally form the A-zone, and the "insignificant many" normally form the U-zone. In Figure 12–13 one pair, route 1–3, seems worthy of the A designation. There are two E's, three I's, and three O's. There are many U's, but none were entered on the from–to chart, and therefore none are identified here.

Nonflow factors. Material flows often dominate layout analysis in manufacturing firms. In offices a variety of nonflow factors may be more important. The relayout of the three Globe County offices is rather more like the typical manufacturing case in that flow (of patrons) is the dominant concern. Still there are several nonflow factors to consider. Nonflow factors are especially important for layout of support areas. In SLP nonflow factors may be combined with flow ratings on an activity-relationship (REL) chart. The REL chart for the three county offices is shown in Figure 12–14.

The chart packs a lot of data into a small space, but it is easy to interpret. The activity on a downsloping line intersects with the activity on an upsloping line at a diamond-shaped box. Each box holds a code. The vowel in the top half indicates how close together activities should be, and the number in the bottom half is coded to reasons why. Vowel and number codes are listed on the figure. Vowel codes are the same in every SLP analysis. Number codes (reasons) depend on the situation.

A few steps leading to the combined REL chart are not included here for the sake of brevity. The omitted steps include separately charting nonflow factors, combining them with flow factors, converting the combined totals to vowel ratings, and finally plotting the vowel ratings on the combined REL chart.[7]

The 120 diamond boxes in Figure 12–14 include one A, one E, 21 I's, 25 O's, 72 U's, and no X's. The A indicates that it is *a*bsolutely necessary for customer-service people in the clerk and treasurer offices to be close together. Reasons why are work

---

[7] See steps in Muther, *Systematic Layout Planning*, appendix 12.

FIGURE 12–13
Conversion of
flow volume to
vowel rating
scale

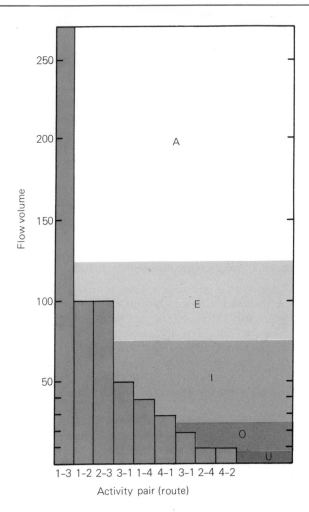

flow (1), employee sharing between departments (3), and share counter (4). The same reasons apply to the E—for *e*specially important—in the box connecting customer-service people in the clerk and assessor office.

The 21 I's—for *i*mportant—include all five reasons: Several I's are for the sharing of counter space between different types of service in the same office. Several I's are for employees from the same office who need to be close only for supervision (same boss) reasons. A few I's are for facilitating personal communication between counter and clerical people. Work flow and employee sharing also explain a few I's.

The 25 O's call for *o*rdinary closeness. Two are for counter people who need to visit the copier room. Three are for personal communication among the three managerial staffs. The rest are for convenience of supervision.

The 72 U's show *u*nimportant relationships between employees in unlike work areas, departments, and so forth.

Activity arrangement.   The combined REL chart is converted to an activity-arrangement diagram. The diagram shows the arrangement of all activities (circles are used

FIGURE 12-14: Combined activity relationship (REL) chart, county offices

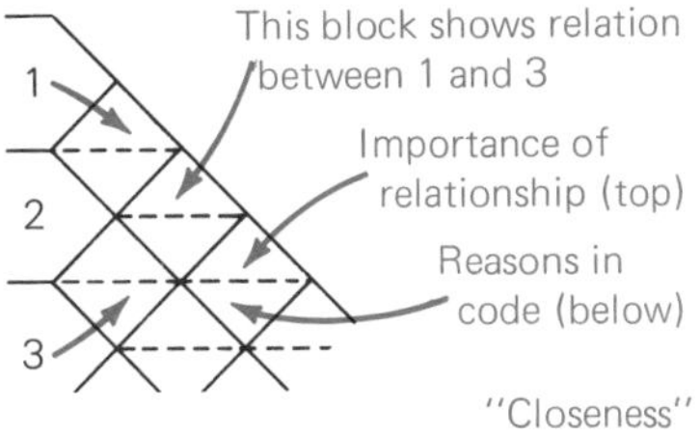

Value	Closeness	Number of ratings
A	Absolutely necessary	
E	Especially important	
I	Important	
O	Ordinary closeness OK	
U	Unimportant	
X	Not desirable	

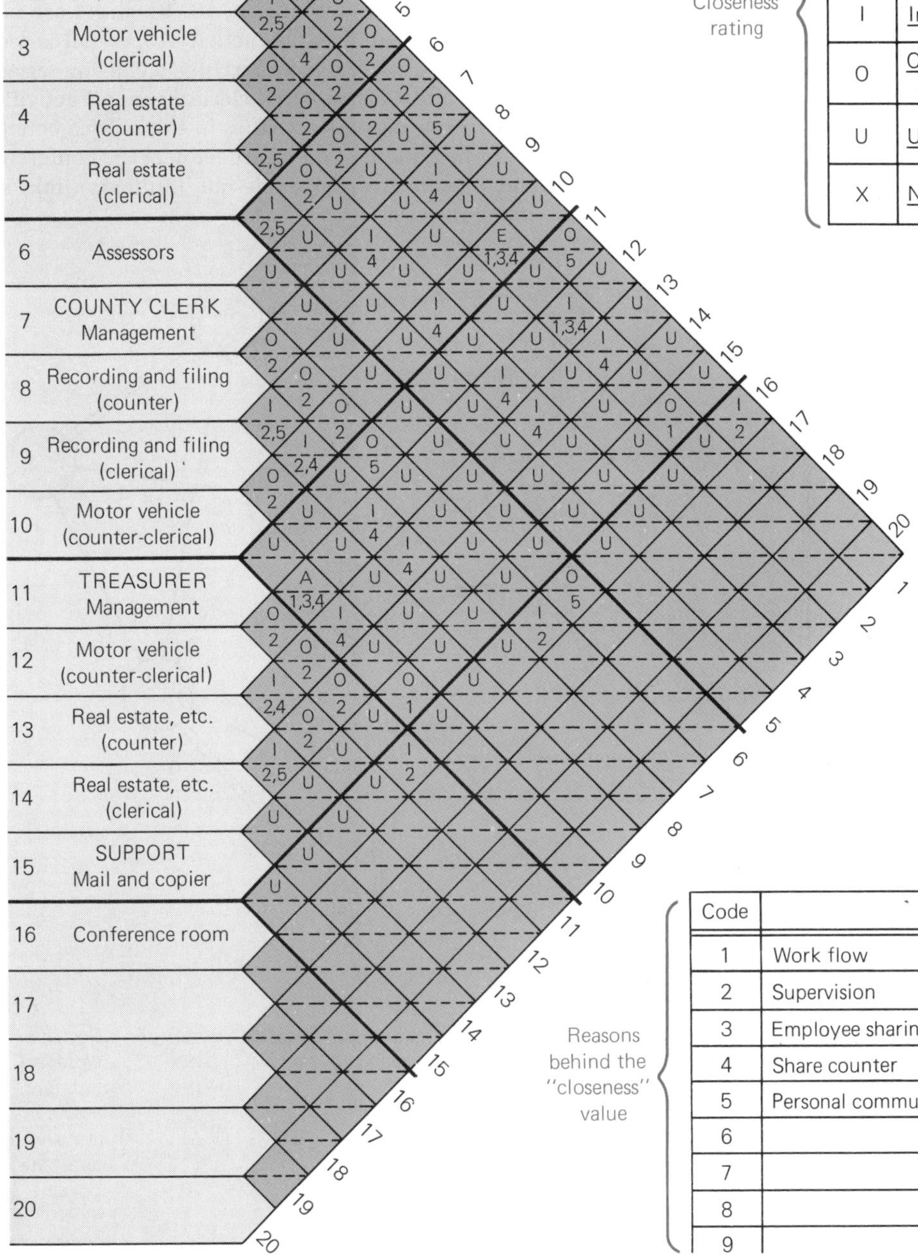

Code	Reason
1	Work flow
2	Supervision
3	Employee sharing (between departments)
4	Share counter
5	Personal communication
6	
7	
8	
9	

Reasons behind the "closeness" value

Source of REL chart form: Richard Muther and Associates, Kansas City, Missouri. Used with permission.

to represent them) without any restrictions on space, shape, utilities, halls, and so on.

Figure 12–15 is the activity-arrangement diagram for the Globe County offices. Lines between circles correspond to relationship codes, as the key on the figure shows. Four lines mean four degrees of closeness for A-codes; three lines mean three degrees of closeness for E-codes, and so on. Distances between circles are set according to degree of closeness as much as possible. Activity 2 is in a central position, because it is the hub of the largest number of flow lines: 15. Activities 8, 10, 12, and 4 are next at 13, 11, 10, and 10 flow lines, respectively. These five, plus activity 13, are all service-counter activities, and earlier ratings placed considerable importance on having service-counter activities together. Activities 3, 9, and 14 are related clerical-support activities; two lines (important) connect them with counterpart activities in the service-counter cluster. The three sets of double lines at the bottom of the chart connect the conference room (16) to the managers (1, 7, and 11). Most of the single-line (ordinary) links are between managers and activities under their supervision.

FIGURE 12–15
Activity-arrangement diagram, county offices

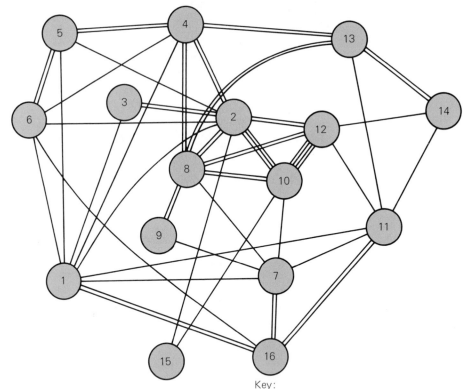

Key:

Vowel code	Closeness value	Number of lines	Degree of closeness
A	4	IIII	Absolutely necessary
E	3	III	Especially important
I	2	II	Important
O	1	I	Ordinary
U	0		Unimportant
X	–1	⋁⋀⋁	Not desirable

Space arrangement. The activity-arrangement diagram is converted to a space-relationship diagram in two steps:

1. Determine space needs (square feet) for each activity. This is done by calculating space needs for each desk, chair, file cabinet, shelf, machine, table, and so on. The organization's own space standards and widely available industry space standards (e.g., 300 square feet per auto in a parking lot) may serve as a guide. Square footage requirements for each of the 15 activities of the Globe County office were given in Figure 12–11.

2. Draw the space-relationship diagram, arranging activities like the activity-arrangement diagram but with activity blocks sized according to space needed. Space between blocks is unimportant at this point, but it is a good idea to try to end up with a shape similar to that of an existing or proposed building.

Figure 12–16 is the result. It is in the generally rectangular shape of the space into which the activities must fit. All of the service-counter activities are together at the top, where customers may have access. The clerical staff is in the middle band of the chart, which is convenient for supporting the service-counter people at the top and the managers at the bottom.

FIGURE 12-16
Space-relationship diagram, county offices

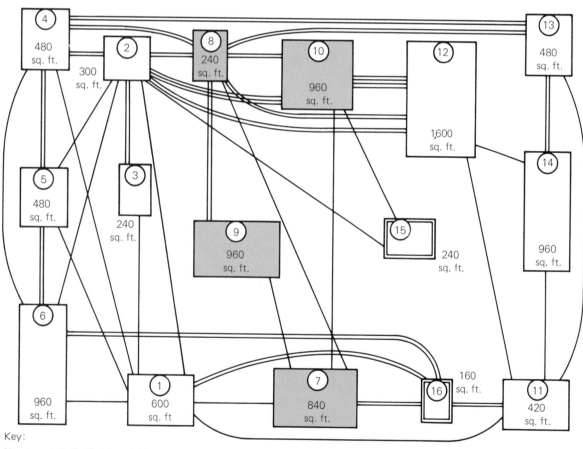

Key:

Numbers 4, 2, 8, 10, 12, and 13 are service-counter activities

County assessor activities are 1–6.

County treasurer activities are 11–14.

County clerk activities are shaded.

Shared activities are are double-bordered.

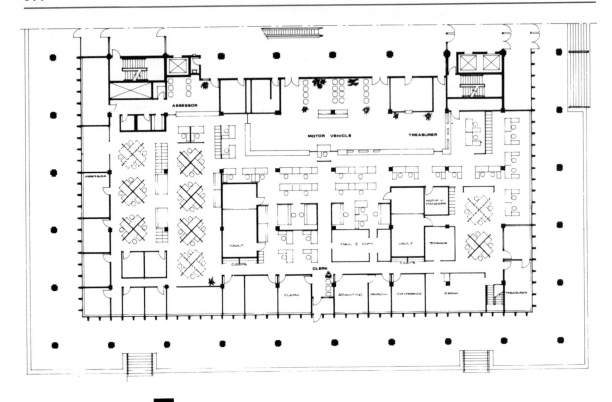

FIRST FLOOR SOUTH PLAN

Source: Greathouse-Flanders Associates, Lincoln, Nebraska. Used with permission.

FIGURE 12-17
Possible final
layout, county
offices

The space-relationship diagram may be regarded as a rough layout.

Layout into available space. In this step open spaces on the space-relationship diagram are eliminated, and the activity areas are fitted in with walls, aisles, utility hookups, and so forth. Activity areas may be shortened and narrowed, shaped into an L, and so on.

After the activity areas have been suitably fitted together, facilities and furnishings *within* each area must be laid out. In a large and complex layout, analysis within activity areas may proceed through the full SLP pattern: *detailed* analysis of material flow, nonflow factors, REL chart, and so on. Templates or two- or three-dimensional models of desks, files, chairs, and so on, are useful in the final stages of detailed layout. These steps are not discussed in this example.

Figure 12–17 is an example of what the final layout (or one of a few alternative final layouts) might look like for our example. The final layout follows the activity arrangement of the space-relationship diagram rather well, but of course activity shapes have been changed to fit the available floor space.[8]

---

[8] While Figure 12–17 is an actual layout of county offices, all the preceding parts of this example were mock designs.

Interior design

Consultants are often hired to perform or assist in-house staffs in layout planning. One may choose an interior-design consultant, an architectural firm or a firm specializing in layout. Layout specialists are more engineering-oriented and more likely to focus on material-flow factors. Interior-design specialists are more likely to focus on appearance, atmosphere, light, acoustics, and so forth. It may be best to deal with layout specialists in plant layout, where function rather than appearance tends to be the dominant concern. Interior-design consultants are more important for office layouts, especially offices in which the public is met frequently.[9] Architects are helpful when new construction or extensive remodeling is involved.

Interior-design consulting for office layout has grown dramatically in recent years. A major reason has been the *open-office concept*, which became popular in the 1960s and commonplace in the 1970s. (Fifteen articles with "open office" in the title appeared in *Office* magazine alone from 1975 to 1980.) The open-office idea eliminates many floor-to-ceiling walls and de-emphasizes the compartmentalization of people. Open-office layouts are thought to foster communication and to provide flexibility for easy relayout. Modular office furniture and movable partial-height partitions aid in achieving these goals.

Maintaining a degree of privacy and cutting noise in open offices have been emphasized in recent years. Means of doing this include the use of wall carpeting, sound-absorbent panels, acoustical screens, fabric-wrapped desk-top risers, and freestanding padded partitions. Office landscaping (the use of plants) has become another important factor in office layout.

The open office is not for all. The Indianapolis office of Peat Marwick Mitchell & Co. (an accounting firm) wanted the feeling of openness but needed privacy for reasons of client confidentiality. Its solution was fixed seven-foot-high partitions with glass extending from them to the ceiling.

Vendors of office equipment often provide interior-design consulting in connection with product promotion.

Computer assistance in layout planning

Developing the activity-arrangement diagram, the space-relationship diagram, and the layout diagram (see Figures 12–15, 12–16, and 12–17) is not a straightforward process. There are a lot of options for arranging circles, blocks, and activities; a good deal of trial and error on an erasable surface is common. Where you decide to place a circle on the activity-arrangement diagram tends to limit your choices for placing blocks and activities on the next two diagrams.

Computer programs are available to eliminate some of the drudgery and to avoid placement-decision errors in this *search* phase of layout planning. Three prominent programs deserve mention:[10]

CORELAP (*C*omputerized *R*elationship *L*ayout *P*lanning).

---

[9] An architectural firm specializing in interior design developed the layout of Figure 12–17.

[10] Copies of the programs are available as follows: CORELAP from Engineering Management Associates of Boston; ALDEP from IBM; and CRAFT from the IBM Share Library System. Enhanced versions of these programs are announced rather often.

ALDEP (*Automated Layout Design Program*).

CRAFT (*Computerized Relative Location of Facilities Technique*).

Each program produces computer-printed layouts.

CORELAP and ALDEP are similar. Both use closeness ratings from the REL chart (see Figure 12–14) as inputs. CORELAP produces a single layout of rectangular-shaped departments; department lengths and widths are set forth in advance. The CORELAP algorithm maximizes common borders for closely related departments. ALDEP produces a number of alternative layouts; each is scored based on the adjacency of departments. A weakness is that irregularly shaped departments tend to emerge.

CRAFT differs from CORELAP and ALDEP in two respects. First, CRAFT requires that an existing layout be input; its job is to improve the layout. Second, CRAFT is based on flow (from–to chart) data but not on nonflow (REL chart) data; the CRAFT algorithm minimizes material handling cost. Generally speaking, CRAFT is suitable mainly for plant layout; because of their flexibility, CORELAP and ALDEP are suitable for either plant or office layout.[11]

ASSEMBLY-LINE BALANCING

Product layouts—for repetitive production—may be developed using SLP. An additional problem is achieving balanced capacity along the repetitive production line. This class of planning is known as assembly-line balancing, or line balancing for short.

Planning a product layout for highly automated repetitive production is mostly a production engineering problem and beyond the scope of this book. Assembly lines, which are usually less automated, present challenging product-layout problems of interest to the operations manager. The major planning problem is assigning balanced amounts of work to *workers* at work stations.[12] (In plants with multiple assembly lines, each line might be balanced as a first step, followed by SLP to locate the assembly lines in the plant.)

Line balancing generally proceeds after division of labor. In division of labor the complete assembly process is divided and subdivided into tasks; division should be carried down to the point where a task would be assignable to only a single worker. The list of subdivided tasks is the chief input into line-balancing analysis.

---

[11] More complete comparison of the three programs may be found in chapter 3 of Richard L. Francis and John A. White, *Facility Layout and Location* (Prentice-Hall, 1974) (TS178.F7).

[12] Line balancing could be applied to balancing work among *machines* in automated production as well as among workers on assembly lines. In practice, machine balancing is largely impractical. The capacities of a collection of machines tend to be inherently unbalanced, because most machines cannot be bought in a wide variety of different capacities at different prices. Also, it is possible for a worker to split time between geographically separated tasks to help balance a line, but machines are not very mobile or flexible. Thus, workers are the main focus in line balancing.

There are a variety of line-balancing analysis methods. Most begin with a precedence diagram. Analysis of data in the diagram may be by trial and error, heuristics, algorithms, and mathematical models.[13] Computer packages are available for some of the algorithms and models. In the method discussed in this chapter a precedence diagram is developed, followed by analysis using a manual heuristic line-balancing procedure.

Precedence diagram

The precedence diagram thoroughly describes work elements and their sequential limitations. The type of precedence diagram considered here shows the earliest stage of assembly in which a given work element may be performed. Assembly stages are designated by roman numerals on the diagram, and each work element is aligned vertically with one of the roman numerals. Element durations, numbers, and perhaps descriptions appear on the diagram, and precedence restrictions are shown by arrows between elements.

The following example demonstrates the precedence diagram. The assembly task is clothing a male doll in a toy factory.[14] All of the work elements for such assembly would probably be done by a single assembler in a real toy factory, because the element times are very short. For the sake of illustration, we shall assume that the work elements could reasonably be divided among a number of assemblers along an assembly line. Precedence diagraming can be elaborated to allow for a variety of special restrictions, but this example is kept simple.

**EXAMPLE 12–3
Precedence diagram for line balancing, doll assembly**

A toy company is coming out with a new male doll. The doll itself and the doll's clothes are parts made off-line. The doll is to be clothed on an assembly line, with different items of clothing put on at different stations along the line. The stations are separately staffed (a typical assembly line). A balanced assembly line is sought. A precedence diagram is to be prepared to facilitate line balancing.

Given data:

Methods engineers have performed the division-of-labor step: They have determined that putting on each of 13 separate items of clothing constitutes a reasonable work element. The elements and element times are listed below.

---

[13] A heuristic is a search procedure that may solve a problem but offers no guarantee of doing so. If it can be proven that an exact solution exists, then this becomes an algorithm rather than a heuristic search procedure.

[14] The example is borrowed, except that the originators of the example called it "how to dress in the morning." It apparently did not occur to the originators that their easy-to-relate-to example might even be realistic if the setting were changed from dressing oneself to dressing dolls in a factory. That oversight may be forgiven, because the book containing the example is one of the better reference books on one of the many specialized topics of operations management: Theodore O. Prenting and Nicholas T. Thomopoulos, *Humanism and Technology in Assembly Line Systems* (Spartan Books, 1974), pp. 131–32 (TS178.4.P73).

Element	Element time, t (in 0.01 minute)
1. Put on undershorts	10
2. Put on undershirt	11
3. Put on left sock	9
4. Put on right sock	9
5. Put on slacks	22
6. Put on shirt	42
7. Put on left shoe	26
8. Put on right shoe	26
9. Put on belt	30
10. Insert pocket items (wallet, keys, and handkerchief)	20
11. Put on tie...........................	63
12. Put on coat	32
13. Put on hat	6
Total work-content time, Σt	306

Solution:

The precedence diagram for the given work elements is shown in Figure 12–18.

In the diagram, work elements are in the circles and element times are beside the circles. Arrows show precedence restrictions. The four elements under stage 1 have no predecessors and can be started anytime. No elements can begin until their predecessors have been completed.

In any one column work elements are independent of one another. Three of the elements—left sock, right sock, and hat—have lateral flexibility; that is, they may be moved one column to the right without disturbing precedence restrictions. With these kinds of flexibility, it is clear that a large number of combinations of work-station layout sequences satisfy precedence restrictions.

It may be noted that precedence diagrams are similar to the activity-on-node networks used in PERT/CPM (see Chapter 7). A difference is that the precedence diagram does not have a single start and a single end point, as is true of the PERT/CPM network. The reason is that assembly lines keep running rather than start and end at finite points in time, as projects do. Another difference is worth mentioning: The precedence diagram is not a sequence plan but only presents sequence limitations (the Roman-numeraled stages in Figure 12–18); the network is intended as a final plan.

Line-balancing analysis

A valid layout—one that includes all work elements and meets precedence restrictions—is a requisite in line balancing. A perfectly balanced line has zero balance delay, where balance delay, d, is:

$$d = \frac{nc - \Sigma t}{nc},$$

where

n = Number of work stations

FIGURE 12–18
Precedence
diagram,
clothing a doll

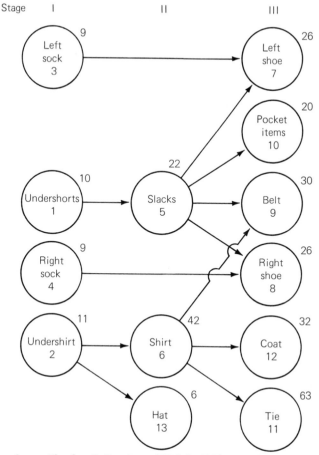

Stage   I   II   III

Source: Theodore O. Prenting and Nicholas T. Thomopoulos, *Human-ism and Technology in Assembly Line Systems* (Spartan Books, 1974), p. 132 (TS178.4.P73). Used with permission.

$$c = \text{Cycle time}$$
$$\Sigma t = \text{Total work-content time for one unit}$$

Manual heuristic method. A manual heuristic line-balancing method is explained below, using a continuation of the doll-assembly example.

EXAMPLE 12–4
Manual
heuristic line
balancing, doll
assembly

Total work content, Σt, for the doll assembly is 306 hundredths of a minute (see given data, Example 12–3). A first step in line-balancing analysis is expressing Σt in terms of its prime numbers. There are four prime numbers:

$$306 = 2 \times 3 \times 3 \times 17$$

The cycle time (the time to assemble one unit) for a balanced line is equal to the product of any combination of these prime numbers. The combinations yield the following possible cycle times:

$$c_1 = 2 \times 3 \times 3 \times 17 = 306$$
$$c_2 = 3 \times 3 \times 17 = 153$$
$$c_3 = 2 \times 3 \times 17 = 102$$
$$c_4 = 3 \times 17 = 51$$
$$c_5 = 2 \times 17 = 34$$
$$c_6 = 17$$

Perfect balance may be achieved by any of the following numbers of stations, each determined by dividing one of the six cycle times into Σt.

$$n_1 = \frac{\Sigma t}{c_1} = \frac{306}{306} = 1 \text{ station}$$

$$n_2 = \frac{\Sigma t}{c_2} = \frac{306}{153} = 2 \text{ stations}$$

$$n_3 = \frac{\Sigma t}{c_3} = \frac{306}{102} = 3 \text{ stations}$$

$$n_4 = \frac{\Sigma t}{c_4} = \frac{306}{51} = 6 \text{ stations}$$

$$n_5 = \frac{\Sigma t}{c_5} = \frac{306}{34} = 9 \text{ stations}$$

$$n_6 = \frac{\Sigma t}{c_6} = \frac{306}{17} = 18 \text{ stations (not feasible since there are}$$
$$\text{only 13 work elements)}$$

We want to see which of these numbers of stations fits the doll-assembly data best. The data from the precedence diagram, Figure 12–18, are rearranged as a table in Figure 12–19. Columns A, B, and D in the table are taken directly from the precedence

FIGURE 12–19
Tabular form of precedence relationships in "assembling clothes"

(A) Column number in precedence diagram	(B) Element number	(C) Remarks	(D) Element time, t	(E) Sum of element times	(F) Cumulative sum of times
I	3	→ II	9		
	1		10		
	4	→ II	9		
	2		11	39	39
II	5		22		
	6		42		
	13	→ III	6	70	109
III	7		26		
	10		20		
	9		30		
	8		26		
	12		32		
	11		63	197	306

diagram. Column C indicates elements that could be performed in a later stage. As has been mentioned, elements 3 and 4—put on socks—could be done in stage II as well as stage I; and element 13—put on hat—could be done in stage III as well as stage II. Column E sums the element times for each stage, and Column F cumulatively sums the stage time totals.

Figure 12–19 is inspected, along with the above data on cycle times and number of stations, for ways to achieve a balanced line. Several conclusions are clear:

1. Option n_5, calling for nine stations, may be rejected: Its cycle time of 34 is exceeded significantly by work element 6 with a time of 42 and by work element 11 with a time of 63.

2. Option n_4, calling for six stations, may also be rejected: Its cycle time of 54 is exceeded by work element 11's time of 63.

3. Option n_3 looks more promising. It calls for three stations, each with work content adding up to a cycle time, c_3, of 102. We can see from Figure 12–19 that the cumulative sum of stages I and II is close at 109. An obvious way to reduce it closer to 102 presents itself: Move element 13, with a time of 6, from stage II to stage III. This reduces the time for stages I–II to 103, which is very close to the 102 that is desired for perfect line balance.

Moving element 13 to stage III increases the stage III sum from 197 to 203. It is desirable to split the group into two stations, with cycle times of 102 and 101. To find a set of work element times whose sum is close to 102 or 101, it is efficient to begin by adding the larger numbers: Adding elements 11 and 12—63 and 32—gives 95; now add 6, the time for element 13, and you have 101. The remaining four elements—7, 10, 8, and 9—total 102.

The resulting solution is displayed in Figure 12–20. It is nearly perfect: Station 1 has a cycle time of 103; station 2, 102; and station 3, 101. This means that one doll

FIGURE 12–20
Improved line-balancing solution for "assembling clothes"

(A) Column number in precedence diagram	(B) Element number	(C) Remarks	(D) Element time, t	(E) Sum of element times	(F) Cumulative sum of times	
I	3		9			
	1		10			
	4		9			Station 1
	2		11			
II	5		22			
	6		42	103	103	
III	7		26			
	10		20			Station 2
	9		30			
	8		26	102	205	
	13	From stage II	6			Station 3
	12		63			
	11		32	101	306	

may be clothed every 103 hundredths of a minute, not counting transit time between stations. Station 1's capacity is fully utilized each cycle; station 2 wastes 0.01 minute per cycle; and station 3 wastes 0.02 minute per cycle. The waste or underutilization of capacity for the whole assembly line is known as the balance delay. It is the time wasted divided by total work time. By the previously given formula, balance delay, d, is:

$$d = \frac{nc - \Sigma t}{nc} = \frac{(3 \times 103) - 306}{3 \times 103}$$

$$= \frac{309 - 306}{309} = \frac{3}{309} \approx 1\%$$

Note that less than 3 stations is not feasible, since the precedence diagram, Figure 12–18, calls for several sequences going from stage I to stage II to stage III (e.g., 1 to 5 to 7). Options in between n_3 and n_4, i.e., 4 or 5 stations, are feasible, but reducing the balance delay below 1 percent seems unlikely. Therefore, n_3, is selected, and the analysis ceases.

Manual heuristic versus other methods. The heuristic method presented above yields good results, but considerable work has been done on developing algorithms and mathematical models that yield optimal results. Algorithms have been developed for mixed-model as well as single-model assembly lines. Mixed model means that more than one model of a product is assembled on the same assembly line. For example, a mixed-model doll-clothing line might accommodate male dolls, female dolls, large dolls, small dolls, and so forth; our example above was of a single-model line since it assembled one type of male doll. Mixed-model line balancing involves (1) determining the sequence of products (model numbers) progressing down the line and (2) balancing the line. Some line-balancing methods allow for various restrictions and special conditions: subassembly lines that feed main lines, distance and direction requirements, safety needs, special groupings of elements, zoning restrictions, maximum and minimum conveyor speeds, and so forth.

A variety of computer programs are available that incorporate some of the line-balancing algorithms and models. The heuristic programs generally yield good results and require minimal computer time. Manual methods, both heuristic and trial-and-error, are probably far more widely used. Computer methods will undoubtedly continue to gain in popularity as more industry people become acquainted with them.

HANDLING

The goals of layout and handling overlap. In layout, there are both nonflow and flow factors to consider; in handling, flow factors, that is, minimizing the cost of resource handling, are dominant. (Were it not for this commonality of goals, handling might just as well be discussed in conjunction with material storage in Chapter 14. As a matter of fact, the functions of the material handling analyst often include storage.) Our limited discussion of handling is concerned with handling concepts and handling analysis.

Handling concepts

The best handling system is that which handles least, for handling adds nothing to the product but cost. A well-established practice that aids in holding down handling cost is the unit-load concept. The simple idea is to avoid moving piece by piece and instead to accumulate enough pieces to move them as a unit load. Common unit loads are truckloads and rail-car loads in the transportation area. In handling, common unit loads are a loaded pallet, skid, drum, tote box, hand truck, and carton.

Handling costs may also be held down through planning aimed at avoiding duplication and overlapping. Apple[15] visualizes three approaches to handling: (1) The conventional approach is concern for point-to-point material flows. (2) The contemporary approach is that of an integrated plan for handling materials throughout a plant. (3) The progressive approach is a broader systems approach that includes incoming raw materials and outgoing finished goods as well as intraplant handling.

A fourth approach is proposed here. It is Apple's progressive (systems) approach, but applicable to *resource* handling, not just material handling. Besides materials, resource handling would include the handling of tools, people, and mail. A few examples of the resource-handling approach may be noted. For example, some multibuilding organizations operate a corporate taxi or courier service. At a given time a courier vehicle may be carrying workers, small parts, tools, and mail. Within a plant one might find an operatorless tractor-with-trailer carrying both materials and tools around a delivery route. In office areas robot "delivery boys" may carry mail and supplies on a circuit through hallways. A pneumatic-tube system serving plant and offices may move documents, small parts, tools, and funds (and, inevitably, pieces of birthday cake and perhaps an occasional insect or rodent—dispatched by the resident practical joker).

The resource-handling approach has evolved partly because of developments in handling technology, such as operatorless delivery devices and pneumatic tubes.[16] A greater reason is the economies gained by planning a system in which several resource types may be moved by a single handling device.

Many firms fail to gain these kinds of economies because planning is separate for each type of resource to be moved. The materials-management organization structure, discussed in Chapter 14, creates organizational links among all material-oriented activities in the firm. This helps bring about the kind of planning needed to integrate raw-material and finished-goods handling with intraplant handling (Apple's third approach). Broader planning is needed for the resource-

---

[15] James M. Apple, *Plant Layout and Material Handling*, 3d ed. (Ronald, 1977), pp. 338–39 (TS155.A58).

[16] But we are nowhere near a handling technology in which a Captain Kirk might say, "Beam up these ore samples, Scotty. And then beam me up."

handling approach. In one organization the solution was to hold occasional meetings on integrated handling. Representatives came from material handling, warehousing, receiving, shipping, motor pool, courier, mail, the parking coordinator (because employee vehicles were sometimes used for employee transportation and deliveries), and the technical librarian (who dispatched books and other technical matter to various employees).

Handling analysis

Handling analysis is in two basic steps: (1) analyzing resource flows and (2) prescribing handling methods. If the first step is well done, the second is rather easy.

The product-quantity (P-Q) chart, mentioned in connection with layout, may also play a role in handling analysis. In Figure 12–21, two sample P-Q curves are graphed. Assume that the shallow curve (light) is representative of all of a plant's material flows. The quantity is low for every one of the products (resources). With such uniform volume a single type of handling (a simple one in this case) may suffice for all products. By contrast, the dark curve is deep. Both high-volume and low-volume products are included. If that curve represented a plant's material flows, there would undoubtedly need to be two types of handling, one for mass handling and another for small quantities.

FIGURE 12–21
P-Q chart indicating type of handling

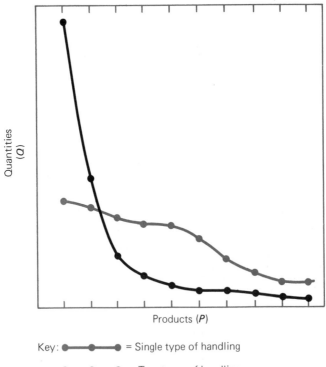

Key: ●——●——● = Single type of handling

●——●——● = Two types of handling

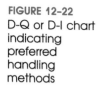

FIGURE 12–22
D-Q or D-I chart
indicating
preferred
handling
methods

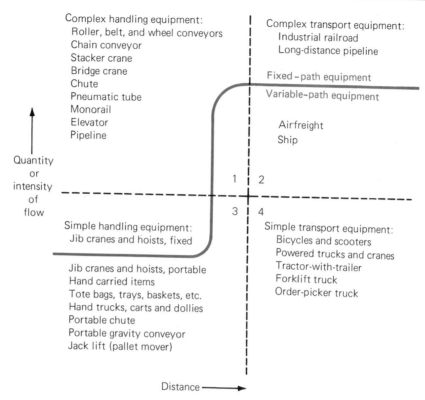

Data collected about each product or resource may be plotted on a distance-quantity (D-Q) chart—or, if products/resources are dissimilar, on a distance-intensity (D-I) chart. Intensity of flow, a measure developed by Muther, equals quantity times transportability. Transportability, in turn, is an artificial measure that may include size, density or bulk, shape, risk of damage, condition, and (sometimes) value of the given item.[17]

The D-Q or D-I chart helps show the types of handling methods needed. Figure 12–22 is a guide to interpreting points plotted on the D-Q or D-I chart. Four quadrants are shown in the figure. A low-distance, high-volume product would plot in the first quadrant, which suggests complex handling equipment, such as conveyors. Low-distance, low-volume calls for simple handling, such as hand-carry or other items in the second quadrant. High-distance, low-volume calls for simple transport equipment—any of the types of vehicles in the third quadrant. High-distance, high-volume, in the fourth quadrant, is sometimes symptomatic of poor layout. Where necessary, the condition calls for complex transport equipment, such as a railroad.

---

[17] A method for determining transportability may be found in Richard Muther, *Systematic Handling Analysis* (Management and Industrial Research Publications, 1969) (TS180.M8).

The solid line cutting through the chart indicates an additional distinction among equipment types. Above the line are fixed-path types of handling equipment; below the line are variable-path types. It is well to be cautious about investing in the fixed-path variety, because it may be too expensive to relocate or modify fixed equipment when conditions change. It is quite common to enter a plant of average age and see unused remnants of an overhead-conveyor or pneumatic-tube system up in the rafters. (But many firms are able to get some benefit from a mislocated overhead conveyor: Use it to store work-in-process inventories!) Operatorless tractors and self-guiding order pickers, popularized in the 1960s, were something of a breakthrough. They have fixed-path advantages, but it is cheap to change their route: Simply paint a new white line on the floor for those that optically follow a line, or embed a new wire in the floor for those that sense a magnetic field generated by a current-carrying wire.

After the preferred type(s) of needed handling have been noted, detailed analysis is necessary. Specific equipment is selected based on such factors as cost, reliability, maintainability, and adaptability. Vendors of material handling equipment are called upon to quote prices and, frequently, to help with detailed design and installation.

It is worth pointing out that systematic analysis, starting with products and product flows, is by no means the only way to resolve handling problems. The piecemeal way—perhaps starting with the notion that "we ought to acquire a powered-conveyor system"—is common. Piecemeal analysis features the *feasibility study,* in which this question is raised: Is it feasible to acquire the given equipment? The feasibility approach often proceeds from some rather blind presumptions. Still, the approach is quick and cheap, because it requires far less data collection than does systematic analysis. Also, a full-scale systematic analysis involves many organizational units, and it is hard to organize the effort more than perhaps once every five years. Handling problems crop up more often than that, which is why piecemeal analysis is popular.

SUMMARY

Deployment of operating resources includes geographically locating a plant, laying out facilities within the plant, and handling resources among the facilities. Minimizing handling is important in all three levels of deployment.

Location decisions must consider markets, labor, taxes, sources of supply, and a variety of other factors. Location decisions become more complex when there are several sources of goods (resources) and several destinations. Some of the complexity may be reduced through use of the transportation method of analyzing transportation costs among the plants.

The transportation method is set up as a from–to matrix with cost per unit shipped in each cell of the matrix. Quantities supplied (from) and demanded (to) are also shown on the matrix. The method calls for (1) developing an initial feasible solution (the NW-corner method or Vogel's approximation method may be used) and (2) improving the initial solution in successive steps (using the stepping-stone or modified distribution method). The idea is to develop a routing pattern that meets supply and demand at minimum transportation cost. When various new plantsites are being studied, the optimal transportation-cost routing pattern can be calculated for each so that relative cost advantages for each site can be seen.

Layout planning is arranging facilities or work activities in order to minimize product/resource flows and generally to optimize propinquity among related activities. Systematic layout planning (SLP) is a useful approach that usually begins with product and quantity analysis and identification. Next a from–to chart may be prepared to show flow characteristics for products (or resources) that move in quantity, and an activity-relationship (REL) chart may cover nonflow factors. The charts are assessed in order to arrange work areas on an activity-arrangement diagram, which does not identify the space needed for activities. That diagram is converted to a space-relationship diagram, which also shows square footage needs for each activity. The next step is to develop the activity-area layout to fit an actual floor plan. The three preceding steps may be manual or computer-assisted (as a single step). Finally, the details within each activity area are located on the floor plan, and the layout is complete.

SLP is suitable for office as well as plant layout. But interior design—furnishings, acoustics, light, color, signs, counters, landscaping, and so on—has become important in office layout, and interior designers tend to rely less on systematic analysis and more on art.

Layout of an assembly line is complicated by the goal of trying to fully utilize the capacity of each work station on the line. This is the problem of assembly-line balancing. Line-balancing analysis often begins with breakdown into work stations and identification of precedences among work stations on a precedence diagram. In a manual heuristic method of analyzing precedence-diagram data, alternatives are calculated for achieving a perfectly balanced line. The alternatives specify cycle time and number of work stations. Manual analysis leads to selection of a solution close to one of the alternatives. A perfectly balanced line is one that has zero balance delay, that is, full utilization of each work station. Promising computer programs are available for line balancing but are not widely used as yet.

Handling analysis aims at minimizing handling costs. Handling of unit loads and development of integrated handling systems that include movement of people, tools, and mail as well as materials are helpful in achieving that goal. Systematic handling analysis proceeds from product-quantity study to distance-quantity study. Distance-quantity (or distance-intensity) data suggest type of handling equipment: simple handling, complex handling, simple transport, or complex transport. Finally, specific equipment is selected. Variable-path handling equipment has the inherent advantage of adaptability. Smaller-scale handling problems may be solved by directly studying the feasibility of a proposed type of equipment, whereas large-scale problems tend to warrant full systematic analysis.

REFERENCES

Books

Apple, James M. *Plant Layout and Material Handling.* 3d ed. Ronald, 1977 (TS155.A58).

Bolz, Harold, ed. *Materials Handling Handbook.* Ronald, 1958 (TS149.B59).

Burbidge, John L. *The Introduction of Group Technology.* Wiley/Halstead Press, 1975 (TS155.B7287).

Francis, Richard L., and John A. White. *Facility Layout and Location: An Analytical Approach.* Prentice-Hall, 1974 (TS178.F7).

Muther, Richard. *Systematic Handling Analysis.* Management and Industrial Research Publications, 1969 (TS180.M8).

———. *Systematic Layout Analysis.* 2d ed. Cahners, 1973 (TS178.M87).

Prenting, Theodore O., and Nicholas T. Thomopoulos. *Humanism and Technology in Assembly Line Systems.* Spartan Books, 1974 (TS178.4.P73).

Sawyer, J. H. F. *Line Balancing.* Machinery Publishing, Brighton, 1970 (TS178.5.S3).

Periodicals (societies)

Factory Management.

Industrial Engineering (American Institute of Industrial Engineers).

Management Science (Institute for Management Science), includes quantitative and computer models for location and layout.

Material Handling Engineering.

Material Management Pacesetter (International Materials Management Society).

Modern Materials Handling.

Office, frequent articles on office layout.

PROBLEMS

Note: **Asterisked (*) problems require more than mimicry. They require judgment, and you should include discussion of reasons, assumptions, and outside sources of information.**

Plant location

1. Recyclation, Inc., has five aluminum-can collection stations located around the metropolitan area. Trucks periodically haul the cans to either of two can-crush facilities; one is referred to as the East facility, the other as the West facility. A third can-crush facility is to be set up, and two alternative sites—a North and a South site—are being considered. The average weekly volume of cans available from the five collection sites is given below, along with the can-crushing capacities of the two present and the two proposed sites. The costs of transportation from each collection site to each can-crush site are also given.

Collection sites	Supply (loads per week)	Routes From	To	Transportation costs per load
1	3	1	E	$8
2	3	1	W	4
3	4	1	N	3
4	5	1	S	7
5	1	2	E	5
		2	W	5
		2	N	7
		2	S	3
Can-crush sites	Capacity (loads per week)	3	E	1
		3	W	3
		3	N	3
East	5	3	S	5
West	7	4	E	6
North	6	4	W	2
South	6	4	N	3
		4	S	4
		5	E	7
		5	W	3
		5	N	5
		5	S	2

a. Develop the minimum transportation-cost solution if the new plant is built at the North site. Use NW-corner or VAM, and stepping-stone.
b. Develop the minimum transportation-cost solution if the new plant is built at the South site.
*c. Which site is preferable—North or South? Discuss in terms of transportation and also possible nontransportation factors. Do all can-crush sites operate at full capacity? Explain.

2. In a large woodshop tubs of sawdust accumulate in four locations (sawdust is sucked to those four locations via a vacuum system with tubes going to each machine). Several times daily the tubs are grabbed by a fork truck and taken to

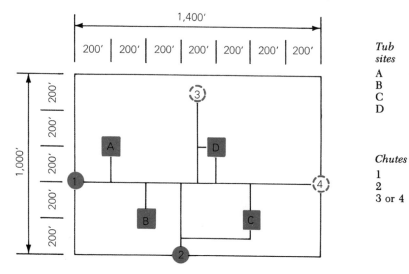

Tub sites	Sawdust produced (tubs per day)
A	10
B	13
C	7
D	15

Chutes	Capacity (tubs per day)
1	22
2	28
3 or 4	12

be dumped at chutes located at two sides of the building. Transportation cost works out to be $1 per 200 feet moved. A third dump chute is to be installed at one of two locations in order to cut move distance. The accompanying floor plan shows the layout with distances. Squares show where sawdust builds up in tubs; solid circles are present chutes; and dashed circles are alternative locations for a new chute.

    a. Create a transportation matrix for the sawdust-movement problem, assuming that a new chute is installed at site 3.

    b. Develop the minimum-cost solution for your matrix from part a.

    c. Create a transportation matrix for the sawdust-movement problem, assuming that a new chute is installed at site 4.

    d. Develop the minimum-cost solution for your matrix from part c.

    e. Compare the results from parts b and d. Discuss the utilization of chute capacities for each location.

3. American Tractor Company machines engine-block castings in three different plants. The castings come from two of the company's foundries, but the supply of castings has become inadequate. A third foundry, either at Toledo or Rock Island, is to begin casting the tractor engines. Its capacity is to be just enough to make up for the capacity shortage.

    The transportation method is being used to analyze transportation costs for the two sites. Transportation costs, demands, and capacities are given below.

Foundries	Plant	Transportation cost (per casting)	Supply (castings)
A	1	$10	Foundry A— 80/wk.
B	1	3	Foundry B—100/wk.
Toledo	1	5	
Rock Island	1	☐	
A	2	7	Demand (castings)
B	2	11	
Toledo	2	☐	Plant 1— 40/wk.
Rock Island	2	3	Plant 2— 90/wk.
A	3	☐	Plant 3—110/wk.
B	3	5	
Toledo	3	9	
Rock Island	3	7	

    a. Three of the transportation costs are omitted above (see three empty boxes). Provide your own reasonable costs, and set up initial transportation matrices for each alternative foundry site.

    b. Use the transportation method to solve for minimum transportation cost, using Toledo as the foundry site.

    c. Use the transportation method to solve for minimum transportation cost, using Rock Island as the foundry site.

Layout types   4. For each of the following types of industry, suggest which types of layout (process, product, fixed, and mixed) are likely to apply. Some types may have more than one likely type of layout. Explain your choices briefly.

Auto assembly   Military physical exams
Auto repair   Small airplane manufacturing

Shipbuilding	Small airplane overhaul and repair
Machine shop	Large airplane overhaul and repair
Cafeteria	Shoe manufacturing
Restaurant	Shoe repair
Medical clinic	Central processing of insurance forms
Hospital	Packing and crating

REL chart

*5. Develop an REL chart for a large discount store or department store that you are familiar with. (You may need to visit the store for firsthand information.) Use the store's different departments as activities. Would the REL chart be likely to be helpful in layout or relayout of such a store? How about a flow diagram or a from–to chart? Explain.

Layout analysis— Flow and nonflow oriented

6. Automatic Controls Corp. is building a new plant. Eight departments are involved. As part of a plant-layout analysis, the activity relationships and square-footage needs for the departments are shown on the accompanying combined REL chart (combined flow analysis and nonflow analysis).

Activity	Area (square feet)
1. Shipping and receiving	600
2. Stockroom	1,500
3. Fabrication	800
4. Assembly	700
5. Paint	500
6. Tool crib	300
7. Cafeteria	600
8. Offices	1,200
Total	6,400 square feet

Code	Reasons
1	Personal contact
2	Paperwork contact
3	Product/resource flow
4	Use same equipment/tools
5	Possible fumes

    a. Develop an activity-arrangement diagram based on the REL-chart data.

    b. Develop a space-relationship diagram for the eight departmental areas.

    c. Fit the eight departments into a 100-foot by 80-foot building in as close to an optimal layout as you can. Include aisles between departments on your layout.

**d.* How necessary is the combined REL chart in this case? If it were not included in the analysis, what would the analysis steps be? Explain. (Hint: Note the pattern of reasons for relationships.)

7. Pharmaco, Inc., manufacturer of a drug line in liquid and tablet forms, is moving to a new building. Layout planning is in process. The data below have been collected on material movements in the drug manufacturing process.

	Unit loads per month	Move distances (feet) in present building
Raw-material movements:		
Receiving to raw-material storage		180
1. Powder in drums	800	
2. Powder in sacks on pallets	1,100	
3. Liquid in drums	100	
4. Controlled substance (heroin) in cans in cartons	10	
5. Empty bottles in cartons on pallets	8,000	
6. Water piped into granulating and liquid mixing (gallons)	3,000	
In-process movements:		
Raw-material storage to granulating		410
7. Powder in drums	800	
8. Powder in sacks	1,000	
9. Controlled substance in cans	50	
Raw-material storage to liquid mixing		300
10. Powder in sacks	100	
11. Liquid in drums	100	
12. Controlled substance in cans	10	
13. Granulating to tableting (granules in drums)	1,500	290
14. Tableting to fill and pack (tablets in tubs)	6,000	180
15. Liquid mixing to fill and pack (gallons piped)	4,000	370
16. Raw-material storage to fill and pack (empty bottles)	8,000	260
17. Fill and pack to finished storage (cartons of bottles and of tablet packs on pallets)	10,000	320

    a. Develop a P-Q chart with each of the material movements plotted on the chart. What does the chart suggest about the type of layout for Pharmaco's new building? Explain.

b. Convert the given flow-volume data to a vowel-rating scale. That is, identify which activity pairs (routes) should be rated A, E, I, O, and U.

c. Develop an activity-arrangement diagram.

d. The layout planners see little need for a from–to chart or an REL chart. Explain why.

e. Develop a P-Q chart (or use the one from part *a* above if it was assigned). Based on the P-Q chart, what is the nature of the material handling system needed in Pharmaco's new building? Explain.

f. One option is to call off the move to the new building and update the material handling system in the present building. Develop a D-Q chart using data for the present building. From your D-Q chart, draw some conclusions about types of handling methods (equipment) that seem suitable for the present building.

Line balancing

8. As a first step in a line-balancing analysis, the following precedence diagram has been developed.

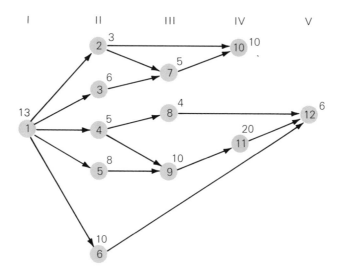

a. Calculate Σ*t*. Now calculate all the possible cycle times and numbers of stations that could be used in a perfectly balanced assembly line.

b. Which of the options develped in part *a* are not worth pursuing further? Why?

c. Balance the line as best you can, and calculate the resulting balance delay.

9. The following precedence diagram has been developed for circuit-breaker assembly.

a. Calculate all the possible cycle times and numbers of stations that could be used in a perfectly balanced assembly line.

b. Balance the line as best you can for three stations. Calculate the resulting balance delay.

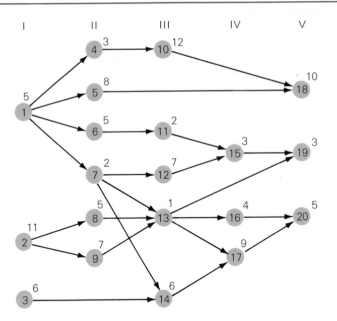

10. The processing of workers' compensation claim forms in a state office is being organized as a production line. Work elements have been divided as far as possible and have been organized into the following precedence diagram.

    a. Calculate all combinations of cycle time and number of stations that would result in zero balance delay.

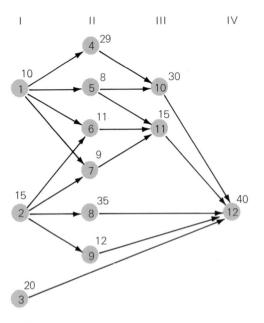

    b. Which combinations (from part *a*) are not reasonable for further analysis? Explain.

    c. Balance the line for five stations, and again for six stations. Which is best? Why?

11. Crow's Eye Foods, Inc., has patent rights to a special type of segmented dish for perfect warming of foods in a microwave oven. The dish permits Crow's to launch a new line of frozen breakfasts. Crow's kitchens are planning for the first breakfast: two strips of bacon, one egg, and two slices of buttered toast.

    a. Develop a precedence diagram that could be used in balancing the production line for this breakfast. Make your own (reasonable) assumptions about work elements and element times. Explain your diagram.

    b. Determine all sets of cycle time and number of stations that would result in a balanced line.

    c. Balance your line.

Layout and handling analysis— Flow-oriented

12. The woodshop building of E-Z Window Co. is undergoing major relayout in order to reduce backtracking and decrease flow distances. A flow diagram of the frame-manufacturing operation and an REL chart for nonflow factors in the operation are given below.

    a. Develop a P-Q chart with each of the material movements plotted on the chart. What does the chart suggest about the type of layout needed?

    b. Construct a from–to chart based on flow-diagram data. What is the meaning of the notation that quantities are in "unit loads"? Explain by referring to a few examples on the chart.

   c. What proportion of total flow on your from–to chart represents backtracking? How does that proportion depend on your chosen order of listing activities on the chart? What does your chosen order of listing activities on the chart imply about the final layout arrangement?

    d. Convert the flow-volume data in your from–to chart to a vowel-rating scale. That is, identify which activity pairs (routes) should be rated A, E, I, O, and U.

    e. Combine your vowel-rating data representing flow volumes with the non-flow-factor vowel ratings on the REL chart. Express the result in a new combined REL chart.

    f. Convert your combined REL chart into an activity-arrangement diagram.

    g. Develop a space-relationship diagram for the eight activity areas.

    h. Fit the eight activity areas into a square building without allowances for aisles, etc. Make your layout as nearly optimal as you can.

    i. Develop a P-Q chart (or use the one from part *a*—if it was part of your assignment). Based on the P-Q chart, what kind of material handling system is needed? Explain.

    j. Based on distances between departments in your layout in part *h* above, develop a D-Q chart. From your D-Q chart, draw some general conclusions about the type of handling methods (equipment) that seem suitable.

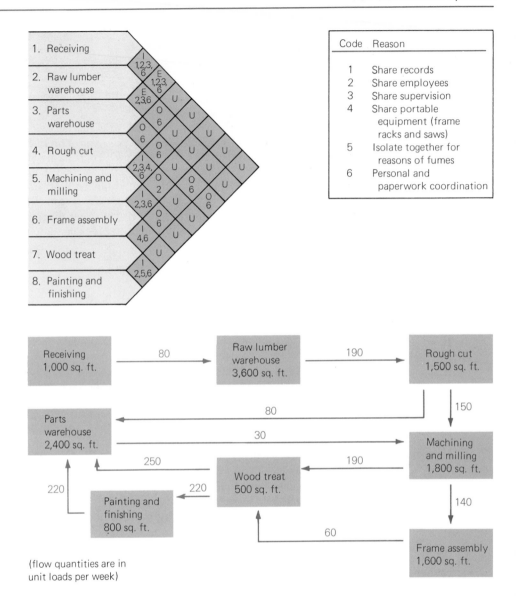

Code	Reason
1	Share records
2	Share employees
3	Share supervision
4	Share portable equipment (frame racks and saws)
5	Isolate together for reasons of fumes
6	Personal and paperwork coordination

(flow quantities are in unit loads per week)

---

* See instructions at end of problems section, Chapter 1.

CASE

St. "M's" Hospital

In 1970 St. "M's" Hospital was built. A unique feature is an automated monorail system to carry linens, food, instruments, medication, and other items all over the hospital from central storage and distribution points. The monorail hauls materials on carts and in baskets. The monorail system, the first of its kind in the world, was justified based on such features as: (1) labor-cost savings, (2) freeing professionals like nurses from various handling tasks, (3) high-quality sterilization of instruments at a site away from operating rooms, and (4) a twin-cart system that provided for one cart to be in loading while its twin was in service. At first the monorail system was feared, ridiculed, misused, and/or ignored by employees. But after about three years, the system realized its potential.

By 1980 monorail technology in hospitals had become fairly common. But newer monorail systems used lightweight materials, greaseless moving parts, and computer controls. By contrast, St. M's has a heavy-duty factory-grade monorail—noisy, bulky, mechanically controlled, and very expensive to maintain. Three options are being considered:

1. *Maintain present system.* The costs include over $20,000 per year for maintenance, including parts. The chain that drives the monorail must be replaced every seven to ten years at $25,000 per replacement. With good preventive maintenance, the system might last 15 to 20 more years.

2. *Introduce manual handling.* It would cost $15,000 to modify three elevators that are now "injector elevators" and part of the monorail system. The other monorail facilities could be dismantled over a long time period since manual operations would not be hampered much by most of the overhead rails. According to one authority,[1] automated delivery systems do not reduce

---

[1] Charles E. Housely, "Distributing the Goods the Right Way," *Hospitals,* June 16, 1977, pp. 103–5.

delivery costs: Manual deliveries take an average of two minutes, whereas unloading/replenishment takes an average of 45 minutes in hospitals around the country. While St. M's was a pioneer in use of the twin-cart system, that system has come into use in hospitals which use manual delivery as well.

3. *Replace the monorail.* The cost is estimated at $1.2 million, including elevators and computer controls. A part of the cost is for tearing out the old monorail—a considerable task since it is such a heavy-duty system.

What should the administrators do?

supplement to chapter 12 ·

VOGEL'S APPROXIMATION METHOD

Vogel's approximation method (VAM) is presented in this supplement. Since most applications of the transportation method are processed by computer, the manual VAM method is not often used in practice. On the other hand, VAM is useful for developing an initial feasible solution to modest transportation problems, such as classroom exercises. Also, an understanding of the VAM procedure helps provide a broader understanding of transportation problems in general.

The problem of locating a printing plant in the Hawaiian Islands, Example 12–1 in the body of the chapter, is used to illustrate VAM. The VAM solution for the Hilo location is presented below.

EXAMPLE S12–1
Initial solution using VAM— Hilo location

The basic data for this problem are given in Example 12–1 in the chapter.

An initial feasible solution using Vogel's approximation method is developed in Figure S12–1. VAM begins with calculation of row and column penalties. The penalties are a way of pointing out the relatively least costly transportation cell in the matrix; that cell represents a route that you want to be sure to traverse. Having eliminated that cell, you consider the remaining cells and again find the relatively least costly cell. This continues until all supply-and-demand constraints have been met. The result is a transportation plan that approaches the optimum, because VAM seeks out relatively least costly routes.

Figure S12–1A shows the penalties calculated for the three columns and three rows. The penalty in each case equals the lowest transportation cost subtracted from the second lowest. For Lanai the lowest is $5 per pallet (from Hana); the second lowest is $7 per pallet (from Honolulu); and the penalty is $7 − $5 = $2. The meaning is this: Lanai's demand can be transported most cheaply from Hana, and the penalty is at least $2 per pallet if Hana is not selected as the source. For Molokai, the penalty is $7 − $7 = 0; that is, it makes no difference whether the cheapest or second-cheapest source is selected, since they are the same. Row penalties have nearly the same meaning. Hilo can send its output for $1 less to Lanai than to Molokai; therefore, there is a $1 penalty for not shipping to Lanai.

Among the six penalties, the largest is $3 in the Kauai column. The largest penalty identifies the row or column containing the relatively least costly cell in the matrix. It is the Honolulu-Kauai cell, at $9 per pallet. Note that the absolute least costly cell is Hana-Lanai, at $5. But the $9 cell, Honolulu to Kauai, is worthier of our attention because it has a $3 relative advantage in its column, whereas the $5 cell has only a $2 relative advantage in its column and in its row as well.

The next step is to allocate resource shipments to that $9 cell. The most that may be sent from Honolulu to Kauai is 25 pallets per week; that is Honolulu's maximum, and it is within Kauai's demand limit of 50. In Figure S12–1B that quantity, 25, is

FIGURE S12–1
VAM initial solution, Hilo location

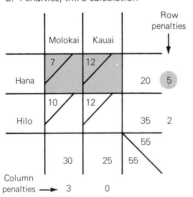

A. Penalties, first calculation

	Lanai	Molokai	Kauai	Row penalties ↓	
Honolulu	7	7	9	25	0
Hana	5	7	12	40	2
Hilo	9	10	12	35	1
	20	30	50	100 / 100	
Column penalties →	2	0	3		

B. First allocation

	Lanai	Molokai	Kauai	Remaining supply
Honolulu			25	2̶5̶ 0
Hana				40
Hilo				35
Remaining demand	20	30	5̶0̶ 25	75

C. Penalties, second calculation

	Lanai	Molokai	Kauai	Row penalties ↓	
Hana	5	7	12	40	2
Hilo	9	10	12	35	1
	20	30	25	75	
Column penalties →	4	3	0		

D. Second allocation

	Lanai	Molokai	Kauai	Remaining supply
Honolulu			25	0
Hana	20			4̶0̶ 20
Hilo				35
Remaining demand	2̶0̶ 0	30	25	55

E. Penalties, third calculation

	Molokai	Kauai	Row penalties ↓	
Hana	7	12	20	5
Hilo	10	12	35	2
	30	25	55	
Column penalties →	3	0		

F. Third allocation

	Lanai	Molokai	Kauai	Remaining supply
Honolulu			25	0
Hana	20	20		2̶0̶ 0
Hilo				35
Remaining demand	0	3̶0̶ 10	25	35

FIGURE S12–1
(continued)

G. Status for fourth allocation

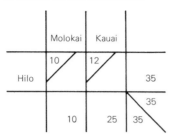

H. Fourth and final allocation

	Lanai	Molokai	Kauai	Remaining supply
Honolulu	7	7	9 / 25	0
Hana	5 / 20	7 / 20	12 / 12	0
Hilo	9	10 / 10	12 / 25	35 0
Remaining demand	0	1̶0̶ 0	2̶5̶ 0	0

placed in the cell, and Honolulu's supply is reduced to 0. Since 25 of Kauai's demand has been satisfied, the remainder, 25, is entered as its remaining demand.

Figure S12–1C shows the new matrix and the new calculation of penalties. Honolulu is no longer part of the problem since its supply went to zero in Figure S12–1B. The new maximum penalty is $4 in the Lanai column, and the Hana-Lanai cell is selected for the next allocation.

All of Lanai's demand of 20 may be met from Hana. Therefore, in Figure S12–1D 20 is placed in the cell. This reduces Lanai's demand to 0 and Hana's supply to 20.

Figure S12–1E shows the new reduced matrix; Lanai is no longer part of the problem and is not included. Of the newly computed penalties, the largest is $5, in the Hana row. This pinpoints the $7 Hana-Molokai cell as being relatively least costly in the reduced matrix.

All of Hana's remaining supply, 20, may be shipped to Molokai, which reduces Molokai's remaining demand to 10. The allocations so far are shown in Figure S12–1F.

Now the problem has been reduced to a single source of newspapers, Hilo, as is shown in Figure S12–1G. In a single-row (or single-column) matrix there are no choices, and so there is no further need to calculate penalties.

In the fourth allocation, Hilo's supply of 35 may be allocated in only one way: 10 to Molokai and 25 to Kauai. Figure S12–1H shows the final VAM solution with no remaining supply or demand to be allocated.

The total weekly transportation cost for the VAM solution is the sum of transportation rates times quantities for all cells in the solution. The calculations are:

Honolulu-Kauai:	$ 9 × 25 =	$225 per week
Hana-Lanai:	5 × 20 =	100 per week
Hana-Molokai:	7 × 20 =	140 per week
Hilo-Molokai:	10 × 10 =	100 per week
Hilo-Kanai:	12 × 25 =	300 per week
	Total	$865 per week

chapter 13

MAINTENANCE MANAGEMENT

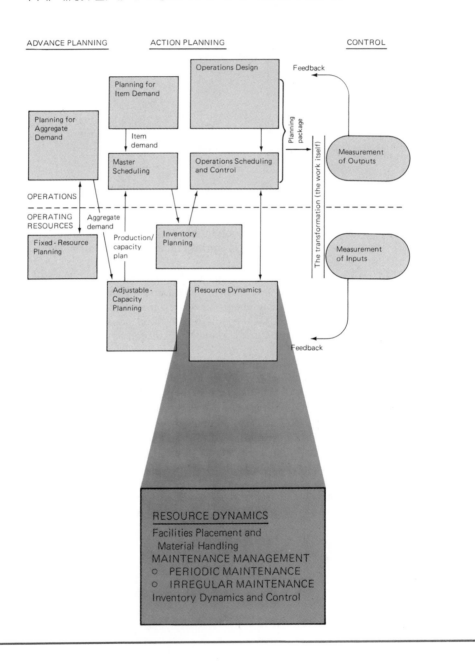

ADVANCE PLANNING   ACTION PLANNING   CONTROL

Operations Design

Feedback

Planning for
Item Demand

Planning for
Aggregate
Demand

Item
demand

Master
Scheduling

Operations Scheduling
and Control

Planning
package

Measurement
of Outputs

OPERATIONS

OPERATING
RESOURCES

Aggregate
demand

Fixed - Resource
Planning

Production/
capacity
plan

Inventory
Planning

The transformation (the work itself)

Measurement
of Inputs

Adjustable -
Capacity
Planning

Resource Dynamics

Feedback

RESOURCE DYNAMICS

Facilities Placement and
  Material Handling
MAINTENANCE MANAGEMENT
  ○ PERIODIC MAINTENANCE
  ○ IRREGULAR MAINTENANCE
Inventory Dynamics and Control

Maintenance is the third of the four stages in the life cycle for operating resources. The stages are diagramed below.

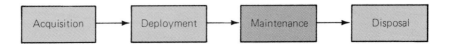

Maintenance refers to keeping operating resources in good operating condition. The term *maintenance* is usually thought of in regard to plant, equipment, and tools, although work force and materials must also be maintained (via training, etc., for people and proper storage of materials). While the maintenance management focus in this chapter is on plant, equipment, and tools, some of the concepts apply as well to work force and materials. For example, a major problem in managing repair crews is uncertainty about when breakdowns will occur; similarly a major problem in maintaining people's health and well-being—via food services, health services, entertainment services, and so on—is uncertainty about when people will arrive for service. The latter part of the chapter, including the chapter supplement, concerns the problems of planning for such uncertainty. The first sections of the chapter are on more traditional maintenance management topics, such as preventive maintenance, group replacement, and standby equipment.

MAINTENANCE ORGANIZATION

A single department sometimes houses maintenance and the other three facilities life-cycle stages as well. The department might be called the facilities department. In practice, it is more likely to be called the maintenance department. The organization structure could look like Figure 13–1.[1] The three major sections shown are *analysis* (planning), on the left; *design* (engineering), in the middle; and *operations*, on the right.

The grouping of functions shown in Figure 13–1 merits some explanation. The common thread is that all the functions shown share the mission of providing for an *efficient* working environment at *reasonable cost*. Our interest in maintenance management centers on analysis of trade-offs among those two goals—efficiency and cost—rather than maintenance operations. Therefore, our discussion of maintenance operations will be brief.

Figure 13–1 shows four types of maintenance operations: custodial services, preventive maintenance (PM), repair maintenance, and millwrights and minor construction. The first two, PM and custodial services, fall into the category *periodic maintenance*. Repair maintenance and millwrights/minor construction may be termed *irregular maintenance*. In the maintenance field much

---

[1] A variety of other maintenance/facilities organization structures may be found in James A. Murphy, ed., *Plant Engineering Management* (Society of Manufacturing Engineers, 1971), ch. 2 (TS184.P435x).

FIGURE 13-1
Organization of
a maintenance
department

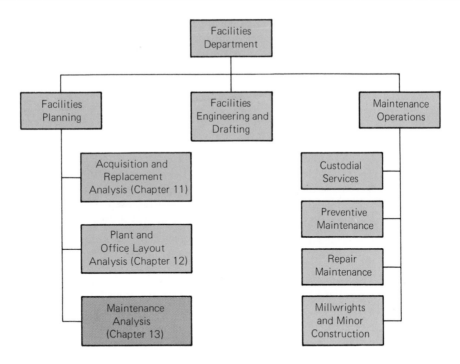

of the analyst's attention has been on the proper use of periodic and irregular maintenance. The sections of this chapter on group replacement and standby equipment include ways of analyzing uses of periodic and irregular maintenance. The final section on waiting lines and roller-coaster workloads is concerned only with irregular maintenance, which tends to be accompanied by rising and falling waiting lines of maintenance jobs awaiting service.

The term *millwright* is a bit archaic today—but just a bit. There are still companies, mainly machining and metalworking, that refer to a millwright shop. The millwright shop employs the tradesmen who move and install machines and other facilities (originally in a mill).

According to an extensive survey,[2] the maintenance hourly work force averages 6 percent of total plant employees in 502 diverse firms. Our concern is not so much with the maintenance tradesmen; rather it is with those who plan and control the work of the maintenance tradesmen and the millwrights. The survey also indicated that the planning staff averages 4 percent of maintenance hourly tradesmen.

The maintenance department may be viewed as a minifactory. As such, it has a full operations and operating resources management system. Of course, the minifactory shares many resources with the parent organization. The par-

---

[2] *How over 500 Firms Manage Their Maintenance Force*, Albert Ramond and Associates, Chicago, 1969.

ent would usually supply the maintenance department with such services as personnel, purchasing, and methods and time standards.

PERIODIC MAINTENANCE

A comprehensive maintenance function generally includes periodic as well as repair maintenance. Periodic maintenance is an appealing idea for at least the following reasons:

1. Periodic maintenance crews may have their time evenly scheduled; repair crews are busy only when there is something to fix.
2. Periodic maintenance tends to forestall work stoppage; repair crews feed upon adversity: breakdowns and stoppages.
3. Periodic maintenance may often be scheduled to avoid work stoppage; with repair maintenance there is work stoppage not only during repair but also, frequently, while waiting for a repair crew.

The custodial side of periodic maintenance does not warrant much discussion here. Custodianship involves few hard choices, because it is not closely linked with work stoppages. Preventive maintenance (PM) is the more issue-laden aspect of periodic maintenance.

There are three types of PM, as follows:

PM based on calendar time.

PM based on time of usage.

PM based on inspection.

PM based on calendar time means performing maintenance at regular intervals. PM based on time of usage means performing maintenance after a set number of operating hours. PM based on inspection means performing any maintenance that seems prudent, as revealed by planned inspections.

Among the most ardent believers in the PM concept are aircraft maintenance people. In aircraft maintenance PM is everything; waiting for a failure is untenable since, if a failure occurs, there is often nothing left to fix.

Preventive maintenance of aircraft is largely based on time of usage. Flight logs recording hours of usage are the basis for thorough overhauls and replacements.

PM based on inspection is also important. Pilots and ground crews have inspection checklists for routine maintenance. Also, critical components are periodically torn down for interior inspections; the U.S. Air Force refers to this as IRAN—*in*spect and *repair as n*ecessary—maintenance.

There are many shining examples of the success of the PM concept in aircraft. The well-traveled B-52 is one. Even more remarkable is the DC-3, now over 40 years old. (The military version, the C-47, was affectionately known as the "Gooney Bird.") A few thousand of this venerable aircraft are still logging mileage, thanks to the thoroughness of aircraft PM practices coupled with good design.

Most auto owners do a small amount of PM based on time of usage; examples are oil changes, grease jobs, and tune-ups. The many recent-model cars in auto graveyards provide mute testimony to the poor job that most of us do in preventively maintaining our cars. In the face of this there is some evidence that applying airplane-style PM to an automobile can yield impressive results: Newspapers a few years ago reported that a taxi owner in Madison, Wisconsin, following a rigorous daily PM regimen, had logged nearly 1 million miles on a limousine. This was achieved without body or engine replacement and only one engine overhaul.

The strong commitment to PM in regard to aircraft extends backward to the design of the product. The military services and private airlines treat *maintainability* as an important design attribute. Airframe manufacturers try to design maintainability into their aircraft in order to have a chance at government contracts.

Operationally, a good PM program depends on records. A maintenance history is needed for each piece of equipment. This permits analysis of breakdown frequency and causes; the analysis provides the basis for improving PM procedures. (Lack of a simple maintenance record-keeping system for the auto owner undoubtedly contributes to poor auto maintenance. Another factor: Consumers have never made it known to auto manufacturers that they care much about maintainability.)

For all its advantages, PM can be overdone. Preventing all failures is commendable for aircraft, but this is far too expensive for most other kinds of equipment; breakdowns must be allowed. The decision on breakdown (i.e., repair) versus preventive or periodic maintenance may be subjected to cost analysis in the case of certain replaceable components; such a cost analysis is found in assessing the merits of group replacement, which means replacing a whole group of components at periodic intervals rather than as they fail individually. Keeping standby equipment on hand, to be used in case of breakdown of primary equipment, is akin to preventive maintenance. That is, the standby equipment serves to prevent work stoppage resulting from equipment breakdown. Group-replacement analysis and standby-equipment analysis are considered in the following two sections. The remainder of the chapter, on waiting lines and roller-coaster workloads, concerns irregular repair rather than preventive maintenance.

GROUP REPLACEMENT

When to replace (or trade in) a machine is a capital acquisition problem; the method of analysis (EAC) was discussed in Chapter 11. When to replace machine *components* is a maintenance problem—to be considered here.

For a few kinds of components, replacement is based on wear and tear. Tires are of this type. For most kinds of components, however, sudden failure is a greater problem than wear-out. Examples include electronic components, relays, light bulbs, shoelaces, and to a considerable extent, bearings. Where

FIGURE 13–2
Probability of
failure over
operating life

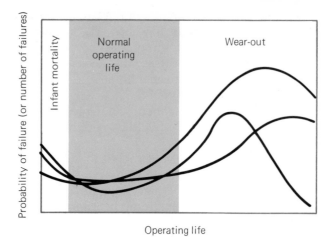

a number of the same type of component are in use, consideration must be given to group replacement as opposed to replacing individual components as they fail.

Calculating the cost of group replacement requires data on the failure pattern for the component.[3] Three examples of a *general* failure probability pattern over component operating life are shown in Figure 13–2. Each would represent the failure pattern for a different type of machine or machine system, and a variety of different components of each machine could be the cause of sudden failure.

Three zones are identifiable in the figure. The first is the infant-mortality zone. Failure this soon may result from improper assembly or from rough handling or shipping. The probability of infant mortality can sometimes be reduced by preuse or by "burning in" components or the whole machine before shipment.

If a component survives the infant-mortality period, the chances of failure tend to be low for a time. Failures occur randomly and for diverse reasons. This is the normal operating period.

After that the component enters the wear-out zone. In that zone the probability of failure rises sharply, peaks, and then falls to zero at maximum product life. In both the normal operating period and the wear-out zone, failure probability can sometimes be reduced by operating the product under lower loads or better conditions than it is designed for. This is referred to as "derating" the product.

The shape of the curve for a given machine or machine system must be discovered by testing. For a given type of component in the machine, a manu-

---

[3] Maintenance managers are in need of a general rudimentary understanding of failure patterns but need not know how to calculate failure rates, mean time between failures, and so forth. Such reliability engineering concepts are important in new-product design, however.

facturer or a trade association may do the testing and publish the results. Otherwise the maintenance department may run its own tests. Examples of each source of data follow.

Light-bulb example

This example is in two parts, one using failure data provided by the manufacturer and the other using data collected by the firm's maintenance department. The example compares two policies on light-bulb replacement. One policy is to allow light bulbs to last as long as they will before replacing them. In this policy a few fail in infant mortality, a few more fail at random for various causes, and the rest (probably the majority) fail in the wear-out zone. The second policy is not to leave bulbs in their sockets long enough for wear-out. Instead all bulbs are replaced at regular intervals (periodic maintenance) when they are partway through their normal life expectancy. It is this second preventive policy, called the group-replacement policy, for which the maintenance manager needs access to failure-rate data.

EXAMPLE 13–1
Group versus individual replacement of light bulbs

At present, light bulbs in Building C are replaced as they fail. Whoever notices a failure phones the trouble-call desk, Maintenance Department. The trouble-call dispatcher sends someone to change the light bulb. The average cost: $3.30 per bulb, including labor.

An alternative policy is the preventive one of replacing all Building C bulbs at regular intervals. In the maintenance trade this is known as the group-replacement policy. For Building C the group-replacement policy would cost $1 per bulb, including labor. There are 1,000 light bulbs in Building C. Therefore each group replacement would cost $1,000. What replacement policy is optimal?

Situation A—Failure probabilities known. It is known that the operating life for the given light bulb has the following probability distribution:

Time until failure	1 mo.	2 mo.	3 mo.	4 mo.	5 mo.
Probability	0.05	0.15	0.20	0.30	0.30

With that probability distribution it is easy to calculate the average life of a light bulb. It is calculated using the expected-value method:

$$\begin{aligned}
\text{Average (expected) life} &= (1 \text{ mo.})(0.05) + (2 \text{ mo.})(0.15) \\
&+ (3 \text{ mo.})(0.20) + (4 \text{ mo.})(0.30) \\
&+ (5 \text{ mo.})(0.30) \\
&= 0.05 + 0.30 + 0.60 + 1.2 + 1.5 \\
&= 3.65 \text{ months}
\end{aligned}$$

Cost of present policy:

Since there are 1,000 light bulbs in Building C, the number that fail per month is:

$$\frac{1,000 \text{ bulbs}}{3.65 \text{ months average life}} = 274 \text{ bulbs per month}$$

Then the cost of the present replace-as-they-fail policy is:

$$274 \text{ bulbs/mo.} \times \$3.30/\text{bulb} = \$904.20 \text{ per month}$$

Cost of group-replacement policies:

Group replacement every month, every two months, every three months, and so on, are other alternatives. If all 1,000 bulbs are replaced as a group at the end of a given period, there are still some failures *during* that period. Those failures must be replaced by the trouble-call process. Thus, the following cost analysis of group-replacement alternatives includes the cost of replacing the bulbs that fail between group-replacement intervals.

If there is a group replacement every month, the costs are:

Group costs:	1,000 bulbs/mo. × $1.00/bulb	= $1,000/mo.
Failure costs:	1,000 bulbs × 0.05 × $3.30/bulb =	165/mo.
	Total costs	$1,165/mo.

If there is a group replacement every two months, the costs are:

Group costs:
  $1,000 per two months
Failure costs:
  (First month's failures from the original 1,000)($3.30)
  + (Second month's failures from the original 1,000)($3.30)
  + (Second month's failures from first month's replacements) ($3.30)
  = [1,000)(0.05) + (1,000)(0.15) + (1,000)(0.05)(0.05)] [$3.30]
  = (50 + 150 + 2.5)($3.30)
  = (202.5)($3.30) = $668.25 per two months
Total costs:
  $1,000 per two months + $668.25 per two months
  = $1,668.25 per two months = $834.12 per month

Next, group replacement every three months is analyzed; then group replacement every four months; and so forth. A table, Figure 13–3, helps simplify the calculations.

Notice that the original quantity, 1,000 bulbs, is entered repeatedly along the diagonal, so that 1,000 appears under each probability; the 50 that fail in month 1 is on

FIGURE 13–3
Calculating optimal group-replacement policy for light bulbs—Tabular approach

Replace every...	Number subject to failure during month					Failures					
	Month:	1	2	3	4	5	Month	Cumu-lative	Cost @ $3.30	Group cost @ $1	Total cost	Monthly cost
	Probability:	0.05	0.15	0.20	0.30	0.30						
1 month		1,000					50		$ 165	$1,000	$1,165	$1,165
2 months		50	1,000				152	202	667	1,000	1,667	834
3 months		152	50	1,000			215	417	1,376	1,000	2,376	792 ←
4 months		215	152	50	1,000		344	761	2,511	1,000	3,511	878
5 months		344	215	152	50	1,000	395	1,156	3,815	1,000	4,815	963

the next diagonal; the 152 that fail in month 2 is on the third diagonal; and so forth. A sample calculation may be shown: In order to find the fourth diagonal value, 215, the calculations are based on failures in the third month: $152(0.05) + 50(0.15) + 1,000(0.20) = 215$. The total cost and the monthly cost are computed and the monthly cost is then compared with the monthly cost of the previous group-replacement alternative. This may cease when the monthly cost bottoms out; it does so for group replacement every three months in this example.

It was shown earlier that the present replace-as-they-fail policy costs $904 per month. Therefore, the optimal policy is group replacement every three months at $792 per month.

Situation B—Failure probabilities unknown.   When light-bulb failure data are not given, they may be collected experimentally. The Maintenance Department may learn about failure patterns by placing 1,000 new light bulbs in the 1,000 sockets in Building C. It is not practical to let the building go dark, so all failures are replaced during the experiment. The following are the experimental results:

Month	1	2	3	4	5	6	7	8	9	10	11	12
Failures during month	46	150	218	360	520	353	387	240	260	330	301	310

It appears that the experiment has been run long enough to achieve a nearly "steady state." That is, all new bulbs put in at the beginning of the year have been replaced, and their replacements have been replaced; the mix of bulbs is now a more uniform mix of ages, and the steady-state failure rate is about 310 per month. Actually, there is no need to run the experiment long enough to achieve a steady state unless a new type of bulb is being used or the building is new. In an existing building the light-bulb failure rate prior to the experiment would have been steady-state.

Cost of present policy:

The steady-state condition applies to the present replace-as-they-fail policy. Its cost is:

$$310 \text{ bulbs/mo.} \times \$3.30/\text{bulb} = \$1,023 \text{ per month}$$

Cost of group-replacement policy:

The cost of group replacement every month is:

Group cost:	1,000 bulbs $\times$ \$1.00/bulb =	\$1,000/mo.
Failure cost:	46 bulbs $\times$ \$3.30/bulb =	152/mo.
	Total cost	\$1,152/mo.

The cost of group replacement every two months is:

Group cost:		\$1,000/2 mo.
Failure cost:	$(46 + 150) \times \$3.30 =$	647/2 mo.
	Total cost	\$1,647/2 mo.
	=	\$823/mo.

The cost of group replacement every three months is:

Group cost: $1,000/3 mo.
Failure cost: $(46 + 150 + 218) \times \$3.30 = \underline{\quad 1,366/3 \text{ mo.}}$
                                    Total cost $2,366/3 mo.
                                           $=$ $789/mo.

The cost of group replacement every four months is:

Group cost: $1,000/4 mo.
Failure cost: $(46 + 150 + 218 + 360) \times \$3.30 = \underline{\quad 2,554/4 \text{ mo.}}$
                                    Total cost $3,554/4 mo.
                                           $=$ $888/mo.

The costs have begun to turn upward; this suggests that the optimum (lowest cost on a U-shaped cost curve) has been found. It is $789 per month for group replacement every three months. That beats the $1,023 per month for replacing the bulbs as they fail, so group replacement every three months is the optimum among the policies considered.

The example may seem to suggest that it is better *not* to know the failure probabilities, because the computations are simpler when experimental data collected by the Maintenance Department are used than when probabilities are provided. The computational advantage is more than offset, however, by the time and cost of collecting experimental data.

Expected-value concept

In the above solution method the expected-value concept was introduced, and it deserves further comment. Expected value is a weighted average. It is the sum of all "payoffs" (bulb life was the payoff above) times respective probabilities.[4] The probabilities must add to 1.0, thereby accounting for all possible payoffs.

The expected-value concept is useful only for probability-distributed input data—and only when records are good enough to yield the probabilities. In maintenance, where breakdowns tend to be probabilistically distributed random events, the expected-value concept is widely applicable. This is especially true since good record keeping on machine failures has become accepted practice in well-run maintenance organizations.[5]

Elsewhere in this book, for the most part, input data are more narrowly distributed, and single-valued estimates (instead of expected values) suffice.[6]

---

[4] Some readers may be aware of an application of the expected-value concept in the behavioral sciences: It is Vroom's expectancy model. In Vroom's model,

$$\text{Motivation} = \Sigma[(\text{Valence})(\text{Expectancy})]$$

One can see that valence is about the same as value or payoff, and expectancy is about the same as probability. Substituting the alternative terms on the right side of the equation, we have $\Sigma[(\text{Payoff})(\text{Probability})]$, which is the general form of the expected-value model.

[5] Thorough discussion of computer automation of this record keeping may be found in J. J. Wilkerson and J. J. Lowe, "A Computerized Maintenance Information System That Works," *Plant Engineering*, March 18, 1971, p. 68.

[6] A point of terminology for those students who have studied decision theory: Use of single-valued estimates is known in decision theory as a condition of assumed certainty; use of probabilistic input data is a condition of assumed risk (or, by some authors, assumed uncertainty).

STANDBY EQUIPMENT

Society is becoming increasingly dependent on technology. We are at the mercy of machines. They break down, and lives are lost, not to mention profits. Sometimes the consequences of breakdowns are severe enough to justify spares. Spares provide comforting backup at some price. Standby facilities are an alternative to paying for a very high level of maintenance in order to reduce the chance of breakdowns.

Machine failures: The Poisson distribution

Analysis of standby policies when there are large numbers of identical machines can be simplified by using our knowledge about patterns of machine failures in this type of situation. In a wide variety of situations in which large numbers of identical machines are used, analysts have found that failures per unit of time are random variables that tend to follow a particular type of probability distribution: the Poisson distribution. The shape of the Poisson is based on a mathematical function, and the complete shape can be developed by simply entering the mean number of failures per time unit into the Poisson general formula.

A characteristic shape of the distribution is shown in Figure 13–4. It can be seen that in the Poisson distribution there is some chance of zero failures per time unit (e.g., per day), but of course there can be no chance of negative failures per time unit. Poisson distributions rise to a peak probability and then taper off (are skewed) to the right. There is a 50 percent chance that in the given time period the number of failures will be fewer than the mean (2.5 per time unit in the sketch), and there is also a 50 percent chance that the number of failures will exceed the mean.

Example of standby-equipment analysis

Sometimes the merits of standby equipment may be judged by a cost analysis. The following example illustrates a type of cost analysis that employs the Poisson probability distribution.

FIGURE 13–4
Poisson probability distribution

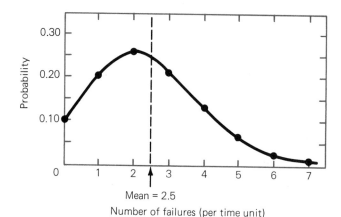

Mean = 2.5

Number of failures (per time unit)

EXAMPLE 13–2
Standby
"scopes" and
Poisson-
distributed
failures

A large electronics manufacturer does testing with "scopes" at each of 100 assembly and testing stations. When a scope breaks down, testing is halted at one station for one day (the time it takes to get the scope repaired). The cost of disruption and idleness is estimated at $100 for each day that a scope is down. That cost is $200 if two scopes are down, $300 if three are down, and so forth.

One way to avert the downtime cost is to keep spare scopes on hand. It costs about $50 per day to own and maintain each spare.

If scope breakdowns are random and they average three per day, how many spare scopes should be maintained?

Solution:

The mean number of scope failures is known to be three per day. From that figure, the probabilities of any other number of failures per day can be calculated or can be looked up in a table or graph. The calculations (and the tables and graphs) are based on the Poisson formula:[7]

$$P(n) = \frac{e^{-\lambda}\lambda^n}{n!},$$

where

$n =$ Number of failures per time unit
$\lambda =$ Mean number of failures per time period $= 3$ scopes/day
$e = 2.7183$
$P(n) =$ Probability of n failures per time unit

For example, zero scope failures per day has the probability:

$$P(0) = \frac{2.7183^{-3} \times 3^0}{0!} = \frac{1}{(1)(2.7183)^3} = \frac{1}{(20.086)} = 0.050$$

One scope failure per day has the probability:

$$P(1) = \frac{2.7183^{-3} \times 3^1}{1!} = \frac{3}{(1)(20.086)} = 0.150$$

Calculating the optimal number of spare scopes requires a number of steps. The table in Figure 13–5 simplifies the bookkeeping. The calculation procedure in the table follows the expected-value concept. For example, for the first row, zero spares, expected cost of failures is:

$E_F = \$100(0.150) + \$200(0.224) + \$300(0.224) + \$400(0.168) + \$500(0.101)$
$\qquad\qquad\qquad\qquad\qquad\qquad\qquad\qquad + \$600(0.050) + \$700(0.022)$

$\quad = \$15 + \$44.8 + \$67.2 + \$67.2 + \$50.5 + \$30.0 + \$15.4$
$\quad = \$290.10$

Each row is calculated similarly. The process stops when the total cost bottoms out and begins to rise. That identifies the optimal policy; in this case it is to provide three spares at a total cost of $210.80 per day.

---

[7] Figure S9–1 (in the chapter supplement) is a table of cumulative Poisson probabilities. Individual Poisson probabilities are not shown in the table, but they may be obtained by successive subtraction.

FIGURE 13–5
Calculating optimal number of standby machines—Tabular approach

Number of spares	Cost of curtailed scope testing								Daily cost of curtailed testing	Daily cost of spares	Total cost per day
	n: 0 P(n):0.050	1 0.150	2 0.224	3 0.224	4 0.168	5 0.101	6 0.050	7 0.022			
0		0	$100	$200	$300	$400	$500	$600	$700	$290.10	$ 0	$290.10
1			0	100	200	300	400	500	600	196.20	50	246.20
2				0	100	200	300	400	500	117.30	100	217.30
3					0	100	200	300	400	60.80	150	210.80◄
4						0	100	200	300	26.70	200	226.70

WAITING LINES AND ROLLER-COASTER WORKLOADS

Repairing breakdowns is an irregular type of maintenance that is difficult to plan for. Breakdown frequencies are somewhat predictable on the average but are random and uneven about the averages. By uneven, we mean sometimes occurring in bunches and sometimes occurring at widely spaced intervals. A suitable metaphor is that of a roller-coaster workload, which is graphically depicted in Figure 13–6. As the figure indicates, the roller-coaster pattern may apply from week to week or from month to month (top panel). And on any given day of one of the weeks or months the workload may show a roller-coaster pattern from hour to hour (or more often).

A critical consideration in planning for roller-coaster workloads is the work-stoppage cost that is incurred when breakdowns bunch up and waiting lines of repair jobs form. Another critical consideration is the cost of the repair crew's idleness when breakdowns are widely spaced. The cost analyses involved in planning for waiting lines and roller-coaster workloads apply not just to maintenance but to services in general.

In many service trades a manager may take some comfort from the knowledge that the service staff is rather low-paid; examples of low-paid service personnel include salesclerks, waiters/waitresses, gas pump jockeys, and computer center I/O clerks. In such cases, mismatches between staff on hand and workload do not cost much. In maintenance, however, there is greater concern about troughs in workloads, especially repair workloads, because repair workers are skilled, well-paid tradesmen. Repair workers need to know more than how to tighten nuts onto bolts. Their troubleshooter role requires diagnostic skills as well as breadth of technical skills.

In fact, a nice maintenance department career ladder, with increasing skills and wage rates, is from custodianship to preventive maintenance to breakdown maintenance or to millwright and minor construction. The steps of the ladder are arranged in just that way in the Figure 13–1 sample organization chart for maintenance operations. The irony and the difficulty of maintenance management is this: Lower-paid custodians are easy to keep busy since they do

FIGURE 13–6
Roller-coaster
workloads

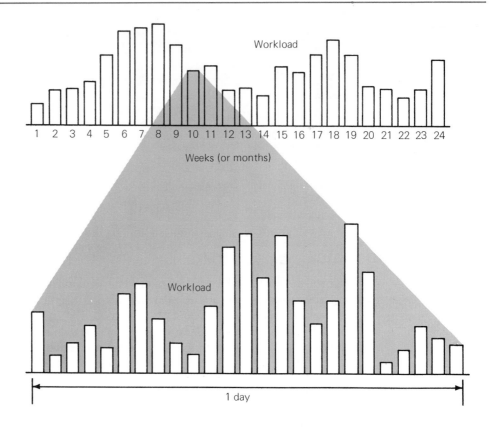

regular, periodic maintenance work; higher-paid repair tradesmen are hard to keep busy since they do irregular breakdown maintenance work.

One requisite in dealing with the roller-coaster workloads found in breakdown maintenance is good record keeping. Breakdown records permit analysis of means, probability distribution, and trends in breakdown frequency. With such information the maintenance manager may come to "know" the maintenance workloads. So armed, the manager may analyze alternative ways of responding to workload variability. Analysis methods include the use of mathematical queuing formulas and Monte Carlo simulation of waiting lines. The application of waiting lines (queues), queuing formulas, and simulation to services in general is discussed in the chapter supplement. Uses of queuing formulas and simulation in maintenance management are considered in the next sections.

Queuing formulas in maintenance

In the maintenance environment, surges in breakdowns are likely to result in queues (waiting lines) of repair orders waiting for repair crews. Long, hard-to-repair jobs are also likely to result in queues of repair jobs unless the maintenance department can find extra repair crews to assign to the new jobs that arrive. We see that maintenance jobs might queue up waiting for service for two reasons. One reason is a surge in breakdowns; that is, the *arrival rate* of jobs needing service increases. The other reason is a slowdown in the time required to make repairs; that is, the *service rate* decreases.

The maintenance manager knows that adding repair crews speeds up average service times and cuts queue lengths, but the manager does not know by how much. A simple, precise way to find out how adding repair crews affects queues is to use queuing formulas. The formulas are simple in that most require only two inputs:

1. Mean arrival rate in units arriving per time period; the Greek letter *lambda*, λ, is the symbol.
2. Mean service rate in units served per time period; the Greek letter *mu*, μ, is the symbol.

A queuing example. Common queuing formulas that use the λ and μ inputs are presented in the chapter supplement. A limitation is the necessary assumption that arrival rates and/or service rates follow the Poisson probability distribution. This and other requisites are more fully discussed after the following example of the use of queuing formulas. (Basic queuing formulas may be found in Figure S13–2 in the supplement.)

EXAMPLE 13–3
Queuing for plumbing service

At present the plumbing breakdown crew can easily handle plumbing trouble calls. The logbook shows that trouble calls come in on an average of one call every 100 minutes; thus the mean arrival rate, λ, is 0.01 calls per minute. The dispatcher's logbook also shows that the average plumbing repair takes 33 minutes; that is a mean service rate, μ, of 1/33, or 0.03 repairs per minute. Thus, the service rate, 0.03, is three times as fast as the arrival rate, 0.01.

This is good service, but it means that the crew is busy only one third of the time. That should be obvious, but for those who like formulas, there is one for calculating "busyness" or utilization rate for a service facility—the repair crew in this case.

$$\text{Utilization rate} = \frac{\lambda}{\mu} = \frac{0.01}{0.03} = 0.33, \text{ or } 1/3.$$

The plumbing repair crew is really not idle the other 67 percent of the time. It has some shop cleanup and tool upkeep work to do between trouble calls. But should well-paid journeyman plumbers be sweeping floors and honing tools? The maintenance manager does not think so.

The maintenance manager is considering reducing plumbing crew size so that things are reversed; that is, his object is to keep the crew busy 67 percent of the time and "idle" only 33 percent of the time. This could be accomplished by cutting the crew size in half, thereby doubling service time. This will halve the wage expense. The manager feels that the change should hardly affect service since mean service rate would still be 50 percent faster than mean arrival rate, which may be proved by using an inversion of the utilization-rate formula:

Since utilization rate, U, $= \lambda/\mu$, then $\mu = \lambda/U$. Since $\lambda = 0.01$ and desired utilization rate, U, $= 0.67$,

$$\mu = \frac{\lambda}{U} = \frac{0.01}{0.67} = 0.015$$

Now μ at 0.015 is 50 percent faster than λ at 0.01.

Is the maintenance manager correct in believing that service would hardly be affected? Further use of queuing formulas may help to answer the question.

Solution:

The manager's belief that service would hardly be affected calls for an analysis of queue times and queue lengths. That is, service responsiveness to trouble calls may be measured by average trouble-call waiting time, which is the mean time that trouble-call orders sit on the dispatcher's desk waiting, in queue, for a plumbing crew to return from previous trouble-call work. In addition, service may be measured by the average number of jobs waiting in the queue.

Queuing formulas are available for the two measures, average (mean) time in queue, T_q, and average (mean) number in queue, N_q. The formulas are:

$$T_q = \frac{\lambda}{\mu(\mu - \lambda)} \qquad N_q = \frac{\lambda^2}{\mu(\mu - \lambda)}$$

For the present size of plumbing crew, $\lambda = 0.01$ trouble calls per minute and $\mu = 0.03$ repairs per minute. Therefore,

$$\text{Mean time in queue} = T_q = \frac{\lambda}{\mu(\mu - \lambda)}$$

$$= \frac{0.01}{(0.03)(0.03 - 0.01)}$$

$$= \frac{0.01}{(0.03)(0.02)} = \frac{0.01}{0.0006} = 16.67 \text{ minutes per job}$$

$$\text{Mean number in queue} = N_q = \frac{\lambda^2}{\mu(\mu - \lambda)}$$

$$= \frac{(0.01)^2}{(0.03)(0.03 - 0.01)}$$

$$= \frac{0.0001}{0.0006} = 0.17 \text{ jobs}$$

The manager has proposed reducing crew size by half, which cuts service rate, μ, from 0.03 to 0.15. Arrival rate, λ, stays at 0.01. For this proposed level of staffing,

$$\text{Mean time in queue} = T_q = \frac{\lambda}{\mu(\mu - \lambda)}$$

$$= \frac{0.01}{(0.015)(0.015 - 0.01)}$$

$$= \frac{0.01}{(0.015)(0.005)}$$

$$= \frac{0.01}{0.000075} = 133.33 \text{ minutes per job}$$

Mean number in queue $= N_q = \dfrac{\lambda^2}{\mu(\mu - \lambda)}$

$$= \dfrac{(0.01)^2}{(0.015)(0.015 - 0.01)}$$

$$= \dfrac{0.0001}{0.000075} = 1.33 \text{ jobs}$$

The calculated results may be compared. Cutting the crew size in half increases mean waiting time from $T_q = 16.67$ minutes per job to $T_q = 133.33$ minutes per job. This is an eightfold increase in waiting time, a considerable deterioration in service. At the same time mean number of plumbing jobs waiting for a crew increases from $N_q = 0.17$ jobs to $N_q = 1.33$ jobs, which is also an eightfold increase. The maintenance manager believed that cutting crew size in half would have little effect on service, but the queuing analysis proves him wrong.

The analysis need not stop here. Even though service deteriorates a good deal when plumbing crews are cut, the wage reduction may be large enough to justify proceeding with the cut. In some waiting-line problems a cost may be placed on waiting time, and the sum of waiting-time cost and repair-crew wages can be compared for each size of crew. (This type of cost analysis is presented later in a waiting-line simulation example.) The costs of waiting for a plumbing crew are hard to estimate, however. It appears that the maintenance manager's decision would need to be based on a mix of service-*time* data and wage-*cost* data rather than complete cost data.

Queuing requirements. The above problem serves to show the high degree of efficiency of queuing formulas: The casual observer sees a rather disorderly process of random job arrivals, queue variability, and service-time variability; yet a few trivial calculations reduce it all to easy-to-comprehend responsiveness statistics. And it is not only the calculations that are simple. There are but two items of input data: λ and μ. These means may be computed based on sample cases from a dispatcher's logbook.

For all this efficiency there are two major requirements or limitations in queuing formulas. One is the Poisson probability distribution requisite; it was mentioned earlier, but it merits further discussion.

Are plumbing trouble calls and service rates sufficiently Poisson for the above solution to be valid? The trouble calls probably are. "Natural" arrival rates, such as "arrival" of breakdowns of mechanical devices, are most likely to follow the idealized Poisson distribution. Anytime people get into the act, their habits and proclivities tend to distort the natural Poisson pattern; examples are the human tendency to *balk* at entering a long queue and to *renege* or leave a queue that is moving too slowly. But distorting human influences seem minor in the case of washbasins, sewer systems, and other potential spots for plumbing breakdowns.

Plumbing service-rate distributions seem more subject to distorting human influences. The natural Poisson shape, shown in Figure 13–7A, has a tail extending (skewed) far to the right. But the plumbers may feel some pressure not to allow the tail to go so far. That is, during a very time-consuming plumbing repair the queue of other trouble calls may lengthen. The dispatcher may then put pressure on the plumbers to get done and move on to the next case. Most of us are quite capable of working far faster than we normally do, at least for short spurts of time. That is what the plumbers might typically do in response to queuing pressure. The distribution is no longer perfect Poisson but is crunched from the right, as in Figure 13–7B.

FIGURE 13–7
Distortions of
service-rate
distributions

A.

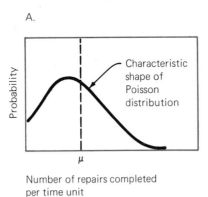

Number of repairs completed
per time unit

B.

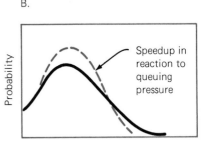

Number of repairs completed
per time unit

D.

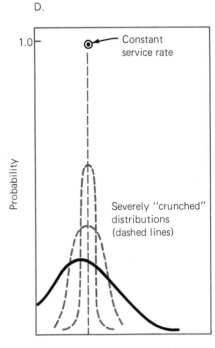

Number of repairs completed
per time unit

C.

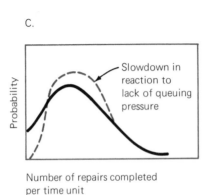

Number of repairs completed
per time unit

There may be an opposite reaction to opposite conditions. Say, for example, that the plumbers are on a minor job and know that there are no backlogged trouble calls. Their reaction might be to stretch out the job. (Stretching out work to fill the available time is a phenomenon popularly—or unpopularly—known as Parkinson's Law.) If this becomes a common response, the Poisson curve becomes crunched from the left, as in Figure 13–7C.

Figure 13–7D shows the effect of crunching on both the right and the left. As the stretching out of short jobs and the compressing of long jobs is increased, the distribution narrows and grows taller. The limit is where distribution (variability) disappears and gives way to a constant service rate. That rate is the single circled point, with probability equal to 1.0.

The second major requirement of queuing formulas is that they be based on a steady-state condition, which means a condition in which average waiting lines no longer change. Before a repair system achieves steady-state maturity, it must, of course, start up. (The transition from start-up to steady state is discussed in the chapter supplement.) At the beginning of start-up there are zero jobs waiting.

During the transition to a steady state, the average number of repair jobs waiting and the average waiting time continually change. A repair system may close down at the end of the day without ever having achieved steady state. If that is so, it is start-up—every workday, for example—and the transient state that are of interest. Queuing formulas are inaccurate in such cases, and their degree of inaccuracy depends on the degree of change from start-up to steady state. In such cases, Monte Carlo simulation is an alternative.

Monte Carlo simulation in maintenance

Monte Carlo simulation is not difficult, but it is time-consuming; it is messy compared with the mathematical simplicity of queuing formulas. But Monte Carlo simulation is versatile; it can capture repair-time distributions distorted by repairmen's proclivities, and it can deal with start-up as well as steady-state conditions in a repair system.

A basic discussion and a simplified example of Monte Carlo simulation are included in the chapter supplement. A more elaborate example of Monte Carlo simulation in a fairly realistic maintenance setting is presented in this section. (The simulation in the supplement is a simple case presented slowly and thoroughly; here a more complex case is presented with less basic explanation.) An intent of the example is to show that simulation of realistic waiting-line situations is difficult and time-consuming—but sometimes promises a high payoff.

A Monte Carlo simulation example. The following example demonstrates a five-step procedure for Monte Carlo simulation analysis. The steps are shown in Figure 13–8. They consist of collecting input data on job arrivals and service times, transforming the data into probability distributions, performing the simulations, summarizing the outputs, and analyzing the alternatives supported by the output information. Each of these steps is demonstrated in the example.

FIGURE 13–8
Monte Carlo
simulation
analysis

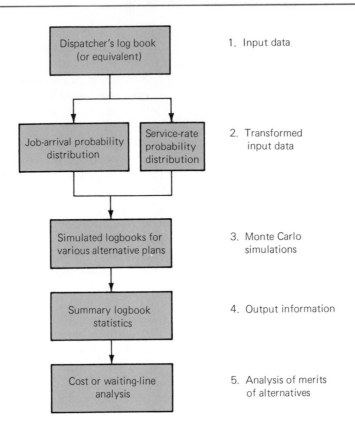

1. Input data

2. Transformed
   input data

3. Monte Carlo
   simulations

4. Output information

5. Analysis of merits
   of alternatives

EXAMPLE 13–4
Monte Carlo
simulation of
repair-crew
sizes

At Echo Engine Co. the most serious and recurring bottleneck is malfunction or breakdown of any of the large number of powered conveyor sections that feed various parts to the engine assembly line. Conveyor failure shuts down the given feeder line, idling its work crew. Crew size is nearly the same on each feeder line, and a flat $50 per hour may be used as the cost of feeder-line idleness.

A four-hour parts inventory is stockpiled at the end of each feeder line. If any feeder line is idle for more than four hours, the parts stockpile is used up, idling the whole assembly line; the cost of assembly-line idleness is $1,000 per hour. A partial layout sketch of the assembly line and the feeder lines is shown in Figure 13–9.

Currently Echo's Maintenance Department employs one mechanic whose main job is to repair and adjust conveyors. The mechanic's wage is $10 per hour, time and a half ($15) for overtime. Overtime is scheduled for any maintenance not completed during the eight-hour workday.

Echo operates only one production shift per day, but an evening skeleton crew builds up parts stockpiles so that the four-hour parts inventories are fully restored by the next morning. That way the regular day-shift production crews are not paid for any overtime.

The question is, Is one mechanic enough?

Solution:

Monte Carlo simulation seems clearly preferable to queuing formulas for the following reasons:

1. Because of distorting human influences, breakdown and service-rate probability distributions are not likely to be Poisson, which is necessary when queuing formulas are used. Monte Carlo simulation is usable with any probability distribution.
2. The system starts fresh each day with empty queues, and average queues grow as the day progresses; queuing formulas require steady-state queue conditions.

Step 1: Input data. The conveyor repairman acts as his own dispatcher, and his trouble-call logbook is complete and accurate. The logbook is shown in Figure 13–10A. Logbook records on breakdown times and repair start and finish times provide the necessary input data for Monte Carlo simulation.

Step 2: Transformed input data. The logbook provides enough data for computing arrival-time and service-time probability distributions. To the logbook in Figure 13–9A, two columns of working figures may be added: an interarrival-time (time-between-arrivals) column and a service-time column. These working figures are shown in Figure 13–10B, just to the right of the raw data in the repair logbook. Interarrival time (IAT) is determined by successive subtraction of trouble-call times. The first trouble call after the 8:00 A.M. opening time is at 9:20, and 9:20 minus 8:00 is 1:20, or 80 minutes, the IAT. The repair time for call number 1 is 9:50 minus 9:20, which is 30 minutes. Each of the other IAT and repair-time working figures is similarly calculated.

The next step is to transform the working figures into frequency distributions. To do this, the continuous distributions must be segmented into intervals; 15-minute intervals will suffice. Then, tallying the number of working figures that fall into each interval produces the frequency distributions. For the single day's working figures, the tallying is as shown in Figure 13–10C. The arrows in the figure show where the tally marks go for trouble-call number 1. The 80-minute IAT falls within the interval 75–89, so one tally is entered in the 75–89 row under IAT frequencies. The 30-minute repair

FIGURE 13–9
Layout sketch of Echo Engine plant

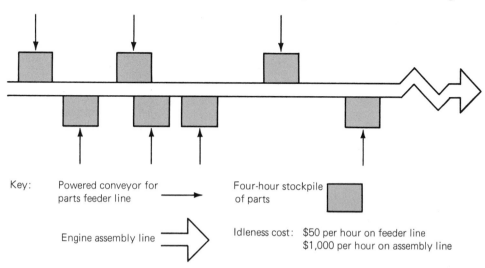

Key: Powered conveyor for parts feeder line   ⟶

Engine assembly line ⟹

Four-hour stockpile of parts ▭

Idleness cost: $50 per hour on feeder line
$1,000 per hour on assembly line

time falls within the interval 30–44, so one tally is entered in the 30–44 row under repair-time frequencies. The rest of Figure 13–10C is determined similarly.

For only seven trouble calls—one day's worth—the frequency distribution table is sparse. It is desirable to gather and tally trouble-call data for a number of days, so that the full range of variability may be captured in the frequency distributions. Let us assume that a total of 100 trouble calls is tallied and that the resulting frequency distributions are as shown in Figure 13–11A.

FIGURE 13–10
Developing IAT and service-time frequency distributions

A. Logbook entries

B. Working figures

Date	Number	Time	Started	Completed	IAT (minutes)	Repair times (minutes)
		Trouble call	Service			
3/12	1	9:20	9:20	9:50	80	30
	2	10:25	10:25	11:35	65	70
	3	10:55	11:35		30	
		Lunch 12:00–1:00		1:05		30
	4	1:05	1:05	1:50	70	45
	5	1:15	1:50	2:50	10	60
	6	3:20	3:20	3:45	125	25
	7	4:35	4:35	5:10	75	35

C. IAT and service-time frequencies

Frequencies

Interval	IAT	Repair times
0–14		
15–29		
30–44		
45–59		
60–74	||	||
75–89		
90–104		
105–119		
120–134		
135–149		
150–164		
165–179		
180–194		
195–209		
210–224		
225–239		

FIGURE 13–11
Transformed trouble-call and service-time data for Echo Engine Co.

A. Frequency distributions

Interval	IAT	Service-time
0–14	‖‖ ‖	‖‖ ‖‖ ‖‖
15–29	‖‖ ‖‖	‖‖ ‖‖ ‖‖ ‖‖ ‖‖
30–44	‖‖ ‖‖	‖‖ ‖‖ ‖‖ ‖‖ ‖‖ ‖‖
45–59	‖‖	‖‖ ‖‖ ‖‖ ‖‖
60–74	‖‖ ‖‖	‖‖
75–89	‖‖ ‖‖	
90–104	‖‖ ‖‖ ‖‖	
105–119	‖‖ ‖‖ ‖‖	
120–134	‖‖ ‖‖ ‖‖	
135–149	‖‖ ‖‖	
150–164	‖‖ ‖	
165–179	‖‖ ‖	
180–194	‖‖ ‖‖	
195–209	‖‖	
210–224	‖	
225–239	‖	
	100	100

B. Probabilities and Monte Carlo number ranges

	IAT		Service Time	
Interval midpoints	Proba-bilities	Monte Carlo number ranges	Proba-bilities	Monte Carlo number ranges
7	0.03	00–02	0.15	00–14
22	0.05	03–05	0.25	15–39
37	0.04	06–09	0.30	40–69
52	0.05	10–14	0.20	70–89
67	0.07	15–21	0.05	90–94
82	0.10	22–31	0.03	95–97
97	0.14	32–45	0.02	98–99
112	0.15	46–60		
127	0.13	61–73		
142	0.09	74–82		
157	0.06	83–88		
172	0.04	89–92		
187	0.03	93–95		
202	0.02	96–97		
217	0.01	98		
232	0.01	99		
	1.00		1.00	

Step 3: Monte Carlo simulations. Figure 13–11B is extended from Figure 13–11A. The midpoints in B are midpoints for each interval in A; and the probabilities in B are the number of tallies in A divided by the total of 100 tallies in the sample. The probabilities are then expressed as ranges of two-digit numbers from 00 to 99; these may be called Monte Carlo number ranges. The sizes of the Monte Carlo number ranges are proportional to the probabilities; for example, 00–02 comprises 3 of the 100 numbers, which is proportional to the probability 0.03.

Now a simulated logbook may be developed by drawing numbers from a table of uniformly distributed random numbers and fitting them into the Monte Carlo ranges. Two-digit random numbers are provided in Table S13–1 in the chapter supplement. The first random number in the upper left corner of the table is 42; 42 fits into IAT range 32–45, representing the midpoint 97 (see Figure 13–11B). Therefore, the first trouble call occurs at 00 (beginning of shift) plus 97, that is, the 97th minute. The next lower random number, 55, is used to simulate the service time; the 55 fits into service-time range 40–69, representing 37. Therefore the first simulated trouble call takes 37 minutes to repair.

These numbers are entered in columns 3, 4, 7, and 8 of Figure 13–12A, which is a simulation of 20 trouble calls with one repairman at Echo Engines. Other times are developed from the IAT (column 4) and service-time (column 8) entries. Column 5 contains trouble-call arrival times, which are the cumulative interarrival times. The IAT for trouble call 2 is 82, which means 82 minutes between call 1 and call 2. Therefore, since call 1 arrived in minute 97, call 2 arrives in 97 + 82 = 179.

Column 9, time service completed, is simply time service started (column 6) plus service time (column 8). For the first call, service time is completed at 97 + 37 = minute 134.

Column 6, time service started, is the same as trouble-call arrival time (column 5) when there is no waiting line of trouble calls. This is the case for calls 1 and 2. Call 3 arrives in minute 291, but we see from column 9 that call 2 is still in service until minute 321. Thus call 3 has to wait. The wait amounts to 321 − 291 = 30 minutes, which is entered in column 10, feeder-line idleness waiting for repairman.

Column 11, repairman overtime (after 480th minute), may contain entries only at the end of the day—if overtime is needed. In this simulation overtime is needed every day when there is only one repairman. In day 1, 150 minutes of overtime are needed because trouble-call number 4 is not completed until minute 635, and the regular shift is only 480 minutes: 635 − 480 = 155 minutes overtime. In day 5 overtime is needed for the last three trouble calls (18, 19, and 20), since all three are completed later than the 480th minute.

Column 12, assembly-line idleness for repair (of feeder line) over four hours, occurs only in day 5 for call 18. Feeder-line idleness for call 18 is 285 minutes (column 10), which is 45 minutes longer than the 240-minute (four-hour) stockpile of feeder-line parts. When feeder-line parts are gone, the whole assembly line stops.

Figure 13–12B and 13–12C show the same simulation data as applied to two and three repairmen, respectively, but only for the busiest repair day, day 5. The random-number and IAT columns are omitted in Figure 13–12B and 13–12C, and a new column (number 5) is added to show which repairman the job is assigned to.

In Figure 13–12B call 15 is assigned to repairman 1, who leaves at minute 82 and returns at minute 194. Meanwhile, trouble call 16 comes in at minute 89, so it is assigned to repairman 2. Call 17 comes in at minute 171 when both repairmen are out. The first to return is repairman 1 at minute 194, so he gets call 17. Call 17 had to wait $194 - 171 = 23$ minutes, which is entered as feeder-line idleness (column 8). Overtime is not needed until call 19. That call is completed in minute 537, 57 minutes after the day shift ending time in minute 480.

Step 4: Summary logbook statistics. Summary idleness and overtime totals are shown for day 5 Figure 13–12A, 13–12B, and 13–12C. The results are no surprise: Feeder-line idleness while waiting for a repairman is drastically cut from 688 minutes for one repairman, to 46 minutes for two repairmen, to 1 minute for three repairmen. And, of course, the 30 minutes of feeder-line idleness in day 1 and the 45 minutes assembly-line idleness in day 5 are cut to zero with more repairmen. Overtime is reduced slightly with more repairmen.

The five-day, 20-call simulation is too short to be precise. Let us assume that the simulation is continued for 100 days. Idleness and overtime data for the 100-day simulation may be averaged. Assume that the averaged data are:

One repairman
Feeder-line idleness . . . . 130 min./day
Overtime . . . . 110 min./day
Assembly-line idleness . . . . 5 min./day

Two repairmen
Feeder-line idleness . . . . 3 min./day
Overtime . . . . 100 min./day
Assembly-line idleness . . . . 0 min./day

Three repairmen
Feeder-line idleness . . . . 0.1 min.day
Overtime . . . . 95 min./day
Assembly-line idleness . . . . 0 min./day

Step 5: Cost analysis of repairman alternatives. The total costs for each repairman alternative are the sum of regular and overtime repairman wages and the cost of feeder-line and assembly-line idleness. Not relevant are the wages of production workers and feeder-line idleness during service; they are constant—not related to number of repairmen. Relevant average daily costs are determined below.

The regular wage rate was given as $10 per hour per repairman. For an eight-hour day, wage costs are:

For one repairman:
$$1 \text{ repairman} \times \$10/\text{hr.} \times 8 \text{ hours} = \$80/\text{day}$$
For two repairmen:
$$2 \text{ repairmen} \times \$10/\text{hr.} \times 8 \text{ hours} = \$160/\text{day}$$
For three repairmen:
$$3 \text{ repairmen} \times \$10/\text{hr.} \times 8 \text{ hours} = \$240/\text{day}$$

Overtime wages are time and a half, or $15 per hour. Simulated overtime per day, from step 4 above, is 110 minutes for one repairman, 100 minutes for two repairmen, and 95 minutes for three repairmen. Therefore, the daily costs are:

For one repairman: $\dfrac{110 \text{ min./day}}{60 \text{ min./hr.}} \times \$15/\text{hr.} = \$27.50/\text{day}$

For two repairmen: $\dfrac{100 \text{ min./day}}{60 \text{ min./hr.}} \times \$15/\text{hr.} = \$25.00/\text{day}$

For three repairmen: $\dfrac{95 \text{ min./day}}{60 \text{ min./hr.}} \times \$15/\text{hr.} = \$23.75/\text{day}$

FIGURE 13–12
Simulation of trouble calls and repairs, Echo Engine Co.

A. One repairman

(1) Day	(2) Trouble-call number	(3) Random number for generating IAT	(4) IAT	(5) Trouble-call arrival time (cumulative IAT)	(6) Time service started	(7) Random number for generating service time	(8) Service time	(9) Time service completed	(10) Feeder-line idleness waiting for repairman (minutes)	(11) Repairman overtime (minutes after 480th minute)	(12) Assembly-line idleness for repair over four hours (minutes)
1	1	42	97	97	97	55	37	134			
	2	24	82	179	179	82	142	321			
	3	56	112	291	321	48	112	433	30		
	4	95	187	478	478	86	157	635		155	
2	5	49	112	112	112	41	97	209			
	6	95	187	299	299	78	142	441			
	7	84	157	456	456	40	97	553		73	
5	8	80	142	142	142	12	52	194			
	9	84	157	299	299	01	7	306			
	10	25	82	381	381	46	112	495		13	
4	11	83	157	157	157	69	127	284			
	12	78	142	299	299	43	97	396			
	13	07	37	336	396	00	7	403	60		
	14	55	112	448	448	17	67	515		35	
5	15	22	82	82	82	57	112	194	105		
	16	02	7	89	194	70	127	321	150		
	17	28	82	171	321	86	157	478	285		
	18	04	22	193	478	95	187	665	115	185	
	19	89	172	365	665	92	172	837	33	172	45
	20	30	82	447	837	86	157	994		157	
								Day 5 totals:	688	510	45

B. Two repairmen

(1) Day	(2) Trouble-call number	(3) Trouble-call arrival time	(4) Time service started	(5) Which repairman job is assigned to	(6) Service time	(7) Time service completed	(8) Feeder-line idleness waiting for repairman (minutes)	(9) Repairman overtime (minutes after 480th minute)
5	15	82	82	1	112	194		
	16	89	89	2	127	216		
	17	171	194	1	157	351	23	
	18	193	216	2	187	403	23	
	19	365	365	1	172	537		57
	20	447	447	2	157	604		124
	Day 5 totals:						46	181

C. Three repairmen

(1) Day	(2) Trouble-call number	(3) Trouble-call arrival time	(4) Time service started	(5) Which repairman job is assigned to	(6) Service time	(7) Time service completed	(8) Feeder-line idleness waiting for repairman (minutes)	(9) Repairman overtime (minutes after 480th minute)
5	15	82	82	1	112	194		
	16	89	89	2	127	216		
	17	171	171	3	157	328		
	18	193	194	1	187	381	1	
	19	365	365	2	172	537		57
	20	447	447	3	157	604		124
	Day 5 totals:						1	181

Feeder-line idleness cost was given as $50 per hour. Simulated feeder-line idleness per day, from step 4 above, is 130 minutes for one repairman, 3 minutes for two repairmen and 0.1 minute for three repairmen. The daily costs are:

For one repairman:

$$\frac{130 \text{ min./day}}{60 \text{ min./hr.}} \times \$50/\text{hr.} = \$108.33/\text{day}$$

For two repairmen:

$$\frac{3 \text{ min./day}}{60 \text{ min./hr.}} \times \$50/\text{hr.} = \$2.50$$

For three repairmen:

$$\frac{0.1 \text{ min./day}}{60 \text{ min./hr.}} \times \$50/\text{hr.} = \$0.08/\text{day}$$

Assembly-line idleness was given as $1,000 per hour. Simulated assembly-line idleness, from step 4 above, is five hours for one repairman and zero time for two and three repairmen. The daily cost for one repairman is:

$$\frac{5 \text{ min./day}}{60 \text{ min./hr.}} \times \$1,000/\text{hr.} = \$83.33/\text{day}$$

The four types of daily costs are totaled in Figure 13–13 for the three staffing options. Comparing the total costs is helpful in deciding on the best staffing policy.

FIGURE 13–13
Total costs for three staffing options, Echo Engines Co.

| Number of repairmen | Wages | | Idleness | | Total average daily cost |
	Regular	Overtime	Feeder-line	Assembly-line	
1	$ 80.00	$27.50	$108.33	$83.33	$291.16
2	160.00	25.00	2.50	0	187.50
3	240.00	23.75	0.08	0	263.83

In the figure the total average cost per day for two repairmen is $187.50. This is over $75 per day less than the next lowest cost, $263.83 for three repairmen. The wage cost alone for three repairmen is $240 per day, considerably more than the total daily cost for two repairmen. The $75 per day saving, when extended to a 250-day year, is a saving of $18,750 per year. On the basis of costs alone, two repairmen is clearly the best staffing policy. An additional intangible advantage of two (and three) repairmen over one repairman is that output on the engine line is more predictable and uniform when feeder-line breakdowns can be repaired without waiting time.

Understanding waiting-line phenomena. The chief limitation of Monte Carlo simulation is cost. Monte Carlo simulation is as time-consuming—to set up and run—as queuing formulas are time-saving. But Monte Carlo can be as realistic as one cares to make it—and as one cares to pay for.

Despite the time and cost it requires, Monte Carlo simulation can pay large dividends. In the preceding simple case of repairing conveyors, the saving—two repairmen instead of one—amounts to $18,750 per year. The cost to set up and run the simulation is a pittance compared to that. But let us not become overly ecstatic. It may be that the maintenance chief and the production chief together would conclude that two repairmen are optimal—*without benefit of simulation,* and without the cost.

The astute manager is able to recognize when a good decision may be based purely on judgment and when simulation or other analysis is called for. What is it that makes for an astute manager, capable of recognizing these things? The answer is, in part, the manager who thoroughly understands waiting-line phenomena. And the best way to understand waiting lines is probably *not* by experience and personal observation; that would provide only limited exposure even in a lifetime. Those who best understand waiting lines are those who have studied many cases—in relatively short periods of time—as students, for example.

It may be true that study is rarely a worthy substitute for the real thing. Let us examine why, in the case of waiting lines, study may well be superior to the real thing.

One aspect that the student may learn about is how waiting lines are affected by different arrival and service-line distributions. These distributions may be wide or narrow, close together or far apart.

In the Echo Engines example the means of the two distributions are rather far apart: The mean interarrival time is 108 minutes between breakdowns, while the mean service time is far faster at 40 minutes per repair. Yet waiting lines form. The reason is that the probability distributions are wide enough to intersect substantially. This is shown in the accompanying sketch.

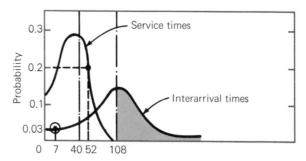

Minutes per repair job

The sketch shows that repair service never takes as long as 108 minutes. Since 108 is the mean, or 50 percent point, on the IAT probability distribution, this means that the 50 percent of trouble calls in the shaded area cannot contribute to waiting lines. But any calls in the unshaded half have a chance of being delayed. For example, 3 percent of all trouble calls arrive at seven-minute intervals; see the circled point on the sketch. And 20 percent of all calls take 52 minutes to repair; see the dot on the sketch. That combination of events—7 minutes between arrivals and 52 minutes to repair—occurs statistically only 6 times in 1,000 ($0.03 \times 0.20 = 0.006$). But since these are random events, there is nothing to stop several such events from occurring in a row. That is generally what happened in week 5 in the Echo Engines example: Arrivals (of conveyor breakdowns) came fast, and service slowed. The result was very long waiting time.

When should you simulate? To repeat, the astute manager might realize all these things without simulation. Simulation may be reserved for trickier cases. Tricky cases are created when the distributions move closer together. The accompanying sketch illustrates.

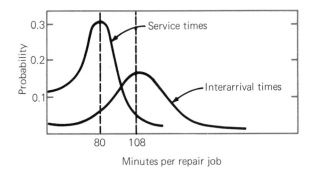

Minutes per repair job

The shapes of the two curves are the same as in the previous sketch, but the service-time curve has moved to the right, from a mean of 40 to a mean of 80. (Such a service slowdown could be caused by greater problems in repairing aging equipment.)

Greater overlap between the two curves causes greater variability in waiting-line length. Greater variability of waiting-line length results in more choices. Assume, for example, that the above sketch applies to Echo Engines. If so, the maintenance manager might be thinking about the choice of one, two, three, four, five, or six repairmen rather than only one, two, or three. One repairman might be enough for the low extremes in waiting-line length, but six might be needed to handle the high extremes. So large a number of choices is difficult to judge, even if the manager is "astute" about waiting-line behaviors. Monte Carlo simulation becomes more attractive.

Various arrival- and service-time conditions. Figure 13–14 illustrates the two cases discussed above: moderate overlap (case C) and great overlap (case D) between interarrival-time and service-time distributions; it also includes three other cases: narrow distributions, no overlap, and "total" overlap.

For case A, narrow distributions, there is no point in simulating. The distributions are too narrow. It is practical to act as if interarrival and service times were not distributed at all. In other words, find the modes of these very narrow

FIGURE 13-14
Arrival- and
service-time
conditions and
effects

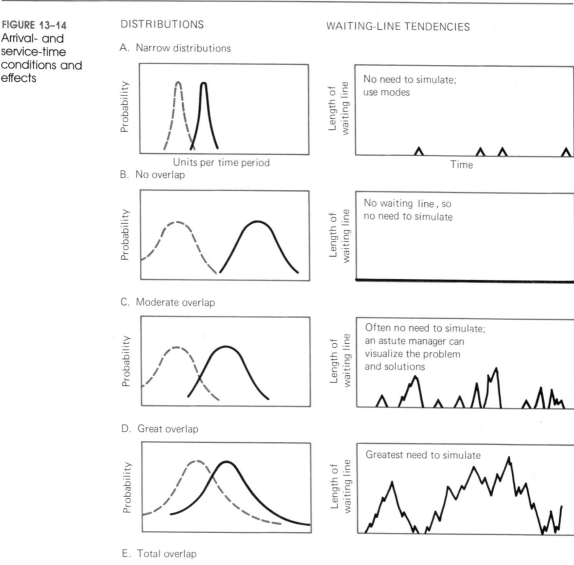

DISTRIBUTIONS

A. Narrow distributions

Probability

Units per time period

B. No overlap

Probability

C. Moderate overlap

Probability

D. Great overlap

Probability

E. Total overlap

Probability

WAITING-LINE TENDENCIES

Length of waiting line

No need to simulate;
use modes

Time

Length of waiting line

No waiting line, so
no need to simulate

Length of waiting line

Often no need to simulate;
an astute manager can
visualize the problem
and solutions

Length of waiting line

Greatest need to simulate

Length of waiting line

No need to simulate;
unstable, so
intervention is
required (can't
simulate instability)

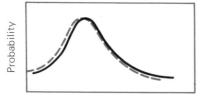

(dashed lines are arrival
distributions; solid lines
are service-time distributions)

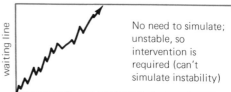

distributions, that is, the most frequently occurring interarrival time and service time; then treat the modes as single-valued estimates. That way, decisions on staffing and scheduling are simple—often self-evident.

For case B, the probability distributions are wide but do not overlap. Without overlap, there are no interactions, no chances of waiting lines, and thus there is nothing to simulate. Staffing and scheduling should be based on the expected values (e.g., average or mean of interarrival and service times).

Case E, total overlap, *could* be simulated. Generally it should not be. The result is a foregone conclusion: growth toward an infinite queue. The *pattern* of growth could be simulated; this might seem valuable in order to learn about waiting-line behavior in the start-up phase. But it would usually not be worth doing, because the conditions leading to an infinite queue are unstable. It is highly likely that management would quickly intervene to reduce such instability. The condition would scarcely last long enough to gather data to simulate it.

We have seen that four of the five cases in Figure 13–14 do not seem to call for Monte Carlo simulation. Considering the cost of simulation, that is good news!

Maintenance managers—and managers of other service units—are not likely to find a lot of uses for Monte Carlo simulation. They should, however, find many uses for a thorough understanding of waiting-line phenomena.

It was noted in earlier chapters that Monte Carlo simulation is a versatile tool. It has some value in inventory management and considerable value in job-shop production scheduling.

SUMMARY

A maintenance department is likely to house both maintenance planning and maintenance operations (and may house other facilities planning and engineering functions as well). Maintenance planning centers on choices between periodic and irregular maintenance.

Periodic maintenance ranges from routine custodianship to well-planned preventive maintenance (PM) to group-replacement and standby-equipment policies. Custodianship and PM warrant careful managerial oversight; an effective PM program also requires good records. Group-replacement and standby-equipment decisions usually require cost analysis.

Group replacement may apply to any large group of identical components that are subject to failure (rather than wear-out). The analyst considers costs of two replacement options. One is replacing components as they fail on a trouble-call basis. The second is replacing all components at periodic intervals, plus trouble-call replacements between periods. Data inputs are: (1) unit costs of each type of replacement and (2) the historical pattern of component lives. The latter may be expressed as a failure probability distribution, or actual numbers of failures per time unit as determined in a live test may be used.

Standby-equipment analysis also applies to large groups—but groups of machines, not components. Failures of machines (in a group) tend to follow the Poisson probability distribution. If the maintenance manager knows the average number that fail per time period, the probabilities of any other number of failures per time period may be found using Poisson tables or formulas. The probability of any number of out-of-service machines may be multiplied by the cost of lost service. The other cost factor is cost to keep standby machines on hand—to avoid lost service. A minimum-cost standby policy is sought.

Irregular maintenance, for example, repairing breakdowns, is a special problem, because breakdowns are random. Like other services, repair services are faced with heavy demand at some times and with light demand at other times—a roller-coaster workload pattern. Waiting lines of jobs (or customers) form at busy times; staff idleness may occur at slow times. Two methods of analyzing waiting lines and idleness (or utilization) are queuing formulas and Monte Carlo simulation.

Queuing formulas are based on the assumption that job arrival rates and service rates are Poisson-distributed (or constant). Only the mean arrival rate and service rate need be known. With those means, a host of waiting and service-facility statistics may be computed. Queuing formulas are most valid when human variability is a minor influence, for example in a machine-controlled situation.

Monte Carlo simulation yields the same kinds of statistics on waiting and on service-facility use/idleness as queuing formulas do. But simulation works in complex cases, whereas queuing formulas do not. Simulation is much more demanding than queuing formulas because of the need to gather and manipulate data on nonstandard (non-Poisson) arrival and service rates. The Monte Carlo process involves drawing random numbers and letting the numbers stand for a certain time between arrivals and a certain service time. The output (often from a computer) is a simulated logbook of arrivals and services, plus summary statistics on waiting and on utilization of service facilities. Simulation is too expensive to use on small waiting-line problems, but simulation studies can help sharpen a manager's judgment about waiting-line behaviors.

REFERENCES

Books

Hildebrand, James K. *Maintenance Turns to the Computer.* Cahners, 1972 (TS192.H55).

Lewis, Bernard T., and J. P. Marron. *Facilities and Plant Engineering Handbook.* McGraw-Hill, 1973 (TS184.L48).

Mann, Lawrence, Jr. *Maintenance Management.* Lexington Books, 1976 (TS192.M38).

Murphy, James A., ed. *Plant Engineering Management.* Society of Manufacturing Engineers, 1971 (TS184.P435x).

Periodicals

Plant Engineering, includes plant maintenance.

PROBLEMS

Note: Asterisked (*) problems require more than mimicry. They require judgment, and you should include discussion of reasons, assumptions, and outside sources of information.

Maintenance (facilities analysis)

*1. Every maintenance *operation* requires facilities *planning* (see Figure 13–1). A number of maintenance operations are listed below:

Replace ceramic tiles in a floor.

Mop floors.

Repair power outage.

Change oil and grease equipment.

Change dies—simply unscrew dirty one and screw on clean one—as they randomly clog up (in a factory full of plastics extrusion lines, each with a die to form the plastic).

Replace drive belts, bearings, and so on, as they fail (among large group of various machines on factory floor).

Repaint walls.

Maintain spare motors for bank of spinning machines.

Remodel president's office.

Repair shoes (shoe repair shop).

Your assignment is (1) to name one or more analysis techniques (if there are any) that apply to each maintenance operation and (2) to list the data inputs necessary to conduct the analysis. (Note: Some of the analysis methods were presented in Chapters 11 and 12.) Three completed examples follow:

Maintenance operation	Analysis technique	Data inputs
Rearrange office equipment	Layout analysis (Chapter 12)	Flow data (types and volume) Relationship data
Replace old lathe with new one	Replacement analysis (Chapter 11)	Purchase price O&M cost Salvage (trade-in) value
Prepare platform with utility hookups for new equipment	None	

PM

*2. With computers (microprocessors) now in common use as automobile control devices, perhaps the same computers or other computers could serve a preventive maintenance purpose. A dash panel could be used to input into a computer every maintenance operation performed on the car, and mileage data could be entered into the computer automatically. A screen could then recommend preventive maintenance whenever a program determines a need.

a. How practical do you think this idea is *right now?* What are some obstacles in the way of implementing such a PM system?

b. What are some important items of historical data that would need to be programmed into the auto's computer? Where would such data come from? Explain.

c. Large numbers of nearly identical autos are sold, which provides a sizable potential data base for gathering failure and wear-out data. For almost any type of factory machine there is not so large a potential data base, that is, there are far fewer "copies" of the same machine. Yet good factory PM is based on good failure records. How can good records be developed for factory machines?

Maintain-ability

*3. Think of three consumer products that advertisers tout as being especially *maintainable*. Distinguish between the maintainability and the reliability of each of those products.

*4. Name two industries in which maintainability is especially important. Especially unimportant. Discuss. What can a maintenance manager do about the maintainability of the facilities in his firm?

Group replacement

5. Diodes in a process control system have the following failure distribution:

Operating hours:	500	1,000	1,500	2,000
Probability of failure:	0.25	0.20	0.20	0.35

The diodes cost $0.10 each, and there are 100 of them. Labor to replace a single diode is $4.90, but it is only $0.90 if all 100 are replaced at one time.
   a. What is the expected operating life of a diode?
   b. For a maintenance policy of replacing the diodes as they fail, what is the replacement cost per 1,000 operating hours?
   c. Calculate the optimal group-replacement policy; assume that any failures between group replacements must be replaced immediately. Is the optimal group-replacement policy superior to the replace-as-they-fail policy?

6. Same as problem 5 above, except for the following changes: The diodes cost $1.10 each, and there are 50 of them; failures between group replacements need not be replaced.

7. There are 50 filter traps in the cooling system of a nuclear power plant. Monitor lights warn an attendant when a filter clogs up, and the attendant alerts the maintenance department. It costs $100 in labor and downtime to remove plates and clean out the filter. Maintenance can remove plates and clean out all 50 filters at the same time for a labor-and-downtime cost of $800.

The maintenance department has collected some experimental data on filter-clogging frequencies. The experiment began with 50 clean traps and ran for 6,000 hours. Results are:

Operating hours:	1,000	2,000	3,000	4,000	5,000	6,000
Number of clogged filters replaced during period:	1	3	5	6	6	6

What is the optimal maintenance policy?

8. A refinery has 50 identical pumps installed in various places. Replacing the seal in the pump motor is a delicate task requiring a visit from a maintenance engineer of the pump company, which is situated in another city. The cost of the trip is $200. The cost of replacing one seal is $20.

a. The refinery has used the 50 pumps for ten quarters (2½ years), which is the time that the plant has been in service. Pump seals have been replaced as they failed. The following is the failure history for the ten quarters.

Quarter	1	2	3	4	5	6	7	8	9	10
Seal failures	0	1	1	2	3	3	2	4	3	3

Analyze the merits of a group-replacement policy.

b. The pump company's engineers estimate the following probability distribution for the operating life of the pump seal.

Time until failure	1 qtr.	2 qtr.	3 qtr.	4 qtr.	5 qtr.	6 qtr.	7 qtr.	8 qtr.	3 yr.	4 yr.	5 yr.
Probability	0.0	0.01	0.02	0.02	0.02	0.04	0.04	0.05	0.25	0.30	0.25

Analyze the merits of a group-replacement policy, using the probability data.

*c. Which results should be used—those of part *a* or those of part *b*? Or doesn't it make any difference? Explain.

Standby equipment

9. A refinery has 50 identical pumps installed in various places. When a pump fails, the product flow rate drops, but the refining continues. The estimated average cost of reduced flow rate when a pump is down is $1,000 per day. If a spare pump is on hand when one goes down, the spare can be installed quickly enough so that flow-rate losses are negligible. It costs $60 per day to own and maintain one spare pump. The maintenance manager estimates that one pump per day fails on the average. How many spare pumps should be maintained?

Queuing

10. Voters arrive at a precinct polling place at a mean rate of 60 per hour during the peak 5:00–8:00 P.M. time period. Their mean voting rate is 61 per hour.

a. Though the line is long, there is virtually no balking or reneging on the part of new arrivals. (Those who make the effort to drive to the polls are apparently committed enough to wait through the lines.) What statistical distribution of arrivals seems likely, and why?

b. The service rates seem to approximate a Poisson distribution. (The distribution is "crunched" on the left just a bit—because voters are hurrying just a bit.) Calculate the mean waiting time in queue and the mean number in queue. Discuss these results.

c. The precinct captain has the authority to enforce a time limit of under five minutes for each voter in a voting booth (there are five booths). If the captain were to enforce the time limit, the voting time would be approximately constant at 4.9 minutes, because few voters take much less than that. What, then, would be the mean waiting time in queue and the mean number in queue? Explain your results—as compared with the results in part *b*.

d. For part *b*, draw arrival and service-time distributions on a single graph, as in Figure 13–14. Do the same for part *c*. Explain your results from parts *b* and *c* by referring to the graphs.

11. Plastic parts for medical syringes are manufactured in a completely automated molding plant. It is at present a one-shift (eight-hour-a-day) operation. That is, there are no production workers, only maintenance crews. Maintenance policies

need to be reviewed, by type of machine. The review begins with the molding-machine crew.

a. Molding machines break down at a mean rate of five per day. When a machine breaks down, the molding-machine crew is sent to fix it. The mean repair time is 45 minutes. Refer to the queuing formulas in Figure S13–2 in the chapter supplement, and make use of two that you feel would yield especially useful statistics for setting maintenance policies. Perform the calculations, and explain their value.

b. Is it reasonable to use queuing rather than Monte Carlo simulation in part a? Explain.

c. If a preventive maintenance (PM) program is established, molding-machine breakdowns would be expected to decrease from five to four per day. The PM crew would get its budget and staff from decreases in the repair crews; the smaller molding-machine repair crew would then require 60 minutes of mean repair time (instead of 45 minutes as in part a). Is the PM program worthwhile? Base your answer on queuing analysis.

Monte Carlo simulation

12. A group of similar machines requires servicing. Preventive maintenance is neither feasible nor economical in this case. Therefore, the problem is to hire that number of repairmen which results in minimizing the sum of the costs of machine idle time and the repairmen's wages. Solve the problem, using Monte Carlo simulation; limit your analysis to about 100 simulated hours. Comment on the validity of your simulation.

Data for solution:

Idle machine time is estimated to cost the company $35 per hour.

The daily wage for one repairman is $36.

Historical data on breakdown frequencies and repair times are as follows:

Breakdowns per hour	Frequency	Probability
0	1,025	0.854
1	156	0.130
2	19	0.016
3 or more	0	0.000
	1,200	1.000

Hours spent on repair	Frequency	Probability
2 or less	0	0.000
3	72	0.072
4	178	0.178
5	281	0.281
6	307	0.307
7	115	0.115
8	47	0.047
9 or more	0	0.000
	1,000	1.000

Suggestion: Set up a simulated logbook. Try simulating one repairman; show the resulting waiting-time costs plus wages for a given number of simulated hours. Then try the same thing for two repairmen, and so on, until the optimal hiring policy is apparent. (No two people should get the same results.)

13. Global Trade Center, a massive office complex retains its own elevator maintenance staff so that elevator breakdowns may be repaired fast. Problems occur when several elevators break down at the same time. A Monte Carlo simulation of breakdowns and service times is being performed based on logbook data. Simulated breakdowns and repair times are shown below, along with the random numbers used in their generation:

Breakdown number	Random number	Minutes between breakdowns	Random number	Repair minutes
1	29	50	95	60
2	01	10	55	40
3	97	130	80	50
4	54	80	66	40
5	19	40	95	60
6	08	20	12	10
7	27	50	15	20
8	61	90	89	50
9	36	60	58	40
10	17	40	49	30
11	00	10	95	60
12	03	10	21	20
13	92	120	72	40
14	62	80	66	40
15	48	70	64	40

   a. Complete the Monte Carlo simulation by setting up a simulated logbook. (The instructor may direct that some of the class base the simulation on the first eight breakdowns, others on the first nine, others on the first ten, and so on.) Assume that the repair crew can work on only one elevator at a time. What is the mean number of elevators that are out of service?

   b. Determine the average number of minutes that an out-of-service elevator waits for repair to begin.

   c. Determine the percent of utilization (percent of the time busy) for the elevator repair crew.

   d. The busy period for Global Trade Center's elevators is the ten-hour period from 7:30 A.M. to 5:30 P.M. Is your simulation of 15 (or fewer) breakdowns adequate to provide statistics good enough for the maintenance manager to make staffing decisions? Explain.

   e. To the best of your ability, reconstruct Monte Carlo number ranges and probabilities that fit the breakdown and service-time data for the given 15 simulated breakdowns. Also, estimate mean time between breakdowns and mean time to repair. With the difference in means, how do you explain the average waiting time statistic that you obtained in part b?

14. Repeat parts a, b, and c in problem 13, except assume that two repair crews are available.

15. The maintenance staff of the local office of Aquarius Computers completes trouble-call maintenance at the rate of about three per day, but the exact number of completions varies above and below three. Jobs not completed on one day are delayed until the next. The pattern of variability, taken from maintenance logbooks, is given below:

Daily job completion rate	Probability
1	0.05
2	0.15
3	0.50
4	0.20
5	0.10

The same logbooks also contain enough data to show the frequency of trouble calls per day. This is shown below:

Daily number of trouble calls	Probability
0	0.12
1	0.16
2	0.18
3	0.25
4	0.20
5	0.09
	1.00

a. Use Monte Carlo simulation to determine the average number of jobs delayed until the next day. Simulate for ten days only. (Each student should get a different answer based on different random numbers.)

b. What other useful statistics may be obtained from your simulation? Provide two other such statistics, and explain their significance.

c. Could queuing formulas be used in this problem? Discuss fully.

IN-BASKET CASE*

Topic: Waiting Lines and Resource Utilization—Tool Dept.

To:

From: Tool Department Manager

For the 400 mechanics in the various shops in our main building we have only one central tool crib. This centralization saves us money (on labor and duplicate tools and equipment), but the production manager claims that we aren't conveniently located for the users. Long walks and waiting lines are common. I'd like you to write up a report spelling out *how we could do an analysis* of the matter. Based on your report, I may assign someone to gather data and actually conduct the study.

* See instructions at end of problems section, Chapter 1.

supplement to chapter 13

WAITING-LINE ANALYSIS

In this supplement an examination of waiting lines in general is followed by discussion of two types of waiting-line analysis; use of mathematical queuing formulas and simulation. The order of discussion is:

1. Waiting lines.
2. Mathematical queuing formulas.
3. Simulation.

Waiting lines   A waiting line (queue, for short) is one or more orders or customers waiting for service. Waiting lines occur increasingly in a crowded, busy environment. Servers are valued, but waiting lines are not, and there is the reason for waiting-line analysis. The analysis provides information to those who decide on the type, number, and arrangement of serving stations. For a given design of the service facility, it is helpful to have information on how much waiting in queues there will be for customers and how much idleness there will be for servers when lines are empty.

Types of waiting lines. A waiting line may be simple, involving only one server (or channel) and one stage of service. A single stoplight on the main highway through a very small village acts as such a server (serving to regulate traffic flow). If the village were to grow and install more stoplights on the highway, autos would pass through what is called a *multistage* waiting line; each light is a stage. Autos may also encounter what is known as *multichannel* (or multiserver) waiting-line situation: An example is a toll station with several lanes that the driver may choose from. The lanes are considered channels, each offering the same service (taking tolls). Students registering and paying for classes may encounter a multichannel, multistage waiting line: There are several choices of lines to get into for registration, each of which may be followed by lines for payment of fees. (Computer-assisted registration has managed to eliminate some of the queuing on some campuses.)

The above four types of service facilities and waiting-line patterns are sketched in Figure S13–1. The four constitute four levels of waiting-line analysis; single-channel, single-stage analysis; single-channel, multistage analysis; multichannel, single-stage analysis; and multichannel, multistage analysis. Distinguishing among the four levels is important in *queuing* analysis, in which mathematical formulas are used. The formulas are grouped into the four levels, and the analyst begins by analyzing the problem to see which level of queuing formulas applies. The four levels are not so important in *simulation* of waiting

FIGURE S13–1
Service facilities
and waiting-line
patterns

A. Single channel, single stage

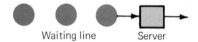

Waiting line   Server

B. Single channel, multistage

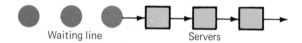

Waiting line   Servers

C. Multichannel, single stage

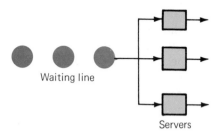

Waiting line

Servers

D. Multichannel, multistage

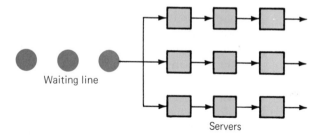

Waiting line

Servers

lines, which can be applied to a multitude of combinations of arrival, waiting, and service patterns.

Timing. In the operation of a service facility customers or jobs arrive, wait in line for a time (a time of zero if the line is empty), receive service, and leave. Two important timing factors that influence the operation of service facilities are the frequency distribution of arrivals and the frequency distribution of service times.

The simplest case is that in which arrivals are evenly spaced and service times are constant. If the evenly spaced arrivals are more frequent than the constant serving rate, the system is unstable. The customer flow must be decreased or the service rate increased; otherwise the waiting line grows without limit (instability). If the arrivals are less frequent than the service rate, the system is stable, with zero customer waiting time. The service facility will, however, be idle some of the time: Merely subtract the constant service time from the constant time between arrivals to get the time of idleness per cycle.

Usually arrivals are not evenly spaced and service times are not constant. In such cases it is no longer so simple to determine customer waiting and service-facility idleness. Mathematical queuing formulas and waiting-line simulation methods have been developed for such problems.

Another timing factor is hours of operation. If the facility operates all of the time, no information need be gathered about what happens to waiting lines and service-facility idleness during start-up and shutdown. The facility that operates all of the time tends to move toward what is called a *steady state*. A steady state is simply a condition in which the average waiting line no longer changes (but the waiting line may vary around that average).

A facility that starts and stops may sometimes achieve steady state. A production line, for example, may begin the day with all machines empty, but in a short time the factory is humming and waiting lines before each machine have come up to some average state—the steady state.

When human customers rather than production job orders are in the waiting lines, the concept of steady-state operation is more complicated. Arrival rates of customers for food service, copier service, entertainment, and so forth, seem to change all the time. It may be conceivable to divide mealtimes into 15-minute periods and look for a different set of steady-state variables (waiting lines and service-facility idleness) for each of the periods. But it is very costly to collect, analyze, and make and implement decisions for the large number of cases that result from so fine a time division.

A final timing factor is human reaction to waiting lines. Some customers *balk* at entering a waiting line that seems too long, and some *renege* or leave a line that is moving too slowly. The server's reaction to a long line is often to speed up, and the server's reaction to a short or empty line is often to slow down. These tendencies make the study of waiting lines still more difficult.

For all the difficulties, waiting lines must be studied. They are all around us, and if not well managed they are a drain on resources—the customer's waiting time and the service facility's idle time. Mathematical queuing formulas and simulation offer some help in waiting-line analysis.

Mathematical queuing formulas

Mathematical formulas or models have been developed for each of the four queuing patterns shown in Figure S13–1. Only the first of the four patterns—single channel, single stage—is discussed here. A few queuing formulas for that pattern are given in Figure S13–2.

Formulas depending on means only. The top two formulas in the figure are for computing the percent of time that the service facility is busy (left formula) and idle (right formula). Percent of time busy, known as utilization rate, is the mean arrival rate, μ, divided by the mean service rate, λ. When the server (service facility) is not busy, it is idle. Therefore, idleness is 1 minus the utilization rate, μ/λ. For example, if customers arrive at a mean rate of

FIGURE S13-2
Queuing
formulas for a
single-channel,
single-stage
service facility

Not dependent on probability distributions

Utilization of server:

$$U = \frac{\mu}{\lambda}$$

Idleness of server:

$$I = 1 - \frac{\mu}{\lambda}$$

Poisson-distributed arrival rate and service rate

Mean waiting time in queue:

$$T_q = \frac{\lambda}{\mu(\mu - \lambda)}$$

Mean time in system (in-queue + in-service):

$$T_s = \frac{1}{\mu - \lambda}$$

Mean number in queue:

$$N_q = \frac{\lambda^2}{\mu(\mu - \lambda)}$$

Mean number in system (in-queue + in-service):

$$N_s = \frac{\lambda}{\mu - \lambda}$$

Probability of n customers in system (in-queue + in-service):

$$P_n = \left(1 - \frac{\lambda}{\mu}\right)\left(\frac{\lambda}{\mu}\right)^n$$

Poisson-distributed arrival rate and constant (c) service rate

Mean waiting time in queue:

$$T_q(c) = \frac{\lambda}{2\mu(\mu - \lambda)}$$

Mean number in queue:

$$N_q(c) = \frac{\lambda^2}{2\mu(\mu - \lambda)}$$

λ = Greek letter *lambda*, standing for mean arrival rate in number of arrivals per time unit

μ = Greek letter *mu*, standing for mean service rate in numbers of customers served per time unit

eight per hour, and the service facility can serve them at a mean rate of ten per hour, utilization rate and idleness rate are:

$$U = \frac{\mu}{\lambda} = \frac{8}{10} = 0.8, \text{ or } 80\%$$

$$I = 1 - \frac{\mu}{\lambda} = 1 - 0.8 = 0.2, \text{ or } 20\%$$

Rate of service, μ, means rate of service *when customers are there.* It is the standard production rate. We are not concerned about whether the rate is based on an engineered or a nonengineered time standard. (See discussion of time standards and their reciprocal, standard production or output rates, in Chapter 8.) But some timing method is necessary to find out what μ is. A simple way is to use a wristwatch to time a few customer-service cycles and average the times; the result, the average time per customer, is then divided into 1.0 to yield mean (average) customers per time unit, μ. For example, suppose that service times for six customers are 5, 7, 5, 6, 4, and 9 minutes. The average is:

$$\frac{5+7+5+6+4+9}{6} = \frac{36}{6} = 6 \text{ minutes per customer}$$

Then, mean service rate is:

$$\mu = \frac{1}{6.0 \text{ min./customer}} \times \frac{60 \text{ min.}}{1 \text{ hr.}} = 10 \text{ customers per hour}$$

Rate of arrivals, λ, is simply a count of number of arrivals divided by the time over which they are counted. For example, suppose that a three-hour study is taken of customer arrivals and that 24 customers are counted. The mean rate of arrivals is:

$$\lambda = \frac{24 \text{ customers}}{3 \text{ hours}} = 8 \text{ customers per hour}$$

Utilization and idleness rates are based only on the means, λ and μ. The pattern of variability distribution around the means makes no difference. The formulas apply for any (or no) variability pattern or distribution. Not so for the formulas discussed next.

Formulas using Poisson-distributed arrival and service rates. The second group of queuing formulas in Figure S13–2 are also solved using only λ and μ. But the results are true only if variability patterns about the means form a particular probability distribution: the Poisson distribution.[1] It is unlikely that λ and μ will ever be exactly Poisson. As probability distributions stray from Poisson, the results become less valid. The analyst needs to be convinced only that the arrival and service rates are reasonably close to Poisson in order to use the second group of formulas in the figure. (The main body of the chapter includes further discussion of the Poisson distribution.)

The first two formulas in the group provide for calculating mean queue time, T_q, and mean time in the system, T_s, which includes both queue time and service time. If customers arrive at a mean rate of eight per hour and they can be served at a mean rate of ten per hour, then

---

[1] It is usually stated that arrival-*rate* distribution must be Poisson and that service-*time* distribution must be exponential. However, an exponential probability distribution of service times (times to serve customers) transforms into a Poisson probability distribution of service rates (number of customers served per time period—when the facility is busy). Since the queuing formulas use mean rates rather than mean times, the exponential distribution of times need not be discussed here.

$$T_q = \frac{\lambda}{\mu(\mu - \lambda)} = \frac{8}{10(10 - 8)} = \frac{8}{(10)(2)} = \frac{8}{20}$$

$= 0.4$ hour, or 24 minutes waiting time per customer

$$T_s = \frac{1}{\mu - \lambda} = \frac{1}{(10 - 8)} = \frac{1}{2}$$

$= 0.5$ hour, or 30 minutes in the system per customer

The second two formulas in the group are for calculating mean number in the queue, N_q, and mean number in the system, N_s. Again for $\lambda = 8$ and $\mu = 10$,

$$N_q = \frac{\lambda^2}{\mu(\mu - \lambda)} = \frac{8^2}{(10)(10 - 8)} = \frac{64}{(10)(2)} = \frac{64}{20}$$

$= 3.2$ customers waiting

$$N_s = \frac{\lambda}{\mu - \lambda} = \frac{8}{10 - 8} = \frac{8}{2}$$

$= 4$ customers in the system

The last formula in the second group is for calculating the probability, P_n, of any given number, n, of customers in the system. For example, the probability of four customers in the system of $\lambda = 8$, $\mu = 10$ is:

$$P_n = \left(1 - \frac{\lambda}{\mu}\right)\left(\frac{\lambda}{\mu}\right)^n$$

$$P_4 = \left(1 - \frac{8}{10}\right)\left(\frac{8}{10}\right)^4 = (1 - 0.8)(0.8)^4 = (0.2)(0.410)$$

$= 0.082$, or 8.2%

We know from the earlier calculation of N_s that 4 is the mean number of customers in the system, but the probability that there will be exactly four customers is just 0.082.

Formulas using Poisson-distributed arrival rates and constant service rates. Two formulas are given in the figure for the case of Poisson arrival rates with constant service rates. The first is for mean waiting time, $T_q(c)$, and the second is for mean number in the queue, $N_q(c)$. Constant service rates are increasingly likely as more services become mechanized in our society. For $\lambda = 8$ and $\mu = 10$,

$$T_q(c) = \frac{\lambda}{2\mu(\mu - \lambda)} = \frac{8}{(2)(10)(10 - 2)} = \frac{8}{(20)(8)} = \frac{8}{160}$$

$= 0.05$ hour, or 3 minutes per customer

$$N_q(c) = \frac{\lambda^2}{2\mu(\mu - \lambda)} = \frac{8^2}{(2)(10)(10 - 2)} = \frac{64}{160}$$

$= 0.4$ customers waiting

The imposition of a constant service rate has dramatic results. T_q and N_q for Poisson arrival and service rates were calculated earlier as 24 minutes waiting time and 3.2 customers waiting. Those figures are eight times as large as $T_q(c)$ and $N_q(c)$. A constant service time reduces waits a great deal (but it does not eliminate them as long as arrivals are variable).

Simulation

Simulation means imitation. As a tool in waiting-line analysis, simulation means imitating a waiting line by use of numbers. Simulation differs from mathematical queuing formulas in that queuing formulas do not imitate a waiting line; rather, the formulas simplify a waiting line so that summary waiting-line data can be easily solved for. Simulation of waiting lines also differs from simulation for training or education. Physical simulators are used to train drivers and pilots. Simulation games (e.g., management games) are used in education to provide students with realistic experience in making decisions. Since waiting-line simulation applies to real situations, its purpose is actual decision making, not education.

Real waiting lines change all the time. Simulation captures these changes with streams of numbers that stand for customers or orders and their progress through a service facility. The numbers can then be examined to find out about maximum, minimum, and average conditions and durations.

One would have to watch real waiting lines for a long time in order to get accurate impressions about such conditions and durations. With the aid of computers a waiting-line simulation can represent a very long time period—hundreds of simulated years if so desired—at rather small expense. The expense is small, at least, in comparison with trial and error on real waiting lines. Even if a simulation is run for a short time, say a few simulated hours or days, a computer may be needed to handle the large streams of numbers necessary to represent the changing flows through the waiting lines and the service facility.

As in queuing analysis, the inputs to simulation are arrival frequencies and service times. Unlike queuing analysis, simulation can handle any distribution of arrivals and service times, not just the Poisson probability distribution. The way in which arrivals and service times are simulated is considered next. The method is known as Monte Carlo simulation.

Monte Carlo simulation. Monte Carlo simulation follows the first four steps of Figure 13–8 in the main body of the chapter—restated here:

1. Gather input data on arrivals and service times.
2. Transform input data into probability distributions.
3. Simulate by matching random numbers against frequency distributions.
4. Extract output information.

These four steps, plus a final assessment, are considered in the following simplified example.

EXAMPLE S13–1
Monte Carlo simulation of a shoeshine stand

A shoeshine stand currently has a staff of one. A Monte Carlo simulation is undertaken during the peak 9:30–11:30 A.M. period. During the peak period, customers often have to wait, and some are too impatient to do so. The goals are to find out what would happen to the waiting lines under other conditions. In the following discussion only the present conditions are simulated, but the data could be modified for simulation of options, for example, cutting service times by adding staff or using an electric buffer, and smoothing out the flow of customer arrivals by allowing appointments. The four steps in simulating—gather data, transform data, simulate, and extract outputs—are considered in turn.

Gather arrival and service-time data. Observers have watched the shoeshine stand for three days from 9:30 A.M. to 11:30 A.M. One set of observations concerns customer arrivals. Observed arrivals are plotted on the time charts shown in Figure S13–3A.

FIGURE S13–3
Customer-arrival and service-time data on time charts

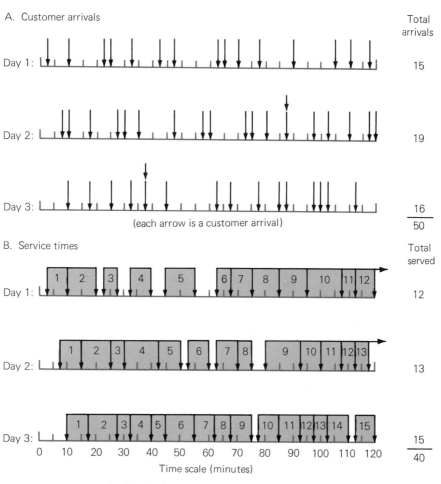

A. Customer arrivals

Day 1: Total arrivals 15

Day 2: 19

Day 3: 16

(each arrow is a customer arrival)
50

B. Service times   Total served

Day 1: 1 2 3 4 5 6 7 8 9 10 11 12   12

Day 2: 1 2 3 4 5 6 7 8 9 10 11 12 13   13

Day 3: 1 2 3 4 5 6 7 8 9 10 11 12 13 14 15   15

0 10 20 30 40 50 60 70 80 90 100 110 120
Time scale (minutes)

40

(each pair of arrows spans service time for a customer, each of whom is numbered)

The time-chart data are examined to assure that the three days are enough alike and that arrivals are spread out over the 120-minute periods. If the days and minutes are not much alike, then it would be best to divide the study into parts and to separately simulate for each part whose arrival patterns are indeed alike. For the data in Figure S13–3A, numbers of customers arriving seem similar enough from minute to minute and day to day to use all of the data in a single simulation.

Figure S13–3B shows the results of a second set of observations, this set on customer service times. Service times are plotted on time charts for the same three 120-minute periods. The total number of customers served is only 40, as compared with 50 customers counted as arrivals in Figure S13–3A. The ten-customer difference includes eight customers who refused to wait in line (lost business) and two customers whose shoes were still being shined at the end of the 120-minute periods in days 1 and 2. (The observer who counted customer arrivals was careful to include even those persons who approached the shoeshine stand but turned away upon seeing a waiting line.)

From Figure S13–3A and S13–3B it is possible to develop summary output data: utilization rate of the server, maximum and average waiting line, and so on. But that is not the purpose of gathering the data. The purpose is to transform the data, such that extensive simulations can be performed for present and proposed operating conditions. Transformation of the data follows.

Transform data into probability distributions. Customer arrivals and service times are variable. Inspection of Figure S13–3 shows that time between arrivals, or interarrival time (IAT), varies from zero (two arrivals at the same time) to 17.5 minutes (which occurs once, between minute 45 and minute 60.5 in Figure S13–3A). The service time to shine one customer's shoes varies from 5 minutes to 12.5 minutes.

The variability may be captured (condensed) in the form of a probability distribution. The procedure is to set up classification intervals and to count the number of occurrences (frequency) in each interval; the midpoint of each interval is used to represent the whole interval.

Figure S13–4A shows the transformation of interarrival times to a frequency distribution. (Time between arrivals is easier to measure from the time charts than is its reciprocal, number of customer arrivals per time period.) Four time intervals are used; the midpoints are 2, 7, 12, and 17. (Division into five or six narrower intervals would work as well.)

Tally marks are used to tabulate frequencies. The arrows in the figure show how this is done for the first three arrivals that were entered on the time chart of Figure S13–3A. The first customer arrived 2.5 minutes after the observer began watching, so 2.5 minutes is the first IAT (interarrival time); one tally mark is entered in the appropriate row, which is the 0–4 row, since 2.5 minutes falls within that classification interval. The second customer arrived 7.5 minutes after the first. Since 7.5 falls within interval 5–9, a tally is entered in the 5–9 row. The third customer arrives 12.5 minutes after the second, and a tally is entered in the 10–14 row.

The tallies are shown separated into days, but they are then totaled for all three days. The interval totals—13, 22, 12, and 3—are each divided by the grand total of 50. The result is the probabilities in the final column in Figure S13–4A.

In Figure S13–4B the probabilities are entered as bars for each of the four interval midpoints. The bar chart shows the shape of the probability distribution of IATs at the shoeshine stand, but the bar-chart format is not necessary for simulation purposes.

The same procedure is followed for service times. The result is the service-time frequency data and probability distribution in Figure S13–5. Since arrival times may

FIGURE S13–4
Developing an
IAT probability
distribution

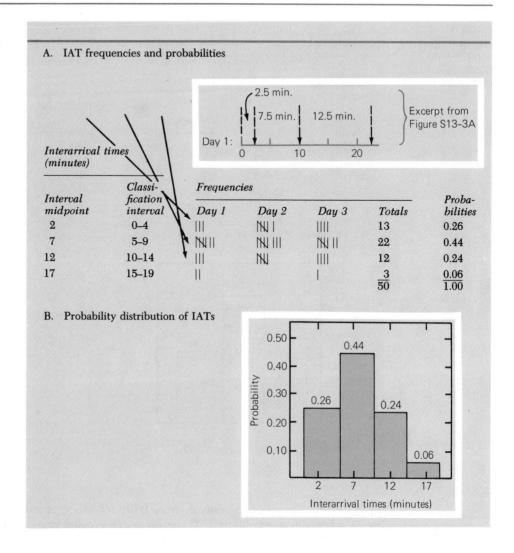

A. IAT frequencies and probabilities

B. Probability distribution of IATs

be parts of minutes, the classification intervals account for decimal parts. By contrast, the intervals for arrivals were in whole numbers only, since there cannot be a part of a customer. The smallest service-time interval is set at 4–6.9, with 5 as the midpoint, since every shoeshine in Figure S13–3B took at least five minutes.

Simulate. The probability distributions in Figures S13–4 and S13–5, plus a table of random numbers, are the inputs needed to conduct Monte Carlo simulation. A preparatory step is to express the probabilities as number ranges, which are sometimes called Monte Carlo number ranges. The number ranges should be the same as the range of the numbers in the table of random numbers—two digits, 00 to 99, for this example. The development of the Monte Carlo number ranges is shown in Figure S13–6A. The size of each number range is 100 times the probability, and the numbers

FIGURE S13–5
Developing a service-time probability distribution

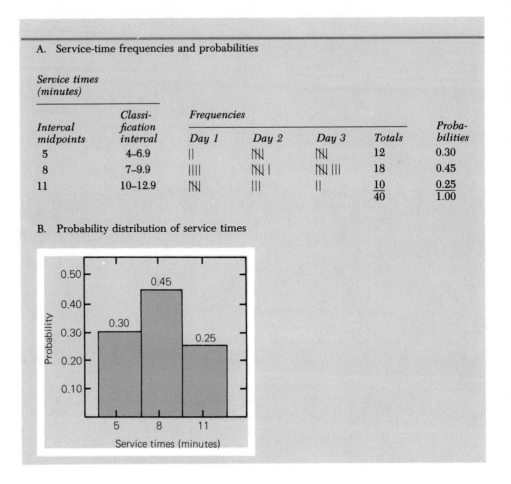

A. Service-time frequencies and probabilities

Service times (minutes)		*Frequencies*				
Interval midpoints	*Classification interval*	*Day 1*	*Day 2*	*Day 3*	*Totals*	*Probabilities*
5	4–6.9	ǁ	𝍸	𝍸	12	0.30
8	7–9.9	ǁǁ	𝍸 ǀ	𝍸 ǀǀǀ	18	0.45
11	10–12.9	𝍸	ǀǀǀ	ǁ	10	0.25
					40	1.00

B. Probability distribution of service times

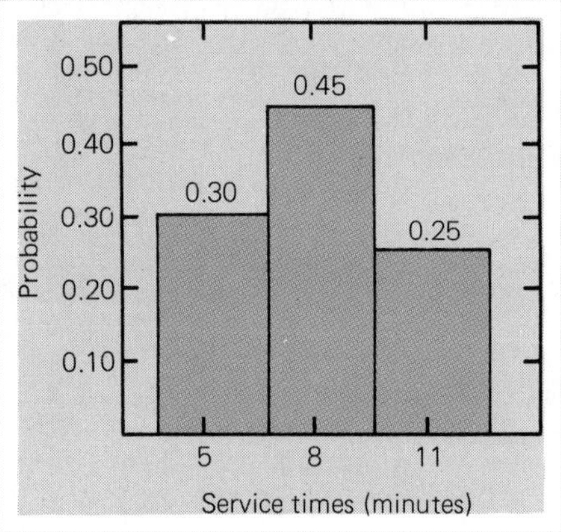

in the ranges increase progressively from 00 to 99. (An alternative is to go from 01 to 00, where 00 stands for 100. Three digits are avoided since a two-digit random-number table is to be used.) Thus, the range for IAT 2 has a size of:

$$100 \times 0.26 = 26 \text{ numbers}$$

The 26 numbers included in the range go from 00 to 25. The next range begins with 26, and so forth.

Figure S13–6B is a small simulation of the shoeshine stand. The random numbers in columns 2 and 6 come from the second column of the random-number table, Table S13–1. The first random number, 27 (in column 2), is used to represent the IAT for customer number 1. Since 27 falls within Monte Carlo range 26–69 in the IAT table in Figure S13–6A, the IAT is 7. Arrows drawn between Figure S13–6A and Figure S13–6B show these steps. The second random number, 39 (in column 6), is used to represent service time for customer number 1. Since 39 falls within Monte Carlo range 30–74 in the service-time table in Figure S13–6A, the service time is 8 (see arrows).

Columns 4, 5, and 8 in Figure S13–6B represent what would be seen by an observer

FIGURE S13-6
Monte Carlo simulation of shoeshine stand

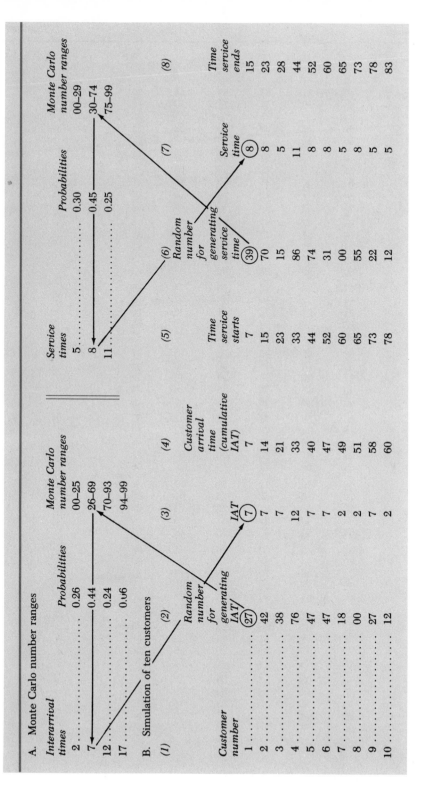

42	27	11	61	64	20
55	39	37	71	35	78
24	42	25	60	61	78
82	70	68	68	28	08
56	38	62	42	05	47
48	15	21	40	25	78
95	76	15	43	63	18
86	86	96	50	43	17
49	47	10	94	14	22
41	74	33	33	28	76
95	47	92	56	95	95
78	31	27	77	66	63
84	18	88	65	46	81
40	00	61	17	82	53
80	00	85	42	64	44
12	55	13	20	74	16
84	27	50	45	97	19
01	22	40	81	36	10
25	12	07	98	82	74
46	12	83	52	30	42
83	02	73	53	18	07
69	18	16	09	93	65
78	22	36	94	45	32
43	18	05	33	44	45
07	34	46	30	49	10
00	50	31	12	42	88
55	34	73	61	96	44
17	39	51	92	64	44
22	81	84	00	95	32
57	00	21	12	36	96
02	20	12	50	71	82
70	15	52	75	67	60
28	36	84	20	73	23
86	60	52	37	46	79
04	34	33	73	42	91
95	35	13	16	75	03
89	14	24	19	29	82
92	46	72	35	17	81
30	28	74	35	87	67
86	31	84	29	75	89
13	21	48	73	40	73
38	87	98	23	72	43
02	42	81	84	08	38
72	22	79	60	26	26
16	05	14	42	74	74
70	03	63	58	32	12
45	45	96	64	49	83
05	38	40	89	75	32
29	24	05	17	03	53
20	87	26	88	06	18

at the shoeshine stand: Column 4 gives the arrival time for each customer. It is simply the cumulative sum of the IATs in column 2. Column 5 is the time that service starts. Service does not always begin when the customer arrives, because some customers must wait. In this simulation customers 2, 3, 5, 6, 7, 8, 9, and 10 must wait (the times in columns 4 and 5 are not the same for those customers). Column 8 is the completion time for each shoeshine. It is the start time (column 5) plus the service time (column 7).

The time that service ends must be examined to see when the next shine may start. For example, the first customer's shine starts at minute 7, takes eight minutes and ends at minute 15. Customer 2 arrives at minute 14 but must wait until customer 1 leaves at minute 15. Therefore, to get a start time in column 5, the previous end time must be compared with the arrival time for the current customer.

Various summary data may be extracted from the simulation, as is explained next.

Extract information. Common information from a Monte Carlo waiting-line simulation includes maximum and average waiting-line length, average waiting time per customer, and percent idleness or utilization of the service facility. All of these statistics may be extracted from columns 4, 5, and 8 of the simulation in Figure S13–6B. Those columns, plus three more columns of working figures and summarized information, are given in Figure S13–7.

FIGURE S13–7
Summary information from simulation

(1) Customer number	(2) Customer arrival time	(3) Time service starts	(4) Time service ends	(5) Number of customers waiting	(6) Customer waiting time	(7) Time of idleness in service facility
1	7	7	15			7
2	14	15	23	1	1	
3	21	23	28	1	2	
4	33	33	44			5
5	40	44	52	1	4	
6	47	52	60	1	5	
7	49	60	65	2	11	
8	51	65	73	3	14	
9	58	73	78	3	15	
10	60	78	83	3	18	
Totals				15	70	12

Maximum waiting line = 3 customers

Mean waiting line $= \dfrac{15 \text{ customers waiting}}{10 \text{ customer arrivals}} = 1.5$ customers

Mean waiting time $= \dfrac{70 \text{ minutes waiting}}{10 \text{ customers}} = 7.0$ minutes

Idleness rate $= \dfrac{12 \text{ minutes idle}}{83 \text{ minutes simulated}} = 0.145$, or 14.5% idleness

Columns 5, 6, and 7 in Figure S13–7 show number of customers waiting, customer waiting time, and service-facility idleness. The first customer arrives after the facility has been idle for seven minutes. The second arrives in minute 14 and waits one minute until customer 1 departs in minute 15. Customers 3, 5, and 6 also find a customer ahead of them when they arrive. Customer 7 arrives at minute 49, but customer 5 does not leave until minute 52, so customers 6 and 7 are waiting at the same time. Each of the other calculations follows the same logic.

The summary information below the table indicates that the maximum waiting line is 3 customers; the mean waiting line, 1.5 customers; and the mean waiting time, 7.0 minutes. The idleness rate is found by dividing 12 minutes of idleness by the 83 minutes in the simulation, which equals 14.5 percent idleness.

Assessment. The above simulation of a shoeshine stand was simplified for illustrative purposes. A real simulation should be elaborated in several ways:

1. The data-collection phase should perhaps run longer than six hours (three days) and 40–50 customers.

2. A reason for collecting more data is in order to narrow classification intervals. The interval midpoints for the IAT and service-time distributions in Figures S13–4 and S13–5 were set rather wide apart (i.e., 2, 7, 12, and 17 for the IAT distribution) because of limited data for narrower intervals.

3. A ten-customer, 83-minute simulation is very short. The simulation period should last 120 minutes, which is the peak period of operation for the shoeshine stand. To have confidence in the final waiting-line and idleness statistics, the simulation should be run for many days. Normally, Monte Carlo simulation is run on a computer, which permits running the simulation for hundreds or thousands of days. With many days of simulation the effects of an unusual selection of random numbers wash out.

4. As was mentioned at the outset, a purpose of simulation is to test various conditions, such as adding staff. Reruns of the simulation with different IAT or service-time distributions are among the options that may be tried. Special computer simulation languages (such as SIMSCRIPT, GPSS, GASP, Q-GERTS, and SLAM) are useful in testing a wide variety of options, including customer balking and reneging.

chapter 14

INVENTORY DYNAMICS AND CONTROL

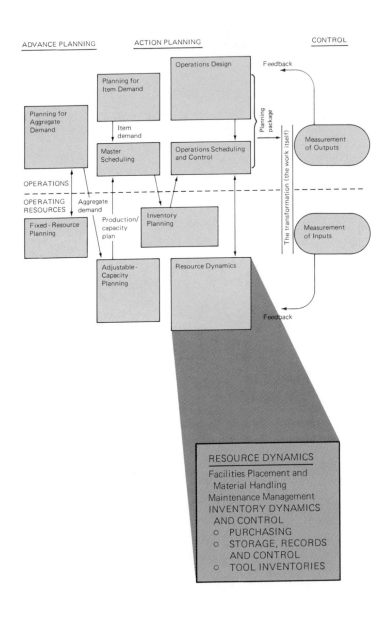

ADVANCE PLANNING   ACTION PLANNING   CONTROL

Operations Design

Feedback

Planning for
Item Demand

Planning for
Aggregate
Demand

Item
demand

Master
Scheduling

Operations Scheduling
and Control

Planning package

Measurement
of Outputs

OPERATIONS

OPERATING
RESOURCES

Aggregate
demand

Fixed - Resource
Planning

Production/
capacity
plan

Inventory
Planning

The transformation (the work itself)

Measurement
of Inputs

Adjustable -
Capacity
Planning

Resource Dynamics

Feedback

RESOURCE DYNAMICS

Facilities Placement and
  Material Handling
Maintenance Management
INVENTORY DYNAMICS
  AND CONTROL
   o PURCHASING
   o STORAGE, RECORDS
      AND CONTROL
   o TOOL INVENTORIES

Inventory dynamics and control refers to actions to carry out inventory plans. Several types of inventories must be managed: capital goods, manufacturing materials, support materials, tools, work in process, and finished goods. Planning for each of these types was discussed in earlier chapters, and some aspects of inventory dynamics and control were also discussed earlier for reasons of convenience.

The life cycle of inventory dynamics and control has been referred to several times. The life cycle is reproduced below:

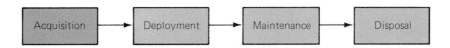

Key aspects of the inventory life cycle remain to be discussed in this chapter:

1. *Acquisition.* As applied to inventories, acquisition refers to purchasing. The purchasing section in this chapter applies to capital goods, manufacturing materials, support materials, and tools.
2. *Deployment.* Deployment of tools (tool loans) is discussed in this chapter. Deployment of capital goods (facilities placement) and materials (material handling) was covered in Chapter 12.
3. *Maintenance.* As applied to material and tool inventories, maintenance refers to physical storage and control of stocks, which is examined in this chapter. Maintenance of capital goods (facilities) was discussed in Chapter 13, Maintenance Management.
4. *Disposal.* As applied to material and tool inventories, disposal refers to getting rid of excess stocks, which is treated in the discussion of item review in this chapter. Disposal of capital goods was partly considered in Chapter 11 under the heading "Replacement of Existing Facilities."

In this chapter the broad issue of organization structures for inventory dynamics and control is considered in the first section. The second section examines a broad concept of ABC analysis for inventory control. The third section concerns the purchasing challenge: why purchasing has become a critical success factor and a challenging career field. The dynamics of purchasing, including the issues of value analysis and sourcing, is the subject of the fourth section. Inventory control, including record keeping, physical inventory control, item review, and procedural controls, is considered in the fifth section. The discussion of material controls concludes with a section on materials management as a profit center. A final section takes up special issues that apply to tool inventories.

MATERIALS ORGANIZATION

Material costs account for much of the operating budget in many industries. Many organization charts give little hint of the large role played by materials and material costs. The major vice-presidential blocks on the organization chart are likely to be manufacturing, marketing, comptroller, personnel, engineering, production control, and quality control. Where is materials management?

That question began to be asked persistently in the 1960s. Computers had become important as a tool for coordinating inventory planning and control. Airfreight had become significant as a means of expediting vital shipments. But organizational coordination of material flows was missing. Materials-management functions tended to be scattered about the organization chart.

New ways of organizing materials-related activities were developed in the 1960s. At one extreme is the *materials-management* structure, in which materials specialties are combined. At the other extreme is the idea of wiping out some of the materials specialties by turning over their responsibilities to line departments, especially the production department; this approach is referred to as *despecialization.* The materials-management structure is considered next, followed by a brief discussion of despecialization.

Materials-management department

Purchasing people were the strongest early advocates of the materials-management structure. *Purchasing* magazine published a series of articles on the concept of a materials-management organization. In such an organization, materials management would be a department at the vice-presidential level, and it would consolidate far-flung materials activities.

Figure 14–1 is a before-and-after example of the effects of adopting the materials-management structure. Figure 14–1A shows how materials activities might be scattered on a traditional organization chart. Purchasing might be under the comptroller. Traffic (shipping) might be in marketing. Receiving might be in quality control. Material handling might be in manufacturing. Stores and inventory control might be in manufacturing, with the counting of physical inventory under the comptroller.

Figure 14–1B shows one possible way in which materials functions might be put into one department. All of the materials activities from Figure 14–1A are included. Production control is sometimes also included in a materials-management department. This is perhaps most likely in highly repetitive manufacturing, because in that situation production control is heavily concerned with feeding purchased materials to manufacturing; in job-lot, job-shop, and project operations, production control is more concerned with scheduling, priorities, and capacity management.

Perhaps the major goal of a materials-management structure is to forge a link between purchasing and inventory control. Inventory control includes planning for what purchasing buys, and in firms using material requirements planning the computer helps link these two functions. A materials-management structure helps assure that the information processing linkages between purchasing and inventory control will function properly—with consistent managerial oversight.

The cause of materials management was taken up by another magazine,

FIGURE 14-1
Organization of
materials
activities

A. Traditional

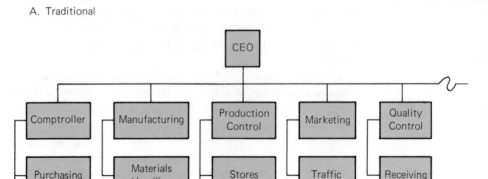

B. Materials management

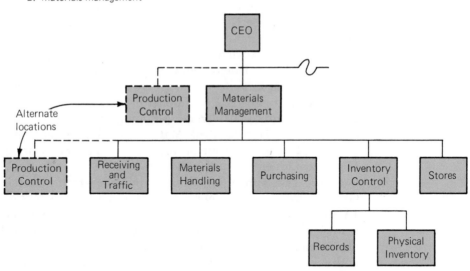

Materials Handling, in the mid-1960s. *Materials Handling* was the official
organ of the American Materials Handling Society. The society and the magazine were so taken with the idea that they changed their names—to *Materials
Management* and the International Materials Management Society.

The reasons why purchasing and material-handling practitioners favor the
materials-management structure may have something to do with their image
as bottlenecks. Neither purchasing nor material handling contributes tangible
value to the product, but both are sources of delay. When schedules are not
met or quality is poor, manufacturing and engineering look for someone to

blame. Purchasing is blamed for buying the wrong items from vendors who can't deliver on time; material handling is charged with being too slow and too careless. The main advantage of grouping all materials activities together is *coordination,* and coordination reduces delay; perhaps it also improves communication in ways that can lead to better service with respect to the *quality* of materials. These real benefits of materials management could dampen criticism. Increased power and improved position are, of course, other reasons why purchasing and material-handling people like materials management.

Today the materials-management structure is quite common. Surveys suggest that most large industrial firms have implemented some form of materials management.

Despecial-ization

The traditional organization, as we have seen, places the various specialties in line and staff departments all over the organization chart. The materials-management department is an extreme in which all materials specialists are together. There is an opposite extreme in which the specialists are done away with.

Robert Townsend partially implemented that extreme, which may be called *despecialization,* when he took over Avis in 1963. At that time Avis had been suffering losses for some years. As Townsend tells it,[1] he found that profit-center managers at Avis wanted to blame failures to achieve profit goals on bottleneck departments like purchasing. Townsend's reaction: He fired the purchasing department. (He also fired the personnel and public relations departments for much the same reason.) Purchasing funds were turned over to the profit centers with the challenge to, in effect, "put up or shut up." In other words, the generalists in the profit centers could no longer blame the specialists in purchasing for delays, unwanted substitute items, poor materials, and so forth. Authority to control their own fate, commensurate with responsibility for results, was in the hands of the profit-center managers.

This extreme, which may have helped Avis get back into the black, has obvious weaknesses. It may be a useful emergency measure in some cases, but most firms would find themselves paying exorbitant prices for shoddy goods to fly-by-night vendors if purchasing experts were not in control of the buying.

ABC ANALYSIS

An old and widely known inventory control technique is ABC analysis. Actually ABC analysis does not control inventory but rather provides a basis for efficient control of inventories. By *efficient* control, we mean more control over key inventory items and less control over lesser items.[2]

---

[1] Robert Townsend, *Up the Organization* (Knopf, 1970) (HF5549.T6).

[2] This idea of giving an item the degree of attention it deserves is sometimes called the *principle of parsimony* (parsimony means frugality). The more general principle, widely applicable in society, is the *Pareto principle;* it is named after Vilfredo Pareto (1848–1923), an economist who observed that 90 percent of wealth is in the hands of 10 percent of the population.

ABC analysis provides for classifying all stocked items according to annual dollar-volume, that is, annual demand times cost per unit. Class *A* items, needing close control, are the high-dollar-volume group. They may include 80 percent of total inventory cost but only 1 percent of total items stocked. Class *B* is an intermediate-dollar-volume group—perhaps 15 percent of dollars and 30 percent of items. Class *C* is the rest—say, 5 percent of dollars and 69 percent of items. Some firms do not stop with *A*, *B*, and *C* but add a *D*, *E*, and so on.

ABC processing and applications

Old as ABC analysis is, modern computer processing makes it more tractable. Item cost is available in the inventory master file. Any measure of annual usage—such as actual usage last year, actual usage last month times 12, or a forecast—may be used. The computer multiples item cost by annual usage, giving annual dollar volume. The ABC formula is fed into the computer so that a complete list of items may be printed; the list is in descending dollar-volume order, with the top group of items labeled as *A* items, and so forth.

Examples of inventory controls that may be based on ABC classification are:

Purchasing. A purchase order for a class *A* item might be signed by the president, for a class *B* item by the chief of purchasing, and for a class *C* item by any buyer.

Physical inventory counting. Count *A* items monthly, *B* items annually, and *C* items biennially.

Forecasting. Forecast *A* items by several methods on the computer with resolution by a forecasting committee, *B* items by simple trend projection, and *C* items by best guess of the responsible buyer.

Safety stock. No safety stock for *A* items, one month's supply for *B* items, and three months' supply for *C* items.

While ABC analysis seems natural for computer-based inventory systems, some authorities take a dim view of including ABC in the high form of computer-based inventory management known as MRP. Orlicky,[3] for example, suggests that the MRP system should treat all items alike (except for especially hard-to-get items). MRP plans priorities (i.e., it plans the order in which parts will be scheduled), and *C* items must contend for productive capacity and purchasing attention along with *A* and *B* items. Including *C* as well as *B* and *A* in the MRP system accounts for all loads on capacity and also helps to assure that all items will be on hand when needed.

ABC example

While ABC is questionable as a component of MRP, it can be valuable in ROP (reorder-point) systems. A wholesaler is a good example, as is demonstrated next.

---

[3] Joseph Orlicky, *Material Requirements Planning* (McGraw-Hill, 1975), p. 161 (TS155.8.O74).

EXAMPLE 14–1
ABC analysis,
wholesaler

Universal Motor Supply Co. has arranged its ten inventory items in order of annual dollar-volume. Figure 14–2 shows the ordered list, with dollar-volume also expressed in percentages. The ordered list is examined in order to arrive at an ABC classification of the items.

FIGURE 14–2
Inventory items in annual-dollar-volume order, Universal Motor Supply Co.

Stock number	Annual demand	Unit cost	Annual dollar-volume	Percent
407	40,000	$ 35.50	$1,420,000	59.5
210	1,000	700.00	700,000	29.3
021	2,000	55.00	110,000	4.6
388	20,000	4.00	80,000	3.4
413	4,400	10.00	44,000	1.7
195	500	36.00	18,000	0.7
330	40	214.00	8,560	0.4
114	100	43.00	4,300	0.2
274	280	1.00	280	0.1
359	600	0.25	150	0.1
		Totals	$2,385,290	100.0%

FIGURE 14–3
ABC classification, Universal Motor Supply Co.

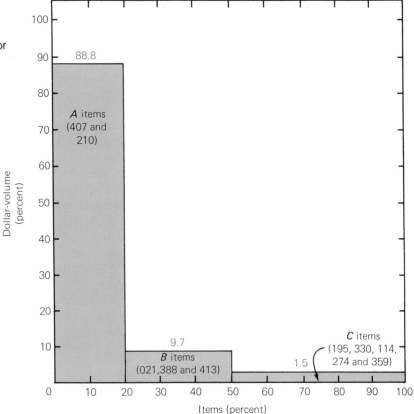

Figure 14–3 shows the same ten items grouped into classes *A*, *B*, and *C*. The groupings seem natural: The three *B* items account for about nine times as much annual dollar-volume as the five *C* items; the two *A* items account for about six times as much as the three *B* items. It is clear that *A* items should receive major attention, *B* items moderate attention, and *C* items little attention.

The ABC concept has broad application in inventory dynamics and control. Purchasing, the first function in inventory dynamics, has a long history of following (formally or informally) the ABC concept of requiring higher levels of control over high-dollar-volume items. Purchasing is considered next.

THE PURCHASING CHALLENGE

The importance of the purchasing function has grown a good deal in recent years. One reason is growing shortages arising from dwindling reserves of the earth's raw materials. Scarcity of primary metals leads to shortages of processed steel, copper, lead, titanium, chrome, and so forth. Those shortages translate into long purchase lead times for machined components and finished goods from bearings to buses to boxcars. Engineers hurry to redesign products from alternative materials, which inflates demand and causes shortages of still other materials. For example, petrochemical scarcities have led to shortages in the materials from which plastics may be made, and the primary metals scarcities have bid up demands for plastics, which further aggravates petroleum shortages. Purchasing departments are in the thick of the scramble to find basic materials and parts sources or substitute materials.

Another reason for purchasing's growing importance is an apparent tendency away from vertical integration as a corporate strategy. The vertical-integration philosophy says, in effect, "Let's not buy it; let's make it ourselves." The gigantic River Rouge plant built by Ford Motor Company in the 1930s is a good example. The plant integrated assembly, fabrication, foundry, tire manufacturing, and even steel refining. Add refineries, oil wells, and mines to the company, and virtually nothing remains to be purchased.

There is an inkling of a trend today, however, toward "doing what you do best and buying the rest."[4] Parts of all kinds may be bought from the thriving specialty manufacturing industry. Even more notable is the trend to buy services: a caterer to run the company food-service operation, a janitorial service to clean the premises, and consultants of all kinds to recommend operating and strategic improvements.

The growing importance of purchasing may be part of the reason for more materials-management departments. An alternative is to move purchasing up to the vice-presidential level—without attaching other elements of the total materials flow. Purchasing has become more attractive as a challenging and

---

[4] See, for example, Wickham Skinner, "The Focused Factory," *Harvard Business Review,* May–June 1974, pp. 113–21.

rewarding career field, and the National Association of Purchasing Management is active in promoting increased professionalism in the field.

Today's aggressive purchasing managers are extending their departments' expediting activities to the point of involvement in suppliers' order-control functions; this trend is considered as the first major topic in this section, *the supplier interface*. Some of the challenges in purchasing are related to the diversity of things to be bought, which is examined as the second major topic of the section, *purchasing goods versus services*.

The supplier interface

Doyle Selden, director of material for McDonnell Douglas and a nationally known speaker on purchasing, has noted that "one of the major problems inpeding manufacturing productivity today is the failure of suppliers to deliver material on the promised date." Must the purchasing manager accept this as a fact of industrial life? Or can something be done about it? Let us examine two views of purchasing activities at the supplier interface.

One view is that the supplier is, in effect, a black box. Figure 14–4 is a diagram of this view. You place the order, it disappears into the supplier's system, and the goods (or apologies) come out. It is not for you to know what happens to the order in the supplier's system. It is like a vending machine or the electronic engineer's black box. You may inquire about the order at any time, and you may request modifications to the order (e.g., an earlier delivery). Such inquiries and requests also enter the black box, and limited replies come back to you, but you do not understand how the inquiries and requests were processed.

A more aggressive view is that the buyer's job includes probing the black box. As Selden's remarks suggest, suppliers have plenty of problems in meeting deliveries. The buyer would like to know about these difficulties in order to take proper actions. Such actions would include notifying production control (in the buyer's own plant) of likely delivery delays, modifying or canceling orders, arranging for alternative suppliers or substitute materials, assisting the supplier in some way, and a variety of order-expediting actions. Order-expediting actions range from impressing the supplier with the importance of the order to your firm to threatening the supplier with loss of future orders. Modifying orders includes reducing the order quantity (if it appears that the supplier could meet delivery for a smaller order), accepting partial shipment, delaying the order, changing to a faster mode of transportation, and paying a premium for more supplier attention. Some buyers go so far as to assist the supplier. For example, the buyer might put pressure on one of the supplier's suppliers

FIGURE 14–4
Black-box view of the supplier's system

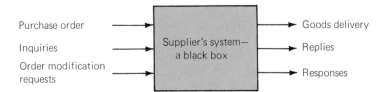

if there is a raw-material problem; and engineers from the buyer's own plant could be called upon to help straighten out an engineering difficulty that the supplier is having. But any of these actions requires knowing what is really happening in the supplier's plant.

A longer-range reason for knowing all about the supplier has to do with better supplier selection. Assume that your firm has dropped an otherwise excellent supplier because of late deliveries. Assume further that the supplier corrects problems that have caused the late deliveries. Under the black-box approach, your buyer selects suppliers mainly on past records (perhaps in a formal supplier-selection system); nothing is known about why suppliers are late and about what they are doing to correct the late performance. Your buyer may pass up suppliers that are becoming good and may continue to order from some whose systems are becoming overloaded.

The aggressive, probing buyer may visit a key supplier's plant, study the supplier's production-control system, and establish personal relationships with the supplier's personnel. Information about less vital suppliers may be obtained by asking the right series of questions over the phone. The following hypothetical exchange is an example.

> **Buyer:** What is the status of my order?
>
> **Supplier's Representative:** According to my current information, it is on time.
>
> **Buyer:** What do you mean by current information?
>
> **SR:** Well, I haven't received a delay notice.
>
> **Buyer:** Do you receive regular delay reports?
>
> **SR:** Yes.
>
> **Buyer:** How often?
>
> **SR:** Monthly.
>
> **Buyer** (mentally noting that month-old delay reports are badly out of date): Could you please check to see where the order is in your shops?
>
> **SR:** No, I've tried that before. Manufacturing tells me there are just too many orders on the floor to go searching for a particular one.
>
> **Buyer:** OK. Then could you just check with your master scheduler to see where my order is on your MPS?
>
> **SR:** MPS?

At this point it is clear that the supplier's representative is not in the habit of checking with production control or manufacturing. The aggressive buyer will press on and will have scored a coup if the supplier's rep is induced to go to production control for order-status information—and succeed in getting it.

The trend seems to be for the buyer-supplier interface to evolve into an information network with benefits both ways. The buyer gains better status information and better deliveries; the supplier, in return, may obtain advance notice of the customer's future materials needs. In one version of this type of information network, MRP-generated planned orders in the buyer's com-

FIGURE 14–5
Buyer-supplier
information
network

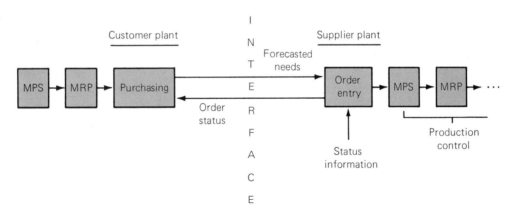

pany are transposed into demands against the master production schedule (MPS) in the supplier's company. As Figure 14–5 indicates, purchasing at one end and order entry at the other manage the information transfer at the interface.

Activities at the buyer-supplier interface lead to a legal contract—the purchase order—requiring the buyer to pay if the supplier complies. Growing difficulties of getting what you bargain for are examined in the following discussion of purchasing goods versus services.

Purchasing goods versus services

A distinction may be made between the purchase of goods, or *tangibles,* and in purchase of services, or *intangibles.* The quality of tangibles is physically measurable; the quality of intangibles is not. The distinction has an impact on purchasing.

Besides *quality,* the objectives of purchasing are *price, delivery,* and *favorable supplier relations* (or service). The four objectives are not independent. A buyer may sometimes deal with a loyal supplier even if that supplier's current prices are higher than, deliveries slower than, or quality not quite as good as that of another supplier.

Tangible goods. Level of purchasing effort may be related to dollar-volume for standard (stocked) goods or to item cost for nonstandard (nonstocked) goods. Thus, low-dollar-volume items, for example, class *C* and low-cost items, do not warrant extensive search for the lowest price; class *A* and high-cost items do.

A class *A* or high-cost item may be an expensive item that is seldom ordered or a low-cost item that is ordered very often or in very large quantities. Common purchasing measures are described below:

Soliciting competitive bids on *specifications.* An *invitation to bid* or a *request for quotation* is mailed to prospective suppliers. The item to be bought is specified in detail; the description may consist of *technical specifications* (physical or chemical properties) and *performance specifications* (mean time until failure, rated output, etc.). Specifications may be necessary because the item is nonstandard or because the buying firm wishes to exclude low-quality suppliers. And specifications can establish a sound basis for determining compliance with the requirements of the buyer. Engineering often plays a key role in developing "specs," as they are called, and engineering blueprints may be attached. Attorneys sometimes participate to assure that contractual obligations are legally clear.

Governments, especially the federal government, intermittently buy based on publicly available specs. Regulations require that, for many types of purchases, the invitation to bid be published in a widely circulated government document.

Negotiation. Where sources of supply are well established, there may be no need to solicit formal bids. Instead, the buying firm may just periodically negotiate with the regular source for better price or delivery terms. Typically, negotiation applies to nonstandard high-dollar-volume items produced to the buyer's specs.

Buying down and speculation. Buying down means trying to buy an item with a history of cyclic price swings when its price is down. Buying down is a form of speculative buying. In pure speculation, purchases are made for price reasons rather than to meet an actual need for the goods.

Hedging. Hedging applies especially to commodities such as wheat, corn, silver, and lumber. Organized futures markets exist for commodities. A buyer can pay cash to buy a commodity now and at the same time sell a like amount of a future of the commodity. Price changes will mean that losses on one order are offset by gains on the other.

Class *B* or intermediate-cost items usually warrant less purchasing effort. Specifications may be necessary if the items are nonstandard. But the expense of soliciting bids is harder to justify for such items than for high-cost/class *A* items. Many items of this kind are standard "off-the-shelf" goods, such as MRO (maintenance, repair, and operating supplies). Simpler order procedures, such as the following, may be used.

Approved supplier lists. For medium-dollar-volume purchasing, buying from proven suppliers is a reasonable substitute for seeking the lowest bid. A formal or informal supplier-rating procedure may be set up. Suppliers who get high ratings on price, quality, delivery, and service may be placed on an approved supplier list. Then, for certain types of purchases, only approved suppliers are considered.

Catalog buying. Perhaps the most common purchasing procedure for off-the-shelf (MRO) goods is buying out of current catalogs, sometimes with salesmen's assistance. Most buyers maintain extensive shelves of suppliers' catalogs for this purpose.

Blanket orders. Where there is a continuous but varying need for one or several rather low-cost items, a blanket order may be drawn up with a supplier. The blanket order covers a given time period, and deliveries are arranged by a "release" procedure. Price and other matters are covered in some fashion in the contract.

Systems contract. A systems contract is similar to a blanket order, but the systems contract is longer-term and more stringently defined. The purchasing department negotiates the systems contract; purchasing then typically becomes a monitor but not a participant in ordering. The contract may designate certain foremen and other managers who may requisition— by mail, phone, or other means—directly with the supplier.

Stockless purchasing. Stockless purchasing is a way for the buying firm to rid itself of the costs of carrying inventories of certain commonly used goods. The supplier assumes the inventories, even when they are physically located at the buyer's plant. The supplier may receive a higher-than-usual price in return for dependability and relief from the financial burden of carrying the inventories. By signing up several stockless purchasers, the supplier consolidates and saves on safety-stock inventories.

Class *C* or low-cost items are worthy of little attention by purchasing specialists. Attempting to buy such items from a supplier on an approved supplier list provides a measure of control. For many items, even that is too much unnecessary control and red tape, and to avoid these, using departments are provided with *petty cash funds* and may buy directly and pay cash.

Intangibility. An intangible item, as the designation suggests, is difficult to specify. Without clear, physically measurable specifications, the buyer is at the mercy of the seller.

Intangibility is relative, as Figure 14–6 attempts to show. The top end of the continuum represents one extreme—high tangibility. Highly tangible items include simple parts, such as screws, diodes, and switches. Commodities, such as tobacco, iron ore, and bananas, are near to the tangible end, but some of their key physical properties may be expensive to measure; less tangible "eyeball" judgments on quality may be used to some extent in evaluating commodities. Simple finished goods may be considered a bit less tangible than commodities; for example, books, furniture, and fabrics have several measurable physical properties, but for items of this kind visual inspection for scratches, flaws, and so forth, may be as important as physical measurements. Complex finished goods (e.g., autos, ships, and missiles) have thousands of measurable physical properties; yet partly subjective judgments as to their effectiveness (e.g., how well the destroyer protects the fleet) are quite important.

Procedures for purchasing or contracting for these mostly tangible goods are rather well established. Purchase contracts may be based to a considerable degree on clear *standards of output*—that is, on physically measurable properties of the end product.

Intangibles, at the other end of Figure 14–6, do not have physically measurable properties. Therefore, purchase contracts may, at best, be based on input and procedural factors. In a contract with a consultant, input factors may

FIGURE 14-6
Tangibility of purchased goods

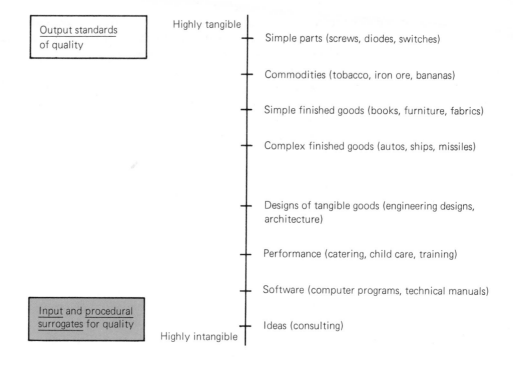

include the consultant's level of education and years of experience; procedural factors may include number of people interviewed and number of pages on the final consultant's report. These do not constitute the quality of the consultant's services, but they are often treated as surrogates for output quality. A consultant may meet all the terms of a contract specifying input and procedural factors and yet end up with totally worthless, incorrect, and irresponsible findings and recommendations. With such poor quality, the consultant does not deserve to be paid in full, but since the specifications of output quality were too intangible to be in the contract, the consultant is legally entitled to full pay.

Slightly more tangible than ideas is software, such as computer programs and technical manuals. You can count lines of code in a computer program and number of words in a technical manual, and the contract may set forth limits on these factors. But no one would suggest that these constitute measures of quality. However, the software firm is legally entitled to full pay, even for a shoddy job, if it has met the input and procedural contract terms.

Contracting for performance is growing explosively; catering, child care, and employee training are prominent examples. Enterprising college students have capitalized on the trend by establishing part-time businesses to provide janitorial service, yard-care service, computer-dating service and a variety of other services. The end products or outputs are good food, well-adjusted children, requalified employees, clean floors, weed-free lawns, and well-matched dating couples. It is difficult to write standards for these outputs into a contract. Consequently, there has been a growing use of measures of compliance such as mean number of complaints by customers and opinion polling involving customers, experts, or impartial panels using some form of Likert scale (i.e., a rating scale from 1 to 5 or 1 to 7, etc.).

This may seem nearly as objective as measuring the diameter of a shaft with a micrometer. It isn't. The weakness lies in the difficulty of securing a representative sample. A random sample of shafts is easily obtained because the shafts have no will and no bias. Selecting people to poll, on the other hand, depends on willingness to be polled, and there are many possible biases that are hard to control for.

In the center of Figure 14–6 is the purchase of designs for tangible goods, such as engineering and architectural designs. The output is like software or consulting reports, and the above remarks on the use of input and procedural contract terms apply. But there is a distinct difference: The engineer's or architect's design *becomes a tangible good.* If the bridge collapses or the roof caves in, the engineer or architect may be legally liable. This makes contracting for these services less risky.

We see that the most serious problems exist in buying performance, software, and ideas. Buying from firms with good reputations (such as the firms on an approved supplier list) would seem to be one helpful measure. But performance services tend to come and go rather than to stay and build clientele and reputation. Software firms and consulting firms are somewhat more stable. Ironically, poor software or poor consulting is not notably destructive to the reputations of firms. The reason is that dissatisfied customers tend not to admit their dissatisfaction *(a)* because of the risk of defamation suits, since bad quality is difficult to prove; and *(b)* because dissatisfaction would be an admission of having wasted a perhaps large sum of money on poor software or consulting service.

Public and corporate officials rely increasingly on consultants to help them with sticky decisions. Inability to write tough contracts leaves the officials at the mercy of the consultants. Fortunately most consultants are professionally dedicated and motivated to maintain a measure of self-respect. Still, contracting for these kinds of intangibles has become perhaps the greatest challenge for people in the purchasing field.

OTHER PURCHASING ISSUES

Other activities requiring professional purchasing expertise have to do with value analysis, sourcing, and receiving. Each of these is a shared activity. *Value analysis* aims at improving the specifications for that which is to be bought. Purchasing and engineering people are jointly involved in value analysis— or value engineering, as it is more often called today. *Sourcing* is deciding whether to make or buy. It is a decision that gets purchasing involved in high-level policy decisions. *Receiving* is accepting delivered purchases and assuring that the supplier complied with the purchase order, which provides closed-loop control over the purchasing function. Purchasing must insure that receiving procedures (carried out by the inventory control or warehouse staff) actually help to assure compliance. These three topics, value analysis/value engineering, sourcing, and receiving, are considered in turn in the following discussions.

Value analysis/ value engineering

Value analysis (VA) was developed in the purchasing department of General Electric in 1947. Since that time it has evolved into value engineering (VE), though the term *value analysis* is still used, especially by purchasing people.

VA is a procedure for analyzing existing specifications with the aim of improving value. In large organizations purchasing and engineering file cabinets may be filled with specifications developed by engineers years ago. New technology makes some of the old specifications obsolescent. Each time such items are reordered, the obsolescence becomes more apparent and purchasing takes some of the heat for not "buying modern." It is no surprise that the VA procedure was developed and promoted by purchasing people. As engineers got more involved, the concepts were extended to include new designs as well as old specifications.

VA/VE procedure. VA/VE studies are done by teams. Initially, VA teams were ad hoc: A purchasing specialist would call together a team to study the specifications for an item that was bought periodically. For example, if the item was a wooden barrel, perhaps a chemical engineer with an up-to-date knowledge of plastics and a mechanical engineer who was current in metals would be invited; others might include an industrial engineer working in the barrel-filling department and an industrial salesman from a firm that manufactured bottles and cans.

Since engineers were nearly always invited to serve, value analysis evolved into value engineering in many industrial organizations. VE today is often done by a department with a permanent staff instead of by ad hoc teams.

The VA/VE step-by-step procedure was developed in General Electric and has been adopted worldwide. The steps (a variation of the scientific method) are:

1. *Selection.* A product that is ripe for improvement is selected for value engineering.
2. *Information gathering.* Drawings, costs, scrap rates, forecasts, operations sheets, and so forth, are collected by the team coordinator before the team first meets. Team members are asked to send in whatever information they have.
3. *Function definition.* The team meets and defines each function of the product. A function is defined in two words, a verb and a noun. (A barrel *contains fluid.*) Only essential functions are included. Next the team determines the present cost of each function. This reveals which functions are costing far too much. (Note: Defining functions in this way is unique and sets VA/VE apart from less formal cost-reduction techniques.)

4. *Generation of alternatives.* Team members suggest ideas for new and different ways to accomplish the functions. This is known as brainstorming. The ideas are recorded, and later they are culled to a list of manageable size.

5. *Evaluation of alternatives.* Alternatives are evaluated based on feasibility, cost, and other factors, which cuts the list to one or two (or a few) good ideas.

6. *Presentation.* The final alternatives are refined and presented to a management committee as value-engineering change proposals.

7. *Implementation.* The approved value-engineering change proposal is translated into an engineering change order (ECO is a common industry abbreviation) and implemented.

VA/VE example. The description of a real VA/VE study helps show how the procedure works.[5]

EXAMPLE 14–2
VA/VE procedure for improving a bearing housing–support

A value-engineering team was given a dust-collector valve as a study project. In the information phase, it duly reviewed the assembly and subassembly parts and their costs. During this information search, the team noted that two bearing housing–supports were listed on the bill of materials, that is, right- and left-hand gray iron castings.

The team found that these bearing housing–supports were used in the main assembly to locate the bearings, which, in turn, supported and located the main shaft of the dust-collector valve. Also, each of these assemblies required a bearing housing–support, a bearing, and inner and outer bearing seals. The direct material and labor costs of the two subassemblies totaled $36. See the part drawing in Figure 14–7A.

In the function definition phase, the team defined the required subassembly basic and secondary functions as "provide support," "provide location," "reduce friction," and "provide seal."

In generating alternatives for the functions "provide support" and "provide location," the team listed steel plate for both. In developing this idea, it found that a steel plate would indeed provide the required support and location but would not "reduce friction" or "provide seal."

FIGURE 14–7
Bearing housing–support undergoing value engineering

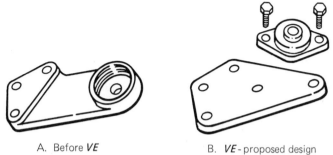

A. Before *VE*   B. *VE*-proposed design

Source: Arthur E. Mudge, *Value Engineering: A Systematic Approach* (McGraw-Hill, 1971), p. 263 (TS168.M83). Used with permission.

---

[5] Arthur E. Mudge, *Value Engineering: A Systematic Approach* (McGraw-Hill, 1971), pp. 263–64 (TS168.M83). Used with permission.

The problem attack now centered on the last two functions. In this part of the problem attack, the team secured and searched a number of bearing manufacturers' catalogs. In each of these it found a sealed, self-mounting bearing listed as a standard item. When the team's solution to the functions "reduce friction" and "provide seal" was combined with its solution to the functions "provide support" and "provide location," the team realized that it had a workable solution.

The team realized that the self-mounting bearing could be mounted on either side of a common piece of steel plate, as shown in Figure 14–7B. This solution reduced the total housing subassembly cost by 33 percent, to $25 per pair. Since only minor engineering changes were required and no tooling was needed, the annual net saving of approximately $3,100 began in the first year.

Impressed by the results of value engineering in private industry, the Department of Defense established VE regulations that were applicable to all DoD contracts costing more than $100,000. In 1964 the American Ordnance Association conducted a survey that randomly sampled 124 successful VE changes in the DoD.[6] The survey report showed not only impressive cost savings but also, in many cases, collateral gains in these areas: reliability, maintainability, producibility, human factors, parts availability, production lead time, quality, weight, logistics, performance, and packaging.

The DoD then implemented a formula for sharing some of the VE savings (usually 20 percent) with contractors; this gave the contractors' VE teams an additional incentive to squeeze savings out of the design specifications. Many private companies that had not previously used VE adopted it in order to get defense contracts, and many began applying VE to their own commercial goods. Value engineering became widespread, and a sponsoring organization known as the Society for the Advancement of Value Engineering (SAVE) was formed.

VA/VE helps to determine the purchasing specifications. Deciding whether to make or buy to those specifications is the sourcing decision, considered next.

Sourcing (make or buy)

The sourcing decision—to make or to buy—is one in which purchasing participates. Sourcing decisions can have major effects on the firm's finances, resources, capacity utilization, productive efficiency, costs, and strategy. The more important make-or-buy decisions may therefore be made by higher-level managers or be governed by company policies.

Analysis of most of the decision factors varies from situation to situation. Make-or-buy costs, however, may be analyzed by means of a common model: the break-even model.

Figure 14–8 is a graph showing how the break-even model may be applied to make-or-buy analysis. This version looks nearly the same as Figure 11–3

---

[6] "Reduce Costs and Improve Equipment through Value Engineering," Directorate of Value Engineering, Office of the Assistant Secretary of Defense for Installations and Logistics, January 1967. (TS168.U5).

FIGURE 14–8
Break-even
graph for make-
or-buy analysis

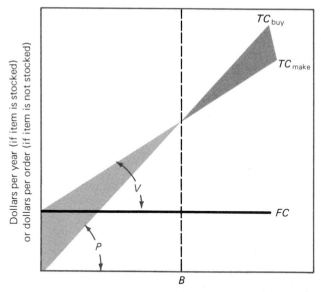

Demand per year (if item is stocked)
or demand per order (if item is not stocked)

in Chapter 11. The main difference is that Figure 11–3 was a cost-revenue analysis of *one* proposal, whereas Figure 14–8 is a cost-cost analysis of *two* competing proposals.

One of the competing proposals is to buy, which involves only a unit price. Price, P, times demand, D, equals total cost to buy:

$$TC_{buy} = P \times D$$

The other proposal is to make, which includes the fixed cost of the production facilities plus the variable cost to produce one unit. Variable cost, V, times demand, D, plus fixed cost, FC, equals total cost to make:

$$TC_{make} = (V \times D) + FC$$

In Figure 14–8 we see that the break-even demand, B, occurs where the total costs are equal. For demand less than B the total cost to buy is lower, so buy is preferred. For demand greater than B offsetting of the fixed cost by the lower unit cost results in a lower total cost to make, so make is preferred. The analysis should be based on annual demand and cost if the item is a stocked item that is bought year after year. The demand and cost of a single order should be used for a nonstocked item that may or may not be reordered in future years. (This is similar to the complete-recovery break-even method in Chapter 11.)

Since the total costs are equal at the break-even point, a break-even formula is easily developed. Using B (for break-even demand) instead of D, we have:

$$TC_{\text{buy}} = TC_{\text{make}}$$
$$P \times B = (V \times B) + FC$$
$$(P \times B) - (V \times B) = FC$$
$$B(P - V) = FC$$
$$B = \frac{FC}{P - V}$$

Examples of the formula's use are reserved for the end-of-chapter problems.

Receiving

Receiving has strong ties to purchasing and is sometimes a formal branch of purchasing. Receiving provides the check on purchased goods that allows the purchase order (PO) to be closed. As Stephen Love puts it, "Vigilance is required to ensure that stock received is accounted for, especially since vendor packing lists are not divinely inspired."[7]

In smaller operations the receiving clerk may check incoming goods against a copy of the purchase order; the clerk then records the count, damage data, discrepencies, and so on, on forms which go to purchasing, accounting, and inventory control.

In a larger operation prepunched cards or on-line terminals may be used, which reduces manual generation of records. The punched-card approach is batch-oriented; that is, receiving transactions are run through the computer in batches, say, once a day. A set of prepunched cards would be created at the same time that the PO is entered into the computer.

Figure 14–9 shows a typical packet of four prepunched cards and their flows out of receiving. In step 1 the goods are delivered and unloaded if the attached documents are in order (correct PO number, etc.). Receiving rough-checks and records the quantity, date, and so forth, on card 1. In step 2 inspectors carefully count, measure, and weigh goods. Sometimes a quality-control representative inspects for quality. Inspection data are recorded on card 2. In step 3 the goods go to stores and are entered into storage. Quantity and location are entered on card 3. In step 4 the goods, or part of them, go to the user. Card 4 goes along to identify the PO (and the vendor) in case the goods prove to be defective.

As Figure 14–9 also shows, management reports are generated periodically: A receiving report summarizes receiving activity from batches of card 1; an inspection report summarizes inspection activity from batches of card 2. Card 3 is processed, perhaps daily, to update stock records in the inventory master file.

There are many variations of the receiving system that has been described, but the four steps shown in Figure 14–9 and the basic types of information are rather standard.

Receiving controls on purchased goods are followed by inventory controls on goods in stock. Inventory control procedures are considered next.

---

[7] Stephen F. Love, *Inventory Control* (McGraw-Hill, 1979) (HD55.L68).

INVENTORY CONTROL

Inventory control is a term that we shall use to mean control over:

1. *Inventory records and files.* Stock records and files show what has occurred and what the current inventory status is.
2. *Physical stocks on hand.* What the records say may be verified by a physical inventory count of what is in storage.

FIGURE 14-9: Batch-oriented receiving using prepunched cards

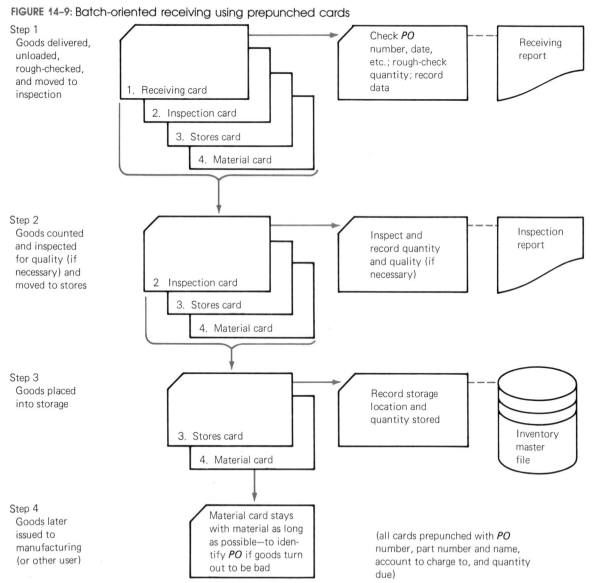

Step 1
Goods delivered, unloaded, rough-checked, and moved to inspection

1. Receiving card
2. Inspection card
3. Stores card
4. Material card

Check *PO* number, date, etc.; rough-check quantity; record data

Receiving report

Step 2
Goods counted and inspected for quality (if necessary) and moved to stores

2 Inspection card
3. Stores card
4. Material card

Inspect and record quantity and quality (if necessary)

Inspection report

Step 3
Goods placed into storage

3. Stores card
4. Material card

Record storage location and quantity stored

Inventory master file

Step 4
Goods later issued to manufacturing (or other user)

Material card stays with material as long as possible—to identify *PO* if goods turn out to be bad

(all cards prepunched with *PO* number, part number and name, account to charge to, and quantity due)

Source: Adapted from Kailash M. Bafna, "Receiving: A Systems Approach," *Production and Inventory Management*, 1st quarter 1973, p. 34. Used with permission.

3. *Number of items stocked or bought.* Item review provides controls over the variety and number of inventory items.
4. *Procedures for controls on inventory movements.* Potential abuses may be controlled by careful procedures.

These aspects of inventory control apply to manufacturing materials, MRO (maintenance, repair, and operating) inventories, and finished goods.

Two other aspects of inventory control are aggregate inventory control and control of work-in-process (WIP) inventories. Aggregate inventory control is really more a matter of planning than control, and the topic has been discussed in Chapter 5. Control of WIP inventory is closely related to production control; thus the topic was discussed in Chapter 6.

Stock record keeping

The very small organization may get by without stock records. The small amounts of stock carried may be mentally and visually managed. Growth in stock brings the need for stock records. Stock records are helpful for reasons of:

Security.
Reordering.
Review (for standardization and disposal).
Valuation (investment in inventories).
Performance assessment (supplier lead times, stockouts, backorders, etc.).

Stock record card. In manual systems some form of index card may be used for stock record keeping. Figure 14–10 is an example. The stock records should (except in very small operations) be processed in a place removed from physical storage and by people other than the storekeepers. This practice provides a measure of security, because discrepancies between stock-record balances and actual inventories will arise if goods are stolen or misallocated.

The record provides the needed data for reordering by the reorder-point method. The balance is checked against the ROP each time an issue is recorded, and order action is taken when the ROP is reached. Balance data are also needed in MRP systems: Net requirements equal gross requirements minus balance on hand. The stock record may also provide usage data—see the monthly usage summary in the figure—which is useful in review for standardization and disposal, for inventory valuation, and for performance assessment. Supplier lead times, stockout and backorder frequency, and other information may also be gleaned from data on the stock record.

Computer files. In computer-based inventory control, stock-record data are likely to be on magnetic tape or in a disk storage file. The file may serve as an *inventory master file,* and its data may be used for many purposes and programs, including forecasting, ROP, BOM explosion, MRP, lot sizing, inventory accounting, item review, simulation, transaction recording, order entry, and management reporting. To serve all of these purposes the inventory record

FIGURE 14–10
Stock record card

STOCK RECORD

Name or description					Location	
Stock number					Order quantity	
Primary users or uses					Reorder point	

Monthly usage summary

Jan.	Feb.	Mar.	Apr.	May	June	July	Aug.	Sept.	Oct.	Nov.	Dec.

Date	Orders or allocations	Qty. on order	Receipts	Issues	Balance	Date	Orders or allocations	Qty. on order	Receipts	Issues	Balance

FIGURE 14–11
Open-order file
record and key
ordering actions

Description of field	Placement of order	Modification of order	Receipt of material	Closing of order
Purchaser ID code	X			
Order serial number	X			
Date order placed	X			
Vendor ID code	X			
Item ordered	X			
Quantity ordered	X	X		
Price per unit	X	X		
Delivery date (promised)	X	X		
"Deliver to" code (department)	X			
Date actually received			X	
Quantity actually received			X	
Receipt document number			X	
Amount charged			X	
Closing flag				X

Source: Stephen F. Love, *Inventory Control* (McGraw-Hill, 1975), p. 255 (HD55.L68). Used with permission.

in the master file would have to contain much more data than that on the simple stock record of Figure 14–10.[8]

A second file that is often added to a computerized inventory system is an *open-order file*. Earlier discussion of purchasing, the supplier interface, and receiving suggests the need for an open-order file; that is, the events related to a purchase order warrant monitoring and recording. Figure 14–11 lists some of the common fields found in each record of an open-order file. The figure also shows how the fields interact with key ordering actions: placement, modification, receipt, and closing.

The inventory master file and the open-order file have some common data fields, such as stock name and number, date of order, quantity ordered, and price. Therefore, certain order and inventory transactions must update both files—and often other inventory-related files not discussed here. Duplication of data fields in more than one file is eliminated by modern data base management systems (DBMS), which are growing in use as repositories of inventory (and other) data.

Closely related to the record-keeping side of inventory control is the physical-inventory side. Physical-inventory concepts and procedures are considered next.

---

[8] Examples of data fields found in inventory master files are listed in Love, *Inventory Control*, p. 272; and (an MRP-oriented list) in Orlicky, *Material Requirements Planning*, pp. 181–83.

Physical inventory

Most of us are aware of retailers or other businesses that are sometimes "closed for inventory." This means closed to count the goods in stock. At one time the main purpose of this operation was to get an inventory valuation; the counting was in dollars. Today counting is mostly in pieces, gallons, yards, boxes, pounds, and other natural physical units. It is easy enough, via data processing, to have the counts converted to dollars for valuation purposes. But unit counts are needed for operations management purposes, which includes correcting discrepancies on stock records. Recently there has been a growing emphasis on more frequent or more accurate unit counts.

Counting. The need for accuracy is especially great in firms using MRP. MRP experts and users seem to be united on the point. A few will say that accurate up-to-date counts (reflected in the item master file) are more important than, say, a good demand forecast. Marketing takes most of the heat when the forecast is wrong, but inaccurate inventory records mean that released orders are often going to be for parts known—by operating people—to be in stock. The likely result is lack of confidence in the MRP system and perhaps failure of the system.

An accurate physical inventory count was also thought to be important in ROP/shortage-list systems. However the physical count is often inaccurate, yet no one panics. If records are inaccurate, the response may be simply to increase safety stock and pad shortage lists—or to increase the staff of expediters. In non-MRP systems, the crisis mode is often normal and inaccurate inventory counts do not seem out of place.

Improved inventory accuracy is being achieved in several ways. One is *cycle counting.* By this method a small fraction of items are counted each week or day, year around. Cycle counting may be tied to ABC classes; for example, *A* items might be counted many times per year, *B* items less often, and *C* items seldom. In general, cycle counting is one method of taking a physical inventory. But in the jargon of the trade the term *physical inventory* is used to mean a complete one-time count of all items stocked—as opposed to sampling by cycle counts or other methods.

Other alternatives to the complete physical inventory are *event-based* counting and *stock-location* counting. One form of event-based counting is counting an item whenever it is issued; thus more active items get counted more often. Another is counting when stock is low, for example, just before a scheduled receipt; the advantage is that there is less to count. In stock-location counting, the counting moves from one storage area to another; an advantage is that "lost" items may be found in the process.

Deterrence. Counting has been valued as an inventory control tool partly because it serves as a deterrent to theft and improper storage or use of materials. This point was made in the earlier discussion of stock records: Matching count totals against stock-record balances reveals discrepancies. To achieve full deterrent value and avoid counting errors, some procedures require that outsiders do the counting; sometimes two outside teams (whose members may be storekeepers from another stockroom) double-count the same items and a third party verifies.

In the MRP mode, deterrence is the lesser purpose and accuracy the greater purpose. Deterrence is less important because MRP inventories tend to be low—zero or close to zero for many items, as opposed to the large safety stocks common in ROP systems. There is therefore less to steal. With MRP, counting procedures tend to be less elaborate, perhaps allowing storekeepers to count their own goods, but counting is likely to be more frequent.

It should be pointed out that physical counting and stock records provide a secondary kind of deterrence. Primary deterrence consists of some sort of stockroom security. Lockable storage cabinets are one type. No-access or controlled-access storerooms are another. Controlled access to buildings in which inventory is stored provides more general security. And perimeter controls—fences, gates, guards, badges, and random searches—provide boundary security.

Item review

While the purpose of item records and physical inventory procedures is to control present stocks, item review has the aim of reducing the variety and number of the goods to be controlled. Item review includes review for standardization and for disposal.

Standardization. Standardization (also referred to as simplification) means reducing a proliferation of similar items to a single standard item that can serve multiple needs. In some cases this is done by creating a new design with the essential features of several old designs. More often, item review reveals that one out of several existing designs is sufficient and that the other designs may be dropped. Some golfers, for example, make standardization decisions to rid the bag of all but a single wood, a putter, and perhaps three irons.

Advantages of standardization include fewer items to design, to buy or make, and to carry as safety stocks, and the larger quantities offer opportunities for quantity discounts and leverage to gain better deliveries and service. These advantages are sometimes overshadowed by maintenance advantages: With fewer parts better spare-parts service can be provided.

Standardization is a hallmark of the industrial revolution. Consider, for example, the work of Eli Whitney in standardizing musket parts so that muskets could be mass-produced instead of handcrafted. But the work of standardization never ends, and in many firms purchasing or design engineering, or a special team, periodically undertakes a full-scale standardization study. Today, computers can assist by performing searches and providing specially formatted listings of parts and their characteristics.

Disposal. Standardization applies to items for which there is a healthy demand; disposal applies to items for which there is little demand. Periodic item review can identify items that need not be carried in stock, and present stocks of those items can be sold off. The benefits of disposal include lower carrying costs, cash proceeds from sales, and tax credits on losses.

The decision to retain or dispose of an item depends on several factors. Two objective factors are unit cost and number of demands per year. High unit cost coupled with few demands suggests disposal of an item in order to save on carrying cost. After disposal, occasional demands for the item would be handled as special orders—with the disadvantage of slower response in providing the user with the item requested.

Annual demand is another factor that affects the decision. Contrary to what one might expect, it is not the low-demand items that should be disposed of. The opposite is the case, because high-demand items tend to be ordered in larger lot sizes, which means more carrying cost.

Data on these three factors would normally be available in a computer-based inventory system. This permits use of a decision model for item review for disposal. One model that serves the purpose balances the annual cost that would arise from retaining an item against the annual order-processing cost that would arise from disposal and subsequent special orders. A decision factor, F, is the ratio of the two annual costs, as is explained below. (All but one of the variables were discussed in Chapter 5.)

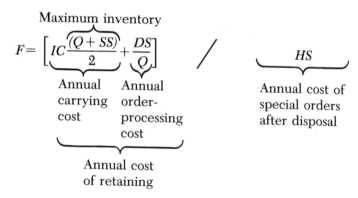

where:

F = Decision factor (1.00 at the point of indifference)
I = Inventory-carrying-cost rate
C = Cost per unit
Q = Lot size (EOQ)
SS = Safety stock
D = Annual demand
S = Cost of processing the order (setup cost)
H = Number of demands per year (measured by tallying number of issues per year)

The decision rules are:

When F is greater than 1.00, dispose of item.
When F is less than 1.00, retain the item.

The model does not consider the subjective factors. For example, a recommendation to dispose of an item might be overruled if the item were rare or hard to get, were a vital replacement part, or were important to some profitable future venture.

Procedural controls

The final topic in this section on inventory control concerns overall procedural controls in connection with materials transactions.

Flows of materials within the organization give rise to flows of information about the materials. Procedures are established to control material and information flows and to perform certain actions at each control point along the way. One set of procedures may concern ordering and receipt; another, storage and issue; a third, work in process; and a fourth, finished goods.

There is not space enough to examine the many possible configurations of procedures that might be found in practice. Instead, two examples are presented here. One is an elaborate set of procedural controls—for just the ordering-receipt activity. The other is a way of avoiding elaborate controls via use of what is called the "supermarket system"; the supermarket system applies only to the storage-and-issue activity.

Order-receipt procedures. For example, Figure 14–12 shows one possible set of procedural controls over ordering and receipt. Six control points, numbered *C1* through *C6*, are shown. The control points are the points at which controllers (in rows) have key decisions to make about the objects of control (information, material, and funds—in columns). Common flow-charting symbols are used in the figure. Each control point is described below:

C1. The inventory planner, who had prepared the requisition for material earlier, now checks to see that the buyer's purchase order matches the requisition. The purpose is to assure that the purchaser is buying the intended goods, that the goods are being bought at the right price, and so forth.

C2. The buyer checks the supplier's invoice. Discrepancies (wrong quantity, etc.) can be passed along to the inventory planner.

C3. The stockroom clerk counts the goods in order to verify the count entered by the receiving clerk (or inspector) on the receiving report. Discrepancies are passed along to the inventory planner.

C4. The inventory planner checks the count against the quantity ordered before updating the inventory records.

C5. The buyer checks the count to make sure that the supplier has complied with the order and also to assess the supplier's performance.

C6. Accounting checks the invoice for reasonableness and for terms (quantity discounts, etc.) prior to payment.

This system of procedural controls provides for a certain amount of duplication—several points at which errors (or dishonesty) may be caught. No firms have exactly the same procedural controls, but Figure 14–12 is representative.

The supermarket system. A disadvantage of procedural duplication is that it tends to act as red tape and to slow down the flow of materials. There are various ways of speeding up material-flow procedures without serious losses in control. The supermarket system is an example.

The supermarket system is a procedure for storing and issuing. The system calls for setting up a storage area as a "supermarket" and allowing employees to "shop" there. These "shoppers" have shopping lists, check the prices that are marked on items displayed on shelves, fill a cart, and "pay" for charges run up at a register at the end. Payment is usually made by entering the employee's department number on the bill, which goes to accounting for later processing. Sometimes employees use a departmental charge plate or credit card.

FIGURE 14-12
System of checks to assure procedural integrity for stock ordering and receipt

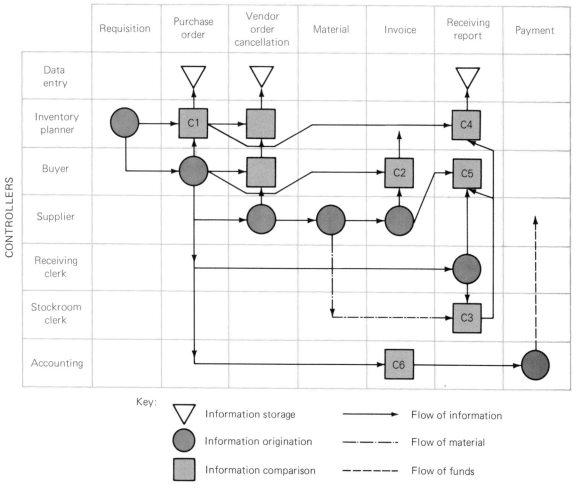

Source: Adapted from Stephen F. Love, *Inventory Control* (McGraw-Hill, 1975), p. 259 (HD55.L68). Used with permission.

The U.S. Navy supply system has set up supermarkets for the convenience of ship-stores people in busy ports. Some larger organizations also use supermarkets for office supplies. The supermarket system allows customers to see what is being bought, and it cuts delivery time, thereby reducing customer hoarding. Information processing is simplified in that no requisition has to be prepared and a number of items can be charged on a single document. Like the grocery supermarket, the supply supermarket can be run on a largely self-service basis and it can respond rather quickly to current demand.

MATERIALS MANAGEMENT AS A PROFIT CENTER

As was stated earlier, materials management does not add tangible value to materials. It does, however, add intangible value, that is time and place value. The materials management (MM) department serves, and their services cost money. MM service costs must be passed along to the using department in some way, e.g., by transfer pricing or by overhead charges. Transfer price means the price charged by MM to the user, and the price would be the purchase cost of the item plus MM's service charge. If transfer prices are held constant from year to year, then the MM department would earn a profit if it were able to lower its service costs or to buy goods for a lower purchase cost. Similarly, MM would earn a loss if its costs or prices paid went up.

To establish MM as a profit center requires a special (artificial) bookkeeping manipulation to set transfer prices. A sound approach is to set transfer prices so that MM earns the same return on capital as the firm does as a whole. The following example will illustrate.

EXAMPLE 14–3
Materials management as a profit center, Energistics, Inc.

Energistics, Inc., earns 20 percent (before taxes) on capital. Therefore, in setting up its materials management (MM) department as a profit center, Energistics provides MM with a 20 percent profit to be used to set transfer prices. The 20 percent rate is applied to MM department capital assets, namely:

Assets:
Facilities (floor space and equipment) $1,000,000
Inventories of purchased goods   5,000,000
    Total $6,000,000

Profits on capital assets = 20% of $6,000,00 = $1,200,000

In the same year MM's service expenses are $800,000 and cost of purchased goods is $40,000,000. Determining transfer prices requires working backwards from the normal way than an income statement is prepared:

MM department profit .... $ 1,200,000
MM service expenses   800,000
    Gross margin .... $ 2,000,000
Cost of goods sold (purchased goods) 40,000,000
    "Sales" (transfer-priced) $42,000,000

That $42 million is the revenue that MM should earn by charging using departments for materials. MM's average markup is 5 percent, that is,

$$\frac{\$2,000,000}{\$40,000,000} = 0.05$$

In the following year, the MM department mounts an internal campaign to (a) lower inventories, (b) get rid of excess facilities, (c) get better prices from suppliers, and (d) lower its operating expenses. At year's end the result is a small increase in MM profitability:

Income statement:

"Sales" (transfer-priced)	$42,000,000*
Cost of goods sold (purchased goods)	40,100,000
Gross margin	$ 1,900,000
MM service expenses	700,000
MM department profit	$ 1,200,000

*Transfer prices and volume of goods "sold" stayed the same as the previous year.

Assets:

Facilities (floor space and equipment)	$ 900,000
Inventories of purchased goods	4,900,000
Total	$5,800,000

$$\text{Return on capital assets} = \frac{\$1,200,000}{\$5,800,000} = 0.207, \text{ or } 20.7\%$$

The 0.7 percent improvement in profitability is in spite of failure to get lower prices from suppliers. In fact, because of inflation, prices paid went up from $40 million to $40.1 million. (If the general rate of inflation had been normal that year, Energistics buyers would have done very well to keep prices paid that low.) Successes were in cutting service expenses (from $800,000 to $700,000), facilities investment (from $1,000,000 to $900,000), and inventories (from $5,000,000 to $4,900,000).

The example shows that treating MM as a profit center has important motivational advantages. The profit-center concept is good for managerial development in that it exposes managers to challenges, risk-taking, investments aimed at operating savings and profits, and so forth.

If the profit-center concept is so great, why not apply it then to capacity management, maintenance, and other operations management areas? In some cases, other operations management areas might be set up as profit centers, but MM is a more natural application of the concept because, commonly, materials constitute a large part of operating costs. Accounting costs are higher for profit centers, and profit centers can result in bickering between departments as well as inordinate time spent by profit center managers to gain accounting advantages. Thus profit-center management is best-applied where the cost impact and potential for cost improvements is great.

TOOL INVENTORIES

Unlike materials, tools do not become a part of the end product. Tools are worn out rather than used up, and tools are issued and retrieved rather than merely issued. In these respects, tools are more like equipment (machines) than materials. But a tool is less automatic, more manipulative than a machine. To confuse the issue there is a class of implement known as a machine-tool. It is what it implies, a cross between a machine and a tool. A lathe and a drill press are examples. They have automatic, or machine characteristics but augmented by manipulative skills of the worker. Machine-tools are generally planned and controlled by a facilities-planning group rather than a tool-control group and need not be discussed further here.

Tools are an inventory-management problem with many of the attributes of materials management: purchasing, lot sizing, reorder points, item review, and so forth. In addition, tools must be retrieved.

Tool issue and retrieval is much like book issue and retrieval in libraries. In fact, library materials are tools of the student and the researcher, and libraries are a type of tool crib. The library analogy is extended below to show four common ways in which tools may be provided to workers:

Industrial and office tools	Library materials
1. Short-term tool loans from tool crib	One-day issues from reserve
2. Long-term tool loans from tool crib	Nonreserve issues
3. Shop has its own tools permanently assigned	Dormitory or other living unit has its own books and magazine subscriptions
4. Workers pay for and bring their own tools to work	Personal libraries

For 1 and 2 above, tool accountability procedures are needed. Three accountability systems are described below. These are the brass-disc system, the paper-slip system, and the on-line-computer system.

An old and simple system is the *brass-disc* system. Each tool user is issued a quantity of small brass discs. The employee's payroll number is imprinted on the discs, and there is a hole punched in each disc. The employee surrenders one disc upon receipt of one tool. The tool-crib attendant places the disc on a hook fronting the bin from which the tool was withdrawn. The brass-disc system is simple and fast, and yet it keeps track of who has tools.

A weakness is that the brass discs provide no records. Tools may be kept out of circulation for overly long periods since there is no accounting for date of issue. Also, without date information it is difficult to determine tool demand rates so that proper tool quantities may be planned.

The *paper-slip* system is more involved than the brass-disc system, but paper slips provide records. When a tool is issued, the date and the name and number of the tool are written on the slip, and the user's payroll number, work center, and signature are entered. The process may be simplified by use of charge plates. The tool crib keeps, say, three copies of the paper slip, and the user may also get a copy. The tool crib files one copy by tool number, a second copy by tool return date in a tickler file, and a third by employee payroll number or work-center number. When the tool is returned, the copy filed by payroll or work-center number is given to the employee as a receipt. At the end of each day current-date slips in the tickler file are pulled for overdue action. Slips filed by tool number may be checked periodically for tool-issue-rate data, which are used to see whether a greater supply or a smaller supply (disposal) of the tool is needed.

On-line-computer accountability is simply the automated version of the paper-slip system. Paper is done away with at the issuing stage, but a typewriter or a visual display terminal connected on-line to a computer is necessary. Advantages of this system are its capability for intensive computer analysis of tool usage patterns and its flexibility in producing a variety of management reports.

SUMMARY

Inventory dynamics and control follows inventory planning. Inventory dynamics involves carrying out inventory plans via purchasing; material handling (discussed in an earlier chapter); and receiving and issuing inventory and recording inventory transactions. Inventory control includes protection, security, and accountability for inventories and review and disposal of excess inventories.

Inventory functions have tended to be scattered about the organization chart. The materials-management department changes this by consolidating many of the functions. The new department, often at the vice-presidential level, may gain in coordination, thereby cutting red tape and delivery time and improving services. The materials-management department might include receiving and traffic, material handling, purchasing, inventory control, and stores; it sometimes includes production control.

An opposite extreme in organizing material functions is to despecialize, that is, to break up specialist units like purchasing and material handling and transfer those duties to line departments. The purposes—which are often related to the rescue of a faltering company—are to cut costs and to give line departments more authority and control.

ABC analysis is a well-known method for managing inventories based on their importance, as measured in annual dollar-volume. High-dollar-volume (class A) goods may be intensively managed, for example, by thoroughly searching for best prices and by carefully matching orders to current needs. Low-dollar-volume (class C) goods may be loosely controlled.

The purchase of intangibles (services) is a special challenge in that services cannot be specified by physical or chemical properties. Thus the supplier could provide poor services and still be legally entitled to payment.

In addition to price and quality, the purchaser's goals are delivery and good supplier relations. Meeting deliveries has been a growing problem, and some buyers have been becoming more aggressive in getting commitments and status information from suppliers.

Value analysis is a procedure that purchasing people developed in order to meet material needs (functions) with lower-cost materials and designs. Engineers were commonly invited to serve on value-analysis teams, and value engineering (VE) emerged. VE has been promoted by the federal government, which offers higher profits to contractors that are able to lower costs through VE studies of government specifications.

An inventory decision that precedes purchasing is the make-or-buy decision, that is, deciding on the source. Cost elements in the sourcing decision may be analyzed using break-even analysis. The break-even point is the point at which total cost to make equals total cost to buy. Below this point buying is cheaper, because there is not enough volume to justify the fixed cost of setting up a manufacturing capability.

Receiving includes the activities involved in accepting delivered goods and checking on compliance with the purchase order. Receiving information may be entered on prepunched cards, which may be used to produce various management reports.

Stock record keeping ranges from none in very small organizations to multi-file computer-based inventory records. Stock records provide data that discourage misuse of materials, assist in reordering and review, and facilitate inventory valuation and performance assessment.

Index cards may be used as basic stock records. Item identification details may be entered at the top, and each transaction—purchase, receipt, issue, date, and new balance—may be recorded below.

In computer-based inventory record keeping, two common files are an inventory master file—a computerized version of the stock record card—and an open-order file. The two files (and any others) permit a wide variety of special studies, simulations, and reports, in addition to displacing clerical labor that is necessary in manual stock record keeping.

Inventory control includes control over the variety and number of the items handled, over the physical well-being of those items, and over procedures for handling stores and inventory information. The variety of items handled may be examined periodically for purposes of greater standardization and disposal. Disposal seems desirable when the cost of retaining an item exceeds the cost of the special orders that would be necessary if the item were not retained. A decision model that takes these costs into consideration may be used as an aid in reviews for disposal.

The physical control of stores includes such security measures as lockable cabinets, doors, and gates and limited-access policies. Conducting a periodic inventory or a continuous-cycle count of stores has value as a deterrent to the theft or misuse of stores. Counting is even more important in MRP systems as a means of making order-release decisions correspond to real need.

Procedures for controlling material and information flows provide for checks and recording at each key stop on the material-flow path. Some duplication is desirable to combat errors and improprieties.

The supermarket system of storage and issue avoids duplication by offering users the chance to do self-service shopping in a storeroom. The system is mainly for supplies and commodities that are used in low volume.

Sometimes materials-management departments are established as profit centers. The profit-center concept provides incentive to seek lower prices for purchased goods, to reduce service expenses, to cut inventories, and to maximize use of facilities.

Tool inventories are managed much like material inventories, except that tools must be retrieved as well as issued. Tool retrieval systems include the brass-disc system (a disc with the tool user's ID on it is placed in the tool bin), a paper-slip system, and an on-line-computer-based system. Tool retrieval is fraught with many of the same difficulties as book retrieval in a library.

REFERENCES

Books

Ammer, Dean S. *Materials Management.* Irwin, 1974 (TS161.A42).

England, Wilbur B. *Modern Procurement Management: Principles and Cases.* Irwin, 1970 (HD52.5.E499).

Love, Stephen F. *Inventory Control.* McGraw-Hill, 1979 (HD55.L68).

Mudge, Arthur E. *Value Engineering: A Systematic Approach.* McGraw-Hill, 1971 (TS168.M83).

Orlicky, Joseph. *Material Requirements Planning.* McGraw-Hill, 1975 (TS155.8.O74).

Periodicals (societies)

Journal of Purchasing and Materials Management (National Association of Purchasing Management)

Production and Inventory Management (American Production and Inventory Control Society)

Purchasing

PROBLEMS

Note: Asterisked (*) problems require more than mimicry. They require judgment, and you should include discussion of reasons, assumptions, and outside sources of information.

Materials organization

*1. From the chapter discussion four kinds of organization for materials activities may be identified: (1) traditional (see Figure 14–1A); (2) materials management, including production control (Figure 14–1B); (3) materials management, without production control (Figure 14–1B); and (4) despecialization. A number of organizational settings are listed below. For each one, state which of the four forms is most suitable. Explain your reasoning. (A reference on materials management is: Jeffrey G. Miller and Peter Gilmour, "Materials Managers: Who Needs Them?" *Harvard Business Review*, July–August 1979, pp. 143–53.)

Aerospace company that is highly project-oriented.

Chemical company.

Foundry.

U.S. Navy shipyard.

Private shipyard faced with severe cost problems.

Fabric manufacturer.

Machine-tool manufacturer.

ABC

2. Below are eight items in a firm's inventory. Add four more of your own, and devise an ABC classification scheme for the items. Show which class each item fits into.

Item	Unit cost	Annual demand
A	$ 1.35	6,200
B	53.00	900
C	5.20	50
D	92.00	120
E	800.00	2
F	0.25	5,000
G	9,000.00	5
H	15.00	18,000

*3. Several examples of uses of ABC inventory classification were discussed in the chapter.
   a. Suggest five more uses, and discuss their value.
   b. How could ABC analysis be used for MRP component parts?

Purchasing

*4. Several types of organizations are listed below. Each has different kinds of purchases to make.

Fashions (apparel)	Car-rental company
Liquor wholesaler	Glass manufacturer
City government	Plastics manufacturer
Major home-appliance manufacturer	Computer manufacturer
Electric power company	Food wholesaler
Furniture manufacturer	Shipbuilder
Construction contractor	Aerospace company

   a. Select any four of the organization types, and discuss how challenging it is to purchase for each.
   b. Discuss some key purchasing techniques that would be useful for each of the four types of organizations that you selected in part a.
   c. Which types of organizations on the list are most likely to be heavily involved in buying intangibles? Explain.
   d. Which types of organizations on the list are most likely to use an approved supplier list? bid solicitation based on specifications? blanket orders? Explain.
   e. Which types of organizations on the list are most likely to use value analysis/value engineering? Explain.

VA/VE

5. The following is a list of products to be analyzed by VA/VE.

A classroom desk	Bookends
A mousetrap	An electric fan
A backpack-style book toter	Handlebars on a bike
The grate in a fireplace	A bike lock

A coaster on which to set drinks

The lamp part shown in the accompanying sketch

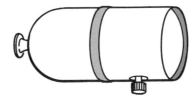

a. Select any four of the above, and define its function or functions in two words, as discussed in the chapter.

*b. Why is function definition an early and precisely done step in value analysis/ value engineering? Explain what this step accomplishes, using some of your examples from part a.

Sourcing

6. A large corporation is considering the establishment of its own travel department, which would earn commissions on airline tickets. The current cost of airline tickets averages $122 per trip. With an internal travel department earning commissions, it is estimated that the ticket cost will drop to $105 per trip. The salaries and expenses of the travel department would come to $40,000 per year.

What number of tickets per year would the corporation need to process in order to break even on "making its own tickets" instead of "buying tickets" from an outside agency? If the corporation projects 2,000 trips per year, should it "buy" or "make"?

Purchasing and inventory control

7. Stock record cards for three inventory items are shown below:

Item: Stock no.: 3688 Location:			$Q=$ $ROP=$			
Remarks	Purchase/ manufacture order no.	Unit cost	Date	Receipts/ issues	Balance	
Adjust for cycle count			2–1 2–17 3–1	−10 −400 −25	1,100 700 675	
Order	P–110		3–1 3–15	−80	595	
Receipt	P–110	$50	3–28 4–4 4–20	+1,000 −65 −100	1,595 1,530 1,430	
Adjust for cycle count			5–1	−5	1,425	

Item: Stock no.: 1011 Location			$Q=$ $ROP=$		
Remarks	Purchase/ manufacture order no.	Unit cost	Date	Receipts/ issues	Balance
Adjust for cycle count			2–1	+2	1,820
			2–10	−500	1,320
			2–18	−700	620
Order	M–88		2–19		
			2–21	−250	370
Backorder 30			2–28	−370	0
Receipt	M–88	$2.10	3–2	+2,000	2,000
			3–3	−30	1,970
			3–11	−350	1,620
			3–16	−650	970
			3–20	−500	470
Order	M–110		3–21		
			3–27	−300	170
Receipt	M–110	$2.20	3–30	−2,000	2,170
Adjust for cycle count			4–1	0	2,170

Item: Stock no.: 7092 Location:			$Q=$ $ROP=$		
Remarks	Purchase/ manufacture order no.	Unit cost	Date	Receipts/ issues	Balance
Adjust for cycle count			2–1	0	15
			2–4	−2	13
			2–9	−3	10
			2–12	−3	7
			2–13	−2	5
			2–18	−1	4
Order	P–78		2–18		
			2–22	−2	2
Receipt	P–78	$1,500	2–23	+20	22
			2–26	−2	20
			2–27	−2	18
Adjust for cycle count			3–1	0	18

a. What are the order quantities and approximate reorder points for each item?
b. What are the average annual demand rates and the average lead times for each item?
c. For each item, make the computation needed for ABC classification of items.

What classes would you expect for each of these items? Why?

d. Discuss the firm's physical inventory policies. Include explanation of the cycle-count adjustments for each item.

e. Assume that manual posting to the kind of stock record cards shown above is used. Then explain how the receiving procedure of Figure 14–9 would be employed to provide information for posting to the stock record cards. Discuss the need for accurate count controls at various points.

f. If the above stock record cards were converted to a computerized item master file, what would probably be done about the remarks column?

g. What transactions would take place in an open-order file (manual or computerized) for the items shown in the three stock record cards? What are some purposes of the open-order file?

Disposal

8. Data for several stocked inventory items are given below:

Item	Annual demand	Reordered annual number of demands	Unit cost	Remarks
A	8,000	40	$ 25	
B	200	20	125	Unstable source
C	40	2	1	
D	200	8	5	
E	1,000	10	300	

Additional data that apply to all of the items are:

Order-processing cost = $50

Safety stock = 0

a. Should any of the items be disposed of? (In your calculations, you pick the inventory-carrying-cost rate.)

b. The inventory manager believes that the recorded number of annual demands understates the true frequency of need for the items (because some inventory users are put off by all the paperwork and lead time in getting their goods from inventory and therefore sometimes do without). If demands were 50 percent greater, would any of your disposal recommendations change?

MM as profit center

9. In Energistics' second year it earned a 22 percent profit. The MM department's new profit target for the third year thus became 22 percent.

a. What revenue and what average markup should MM plan for in the third year? (See Example 14–3 for second-year results which are used in third-year planning.)

b. Assume that MM's "sales" to other departments drop to $40 million and that aggressive buying yields a 5 percent improvement in the purchase cost of goods "sold." If service expenses and assets are unchanged, what is MM's third-year profit performance?

*c. In part b it seems that purchasing carries most of the load in achieving a given rate of profitability in MM. But purchasing is only one of several MM divisions. Discuss the effects on MM profitability that can be attributed to other divisions normally found in an MM department.

*10. Tool inventories are not normally a responsibility of a materials management department. Why not?

IN-BASKET CASE*

Topic: Inventory-Taking—Aerospace Products

To:

From: General Manager, Aerospace Products Division

Every year we have each of our warehousemen take a thorough physical inventory count of the goods he is responsible for. These counts are compared against stock balances in our inventory records section. The agreement between the count and the record balances is generally good; but we have so many stockouts during the year that I'm beginning to question our inventory procedure. I'd like you to study the proper ways of *taking an inventory* and report to me.

---

* See instructions at end of problems section, Chapter 1.

index

639

*This book has been set VideoComp in 10 and
9 point Gael, leaded 2 points. Part numbers
and titles and chapter numbers and titles are
Avant Garde Gothic Extra Light. The size of
the type page is 37 by 47 picas.*